SAKHALIN
SOYA STRAIT (LA PÉROUSE)

P9-CLD-909

HOKKAIDO

KURILE ISLANDS
ETOROFU

KUNASHIRI

SHIKOTAN

Sapporo

HABOMAI
ISLANDS
(Occupied by U.S.S.R.)

Hakodate

PACIFIC OCEAN

Aomori

Asahikawa

Otaru
Sapporo

Akita
Morioka

Oshamambe
Muroran

Sendai

TUNNEL UNDER CONSTRUCTION

Aomori
Hachinohe

SADO

iigata

Morioka

Akita

HONSHU

Yamagata
Sendai

Niigata
Fukushima

MT. FUJI
Tokyo
Yokohama

Nagano

RIDOR

Toyama
Kanazawa

Takasaki
Narita

hizuoka

Fukui
Tsuruga

Kofu

tsu

Obama

Gifu-
Hashima

Tokyo

Matsue

Nagoya

Tottori

Okayama

Nara

Hiroshima

Osaka

Shimonoseki

Takamatsu

Tokushima

Fukuoka

Kochi

ROUTES OF THE SHINKANSEN
(Japan's high-speed bullet trains)

Saga

Matsuyama

Nagasaki

Oita

In operation

Kumamoto

Under construction

Miyazaki

Already decided

Kagoshima

Planned routes

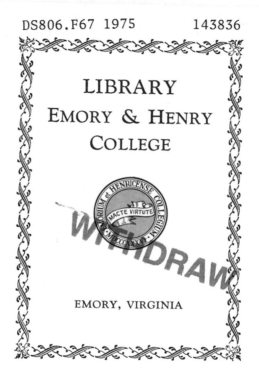

JAPAN TODAY

A  BOOK

William H. Forbis

JAPAN TODAY

PEOPLE, PLACES, POWER

Foreword by Senator Mike Mansfield

HARPER & ROW, PUBLISHERS
NEW YORK, EVANSTON, SAN FRANCISCO
LONDON

The line on page 4 from T. S. Eliot's *The Waste Land* is reprinted with permission from Harcourt Brace Jovanovich, Inc., and Faber & Faber, Ltd.

JAPAN TODAY: PEOPLE, PLACES, POWER. Copyright © 1975 by William H. Forbis. All rights reserved. Printed in the United States of America. No part of this book may be used or reproduced in any manner whatsoever without written permission except in the case of brief quotations embodied in critical articles and reviews. For information address Harper & Row, Publishers, Inc., 10 East 53rd Street, New York, N.Y. 10022. Published simultaneously in Canada by Fitzhenry & Whiteside Limited, Toronto.

FIRST EDITION

Designed by Sidney Feinberg

Endpaper maps by Jean Paul Tremblay

Library of Congress Cataloging in Publication Data

Forbis, William H
  Japan today.
  (A Cass Canfield book)
  Bibliography: p.
  Includes index.
  1. Japan. I. Title.
DS806.F67 1975   952.04   75–6336
ISBN 0–06–011311–1

75 76 77 78 79 10 9 8 7 6 5 4 3 2 1

Contents

Foreword

Japan continues to be a subject of compelling fascination for American journalists and scholars, not simply as an object of cultural curiosity, but because popular understanding of the Japanese phenomenon has become essential to the public support of an effective foreign policy. The rusting mementoes at Pearl Harbor and the more recent invasion of American streets by vehicles bearing the names Datsun, Toyota, Honda, or Yamaha all serve to remind us of the need to comprehend and make allowances for the forces which motivate our most extraordinary neighbor in the Pacific.

To understand and interpret such a phenomenon is not an easy task. Lafcadio Hearn, that exotic American expatriate who settled in Japan at the end of the last century, thus becoming the first of a long line of journalist-scholars to rise to the challenge, wrote in 1904 of "the immense difficulty of perceiving and comprehending what underlies the surface of Japanese life."

> No work fully interpreting that life—no work picturing Japan within and without, historically and socially, psychologically and ethically— can be written for at least another fifty years. So vast and intricate the subject that the united labour of a generation of scholars could not exhaust it, and so difficult that the number of scholars willing to devote their time to it must always be small.

Hearn could not foresee the circumstances which would compel so much attention to Japan in the half-century which followed, but his estimate of the scope of the subject was quite accurate. The generation of scholars has come and gone and done its work many times over, but the inexhaustible subject remains and renews itself, demanding continuing reexamination.

Now to the distinguished roster of journalists and scholars who have been called to the task—Edwin O. Reischauer, John Hersey, James Michener, John Gunther, to name only a few—must be added the name of my fellow Montanan, William H. Forbis. I am especially proud to be able to claim a remotely inspirational role in his work, inasmuch as he was a student in my classes in Far Eastern history at the University of Montana back in 1938. So many cataclysmic events have intervened since that time as to totally reshape the subject we then considered together, and time and circumstances have taken each of us far afield. But now we come full circle and our interests again focus on Japan and the Far East at a most timely juncture.

My most recent travels in Asia have impressed upon me the fact that a new order is at hand in that part of the world. History will probably date the beginning of this new era as the year 1972, when the United States initiated contact with the People's Republic of China. That step had the effect of releasing a whole set of pent-up forces which had been frozen for a quarter-century by that paralysis of ideology which we know as the cold war. Japan quickly followed suit in opening its doors to Peking, as did other nations of Asia, often to accompanying internal political stress; the exiled government on Taiwan became progressively isolated; new trade patterns began to emerge, and with them new prospects for a broader base of interdependence and stability.

Bill Forbis now informs us in astonishing detail of the nature of that new order within Japan itself. He describes the period of almost unbelievable economic growth through which Japan has passed during the last two decades—a period in which the gross national product increased at an annual rate two or three times that of the Western countries, while per capita income rose from $17 to $3,400 and trade volume swelled from $7 billion in 1964 to $38 billion in 1973.

Now that the economic miracle has been achieved, Japan is at a crucial turning point. The Japanese are surveying the social costs of success, which include, most notably, some of the world's worst industrial pollution of air and water. There is a growing sense, Forbis tells us, that the boom time may be about spent; that the sources of the miracle—cheap raw materials, cheap labor, easy access to foreign technology—are diminishing; and that the spirit of national dedication to economic growth as a positive goal is being critically reexamined.

Out of all this could come yet another phenomenon, Forbis suggests: a society which is deliberately planning for itself a "post-industrial" future avoiding many of the snares that entrap the rest of the world. Japan alone among the major industrial states has so far rejected the temptation of costly nuclear armaments, substituting the positive promise of economic gain in lieu of negative deterrence by military threat. And the measure of future progress might well become "net national welfare" rather than gross national product, with industries increasingly diverting to "knowledge-intensive" electronic and computerized services in health, transportation, and banking, as well as in pollution control. If it all should come to pass, Japan may well be showing the rest of the world not only how to survive the twentieth century but how to prepare for the twenty-first. America might profit from watching closely.

Bill Forbis has managed to give us a remarkably interesting and readable account of the current Japanese phenomenon. No part of the contemporary scene escapes his trained journalistic eye, and he tells the story not with graphs and charts and statistics but by a lively narrative account of the sights and sounds and smells of Japanese life. He has grasped the whole of what Lafcadio Hearn described as a "vast and intricate subject" and done it great justice.

MIKE MANSFIELD
Majority Leader
United States Senate

PART ONE   *People*

1/

Japan: Its Strength and Tang

For THIRTY YEARS now, the world has been hearing—without widely comprehending—the rumble of great cultural, social, and economic explosions in modern Japan. Suddenly the Westerner becomes aware that Japan has more universities than all of Western Europe: soon half of Japanese youth will be able to get a higher education. Equally suddenly, the world begins to see Japanese everywhere: proportionally to population, they have become the globe's most assiduous travelers. In the process of vastly improving the quality and quantity of their food and health care, the Japanese, who three decades ago died at fifty, have joined the Scandinavians as the world's longest-lived people. In a cadenced *boom-boom-boom* of other explosions, the Japanese have acquired the world's fastest railroad, put together the world's largest steel company, and become the builders of not only the world's biggest and most modern ships but also the great majority of *all* ships. Japanese automakers whose names the world scarcely knew in the mid-1960s have since then surpassed all others except the two biggest American companies. The only explosions that Japan conspicuously lacks are—blessedly—a population explosion and a military explosion.

As a sort of cumulative *boom* to all the other *booms*, Japan has advanced from a war-end standard of living not much above that of Andean Indians to its affluence of today, which measures ahead of most of Europe, and not far short of the United States. From their thin strand of islands, $\frac{1}{360}$ of the world's land area, a country without any major natural resources, the industrious and intelligent Japanese, comprising only $\frac{1}{36}$ of the world's population, produce

3

goods in quantities surpassed only by two giant nations, the United States and the Soviet Union. In 1975, Japan's gross national product is approaching half a trillion dollars a year, more than one-third that of the United States, and two-thirds of Russia's.

Yet if what is new in Japan is astonishing, what is old contains even greater wonders and marvels. At some quiet, still, central place in the Japanese psyche, the people of Japan hold, without concession, to esthetics, ideals, and societal bonds unchanged in twenty centuries. More than any other nation of the East, Japan has adopted, adapted, co-opted, or even stolen the best of the West. But also more than any other nation of the East, Japan has remained itself. The Japanese do not admit the West is best. Japan is ineluctably and intractably alien, not in the sense of hostile but in the sense of different. Persia, Greece, and Egypt cling only to shards of their old distinctive styles, "fragments . . . shored against my ruins," in T. S. Eliot's phrase. In their inner hearts, these nations have conceded the failure of their old cultures. China has embraced the political philosophy of the German Karl Marx; India seems chiefly embarrassed by its traditions, from sacred cows to erotic art, as it tries to industrialize and become a "modern" nation. But Japan, while shopping the Western supermarket for technology and comfort, has resolutely refused to let the importations displace the tough, calm core of Japanese tradition. At some final point the Japanese are incorruptible—undismayed, and even unimpressed, by the arrogance of Western materialism. Japan has confidence that its past is valid in the present.

Understandably, the Japanese take a bursting pride in their latter-day accomplishments—what other nation ever achieved so much so fast? But those accomplishments accomplished, the Japanese are beginning to see that they can make a better mix of past and present. For one thing, growth at such recent rates as double every four years leads to the absurd: in theory the economy would grow 1,024-fold in forty years. No Japanese wants that, and none expects it. And so it is that in the middle of the 1970s, while everyone else is still trying to ingest and comprehend the already accomplished Japanese miracle, Japan is busy devising what may turn out to be an equally astonishing new miracle, a truly better way of life. Since the body will have been given its due in material well-being, the stress will be on the mind and spirit. More emphasis on the arts and art appreciation. Universal higher education, probably. In expanded leisure time, a new cultivation of great ancient traditions. And, in the economy, a "postindustrial," "technetronic" utilization and export of brainwork instead of hardware.

As the world moves into the latter 1970s, increasingly short of food and energy, vulnerable to brush-fire wars that could turn into conflagrations, such goals may be beyond the reach of the Japanese or any other people. In 1974–75 the Japanese saw their economic growth touch zero for the first time since World War II, which was more than the proponents of slower growth had bargained for; luckily, it soon turned up again. Recession in the United States and Europe inevitably hurt Japan to some degree (although even in adversity Japan managed to increase exports to record highs—cars by 47 percent, ships 54 percent, steel 99 percent). Quadrupled oil prices in a nation that gets virtually all of its oil abroad contributed to the world's highest burst of inflation among industrial countries, and it took an inflexible tight-money policy to bring prices back under control. In sum, hazards abound, and Japan could suffer seriously.

But it is always worth remembering that the Japanese, 111 million of them living 800 to the square mile (as compared to 64 in the United States), have an unmatchable combination of qualifications for carrying out their goals—not to mention an unexcelled track record of achieving goals in the past. Taken one by one, they are ordinary people, with ordinary failings; there are few individuals of flair or brilliance. It is as a totality that the Japanese excel. Their collective characteristics—diligence, thrift, courage, unity—add up to more than the sum of the parts. At work they are steady, intelligent, and loyal.

"Japanese energy is like a typhoon," says the sociologist Chie Nakane. Workers and employers are basically collaborators rather than adversaries. Even school-age children work hard, sometimes to the point of suicide; high school students do three hours of homework a day, as part of the formidable education system. The Japanese also save prodigiously, 17 percent of disposable income, as compared to 7.5 percent in Great Britain and 5.7 percent in the United States. Via banks that are not afraid to take risks, these savings go directly into productive machinery and other capital goods. And the Japanese are remarkably persistent and dutiful—witness the Japanese soldier who fought on alone in the Philippine jungles for thirty years after World War II because he never got the word to surrender. Finally, the Japanese share with the Communist Russians and Chinese the concept of placing the group ahead of the individual (rather a shock for American, French, or British individualists).

It is one of the extraordinary facts of postwar Japan that a conservative government in a capitalist society devised the unique (and uniquely powerful) planning institution known as MITI (Ministry of International Trade and Industry), which has drastically reshaped Japan. It abolished some industries and established others, directed what companies should put their plants where, ordered up docks where there were none and scrapped others. In short, it turned Japan into an advanced industrial nation, with a peculiarly Japanese orchestration of government, business, and labor in a great national effort that the people typically accepted without a murmur of protest. For Japanese conformity is not static; it is conformity to change. "When people are unanimously changing in the same direction, opposition to change is failure to conform," explains one Tokyo University political scientist. The result is a society with low crime and divorce rates, few slums, near-absence of racial divisions, and full employment.

As Northwest Orient's Flight 7 taxis out to the runway in Seattle every day at 2:05 P.M., the pilot announces, "If you'd like to set your watch, the time in Tokyo is now five after six tomorrow morning." For hour after sunny hour—nearly ten of them altogether—the jumbo jet flies westward. At the date line, a day disappears from your life, a pawn that you can redeem when you fly east again. You touch down at Haneda Airport at 3:40 in the afternoon, Tokyo time. At the exit of the terminal, a cab rolls up and, just as you reach out to open the door, it springs open by itself, a little touch of Japanese automation. As you drive to the city, first impressions of Japan pour over you in waves.

What is Japan? During your first days there, your eye and your ear force you to begin by asking whether it is the farthest west of the Western powers or the farthest east of the Eastern cultures. At the post office in exotic Kyoto, the man at the window weighs your letter to a snatch of tune from an old American pop song ("I wore a big red rose") on the Muzak. More Western than the West! But the most visible inscriptions on every hand are the Chinese ideographs in signs and other advertising. Ah yes, you remember, Japan is the cultural daughter of China—took over Chinese writing, for example, in one fast swallow. Just a lazy borrower, that's Japan. An imitator, as Americans tirelessly charge. But further thoughts and observations begin to intrude on this pat conclusion. Japan, you recall, refused to borrow Western religion on any great scale, or Western philosophy, or psychotherapy. And for all her borrowing from ancient China (Buddhism, coinage, art styles), Japan is utterly unlike China. Many of the most Oriental-seeming trappings of

Japan's culture—sliding paper walls, incessant hot baths, the taste for raw fish, the Shinto religion—descend from nowhere else but ancient Japan.

And as for borrowing, who hasn't? Rome from Greece, northern Europe from the Mediterranean, America from Europe. The whole world is in debt to China for paper, printing, the wheelbarrow, canal locks, the sternpost rudder, the compass, gunpowder, and porcelain. Thus Japan is indeed a bicultural borrower, the world's first and only Eastern-Western nation. But the components mingle unschizophrenically, both because borrowing is not an unnatural process and because the Japanese have the racial unity to absorb it without strain. By virtue of Japanese adaptivity, the country will probably continue to borrow a great deal more without losing its uniqueness. Kentucky Fried Chicken will not drive raw fish from the Japanese diet, nor will blue jeans obliterate the kimono. I came to believe that Japan is an infinitely replenishable vessel, into which unending amounts of both Eastern and Western culture can be poured without either displacing the other.

So, back to the question: What is Japan? To begin with, it is the colossus of Asia, producing more than the entire rest of the continent, including China, put together. As a trading power, it is second only to the United States in global impact. It is the world's most integrated nation-family, not a collectivity of individuals but a homogeneous identity transcending time and space, as is significantly symbolized by its emperor, Hirohito, the 124th in an unbroken line. It is Asia's best-working constitutional democracy. It mass-educates its youth more thoroughly than any nation but the United States. With the world's largest public television system, amplified by five private systems, Japan provides the most varied, informative, and educational TV on earth. Its Nippon Steel Corporation, the world's largest steel company, supplied all the structural steel in New York City's World Trade Center and all the pipe for the Alaska pipeline. And Japan has what are beyond dispute the world's prettiest and most intricate barber poles.

Japan is an archipelago of four main islands and thousands of smaller ones. Of the main islands, arc-shaped Honshu, centered on Tokyo and the home of four-fifths of the Japanese people, is nearly twice as big as the others taken together. Next in significance, though far less important, comes Kyushu, separated from Honshu's western headlands by a strait no wider than the length of a tanker. In similar propinquity, the island of Hokkaido nearly touches the northern cape of Honshu, and its northerliness gives it some snowy distinction in a nation where the land is almost as homogeneous as the people. The fourth island, little Shikoku, nestles under western Honshu and thus serves to enclose the scenic and tranquil waters known as the Inland Sea.

The Japanese archipelago is four-fifths mountains and one-fifth alluvial plain, but, mountain or plain, the hand of man has groomed almost all of it during the passage of twenty centuries. Rice paddies, leveled and terraced, fill the lowlands; straight-rowed tree farms clothe the knobby mountains. Its temperate climate, its plentiful rain, and its carefully tended vegetation make the archipelago into an abundance of emerald islands, a uniquely lovely part of the earth. Many are man's ugly scars on this landscape, but the doom criers' much-heard wails over Japan's lost natural beauty sound like the reports of observers who never got beyond the Tokaido corridor, the industrial belt between Tokyo and Osaka.

Though Japan is overpopulated (in terms of congestion and ability to feed itself), most people live in cities of fewer than 1 million population. Only four cities—Tokyo, Yokohama, Osaka, and Nagoya, all on Honshu—contain more than 2 million. Tokyo, stately in places and slatternly in others, forms the most populous metropolitan area in the world, with 11.6 million people. Sophisticated, pleasure-loving, bustling, and the site of 102 universities, it draws young men and women from the hinterlands in droves. Yokohama is Tokyo's port; Osaka and Nagoya are, roughly, Chicago and Detroit. Japan's true second city, however, distinguished by age, temples, gardens, and a Florentine air, is Kyoto, population 1,450,000, two and three-quarters hours on the bullet train west from Tokyo. Modeled on the ancient Chinese city of Ch'ang-an, and capital of Japan until a century ago, Kyoto has had eleven hundred years to accumulate its beauties, and many a prince and emperor and shogun to patronize the arts. Kyoto has foundries for temple bells, doll-making shops, an ineffable Garden of Nothingness. It also has a thriving McDonald's hamburger stand.

The lesser main islands, though they grow rice and run factories just like Honshu, are inevitably mere provinces that stand in some awe of Honshu's size and economic power. Northerly Hokkaido, not really settled until a century ago, reveals by its cowboys and its land-grant-style university the influence of the Americans who were imported to help with the colonization. Little Shikoku takes stout pride in the fact that of its youngsters who go off to get jobs in Tokyo, many choose to return. Kyushu prizes Nagasaki, a Japanese

Naples or San Francisco, where Madame Butterfly would have lived, had there ever been a Madame Butterfly. And, below the horizon, there's Okinawa, the forty-seventh prefecture of Japan since the United States returned it in 1972, but still the site of the biggest American military base in the Far East, and hence of an unhappy American-Japanese relationship.

Japan is tied to Asia, but not of it. Its islands are actually the summits of a mighty mountain range that lies off the edge of the Asian alluvial lands. And so the Japanese have always been a moated people protected by the sea, relatively immune from invaders of other races or characters or colors. As a result, no other major nation has such a homogeneity of face, skin, and hair color. From this flows the Japanese sense of nationhood and unity—and perhaps also the sense that any individual's first loyalty is to his nation, not to his individual welfare. When Japan has imported ideas or styles, it has done so as a nation, not as individuals introducing independently some eccentric idea from abroad. And since isolation has spared Japan from invasion, it has also resulted in a pride in the nation's long, uninterrupted history, and produced a singular culture.

For something over two thousand years, an emperor or an empress belonging to the same family as Hirohito has ruled or reigned over Japan. Beginning in the twelfth century, however, a series of military shoguns (which at first was just another name for "general") seized and exercised real power, in the name of the emperor. The dynasty that left the most definitive print on Japan was the shogunate of the Tokugawa family, who, governing from 1603 to 1867, sealed Japan off from the rest of the world. This was a gesture unique in world history—a gesture of a nation that felt so complete in itself that it wanted no outside advice or advantage, a gesture stemming from a confidence that it knew all it needed to know and from a fear that whatever intruded would upset its order and its peace. This declaration of self-content shaped much of the unique integrity that maintains and informs Japanese society today.

Because it is such a tidy historic fulcrum, the Tokugawa period provides a point in time from which the Westerner can study what went before and what followed. And what went before is singularly unknown outside Japan, probably because only once did an event affect the course of world history. Toward the end of the thirteenth century, Kublai Khan, leader of the Mongol Empire that stretched from Korea to Poland, tried to invade Japan and met defeat from samurai swords, marking the end of the long expansion of the khanate of the Golden Horde. Thus it is that Japan was never a colony or (with some exceptions in the past century) a colonizer, and this is a source of the country's historic sense of pride and distinction. In fact, not until the 1540s did any Westerner lay eyes upon Japan. Even then, the only notable visitor was St. Francis Xavier, who in a report to his Jesuit superiors wrote: "The people whom we have met so far are the best who have as yet been discovered, and it seems to me that we shall never find among heathens another race to equal the Japanese."

But though Japan's early history sometimes seems to be almost a private matter among the Japanese, it was the brilliant formative stage of a civilization and of values still held high. The populators of Japan were central Asian Mongoloids who reached Kyushu via China, but even as they were spreading into Honshu and Shikoku, they were already sending emissaries back to China to borrow the best features of that old land's arts, religion, and government. This flow of culture continued from just after the time of Christ until the ninth century. Particularly under the sensitive and learned Prince Shotoku (574–622), Chinese-style Buddhism and Chinese Confucianism came to dominate (but not displace) Japan's native, primitive, spirit-worshiping Shintoism. Japanese artists learned those deft Chinese brush strokes that tell more in a landscape by what they omit than by what they depict. Via China, Japan got the tiger—not the animal itself, but the alluring concept of a ferocious beast, which endures today in temple paintings and in avidly attended tiger-dance festivals in small towns. At the end of this long borrowing period came a time of altering, elaborating, and Japanizing the Chinese influences. From this evolved the unique Japanese tea ceremony, the tatami straw floor mat, the romantic novel, the two-sworded samurai, and a European-like feudalism that prevailed through the Tokugawa period.

When the Tokugawas slammed shut Japan's doors to the world in 1639, their motive was to perpetuate a stable society unaffected by the winds of change from the rest of the world. From the highest rank of society, the lords and the samurai, down through the farmers and the artisans to the lowest class, the merchants, men were to keep their place and do their duty. In point of fact, as the centuries passed, society slowly changed, developing commerce and the arts (the Kabuki theater, for example) and often enjoying itself in the process (with the geisha, for example). Finally, in 1853, a firm-willed American sailor from Rhode Island and a painted Japanese princeling from Kyoto came into conjunction to revolutionize Japan.

Commodore Matthew Calbraith Perry, steaming into Tokyo Bay,

coolly opened the doors to Japan and forced the shogunate to accept the establishment of an American consulate. Nobody consulted the incumbent emperor, secluded in remote Kyoto, and Perry never even discovered the existence of the future Emperor Meiji, a baby eight months old when the commodore arrived. But this prince needed only fourteen years of growing up to be ready to give his name to the nation-shaking Meiji Restoration, which, beginning in 1868, reasserted the primacy of the imperial family, abolished the Tokugawa shogunate, reversed its seclusionist policy, and committed Japan to a course of modernization by openly embracing the whole world. Moving to Edo, the seat of the shoguns, the emperor renamed it Tokyo and made it his capital. His ministers sent missions to Europe and the United States to bring back knowledge of Western medicine, banking, government, railroads, and electric power.

One Western practice that the Japanese caught on to quickly was war and foreign conquest: by 1905, having sunk the Russian fleet in the strait between Japan and Korea, Japan ruled or controlled Taiwan, Korea, and northern China's Liaotung Peninsula. Such success for her arms prefigured Japan's conquest of Manchuria in 1931, the invasion of the rest of China in 1937, and the disastrously miscalculated decision to bomb Pearl Harbor in 1941, leading to the war in the Pacific that left Japan the most thoroughly bomb-destroyed of any of the combatant nations. Many Japanese liked to believe, incidentally, that the war was really waged on behalf of all yellow Asians against the oppression of white Westerners, and in point of fact Japan's effort led to the collapse of colonialism in Indonesia, Malaya and Singapore, the Philippines, Burma, and ultimately in Indochina (Cambodia, Laos, and Vietnam).

This many-centuried story demonstrates a singular characteristic of the Japanese: U-turn history. Japan rushes to borrow from China, then abruptly turns off on China; Japan isolates itself from the world, then suddenly takes the world for its model. Such switches arise from a candid recognition that an old policy no longer works. Thus, after World War II, Japan readily abandoned totalitarian government, military forces, nationalistic education, and emperor worship—all factors in what had gone wrong. The American Occupation authorities wrote (audaciously starting out with "We, the Japanese people") a democratic constitution that the Japanese live by to this day. And the merchant, the businessman, was resurrected from a thousand years of disrepute and put in charge of rebuilding the country.

Taking a course nearly opposite to China's under the Marxist Mao Tse-tung, Japan proposed to advance to prosperity under "guided capitalism." The motto was "GNP First." Japan, lacking iron ore, coking coal, petroleum, and bauxite, would nevertheless become a workshop producing nearly everything. Japan would import raw materials and, to pay for them, export finished goods, earning its living from the value added by Japanese fabrication. Everyone knew that Japan had silkworms but not sheep; Japanese tycoons dispassionately concluded that silk was noncompetitive with synthetics, and, importing Australian fleece, turned Japan into one of the world's major weavers of woolens. The United States, shifting under cold-war pressures away from Secretary of State James Byrnes's vindictive 1946 proposal to leave Japan impoverished for forty years, undertook to supply raw cotton and soybeans and to buy Japanese textiles and radios. By the early 1960s, thanks mainly to the productivity of the Japanese people, growth in GNP was hitting as much as 15 percent a year, while other major countries averaged 5 percent.

By the early 1970s it was becoming evident that the Japanese had overproved themselves. Japan had moved so fast and aggressively into other peoples' markets that even the Japanese could see the need for slowdown and less disruption. Worse, industrial pollution in Japan began to kill people by the hundreds and make others into permanent invalids—even cats were to be seen dancing a tottery gavotte suggestive of the incurable "Minamata disease" caused by mercury poisoning. The huge Japanese consumer society had more color television sets (70 percent of all households) than Americans (58 percent), but its values were plainly out of kilter. The country set out upon an "introspection boom" that is still going on, in search of a better cultural-economic balance.

The economic great leap forward dominates the story of Japan since the war, but Japan is not turning into a California. One of my most vivid memories is of an eerie night in Nagasaki, where on a dim little street two dozen breechclouted young men—by day clerks and shipyard workers—were practicing for some forthcoming festival. Shouting, stamping, belligerent, they wheeled this way and that, bouncing a heavy wooden palanquin that contained young costumed boys beating the drum that provided the rhythm for the dancer-bearers. Such festivals go on all over Japan, carried out with zest and a deep respect for myth and legend. Japan is still, and always will be, an exotic country. The devotees of Shinto can see a spirit in a stone, and after a few months of residence a Westerner begins to see a spirit in a stone—for the simple reason that there *is* a spirit in a stone. Japan has, and always will have, Fujiyama, exquisite calligraphy, moon viewings, chopsticks, virgin priestesses, gargantuan sumo wrestlers, begging monks, sake, polished cedar, chrysanthemums, soy sauce, plum blossoms, and hara-kiri.

"Japan," the word, derives from the Chinese pronunciation, *Jih-pen,* of the characters (common to both languages) that in Japanese come out as *Nihon* or *Nippon.* The first connotes warmth, homeyness, and softness; the second connotes size, importance, and prestige. Nippon was the preferred term in the Meiji era and during the militaristic 1920s and 1930s; Nihon came in as part of the postwar U-turn. Now, as a glance through a business directory shows (Nippon Steel, Nippon Oil), Nippon is coming back. If Nippon's connotation of importance means belligerence—as we shall discover if Japan builds nuclear weapons, or surpasses the present 1-percent-of-GNP limit on arms spending, or sends troops beyond its borders— the world may have cause for worry. But that is unlikely. Says Robert Guillain, the veteran Tokyo correspondent of *Le Monde*: "Japan knows far better than we do that from now on war is unthinkable unless we want civilization to vanish." So the probability is that Nippon's importance will be expressed as the strength of stability, as postindustrial power, as exports of brains, technology— and Japanese tourists. For thirty years, as it grew in importance, Japan has astonished the world by the focused energy of its able people. For thirty more, as its importance increases in new directions, it should provide an irresistible drama.

Does the world have something to learn from those tireless imitators, the Japanese? In many ways—art and architecture, cuisine, Zen, business organization, social cohesion, the martial sports, theatrical technique—the world can learn, or is already learning. Much else may be too tightly locked within the unsharing Japanese mentality to be learned. But even if that is true, Japan still remains to be cherished as adding tang and the excitement of the exotic in an averaged world. It is the single rival culture to the West that seems both totally different and totally viable.

2 /

A Not-Too-Inscrutable Race

"IT SEEMS I'll never understand Japan," an American friend of mine who lives in Tokyo wrote not long ago. "But that's okay, I suppose," he added jovially. "Being inscrutable isn't the worst thing in the world." My own conclusion, after traveling the length of the country, conversing with hundreds of people, and peering into innumerable faces on street and subway, was that at bottom the Japanese are scrutable enough—they bleed when pricked and laugh when tickled—but nonetheless are quite sufficiently complex and distinct to merit my friend's furrowed brow. It is how traits common to all humanity are stressed and paired in Japan—how kindness coexists with brutality, silence with communication, emotion with logic—that makes the Japanese different from any other nationality or ethnic group, including the Nisei Japanese of the United States and Brazil.

The characteristic of the Japanese that lies under all the other national traits is the submission of the individual to the society. Nobody wants to stand out. The need to make heroes or to be heroes is not strong. Statues of ancient worthies are nearly nonexistent. Charisma is considered *outré*, even rather vulgar. Politicians, golf champions, actors, crime-gang leaders, and businessmen can all win recognition, but not adulation. I asked a history-minded writer to name Japan's greatest heroes, and he hesitantly offered just one: the Buddhist monk Kobo, the ninth-century "Great Teacher" who was poet, calligrapher, artist, and religious leader all at once.

Japan lacks Churchills, Gandhis, Lincolns, Lindberghs, Mao Tsetungs, Bonnies and Clydes. Few Japanese have ever achieved world

14

fame or attempted lonely excellence. The Japanese have never fought for their own freedom or anybody else's. Instead, a Japanese aspires to achieve importance only as he contributes to—or sacrifices for—his nation and his race.

The root of this attitude is a natural and unconscious conviction that Japan is a unique nation-family, a concept that in turn comes from the country's racial homogeneity and isolated geography. Japan has no shared borders, no common frontiers with any neighbors. Other nations may be melting pots, but from Hokkaido to Kyushu the Japanese derive from more or less the same sets of genes. Regionalism is feeble; there's no Wales or Scotland in these isles, no areas where one cannot be understood speaking standard Japanese. Among other assets, this soaked-in Japaneseness spares the country, at least when not under pressure for survival, of any need for rampant jingoism. Other lands, less sure of their identities, may feel required constantly to whip up patriotism; Japan, confident of being a true nation (and having long since recovered from prewar chauvinism), scorns such action.

The measuring of a man's actions against the needs of the nation-family rather than his individual conscience brings with it a whole train of corollaries. The one that Westerners most persistently note—first widely publicized by Ruth Benedict in her 1946 book *The Sword and the Chrysanthemum*—is that in Japan a sinner feels shame, brought on by the judgment of society, rather than guilt, inflicted by his own conscience. Carried to the extreme, Benedict argues, this implies that to a Japanese a crime is wrong only if society catches the culprit in the act. Japanese scholars tend to agree with Benedict's observations, although the psychiatrist Takeo Doi takes two exceptions: that shame should not be thought to be less worthy than guilt, as Benedict implies, and that the Japanese do indeed feel guilty when they perform an act that betrays society as a whole.

One way of betraying society, I suppose, would be laziness, and the Japanese, as the world has learned in awe, are what have been dubbed "workaholics." The Japanese face holidays, says a Tokyo newspaper editor, as "a time of life to be enjoyed at breakneck speed."

A subtle point here is that the Japanese yearn to be best in a nonrelative way—not to be better than some other nation, but simply to be at the top. Father Maurice Bairy, a Jesuit who teaches at Sophia University in Tokyo, contends that Japanese psychology is centered on the notion that higher is always better, originating in the fact that life itself comes from above, in the form of sun and rain, and expressed in reverence for heights, particularly Mount Fuji, and in wearing elevated wooden clogs. By inversion, the custom of bowing expresses a polite effort to make a respected person taller relative to oneself.

Such obsessive energy and solemn aspirations make the Japanese a serious people. There's hardly a smidgen of just-for-the-hell-of-it in the whole country. Laughing at a person to his face is virtually forbidden, because to ridicule a person is to shame him. But seriousness at work does not have to stand in the way of fun elsewhere. There's lots of gaiety and laughter—often silly, tittery laughter, over puns, or mimicry of absent acquaintances, or merely over a snootful of sake —in the bars and restaurants.

The fit between the individual and the society is mostly a good one, and the sense of pleasing society, of having a place in it, seems to provide satisfaction. The Japanese take a warming joy in the beautiful children of their nation-family. A mother I knew who frequently carried her baby son on her back in trains and elevators told me that the child was constantly getting gifts of candy and toys from kind people that she could not even see. Similarly, the Japanese get a great deal of uncomplicated pleasure out of festivals, shopping, zoos, fireworks, amusement parks. The secret of the uniquely Japanese Morita school of psychotherapy-by-isolation is that, rather than "freeing" the ego of the patient, it deprives him of society for a while and then lets him get back happily into the relationships that sustain him. A successfully treated Japanese psychiatric patient will perhaps say, "I am pleasing my father better now."

The submission of the individual to society, however, requires an uncomfortably heavy stress on authority. "In courtesy and submission to their superiors, few nations can be compared to them," wrote a German doctor who visited Japan in the early 1800s, and the observation still goes. Mothers make children obedient by threatening that bad behavior "will make people laugh at you," or—very commonly—by threatening to call a policeman. The psychologist Hiroshi Minami contends that this threat ultimately creates an excessive awe of government officials and a proneness in anyone accused of wrongdoing to bow and apologize rather than put up a defense.

Tough school entrance examinations further regiment the Japanese, and the slow process of learning the thousands of complex Chinese characters in the Japanese written language firmly implants the image of the teacher as an authority whom the student must accept if he is to receive vital knowledge. After graduation, the hierarchical structure of Japanese business provides a similar discipline. This all produces the kind of people who stand waiting for traffic lights to turn green even on deserted streets late on rainy nights. The government's Administrative Management Agency has put forth (though so far unsuccessfully) an individuality-destroying proposal to allocate to each citizen a fourteen-digit computer code number that would reveal his birth date, income tax, criminal record, and venereal diseases, if any. Authoritative admonitions fill the air in Japan, such as the tape-recorded Big Sister voices in buses that endlessly prohibit smoking and other misdemeanors.

Still, Japan is not a nation squelched and suppressed. Most people respect their bosses and obey them, but do not stand in awe of them. The Japanese bow, but don't scrape. Twice, after interpreted interviews with VIPs, I fell into conversation with the translators, who proceeded to explain in detail how they disagreed with what the boss had told me.

Japan has never had a revolution like the French or American or Russian or Chinese revolutions, and the reason, again, lies in the relation of the individual to society. "The Japanese are nonrevolutionary because they care so much about society and harmony," one professor told me. The Tokyo University sociologist Chie Nakane holds that individuals never give up faith that society will ultimately let them rise a step or two, and therefore do not share the desperation of the true revolutionary. A television producer surmised that Japanese homogeneity also plays a significant role in suppressing revolution, because even the rich and powerful, however oppressive, remain an accepted part of the "Japanese family." For Japan, evolution is good enough. University students often rage and battle against the system, but this rebellion is followed by a phenomenon so consistent that the Japanese have a word for it: *tenko*, a 180-degree reversal in which the rebel after graduation ardently embraces the whole Establishment that he has been violently fighting.

Defining how a man should act by what society demands of him requires a code of ethics that can cover many different situations. The Japanese code resembles the "situation ethics" preached by certain Western moralists, in which the specific factors of a given plight, rather than a few universal principles, determine the individual's actions. But it differs in that the individual is expected to follow the exact rules for the situation and cannot make up his own rules depending on the factors. Since it is impossible to write rules for every conceivable human situation, the Japanese are often left without the guidance that a universal standard would provide.

In actuality, the rules resulting from Japanese situation ethics are broadly like the rules elsewhere: thou shalt not kill, steal, swindle, commit adultery, and so on. It is the specifics that are intriguing. An example is resistance to the concept of contracts, which are "a really bad idea," according to a thoughtful young company executive I met in Kure. "A contract smacks too much of a crude deal—this for that, eliminating all human values." Japanese businessmen regularly make written contracts, as elsewhere, but they are more ready to drop or change them without compunction if conditions change. Taking contracts lightly seems to cut down, rather than heighten, petty squabbling. "There are only sixteen thousand lawyers in Japan," a rich businessman told me. "We get along and don't need to fight over every little point." In routine money matters, cash purchases and the like, Japan's social contract works out as unvarying honesty: one never needs to count the change, and foreigners need not fear that they are paying more than the Japanese.

Human values again rule the questions of debt and obligation—a touchy issue in both Japan's society and economy. Lifelong debts are those owed to revered parents, teachers, and benefactors, with endless repayment due. Lesser debts arise from the Japanese compulsion for gift giving. Even on such routine occasions as social visits, the guest presents the hostess with a gift, and the hostess must later reciprocate with a return gift of exactly gauged value; "thank you" is not enough. Imbued with the notion that gifts repay obligations, the Japanese are notoriously unwilling to give altruistically; big corporations are just beginning to make philanthropic gifts to colleges and other institutions, and then mostly for public-relations purposes.

Other clauses in the code of ethics control the peculiar responsibilities of leaders and the vast field of behavior that concerns itself with apologies. A while back, some Japanese volleyball players who had won gold medals at the Munich Olympics committed several minor infractions of the rules of amateurism. These acts promptly produced the resignations not of the players but of two top officials of the Japan Volleyball Association. In the Japanese code, the leader has to take the blame for the wrongdoing, errors, or even small missteps of people over whom he has charge. Regularly, the heads of large corporations resign solely because they accept the blame; almost always, the leader's confession of insufficient attentiveness compensates for whatever went wrong, even something so serious as a bad train wreck. Those who resign seem happy to do so. Loss of honor comes only from failure to perform this duty of the individual to the society.

When resignation would be too drastic, apologies will serve. After a deranged youth stabbed U.S. Ambassador Edwin Reischauer in 1964, Prime Minister Hayato Ikeda took advantage of the first television transmission by satellite from Japan to the United States to make apologies to the American people. A year or so ago, a movie-making company, having been caught "inconveniencing visitors" by filming nude scenes in a national park, humbly apologized to the government's Environment Agency.

In several interesting and specific ways, the Japanese concept of the individual in society answers a disturbing but important question: How did the traditionally humane and sensitive Japanese turn themselves in the 1930s and 1940s into the "Japs" who tossed Chinese babies into the air and caught them on bayonets, brutalized Bataan death marchers, hurled themselves at Allied ships in Kamikaze planes, and sacrificed three million of their own lives? And would they do it again?

They would, to answer the second question first, and to answer it in psychological rather than political terms. I asked many Japanese about this balance of benignity and ferocity, hoping, I suppose, to hear that the war had removed belligerence from the national character. The respondents stressed that no hero-size individual is likely to rise up and take Japan to war, but the decision for war could be made precisely because no heroic individual would come forth to take charge of stopping it, especially if (as before Pearl Harbor) the Japanese felt that things had come to an unbearable state.

As for brutality, the Japanese have no monopoly on it, because war itself is brutalizing, but they do have some traits that tend to heighten it. To begin with, the ingrained national habit of obedience can make masses of men unquestioningly commit atrocities on orders from a few cold-blooded or even irrational officers. And although society in peacetime Japan provides a "web" relationship of behavior that holds down violence, when the constraint is off in battle on some foreign shore—when the soldier gets into a situation for which there is no specific ethic—the animalistic barbarity that resides in every man can come out. The Japanese also fight all the harder because of the shame that cowardice or surrender causes in the eyes of society. They were cruel to prisoners of war partly because they were contemptuous of them for *being* prisoners.

Moreover, the Shinto tradition makes dying for the country not merely honorable but sometimes positively attractive, while Buddhism supplies a sense of inevitability and an understanding of the underlying harmony of contradictions (a man may be good and bad, sensitive and brutal, at the same time). This creates a hara-kiri mentality, lessening the trauma of death, which helps explain the joyful Kamikaze. Seen another way, diminishing the importance of the individual diminishes the importance of his death, even in his own eyes. A corollary of this attitude toward death is the Japanese soldier's saving conviction that wounds do not hurt beyond a man's capacity to bear pain. Finally, the homogeneous Japanese may have a particular sense that their victims are lesser people, and don't really count.

Not only are the Japanese determined to make their society work, at the cost of individuality, but they are also determined to make it work despite the friction of living in an overcrowded land. Friction seems to be the imperative behind that celebrated Japanese idiosyncrasy, the blank fixed smile, the smile that hides emotions by making its wearer seem permanently pleased, the smile too toothy to be stoic, though stoicism may lie behind it. Disturbing and even tragic news is often delivered with a smile, even when the person most affected is the smiler, announcing, perhaps, that his wife has just died. Chattering schoolgirls smile, bill collectors smile, waiters and waitresses smile, businessmen smile. A scene that repeats itself endlessly is this: girl scurries toward waiting train; train door closes in her face; girl smiles radiantly, as though to say, "How funny and delightful to have missed the train!"

The correct and tireless Japanese bow is another obligatory civility, serving for both greetings and departures. No mere inclination of the head will do: the Japanese bow is performed on the axis of the hips, with carefully graduated angles, running from five degrees to thirty, depending on what one Japanese describes as "mutually recognized inequality." No single bow will do, either: two or three is the minimum, and particularly on farewells people will back away bowing alternately like automatons, each trying to get in the last bow. Usually each opening amenity in a conversation ("How nice of you to have invited me!" "How nice of you to have come!") is accompanied by a bow. Men bow with hands at sides and arms rigid; women place their palms on their thighs. The Japanese bow is essentially stiff and formal, but it has some interesting varieties: the unison bow, in which six executives from Firm A face six from Firm B, and flex together as though choreographed; the over-the-shoulder bow, in which two ladies walking away from one another repeatedly half-turn and kowtow; and the telephone bow, when the participants bow with each spoken *arigato* (thank you) even though they cannot see one another. Once, as a bus moved away from a stop,

I saw a woman passenger standing near a window bow repeatedly in farewell to another woman, also bowing, on the sidewalk. Another time the driver of a car in which I was riding let two little girls scamper across the street in front of him; when they reached the curb they turned and bowed to him. Do the Japanese, then, also greet one another by shaking hands, as they do with Westerners? Yes, they frequently do, even while simultaneously bowing.

And do the Japanese really hiss, as they are shown to do in movies and television shows? The answer to that question, too, is yes. Sucking in the breath between clenched teeth is both a way of being obsequious to important people and a prologue, embarrassed and yet eloquent, to refusing to do some requested favor. The smile and the bow and the hiss are fundamentals of the famous Japanese politeness, so charmingly colored with sensitivity and consideration. An Englishman whom I met went with much trepidation to a Tokyo police station on summons for numerous and flagrant parking violations; the cops, before collecting the fines, courteously seated him and gave him a cup of tea.

Without disparaging either smiling or courtesy, we can justifiably examine the motivations for both. Chie Nakane traces the facial expressions, postures, involuted phraseology, and "extremely sensitive manners" of the Japanese to the "high degree of involvement in interpersonal relationships." Thus, she says, "ambiguity of expression . . . is used to avoid confrontation, for self-defense and to conceal hostility. The flattery, the insinuation and the smile are used to gain advantage, while at the same time they conceal the precise nature of desire or feeling."

The use of the smile to conceal hints that there is much to conceal. Historian Reischauer points out that the Japanese "have seen fit to bridle their free emotional expression as severely as any major people in the world, thus establishing a tension . . . sufficiently strange to us to create in our eyes many apparent inconsistencies in their conduct." For instance, courtesy goes out the window when a situation does not require face-to-face dealing. Japanese public manners, in great anonymous crowds, are singularly rude. I once saw a man, bulling his way out of a train, knock a bottle from a baby's hand.

Observers up to and including Henry Kissinger have commented that with Japanese abundance of buried emotion goes a proportionate lack of logic. "They don't distinguish between the subject and the object," it is said. "They have no notion of causality; you can't demonstrate anything. They have no conceptual thought. They can't make an outline." But such criticisms are contradicted by the phenomenal industrial success of the Japanese. The answer to the contradiction seems to be that the tidy logic of, say, the French is just not needed to achieve overall results that are in themselves well conceived and logical. The Japanese don't get so caught up in causality that they forget the ultimate goal. They "are concerned with life and survival, not with the literals of yes and no," a Tokyo professor of business told me.

The depths of Japanese emotion certainly include an extraordinary measure of sensitivity—toward art, toward nature, in communicating, and in other ways. I heard of a man in Tokyo who could taste a glass of water and identify the aqueduct through which it arrived. Cherry-blossom viewings stir deep emotions every spring. Westerners are prone to think that if you've seen one cherry blossom you've seen them all. But the Japanese notice differences between orchards, and between trees in orchards, and between blossoms on trees, and between the petals of the blossoms—differences caused by the stoniness of the soil or the strength of the sun or the chilliness of the breeze— and these differences give them billions of petals to exclaim about. Fireflies cause equal frenzies. Lacquerware viewed by candlelight, ancient swords seen as fine art, jade rather than diamonds, Noh robes that "set off to almost erotic effect the dark ivory of the Japanese skin" (as novelist Junichiro Tanizaki put it)—these and a thousand other experiences enchant the Japanese. Ten centuries ago the Lady Murasaki, author and lady of the court, could fold a letter so that even the creases had a message, and that art is not yet lost.

Nyosekan Hasegawa pointed out in *The Japanese Character: A Cultural Profile* that such extremes of climate as produced Egypt's deserts or Russia's arctic lands are absent from Japan, which allowed the Japanese to "accept nature as it was and develop a disposition that was moderate, averse to extremes and exaggerations." Others contend that if nature has had any effect on the Japanese character, it has been a fatalism brought on by recurring and devastating experiences with typhoons and earthquakes. My own guess is that Hasegawa's hypothesis is closer to the mark. "Japan doesn't fight nature," a Japanese acquaintance of mine argues. "Japan tries to huddle against the wind." The Zen expositor D. T. Suzuki contended that the Japanese poets "love nature so much that they feel one with nature, they feel every pulse beating through the veins of nature."

Obviously, the subject of the Japanese and nature is an interminable one, stretching through landscaping, flower arranging, bonsai (miniature trees), the animistic Shinto religion, and Zen Buddhism. (Zen monks used to try to avoid stepping on bugs, and one of them slept with a leg protruding from his mosquito net, to give the insects something to bite.) The main point is that the Japanese traditionally regard nature as an object of appreciation, not mastery—something to be lived with, not conquered. I noticed, however, that this love of nature usually translates as love and attention for one's own garden; the Japanese are more careless than the Americans about public littering. "Outside is a non-place . . . to be spat on, an unpossessed realm to be defiled by orange peel, pear cores, and loquat seeds," wrote the Australian critic Hal Porter. This attitude goes for animals, too. One's own pet gets lavish care; ownerless animals get kicks and hunger. Ducks and geese in parks are occasionally beaten to death with sticks, and swans shot and barbecued.

Indifference to vagrant animals may be a corollary of the "contempt for the damaged" that Ruth Benedict noted among the Japanese, citing the abandonment of wounded soldiers during World War II. "You can't be blemished in Japan," an editor whom I met in Tokyo commented. "The retarded and the crippled are kept out of sight." Even dented cars are rapidly repaired—the vehicles that roll on Japanese streets look newer and cleaner and shinier than those I've seen anywhere else.

The fullest measurement of the delicacy of interpersonal relationships can be taken from the indefinite, suggestive, between-the-lines manner in which the Japanese speak to one another. "Speech is at best eighty percent specific—you have to guess at the other twenty percent," says a Tokyo cultural anthropologist. And the unspoken 20 percent is understood to be the most important. One politician had to scrap his chosen slogan, "A man must live by the truth and die by the truth," because voters took it to mean that he would commit suicide if not elected.

Avoid confrontation—at all costs, under any circumstances. This is a tenet, and a dictum, and an unacknowledged binding of the Japanese social contract. Confrontation leads to argument, and argument leads to decision, and decision creates a winner and a loser, and losing brings unacceptable shame. Avoidance of confrontation explains the common Japanese custom of using go-betweens to arrange introductions, business contacts, and marriages: one person can reject another's overture without having to face him. Almost every formal interview I had in Japan was fixed up for me by a go-between, that is, someone (whom I may also have met via a go-between) who had enough confidence in me to arrange the contact. To avoid confrontation, the Japanese resist spelling things out or explaining themselves—such candor and forthrightness insult the hearer by implying that he is insensitive to nuance. In the last months of World War II, when Hirohito summoned Admiral Kantaro Suzuki to form a cabinet, the emperor's audible words were: "There is no one but you for this task." His unspoken message (as Suzuki correctly understood) was: End the war as soon as possible.

Professor Reischauer pointed out to me that while Westerners often make conversation into an adversary game, staking out big areas of claims from which to retreat if necessary, the Japanese cultivate harmony, modesty, and the avoidance of blunt declarations. No Japanese tells another that he is wrong, even if he is. Nor does one Japanese curse another, for their gentle, obscenity-free language contains no viler malediction than *chikusho*, beast. These inhibitions lead to a certain amount of lying—lying not intended to deceive (though it often deceives Occidentals) but to dodge unpalatable truth or to keep from disrupting harmony. The accepted way for one Japanese to dispute another is to start by agreeing with everything that has been said, and then make a dissent prefaced by "But, maybe . . ." Japanese speech can become excruciatingly roundabout even in the most common courtesies, with phrases like "Excuse my not being able to have had the pleasure of meeting you earlier."

Sometimes I thought, watching the Japanese in tearooms or coffee shops, that they were not talking to one another, but merely in the presence of one another. Restrictions on what can politely be said also lead to certain silences. Japanese psychotherapists reportedly extract very little orally from their patients. But, given the Japanese understanding that words are awkward, merely mechanical contrivances for doing what intuition does better, the silences can be deeply meaningful. One professor who feels close to his students says that occasionally a boy or girl will visit his office, stay two or three hours reading, sitting, talking a little, and, having had an "affective relationship," go away content. The professor believes that these students want counsel, and, without need for words, they get it.

The Japanese are imitators—no question about that. The suppression of individuality, together with the power of tradition and conformity, have led the Japanese to put small value on originality and inventiveness. All the major institutions of Japanese life— government, art, religion, architecture, writing—were copied, centuries ago, from China. "In Japan there has been little need for adventure either in action or in thought," wrote the physicist Hideki Yukawa, although he himself thinks so adventuresomely that he won a Nobel Prize.

The Japanese genius is to receive an innovation, whatever it may be, and elaborate upon it until it becomes Japanese. Tea drinking was tea drinking in China; the Japanese devised the complex and esthetic ritual that constitutes the tea ceremony. And though each master of the tea ceremony tries sincerely to copy exactly the gestures of his predecessors, his Japanese nature inevitably leads him, in the course of performing the gestures thousands of times, to make them his own. "The Japanese have always managed to take over foreign culture in an imitative fashion yet at the same time, sometimes even discarding the borrowings, to think and act according to their own unique character and eventually to create their own unique culture," wrote Hasegawa. And, as Donald Keene asks in *Modern Japanese Literature*, is there anything wrong with a genius for imitation? It is ridiculous to consider this skill a discredit, "as if it were somehow more admirable to imitate badly." One proof of Japanese skill in imitating lies in what they have refused to imitate—Chinese foot-binding, for example.

An unignorable aspect of the Japanese national character is its utter absorption in studying the Japanese national character. In fact, the Ministry of Education has a formal Committee for the Study of the Japanese National Character, which made three major polls of Japanese self-scrutiny between 1953 and 1968. The results emphasize some permanent Japanese traits, and tell how some others are changing.

Choosing from lists of adjectives denoting positive characteristics, the Japanese perennially pronounce themselves to be diligent, persistent, kind, and polite; in negative ways they think themselves insular, impatient, and too quick to lose enthusiasm. One question asked in the polls was: "If you think a thing is right, do you think you should go ahead and do it even if it is contrary to usual custom, or do you think you are less apt to make a mistake if you follow custom?" A remarkably high one-third put "follow custom" ahead of doing the right thing.

Some answers shed light on how the individual is shaped and molded in Japan. Roughly two-thirds of the Japanese people think that discipline should be stressed in teaching children, and fewer than one-fifth would stress freedom. Almost two-thirds think that children should be taught that money is the most important thing. Practical work is held to have greater value for society than scholarship and art, by about two to one. A substantial majority contend that "it can't be helped if individual rights are somewhat sacrificed for the sake of the public interest."

The study confirms the need for thoughtfulness in personal

relationships. Seven to one, the Japanese prefer a boss who "demands extra work in spite of rules against it, but looks after his employees personally in matters not connected to work" over a boss who "sticks to rules, and is never unreasonable, but never does anything for his employees personally." Faced with a choice of hiring the person who scored highest on an employment examination or a relative who scored second highest, 78 percent said that they would hire the high scorer. But suppose the employer's choice is between the high scorer and the son of a benefactor (for example, a much-respected teacher)? In that case, only 54 percent would choose the high scorer, and 39 percent would give the job to the son of the benefactor. The Japanese debt-and-obligation system applies powerfully to benefactors. The poll posed the question: "Your company is having a crucial meeting, and you get word that your father is dying—would you go to his bedside?" About half the respondents said that they would go to the bedside—and equally as many would go to the bedside if a benefactor, rather than a father, were dying.

The accurate adjectives for the West, wrote D. T. Suzuki, are logical, inquisitive, concrete, shallow in feeling, analytical, discriminative, inductive, individualistic, intellectually objective, scientific, generalizing, conceptual, schematic, impersonal, legalistic, organizing, power-wielding, self-assertive, and impositional. His adjectives for the East are: synthetic, totalizing, integrative, nondiscriminative, deductive, nonsystematic, dogmatic, intuitive, affective, subjective, group-minded. A fine list of human qualities, that; and, as Tennessee Williams might put it, "Nothing human is inscrutable to me."

3/

111 Million Overachievers

Oɴ ᴀɴ ᴇʟᴇɢᴀɴᴛ Tokyo boulevard, a black Toyota Crown Super Saloon glides by, offering just a glimpse of the white-gloved chauffeur and the well-tailored business executive in the back, his eyes closed, his head against a lacy antimacassar. One glances at him, and questions stir in the mind. Is he a member of the upper classes? Does Japan *have* classes? Who's rich, who's poor, who's up, who's down? What kind of society is this, anyway?

In talks with professors, doctors, writers, and government officials, I asked these and similar questions, and gradually sifted out some common themes. The main gears in the Japanese clockwork, they said in substance, are:

A profound sense of national unity and shared goals.
A clear understanding of where each person fits in society.
An abiding faith in the family.
A pragmatic ability to draw strength from both internal and Western sources.
A simple but extraordinary dedication to work.

To put it in five words: consensus, hierarchy, family, eclecticism, energy.

A few years ago, the business consultant James Abegglen wrote a little book called *Japan, Inc.*, a title that neatly summarized the Japanese capacity for agreeing on goals and carrying them out with purpose and dedication. Other nations may fall short on five-year plans or fail in great leaps forward, but when the Japanese do not accomplish exactly what they set out to do, it is usually because

27

they have accomplished even more. Flattened by World War II, the Japanese corporately resolved to build a new nation, and in twenty years constructed the world's third-strongest economy. In 1962 they decided specifically to double the gross national product in seven years—and did it in five. An earlier instance was the deliberate, single-minded modernization of the country in the decades after the opening of Japan to the West. Faced now with bad pollution, the Japanese will, I am sure, proceed without deviation to make their land the cleanest on earth.

What accounts for this unity, zeal, and sense of participation? Minister of Education Michio Nagai, with whom I dined one evening, argues that the Japanese are instinctive practitioners of Social Darwinism, the survival-of-the-fittest-society concept that prevailed in the United States in the late nineteenth century. This concept presupposes a process of natural selection among societies analogous to Darwin's natural selection among individuals and species. Certainly the Japanese stress society. The American notion, not a bad one, proposes that societies are founded among men to make the individual more comfortable. The Japanese propose that only by making the society more successful can the individual justify himself— and incidentally make his own lot happier. The American (or, more broadly, the Westerner) considers his own prosperity self-made, and supports the society with a mixture of duty and suspicion. The Japanese considers his own prosperity a spin-off from society's prosperity.

The Japanese have an energy that is almost terrifying to incentive-trained Westerners, because it is induced less by a sense of personal gain than by some compulsive sense of duty or, more remotely, the betterment of Greater Nippon. They are, as perhaps no other people are, with the possible exception of the Israelis, driven men, driven by some mystic sense of nation or purpose that is bigger than any individual. It is a belief that is in itself antithetical to American thought.

As a consequence, present-day Japan, far from being a society of divided classes, is a remarkable "meritocracy," in which for the most part men rise into the Establishment by dint of their own achievements. Even more pronouncedly than the United States, Japan is no longer a society of birth. Masaya Miyoshi, an astute official of the influential Federation of Economic Institutions, told me that "descent from an ancient family, for example, simply does not matter much in modern Japanese life—just something to take a little rueful pride in." Some families can trace their genealogies back to the sixth century; some descend from the peerage set up under the Emperor Meiji in the nineteenth century and abolished by the American Occupation—but nowadays, I heard, "a son doesn't mention that his father was a viscount." In polls, nine out of ten persons say that they regard themselves as belonging to the middle class, which therefore becomes virtually the only class.

Such meritocracy encourages equitable distribution of wealth—more nearly so, says futurologist Herman Kahn, than in the United States. The wretchedly poor are now happily few in Japan; even the war-veteran amputees who plied their accordions on trains ten years ago are gone. Japan has "more or less solved the problems of absolute poverty," said the late Prime Minister Eisaku Sato. "Who are the poor?" I asked one government official. "Day laborers," he answered. "Carpenters." Then he muttered, "Well paid and hard to get." A major factor in eliminating destitution is the national policy of full employment—the Japanese people insist on it, the economy is set up to provide it, and businessmen accept the responsibility for it. Many unproductive jobs, such as chauffeuring cars, are tolerated out of the national conviction that all men, and most women, who want work should have it. Japan simply would not stand for the 5 or 6 percent unemployment that Americans take for granted.

Also as a consequence of meritocracy, wealth in Japan is mostly new wealth. The old rich—notably the owners of the infamous prewar family trusts called *zaibatsu*—lost their fortunes after the war in a capital levy ordered by the American Occupation, and the corporations that descend from the zaibatsu are run by salaried managers who got their jobs on merit. There are no Rockefellers or Du Ponts or Mellons. The only exceptions are certain old-rich families who managed to squirrel away art treasures—pottery, manuscripts, scrolls, screens—that they now sell off for fat sums while inflation pushes the value of what they keep higher than ever.

The new rich make an astonishingly assorted group. At the top of the tax office's report of the nation's biggest incomes in 1973 was Manji Hasegawa, eighty-one, a lumber dealer who made $17,150,000 by selling a piece of Tokyo land that he had bought in 1937. "I think I will buy a mountain and plant trees there," he said. Ninety-eight others in the top one hundred also made their money in land speculation. Others lower down on the list included former Prime Minister Kakuei Tanaka and most of the members of his cabinet, golfer Masashi Ozaki, first baseman Sadaharu Oh, flower-arrangement master Sofu Teshigahara, music composer Masao Koga, tea-ceremony master Soshitsu Sen, wood-block printer Shiko Munakata, novelist Seicho Matsumoto, painter Saburo Miyamoto, movie actor Kazuo Hasegawa, and pop singer Shinichi Mori.

Some of this wealth is spent blatantly and tastelessly. Stores commonly exhibit such gifts as two large cantaloupes in a wooden box for $37, or a bonsai pine for $60, or an Abyssinian cat for $750. One Tokyo chiropractor gives regular parties for his staff and patients at which two string quartets provide music while the guests eat choice *sashimi*, raw fish, that costs $24 a pound. Hyoma Seki, the real estate dealer who topped the 1971 list for high income ($12.6 million), lives in northern Honshu in a two-story Western-style reinforced-concrete house covering 5,700 square feet. His Momoyama-period ("Japanese Baroque") garden contains shapely rocks brought from Hokkaido and an artificial waterfall, all lying next to an eighty-foot swimming pool. He owns nine light planes, a Rolls-Royce, a Jaguar, and two Mercedes-Benzes.

Not all conspicuous consumption comes from the rich. Japan's lavish corporate expense accounts (which in their aggregate, according to the *Times* of London, equal the entire gross national product of Northern Ireland) allow employees with small personal assets to buy expensive gifts, food, drink, and entertainment, though not for themselves. But naturally they get a good deal back in return, as the recipients of other people's expense-account generosity. Contrariwise, men with fortunes equal to millions of dollars often refuse to live on a grand scale. Their residences are luxurious but not large apartments in central Tokyo or Osaka, solidly built houses tucked behind walls in undistinguished residential areas, or small estates, an acre or so, on the outskirts of cities—all these usually supplemented by a villa in the mountains.

The Japanese meritocracy, though egalitarian in opportunity and in its abandonment of hereditary social classes, does not by any means make all men equal. Deriving from the ancient Chinese ethic of the precedence of the elder over the younger, the Japanese have an intense psychological need for everyone to know where he belongs in relation to others. The result is a rigid system of social ranking. The hierarchy principle does not necessarily stand in the way of social relationships among all kinds of people, nor does it prevent good friendships based on mutual appreciation, but the sense that each person must relate to another as inferior or superior pervades all of life. A man who receives a business card from another does not merely glance at it, but rather pores over every ideograph for the clues that it offers (position, firm, address) to establish who's up and who's down in their relationship. The organization charts of Japanese business firms are fixed and uniform, permitting such calculations as that the assistant shipping manager of a large trading company has more prestige than the manager of the general affairs section of a medium-size manufacturing company.

One businessman, explaining these matters to me, provided a tortuously helpful example. "Did you notice," he asked, one day after we had made the rounds of some offices, "how I bowed lower to former Ambassador Y than I did to former Ambassador Z? That was because Ambassador Y did not graduate from Tokyo University and barely made ambassadorial rank, to Norway, before retiring, whereas Ambassador Z is a Tokyo U. man and rose to be ambassador to Washington. I bowed a little lower to Ambassador Y to show him that I respect him even if we all know that Ambassador Z is his superior."

Ranking applies rigorously to politics (where the leading politicians head factions of leaders of subfactions), to sports (where sumo wrestlers are ranked by number), and even within families (where the order of taking baths is carefully worked out). Rank penetrates conversation, with inferiors reluctant to challenge superiors, which makes for windy narrations that will not lead to confrontations. In fact, the tendency to fit oneself into one's proper rank is utterly unconcealed. A foreign businessman in Tokyo a few years ago, having outworn his old company car, needed advice about what model to buy for a replacement. "How is your Mercedes-Benz 280SL?" he asked his chief Japanese aide. "Very good," replied the Japanese. "But if you buy a Mercedes, get a 300SL. Your position requires that your car be better than mine."

Americans are no strangers to the niceties of hierarchy, as anyone can testify who has observed corporate kowtowing, or even hostesses arranging guests at a dinner party. But the Japanese subtleties and corollaries go much further. For one thing, ranking compels the organization of society along vertical lines, rather than horizontal. Typically, the company union, comprising workers who perform all the functions of a given enterprise, prevails over the American-style industrial trade union, comprising workers performing identical functions for many companies. As Professor Chie Nakane points out in *Japanese Society*, the new bible of Japanese social anthropology, vertical ranking rules the lives of those archetypes of city life, the *saraiimen* (which is now a built-in Japanese word but derives from the Japanese pronunciation of "salary men"). The saraiimen are the ubiquitous organization men. The ranking principle leads them dutifully to form groups and subgroups, built pyramid-style around a boss and his several underlings and their several underlings.

The company itself is a group of such groups. People in this structure of "work-place friendship" get to "know each other exceedingly well—one's family life, love affairs, even the limit of one's capacity for cocktails," says Miss Nakane, a delightfully positive and quick-minded conversationalist, whose many years in London, the United States, and India give her a broad background for making comparisons. The group becomes the dominant factor in a man's life —which fits the Japanese penchant for submerging the individual in the society. "In most cases the company provides the whole social existence of a person, and has authority over all aspects of his life," Professor Nakane writes.

The warmth of relations within groups is matched by the frigidity of relations between groups. The situation becomes "us" against "them." Business mergers are rare because joining together groups is so difficult; when Yawata and Fuji merged to become Nippon Steel, it took a long history of friendship of the men at the apex of each group to tie them together.

This kind of organization provides great stability—"the major strength of the Japanese system"—because it requires loyalty down as well as up, most notably in the form of guaranteeing lifetime employment. Thus a young person entering a company at the bottom soon begins to acquire "social capital" in the form of certainty of promotion and membership in a group. The penalty of quitting is sacrificing the social capital. "Here, if you change your factory, you have to change your friends," I was told. "If you move you cannot ask your old friends for a favor, because it will be refused."

A man who does a good job does not get the credit; honors go to the group and the leader. This frustrating "defiance of individual quality and achievement . . . often leads a capable man with no immediate chance of attaining leadership to leave the group and establish himself independently," Miss Nakane writes. The seniority system "dominates Japan more strikingly than nepotism in other societies." But seniority does not cancel out meritocracy; companies find ways of advancing mediocre men by small steps, or moving them sideways, while letting meritorious juniors move up without seeming to jump over the heads of seniors.

Paradoxically, vertical ranking does not in the least mean that Japanese bosses are all-powerful: just the reverse. Decisionmaking in Japan is actually a function of the lower levels of management. Toyosaburo Taniguchi, former chairman of Toyobo Company, and grand old man of the Osaka textile industry, told me candidly: "The big fellow sits there waiting for those down below to make a decision. Quite unlike the United States." He added, by way of corollary, that "once he reaches the top, a great man does not work too hard, because that would deprive someone else of work."

The mechanism of decisionmaking is the *ringi,* a plan of action developed in an organization's lower echelons. This document climbs the chain of command, from one desk to another, acquiring modifications and, at each point, a signature seal of approval. "The ringi may finally reach the president's desk with fifty different seals on it," Taniguchi told me. "It is a system that grew out of our society, and people feel close to it and get a sense of participation out of it." Almost invariably the top man merely adds his approval. As Professor Takeshi Ishida puts it, "The most important qualification for a leader is that he understands what is desired by his followers without explicit discussion."

Says Taniguchi: "This system is so set up that it is difficult to come up with a wrong decision," but he adds that group-think may well fail to produce the best decision. For one thing, it hampers innovation. "It's based on the idea that things do not change, and if you propose a change you are in danger." Obviously, the system is also painfully slow, but once a decision is made, implementation comes fast, because the whole organization is on record as favoring the decided course.

These rules of the game provide a key for understanding the part that ranking and the group play in the workings of Japanese society. I found, though, that not all Japanese play by the rules. The very first young businessman I encountered in Japan was one who had cut loose from Mitsubishi Corporation to start an enterprise all his own. Japanese society is not so simple that everyone fits into a stereotype.

The Japanese family, in its loyalties, its durability, and its vertical structure, is a microcosm of the larger national structure. It has taken jarring blows in the last thirty years. Feverish urbanization, the swift growth of affluence, and the discrediting of authority caused by defeat in war all hit at the old "extended family" concept—the elaborate, many-generationed structure of siblings and in-laws and adopted sons, of "main families" and "branch families" ruled by paterfamiliases on the principles of unbroken family line and inheritance by the oldest son. The American Occupation imposed a constitution that banned any discrimination on account of "sex, social status or family origin," which in effect struck down the "rights of the head of the house" (including the patriarch's right to forbid any member of the family to leave home) and gave women equal rights (meaning principally that they gained rights to inheritance, divorce, and the vote). Away went such verities as "If you love your wife, you spoil your mother's servant," for in the old dispensation a son's new wife was virtually her mother-in-law's maid. In came the "nuclear family"—mother, father, children, and perhaps a grand-parent or two allowed to live in the spare room.

But one statistic makes it clear that the Japanese family did not collapse: the divorce rate in Japan is only one in ten marriages (as compared to one in three in the United States). The new cement for the family, replacing extended-family authoritarianism, is something called *maihomushugi*—one of those Japanese words constructed from English: "my-home-ism," denoting great attachment to the satisfactions of the nuclear family.

To quote Chie Nakane again: "The core of the Japanese family, ancient and modern, is the parent-child relationship, not that between husband and wife." As wives, most Japanese women are submissive but far from slavish toward their husbands. Their rueful word for marriage is "eternal employment." By their actions they give assent to the consensus that men should dominate Japan, but at least the younger wives manage to seem cheerful and unconfined. Japan never came anywhere close to such outrages upon feminine dignity as Islam's veils, and the old custom of a woman's walking three steps behind her husband is dead and gone. When, a few years ago, the Tokyo branch of Maxim's of Paris proposed that a Japanese husband could perfectly well disregard tradition and take his wife out to dinner tête-à-tête, the suggestion swiftly became a custom all over the country. A surprising number of Japanese women lead genuinely independent lives, touring Africa on a whim, or climbing the Himalayas, or running their own businesses. A wife usually takes over her husband's entire pay envelope and gives him back pocket money.

On balance, however, women clearly come second to men. Within five days after first reaching Japan, I was guest for dinner in a Japanese house at which the wife did not feel entitled to eat with the men, talked animatedly with her husband but said "yes" to his every remark, and trotted rather than walked back and forth to the kitchen. American women newly arrived in Japan discover that if they board elevators first, as is the custom at home, they bump into men who are boarding first, as is the custom in Japan. The Ministry of Education's Study of the Japanese National Character shows that men and women overwhelmingly agree that men get greater pleasure out of life. Sex customs commonly tend to benefit the man; in a survey made by Teijin Ltd., a textile maker, only 6.8 percent of Toyko women could bring themselves to say that they were "deeply interested" in sex, and only 34.5 percent confessed even to being "rather interested."

Male chauvinism pervades even the simplest levels of behavior. One Tokyo woman gives this example: "In a subway one day, I let out a hearty yawn. The elderly man facing me on the seat below reproached me in a fatherly way. 'That wasn't feminine. You must always cover your mouth when you do that; otherwise it is improper behavior.' Here is a country where men will spit, piss, and vomit without the least restraint in the most visible public places—but let a woman yawn openly, and her conduct will be viewed as 'improper.' "

Japanese women suffer from discrimination in jobs, politics, the law, and education. Women at work in 1970 numbered 20 million, which was two-fifths of the country's labor force, and included half of all women more than fourteen years old; proportionally more women work in Japan than in the United States. But the pay of Japanese women averages only one-half that of men, and men get all the choice positions. Predictably, women dominate such jobs as nursing, stenography, textile spinning and weaving, and telephone operation, but they constitute only 8 percent of doctors, one-half of 1 percent of lawyers, and 1 percent of civil servants in managerial jobs. Women comprise half of elementary school teachers, but only 1 percent of all elementary school principals. One field opening up for women is service in the Self-Defense Forces, chiefly because men dodge it, but only one woman has risen to colonel (in nursing). Policewomen directing traffic are common. More than half of Japanese farmers are women, a consequence, I suppose, of all the mom-and-pop rice paddies that one sees in the countryside.

Since they got suffrage in 1946, women have taken to voting at rates equal to or higher than men, but the number of women in the House of Representatives has declined from 39 in 1946 to 7 in 1973, even as the House itself grew from 466 members to 491. In education, women fare better. Just as many girls as boys (85 percent in both cases) move from junior high school, the last stage of compulsory education, to senior high school; similarly, about one-fourth of both women and men go on from senior high school to college. But girls go mostly to two-year colleges, where they study home economics, literature, and teacher training, while men fill up the four-year universities.

One day I visited the Tokyo College of Domestic Science, where several hundred girls were making pottery, dyeing cloth, cooking sixty at a time with modern electric stoves and traditional bamboo utensils, and—most impressively—weaving wall hangings in the *kasuri* style. A stunning example of this art employed black threads woven as various-size dots into a creamy white ground, on the same principle as a newspaper half-tone, to make a representation of an old man. A woman teacher told me that weaving kasuri not only teaches an art but also forms a girl's character. I could see that the school aimed higher than training housekeepers. What was the goal, I asked. Her reply was simple and large-minded. "To create an excellent woman," she said.

That led me to ask her opinion of the feminist movement. "I spend most of my time here at the college; my husband, who is a plastics-arts designer, works at home; so he does the housework," she answered. "We have no trouble, without having had a revolution."

"You *are* a liberated woman?"

She smiled. "Yes, but I did not realize it. It's all very natural." I noticed that, like many Japanese wives, she wore no wedding ring.

The director general of the Women's and Minors' Bureau of the Ministry of Labor when I was in Japan was Mrs. Nobuko Tomita Takahashi, birdlike and serious behind her large-lensed glasses. She pointed out to me that, based on the 1946 constitution, Japan has laws to make women the juridical equals of men, plus protective laws allowing maternity leave, banning underground labor, guaranteeing twice-daily nursing periods for mothers of babies, and providing for menstruation leave. "We have plenty of law," Mrs. Takahashi said. "It's a matter of putting it into practice." The most scandalous evasion is the "thirty and out" custom, whereby employers fire white-collar women at that age or earlier on such grounds as that girls are just "office flowers" whose job (as one feminist puts it) is "to meet guests, to be charming and young, and to pour the tea." The net effect is that women rarely move on to senior jobs and are often denied promotions equal to those of men. This discrimination explains the pay differential between the sexes, for the principle of equal pay for equal work, which is the law, applies fairly among newly hired men and women if they are equally qualified.

The recent rise in the number of employed married women, Mrs. Takahashi observed, has exposed some other injustices. Lack of provision for joint income tax returns keeps workers' wives from sharing exemptions. Women are legally limited in overtime and night work, which further cuts their take-home pay. And men customarily get much more in allowances, notably expense-account entertainment.

Women's lib in Japan has caught on enough to take the predictable Japlish name of *uman ribu*, with *ribu gurupu* (lib groups) of about ten women each scattered around campuses, offices, and factories. But the weight of tradition that casts women as mothers and wives has so far been an insurmountable block to a big and radical liberation movement. Ribu's rather defensive main goal is to preserve Japan's liberal abortion law (which is under attack from rightists in the government) on grounds that to keep control of their own bodies women must be able to make the basic decision about whether to give birth. The passion that sparks the American feminist movement is missing in Japan.

Every young Japanese married couple wants a son, a daughter, and a Datsun (or equivalent). Actually, according to the exhaustive surveys made by the *Mainichi* newspapers, nearly half of all couples would like to have three children. But small houses, the cost of college educations, the reduced importance of numerous children in nuclear as compared to extended families, and finally the heightened modern desire of parents to enjoy life rather than slave over kids, all combine to produce an average of very close to two children per family.

The tendency toward smaller families in Japan will determine the most crucial factor of this crowded nation's future: the total population. A hundred years ago, with Tokyo already the biggest city in the world, Japan felt crammed with 35 million people. In the early decades of this century, when the Japanese government was encouraging its citizens to emigrate to the United States (the "yellow peril") and the world thought of Japan as the archetypal teeming Asian nation, the population was still only 44 million to 55 million. Japan entered World War II with 72 million, and all the carnage, balanced against births, reduced that number by only 340,000. The baby boom after the soldiers returned boosted the population to 83 million by 1950 and 89 million by 1955. By then the nation was alarmed, and the rate slowed down, but nevertheless in 1967 the population hit 100 million, and today Japan has 111 million people.

How many people does Japan need? Its present population places it sixth in the world, but since three more populous countries (China, India, Indonesia) are underdeveloped, Japan stands third among industrial nations, after the United States and the Soviet Union, just as it stands third in gross national product. Thus Japan's present population is no more than enough to provide the work force that it requires, and minimal for the heft that it aspires to attain in world affairs. Should another great world war take place, Japan might wish for either (1) more people, for armies and colonizing, or (2) fewer people, to lessen its need for foreign raw materials, particularly food. Right now, a good theoretical argument could be made for a population about half as big as at present. Not only has Japan only half enough land to feed itself, but it hardly has enough space to provide housing room. This mostly mountainous country has a population in its plains and basins of about 3,100 persons per square mile, as compared to 830 in the Netherlands, which is all flat. Japan is the fifth most densely populated nation in the world, after Bangladesh, South Korea, the Netherlands, and Belgium.

Sitting in his office in the Ministry of Health and Welfare—the building of the old Imperial Navy Ministry where the brilliant Admiral Isoroku Yamamoto planned his attack on Pearl Harbor—Yoichi Okazaki of the government's Institute of Population Problems talked to me about some of the consequences of overpopulation. Obviously, two bad effects are pollution and overcrowding in housing, land, and transportation. "People spend an hour and a half or two hours on commuter trains—a great waste of their own energy." Importing food for a people who cannot grow enough for themselves makes Japan dependent on the weather and the whims of other countries. But at least, in Okazaki's view, this dependence makes Japan pursue a policy of peace in the world: "Otherwise, we cannot live."

Before the war, the government had a population policy, which was to promote a high birth rate to produce more soldiers. Now the government is combating pollution and overcrowding, says Okazaki, but it avoids adopting a policy for an optimum population. Despite this taboo, the mysterious workings of society that cause low birth rates in industrialized nations—or perhaps just some gut decision of the Japanese people at large—have brought population growth well under control. Okazaki predicts that Japan will grow at 1 percent a year for thirty years, chiefly by reason of the children now being born to the men and women born in the postwar baby boom—the "echo effect." Then the population, having reached 140 million, will level off. In contrast, the population of the world at large is growing by 2 percent. And Japan performs this miracle virtually without taking the Pill.

The objections to birth-control pills are not personal but political. In the early 1960s, Japan, like West Germany, authorized the use of the tranquilizer thalidomide, the side effects of which caused the birth of nearly one hundred deformed babies from Japanese mothers who took it. The shock in child-cherishing Japan was shattering, inspiring the Ministry of Health and Welfare to forbid the sale of birth-control pills for fear of side effects. Nevertheless, the pills are sold in Japanese drugstores, labeled as hormones for regulation of the menstrual cycle. "But anyway," Yoichi Okazaki told me, "the condom and abortion are effective enough." These are the old reliables of Japanese birth control.

However, only three out of five Japanese wives do use contraception, and the remainder who do not want babies rely on abortion. In polls, nearly 40 percent of women say that they have had an abortion, and 30 percent have had at least two.

In 1948, the government, having come around from banning abortion to permitting it for "MCH" (mother-child-health) considerations, opened the doors by allowing it for "economic" reasons—which in effect let the unwillingly pregnant mother define her own reasons. Japan's confidence that it could control its population explosion dates from then. Aided by propaganda both official (post-office posters showing small, happy, well-fed families contrasted with large, miserable ones) and unofficial (the activities of the Western Pacific Region of the International Planned Parenthood Federation), abortion and condoms forced the birth rate down from 34.3 to 17.2 per 1,000 population between 1947 and 1957—the steepest drop in world history. For a time, the proportion of abortions to live births was seven to three. Now, with contraception commoner, it is three to seven. Incidentally, Japanese men greatly dislike vasectomies, which they call "tampering with the body."

In past centuries, an effective Japanese way of holding down family size was infanticide, which was called *mabiki*, meaning "thinning," in the agricultural sense. "The method was harsh but the idea was modern," commented Dr. Minoru Muramatsu, chief of the population division in the Ministry of Health and Welfare, when I talked to him. "Japan has been historically conditioned to the problems of overpopulation. In the last fifty years, the rate of infanticide has been very small. But now it's as if the tradition were coming back." Since 1965, around two hundred newborn babies a year have been killed by their parents.

While the birth rate in Japan has been sinking, the proportion of the aged in the population has been growing. A quarter of a century ago, life expectancy was 45 to 50 years; the practical effect was that people died shortly after they retired. Now the average newborn boy in Japan can expect to live to the age of 70.7 and the average girl to 76.01, compared to 71.85 and 76.54 in Sweden, the nation with the highest longevity, and 68 and 75 for American whites. This dazzling jump in Japanese longevity is to some extent a statistical illusion. Life-expectancy computations have to average out the probability of death at all ages, including infancy, and by good health care Japan has in recent years cut its infant mortality rate to 12.4 deaths among children under age 1 per 1,000 live births (as compared to 11.1 for Sweden, which has the lowest rate, and 19.2 for the United States).

Those sixty-five or older now form 7 percent of the Japanese population (as compared to 13 percent in Western Europe), and they create a problem still so new that Japan has no comprehensive formula for handling it. It is among the aged, if anywhere, that poverty is to be found. One day a frail seventy-two-year-old in an old-fashioned striped suit struck up a conversation with me on the railroad platform at Kamakura, south of Tokyo. He was headed for the city to try to get a job. "There are many poor people right here in Kamakura—including me," he said mournfully. The customary retirement age, now as in the past, is fifty-five—quite an abridgment, when you come to think of it, of Japan's boast of providing "lifetime" employment for its people. In bygone Japan, most people were dead by fifty-five, and Japanese social security has not fully caught up with the fact that now they survive and need help. A mishmash of two government insurance plans and private retirement allowances pays $190 a month to most people who have contributed from their salaries for twenty-five years. Those not covered receive a dole of $40 a month. Only 5.4 percent of the Japanese national income goes into social security, as compared to as much as 22 percent in Europe.

As one consequence, while big American corporations toy with the idea of pushing the retirement age *down* to sixty, big Japanese corporations, such as the major auto companies, are pushing it *up* to sixty. Early retirement seems to signify a waste of good experienced men, but corporations in Japan as in the United States often like to shove a high-paid senior out the top and put a low-paid newcomer in at the bottom. Thousands of Japanese men in their mid-fifties have to retire unwillingly, and then, to stay alive, take jobs with less pay, tenure, and importance. They are often forced to *arubaito*, the Japanese-from-German (*Arbeit*) word meaning "part-time work." Pushed out of company houses, they have to find new places to live.

Company presidents form a conspicuous exception to the early-retirement problem. They stay on and on. The average age of leaders in the Federation of Economic Organizations, which roughly resembles the National Association of Manufacturers in the United States, is seventy-four. When Riichi Ezaki retired from the presidency of his confectionery company at ninety-one, a year or so ago, he promised to continue to go to the office every day.

Japan still lacks any sizable number of retirement homes, and three-fourths of all people over sixty-five live with their children—a situation that runs against the trend toward nuclear families and small-apartment living, and creates increasing friction. A professor and his wife in Kawasaki share a duplex with their son and daughter-in-law, paying their own utilities and half the mortgage—a far cry from the old paterfamilias pattern. The professor says that he has to ring up his son's wife on the interphone and ask, "Is it all right if I come and talk to the baby?" The last blow to patriarchal hegemony came in 1973. The Supreme Court, considering an ancient law that provided heavier punishment for killing one's parents than for other murders, ruled it unconstitutional. Now a man can kill his own father with as much, or as little, impunity as he might kill any casual acquaintance. Father has lost, forever, his special status.

If an untraveled citizen of Dubuque or Leeds were plunked down by flying carpet on Christmas Eve in front of the Mitsukoshi department store on the Ginza in Tokyo, and if his eyes were somehow blinded to the slanted eyes of the pedestrians and the lettering on the neon signs, he might well spend five minutes figuring out what country he was in. The architecture, the traffic, the clothes, the six-story neon angel over the door of the department store, the strains of "Jingle Bells" from the store's loudspeakers, and the inevitable McDonald's hamburger stand could easily lead him to guess that he was in some fairly large American or European city.

Yet the temptation to detect Westernization in Japan can easily lead to false conclusions. Historian Reischauer supplies the insight that what seems to be Westernization is often more essentially modernization. The railroad, for instance, though it was developed in England, has been used in Japan for a century, which is about two-thirds of the history of this invention. The Japanese have, moreover, modernized the railroad to its highest state and made it much more a part of national life than it is in, say, the United States. But just as the spread of printing from China to Europe did not make Europe Chinese, so the spread of the railroad from England to Japan did not make Japan English. Japan builds most of the world's mammoth tankers—are they therefore to be classified as quaint Oriental products? The

Japanese have been playing baseball, their national sport, since the time of Abner Doubleday. And they used the equivalent of Kleenex long before the West.

Nevertheless, the reason the Ginza resembles an avenue in Paris or Buenos Aires rather than a Kyoto temple grounds is that Japan deliberately and selectively imported massive elements of Western culture during the past century. Importing culture is an old Japanese custom. Most of the traditional institutions of Japanese life were brought in from China between the sixth and ninth centuries, and not by conquering Chinese armies but by culture-thirsty Japanese travelers.

In the judgment of Chie Nakane, the Japanese system "is like a language with its basic indigenous structure or grammar which has accumulated a heavy overlay of borrowed vocabulary." But, she stoutly contends, "the basic social grammar has hardly been affected."

The basic grammar and the borrowed vocabulary make for an outwardly clashing but inwardly harmonious civilization. Visiting a Japanese house is likely to be an unsettling experience in double acculturation: by unbreakable tradition you must remove your shoes at the door, yet the room you enter may turn out to be furnished in Danish modern, while the bedroom beyond is fitted with quintessential Japanese paper walls and straw-mat floors. But the plain fact is that the Japanese find nothing in the least discordant about this kind of blending.

Much murmuring, worrying, and even wailing is expended on the proposition that Westernization will in the end wreck Japan. How can the Japanese stand such a dual culture without having an "identity crisis"? Yet it is strange, as Zbigniew Brzezinski points out, how lists of traditional Japanese traits (personal dignity and worth, dignified acceptance of fate, spirituality, poetic expressiveness, and so on) and of American traits (worship of success, cult of the efficient, work for work's sake, genius for organization, and so on) *both* describe the modern Japanese. Perhaps it is true, as a certain Dr. Ainslie wrote in Nagasaki in 1814, that "the Japanese are a nervous, vigorous people, assimilated by their bodily and mental powers much nearer to Europeans than Asiatics."

The Japanese, in short, are good at combining cultures because they do not take what they do not want. They imported Christmas wholesale, but not Christianity. They imported thousands of Western words, but kept their own syllabary to write them. They imported the chair, but still like to sit on the floor. They imported Western physiological medicine, but not Freud or Jung. "The least successful grafts were those in art and philosophy," wrote Arthur Koestler. The rejected aspects of Western civilization, the Japanese felt, "did not fit with the national character."

With all Japan's clever synthesis of East and West, however, there remain illuminating distinctions between the two cultures. Both to help himself understand the Japanese society and to understand the Japanese society's misperceptions of American society, a U.S. Embassy official compiled a list of differences. The Japanese prize harmony; the Americans healthy friction. The Japanese avoid differences; the Americans confront differences. The Japanese use the language of indirectness, "understandings," and self-effacement; the Americans use the language of directness, "agreements," and forthrightness. Japanese opinions develop from "feeling"; American from "rational analysis." Culturally and racially, the Japanese are happy to be homogeneous; Americans are proud to be heterogeneous.

All these differences come frequently into play in the lives of Americans and other Westerners who reside in Japan. These foreigners are the *gaijin*, a racist word that the newly arrived Westerner learns at once, because giggling schoolchildren, embarrassingly but unmaliciously, shout "Gaijin!" at him on the streets. Some Japanese blandly insist that gaijin means simply "foreign person," which is rather like arguing that "Jap" is just a harmless diminutive for "Japanese." One overtone of "gaijin" is that it applies only to Caucasians; Japanese refer to other Asians as Chinese or Filipinos or Malayans or whatever. Westerners in Japan call one another gaijin for convenience, but nevertheless the label puts them on edge. Says one gaijin: "In this way, the Japanese indicate that you are a foreigner and that no matter what you learn or do you will never understand as much about Japan as the lowliest Japanese."

The ways the Japanese treat the gaijin range from warmth, kindness, and respect to aloofness, reserve, and indifference—not much actual hatred, even though wartime training manuals pictured Westerners as "haughty, effeminate and cowardly." Father Pedro Sagaseta, a Spanish Jesuit priest in Hiroshima, told me that his Japanese friends will often confide to him something that they will not tell one another. "It's easier to speak to foreigners," they say. Students like to try out their English on gaijin, and ask them for autographs not because they are famous but because they are foreign. Most of the mannequins displayed in stores have blue eyes, Western features, and even blond hair; and no less than twenty casting offices in Tokyo supply actors of half-Western, half-Japanese parentage for television commercials. Admiration for everything Western, though declining in proportion to the increase in Japanese self-confidence stemming from its boot-strap rise since the war, remains high.

Although the gaijin generally feel comfortable in Japan, they rarely feel that they can penetrate deep inside Japanese society. Frank Gibney, the president of TBS-Britannica in Tokyo, an American who did penetrate, writes that American diplomats, most of the American business community, and the great bulk of the American press corps "remain largely sealed off from the life around them, for social as well as linguistic reasons." A Japanese businessman told me: "Those American Embassy people at parties are always asking Japanese men 'Who are you *with*?' and it usually turns out that they are talking to the president of Mitsubishi trading company, or some other person too important to be *with* anything." Most U.S. Embassy people in Tokyo live shut away from the Japanese in a compound of big apartment houses.

Japan is diligent in fencing out Westerners who are willing or eager to break the barriers. A trifling but classical example, repeated endlessly, is the reluctance of ordinary Japanese-style inns to accept Westerners. Innkeepers, except some in cosmopolitan cities, have an unshakable conviction that the foreigner will not like the raw fish at dinner, will be unable to sleep on the floor, and, above all, will get into the communal bath without scrubbing himself first, and thereby pollute the water. I well remember an unhappy travel agent in Kobe, on the phone to book a room at an inn for me. "Forbis-san is a gaijin," he told the innkeeper glumly.

More significantly, foreigners who genuinely want to study the country—as scholars or as members of a large clan of travelers and students and writers (mostly Americans) who develop a tortured love for Japan—must surmount high obstacles, even after they master Obstacle No. 1, the stunningly difficult language. To the Japanese, their foreign bluntness and candor seem merely rude. Conversely, Japanese indirectness and self-effacement seem devious and baffling to the gaijin. Foreigners find the Japanese stress on "feeling" to be childish and ambiguous, while the Japanese find the logic-chopping foreigners to be appallingly insensitive. Foreign women who marry Japanese men find it impossible to "become Japanese," largely because their husbands and all other Japanese think such a switch to be inconceivable.

Lafcadio Hearn made a career out of attempting to understand the Japanese, and professed to have failed—leading Professor Edward Seidensticker to label this since-frequently-repeated frustration as "hearnia." "We linger like spurned lovers about the golden door, able to gaze on the riches and beauty and warmth inside, but never able to cross the threshold," wrote Kate Millett after two years in Japan. Still, these generalizations, valid enough as such, never rule over individual cases, and many gaijin have intimate and rewarding relationships with Japanese.

Japan has its own variety of racism, which is different in kind and intensity from the rather polite resistance to the gaijin. It is directed against two specific groups. One is a mass of two million outcasts, of whom the world at large is almost ignorant. The other group is the six hundred thousand Koreans who live in Japan. ("Although they may not realize it themselves," writes Reischauer, "the Chinese, Japanese, and many other Asian peoples are as strongly racist in their basic feelings as any people in the world.")

Japan's outcasts were historically called *eta*, "full of filth." In fact, the word is still in use, but it gives offense, and politer people use the euphemism *burakumin*, "village people," derived from the outcasts' custom of living together in communities called *buraku*, which are often much like ghettos. The most striking difference between Japanese and American racism is that the objects of prejudice in Japan do not differ in physical appearance from the rest of the Japanese. Any given group of outcasts (or of Koreans, for that matter) looks to the innocent eye like a sampling of the general population. This might surprise some Alabama black-hater, who builds his prejudice around difference in skin color, but social anthropologists know that the psychological foundations of discrimination based on physical differences or on alleged caste impurity are one and the same. George De Vos and Hiroshi Wagatsuma, in their book on the outcasts, *Japan's Invisible Race*, define racism as "a deep-seated, psychologically primitive, vaguely conceptualized fear of contamination and loss of purity as a result of possible interbreeding." In sum, a sexual matter.

The alleged impurity of the outcasts, going back ten centuries, is that they have always worked at jobs involving death and the slaughter of animals (which, by way of curious contrast, was the task of priests in the Jewish culture). The fact seems to be that about half of all outcasts at all times were farmers, and they still are, but they have also formed the bulk of the country's butchers, leatherworkers, tanners, shoemakers, furriers, undertakers, gravediggers, cremators, and tomb guards—jobs variously bloody, grisly, menial, or in violation of Buddhist precepts against taking life. In ancient times the outcasts were thought to be of strange un-Japanese descent, not even human, genetically defiled by their contact with blood and death.

They had to wear an identifying patch of leather on their kimonos. Maps made a couple of centuries ago deliberately omitted outcast villages. The Meiji Restoration legally emancipated the outcasts in the same years that the American government was emancipating black slaves, but the Japanese majority clung to such superstitions as "outcasts have one dog's bone in them" or "have distorted sexual organs."

The need of ancient lords for the services of outcasts drew them to the castle towns of western Japan, and that is where most of them are still to be found; only twenty or thirty thousand live in Tokyo. For an idea of outcast life, I visited the poverty-ridden ward in Kyoto that lies just south of the main railroad station. There I met Mitsuo Takeguchi, local district chief of the Buraku Liberation League, and his friend and fellow outcast Tamotsu Shigeno, who is business manager of the well-built, attractive public grade school in the area. From the school's windows we could see the lofty shaft of the Kyoto Tower Hotel a few blocks away on the "good" side of the tracks.

The Buraku Liberation League is a left-wing group, and Takeguchi, emphatic and unsmiling, began by blaming big industry for the perpetuation of racism in Japan. The existence of masses of outcast laborers whose wages can be kept low without exciting general sympathy, he said, works as a weight to keep all wages lower than they might be, to the benefit of employers. Carrying that idea a step further, he argued that the "motive of the league is the liberation of everybody everywhere, because we're all involved in man's freedom." The league's work, said Takeguchi, is giving lectures to people outside the burakus, pestering city hall for housing and job opportunities, and pressing for better education for outcasts at the senior high school and college levels. It was an uphill job, he felt: "Even intellectuals and professors do not want to get involved with us because they would be branded by society as interested in 'dirty problems.'" I asked how the ghetto we were in was geographically defined. Takeguchi said that it was limited by well-known border streets, "but not everybody within it is a burakumin. For example, at this school, out of five hundred and sixty pupils, eighty are not burakumin. This is a slum, and outsiders, poor day laborers, come here because it's cheap."

Shigeno, a former teacher, after narrating the ancient history of the outcasts at scholarly length, described the telltale signs that reveal a man's caste. Accent is one, address another, and place of birth a third. Nevertheless, Shigeno added, "some outcasts become very eminent. One is a professor at Kyoto University, although still not accepted by stiff Japanese society. He does not confess his outcast background—he tried to 'pass.' But it doesn't work." At this point I asked Takeguchi and Shigeno about the significance of holding up four fingers, a gesture that I had been told was common in Japan. It was an unkind question. "Where did you hear about that?" Shigeno asked unhappily. But he admitted that the Japanese flash four fingers behind a man's back to signify that he is an outcast—that is, associated with four-footed animals. Shigeno, in contrast to Takeguchi, was a humble, constantly smiling man, but he ended the interview with a ringing statement: "The problem of Japanese racism has to be solved, or this will never become a first-class nation."

The predicament of the outcasts in Japan brings up a number of questions:

What is the attitude of the majority to this minority? Above all, most Japanese pretend the outcasts do not exist—an amazing conspiracy of silence. When pressed, they say in effect: "I feel sorry for the eta, because of their lowly position, but I will have nothing to do with them until they learn to live like other Japanese, that is, give up their occupations, marry outside their small community, clean up their villages, homes and themselves, and drop their hostile, clannish attitudes." Non-outcasts and outcasts work together in factories, take part together in public events, and mix on the streets even inside burakus, but hardly ever meet socially, except that children from both groups play together.

How do majority people recognize outcasts? Chiefly by occupation. It is a good guess that butchers, shoemakers, ragpickers, junk collectors, day laborers, shoeshine boys, rabbit hunters, goldfish vendors, and flower peddlers are burakumin—but it is not certain. The rise of meat consumption in Japan has brought many non-outcasts into the butcher business, for example.

Are the outcasts decreasing in number? By no means. Not only do they have children at a higher rate than the rest of the population, but they also create new outcasts by marrying spouses from (usually) the poorer levels of non-outcast society. Whereas a century ago they comprised 1 percent of the population, they now comprise 2 percent. And few outcasts pass into the general population: most depend on the support and security that they derive from their communities, despised though they may be; and Japan's intensive registration of births and residences makes it easy for the passer to be caught, so that he lives in terror. Japanese families commonly employ private detectives to check prospective brides and grooms, and these gumshoes have only to check the public records to turn up an outcast background.

How does the church treat outcasts? Buddhism establishes special temples for them.

What is the political status of the outcasts? They vote with no hindrance, and politicians court them. Slum clearance was once tried as a means of dispersing the burakumin, but it did not work. Schools attempt to teach tolerance, but no measure as strong as American-style busing is in effect or contemplated.

Years ago an outcast leader, Jiichiro Matsumoto, a Socialist, was elected to the House of Councillors (the Japanese senate) and caused a sensation by refusing on party principles to bow to the emperor at the annual opening of the Diet. Far from disciplining him, the other Diet members saw his point and thenceforth they all refused to bow. The American Occupation purged Matsumoto as too radical, but when the Occupation ended he was reinstated on a vote of two-thirds of the Diet, backed up by a million petition signers, who thought him the victim of a bum rap. The prevalent anti-American attitude of the outcasts stems from this incident.

If majority Japan mistreats its outcasts in a veiled, unacknowledged way, its mistreatment of the six hundred thousand Koreans who live there is quite aboveboard, frankly peevish, and sometimes appalling. "The Koreans are the Chicanos of Japan," a Tokyo newspaperman told me, hastily adding, "except that the Koreans have historically had a great culture." (So have the Mexicans, but that is what the man said.) Going back to Japan's 1910 annexation of their country, the Koreans have had a lot to resent about Japan, but two events stand out. In 1923, just after the great Tokyo earthquake and fire, Japanese mobs went berserk and massacred about six thousand Koreans on the basis of rumors that the Koreans would take advantage of the quake-caused confusion to stage riots. During World War II, Japan imported three million Koreans as workers, and many died in labor camps and mines, while others were shot to prevent them from revealing secrets about military installations that they were forced to help build. When the war was over, Japan returned most of these workers to Korea; those who remained—plus many who sneaked back to Japan—formed the base of the present Korean population.

The Japanese raise many loud objections to the Koreans, alleging that they were heartless black marketeers after the war and are now heavy in rackets and gangsterism and profiteering businesses. More important, the Koreans do not "fit" in the great Japanese nation-family; they do not belong and must be shunned. And shunned they are. The Japanese will rarely be friends with Koreans; universities find ways to exclude Korean applicants (which led the Koreans to found a university of their own); large corporations rarely hire them. Frozen out of many forms of employment, Koreans have gone in for running restaurants (the savory Korean barbecue), bars, Turkish baths, and pinball parlors, and for building and renting offices. Many lowlier Koreans engage in an occupation peculiar to fire-prone Japan: selling fire extinguishers from door to door.

The Koreans stay in Japan to earn their livings pending what tomorrow may bring in their divided homeland. They cling to their culture, Korean citizenship, and national pride, although now that three-fourths of them belong to the second or third generation, and in some cases have never been to Korea and can scarcely speak Korean, this patriotism is weakening. For the Japanese, Koreans are easy to recognize, clues being Korean speech or accent, the high-waisted gown that Korean women continue to wear, and Korean names like Kim, Dong, or Lee—although to cover up their nationality in seeking jobs, most Koreans have also assumed Japanese names. The Koreans are gayer, noisier, and more openly emotional than the Japanese, but the clues are not infallible. At a big luncheon one day I spent some time admiring the classical Japanese features of a man who looked as though he might be a Kabuki actor specializing in samurai parts or the model for an ukiyoe print. He turned out to be a Korean.

4 /🌸

Life in a Paper House

SO JAPAN IS GOING modern. Yet at its heart there remains an image of itself—an image in which men and women marry not for love but through arrangements made by their parents, move into wooden houses with straw-mat floors and paper walls, and subsist on rice and radishes and dried fish. In fact, this quaint picture of home life represents . . .

Just about what happens to the majority of Japanese families, to this day.

Beyond doubt, life styles are changing, rapidly and in ways both commendable and dismaying. In housing, the last twenty years have brought the fast-growing phenomenon called the *danchi*, tall concrete apartment buildings, built in great clusters in the suburbs, and not too different from those of Moscow or London or New York or Buenos Aires. Also gaining ground is the purely or partly Western-style dwelling—picture window, two-car garage, air conditioning, and all. But the actuality for the majority of the Japanese is a single, detached house that would blend easily into the Kyoto of five hundred years ago—a house made of wood (cypress, cedar, or pine) and of that unlikely building material, paper. Such construction does not necessarily make economic sense, since Japan has to import half its timber needs. But no matter. "We love the warmth of wood," a young broadcasting executive told me, in what he regarded as all the explanation that could possibly be needed.

The house is assembled by the half-man, half-cat known as the Japanese carpenter. He does not use hard-toed shoes, which would protect his feet from a dropped board; rather, he wears a sort of stocking with a limber leather sole and the big toe divided from the rest, so that he can walk along a high, narrow beam with feline assurance. He employs modern power saws and planes and drills, but he remains adept at fine joinery using a handsaw that is like a large, square-ended spatula serrated on both edges. When his rough-sawed lumber needs hand-smoothing, he moves his wooden plane by drawing it toward him, rather than by pushing it away.

Building a Japanese house resembles cabinetmaking more than the West's rude, hurried carpentry. Heavy posts and beams, instead of the light, close-spaced two-by-fours of American construction, hold up the house. The timbers are joined by mortises and tenons, notches, scarfs, and pegs, sometimes requiring bolts but hardly ever nails. Particularly up under the weighty roof there are intricate, nicely made trusses. The most important timbers reach the building site carefully packaged in heavy transparent plastic, to protect them from dents and discoloration. Of these select spars, one becomes the traditional post at the corner of the alcove of the living room, and others serve for various partly visible structural members. The poles are often made of cedar, sawed flat on four sides, but with the natural round showing at the corners; this wood takes on a satiny finish without any treatment except planing. Outer walls of the traditional style are of thin boards laid shiplap, with vertical battens to fix them; they weather to a rich cinnamon color, rather than gray—a cottagey brown that to my mind is one of Japan's greatest charms. Traditionally, builders have also used much stucco, and nowadays, alas, they also employ steel, plastic-coated plywood, and corrugated asbestos. Roofs, praise be, are still mostly made of heavy, curved ceramic tiles, topped by ornate half-rounds on the hips and ridges. Iron gray is the standard color, but brighter tones—ultramarine, a leafy green, maroon—are growing popular.

One autumn morning, early in our first visit to Japan, some friends invited us to breakfast, and in the process gave a lesson in the virtue of the famous Japanese paper wall. One whole side of the room glowed softly with daylight penetrating the white rice paper glued to the latticework of the *shoji*, the wall panels. We sat down at a low table, and then our hostess quietly parted the shoji, which slid easily in wooden guides, and opened a view to the misty, mossy mini-garden —a gnarled tree trunk, some ferns, and an iridescent pigeon strutting by against the enclosing background shrubbery. Exquisite! But paper walls are used mostly as interior partitions. Where they form part of the side of a house, they have to be protected from the weather and from burglars by deep eaves and by wooden shutters that slide in parallel grooves.

The inside dimensions of a Japanese house are always multiples of three feet, so that the floor can be laid out in modules three feet by six. Yes, modules: the Japanese centuries ago adopted this sensible, seemingly modern system. The fact that the module (though it differs slightly in size in various parts of Japan) comes out almost evenly in English feet derives from Japan's pre-metric use of the *shaku*, a measure equal to eleven and fifteen-sixteenths inches. In human terms, the module is derived from the size of the space a man (or anyway, the Japanese man of some centuries ago) needs to sleep, and Japanese houses are accordingly floored with module-size mattresses, the well-known straw tatami.

Tatamis are two-inch-thick pads of matted rice straw, covered with finely woven, slick-to-the-touch reeds, and bound at the edges with black cloth. The reason the Japanese remove their shoes at the doorway is that tatami cannot take the abrasion of leather. Chafed only by stocking feet, however, it is surprisingly durable, but house owners who can afford the cost replace tatamis once a year. They buy the mats from craftsmen in small street-front shops, who compact the straw on a steel framing machine and then sit down on their own tatamis to sew on the surface and binding. Many other house owners preserve the tatami of living rooms by laying a carpet on top, but they still avoid walking on the carpet with shoes. All room sizes are computed in "mats." A room nine by twelve feet, for example, is a "six-mat room."

The interior dividing walls are made, like window walls, of shoji, paper glued to thin wooden strips that form panes about four by seven inches in size. This is the essence of the paper house—the paper providing a magical light and a geometrical charm, even though it scarcely protects against either heat or cold, punctures readily when poked by children's fingers or broom handles, transmits sounds, and makes a peephole when moistened by a wet fingertip. Shoji panels, as well as the solid, double-sided, opaque paper or plastic panels that also serve as interior walls, not only slide aside, but also lift readily out of their guides to leave the house as one big room for special occasions.

This is the grace of the classical Japanese house; it also has another side. Only one in six of the country's houses are connected to street sewers; the rest are serviced by diligent little tank trucks, equipped with pumps and hoses, which come around once a month to empty the pit toilets. In some corner of each house there is what amounts to a privy, with a hole cut directly into the floor and fitted with the Japanese toilet, an oblong of porcelain with a centered hole over which one squats. The odor of these toilets, even though allayed with lime, faintly permeates the house—an unpleasantness that most Japanese simply have to live with.

"We don't like the thought that the skin of our buttocks could touch a surface that someone else has touched," someone told me, in explaining the Japanese toilet. In point of fact, however, Western toilets are common in Japanese hotels, ships, bullet trains, department stores, and many houses. A typical men's room in the modern office building of Mitsui Trust and Banking Company in Tokyo has one Western and two Japanese toilets. Public facilities occasionally display helpful little stick-figure diagrams showing the correct positions for using the Western toilet. Stores that sell seats for Western toilets offer a decal, to be stuck to a nearby wall, with similar information.

The love of—or rather, art of—bathing in Japan requires that the bath be separate from the toilet. The Japanese are fanatic about personal cleanliness. The bath is a room by itself with a tiled and drained space for several people (such as a mother and her children) to scrub and rinse, and a deep, sit-down tub for subsequent soaking. Sometimes the bathroom is a small building detached or semidetached from the main house. The old-style bath, which is still common, has an iron or cypress tub with a wood-burning iron stove built into the bottom; a curl of blue smoke from the stovepipe is the signal that the bath is ready. The water must be made ferociously hot—up to 110° F. More modern baths use gas or electricity. But millions of houses have no bath at all, and whole families ritually traipse off to the public baths at least once a week. One function of the bath is to warm the body in winter. Japanese houses rarely have central heating. Stoves fueled by kerosene (in four-fifths of all houses), propane, or electricity, as well as old-fashioned charcoal-fired hibachis, cut the chill with varying ineffectiveness. In one place where we stayed, we were supplied with a *kotatsu*, a low table with a cloth skirt and an electric radiant heater glowing orange inside this tent. On the theory that if your ankles are warm, your whole body is warm, you stick your feet under the table while eating or reading or talking.

When the Japanese dream house is properly realized, the tatami floors are nearly bare, the rooms are spacious and free of clutter, and the alcove displays a single scroll (an ink-brushed painting or a piece of calligraphy) and a work of flower arrangement. The only furniture is supposed to be a dining table about fourteen inches high and some thin cushions to sit on. Unluckily, the ideal is rarely achieved, for a number of reasons. The most pressing of these is that exploding Japan is a jam-packed land. The view from an airplane of most old residential areas in the cities is one of roof tiles and street pavement, unrelieved by lawns and open space. Where rambling streets form a block, not only do houses line the edges of the block, right up to the street, but they also fill the core of the block, with tiny alleyways giving access. The new towns of Hishino and Tokadai near Nagoya, which are spacious for Japan, allot eighteen units per acre. And not only are the urban houses of Japan set cheek by jowl, but they average out tiny. I know a retired Japanese brigadier general who lives in a home that seems no bigger than a dollhouse.

Prices of building land, though jacked up by speculation, are necessarily high. The size of houses is limited less by the cost of construction than by the cost of the land. Thus it is that the whole floor space of an average Japanese house measures 712 square feet—not much more than a large American living room. Houses have as few as two rooms, and rarely more than five.

Because of this crowding, the Japanese dream of chaste domiciliary beauty—austere and uncluttered—generally fails in practice. Small houses cannot spare rooms for any single purpose. Living rooms have to double as sleeping rooms, which precludes permanently positioned beds. Each night the housewife opens a closet and pulls out thin foldable mattresses, sheets, quilts (or electric blankets), and little hard pillows (sometimes filled with beans—surprisingly comfortable), and makes up pallets on the tatami. The parents may sleep in one room and the children in another, but in tiny houses they all sleep together.

Toys, clothes, books, newspapers, ashtrays, and pillows clutter floors. Crumbs of food filter into straw mats despite the special "tatami suction" provided on Japanese vacuum cleaners. A color television set and a telephone occupy the place of honor in the alcove where flowers or a vase should be. Western furniture inevitably intrudes. "My daughters insist on it," one father told me. "Personally, I'd rather sit on the floor." Taking an informal inventory of a six-mat living room in Tokyo, I noted a piano, two dolls in glass cases, an electric organ, a stereo hi-fi set, a Western dining table with chairs, a bird cage, and a telephone. I also peered into many kitchens, not much bigger than closets, which turned out to be jammed with rice cookers, refrigerators, electronic ovens, stainless-steel sinks, clothes washers, and sometimes dishwashers—all built small to fit. The narrow margin of land surrounding little houses is usually littered, at least in back, but all houses have gardens, even if they are no bigger than card tables and accommodate but a single tree, shrub, esthetic stone, or potted plant.

Multiply this picture of a Japanese house by 18 million, and you get a broad notion of the country's non-apartment dwelling places, where most of the people live. Of course, the variations are infinite, ranging from the packing-box hovels some outcasts live in to the modernistic houses of the rich. A rule of thumb is that the more a house costs, the more Western it will be. White-collar people create in their houses at least one "Western room," with upholstered chairs, carpeting, and perhaps permanent plaster walls, which they use for receiving guests. For costlier houses, architects perform some wondrous feats of "bicivilization," artfully combining thoroughly Western living, dining, and kitchen areas with tatami bedrooms and hideaways (Western beds are growing more popular every year— more than one-fourth of all Japanese use them). A university professor, showing me his lovely Eastern-Western house on a hillside overlooking Kyoto, explained this sort of two-culture style by saying that his public life—entertaining colleagues or conferring with them at his home—demanded Western surroundings, while his private life required a Japanese atmosphere.

Semi-Westernization also changes the outward look of the house. Right next to Japanese houses as quaint as old temples you can see examples of Le Corbusier's 1920–1930s cubical "machine-for-living" functionalism made of poured concrete or unadorned stucco, with flat roofs. Postwar Japanese houses tend to use hipped roofs, prefab panels, post-and-beam construction, and expanses of glass in aluminum sash to achieve a look both Western and Japanese. I inspected a dozen such houses, and noticed that however modernized the rest of the house might be, the bath kept its old form and style as a sacrosanct place, even though in some cases tubs, walls, and floor were prefabricated in one piece out of plastic.

Japan does not have great palatial residences on the scale of Europe and America, but there are a few extravagant houses. One sweltering day in Tokyo a rich businessman showed me through his four-story, poured-concrete house, built all in Western style. He had half a dozen parlors, a dining room that could seat forty, two kitchens, manorial bedrooms, and several small apartments to accommodate visitors. An elevator connected the floors, and a television camera, which could be tuned in by any of the house's receivers, kept vigil on the area just outside the power-operated main door. Two pedigreed Great Danes romped in the spacious garden bordered by lofty trees, but we stayed inside to relish the host's excellent air conditioning and his tall gin-and-tonics. He was proud to tell me that there wasn't a tatami room in the place.

The tatami way of life, though, remains the choice even for the 8 million Japanese families who cannot swing a house and have to live in rented apartments. A third of Tokyo's residents live in wooden apartment houses, in the shoji-tatami style, and these apartments can be dreadful: single rooms as small as four and one-half mats (nine by nine feet) with a kitchen sink and a portable cooking stove, and out in the hall a more complete kitchen and a lavatory for communal use. A better type of apartment has two rooms, kitchen, lavatory, entrance area, and bath. Such flats vary from an apartment in the landlord's house to nondescript two- and three-story buildings containing a dozen units. Tokyo also has 590 buildings, running two to ten stories high and containing a total of 28,000 luxury, Western-style apartments known by the genial, transplanted English term "mansions." First built in the year of the Tokyo Olympics, 1964, and run as condominiums, mansion apartments cost upward of $40,000 and average 800 square feet of floor space—not much. I visited one whose well-to-do occupants limited their entertaining to six people at a time for lack of space. Nearly 2 million Japanese families, incidentally, live in housing, mostly suburban apartments, provided at minimal rent by employers as an incentive to stay with the company.

Taken altogether, Japanese housing is—despite the architectural charm of many individual dwellings and the high level (about seven out of eight) of owner occupancy—unacceptably cramped, uncomfortable, and unhealthful because of the primitive sewage systems. Pollution of all kinds is Japan's worst scandal; but housing is certainly second, because of government neglect. The United Nations puts Japan in a class with Barbados and Malta for housing quality. The supposed cure for this disgrace is the danchi, the publicly built apartment house. Reinforced-concrete apartment buildings, four to fourteen stories high, now tower in legions over low-rise residential Japan. I particularly recall the view at Mukaigaoka, a western Tokyo suburb: a vast valley of thousands of individual houses, serving as a kind of teeming lawn for a large number of danchis with quilts and laundry hanging from their balconies. Battles rage between housewives and building managers over permission to air bedding like this, but the housewives usually win, and their bright comforters give these gray buildings a touch of color, untidy but human.

Danchis are providing Japan with a whole new sociology, in fact. People in aging, costly tenements want the solid construction and convenience of danchis so much that the government must stage lotteries to pick new tenants. Once in, these tenants soon yearn to move out, into a real house. Life in a danchi is too monotonously uniform even for the conformist Japanese. Many a husband, the stories go, mistakenly enters the wrong building out of a group of identical buildings, opens a door just like his own, sits down with his newspaper in a stereotyped room, and fails to notice that the woman making dinner is not his wife.

Danchis have modernity, handy shopping, playgrounds, and access to city centers by train, but they are even more cramped than the average single house. Apartments are classified as "2DK" or "3DK," meaning that they contain two or three small bedrooms and a dining–kitchen room. This encourages nuclear families—no room for grand-parents here. The sturdy concrete walls separating one apartment from another permit the danchi dweller to choose not to make friends with his neighbor, which leads to a more private form of life than Japan has been used to. Many young couples delight in this excuse to be cut off from in-laws, which tends to fill the danchis with people aged from twenty-one to forty.

Unless they work for high-paying corporations, such relatively young people cannot meet the Japan Housing Corporation's stiff requirement of a salary five and one-half times as great as the rent (typically $60 to $110 a month). And since these corporations de-mand good educations of their employees, the vast majority of danchi dwellers are college graduates.

Danchi living is far from ideal, but out of sheer necessity Japan has been building these apartments so fast in recent years—about 1.5 million units annually—that it has stayed neck and neck with the United States, and far ahead of the rest of the world, in new housing starts.

Arranged marriages persist in Japan because many young brides and grooms prefer them to "love" marriages. "To begin with, arranged marriage is really just an introduction system. The couples are never forced to marry against their will," one young husband explained to me. "If the boy and girl don't like one another, they won't marry. It's a safe system. Each person is all checked out. It's especially good if you're shy."

Polls taken by the Ministry of Health and Welfare report that more than three out of five Japanese couples now say that they marry "for love," and the rest marry by arrangement. But close observers contend that in fact the big majority of couples rely on marriage arrangement, even though they may later report their motive as love. The key figure is the man or woman who serves as go-between for the parents—or, in recent times, for the friends or employers—of the boy and girl. Traditionally this operator is a professional.

The writer Lewis Bush cites a certain pro, known as the "god of matchmaking," who has arranged more than 3,100 marriages, so well paired that only five ever got divorces. "You have to be careful," this man says. "For example, you don't bring together a couple each with a long face. Oh, no! A long-faced man should marry a round-faced woman, and vice versa. Otherwise you'll have long-faced children, even grandchildren." But matchmakers can also be almost anyone who happens to think that a certain boy and girl belong together. A prominent businessman, speaking of an associate, told me quite casually: "He's a sort of protégé of mine—I arranged his marriage."

Once a match is suggested, the parents or proxies mull over the young couple's tastes and traits, and schedule a *miai*, a party or dinner where boy and girl are introduced. The sponsors then retire, and the young people can decide whether to meet again, looking toward marriage. The beauty of it is that if either one nixes the deal, the other gets out without much ego damage, although if a girl goes through a dozen miais without being asked for a further meeting, she may well feel bruised.

In the most formal arranged marriages, the go-between and the parents pry deeply into each candidate's background, often using private detectives, and turn off the negotiations if they find, say, bastardy or a streak of mental illness. The investigators also search for positive traits. One Japanese wife, who views herself as a liberated woman and looks with scorn on the old ritual, told me with disdain about how a proper wife under the old dispensation is supposed to be trained to perfection in special schools. "She comes with a flower-arranging certificate, a cooking certificate, a piano certificate, a paper-folding certificate, and a sewing-kimono certificate. Boys ask girls, 'How many certificates do you have?'" A proper bride should be a virgin, too, but in case she is not, and her future husband seems insistent on the point, many Japanese plastic surgeons will perform a discreet hymen-replacement operation.

As a consequence of arranged marriage, presumably, few Japanese husbands seem to feel that they must pamper their wives with incessant attention. "Japanese men value friends more than wives or romantic love. But they move to friendship cautiously and self-protectively—no heart-on-the-sleeve stuff," a British diplomat, long acquainted with Japan, told me. A survey by the Taiyo Bank showed that a majority of salaried managers return home each night after eight o'clock, and that all salary men like to spend an hour or two in the bars after work. Any evening in big railroad stations, scores of these men, reeling in pairs, arms around each other's shoulders, happy, harmless, and silly drunk, head unsteadily for the trains that will take them home. "It is rare for a father to be in time for an evening meal with his children," says Professor Ishida.

Those who claim to know say that Japanese husband-and-wife sex is more satisfactory than it is in the United States and Europe, partly because puritanical guilt is so foreign to the Japanese psychology. Dozens of "the way to married love" sex manuals are published in Tokyo, illustrating the forty-eight "Japanese" sex positions with photographs of wooden dolls, and the like, all as impersonal as instructions for assembling Tinker Toys. But crowded houses and paper walls impose their own inhibitions on enthusiastic marital sex; in fact, the many two-hour trysting-place hotels in Japanese cities are used as often as not by married couples in search of privacy.

Husbands and wives in early marriage are at least equally eager to establish a family—two children, to be born while the wife is young. Yet husbands can be casual about the actual births of children. Young businessmen-students living at the Institute for International Studies and Training near Mount Fuji told me that new fathers among them rarely bothered to go as far as Tokyo, two hours on a bus, to be present when a child was born. An arranged marriage is more a partnership, with chores assigned to each spouse, than a romance. It often works out stiffly. One young man said to me: "My father's conversation with my mother consists of, 'Where is my paper?' and 'When will the meal be ready?' "

Taking a mistress in Japan is still something of the institution that it is in France, or was in England. The freedom of men to spend evenings as they like and the presence of hordes of "hostesses" in bars —not to mention free-and-easy office girls and department-store workers and so on—makes a mistress feasible when a man starts to earn enough money. Wives tend to expect this, and demand only to be spared embarrassment. One wife I heard about got so chummy with her husband's mistress that they arranged to carry on a correspondence by inserting notes under the lining of the heel of the man's right shoe. He carried these notes back and forth for years, and never learned he was a mailman.

Gossip and surveys and even serious sociology make the Japanese husband at home seem pretty much of a boor—more so, I think, than he really is. He hates to invite friends home, and when he does, he is uneasy talking with them in the presence of his wife. Everyone notices that on social occasions wives are shy about mixing with guests, preferring to hover around the kitchen. I met an American girl who, as a student, had arranged to live with a Japanese family in Kyoto. In the first day or so of her residence, she learned not to sit on the cushion customarily used by the father of the family, to take her bath after both the father and his eighteen-year-old son, and to expect to be served meat only after these two had picked the best morsels for themselves. The son, she noted, was sassy to both his mother and his sister, but not to his father. A governmental entity called the Human Capacity Development Division, worrying about how the Japanese might spend the extra leisure they are expected to have in the future, made the dismaying discovery that the Japanese male spends two-thirds of his free time watching television or dozing.

These observations probably overstate the case against the Japanese father. At any fair or festival or fireworks display, fathers by the hundreds can be seen happily shepherding happy kids. More and more on Sundays fathers, visibly relaxed and proud, take their wives and children out to lunch at the zoo or a museum—jabbering, giggling occasions of clattering spoons and chopsticks.

Yet, relative to the United States at least, father is the family's missing figure—worrisomely so, some think. Wataru Hiraizumi, a leading conservative member of the House of Councillors, told me of his concern that "children are left too much without fathers, and women all by themselves cannot properly raise children"; boys need examples, and girls need male authority. Be that as it may, mother is in charge.

Watching Japanese families, I often thought that the main institution of the country must be the Japanese mother, who may once have been a working woman and may become one again, but for fifteen or twenty years devotes herself to her children. The mother who sleeps with her children until they are six or seven, the mother who carries her baby on her back when she goes shopping, the mother who early instills obedience and a sense of what-you-do and what-you-don't, the mother who gently restrains individualism and exuberance, the mother who makes sure that her small son gets to sit down on a bus because he is male and therefore important ("There's a seat! Go get it!"), the mother who takes the child to his first school exams and helps him pass all the later ones, the mother who focuses on her children and is happy enough to have a husband who is healthy and working, the mother who teaches the daughter that she must grow up to be a mother too. These are serious women: the books that they read to children of two or three contain elaborate pedagogical prefaces instructing the mother on how to make the volume teach and advance the child.

The American mother, seeing her child as dependent, feels compelled to develop his independence; the Japanese mother sees her child as an independent creature, who must be shaped into a dependent role. I was fascinated, one day while watching a theatrical for children in a public park, to note that when the juvenile superman character got into a bad jam with some monsters and dragons, he summoned his mother for help.

One mother told me that what Americans call the "terrible twos" occurs among Japanese children at the age of four, because the discipline of school (kindergarten) looms and the kids seem to realize that "this is their last time for revolt before a life of servitude." Whatever the case, Japanese children under four rank with plum blossoms and Fuji on a clear winter day as the country's loveliest treasures. They are (mostly) high-spirited but not raucous, well-behaved but not downtrodden, enchantingly beautiful, and as bright as new coins.

Bringing up children, especially for a mother who adopts the popular "two and no more" credo, does not consume a woman's whole day. The children are off to school at an early age, and taking care of a small house is not all that time-consuming. Most Japanese wives are women of considerable leisure, who get out a lot and make marketing late in the afternoon, a time for gossip and sociability. Preparing meals is a relatively easy task. The food the modern Japanese eat at home—as compared to the many-course meals at inns and gourmet restaurants—is bought half-ready, or is quick and easy to make.

The great simplifier of the Japanese home cuisine is its reliance on rice, which is everywhere cooked in a fast and convenient electrical appliance invented some years back. Breakfast, lunch, and dinner, rice is half the meal. At breakfast, the other main dish is *miso* soup, a broth made quickly by boiling dried fish in water and adding bean paste, or even more quickly by pouring a modern dried-soup mix into hot water. Some pickled vegetables (which can be bought that way) or an egg (raw, broken over the rice) and tea complete the meal. Quite a few Japanese prefer a Western breakfast—dry cereal, or bacon and eggs. A typical lunch is a bowl of rice with a little meat or shrimp or chicken in a sort of stew. With the rice for dinner go vegetables like sliced big white radishes, leeks, spinach, eggplant, or cabbage, parboiled or braised in hot oil, plus fish or a pork cutlet. Variations on meals bring in seaweed, bamboo shoots, ginger, curry, lotus, and bean curd. Japanese housewives do spend a lot of time slicing vegetables, but they can often buy meat already cooked, and baked sweet potatoes. In fact, about 250 kinds of precooked, quick-frozen foods, from hamburger steaks to fried oysters to croquettes to cakes, are available.

Between 6 and 9 percent of the meat the Japanese eat comes

from the whale, consumed as steak, raw slices, or sausage, often in special whalemeat restaurants. Conservationists elsewhere, particularly in the United States, argue heatedly that Japanese (and Russian) whaling puts four species of the whale—fin, sperm, minke, and sei—in danger of extinction. These objectors are joined by the United Automobile Workers Union, since the conservationists have tried to start boycotts of Japanese cars (among other products) to force Japan to stop whaling. They have also tried to boycott Japan Air Lines to the same end. Third-party boycotts—in this case, forcing the Japanese auto industry or JAL to put pressure on the Japanese whaling industry on behalf of Americans whose goals are both disinterested and interested—seem unfair to me, but at any rate Japan has finally agreed to abide by a selective moratorium on whaling set up by the International Whaling Commission.

Better diet—more protein in meat, eggs, and milk, more calories (an average of 2,500 a day, compared to 3,300 in the United States), partly from increased consumption of bread—is helping to make the Japanese into a taller and heavier race, although a more basic reason may be the genetic effect of crossbreeding (because of greater social mobility of formerly isolated communities). In the decade of the 1960s alone, the average weight and height of twelve-year-old boys increased by nearly nine pounds and two inches, and of girls nearly as much. Fatness among children has for the first time become a worry in Japan. But obese adults are hardly to be found; a note that I was moved to jot down in Kyoto reads: "Rare in Japan—display of the flag, unshaven men, fat people."

The bodies of the majority of the Japanese people are in fact notably well knit and compact, the most frequent imperfection being the heavy legs of many of the girls. Such corpulent limbs are so common that the language has a slang name for them, "*daikon* legs," after the giant, elongated white radish that is one of Japan's most popular vegetables. A deformity that is disappearing, but still part of the Japanese street scene, is the permanently bent back. The backs of old men, and even more conspicuously, old women, become ossified at right angles in the lower spine, supposedly from bending over to plant and tend rice. This condition requires that they walk with one arm outstretched to grasp a supporting cane, and their heads are scarcely three and a half feet above the ground.

The basic racial structure of the Japanese is what anthropologists call Mongoloid, like the Chinese, Koreans, Vietnamese, Thais, Burmese, and even American Indians. But these islanders probably also have some of the genes of the Ainu, the hairy, primitive, proto-Caucasoid, Neanderthal-like people who were in Japan before the Mongoloids arrived, and of the Negritos, who came from Malaya and the Philippines. The strong Mongoloid strain gives all Japanese straight black hair, brown or black eyes, and the epicanthic fold of skin that extends from the upper eyelid down over the inner corner of the eye. Japanese drivers' licenses have no space for recording eye and hair color, because everybody's is the same. The other blood mixtures may account for the more luxuriant beards and mustaches among the Japanese than among the other Mongoloids, and for an average skin tone slightly darker than theirs. In cities such as Hong Kong, where Japanese and Chinese mix on streets and in hotels, it is a tantalizing game to try to tell them apart—not even the Japanese and Chinese themselves, much less Westerners, can be very certain.

To an American used to living in a population that includes every race and nationality, Japanese features and physical characteristics seem awesomely homogeneous. On the pate of each and every Japanese child grows an abundant crop of straight, black, shiny filaments (the whorls of which, I learned from a little book called *Japan in a Nutshell*, go 63 percent clockwise and 37 percent counterclockwise). Glancing over the top of the seat in a railroad coach, one sees row upon row of black bristles and dark tresses, broken only rarely by the gray of the aged or the winy red that a Japanese girl's hair turns when bleached. To see a Japanese with Afro hair, as I did just once, is startling.

But within these uniformities, Japanese faces exhibit immense variety. I kept seeing resemblances to Occidental movie actors and actresses. One day in a restaurant I saw two lunchtime companions who looked like Marcello Mastroianni and Liv Ullman. There are burnished Jeanne Moreaus, coppery Anthony Quinns, jasmine-pale Jane Fondas, swarthy Lee Marvins, and many ivory Anouk Aimées. The Japanese, incidentally, do not call themselves "yellow" but rather "wheat color"; and in fact skin colors range from café au lait to chalky. Some girls Westernize their eyes by getting "round eye" plastic surgery. The generally thick-textured Japanese skin also produces abundant and often marvelous dimples.

The kimono is alive but not well in Japan. True, department stores have them in dazzling assortments: kimonos made of silk, cotton, synthetics, and gold-threaded brocades; patterned or painted; priced from $40 to $600. True, too, that no Paris couturier can match the splendor of these garments; the bridal kimonos, in magentas, tangerines, and lemon colors, are especially stunning. For older women there are quiet grays and indigos. From these stores, or from smart little specialty shops, or from their own sewing machines, almost all Japanese women acquire from two to two dozen—or even more—kimonos in their lifetimes. Kimonos hide bad legs and de-emphasize the breast, and expose what the Japanese regard as the sexiest part of the female body, the nape of the neck, a fetish that is supposed to be the consequence of mothers carrying small boys on their backs.

Weddings, funerals, tea ceremonies, graduations, receptions, the theater, and evenings in elegant restaurants bring out kimonos. Tradition-minded women, middle-aged or more, wear kimonos regularly on the street. Among the clusters of suburban housewives waiting on a train platform at midmorning to go to Tokyo, several will be wearing kimonos. For the geisha and for the waitress in good Japanese-style inns and restaurants, the kimono is the working costume. Schools offer thrice-weekly lessons in kimono wearing, at $6 to $8 an hour; the main knacks are dexterity in tying the *obi*, the sash, and taking the quick, short, trotting steps which are all that the hobble skirt allows.

But for most of the occasions of her life—for school, for work, for shopping, for parties, for movies, for travel—the Japanese woman leaves her kimono in her closet. The great majority of Japanese women much prefer to wear Western clothes most of the time. Even on special occasions, women more often opt for what they still call "foreign" clothes than for Japanese. In Kyoto, we made friends with a woman in her forties and several times went out to dinner with her and her husband. It was always a cliff-hanging question whether she would appear in a kimono or a dress, although she looked equally appealing either way. Yet for shopping, this attractive woman wore neither kimono nor dress, but rather a blouse and *monpe*, baggy flannel trousers caught at the ankle with elastic—a farmer-woman getup. She also found monpe useful for climbing trees; her household duties included pruning and gardening.

Some say that the Western clothes preferred by Japanese women are more French in style than American. But Japanese styles seem to have an un-Gallic modesty. Décolletage is rare, colors are muted, long sleeves and stockings are common even in summer, and mini-skirts are unusual.

Extremely popular is the *ji-pan*, jeans pants. The worldwide unisex vogue for blue denim is as pervasive in Japan as anywhere; it started during the American Occupation but caught on big only a couple of years ago. The best jeans boutiques sell only the top brands of American-made jeans, seven or eight million pairs a year. Those who can't afford Levis take jeans made in Japan of American denim; and those who have to settle for third-best take jeans made in Japan of Japanese denim.

The Emperor Meiji took to Western clothes a century ago as one of his first steps in the modernization of Japan; the males of the country have mostly dressed in Western style ever since. Stores are filled with suits made in France, England, the United States, and Japan, and the customer can have anything he wants as long as it's plain, dark, and sober. Actually, sobriety and uniformity seem to be the choice of the customer rather than the merchant, for the conforming salary man likes to look like all other salary men. Stores offer pink shirts, but men buy white shirts. It is astonishing to visit shops and see how many varieties of drab neckties can be designed and sold.

Little old professors, eccentric intellectuals, book publishers, super-nationalists, grandfathers—these kinds of men sometimes go out on the street or to offices in men's kimonos of gray or black, often worn with berets. More commonly, men come home and change from suits to kimonos to relax in, unless they have been converted to slacks and a loose shirt. Japanese inns provide both men and women with the *yukata*, a light cotton kimono suitable for going to and from the bath, or for sitting down to dinner, or, on a nice summer evening in a small town, for a stroll in the streets. Men must wear the kimono with the right side over the left, and women vice versa; the maids in several inns corrected me sharply when I did it wrong. Another Japanese garment for men is the informal *jinbei*, a loose cotton jacket held closed with string ties, and shorts, invented in the fifteenth century as underwear for samurai.

Are the Japanese well dressed? They are tidily, cleanly, soberly, warmly—and in kimonos, beautifully and exotically—dressed. Another of my jotted notes says, "Very few people dirty, ragged, or disheveled."

5 /

Tea and Suicide

ONE MORNING at five thirty, we arose at our hotel in Kyoto, waited while the clerk figured our bill on his abacus, then caught a clanking streetcar to the railroad station. The date on the train tickets that we bought showed that it was September 9 of the year Showa 48. Reaching Kobe about an hour later, we climbed into a cab through the left rear door. From his position on the right-hand side of the front seat, the driver operated a lever that closed the door, and we moved off down the left-hand side of the street. By now schoolchildren were abroad, and we stopped as some little girls, uniformed in long navy-blue skirts, white blouses, and yellow caps, plucked yellow flags from a canister on a telephone pole and waved them to halt traffic as they crossed the street. Nearby, a man bought a can of Suntory beer from a sidewalk vending machine, which responded with a tape-recorded "Thank you very much."

By the time we arrived at the waterfront, the fare on the meter read 300 yen ($1). Into the driver's white-gloved hand I placed a 500-yen bill, the one that bears the likeness of Tomomi Iwakura, who in 1872 led a famous mission from just-opened Japan to the United States and Europe. The driver returned two 100-yen coins, which are finely stamped with a trio of cherry blossoms. I gave him no tip, and he would not have taken any. In the lobby of the pier building, we spotted over a door the short, triple-segmented curtain, *noren*, that symbolizes a restaurant. Even before we ordered our coffee, the waitress brought us those balmy banishers of weariness, steamy little towels in glassine bags that explode open at a light blow. Half an hour later, we boarded our ship, a large white Inland Sea ferry, tossed our suitcases into a tatami-floored stateroom, and watched the sailors cast off while loudspeakers played that beloved old Japanese air, dear to all departures in these islands, "Auld Lang Syne."

The Japanese cherish custom. It gives them a sense of security and identity and history. True, some old rituals are dying. Hospitals no longer give a new mother a small paulownia-wood box containing the umbilical cord of her baby, to be kept as the "uncontrovertible bond between mother and child." But the Japanese remain the heirs and defenders of a great body of other customs. The Japanese eat and drive and dress and wed and give and shop in thoroughly Japanese ways.

Yellow, the color of those little girls' flags, is in Japan the color that means "watch out"; towels are for wetting and not for drying; ships as well as houses must have tatami floors. Abacuses, white gloves, cherry blossoms. Customs as old as noren, as eclectic as adopting Robert Burns, as modern as automatic cab doors and talkative vending machines.

To a Japanese child the question, "What year was Expo '70?" is not a riddle for simpletons but a legitimate query, to which the answer is, "Showa 45." The Japanese number years not from the birth of Christ but from the succession of the incumbent emperor, whose reign takes on a "year name." Hirohito's era, begun in 1926, is Showa, meaning Bright Peace (remember Pearl Harbor?). His father's (1912–26) was Taisho, meaning Great Righteousness. But of course, the eclectic Japanese also use the Western dating system. English-language newspapers and businesses with strong foreign ties use anno Domini; and the Japanese share the Western mentality enough, for example, to speak of centuries and to be concerned about what the nation will amount to by the landmark year A.D. 2000.

The Japanese also find it natural to be one of that small and diminishing band of countries which drive on the left. This custom was the work of Sir Rutherford Alcock, who as Queen Victoria's "Minister Plenipotentiary at the Court of the Tycoon" set up the first British legation in old Edo in 1859.

And there's tipping: virtually taboo throughout the land. Some Western tourists just can't shake this abominable custom, and a few Japanese waiters or bellboys will take a tip; expensive hotels and restaurants, moreover, add a 10 percent service charge to bills. It is true, also, that cab drivers are not above gouging stranded people late at night for what amounts to a fat advance tip. But as for the overwhelming majority of Japanese servitors, in contrast to their European and American counterparts, this is the Country Sans Outstretched

Palm. What a credit to Japanese dignity—a man gets an honest wage and does not truckle for more.

Eating has always been a ritual for the Japanese, and an elegant one. Even a dish of radishes is arranged in a traditional geometric pattern. In fact, the presentation begins well before the meal. On the street in front of nine out of ten restaurants in Japan stands a glass showcase exhibiting samples of the food to be had inside. In the most artful of these displays, the food looks so delectable—curly noodles, salads with moist red tomatoes, dishes of sweet-and-sour pork, fresh-grilled fish, chilled foamy beer—that the impulse arises to smash the glass and gobble it up. The urge must be resisted. The chief ingredient of these enticing dishes is vinyl plastic, and they are the product of a large, weird industry in Japan, a fantastic triumph of mass trompe l'oeil.

One day in the Kappabashi section of Tokyo, I visited out of curiosity a plastic-food factory called Tokyo Biken (meaning "Study of Beauty") Company, Ltd., run by a man named N. Majima. Though a taciturn fellow, he allowed me to extract from him the information that the use of imitation food for advertising began when Japan was first opened to the West, but became big business only after World War II. "When restaurant operators began to adopt many kinds of Western food and create new varieties of Japanese food, they found they could not describe them all in writing on menus, so we took up making models of the dishes," he explained. The idea is a blessed help to the foreigner who cannot speak Japanese, for he can summon a waiter and point out the meal he wants; but the basic purpose is to advertise the food to Japanese customers and illustrate it for them.

In Majima's factory that day, one worker was producing a run of vinyl squids, whose floppy tentacles pulled reluctantly out of the mold after the heat of an oven had set the white liquid plastic. Another man was wiring a fork with a heap of white vinyl tubing to create the illusion of spaghetti being lifted to the mouth. A third was delicately spraying green paint on little nubbins of plastic—presto! Brussels sprouts! On a bench were mugs of bubbly beer made of jelled glycerine topped by wax foam, iced coffee with glass for ice and cream appearing to pour in from a suspended metal beaker, goblets of lemonade, a basket of half-painted prawns, and a few banana splits. Another floor of the building contained nothing but assorted pizzas. Majima explained that the originals for these works of art were the real thing—real sliced hard-boiled eggs, leaves of lettuce, pig's feet, hot dogs, filet mignon. A wax mold made, for example, from a peeled banana served to form a hard plastic banana, from which was shaped a metal mold suitable for casting bananas by the hundreds. A coat of paint completed the illusion. Majima's factory is not large; he subcontracts entire batches of plastic-molded shrimps and peas to cottage industry in the town of Koshigaya, north of Tokyo, where housewives meticulously dab on the paint that gives verisimilitude.

Near Majima's factory, in block after block of stores dealing in restaurant supplies, were a number of shops specializing in retailing plastic food. Their showrooms looked like restaurants whose chefs could effortlessly turn out all the world's cuisines at once: the range went from little cocktail sandwiches through chicken Cantonese and *boeuf à la mode* to roast turkey and a succulent Japanese sea bream, head and all, resting in a wooden boat among daisies, pebbles, and spiny plants, and sauced with tiny shrimps, crabs, and caviar. This *oeuvre*, worthy of any gallery that has the courage to show such works as Claës Oldenburg's baked potatoes made of cloth, sold for $120. But prosaic items needed by restaurants—pork chops, sukiyaki, curry rice, and so on—were cheap enough, $10 or less. Majima said that many foreign tourists buy these "appetite producers" as *objets d'art*.

The generally inexpensive restaurants that use these inedible edibles to seduce the hungry come in half a dozen types: the *soba* shop for noodles; the *sushi* shop for rice and raw fish; the variety restaurant that provides a big choice of dishes made with meat, cooked fish, bean curd, and vegetables; the Chinese restaurant; the mixed restaurant that offers some noodle dishes, some rice dishes, some Chinese food, and some Western cooking; and the restaurant that concentrates on one item only.

The noodle shops' main dish is a product of buckwheat flour, resulting in a gray-brown color. Noodles come in bowls, swimming in broth, and topped with countless variations of meat and vegetables. I usually ordered *gomoku soba*, "five-things noodles," with egg, onion, pork, ham, and fish paste on top. Tolerantly enough, noodle shops will substitute rice for noodles if the customer wishes. In summer, noodles are often served not only cool, but actually mixed with chunks of ice. In sushi shops, the food comes in shallow, lacquered wooden boxes; the staple is a small fat patty of boiled rice, variously plain or wrapped with a strip of seaweed or rolled around a bit of radish or cucumber, seasoned and sprinkled with vinegar, and topped with a slice of raw, marinated, or cooked fish, which may be horse mackerel, tuna, cuttlefish, shrimp, eel, or clams, all served cold. The pleasure of eating sushi depends mostly on combining the morsels with the proper amounts of horseradish and a special soy sauce.

At the variety shops, one can get forty or fifty of the 189 dishes of the Japanese cuisine listed in a clever little book called *Eating Cheap in Japan*. Samples: "Pork slices marinated beforehand and then cooked in the same sauce, which is made from soy sauce and freshly grated ginger." "Whole or sliced mushrooms, bits of chicken, gingko nuts and a few vegetables in a soup made from fish bouillon seasoned with sake and sweet wine." "Fried burdock root and carrot strips seasoned with soy sauce, sugar and red pepper." "A small dish of seasonal, mountain flowering fern which has been boiled in fish bouillon seasoned with soy sauce and sweet wine." It is in these variety restaurants that one eats the mouth-watering *sashimi*, slices of raw tuna or sea bream. Many dishes here involve *tofu*, which is the custardlike curd made from fermented soy beans, and which forms an inescapable part of the Japanese diet. The last course is usually miso soup, the same bouillonlike, bean-paste broth that is popular for breakfast.

These dishes typically are the lunches for the average salary man and for his secretary too. They are cheap and good. But the casual visitor seldom finds them, or dares venture into the restaurants that serve them. Thus Japan maintains an international reputation for expensive eating. The reputation is founded on the sumptuous teahouse meals, commonly running to $100 or more per person, that are served to the rich and the guests of businessmen with expense accounts. On such an occasion in Kyoto, I took a few course-by-course notes on this kind of meal. My host was Toyotaka Murata, president of the city's leading advertising agency and a former Kamikaze pilot who—obviously and fortunately—was never called upon to perform his specialty. This kind ex-enemy invited me to the Beautiful Rich Deep Happiness Restaurant, which has been running for more than a century.

That seems to have been sufficient time to settle a few of the more elementary questions of cuisine and service. We sat on the floor, in a room to ourselves, I with my back to the traditional alcove because I was the guest of honor. One side of the room opened to a softly lighted garden of damp moss and stone. The bean-curd sweet that started the meal was served with a knife-shaped toothpick made not of pine or bamboo, but of a special black willow. The bowl of tea that followed, whipped, foamy, and thick, was designed to clear the mouth of the taste of the sweet, pleasant as it may have been. The tongue was thus tempered for the subtle savor of the root of the mountain lily in the next dish, served with a small heap of inch-long fried Kamo River fingerlings and a pair of tiny shrimp coated with a paste of seasoned sea-urchin eggs, all bedded on a chrysanthemum leaf, which was itself edible. Then came raw fish, to be dipped in soy sauce.

The next dish contained half a fish head. This morsel had been decapitated from a sea bream, *tai* in Japanese, a saltwater goldfish, and it was so big that the up-staring eye looked as large as a marble. The eye itself was not to be eaten, but the musculature back of it, in a loose bony socket like a clamshell, is prized as the most succulent part of the dish. The experience is likely to cause one to reach for his cup of sake, kept filled by the kimonoed hostess. She was a woman whose calculating eyes reflected perhaps forty years of sizing up the human race; her name translated as Quiet Old River. Under my chopsticks, bits of tasty white meat came reluctantly off the fish head; the flavor is traditionally attributed to the exertions that the tai has to make to stay alive in a certain whirlpool in the Inland Sea. A hot towel, patted on hands and mouth, removed the lingering memory and taste of the fish head. (There is nothing more restorative than the Japanese towel, damp but not soggy, handed to you with tongs because it is very nearly too hot to touch, and provided even in the cheapest railroad-station cafés.) Next came sliced pork with a plump edging of fat, on a little plate with a piece of raw salmon. More sake, too. Then a pair of large shrimp fried in batter, accompanied by a bowl of delectable sauce. The meal ended with a perfectly ripened Catawba melon, cool and thirst-quenching.

Meals of many courses are also the custom in Japanese inns, where a multitude of maids brings the food to one's room. At a Hiroshima *ryokan* one night we had these dishes: chicken and eggplant and green pepper; a pickled radish and Brussels sprouts; seaweed; pickled fish with onion and a red leaf of some kind; sashimi; miso soup; cooked fish; sweet potato; ginger; rice; oranges and bananas. At breakfast in a Kobe inn we had bamboo shoots, meat, and carrots served in a sort of bower; cold raw eggs, to be sucked or broken over rice; miso soup with slices of onion floating in it; a tiny dish containing seaweed, cabbage, and orange-colored radish; a separate strip of dried seaweed; rice; tea.

And all this still fails to bring up some of the most salient experiences of Japanese cooking. There is the beef from cattle raised north of Kobe, which trusted informants say is rarely fed with beer or hand-massaged, as legend has it, but is so well marbled that Italian sculptors reportedly derive pleasure from merely looking at it. Eels, served broiled, are another specialty of many restaurants, and consumed heavily by men in midsummer in the belief that eels "rejuvenate," that is, increase sperm production. There is *konnyaku*, a root of no taste or food value whatsoever, but thought to be healthful because it absorbs the bad from the body. There are fine cidery apples from northern Japan. There is lotus root, which makes a person see well because it has holes in it, but must be eaten with noodles and not rice, for rice plugs the holes. There is sukiyaki—beef, pork, or chicken cooked at the table. There is tempura, deep-fried shrimp in batter. There is tea, green tea, too much tea, tea in bottles for babies, enough tea every year, surely, to fill the Sea of Japan. There is laver, edible seaweed, a duty food equivalent to spinach ("Eat your seaweed, it makes your hair grow black and bushy"). There is *ebi odori*, the "dancing shrimp," shelled, gutted, and split down the middle, but still twitching vigorously as the epicure presses a ball of rice around it and pops it into his mouth. There is superior chocolate, coffee-flavored chewing gum, pansy ice cream, pumpkin leaf, and a shellfish like a nautilus.

And there is the *fugu*, puffer fish, which must be cooked by licensed chefs who with surgical skill remove every particle of the liver and ovaries, because these organs contain a poison, tetrodoxin, so powerful that one ounce (it is unreliably reported) can kill 56,000 people. Japanese emperors are forbidden to risk eating puffer, but gourmets go ecstatic over it, and about a hundred of them die each year of chefs' mistakes. Early in 1975, Mitsugoro Bando, a Kyoto Kabuki actor designated as a Living National Treasure, died of eating fugu liver. A haiku about a puffer eater says—

> *Last night he and I ate fugu.*
> *Today I help carry his coffin.*

The essence of Japanese cooking is to start with the finest raw materials and bring out the original taste. The Japanese say that the West stresses "big flavor" while Japan stresses "small flavor." Another distinction is that the Japanese are indifferent about serving food hot; a little chill in the soup is acceptable, and rice can be downright cold. The reason Japanese teacups have no handles is that the tea is never hot enough to require one. I put the Japanese cuisine behind the French, the Italian, the Chinese, and perhaps several others, but it *is* a cuisine, sensitive, well thought out, and deeply traditional. At the 1972 Frankfurt "Olympics of fine cooking," Japanese chefs won high acclaim for their teriyaki and ginger steak, and a gold prize for their "symphony of pastries."

"It is not absolutely necessary to slurp noisily while eating in

Japan," a Kyoto doctor told me one evening as we dined together. "But," he added, slurping noisily, "it is much better manners if you do." Slurping shows appreciation, like the authorized belch after Middle Eastern meals. In eating long, wet, floppy noodles, one is virtually forced to have good manners—that is, nip up some part of the noodle with chopsticks and loudly suck in the rest of it.

The restaurant to which the doctor took me was deliberately inconspicuous, its tiny doorway garden opening on a back alley—a place where one had to be known to be welcome. The proprietress and several waitresses, in kimonos, dropped to their knees as the doctor entered, bowed until their foreheads touched the polished floor, and repeatedly murmured their ecstasy that he should once again favor them with his custom. They helped us remove our shoes and gave us slippers. It is more than a custom, it is a rule, a law, an ironclad decree, that shoes get no farther than the vestibule of a Japanese restaurant or inn. Grimy soles must not defile the polished wood of hallways, and only stocking feet can touch tatami. A well-run establishment requires hall slippers, kitchen slippers, and bathroom slippers. I estimate that Japanese life would run 10 percent faster without the endless changing of footgear, although people are deft at stepping in and out of slippers with scarcely a change of pace.

Slippers slapping, we followed the proprietress through twisting passageways. By the custom of the house, we had a preparatory sake in one private room and the meal in another. We ate, of course, with chopsticks. A Chinese who lives in Tokyo told me how these useful, sanitary, and efficient implements were devised. "Many centuries ago," he said, "the wise men of China developed remarkably effective eating utensils, the knife and fork. Then, determined to do even better, they invented chopsticks." The Chinese like long, rounded, lacquered-hardwood chopsticks, but the Japanese, in what seems to me to be a further improvement, customarily use short, cheap, square-sectioned chopsticks made of pine, which are thrown away after one meal. They are manufactured in pairs joined together at one end and have to be snapped apart, an act that proves they were never used before. The Japanese, like the Chinese, use chopsticks so skillfully that, even allowing for the messiness of slurping, they see no need for napkins in traditional eating places—in fact, find them disgusting, all stained with food. But all Japanese are also deft with knife, fork, spoon, and napkin, for eating Western food.

When the meal was over, the doctor picked his teeth, concealing the operation with his left hand, in the manner of the Latin Americans, or of the Americans in Victorian times. Like so many trivial objects in this tasteful country, Japanese toothpicks are not mere slivers, but rather little creations of the lathe, with a finial at one end. At the door, the waitresses gave us our shoes and shoehorns as long as an arm—a practical tool that lets one slip into his shoes standing up. We left in a drumfire of *domo arigato gozaimasu* ("Thank you very very very much"), while heads again knocked floors. Outside, I thought it might have rained, but the wetness was only water sprinkled on the pavement by a restaurant flunky to hold down dust. Japanese stores and restaurants practice this custom universally, and almost hourly, with a fervor that far exceeds the effect.

In this show of hospitality, the doctor took pride in going to a restaurant that stresses Japanese tradition, but when his wife wants to feed the family quickly and simply at noon on Sunday she pops out to a store in front of which stands the familiar white effigy of Colonel Harland Sanders. Kentucky Fried Chicken, a joint venture in Japan between Heublein and Mitsubishi Corporation, has grown to be a chain of nearly 150 shops, partly because every Japanese knows about Kentucky from learning "My Old Kentucky Home" in school. Similarly McDonald's, with more than sixty outlets for hamburgers, french fries, and milk shakes, does more business per day at its Ginza shop than in any of its American stores. Yet fast food is really nothing new in Japan. Since 1884 railway-station shops and vendors have been selling travelers the tasty lunch called *obento*, which comes in a light wooden box wrapped in decorative paper, that contains fish or beef in soy sauce, well-cooked seaweed, a bit of omelette, pickled radish, ginger-flavored rice, a tangerine, and chopsticks.

The Japanese can't hold their booze—there's no denying that. The intolerance of the Japanese (in fact, of all Mongoloids) for alcohol is apparently due to a genetic factor. A Boston psychiatrist recently proved in experiments that Mongoloids turn red in the face (a spectacle familiar to every visitor to Tokyo) and suffer palpitations, fast heartbeat, dizziness, and sleepiness from amounts of liquor so small as to have no effect on Caucasians.

Nevertheless, the Japanese do drink. One ancient Chinese chronicler, after visiting Japan in the third century, wrote that "the people of Wa [Japan] are very fond of strong drink." Today, the Japanese drink the equivalent of four and three-fourths quarts of pure alcohol per capita each year, almost exactly as much as Americans and a little more than the British, although less than most Europeans. Many Japanese, particularly women, are well aware of their race's inability to guzzle, and fear of getting sick or giddy restrains them. But no moral objections, WCTU style, prevail in Japan. An unembarrassed "I was drunk at the time" excuses bad behavior or even crime. The motto over the desk of Akira Imamura, the police deputy inspector in charge of the Tokyo drunk tank, is "Treat your fellow men as softly as the spring breeze." Imamura reported that in 1972 "no less than 32,700 drunks were taken into protective custody in the Metropolitan Police area alone. That is enough to fill 163 coaches of the Japanese National Railways."

Sociologist Nakane says drinking is essential to relieving the tensions that come from the complexity and delicacy of Japanese personal relations. "Many Japanese will say without a scruple, 'I can't live without a bar.' . . . When a formal meeting faces deadlock or when difficulties arise in personal relations a chat over drinks often proves effective. . . . A gathering of intimate and life-long friends to drink together is one of the most enjoyable occasions for Japanese men; here they can find complete relaxation and can talk and laugh from the heart." The little six-stool bar, almost a club, where perhaps a hundred regular customers and the woman owner-bartender are dearly known to one another, is a Japanese institution. The custom in such places is never to fill your own glass, but rather hold it up for your companion drinker to replenish. Vending machines supply whiskey, cocktails, canned beer, and canned sake in many hotels, and even on the street.

Sake, sold often in jeroboams and served at a temperature of 110° to 120° F. in tiny ceramic cups, is Japan's historic drink. It originated as a food, a yeasty, pasty rice. Some shrewd Japanese entrepreneur discarded the rice part, extracted the elixir that made people high, and thereby invented sake. One brand is called Gekki Ikan, and it comes in grades known as *tokkyu, ikkyu,* and *nikyu.* Gekki Ikan ikkyu, some wag said, perfectly describes the morning-after feeling that too much of the stuff provides. But it takes a lot to make too much, for sake is more akin in strength and taste to wine (though it is brewed somewhat like beer) than to distilled liquor; the percentage of alcohol runs from 15 to 20. The sludge left over from making sake is edible, a heat-and-eat pancake or, with water, sugar, and salt, a dish like oatmeal.

But today, sake accounts for less than a third of all liquor the Japanese consume. Far more than sake they drink beer—beer that in my judgment is heartier and tastier than almost any American or European beer, and nearly as good as Australian, for it is neither dry nor watery. Japanese beer has a sound tradition; they have been making it for a hundred years. The major brews are Kirin, Suntory,

Sapporo, and Asahi. Beer comes mostly in generous pint-and-a-half brown glass bottles, and the Japanese drink thirty-five of them per adult per year. Kirin Brewery, the biggest, sells well over a billion dollars' worth of beer annually.

Whiskey is the prestige liquor in Japan, and, as elsewhere, the best imported Scotches rank highest; Japanese distillers try to emulate Scotch rather than bourbon or Canadian. Suntory's Imperial, at $40 a bottle, comes close to matching imported Scotch, say Dewar's or Red Label, both in price and quality. But Suntory, unlike the Scottish distilleries, is quite willing to trade off quality for cheapness in its other labels through a long series of progressively worse products. One night in a Tokyo bar some fellow drinkers put their heads together and listed for me the whole Suntory line, using the English names that the company gives its whiskeys: Imperial, Excellence, Royal, Reserve, Very Rare Old, Square, White, Red, and Torys. These connoisseurs agreed that anything down to and including Very Rare Old, which they call *Orudo*, was tolerably drinkable.

Japanese wines are at best so-so. The vines suffer from acid soil and rainy Septembers; that is the month when grapes need sun to bring out the sugar, and instead they get a juice-thinning drenching from the seasonal typhoons. Winemakers have to add grape sugar to increase the alcoholic content. Nevertheless, winemaking and wine drinking are greatly on the rise.

In the middle of 1973, I read in *The New York Times* that Soshitsu Sen, a handsome and forceful man of forty-nine who looks as though he might be a hard-driving top executive at Toyota Motor Company, had gone to New York City and performed a Japanese tea ceremony at what used to be known as the Murray Hotel, on Park Avenue at 38th Street. With that ritual he symbolized the transformation of the old Murray into the new Kitano Hotel, Japanese-owned, tatami-matted, and catering to tourists and businessmen from faraway Nippon. The item intrigued me. I had met Sen, Japan's foremost tea master, in Kyoto the year before. He is a man of unique qualifications, being the fifteenth-generation descendant of Sen Rikyu, who in the sixteenth century made himself the chief synthesizer of Japan's most durable, pervasive, and mysterious custom, the tea ceremony.

Tea was brought to Japan from China in the eighth century, and its potentialities gripped Japanese sensibilities from the first. Ancient accounts make it seem that tea's tannin, caffeine, and vitamin C liberated minds and lent physical strength in a way hard to imagine in the present era of more zingy drugs. Gradually Japan developed a hybrid, green tea, then and now unique to this archipelago. For ordinary meals and hospitality, the Japanese have always made this tea into a beverage by the commonplace process of steeping the leaves, but for tea ceremonies and extravagant meals they adopted the Chinese Sung Dynasty method of powdering the leaves to make a mixture of water and tea that looks like thin pea soup.

In ancient times of tumult, tea was found to have extraordinary powers to console the distressed, calm the angry, soothe the frustrated. It became associated with Zen as a way of purging the mind of the trivial and creating a tranquility suitable to the observation of art. Zen masters, as is their wont, made a ritual out of it. The ritual was advanced and refined by a cultivated fifteenth-century shogun, Ashikaga Yoshimasa, whose distress and frustration was his henpecking wife. He devised the tea-ceremony room as a kind of male sanctuary, fixing its size at a modest four and one-half tatamis, the area that it retains to this day.

The maturing of the ritual naturally created a need for a profession to teach and perfect the ceremonies—the tea masters. The first and most revered of these was Sen Rikyu, who lived from 1521 to 1591. He was a man of exalted taste, and this taste spilled over into garden design, architecture, flower arrangement, calligraphy, and religion. He took Shogun Ashikaga's tearoom and made it a special teahouse separate from the main dwelling, with its own garden and stepping stones leading to a door built low to enforce humility by entering the house on hands and knees. The ideas in this teahouse became basic to Japanese design: asymmetry, stress on wood and textures, humility, and the refinement of the primitive. This style expresses what the Japanese call *wabi*, whose meaning cannot be defined in one English word, but can be bounded, according to the architectural writer Teiji Itoh, by the connotations of "loneliness, desolation, rustic simplicity, quiet taste, a gentle affection for antique, unostentatious, and rather melancholy refinement." Taken together, the notions that coalesced in Sen Rikyu's teahouse shaped Japanese architecture for centuries to come, and form the basis of the popular *sukiya* style of today; indeed, through the visits of Frank Lloyd Wright to Japan, they have influenced the whole world.

Rikyu's lofty repute led him to become counselor to the military dictator Hideyoshi on matters of tea and, soon after, on governmental affairs. Thus Rikyu made enemies. One of them whispered to Hideyoshi that Rikyu was plotting to poison the dictator, and Hideyoshi, determining that Rikyu must die, gave the tea master a choice of being executed or killing himself. Rikyu presided over one last ceremony with old friends, then removed his tea gown to reveal a white death robe underneath it. Addressing a dagger in his hand, he murmured, "Welcome to thee, O sword of eternity," and plunged the knife into his belly.

There are three lines of descent from Rikyu, all based in Kyoto, though Rikyu lived in Sakai, a port near Osaka. The most important is Soshitsu Sen's school of tea, called Ura-Senke. It is headquartered in large new buildings, and the training that this modern tea master gives is in such demand that he has set up branches all over Japan and as far away as São Paulo and New York, growing rich in the process. He himself lives nearby in a building that is a maze of rooms and crannies and corridors, begun in the sixteenth century and added to since, that practically pulses with wabi.

When I entered, early on a cool, rainy morning whose gloom darkened the already dim interior, I caught glimpses, as I was guided to a rough equivalent of a throne room, of elderly women in kimonos kneeling in corners or doorways, silent and a little spooky. Waiting for Sen, I too felt required to kneel. The women, advanced teachers of the tea ceremony, began to converge on the room where I was; old manservants of Sen's, mostly with gestures but sometimes with scolding, arranged the women in kneeling rows in front of the cushion where Sen would sit. Some of the faces of the women were lively and sensitive, some truly beautiful. But most were suffused with the look of people whose pleasures (for the tea ceremony is supposed to be a pleasure) are tense and trying. Perhaps this was because Sen, who himself occasionally makes small changes that modernize the tea ceremony, is known to go into tantrums when his students, such as these teachers, try even the slightest variations.

Sen, in kimono, arrived, drew me aside, and showed me a book, "written by my ancestors," that was to serve as a text for that day's lecture to the teachers. He thought that before interviewing him I should attend a tea ceremony, which he agreed to arrange. A few days later, in the afternoon, I went to one of Sen's teahouses, where a lesser Ura-Senke master was to preside over the ceremony. The road into the place led through thronging schoolgirls going to and from Kyoto Women's University and up to the soaring Shinto gate of a shrine built in honor of none other than the dictator Hideyoshi. But the guide whom Sen sent with me led me off through an opening in a hedge, and, in a quick and typically Japanese transition, the bustle was gone and tranquility took over. Here, in a garden, were a rambling house and, off among trees, a teahouse.

We entered the vestibule of the big house, taking off our shoes, and the host gave us a folding fan and a packet of small white papers with which to dab at mouth and fingers. In the doorway of an eight-mat waiting room, where some early arrivals were kneeling in a row, we dropped to our knees, placed the folding fan before us, flattened our hands against the floor, and bowed until our heads nearly touched it; the kimonoed ladies inside responded by doing likewise. Rocking back and rising, we stepped quickly to the alcove of the room, to kneel again and bow in respect to the scroll on the wall and the flower arrangement below it. We then retired to kneel and wait. Some girl students, in kimonos as lovely as themselves, joined us after softly exclaiming over the beauty of the scroll and flowers.

In gentle argument, with elaborate politesse, an elderly woman and man were each protesting the other's superior worthiness to lead all of us on the way to the teahouse. The man at length agreed to start, stepping into the garden on straw sandals placed by a manservant in front of him and the other guests, one by one. My Western socks, not divided between the big toe and the others, made it difficult for me to keep the sandals on from one wet stepping stone to the next, but I managed to seem duly stunned by the artful pruning of the shrubs and trees. Creeping through the doghouse door into the tea-room, we again knelt, flattening our hands to the floor.

The etiquette then was to keep inside that zone where the Japanese traditionally spend most of their lives indoors, that is, within three feet of the floor. We moved either by using our arms like crutches, while still kneeling, or by rising for a quick, hunched, short trot. The guests moved around to admire the teahouse's scroll, flower arrangement, and, above all, the utensils of tea making: brazier, caddy, bamboo whisk, bamboo dipper, and pottery bowls. We all arranged ourselves at the edges of the room. A wall parted, and a shuttle of servants brought in bowls of bean cakes and sugar cakes. We accepted the service with a bow of respect for the cakes. The guests nibbled a little and conversed in the stilted, near-memorized phrases appropriate to the tea ceremony. The tea master, his gestures ritualized and formal, heated water, spooned the powdered tea into bowls, dipped in enough water to cover the bottom, and whirled the whisk between his hands to make the mixture frothy.

Each guest bowed low to his bowl of tea, picked it up in both hands, and tossed down the thick, bitter, opaque liquid. The servants removed the bowls and brought in half a dozen others, old and rich in wabi, in the refinement of their humility, irregular of shape and dark in glaze, intended not for use but to be marveled at. These objects earned bows and scrutiny from guests who, feeling or pretending awe, leaned clear to the floor to inspect details. Following the bowls came tea containers and bamboo dippers. "Five hundred years old!" "Chinese work—see the mosaic of shell!" "Black and gold lacquer; it took months to make!" The host, from whose collection these priceless objects came, smiled and nodded. One account of tea-ceremony etiquette says that at this point the guest "may even venture to compliment the host on the delicious taste of the water, and may perhaps enquire from which spring or river it originated."

In less than an hour, the drinking and viewing came to an end in a great round of bowing. Out through the little door we crept, and took another path to an eight-mat room in the big house, looking out on the damp verdure of the garden. Again, all knelt and bowed to the alcove of this room, which had a scroll 350 years old and a flower arrangement that left some of the ladies speechless, except for faint "ah's" as they touched this petal or that frond with their fans to single out some especially artless artfulness. When at length everyone was seated on his heels against the walls, the servants, gray-kimonoed elderly men and a pretty girl in brighter colors, brought in trays of food. Each of us bowed as we received our little assortments of sushi, raw fish, and pickled radishes in a small straw scoop. The wife of the host, kneeling before each guest in turn, served sake, which required an exchange of several bows. Then, turning at the door for a final bow, my guide and I departed.

Tea is the "religion of the art of life," and nobody is expected to grasp the profundities of the ceremony in one experience with it. Soshitsu Sen—dressed in a stylish, brass-buttoned navy jacket and powder-blue trousers—enlarged on the meaning of the ceremony when I saw him a day or two later. "The tea ceremony involves deep, true friendship. Christ said: love God and become the son of God. Buddha said: everyone can be a Buddha. Tea combines this in its love of all humanity," said Sen. "In tea, you're always concerned with others. No matter how great a man is, he loses his status in the tea-house. You can make a Mitsubishi executive humble by getting him to go through that small entrance. Tea supplies the innocence of childhood. Don't think of it as a ceremony, think of it as a communing. The ceremony is not the point; it's what it does to you inside. Morals, religion, philosophy, sociability—they're all in tea. And you can't do that with coffee or sake—just Japanese green tea."

Whether or not ceremony is the point, Sen can be exquisitely ceremonial. Later I saw him perform a tea ceremony in a temple, on some great occasion. His movements were like a slow ballet, every footfall calibrated, even the scuff of the slippers carefully contrived.

The mere act of folding the cleaning cloth was a legerdemain of quick, sure movements, thumbs and forefingers making rectangles and triangles of the cloth, and finally a foxtail shape suitable for a flick at the already spotless bowls.

A finishing-school grace essential among wives in conservative Japanese society is the ability to do the tea ceremony at home in the form sanctified by a great master. One day at Sen's school I saw thirty young girls (plus six young men) learning the ceremony. It was a dainty tableau: girls in the golds and blues and tangerines of their various kimonos, all sitting on the floor on the backs of their heels, toes crossed and knees together, in that most traditional of postures, which seems to be tolerably comfortable to the Japanese but rapidly brings on gangrene in foreigners. The custom of sitting on heels originated with the tea ceremony, since sitting cross-legged required too much space on the teahouse floor. The room, the size of a tennis court, was a pleasing setting of blond tatami, blond wood, and paper walls.

Four submasters, strict and stern in black kimonos, were giving instruction to groups of nine students each. My eye fell on a plump girl trying to learn the intricacies of serving herself from a bowl of bean-paste sweets. She had barely set the bowl down and bowed low to it, hands flat on the floor with the tips of the forefingers touching, when the master corrected her with an impatient half-turn of the bowl. She had the wrong side toward her, though all sides looked the same to me. Her expression showed how intensely she was concentrating on control of her whole body—posture, eyes, especially hands. She picked up chopsticks with her left hand, transferred them to the right, lifted one of the marshmallowy sweets to her mouth, replaced the chopsticks in her left hand, and laid them parallel on the bowl's rim. Each movement was as measured and prescribed as the gestures of a Balinese dancer, and only part of a long ritual. Nearby, another girl was trying to take off the lid of a teapot, and quite unable to meet the master's requirement of making a circular movement while holding the lid at a geometrically exact angle. Silence prevailed, except for the master's occasional snapping criticisms and (for the occasion was not too solemn, after all) some tittering among the girls.

For tea-ceremony utensils, "the jewelry of Japan," connoisseurs regularly pay prices higher than Westerners pay for old Meissen. In Kyoto I saw tea bowls priced at $6,000, black-and-gold-lacquered tea containers at $10,000, and waste-water bowls at $5,200. And women were buying them.

Even common, or steeped, green tea has its fine points. It divides into three grades, all from the same bush. The best comes from the three buds on the outermost ends of the branches, plucked by hand just after they have budded under cover to protect them from sunlight and dew. The second grade comes from such buds left uncovered, and cut off rather than plucked. The cheapest comes from the rest of the leaves.

A good many well-known, immemorial Japanese customs are practiced with odd new switches. Government genealogical records are kept with inquisitorial zeal, so that the whole citizenry is registered, no one is anonymous, and all ancestries and relationships are matters of public record. "You need your family records when you move, and when you register in school, and when you get a job," a young man told me, as if this Big Brotherism were natural and universal. What is surprising is to see how this ancient custom works out in modern practice: city halls with galleries of clanking, motor-driven Diebold Power Files (made in U.S.A.) that rotate the records into view so that all kinds of snoopers can, for a fee of fifteen cents, pore over anyone's private life.

The art of paper folding, *origami,* has not only reached perfection in Japan, but is also as routine as doodling. On a ferry once, our small son ripped the jacket off my pocket atlas; two girls with whom we were talking almost automatically converted the scrap of paper into tiny cranes, boats, and feudal helmets. As a matter of fact, butchers wrap bacon in complex folds allied to origami. Flower arranging, *ikebana,* is classically supposed to involve only three flowers and some foliage, all artfully disposed to stress the high esthetics of what is omitted; but in practice great flower arrangers today are using not only as many flowers as they wish, but also eggshells, fruit, and vegetables ranging from spinach to cucumbers to chartreuse celery.

The folding fan, that symbol of coyness to the Western eye, is carried and actually used, by men as much as women—a reminder that the ancient samurai packed a fan as well as two swords and a dirk. The quaint old peddler of hot yams—to be consumed on the spot like knishes in New York—still plies his trade but now bellows his wares on an electronic bullhorn in the caverns of Tokyo's modern financial district. A Kyoto "umbrella master" (fifteenth generation, of course) every month sells a thousand *bangasa,* hand-made on frames of bamboo ribs and canes with heavy oiled paper in place of fabric; this picturesque and smelly bumbershoot is particularly favored by students. Incense sniffing remains a ceremony with some of the mystique of tea; the participants identify the fragrances by an inhalation so subtle that it is called "listening" rather than "smelling." Even door knocking has its rules, based on utmost consideration for whomever may be startled; over and over I saw businessmen tap on the doors of their own offices before ushering me in.

Traditional weddings require the bride to wear not only the most formal kind of kimono, but also a high, glossy wig skewered with long ivory hairpins, with a white headband to conceal her "horns" (which represent not cuckoldry but female jealousy). The bride and groom are joined in marriage by the Shinto ceremony of three-threes-are-nine: each takes three sips of sake from each of three separate sake cups. But, as anyone can tell from a glance at the advertisements for bridal gowns on billboards and in the subways, in a sizable share (about one-tenth) of modern weddings the bride wears Western white silk or satin, with veil and flowers, the groom wears what the Japanese call *morningu* (striped pants and tails), and the ceremony is performed—regardless of the couple's religious persuasions—by a Christian priest or preacher in a church, with music from *Lohengrin*. It's fashionable.

But some women, even in these modern times, suffer a severe handicap in the marriage market: they are blackballed by the zodiac. Those born in the Year of the Fiery Horse, which comes every sixty years, are said to be prone to kill their husbands. Apparently quite a few Japanese still put some store in this ancient superstition. In the most recent such year, 1966, the birth rate in Japan dropped by an astonishing one-third, the result of parents trying to cut down, the year before, on the possibility of conceiving ill-omened, unmarriageable women.

When a person dies, a hearse with a roof like that of a pagoda and black-lacquered sides, fitted with cut-glass windows and covered with ornate gold bas-reliefs, carries the body not to a cemetery but to a crematory. After cremation, the canister of ashes is placed under a tombstone that stands side by side with others thick as chessmen— Japan has always been too crowded to give each man six feet of earth.

More than half the people in Tokyo, and proportionately more in the rest of Japan, still do their bathing in public baths, for lack of tubs at home. The capital has about 2,500 public baths, mostly one-story buildings with tall smokestacks for the furnaces that heat the water, but the number is slowly declining as more homes with baths are built. The high price of heating oil has lately forced the municipal government to subsidize these useful social institutions. In these city baths, the sexes are segregated by law. The one I went to in Kyoto was divided into left and right halves, which in turn were partitioned into dressing rooms, front, and baths, rear. From her position at the admissions counter, which was just through the curtained door of the building's windowless front wall, the woman who managed the place could survey both dressing rooms—and so could the entering customer, as he paid his forty yen (fifteen cents). I turned to the left, where an old woman, circulating among two dozen men who were dressing or undressing, handed me a basket in which to store my clothes on a shelf. Some of the men, I noticed, wore knitted belly bands—there is a peculiar superstition among the Japanese that the male navel has a special need to be kept warm. Stripped, I entered the bath area, which was steamy, tiled, and half the size of a tennis court.

Three rectangular pools, as big as dining tables, abutted one wall. They varied in depth, to match the statures of the men and boys sitting in them. Around two sides, a foot or so above the floor, were faucets in pairs, one with a red dot (hot) and the other with a blue dot (cold). Taking my cue from the other bathers, I sat down on a low milkmaid stool, lathered up from toes to hair, rinsed with basins of hot water—and repeated the process, and repeated it again, taking twenty minutes. The Japanese scrub, rub, and massage; they paint their bodies with soap with the same loving care that a painter strokes his canvas; and they rinse in torrents, since the water of the tubs must never be contaminated with lather. My teachers-by-example then showed me how to lower myself inch by inch into the pool—the essence of survival in scalding water is not to agitate it. This very necessity kept me from leaping out, and in a minute or two a marvelously benign feeling, a sensation of relaxation to the point of limpness, spread through my muscles and tendons. When I got out, a new small miracle took place: the warmth of the bath persisted through the process of drying with a tiny towel, through dressing, through the chilly walk home, and through the rest of the evening.

My wife, in the women's bath, enjoyed not only the glow that comes from scalding, but also the "unabashed bedlam, the unaffected congeniality, the egalitarian uniform of nude humanity"—which is a good way of suggesting how naturally the modest Japanese accept the balneal nakedness that Westerners feel obliged to seal off with curtains and stalls. Many women like to go to the bath at three o'clock in the afternoon with their sons (to the age of twelve) and daughters and spend hours soaking in tubs (some with jets or electric currents), using the hair drier, getting a massage from a machine, and drinking milk and sodas at the snack counter.

The classic Japanese bath, of course, was always a mixed affair, whether at home or in public, and stirred the prurient interest of foreigners. The Japanese themselves overcame prurience by adopting a philosophy that the naked person is "seen but not looked at." Nowadays the mixed bath is confined to inns at hot-spring resorts, and the few women that take part are mostly over forty. Even as the old Western sense of bodily shame is weakening in the West, the Japanese are adopting it, in a confused and confusing way. Nudes are permissible, for example, in the advertising of movies, photographic film, and even banks, but any representation of sexual organs or even pubic hair is forbidden in all publications. The Japanese post office employs young men working their way through college to go through imported copies of *Playboy* and *Penthouse* one by one and ink out pubic hair with felt-tip pens.

The impulse to make a ritual out of an ordinary human requirement prevails in the barbershop as well as in the bath. The first delight of these places is the barber pole outside, under a sign that almost always says, in fractured English, BAR BER. The pole's design is Western: a red-and-white spiral, representing a bandage around a bleeding arm, symbolizing the barber's ancient role as bloodletter. But the Japanese alter this whirling spiral with their typical skill at improving what they are imitating: they add blues and greens to the spiral, and make it run both up and down, and place it behind various magnifying glasses of equal fantasy, so that the colors leap and swirl and meld like a fun-house mirror.

Once I was in the barber chair, which could be electrically tipped and vibrated, I found that the haircut was to be a strict ritual of correct attire, both for the barber (who was a woman) and me. She did the initial clipping in a white gown, while I wore a chest cloth topped by a towel topped by an ample wrapper. She whipped off the wrapper while shaving the neck and sideburns, then added a plastic cloth for the shampoo, which included a sensationally pleasant scalp massage and a trip to the washbasin for a rinse. Off came the plastic for a brain-jarring massage of the neck and shoulders. I skipped the shave, but noted that other barbers donned face masks for this operation, and removed even the tiny hairs on the customer's forehead. For tinting hair, that is, restoring gray to black, I noticed that barbers wore dark blue smocks. The barber goes back to his gown, and the customer to his wrapper, for the finale, the coiffing of the hair with electric drier and comb. Price: $3.60.

Students often wear shoulder-length hair, Cantínflas mustaches, and Ché Guevara beards; but salary men, who feel that the boss would prefer them to wear their hair short, go through the ceremony of the barbershop once a week.

This land of workaholics loves holidays with a paradoxical passion. There are twelve national legal holidays a year (compared to nine in the United States). Most of the legal holidays have a dutifully manufactured sound: Adults Day, Respect for the Aged Day, Health Sports Day, Culture Day, and Labor Thanksgiving Day. But the most important are firmly embedded in tradition: New Year's is the time to pay debts and repaper shoji walls; February 11 commemorates the nations' founding; the vernal equinox is dedicated to nature; the fall equinox is a sort of Halloween of worship for the dead. Conversely, three major holidays—the Emperor's Birthday, April 29; Constitution Memorial Day, May 3; and Children's Day, May 5—are shuffled together with May Day and two Sundays to give a large part of the population a week off from work with no emotional overtones at all; it's called "Golden Week."

These official holidays are interspersed with seventy or more local festivals. They range from Igloo-Building Day in snowy northern Japan to a holiday for work horses in Morioka. They are all unexceptionably splendid. Out come costumes, torches, floats, banners, dragons—and the atavism of the salary man. In the fall of 1972 I attended the Fire Festival in Kurama, in the mountains north of Kyoto. The train up was packed, and the crush was even worse among the toppling throngs of spectators who lined the little town's main street. Conflagration-size bonfires, plus faggots shaped into huge torches, gave the only light. Young men, dressed in kerchiefs, corded skirts, and shirtless sleeves, tirelessly and drunkenly chanted four or five syllables over and over, and tugged thick ropes tied to heavy, swaying, jingling litters bearing images of Shinto gods. Spiritually it was light-years distant from the Japan of the Ginza, baseball, television, Mitsubishi Heavy Industries. Do the Japanese descend partly from the same ancestors as the Melanesians and the Polynesians, as some say? On nights like this, it seems so.

Since ancient times, holidays have been the occasion for pilgrimages to some shrine, festival, or rite, and they still are. Three hundred thousand people turned out one February day in 1973 to see the select plum trees that bloom in late winter near Mito, sixty miles north of Tokyo. Thousands of tourists go to the village of Karasaki to view a venerable pine tree with limbs held up by crutches. On summer nights on the Nagara River, aficionados enjoy watching an old Chinese custom, cormorant fishing. The goose-necked cormorants, tethered to picturesque boats, gulp fish attracted by a fiery flare, but are forced to regurgitate them for human consumption. Rings around the cormorants' necks keep them from swallowing the fish. Japan's Easter parade is the November 15 Seven-Five-Three Festival, when girls aged three and seven and boys aged five, dressed in showy kimonos or ancient warrior costumes, visit shrines to give thanks for good health and pray for more of it.

One detects a certain mindlessness in such festive mass excursions, but also real comfort and pleasure in keeping up old traditions. And in recent years, such pilgrimages have shown no signs of abating. Thirty million Japanese went touring during Golden Week in 1974, mostly by train but a good share of them by car. In fact, mass motoring may be Japan's newest custom, and the energy crisis has not curbed it much.

Car accidents in Japan kill about eleven thousand people a year, a rate about equal to that of the United States proportionally to the car population. Efforts at safety seem strangely slack in some respects. The use of seat belts is just beginning. In a Toyota plant I saw stout bumpers installed on cars for export, and flimsy ones on cars for sale in Japan. In other ways, safety measures are stern. Applicants for driver's licenses have to pass a tricky psychological questionnaire and a rigorous eye test, and take thirty hours of lectures on driving technique, auto mechanics, traffic law, and safety. The law requires a minimum of twenty-seven hours of behind-the-wheel instruction. Learners cannot start out on the street, but instead must spend the first twenty hours on a privately operated practice course, of which Tokyo has sixty-three. All this instruction costs at least $240, and for slow learners more than $1,000.

Liability insurance is compulsory, and so is a biennial inspection, which, with the repairs generally entailed, may cost around $100. Trucks and buses must have rear-end beep-beep horns that sound automatically when they are backing up; this warning noise has become one of the characteristic sounds of Japan. Drivers convicted of vehicular manslaughter are sentenced to terms of three months to two years in "traffic prisons" such as the one at Kakogawa, which serves the Osaka-Kyoto area. The motive is reform. "Monetary penalties alone are not enough to make such drivers reflect on their behavior," says Takeshi Ohumi, the warden. The hundred-or-so prisoners get driving training every day during their incarceration. Each morning and evening they go to the prison's "Park of Introspection," bow, and recite: "We apologize to the victims of traffic accidents for our faults, and we swear we will never make such mistakes again."

The Japanese sense of order and social responsibility seems to desert most drivers the minute they get behind a steering wheel. The hurtling taxi drivers have won the nickname "Kamikaze," although in fact only 6 percent of the inmates at Kakogawa Prison are cabbies. Yet perhaps the true culprits in the auto death toll are the old, narrow streets without sidewalks in every Japanese city and town. Streets occupy only 9 percent of the surface area of Osaka, for example, as compared to 35 percent of New York City. Drivers race through tiny lanes on the brazen presumption that if anyone on foot gets in the way he deserves to be killed. Japan is the only major country in the world where more pedestrians than motorists are killed in auto accidents. Predictably, children and the aged are the principal victims. Most of the children are hit within one hundred yards of their own homes.

As elsewhere, bus and truck drivers are far and away the safest and most skillful, and a joy to watch in action. Descending the corkscrew highway from Hakone to Atami once, I marveled at how our driver, his hands and eyes seemingly monopolized in hurling his huge vehicle around the switchbacks, nevertheless managed a leisurely salute for every driver of a bus of the same line that approached. These sober, formal, competent men form a community of professionals. Bus drivers all wear white gloves, and so do many of the truck drivers that one sees on the expressways, sitting high in their air-conditioned cabs.

The same narrow roads that cause accidents make parking and housing cars a problem to be met with drastic solutions. You cannot buy a car without proving that you have off-street parking space for it, which requires presenting the deed to your house or your rental contract if the space is on the premises of your home. A rented space must be within five minutes' walk of home, and all these arrangements have to be verified by the nearest police office. Rent on spaces in central Tokyo runs from $100 to $300 a month. The surge of car buying in Japan has also produced such pains in the eye as heaps of junkers next to lovely old temples.

A number of the most famous and fascinating prints made by the talented wood-block cutter Ando Hiroshige in the first half of the nineteenth century depict the twin buildings of a great dry-goods store in what is now Tokyo, with Mount Fuji rising in the background. In Japan as in the United States, shops like this eventually branched out from drapery and became department stores. But those in Japan are bigger, more elaborate, more varied, and more ubiquitous than elsewhere. Department stores are the cornucopean cathedrals of Japan, validations of the modern, materialistic Japanese Way of Life. Takashimaya, Mitsukoshi, Daimaru, Parco, Seibu, Matsuya, Matsuzakaya—these are mighty institutions in Japan. What other department stores in what other country have built whole railroads extending for miles into the suburbs and ending with terminals in their own buildings, for the convenience of the customers and the enhancement of their own incomes?

Eight stories and two basements is average size for these fortresses of consumerism. The decor runs to the most elegant, colorful, extravagant, opulent, overmuchness imaginable. From the ceilings of lobbies four stories high hang ropes of crystal and twinkling lights. One store on the Ginza a year or so ago mounted on its façade a six-story-high display of "electronic fireworks," in which twelve thousand colored light bulbs made rockets appear to rise and explode, while loudspeakers reproduced the *boom* of real fireworks. Inside, Muzak plays "Tea for Two," "C'est si bon," "Chattanooga Choo Choo," "The Girl from Ipanema." Moon-faced girls with mouths lipsticked into cupid's bows stand at the foot of each escalator, bowing and murmuring "Welcome to our store" and occasionally wiping the moving hand rail with an antiseptic cloth. The rooftops are small Coney Islands, playgrounds for children complete with Ferris wheels, merry-go-rounds, and an occasional zoo. The basements are veritable country fairs, with fish vendors howling, butchers cleaving, women selling celery. Somewhere near the top of each store are a pair of art galleries, one selling paintings and sculpture and pottery, and the other putting on month-long shows of fine art, ancient and modern.

The department stores of Japanese cities serve a function somewhat like that of the art museums of other big cities, and newspapers carry prominent listings of what's on in the stores. For further satisfaction of the senses, there are restaurants: sushi stands, cavernous dining rooms, cafeterias, and coffee shops, variously offering Western and several kinds of Japanese food. And then, of course, there is the railroad. One of the most prominent signs in Osaka, lettered in English on a tall building, says HANKYU DEPARTMENT STORE AND RAILWAY.

A top-to-bottom tour of the great Odakyu department store in Tokyo produced this inventory: fourteenth floor—two restaurants back to back; thirteenth—two more; twelfth—barber shop, beauty parlor, dental clinic, bookstore, photo studio, two restaurants; eleventh —sewing school, cooking school, art gallery (showing marvelous

Japanese tattoo designs, including a patch of real skin from a corpse); tenth—*ten* restaurants, big and small; ninth—four restaurants; eighth—an acre of cheap clothes being pawed over; seventh— watches (Seiko, Citizen, Timex), jewelry, cameras, lamps, fabrics, Singer sewing machines, rice cookers, air conditioners, electronic ovens, washing machines, silverware, crystal, china, coin-operated electric massaging chairs for exhausted shoppers; sixth—a throng of children, both real ones and mannequins, and clothes and de- lightful toys for them; fifth—kimonos as far as the eye could see, plus dresses for large ladies; fourth—women's Western clothes; third— men's suits and shirts; second—shoes enough for armies, handbags, travel bags, thousands of ties; first—terminal of the Odakyu Electric Railway. The store also featured a pet shop, with three girls shear- ing, brushing, shampooing, and electrically drying Pomeranians and miniature poodles, a Mayan ceramics show with a bowl priced at $2,300, and a garden shop offering a mower with blades ten inches wide, for tiny Japanese lawns.

Gift giving is a traditional Japanese obsession. Weddings, gradua- tions, birthdays, holidays, the eves of journeys, and simple sociable home visits all prompt gifts. Every gift must be wrapped with an artfulness that amounts to a display of origami, and the string around it tied in pretty, traditional knots. Summer gift giving started centuries ago as a consolation for the relatives of a person who died in the first half of the year, but has turned into a Mother's Day style of orgy without much heart in it. Businessmen ingratiate themselves with other businessmen by sending midsummer gifts. In earlier times, a live fish used to be a sufficient gift, but now French wine, British whistling teakettles, Italian socks, and Hawaiian papayas are more on the mark. Twice annually, in June-July and before Christmas, de- partment stores artfully capitalize on this ancient tradition to promote spasms of gift giving, fortuitously timed to the dates when com- panies give employees their semiannual bonuses (which in a typical recent year-end totaled $21 billion).

Credit cards—Mitsubishi's Diamond Credit, Japan Credit Bank's JCB, and Union Credit's UC, as well as various American charge cards —serve to pay for a lot of department-store purchases. But the bulk of the dealing is done in cash. The clerks in these ultramodern stores do not, for the most part, add the charges on a cash register or electronic calculator; instead, with fingers flying, they make their calculations on the beads of that ancient device, inherited from Rome via China, the abacus. For quickness, this makes sense; in a famous contest during the Occupation, a certain Kiyoshi Matsuzaki, champion abacus operator of the Ministry of Postal Administration, went up against the electric calculating machine of Private Thomas Nathan Wood, of the American 240th Finance Disbursing Section, and won eight out of eleven heats in addition, subtraction, multiplication, and division. Learning the abacus well takes two years of practicing one hour a day, but produces an extraordinary payoff: the operator learns to calculate merely by visualizing the abacus. An abacus master named Yoshio Kojima once added ten numbers of ten digits each in 13.6 seconds, all in his head.

Banks also do much of their business in cash, and there's an abacus on every desk. Checking accounts are uncommon. Banks will pay utility bills by checkoff from savings accounts, but many housewives keep plenty of cash and pay it out directly to itinerant bill collectors. Yet, oddly, the Japanese like to keep their distance from the crassness, the actual touch, of cash. The samurai of old received their stipends by holding out an open fan on which the money could be placed. Nowadays small fees of various kinds are enclosed in envelopes. Banks and restaurants present change in lacquer trays. The same reticence about money banishes from Japan that deplorable custom of other Oriental countries, haggling. Prices are fixed and followed. Neighborhood stores give easy credit, allowing payment by installments, without interest and without a written contract, even on such a trivial item as a pair of shoes.

> He allowed his upper garments to slip down to his girdle, and remained naked to the waist. Carefully, according to custom, he tucked his sleeves under his knees to prevent himself from falling forward. Deliberately, with a steady hand, he took the dirk that lay before him; he looked at it wistfully, almost affectionately; for a moment he seemed to collect his thoughts for the last time, and then, stabbing himself deeply below the waist on the left-hand side, he drew the dirk slowly across to the right side, and, turning it in the wound, gave a slight cut upward. When he drew out the dirk, he leaned forward and stretched out his neck; an expression of pain for the first time crossed his face, but he uttered no sound. At that moment, the *kaishaku*, who, still crouching at his side, had been keenly watching his every movement, sprang to his feet, poised his sword for a second in the air; there was a flash, a heavy, ugly thud, a crashing fall; with one blow the head had been severed from the body.
>
> A dead silence followed, broken only by the hideous noise of the blood throbbing out of the inert heap before us. . . . It was horrible.

It may be a shock that suicide is an acceptable custom in Japan— at its most stylized in *hara* (belly) *kiri* (cut). To the Englishman who in 1868 witnessed and described this one, it was horrible not only because it was gruesome, but also because it violated his Judeo-Christian belief that killing oneself is immoral. The Japanese see the matter in an entirely different light. To them, the stomach, rather than the heart, is the seat of the emotions, and to cut into it, however painful, is proof of the sincerity of the suicide's intentions. Only after agony demonstrates this sincerity can the kaishaku, the second, lop off the head. Hara-kiri is now rare, but suicide remains common, free of shame, and even admirable. With a current suicide rate of 15.2 per 100,000 population, about the same as France, Japan is well down on the United Nations *Demographic Yearbook* list of national rates, which goes from Hungary (34.7) through the United States (10) to Israel (5.2). Nevertheless, suicide is a Japanese obsession, practiced 18,000 times a year, with singular motives and methods.

In these times, the most unusual Japanese custom in the field of self-destruction is the one called "forced family suicide." A typical news story goes like this: "The wife of a pear orchard operator was reported Saturday to have committed suicide after killing her three children at a workshop here. Mrs. Masaka Sato, 32 . . . disappeared from the house with her children [aged 9, 6, and 3] Friday night after she had a quarrel with her husband." A mother in Itami leaped from an apartment-house balcony with her daughter in her arms after her husband chided her for not clearing the table. A Mito mother jumped into a well with her five-month-old daughter—she had desperately wanted a boy as her third child. A former geisha poisoned herself and her two daughters, aged eight and seven, and left a note to her husband that asked: "Do you like bowling and sake more than us?" In San Francisco, the homesick wife of an expatriate Japanese businessman beheaded her son with a cleaver and urged her husband to join her in a family suicide.

In this manner thousands of children who presumably want to live are carried to death with their parents. Psychiatrist Kenshiro Ohara, an authority on suicide, found that the Japanese regard forced family suicide to be a "beautiful act," and think that women who kill themselves without also killing their children are "demons."

The next most notable form of Japanese suicide is self-destruction among adolescents. A fourteen-year-old Kobe boy, whose mother provided him with an apartment where he could live and study alone near his exclusive and demanding high school, gassed himself to death in his flat. A Tokyo schoolgirl of fourteen burned herself to death with gasoline or a similar combustible on the eve of an entrance examination to a senior high school, and left an ambiguous note: "I do not know the reasons why I am committing suicide. I would really rather die after the examination and learning whether I could succeed in it." An eleven-year-old boy in Hiroshima hanged himself when his mother left him home and took his sister out to a restaurant.

Many suicides have peculiar motives. A housewife, told by a fortuneteller that she was born unlucky, jumped with her three small children in front of a train (a form of suicide so common that public announcements on some Tokyo subway lines urge the despondent not to jump during rush hours). A student, whose thesis had been rejected by the faculty, fought back so long and so hard that he forced the resignation of the dean and got his doctor's degree at the age of twenty-eight—whereupon he poisoned himself because (his note said) he was "too tired." A mandarin-orange farmer drank agricultural chemicals because crops were too good, causing prices to drop.

At least five great Japanese novelists in the past fifty years have chosen to end their lives by suicide. Nobel Prize winner Yasunari Kawabata, who gassed himself to death, once wrote, "There is no art superior to death." Yukio Mishima was a special case. His whole life was a preparation for suicide. Disdainful of death and even more of democracy, he stood for a warrior Japan, centered on the emperor. He would have fought sincerely in World War II, but, to his unending shame, he was too thin and too sickly to be a soldier. During the Occupation, he gave free play (to judge from his novel *Forbidden Colors*) to his leanings toward homosexuality. He mixed a boundless literary creativity (twenty novels, thirty-three plays) with unremitting physical activity—the artist as man of action. Learning swordplay and karate, he built his body until he could have posed for Charles Atlas. His reason, as he explained it in *Sun and Steel*: "I cherished a romantic impulse towards death, yet at the same time I required a strictly classical body as its vehicle; a peculiar sense of destiny made me believe that the reason why my romantic impulse towards death remained unfulfilled in reality was that I lacked the necessary physical qualifications."

Mishima talked unceasingly of death, reincarnation, masochism and sadism, honor, tradition, the emperor. He wrote and played in a movie in which he acted out a self-disembowelment for reasons of patriotism and loyalty. At length, he formed the quasi-military Shield Society and designed green, gold-braided uniforms for his followers. At some point a friend, Hiroshi Funasaka, gave Mishima an ancient samurai sword. When Mishima and the Shields failed (as Mishima certainly knew they would) in their attempt to incite the troops of Tokyo's Eastern Army Headquarters to rise up and overthrow the government, he duly committed ritual hara-kiri. The samurai sword served, in the hands of a helpful kaishaku, to deliver the *coup de grâce* by beheading him. Mishima wanted a "glorious death," but the soldiers to whom he appealed had only cursed and ridiculed him, and the Japanese Establishment, to stamp out any spark of the dangerously jingoistic fervor he had hoped to arouse, moved in massively with the explanation that he was insane.

When psychiatrist Ohara returned to Japan a couple of years ago from a visit to the Suicide Prevention Center in Los Angeles, he suggested that Tokyo might try some suicide prevention of its own. People simply scoffed at him: "Let them die if they want to." The Japanese, like anyone else, prize life, but at the same time they may be rather free of the cowering fear of death that afflicts much of the West. Certainly suicide not only carries little stigma but is often thought to demonstrate courage; and neither Buddhism nor Shintoism prohibits it. And suicide is literally the last word in sincerity, proof that one believes in what he is doing and is willing to make a point that sticks.

6/

Religion—and a Spoonful of Medicine

THE ENGLISH WORD "religion"—loaded with Western connotations of theology, spirituality, dogma, apologetics, bibles, churches, proselyting, instruction, and congregations—does not sit comfortably on Japan. Buddhism, Shintoism, and Confucianism cannot be called anything other than religions, but the first is too untheological to fit the Western usage nicely, the second too primitive, and the third too much a code of behavior. All three lack the sense of fierce adherence and exclusivity expected of Christians, Jews, and Moslems. Moreover, the Japanese think nothing of drawing freely from *all* their beliefs. The central concerns of these creeds have little to do with heaven-and-hell or with religion as a force for social good. They deal, rather, with self-perfection, overcoming suffering, setting aside desire, phallicism, pantheism, the coexistence of opposites, the diversity of truth, relativity, timelessness, the indescribability of God.

The polls of the Ministry of Education's Study of the Japanese National Character regularly show that two-thirds of the respondents answer no to the question "Do you have a personal religious faith?" When the one-third who replied yes were pressed to tell of any activities by which they expressed their religious feelings, nearly half reported no activity, and only 3 percent said that they were deeply engaged. But these figures are deceptive. For the Japanese are strongly imbued with what has been called "irreligious religiosity," an abiding concern with that which transcends daily life.

Most ancient, most pervasive, most persistent, but least articulated is Shinto. It is Japan's primordial religion, rising nameless out of prehistory, animistic, as mythic as the faith of the old Greeks in their

95

gods. It is profoundly based in the Japanese passion for their own land and their own tradition: ancestor worship is a fundamental tenet of Shinto. Whatever faith a Japanese professes formally today, a part of him at the deepest level retains a sense of Shinto.

Birds, beasts, celestial bodies, mountains, rivers, and stones were held in awe as being inhabited by some of Shinto's eight million gods, with the sun goddess Amaterasu-Omikami, ancestor of the imperial house, most sacred among them. Thus, by extension, Shinto was perennially linked to the emperor. The early Japanese worshiped their gods by gifts, music, dances. Sin, rather than being a moral evil, was whatever seemed to be in opposition to nature, dirty, or tainted—illness, wounds, a corpse—and by extension whatever was antisocial, such as robbery or murder. A tainted person put himself out of touch with the gods, and required purification before he could resume contact. Purification, by washing hands at a font near the oratory of a shrine, is to this day a major Shinto ritual.

As an official creed, Shinto has had its ups and downs. The sixth-century arrival of Buddhism in Japan put Shinto into the shadow until about a hundred years ago, when nationalists under the Emperor Meiji officially revived it and restyled it as pure and simple worship of the Japanese state. Shintoism thus served to whip up the fanatic patriotism of the era before World War II, and the American Occupation took particular pains to disestablish it, cutting off its government funds and stripping the divinity from its titular head, the emperor. But Shinto was not so easily extirpated, though it exists now chiefly as a sort of convenience religion, with 88,000 shrines and many little street altars, into which a student, for example, can duck and pray without much conviction for luck in examinations. Business-men, putting up skyscrapers, are careful to bring in a Shinto priest at the groundbreaking, to gain permission for construction from the god of the land, and the Coca-Cola (Japan) Company invariably gets a priest to dedicate new neon advertising signs.

Shinto is more a feeling than a creed. It has no professions or precepts, no hades or paradise, no clear distinctions between what is godly and what is human. "It's an Epicurean religion, and that's why the Japanese admire money and success without guilt," says Fosco Maraini, an Italian writer who has lived in Japan for four decades. Its shrine gates, a pair of phallic columns with double crosspieces representing the female, are the trademark symbols of Japan, and many shrines contain phalli of stone or wood or straw as objects of veneration, symbolizing the principle of life. Besides priests, who dress in white and sometimes in paper, Shintoism em-ploys virgin priestesses, who wear red, divided skirts topped by white chemises and gauzy capes. They enter this profession at fourteen, and usually retire at twenty to marry.

Ise shrine, which has been functioning for thirteen hundred years southwest of Tokyo, is the most venerable and sacred of Shinto's shrines, and one day late in 1973 it presented a startling aspect. Deep in a forest, on a plot of several acres surrounded by four low wooden fences, lay the sanctuary of the inner shrine, flanked by two small treasure houses, and attended by various gatehouses and the out-buildings of the outer shrine. Just next to this rectangle of struc-tures stood . . . exactly the same thing, a perfect duplicate. The first was twenty-four years old, the second spanking new. Shintoists know that their buildings, made of wood and thatch that rot, cannot last much more than two decades. So they simply replace old shrines with identical new ones, constructed alongside. In times past, the abandoned buildings were burned. These days, they are dismantled and made to serve other purposes—although the replaced shrine at Ise is to be left standing for a few years and opened to the public. The Ise shrine has now been reduplicated sixty times.

That night, by the light of a sliver of a moon, high priests, wear-ing black-lacquered sabots and the black-plumed headdress that one sees in old scrolls, transferred sacred objects from the old sanctuary to the new. To shroud the holiest of these relics, the mirror that represents the spirit of Amaterasu-Omikami, several priests carried a silken canopy under which the mirror bearers walked.

Rebuilding Ise cost $20 million, for it required the felling and sawing of 13,600 huge cypress trees to reconstruct the 123 structures of the shrine complex. Priests got the money easily enough, because 6 million people visit Ise every year and their small contributions add up fast. Much more difficult was finding craftsmen who could shape and join the columns, the beams, and the gable-end rafters that shoot beyond the ridgepole into the air. The main sanctuary at Ise shrine is a small, single-story building with nothing of the grandeur of great Christian cathedrals, but it is flawless in proportion and elevating in architecture. Its importance lies in its significance as symbol of the original Japanese religion, the link of man to nature. One of the shrine's priests says: "Send a Western-educated, modern Japanese to Ise, and he will feel Japanese again."

Buddha (the Indian prince Siddhartha, who lived from circa 566 to circa 480 b.c., and is also known as Gautama, Gautama Buddha, and, in the Japanese pronunciation, Butsu) did not bother about such problems as whether the universe is finite or infinite, or whether the soul and the body are identical, or whether there is life after death; he was "neither God nor a person who has some relationship to God." Buddhism, as its founder laid it down, simply looked at man's life, observed that he suffered, and put forward a way of overcoming suffering. "Life is suffering, death is suffering, old age is suffering, to have to meet someone you cannot love is suffering, to have to be separated from someone you love is suffering and not to be able to obtain what you want is suffering," says one text, setting out the first of Buddha's Four Noble Truths. This suffering derives, according to the second truth, from ignorance of the principle of the changeability and impermanence of things. The third truth is that the only way to be free of suffering is to annihilate the passions, creating the state known as nirvana, in which existence is happy and pure. And, fourthly, the way to annihilate the passions is the Eightfold Path: right aims, right views, right speech, right conduct, right living, right effort, right mindfulness, and right concentration.

Buddhism spread to China in the first century, to Korea a couple of centuries after that, and to Japan in the year 552, when travelers brought in some sutras and a resplendent image of Buddha. Its ritual, metaphysics, and impressive temple architecture overwhelmed primitive Shinto, and within fifty years Prince Shotoku took it for the court religion. Later, many priests devised numerous brain-numbing variations of Buddha's founding ideas, but by the thirteenth century they could be divided into two main sects.

The Pure Land concept postulates a paradise of that name ruled by a neo-Buddha named Amida. The Pure Land sect made Buddhism, hitherto the property of the nobility and the intellectuals, a simple and popular belief that guaranteed new birth in heaven to any ordinary man (the more sinful the better) who would recite the name of Amida often enough and fervently enough. This theology is a far cry from proto-Buddhism; in fact, as Professor Reischauer has written, medieval Japanese Buddhism "had come to resemble Christianity more than original Buddhism," in emphasizing salvation through faith in a single deity, zealous preaching and chanting, heaven and hell, scripture in the vernacular, even the married clergy that came to Christianity centuries later. Circumstantial evidence suggests that the resemblance was not accidental: in 804–806 the monk Kobo, founder of a forerunner of the Amida sects, visited Ch'ang-an, the capital of China, where he could have had contact with Nestorian Christians from Assyria, who flourished in China for a while. Some scholars say Kobo brought back a copy of the Gospel of Matthew and the Ten Commandments.

The other main current was Zen. Precisely contrary to the Pure Land doctrine of salvation by utter faith in the grace of another being (Amida), Zen proposed "self-powered Buddhahood" by meditation during the four basic activities of walking, stopping, sitting, and lying down. One of its two Japanese expounders, who got the principles of Zen from China, stressed that every human being is weighted with consciousness of the self, and the Way requires him to shuck off such causes of self-attachment as property, reputation, and sex. To the workaday Western mind, Zen seems inscrutable indeed.

At Tenryuji temple, near Kyoto, I talked one afternoon to the Zen Buddhist master Seiko Hirata, as he sat on the tatami of his four-room, classical-Japanese apartment, surrounded by tea utensils, a brazier for hot water, papers and documents, and a bottle of Suntory Very Rare Old Whiskey. The master's task is to train monks, a fourteen-year process. Formerly masters taught by use of scorn, abuse, blows, laughter, incoherent grunts—all indications to guide a student toward knowledge that cannot be transmitted by exposition and logic. Hirata uses gentler methods, but the goal is the same. Both then and now, Zen masters give novices, early in their training, a koan, an intellectually insolvable question, to meditate upon. An ancient koan goes, "What will you do when you and the whole world are destroyed by heat?" For my own meditation, Hirata offered me a modernized version, "What will you do when you and the world are destroyed by nuclear bombs?" Sufficient instruction and meditation will lead to the abrupt perception of enlightenment called satori, which comes after many years (although in practice only a few monks ever actually achieve it).

"Zen is not a way of life," Hirata told me. "It has passed beyond that. Christianity is a religion of morals, quite different from Zen. Zen tries to find the bases of human nature, the bases of art, morals, and religion. The Zen world is an undivided world." Of Japanese Buddhism, Zen, though not the largest, is the form historically most attractive to Westerners. Though Indian-Chinese in origin, Zen was elaborated by Japan, and in turn molded much of the present national character and culture. Zen draws together architecture, the tea ceremony, flower arranging, the martial arts, the game of *go*, symbolic gardens, and handicrafts. Its followers are not merely monks but intelligent youths, foreigners, businessmen, and statesmen.

The making of a Zen monk, Hirata explained, begins with an applicant's presenting himself at the gate of a monastery. He is admitted for a night, to be spent sitting facing a wall, but in the morning is cast out to wait several days near the gate, as a test of persistence. Then, if he seems promising, he is readmitted for an interview. D. T. Suzuki in his *The Training of the Zen Buddhist Monk* provides a sample of such an interview. The master Ganshu begins by asking an applicant his name.

APPLICANT: "When the River Han reverses its downward course, I will tell you."

GANSHU: "Why not now?"

APPLICANT: "Has the river reversed its course, or not?"

GANSHU: "You may join the monastery."

I asked the master Hirata whether many prospective monks were hammering at the gates of Tenryuji these days. He lamented that sometimes two weeks go by with only a single applicant. Nevertheless, the temple is thriving, one source of income being the retreats that it provides for the spiritual enrichment of young business executives. Many temples supply this sort of service. Enkakuji, in Kamakura, south of Tokyo, contracts to provide Zen training for new employees of Matsushita Electric and the Victor Company of Japan, and gives a summer school for six hundred people who start with meditation at five o'clock in the morning and end their last lecture at nine thirty in the evening.

In any case, it does not cost much to support a monk. Monks beg on the streets, wearing straw coolie hats set low so that their eyes cannot meet those of the givers, making the gift impersonal. The bowl they hold out is for rice, but money is acceptable. Neighboring householders give rice to the *zendo*, a kind of dormitory where the monks live. Hirata let me visit the zendo at Tenryuji, a spare, high-ceilinged room like a handball court, with raised platforms along both sides that provide each of some thirty monks with the space of a tatami mat for sleeping and stiff-spined, cross-legged meditation. Zendo life is "altogether out of keeping with modern life," says Suzuki. "Instead of labor-saving machinery, what may appear as labor-wasting is encouraged"—for example, pulling carts by hand. "Scientific, intellectual education is interdicted. Comfort, luxury, and womanly kindness are conspicuous for their absence."

Church-style services, and even the concept of a regular day of worship, have no place in Buddhism, but Zen has occasional ceremonies, attended by laymen. In the Myoshinji temple compound in Kyoto, I had a chance to see one of the three major events of the year, a ceremony of reverence to Bodhidharma (died circa A.D. 530), who is said to have stared at a wall in India for nine years while conceiving the principles of Zen. The mystery and drama of this performance required a sizable cast: the red-and-gold-robed abbot, eight monks poised on the 30-by-30-foot central floor, another attend-

ing the statue of Bodhidharma on top of the high-railed altar at the
back of the room, and two dozen others kneeling on the low, tatami-
covered platform that bordered the stone floor to the left. Spectators,
who numbered only about twice as many as the cast, sat on their
heels on platforms to the front and right. Incense smoldered in a
corner of the room. On the ceiling, of great span for a wooden building, a painted dragon afforded protection for the humans below.
Between the thick pine trunks of the surrounding colonnade hung
bannerlike curtains of brilliant green, yellow, orange, silver, and
black, brocaded with the crest of the Myoshinji temple.

The abbot, short, stocky, and slit-eyed, unfolded from his left arm
a square of cloth the colors of his robe, and with elaborate delibera-
tion spread it on a straw mat laid before him by a monk. Facing the
altar, the abbot, hands now in a position of prayer, bowed low and
then dropped to the mat, his back hunched, his knees drawn up under
him, his forehead touching the floor, and his hands upturned beside his temples. Slowly he lifted his hands and suddenly rose to his
feet in a nimble backward roll. After three such prostrations, the
abbot approached a table, covered in rich cloth, at the foot of the
altar.

There he held a gilded, black-lacquered cup while a monk filled it
with tea. Turning, the abbot swished the cup over the smoke of the
incense, to purify it, and returned it to the monk, who handed it to
another, who gingerly—as though the tea might spill and scald his
hands—carried the cup up the steep stairs to the top of the altar. The
monk attending that position placed the cup in front of the statue.
In this way rice and cakes were also conveyed to the Bodhidharma,
the abbot occasionally returning to the cloth for further triple
prostrations.

Until then, the only sounds had been the shuffle of the monks'
canoelike slippers on the stone and the laughter, from outside, of
passing schoolchildren. Now comes a tattoo of drumsticks and a
thumping boom. More tea is dispatched up the altar. The kneeling
monks arise. *Boom. Boom.* Through the doors comes the ringing
of Westminster chimes that emanates from somewhere in the neighborhood. Inside, a monk begins to clash cymbals—five times, ten,
fifteen. Another monk, with a peculiarly cruel face, busies himself at
the altar table. Five more times the cymbals clash; then a monk
strikes a barrel-size gong that reverberates for an entire minute.
All the monks spread their arm-draped prostration cloths on the
floor and flatten themselves, while the gong continues to keep the
air aquiver.

When they rise, all the monks face the Bodhidharma, and, in the ancient Indian language called Pali, the abbot begins singing a sutra (sermon of Buddha) to the statue—long, high, keening vowels that end on a descending note, like a phonograph record slowing down. As he stops, and shuffles to the table, there comes another sound, wordless, low and groaning. Has the abbot shifted register? Is this noise human, or some electronic trick? One sees with surprise that the singer is the monk with the cruel face. He seemingly tries to make the lowest sound possible to the human larynx, breaking off each phrase with a grunt.

Now the gong signals a new tempo for this Oriental mass, and the low-voiced monk makes a rasping, hiccoughing sound. The other monks take it up, thrumming like a beehive, their buzzing punctuated by blows on the gong. The sound grows louder, takes on rhythm and harmony, pounds faster and faster, turns into a mumbled chant. With the abbot in the lead, the monks start a twisting, turning parade, around the floor and back and forth across it. Sometimes this sutra breaks off and a single rasping voice supplies a counterpoint. As they wheel by, one notices their robes: white kimono topped by black kimono, and over that a toga—of maroon, purple, black, or buff—secured at the left shoulder by a cinch ring. A mysterious flap of the same garment, flung over the same shoulder, ends in a pair of tassels.

The passing faces, their character more evident because the heads are shaved of distracting hair, are by turn pained, proud, haughty, serene, solemn, fanatical, simple, angry—above all, supremely Japanese. One monk sings loudly and joyfully. An old man, weighing surely no more than eighty-five pounds, fragile and antique, is so far bent over by age that his lower jaw hangs like a towel on a clothesline, waggling from his effort to chant, or perhaps merely flapping in time with his tottery gait. The abbot, eyes unseeing, lips barely moving, leads the procession out of the hall by a rear door. Sudden silence. One of the spectators rolls to one side and gratefully kneads his thigh, to get the blood running again.

To this day, Zen is the subtlest and most developed of the Japanese religions, but after the nation's defeat in the war, 171 "new religions" arose to offer new solutions—sometimes bizarre, such as the worship of electricity—to people's anxieties. Far and away the biggest of the postwar faiths is Nichiren Shoshu (meaning "the orthodox sect of Nichiren"). In the same mid-thirteenth-century years when Zen and the Pure Land sects were getting established, a fiery priest named Nichiren was abroad in the land preaching, with all the passion of a Savonarola, a breakaway Buddhism that held all other religions to be false. He contended that merely reciting the words "Praise be to the wonderful Lotus Sutra" could bring Buddhahood, since all truth was contained in this theme of an ancient sermon by Buddha. Nichiren's movement split several ways when he died, but his forceful creed survived well enough until the seventeenth century, when the Tokugawa shogunate suppressed it as disruptive.

With its traits of self-righteousness, proselyting, incontrovertibility, revival-meeting fervor, and positive thinking, Nichiren Shoshu has made itself in two decades into the world's most successful energizer of whole-family, whole-life mass religion. It is the inspiration and faith of the 17 million members of the frenetic lay organization called Soka Gakkai, which in turn is the sole membership of Japan's No. 4 political party, Komeito (meaning Clean Government Party). The concept of a "value-creation society," which is the meaning of Soka Gakkai, was the work, in the 1920s, of a Tokyo geographer-anthropologist-educator named Tsunesaburo Makiguchi. In years of writing and meditation, the three values that he singled out for stress were beauty, gain, and goodness. While he was propounding what became Soka Gakkai, a chance acquaintance converted him to the then moribund Nichiren Shoshu belief. His ideas did not prosper in the 1930s, coming increasingly into conflict with the Shinto emperor worship fostered by the Japanese militarists, and he died in prison in 1943. It took his postwar successors, who sometimes proselyted by chanting the Lotus Sutra phrase in front of a prospective convert's house day and night for a week, to build the sect to its present strength.

In the process, Soka Gakkai established a system of parochial elementary and high schools, a university, a big publishing house. It started golf courses, a mass drum and bugle corps, a mass ballet, a paramilitary drill team. In culture festivals at Japan's enormous stadiums, 42,000 flash-card manipulators, working from computerized patterns, reproduce such uplifting spectacles as views of the Roman Colosseum, scenes from *Carmen,* paintings by Renoir, the words "world peace" in Vietnamese, and even spectacular animations.

The greatest monument of Soka Gakkai is Nichiren Shoshu's Grand Main Temple, standing near the sect's small, seven-hundred-year-old wooden headquarters temple on the southern slope of Mount Fuji. The Grand Main Temple is longer than three football fields. Its design derives from no architectural tradition whatsoever, but rather from the possibilities of modern technology. Between flaring towers at each end of the sanctuary are stretched the cables of a suspended roof, covering an area big enough for a baseball game. A color-coded floor enables crowds of more than five thousand to move in and out of this dramatic space without milling.

The focus of the sanctuary is an altar containing a wooden

mandala supposedly painted by Nichiren himself, with "Praise be to the wonderful Lotus Sutra" written in the center and the names of lesser Buddhas and Bodhisattvas (divinities who postpone entering nirvana in order to do good on earth) arranged around it. The sect gives a printed copy of this mandala to each new member as an object of home worship, to be offered incense, candles, water, and rice. Conversion requires the believer to throw out all images, scrolls, and tablets of other faiths, in a "removal of evil religion." Daily prayers require chanting the phrase of praise to the sutra (sometimes giving the vowels double duration) while all the members of the family sit on their heels before the house's altar, each with palms together and a rosary caught on the middle finger of the left hand.

The religious appeal of Nichiren Shoshu is marvelously direct and untheological: join, say your Lotus Sutra phrase daily, convert others to the faith, and you will be *healthy* and *rich*. One of the founders of this religion, Josei Toda, called the Nichiren mandala "a machine . . . to make everyone happy." He did not blink at saying, "I want you to become rich by having a firm faith in a mandala." One can almost visualize Buddha rolling his eyes upward at this. Soka Gakkai looks for converts among ailing old people, struggling small businessmen, laborers unwanted by the big unions, families making the switch from the security of ancestral farms to the rootlessness of large cities. To these outsiders, Soka Gakkai becomes a social support, worthy of feverish loyalty.

Any mass movement allied to politics inevitably stirs fears of neofascism, and Soka Gakkai feeds these fears in several ways. In 1969 it made a censorious effort to suppress a book that criticized it. Its mass dances and gymnastics and its stress on blind obedience have a paramilitary smell. Its proselyting is too forcible. Nichiren set for his goal the conversion of everyone everywhere, which Soka Gakkai seeks to attain by giving members quotas of prospective converts to "break and subdue." On balance, however, Soka Gakkai appears to have absorbed most of its natural social constituency, the underdogs of the country, and lacks the theological depth to move much further.

Fewer than one in a hundred Japanese are Christians nowadays, but there was a time four centuries ago when Christianity took a strong hold on Japan, resulting in a strange and violent history. The first Christians in Japan (apart from some Nestorians who visited in the eighth century) were Jesuits, most notably the great Francis Xavier, the later sainted Apostle to the Indies. Having heard of Japan from one of the Portuguese sea captains who "discovered" it for the

West, Xavier scented good mission territory and made his way there in 1549, using a Chinese pirate junk for the last leg of the voyage. He and his Jesuit companions, dressing like Buddhist monks, readily converted some of the greater and lesser lords of Kyushu, the western island, who seem to have reckoned that being Christians would open the way to large profits in trading with the West. Many samurai followed the lords.

Within fifty years, three hundred thousand Japanese were Christians, and Nagasaki had been transformed from a fishing village to the predominantly Christian chief trading port of Japan. In fact, the seed planted by Xavier prospered too well. Buddhist priests hated this dangerous competitor, and the shoguns eventually came to fear that the new *kirishitan* might be more loyal to the Pope in Rome than to themselves. Beginning in 1587, the authorities exiled or executed the Western missionaries, and forced converts to recant by trampling on plaques showing Christ or the Virgin Mary. Some six thousand refused, and were put to death in what the dictator Hideyoshi deemed an appropriate manner: crucifixion. The persecution caused 37,000 peasants around Nagasaki, whose Christian tradition by then went back three quarters of a century, to rise in revolt. They were all slaughtered in 1637 and 1638, just after Japan broke off contact with other nations. But thousands of others went underground, and they and their descendants practiced their faith in secret for 235 years, at risk of their lives.

"So long as the sun warms the earth, let no Christian be so bold as to come to Japan," said an official decree in 1825. "If the great King Philip or even the very God of the Christians contravene this prohibition, they shall pay for it with their heads." But when Japan reopened to the world, the underground Christians reappeared. To the astonishment of most of Japan, and of Christians everywhere, they were still twenty thousand strong. A month after a new Roman Catholic church opened in Nagasaki in 1865, thousands of hitherto secret believers appeared to make open profession of their religion— an event known as "the finding of the Christians." The government formally ended bans against Christianity in 1873, but some of the Christians could not drop the habit of concealment. Even now, thousands of them in islands near Nagasaki worship the Christian God privately and without any ties to the church elsewhere.

Christianity never penetrated Japan again as deeply as it had under Xavier and the Jesuits who followed. About one million Japanese are Christians now, one-third of them Catholics, the rest the product of a stout conversion effort by Protestant missionaries, mostly

Americans, in the last four decades of the nineteenth century. Strong-est among the Protestants are the United Church of Christ, the Anglican Episcopal Church, the Evangelical Lutheran Church, and the Baptist Convention. The Roman Catholic Church divides into sixteen dioceses—"with enough Catholics for two," one priest told me ruefully. The all-Japanese bishops are headed by Paul Cardinal Taguchi, bishop of Osaka.

But Christian membership in Japan is not keeping up with the growth of the population as a whole. The mood of Catholic priests to whom I talked ranged from stiff-upper-lip to downright discourage-ment. One said: "The Japanese have three religions already; it simply overloads the mind to take on a fourth." Another, commenting on the marriages he performs, said: "They want to get married in the Chris-tian church. They make the promises, you know, and they really mean it, but I never see them in church again." Yet Japan keeps a per-manent, bedrock interest in Christianity. A big best seller in the fall of 1973 was *The Life of Christ* by Shusaku Endo, a Catholic novelist sometimes called "the Graham Greene of Japan."

Confucianism, philosophical and humane, does not worry itself about the mystical, the supernatural, the theological, the possibilities of afterlife—or even about death. Like Socrates, Confucius (551–479 B.C.) concerned himself with personal ethics. Working from con-cepts of harmony and order gathered from the study of music, he postulated the concept of the virtuous man, whose responsibilities are to his own orderly life, the welfare of his family, the rule of the country, and the preservation of peace. His version of the golden rule is the obverse of Christ's: "Do not do to others what you would not have them do to you"—a precept that does not require one to return good for evil. Confucianism came to Japan at the same time as Buddhism, and was equally welcomed by Prince Shotoku. But it lay dormant until it was seized upon as a code of ethics for the nation by the Tokugawa shoguns when they sealed off Japan from the rest of the world. It served the Tokugawa feudalism well by inculcating the concepts of unconditional loyalty, filial piety, self-denial in the service of others, and acceptance of one's place in the four social classes. Confucianism is the fount and shaper of Japanese morality. But in all of Tokyo there is only one Confucian temple.

What is the net impact on the Japanese of being the heirs to one native religion, one Indian, one Chinese, and, in lesser degree, one Western? Japanese schools, though conforming to the principle of separation of church and state, nevertheless teach a great deal about religion, and their students generally believe that religion instills peace, is morally excellent, fosters human love, and would be a loss to mankind if it disappeared; but also that it is unnecessary for those who have self-confidence, and not really necessary for a person who is satisfied with his life. In the long history of Japanese religion, many concepts of heaven have been put forth: the "other world," the abode of the gods, the abode of ancestors. Simple people accept the idea of an afterlife in a place in the skies where water lilies grow and Buddha sits in a corner, and others believe that the spirit lives on after death; but many Japanese, in the Japanese way, "harmonize" their doubts, and neither believe nor disbelieve in an afterlife.

The syncretism of the Japanese is demonstrated over and over. People marry in a Shinto ceremony because it stresses purification, live by Confucian ethics, and go to the grave in a Buddhist rite because this guarantees that one will be remembered for a few generations. The edifices of Japanese religions are often built side by side. Standing in a Shinto shrine in Kyoto, I noticed that I could look directly into the main hall of the Buddhist Kiyomizu temple. The rooms of the Nagoya Castle Hotel provide both the New Testament and *The Teaching of Buddha*, published by the Buddhism Promoting Foundation of Tokyo. As if to clear all this up, one bus guide customarily explains that "Japan is 80 percent Buddhist and 70 percent Shintoist."

Buddhism and Shintoism have always been more compatible than competitive. As early as the eighth century, the monk Gyogo, planning to build a huge statue of Buddha, felt called upon to visit the Shinto shrine at Ise and for a week pray to Amaterasu-Omikami for permission to carry out his project. From Shinto some sects of Buddhism picked up ancestor worship and a set of thirty gods (for wind, fire, thunder, and so on), whose sculpted effigies stand in a heroic row behind Sanjusangendo Hall in Kyoto.

Among nations practicing Buddhism, Japan is now the largest, for this religion, though predominant in such smaller nations as Burma, Sri Lanka, Thailand, and South Vietnam, is minuscule in its birthplace, India, and preserved mostly as a "cultural value" in antireligious China.

In Japanese superstition, the number to be wary of is 4, pronounced *shi*, which has for a homonym the word for "death." Next after 4 comes 9, *ku*, homonymous with "pain." Third comes 2, *ni*, because combined with 4 it makes *shi-ni*, homonymous with "dead." Even such a scientific institution as Tokyo University Hospital omits the numbers 4, 9, 14, and 19 (the 1 in these last two figures is regarded as irrelevant) from sickroom numbers in its older buildings. Kyoto University Hospital shuns 4 as a room number and also 420, which would sound out as *shi-ni-rei,* "dead spirit." Osaka University Hospital skips 4, 42, 44, and also 24, which could be read as "double death." The obstetrics section of Sumitomo Hospital in Osaka shuns 43, *shi-san,* which is close to "stillbirth." All hospitals use 13, the Christian number of bad luck, but the Imperial Hotel in Tokyo combines the superstitions of East and West: no rooms numbered 4, no bellboy numbered 13. The telephone company assigns numbers with 42 at beginning or end mostly to service phones and public phones.

Good dreams concern Mount Fuji, a hawk, a cow, a snake, a fire, and a sword. Bad dreams concern a horse, a fish, a star, an earthquake, a tooth coming out. People should avoid sleeping with heads to the north—that is the position for corpses. An itchy left hand foretells bad news. Broken sewing needles should be stuck in a cake of bean curd beside a lighted candle and given a small offering of food in return for service rendered.

The Japanese believe these superstitions in about the same proportion that Westerners believe theirs—or perhaps a little less. Japan Air Lines, like most airlines, omits 13 in numbering the rows of seats on planes, because presumably some Westerners would not sit in a thirteenth row. But the same airline disregards the superstitions of its homeland and fearlessly includes a Row 4 on every aircraft.

One evening in a public bath I saw a man whose back displayed the angry scars of four small, round burns, such as a cigarette might make, arranged with precise symmetry on his shoulders and kidney area. Later, meeting Dr. Isamu Hashimoto, professor of surgery at Kyoto Prefectural University of Medicine, I asked what the burns might be. "Moxibustion," he answered, and although he is a conventional M.D. who would never practice moxibustion, he proceeded to tell something about it.

The substance burned in moxibustion is the downy covering of the dried leaves of *Artemisia moxa,* Japanese or Chinese wormwood. In the form of a small cone, it is applied to any of the same 657 sensitive points of the body that are used in acupuncture, and ignited with a punk. Burning makes a permanent scar, but this at least marks the place for future treatments, if needed. The commonest illness for which it is specified is neuralgia, although moxibustion doctors claim to be able to cure a range of diseases including adult bed-wetting.

Moxibustion is not unknown in the West; the English used to use it as a counterirritant for gout. Japan has for centuries relied as well on Chinese-style acupuncture, with perhaps greater justification. Dr. Hashimoto, though not an acupuncturist either, cited cases of a baby who stopped incessant crying after needles were inserted between its knuckles, and of an older child who had a painless tonsillectomy after acupuncture in the ankles.

The true strengths of Japanese medicine have little to do with moxibustion or acupuncture. Even during the centuries when Japan sealed itself off from the world, learned men managed to acquire and study Dutch anatomy texts, and after the Meiji Restoration in 1868 Japanese leaders looked around the globe, picked German medicine as the best, and imported it in great draughts. Partly as a consequence of better health measures, the population doubled, to 60 million, in fifty years. The first world-famous Japanese doctor was a product of American, rather than German, medical education. Hideyo Noguchi (1876–1928), a Rockefeller Institute fellow, was the first man to obtain pure cultures of the spirochete of syphilis and the first to discover the parasite of yellow fever.

Currently Japanese medicine has a good reputation for cellular histology, public health, and microsurgery. The country's main contribution to the world's science of public health, I was told, is development of ample and informative statistics. The most interesting current development in microsurgery is the operation, developed by Dr. Morio Kasai, to cure biliary atresia, which is the absence of ducts leading out of the liver, in newborn babies. Working under forty-power magnification, pediatric surgeons make new ducts with snipped-off sections of the patient's small intestine. The procedure has been successful enough (saving about one-fourth of the disease's victims from certain death) to induce some American parents to fly stricken babies to Tokyo for the Kasai operation. Another Japanese surgeon, Dr. Susumi Tamai, in 1971 managed a successful transplant of a big toe to the hand of a woman whose thumb had been severed in an industrial accident. The gastrocamera, which can photograph the interior of the lungs, the stomach, the intestinal tract, and blood vessels, and thereby spot early cancer, is a development of Tokyo University Medical School and the Olympus Optical Company. The ratio of hospital beds to the population in Japan is about the same as it is in the Soviet Union or Italy, and the number of doctors, 119,000, is also proportional to those of Europe.

But on balance, "Medicine is the forgotten aspect of our rapid progress," says one young surgeon. A Ministry of Health and Welfare official explained to me that, though Japan produces a number of stars like surgeon Kasai, the system works against high general quality. Tokyo University and Kyoto University medical schools, the best, still follow the old German model, which concentrates on the academic research aspects of medicine rather than everyday practice, such as knowledgeable reading of x-rays. The middle-level med schools cater to the Japanese tradition that the son of a doctor must be a doctor, whether or not he wants to or has qualifications. The reason for succession is that most doctors own and run small hospitals, perhaps with only three or four beds (often cramped and none too clean), and want to bequeath this property and equipment to their sons, because the doctor-plus-hospital setup is a "guarantee for getting rich." In this cozy system, doctors are allowed to make a profit from selling the drugs they prescribe.

The medical schools that cater to training this kind of doctor are generally private ones, hungry for funds, and not above advising the parents of an applicant whose entrance exams are on the borderline that he will get in if they make a gift to the school of, say, 15 million yen ($50,000). The Ministry of Education's licensing examinations, though tightened lately, have been notoriously easy. These one-doctor hospitals perennially lack nurses, and the physician's wife must spend long nights tending patients. "Girls don't like to marry doctors," my informant said. The system leads doctors to prefer to practice in heavily populated areas, and Japan has the universal problem of insufficient doctors in the countryside. Doctors rank with real estate dealers and moneylenders as Japan's worst tax evaders, according to the Tax Administration Agency. The Japanese accept these shortcomings among their doctors with a stoic proverb: "Medicine cures only those who will not die."

The Japanese are insured against medical expenses almost as well as the British, Scandinavians, or Canadians, and better than the Americans. "It's pure socialized medicine," Dr. Osamu Hayaishi, chairman of the department of medical chemistry at Kyoto University, told me. Doctors are reimbursed on a point system—eleven points for an injection, for example, or 1,290 for an appendectomy. The system thus puts a fixed value on all medical services, regardless of skill, and on all medicines. The system underpays talented doctors worth more than the points allow, and overpays "point getters" who cram as many as fifty patients into their daily schedules. But it does protect the individual Japanese against calamitous medical bills.

Two kinds of death afflict the Japanese more than Americans or Europeans: brain strokes and stomach cancer. Stomach cancer is blamed on rice, salt, soy sauce, pickles, and, most provocatively, on what the Japanese call the "stomach strategy," keeping the face straight and the demeanor calm while the stomach churns in anguish over some emotional problem. But no one knows for sure.

Dr. Hayaishi said that back pains and hernia, the banes of so many Americans, are rare, and made a guess that the still relatively short stature of the Japanese is the reason: the spinal disks are flatter and bear weight better, and internal abdominal pressure is less. He notes, and the Ministry of Education concurs, that the increase in size of Japanese children in recent decades has not been matched by improvement in health: they suffer pronouncedly from decayed teeth, near-sightedness, and asthma. The Japanese fight the spread of colds by large-scale wearing of surgical-gauze face masks that hide the mouth and nose. Sometimes, at the height of the cold season, a whole elevatorful of people in an office building may look as if they were going up to assist at a major operation.

Japan combats the medico-legal disease of drug addiction with no-nonsense force—and always has. When the British, Portuguese, Dutch, and Americans were pushing opium in China in the nineteenth century, Japan, upon opening up to the world, made a particular point in its first treaty that the drug must be kept out. An anti-drug law in the 1880s ordained decapitation for trafficking in narcotics. Americans play a leading role in drug pushing in Japan; two of them recently got ten years at hard labor in Okinawa for dealing in narcotics. When heroin addiction reached the proportions of a small epidemic a decade ago, narcotics agents and courts cracked down with life sentences for anyone caught selling the stuff and thirty days of excruciating cold-turkey withdrawal for addicts. Dr. Yoshio Ishikawa, a specialist in drug problems, says that heroin addiction has now become "a subject without a living example for study, like smallpox." Japan contains drug addiction chiefly by policing, but I suspect that, more than other nationalities, the conscientious Japanese people simply abhor habits that would be hard on their bodies, jobs, and duty to the nation, and bring shame to themselves and their families.

7 / 🎌

Education Fever

EUROPEAN RIGOR, American scale, Japanese intensity—those words capsule education in Japan, possessor of one of the world's most advanced and successful school systems. Few other nations have such faith in learning; few other peoples believe so deeply that one's well-being comes from one's schooling. "The most characteristic Japanese trait is the eagerness to learn," a German who teaches in Tokyo told me. "It's an honor to get ahead, and education is known to be the key."

Nine hundred and ninety-nine out of a thousand eligible children attend the first nine grades; nine out of ten get through senior high school; one out of three goes on to college—and the Japanese are soon going to make it one out of two. All of these figures surpass those of any European country. Britain, which has worried in recent years about the Japanese "economic invasion," might well contemplate the fact that the college-attendance rate in Japan is five times as high as the rate in the United Kingdom. Japan has stolen shipbuilding from Britain partly by graduating three hundred naval architects a year, as compared to Britain's twenty.

After Japan opened to the West, it seized on Western education as a tool for advancement with such conspicuous vigor as to obscure the fact that it had long before come to admire learning. The Confucianism that the feudal shoguns favored as a moral force also taught that education was essential for government and for the proper operation of society. The samurai of the hermetic period, warriors-turned-administrators, had to know how to read and write, as did many members of those lower classes of the era, the artisans and the merchants. By the time of the Meiji Restoration, Japan had fifteen thousand schools (mostly taught in temples, as the only available public space), with 1.3 million pupils—not many fewer than those in a nation of similar contemporaneous population across the Pacific, the United States. Two out of five Japanese males (as compared to four out of five American adults at that time) could read and write.

In adopting foreign models after the opening, the system that the Japanese at first chose for education was French, rational and exact. But a chance encounter, by a visiting Japanese mission, with the works and thought of Horace Mann soon led the Japanese to switch to the American elementary-school plan. By 1880, desks and blackboards and wall maps had replaced the tatami floors and scrolls of the old temple schools. The Japanese could not adjust to the American school-board system of administration, however, and switched again, this time to German models. With the German influence came school uniforms, military calisthenics, a central Ministry of Education, and the principle that schools were "not for the sake of the pupils but for the sake of the country," as the first minister of education phrased it. Be that as it may, it was education that in a couple of generations changed Japan from a society based on birth and position to one based on knowledge and ability. From 1930 to 1945, the school system was "a gigantic factory for the production of soldiers or of well-indoc-trinated workers on the home front," in the words of historian John Whitney Hall. The postwar Occupation hauled education back to the American model, but changes since then have made the system eminently Japanese. The inquisitive and flexible Japanese ultimately absorbed a large body of Western ideas into their schools without impairing their national identity.

In the modern grade-school classroom, the teachers are firm but warm, the pupils high-spirited but deeply work-oriented. To get some of the flavor, I visited a Buddhist parochial school in Kyoto. The first-graders, having hung their identical gray coats, caps, and book bags on hooks along the back wall of their airy, modern classroom, were working intently. One child read aloud while the others, sitting on little chairs around big wooden tables, followed the large, simple characters in their illustrated textbooks.

The white-smocked second-graders were learning to write, employ-ing ink slabs with water trays, brushes shaped like tadpole tails, and heavy concentration. On letter-size paper pinned down with chrome-plated bar weights, they copied from the blackboard three characters that can be formed with two or three strokes—those for the sound *su*, the sound *te*, and the figure 2. In the fifth grade, pupils were reading aloud, holding up hands for permission to recite, and rising when they did. "Page thirty-six, line five," said the teacher, a kindly-looking, middle-aged man. The lesson was the usage of *nanishiro*, "anyhow." A girl tried, but stumbled. "That's not so good," the teacher commented mildly, and nodded to a fat boy, who recited. "That was better," said the teacher. "Yes, that was better," the girl acknowledged in a small voice. The children, who numbered thirty-four, then discussed the meaning of the word, seeming acutely interested.

The principal, a man in his late fifties dressed in a neat gray suit, starched shirt, and a pearly blue tie, told me of some of the changes he had observed during his career. "When I first started teaching," he said, "the children sat rigidly, with their hands behind their backs, and learned their lessons by heart. Now it's much more relaxed, and that's better. We make them find out things for themselves." Knowing that the teaching of "morals" by schools was a controversial issue, I asked what he did. "We give one hour a week," he replied. "We teach the difference between big and small children, not causing trouble for others, kindness, respect for parents, how to greet people, don't think only of yourself, put yourself in others' shoes. The formation of the child is chiefly up to the parents, but the school also helps them in teaching how to eat, how to say grace at meals, how to say 'hai, hai' ['yes, yes'] instead of merely grunting. There is much contact between the parents and the school."

The school seemed fun for the children, I thought, but in no way frivolous—everyone understood that learning was serious, important, vital. This good-natured intensity carries over into several other activities that characterize Japanese lower schools. One is homework. The Japanese require one to two hours a day in primary grades, two to two and one-half in junior high schools, and more than three in senior high schools. Another is travel. The cheap and ample services of the Japanese National Railways and the propinquity of the major places in this small nation make it possible for Japanese children to learn their country's geography firsthand. Ancient Kyoto swarms with centipede-like columns of children from all over the nation, walking two by two and holding hands, yellow-capped and dressed usually in the blue-and-white uniforms that are the heritage of the German phase of Japanese education. A third activity is sports, mostly Western: baseball, volleyball, basketball, lawn and table tennis, track and field. On a Sunday morning in a schoolyard in downtown Tokyo, I saw a hilarious tug of war between groups of small boys, in red-and-white hats, and girls, in hair ribbons, fought out to a loudspeaker blaring tunes from *The Sound of Music*.

Japanese schools operate on the six-three-three plan: six grades followed by three years each in junior and senior high schools. Students get into the best universities by passing severe exams, in preparation for which they got into the best senior high schools by passing severe exams, in preparation for which they got into the best junior high schools . . . and, yes, they got into the best kindergartens the same way. Obviously, the bulk of students cannot afford to dream of being the best, and simply go to neighborhood schools. But promising children with mothers affected by "education fever" get pushed along without mercy. "Mama monsters" who pressure children beyond their capacities are a leading cause of runaways, according to the Tokyo police. The hardest crunch comes in the last two years of senior high school, for students aged about sixteen to eighteen. Mothers say to sons: "Four hours' sleep, pass; six hours' sleep, fail." The February-March period of entrance tests for universities is known as the "examination hell." The exams demand sheer memorization of innumerable facts; a typical question, on geography, required high school seniors to name the most direct railroad routes between Nagoya and four towns of various distances and directions from that city.

The university system is now big enough to accept well over half a million students a year (as compared to 1.3 million in the United States), which is more than three-fourths of the high school graduates who want to go to college. The bind, predictably, is that most of them want to enter the dozen universities of highest reputation, which have ten aspirants for each place. Competing for these same places in any given spring are approximately two hundred thousand repeaters—earlier high school grads who failed in their first try at entering college and, having crammed seven days a week for a year or two in private tutoring schools, apply again. I have it on the word of Professor Nakane that "the university entrance examination is an open and free competition, and universities, particularly those of the highest rank, resist any form of bribery or special favor. The wealth, status and so on of parents are completely disregarded (although this is not always so in the case of second-rate universities)."

In the United States, it takes an average of six minutes (my estimate) for a Harvard graduate whom you've just met to work that fact about himself into the conversation. In Japan, graduates of Tokyo University will let you in on this information even quicker. Once, in hopes of being provocative, I asked a leading political scientist, "Who runs Japan?" He answered, only half humorously, "NHK, *Asahi Shimbun*, and Tokyo University"—the pervasive public broadcasting system, the biggest newspaper, and the most prestigious school. Four out of five ranking civil servants are Tokyo University graduates, as have been seven out of twelve postwar prime ministers. Forty percent of all prominent Japanese businessmen are from Tokyo University. One of them told me that once, having overdrawn his bank account by a large amount, he phoned excuses to the bank manager— and found that the fellow, far from being angry, was embarrassed to be getting an apology from a Tokyo University man. "You can even be proud of *not* getting into Tokyo University, if you *almost* passed the exam," my friend said. He found, when he started his business, that the old school tie was a sort of passport. "I'd go to Hitachi, the big electric company, for example, and they'd say, 'There's a fellow from your class in such-and-such a section.'" Even many Communist party leaders are Tokyo grads.

Kyoto had what might be called a university thirteen hundred years ago, well before Cairo, customarily cited as oldest in the world. But Tokyo University grew out of the Astronomy Office, founded in 1684 to study books that reached sealed-off Japan through the single loophole in its walls, the Dutch trading post at Nagasaki. This institution, later renamed Office for the Interpretation of Barbarian Books, merged with a Confucian "university" and a medical school in 1869 and became known as Tokyo University in 1877. In the heyday of the Japanese empire, 1885 to 1945, it was Tokyo Imperial University. The American Occupation excised that overweening word, and at the same time made the school coeducational.

The main campus of Tokyo University, mostly built or rebuilt since the earthquake of 1923, stands on 103 spacious acres. This quiet haven, a couple of miles north of the Imperial Palace and the office buildings of central Tokyo, was once the estate of the Maeda family, greatest of Japan's feudal lords, and the Maedas' Garden of Virtue, wonderfully secluded around its pond, is still the area's hub. The campus is walled, and its main entrance, the Akamon (Red Gate), built in 1827 in temple style, is officially designated as an Important Cultural Property. The newer buildings, of glass and concrete, rise eight stories, no more. A subsidiary campus, miles away in the part of Tokyo called Komaba, gets students started with two years of general education. The university library has 2.4 million volumes, more than 500,000 of them in Chinese, English, or other foreign languages.

"Tokyo University is exceptional because the students are exceptions," says Japanologist James Morley. "They're hard-driving— they expect to run the country." They divide into ten thousand undergraduates and two thousand graduate students. Only a few hundred foreign students, chiefly Chinese, get into this university—the language is too hard—and of all the students who entered in 1974, only 5.8 percent were women. Even though students are accepted on merits after passing entrance exams, a disproportionate number of them come from families with higher-than-average incomes; three out of five fathers are senior officials in big business or government. Such men can pay for the tutoring or the private prep schools that enable their children to get through the tests. Most graduates of the much-respected law school end up in arranged marriages with the daughters of rich and prominent families. "If you make it to Tokyo, you've made it socially," the head of another university told me. A sizable number of students drive their own cars and live off-campus in two-room apartments.

The teaching staff numbers 3,500 with 700 full professors, which gives Tokyo an estimable student–teacher ratio of four to one. Rarely does the university hire a teacher who is not a Tokyo graduate.

The relative quality of private and state universities is a tossup in the United States (Harvard? Berkeley?); in Japan the best are unquestionably the government schools. The Japanese Ivy League is made up of the former imperial universities founded in succession to and on the model of Tokyo: Kyoto University (1897), Tohoku (in Sendai, 1907), Kyushu (in Fukuoka, 1910), and Hokkaido (in Sapporo, 1918). Later additions, including specialized universities, built the government system to 111 schools. Fat packets of government money pour into these institutions, Tokyo University in particular benefitting from the favors of its numerous alumni in the Ministries of Education and Finance. Bustling Kyoto University, No. 2 in Japan, is strong in history and physics, and deserves the qualified gratitude of mankind for its brilliant pioneer work in developing the seedless watermelon.

But though they are brimming with prestige and money, the government universities cannot come near meeting the demand for higher education. Japan, which in 1950 had fewer than 250,000 students in college, now has 2 million, a third of them women; of these, 300,000, mostly women, go to two-year junior colleges. This compares to 8,265,000 university students in the United States, 4,549,000 in the Soviet Union, 615,000 in France, and 346,000 in the United Kingdom. The government schools comprise one-fourth of all universities, and take one-fifth of the students. Japan's 299 private universities educate the rest.

Private universities have to buck the Japanese attitude, ingrained for centuries and contrary to American ideas, "of viewing anything governmental high and anything private low," as one private university official put it. But in doing so they win the gratitude of the "ordinary" student, who cannot make the great government schools. Moreover, the oldest and best of the private universities come close in quality to their public rivals, and possess distinctive characters and histories. Tokyo's Waseda, founded in 1882, and with 45,000 students a large and bustling school, pumps graduates into the middle levels of government and business, into politics, and into newspapers and television. "Tokyo University is simply not as strong as Waseda on the creative arts," boasted a young TV producer who graduated from Waseda. Tokyo's Keio University—or rather, the school for teaching English out of which it later grew—was founded in the 1860s by Yukichi Fukuzawa, one of the first Japanese ever to visit the United States. While most government universities took German or French models, most private universities followed American or British examples; Keio even taught medicine in English rather than Japanese. Super-Establishmentarian Keio now produces more business leaders than any other private university. Another early Japanese traveler in the United States, a stowaway named Jo Niishima, attended Amherst College and returned to found Kyoto's distinguished, Christian-oriented Doshisha University in 1875. Amherst and Doshisha still maintain many intimate links.

Lacking the huge endowments and foundation support that American private colleges get, Japan's private universities operate on tuitions and a pinch of government subsidy. Shortage of funds forces them to saddle teachers with an average of twenty-nine students, as compared to an average of eight in the government universities. While charging students three times as much in tuition as government schools, private universities can spend only one-third as much on each student. Private schools concentrate on social sciences for the pragmatic reason that natural sciences, requiring more equipment, are more expensive to teach. And thus the ratio of science and engineering students in Japan is less than in the United States or Europe, and much less than in the Soviet Union.

Overall, Japanese universities have interesting strengths and persistent weaknesses. Mathematics is unsurpassed ("Something to do with the abacus," my consultant on this subject muttered). The sciences in the government universities are taught with talent, flexibility, and sufficient funds. This flair pays off particularly in physics. Leona Esaki, co-winner of the Nobel Prize for Physics in 1973, was the third Japanese to achieve this honor, others being Hideki Yukawa, in 1949, and Shinichiro Tomonaga, in 1965. Historian Hall credits Japanese education with publishing a range and volume of scholarly journals "perhaps unmatched by any other country."

Critics contend that throughout the system education is unadventuresome, rigid, even stodgy. Yet the draconian entrance-exam system forces teachers to stress memory work, with commercial publishers selling 410 million copies of test and drill books every year. The kind of exam passers thus encouraged are too uniform for the nation's health, as Esaki points out, urging new policies to encourage greater diversity. Few universities have art galleries, symphonies, visiting lecturers. "You can find forty American universities with better wood-block printing courses than any in Japan," an American government official assured me.

The Occupation planted the concept of general education in college curriculums, but it is not thriving. The lingering German tradition still gives faculties control of universities, and they continue to stress research and specialization. Minister of Education Michio Nagai contends, furthermore, that as Japanese universities tried to compress the transition from the European medieval model to white-collar general education, the schools "came to be characterized by the easy adaptation to the practical needs of society rather than by their long-term contribution to the formation of culture through the detached pursuit of truth. Education designed to develop men who think for themselves has already been abandoned."

Another defect is that higher education has concentrated too much in big cities. Students—nearly a million of them—are a major factor in the overpopulation of the Tokyo area, site of one-fourth of the nation's universities. Nagai also holds that the pay of professors is too low, so that nearly two-thirds of them, even at the well-heeled government universities, have to moonlight. This belittling of the value of professors leads many of them to the disillusionment and cynicism that lies behind the Marxism and other revolutionary thinking endemic in Japanese universities.

Something ominous was going on in Room 127 of the Faculty of Literature at Waseda University one fall evening in 1972. Several teachers tried to investigate, but students shoved them back. Inside, other students, armed with steel pipes and clubs, whacked away at sophomore Daizaburo Kawaguchi, who was tied to a chair, until they covered his body with scores of long, narrow welts. "Around 8 P.M. that day, the victim stopped responding to the blows," said the student who was subsequently convicted of the murder, in his confession. The assailants took Kawaguchi's body to the grounds of Tokyo University Hospital, a few miles away, and dumped it among weeds. Kawaguchi's alleged offense (mistakenly alleged, it later turned out) was that as a member of the Middle Core faction of the Federation of Student Self-Government Organizations (Zengakuren), the left-wing association of about half of all Japanese university students, he had spied on the Revolutionary Marxists, another faction.

Strange events followed. Thousands of "nonaligned" Waseda students censured the Revolutionary Marxists with curiously restrained anger, declaring the killing a very naughty act. Toshio Tanaka, head of the student self-government association at the First Literature Department, said: "We Revolutionary Marxists have seriously criticized ourselves over the murder of a fellow Waseda University student. This shame will haunt us all our lives. But we will not let our members surrender to the police." Tanaka bowed in humble apology before Kawaguchi's mother at the campus funeral. Riot policemen kept vigil at the university, but their only act was to rescue seven Revolutionary Marxists hemmed in by protesters. A year later four Revolutionary Marxists were indicted on a lynch charge, but in the meantime the Marxists and the Middle Core had zapped one another again and again, usually in predawn raids on apartment houses occupied by one group or the other. The Middle Core's weapon of choice was an iron pipe wrapped in vinyl. The Marxists used axes, hammers, bamboo sticks, and oxygen torches, and protected themselves with helmets, gas masks, and leg guards.

This feud is only a sample of student violence in recent history. A decade of riots and demonstrations peaked in 1969 with the arrest of twenty thousand people, mostly students. Rebellious students seizing buildings at Tokyo University in 1968 virtually shut the school for a year, with the result that in 1972 the number of its graduates landing choice government jobs slumped sharply. The right-wing students at Kokushikan University a couple of years ago beat up a seventy-year-old woman and a number of Korean high school children. Students roughed up pedestrians for the peculiarly Japanese offense of "looking" at them.

The standard demystification of such ugliness as Kawaguchi's murder holds that students are violent because frustrated—a psychological matter. To the disillusionment with a dehumanizing world that afflicts students elsewhere, the Japanese add some neuroses of their own. With "examination hell" behind them and "lifetime enslavement" (a permanent-tenure job) ahead, they feel cut off from the wonder, joy, and variety of life. All but the best may be bitter that they did not get into a top-rank school. "They kill each other out of desperation," one government official explained to me. "They can't fight the police because the police are so strong." Taken together with Japan's dark, enduring love affair with death, and such triggers as classroom boredom, tuition boosts, or political dissent, this frustration becomes, I think, a believable explanation. One more point: the story of the last decade's Japanese student protest is roughly the story of American student protest—they went out, they battled, they went back to the classrooms. The Establishment turned out to be too tough. Japan's Special University Governance Law, permitting riot police to move in on the campuses, greatly dampened rebellion. What will come next, in both countries, will be a product of cyclical forces not well understood anywhere.

Though Japanese student protest was brought under control by repression, plus some cosmetic reforms, the government's more radical answer was to devise and build a tougher sort of university. At the southern foot of Mount Tsukuba, a pretty little (2,660 feet) prominence rising out of the Kanto Plain forty-six miles northeast of Tokyo, workmen are putting up, at an eventual cost of $3.3 billion, a city for two hundred thousand built around a modernistic, up-from-scratch campus for the University of Tsukuba. Reflecting the ruling conservative party's fear of academic disruption, the organization of this new school is deliberately authoritarian. The minister of education is empowered to appoint not only the president of the university, as in other government schools, but also five powerful vice-presidents and an advisory board of councillors made up of outsiders. Staff appointments, a function of faculties in existing universities, fall to the president and the councillors at Tsukuba. Furthermore, the government will apply this scheme to no less than one hundred other new universities to be built by 1986—and perhaps even to existing universities.

Apart from what seems like ominously powerful control by the central government, Tsukuba offers Japan some provocative educational innovations. To dissolve the student's perennial doubts about whether his professor cares more about research than instruction, it simply separates the two functions. Teachers teach not in faculties but in "clusters": basic sciences, social and biological sciences, business administration, engineering, physical education, fine arts, and medicine. Researchers research, in twenty-six fields. Tsukuba will move deeply into graduate work, so far neglected in Japan, and give undergraduates a broad, interdisciplinary education. It will offer reeducation for adult professionals. Such potent government think-tanks as the High Energy Physics Institute and the National Disaster Prevention Institute are moving to Tsukuba. And, as a final cultural flourish, the United Nations University, which Japan cornered by offering $100 million as basic endowment, will rise in Tsukuba, with

Buckminster Fuller as one of its architects and James Hester, longtime president of New York University, as rector.

The same trend toward more authority for the Ministry of Education is at work as well in lower education. The American Occupation, determined to smash the nationalistic indoctrination function of prewar Japanese education, transferred controls of schools from the ministry to local boards, imposed coeducation, gave teachers wide individual freedom to replace the old set curriculums, played down German-style rote learning, and otherwise "democratized" the system. The new freedom encouraged teachers to organize into a union, which they did with enthusiasm, speed, and large gulps of Marxist theory.

In mid-1973, two-thirds of delegates to the national convention of the Japan Teachers Union voted to support the Socialist Party— and the other third voted to support the Communists. Thus the union has constantly been at odds with the conservative Ministry of Education. In the battle between the two, the ministry is slowly winning. By publishing criteria for curriculums, the ministry gradually regained control of this matter from local boards. By contributing funds for school administrators' salaries, it put over a system for rating teachers so that dissidents can be fired. Throughout all this, the Marxist teachers have sustained the original American reforms, while, in an even greater irony, the ministry's position has been buttressed by the fact that the cold war and Vietnam discredited things American. In a parallel development, the government found a legal loophole to give funds to private schools, despite a prohibiting clause—copied word for word from the original constitution of the state of Montana—in the 1947 Japanese constitution. "In 1970, an education survey mission for the Organization of Economic Cooperation and Development wrote in its report to the Japanese government that nowhere else in the world has a government intervened in the selection of textbooks and the conducting of education so much as in Japan," said *Asahi Shimbun.*

The bitterest battle over the shape of lower-school education has been fought over the teaching of "morals." Until the end of the war, morals meant *kokutai,* the exaltation of the state and the emperor. "I was taught 'Die for duty—you're not a good Japanese if you think about your own welfare,'" recalled the principal of the grade school that I visited. The Occupation banned morals instruction, but no sooner had the Americans gone away than the Ministry of Education revived the subject in another form. Now "social ethics" courses, made compulsory in 1958, inculcate codes that vary with the teacher's inclinations, though they shun indoctrination prewar-style. Typically, students get a fast run through Plato, Aristotle, the Christian church fathers, the Benthamites, and democratic thinkers. The issue still stirs strong emotions. Masami Sakurai, twenty, student: "The kind of moral education enforced by the state is designed to create character-less people who are obedient to the Establishment." Takao Kusu, fifty-six, company president: "If in our society everyone starts doing what he wants to and slacks off whenever he wants to, believing, erroneously, that this is the way to guard one's privacy, can any organization ever attain its purpose or realize its ideals?"

The Japanese love the English language just about as intensely as they hate it. They know they must learn it, because the world will never go in heavily for learning Japanese, which is more difficult even than such brain-numbing tongues as Magyar or Finnish, and ranks tenth in users (after Portuguese and Bengali) among the world's language groups. They also adore the cachet of English; the Japanese language now contains twenty thousand English-derived words. Residential mailboxes are commonly labeled with the English word LETTERS, as though otherwise the postman would not know where to leave the mail. In other ways, the Japanese want to keep English at arm's length: it must not become too wide a doorway to the sometimes dubious temptations of the West. Luckily for this point of view, English is damnably difficult for the Japanese. No one knows for sure whether it is difficult because it is taught badly, or whether it is taught badly so that it will be difficult.

The English-speaking foreigner in Japan, his eye hungry for intelligible reading matter, blessedly finds English words on every hand. Amidst the profusion of Japanese characters in billboards and subway advertising, English phrases leap out. Sometimes they make sense: ENJOY PIPE! More often they are baffling: MOM INPUT FAIR, SUMMER SEX Q & A, NICE ON. A movie marquee shows two nudes and translates the title as TOILET TALK. For some jaunty reason, shopping bags carry such phraseology as FIVE OF YOUNG SOUL, NEW ROCK, or just SEX. Department-store boutiques and sales campaigns take names in English that are inscrutable on purpose, since the merchandisers know that chic obscurity sells goods: HIS-HERS IN SHOP, FEELING ZONE EIGHT, BIG EXCITE, YOUNGER OF BRAVE. In fact, English has penetrated advertising more than any other field; in hundreds of station plazas the Japanese National Railways displays lofty signs that urge the Japanese to DISCOVER JAPAN. The labels on bottles of Yoro Beer carry the enigmatic encircling motto "Yoro's Goal is Two Thousand Restaurants."

Perhaps the most piquant focus for the English-habituated eye is children's T-shirts. Some I saw said DRUNK ST. BERNARD and BANG GOOD LAUGH PERSON. One read LOVE LOVE ANT and depicted two ants, presumably in love. A two-year-old wore a shirt that asked WHO AM I? on the back and replied I AM A DOG on the front. A hapless mother taking her children through a museum wore a blouse printed round and round, over and over, with the word FUCK (the wearers and even the makers of these shirts are mostly ignorant of the meanings, or at least the nuances, of these phrases, according to a professional interpreter I talked to).

To name a store in English is considered "groovy," which inspired me to compile My Own Business Directory of Japan. Some entries:

OUR BEAUTICIAN CAR WASH

ENVIRONMENT HYGIENE'S HOTEL

RESORT INN JOY CLUB

CAR ACCESSORILY

NIPPON SHAKEPROOF CO., LTD.

SNACK ALLEY CAPOO

HALLELUJAH BEAUTY SALON

CLUB THAT MAN (a bar)

TRADITIONAL WITH GUTS (a mod men's shop)

In point of fact, the Japanese have always doted on foreign words. "It would be difficult to find another language in the world—excepting perhaps English during the first few centuries after the Norman invasion—which has been as hospitable to loanwords as has Japanese," writes Roy Andrew Miller, professor of Far Eastern languages at Yale. Ancient borrowings from Chinese and Korean are now so Japanese as to be almost impossible to trace, but words dating from the sixteenth-century Portuguese contact are self-evident. Samples: *pan*, bread, from *pão*, and *tempura*, fried shrimp, from *têmpera* (meaning "seasoning"). Later the Dutch contributed such utilitarian words as *kohi*, coffee, from *koffie*, and *biiru*, beer, from *bier*. Some other borrowings: *ideorogi*, ideology, from German *Ideologie; baikingu*, food served smorgasbord style, from Scandinavian roots for "Viking"; *abekku*, a boy-and-girl date, from French *avec;* and *barikan*, hair clipper, from Bariquand & Marre, erstwhile French makers of this tool.

English began to get into Japanese shortly after Commodore Perry stepped ashore with words like *boto*, boat, and *naifu*, knife, but the anti-American militarists of the 1930s put the naifu to a lot of this lingo. "The end of the war suddenly transformed English from a strictly prohibited enemy language to a license for driving on the highway of life," says critic Daizo Kusayanagi. As part of the process, English words entered Japanese in droves. Some beauties: *teipukoda,* tape recorder; *yangu pawaa,* young power; *wanmanka,* bus operated by driver without assistant (from one-man car); *piiaru,* P.R. (public relations); *tsupiisu,* two-piece suit. To start a bus, conductors learned to yell to the driver, *"Orai!"* (All right!).

As these samples show, Japanese simply does not contain enough sounds to render borrowings accurately. The classic and continuing case is the confusion between *r* and *l.* They sound too much alike to most Japanese to bother making a distinction over. I heard scores of people whose English was otherwise flawless say "recentry," meaning lately. The stewardess on one Japan Air Lines flight said, "I hope you have a preasant fright." The confusion shows again and again in signs and labels. The church bombed at Nagasaki was "Cathoric." An inn there has a "robby." An official book about Tokyo shows a picture of "St. Ruke's" Hospital. The *l* sound does not occur in Japanese, which explains why so many Japanese change it to the nearest thing. But then, recognizing their proneness to this mistake, the Japanese overcompensate by making the reverse error in writing. A restaurant serves "Bulgalian" coffee. On containers printed by the millions and reused for years, one reads: "Flesh Egg." The illustration for *R* in a children's alphabet book shows a lion. The generally meticulous magazine called *The East* writes about the publishing firm of "Harper and Lowe." A further confusion occurs between *b* and *v,* because *v* is another missing consonant in Japanese, and *b* is made to work for both. Japanese has both *f* and *h,* but the English *f* mysteriously turns to *h* when a word is transformed into Japanese, as every foreigner discovers when he first enters a "kohi" house.

Whole chunks of English invade the conversation of educated Japanese. I heard, floating out from the speech of a businessman on the phone, such phrases as "up to 50 percent" and "worldwide marketing." He later explained to me that the English may still have a slightly different meaning: "Cooperate whenever possible" means "Back them all the way!" English is strong in business and trade names. Every other little store offers a service advertised as D.P.E., for "developing, printing, and enlarging." Official forms use "No." in front of the space for the number. A typical list of the brands of Japanese cigarettes goes like this: Hi-Lite, Current, Hope, Luna, Seven Stars, Cherry, and Peace. Model names of cars are all English, too, but a far cry from the Marauders, Jaguars, and Furies of the West. The names of the Datsun line, mostly devised by a former president, include: Cherry (for the favorite Japanese tree), Sunny (it has big windows), Violet (for a beautiful flower), Fairlady (because the former president was much taken by *My Fair Lady* when he saw it in New York), Cedric (well, we must remember that an American company once named a model Edsel), and President (the luxury limousine). Even for the Japanese market, the dashboard controls of all cars are labeled in English.

Similarly, famous corporations are known by their English names inside Japan as well as abroad: Sharp, National, All Nippon Airways. The name of the world-famous Bridgestone tire comes from the name of the company's founder, Shojiro Ishibashi (*ishi* equals stone, *bashi* equals bridge). Computers at the Toyota plant near Nagoya print out instructions in English, typically to build a car in the "L.A. Mode," that is, with emissions controls suitable for Los Angeles. Physicist Yukawa says he cannot think scientifically in Japanese—has to use English. The Russians used to write in French for the Russians; the Japanese, through their thriving English-language book- and newspaper-publishing industries, often write in English for the Japanese. But people who flaunt their expert English too blatantly are called *Eigo-ya*, English-mongers.

Since the Japanese are so deeply involved in English, so clearly seduced by it, the obvious course for the country is to plunge ahead and make English a true second language, as it is in Scandinavia or Quebec. But here Japan is of two minds. To communicate with the world, and particularly to tap the technical literature of the West, Japan needs widespread knowledge of English. Yet the Japanese also feel that learning to speak English universally and well would in some critical way weaken the Eastern component of their culture. Brainy people, able to function easily abroad, might emigrate. The contradictory solution to this dilemma calls for four to six hours of English a week for eight to ten years before graduation from senior high school, taught boringly and abstractly by teachers incompetent in spoken English, producing students who can read the language for knowledge but hesitate to converse in it.

A Nisei friend of mine, who attended an upper-grade English class, brought back a report that briefly summarized the whole problem: "The teacher began by saying, 'Gudu afternoon, boizu andu garuzu,' and I knew that they'd never learn to speak intelligibly." Yoshiaki Yamada, one of the few fluent high school English teachers, comments, "Japanese teachers know a lot *about* English and its grammar, but they do not know English itself." Teachers sweat unnecessarily over such points as the distinction between "in" and "on."

The best Japanese-English dictionary in print exemplifies "scold" with this unlikely rebuke from a father to a son: "A pretty fellow you are to idle away all day!"

Some signs suggest that Japan is growing disgusted with the failure of its vast English-teaching effort. Language labs and tapes are coming into the schools. Corporations send thousands of executives to total-immersion schools to convert their textbook knowledge of English into fluent speech. Young American college graduates earn as much as $50 a day tutoring; this seems to be the commonest employment among Americans in Japan. I trust that they will ultimately erase those persistent Briticisms heard in the talk of Japanese English-speakers of the old school: "so-called," "actually," "and so on and so forth," "that sort of thing." Japlish—English mangled by a Japanese—is less common than before, but not wiped out. The self-service carts at Haneda (Tokyo) Airport baggage-delivery area carry signs with the cheerful advice, "Take care of yourself." I saw a hotel ad that read: "Wonderful nice view Kyoto and the Lake Biwa How does this full of rural beauty barbecue eat taste in a grassplot!"

Japanese, anciently an Altaic language (like Turkic and Mongolian), and a distant cousin of Korean, is otherwise totally different from any other tongue in the world. Spoken Japanese is in some ways simple: it uses only five vowels, *a e i o u*, and each is pronounced with a single specific sound, respectively *ah eh ee oh oo*. Combinations of vowels, *ei* and *ai*, provide two other vowel sounds, *ay* and *eye*. The consonants are *b d f g h j k m n p r s t w y z*, plus *ch sh* and *ts*. "No major modern language uses so few sounds as Japanese," writes Douglas Haring. These sounds are mostly combined in syllables consisting of one consonant and one vowel, although occasionally one vowel stands alone as a syllable, and occasionally a consonant sound (*n m k p* or *t*) is added to complete a syllable. In general, each syllable is pronounced with equal stress (Yo-ko-ha-ma, not Yo-Ko-*ham*-a), but often, for reasons too baffling to go into, *u* or *i* gets demoted to silence: Matsushita, the electronics firm, is pronounced Matsushta. There are no consonant clusters, as in "strike," which is why Japanese baseball announcers say *sutoraiku*. The result of all this is a language more pronounceable and audible than, say, French or Chinese. Donald Keene contends that Japanese "sounds rather like Italian, at least to those who do not know Italian." Since almost every word ends monotonously in a vowel, and since words have no heavy stresses, rhyme and meter cannot be used in Japanese poetry.

But the basic simplicity of the word units belies the devilish complexity of the grammar. Verbs can be inflected—that is, the suffixes changed according to usage—in dozens of ways; and adjectives are inflected like verbs. Nouns, however, are not inflected at all, not even to make them plural. In counting, the basic Chinese-derived numerals (*ichi*, one; *ni*, two; *san*, three; and so on) change in at least twenty-six ways according to what is being numbered: *sanchaku* for (three) suits or dresses; *sandai* for pianos or beds; *sambon* for long, round objects like trees, cigarettes, ropes, legs, needles, pencils, bottles, or fingers. The syntax places the verb at the end of the sentence and uses connectives to sort out the subject–object relationship of nouns. Personal pronouns are in disrepute in Japanese, because they raise touchy questions of hierarchy; but by the same token, when used they take many forms to fit the positions of the speaker and hearer. "The writer can easily mention over twenty Japanese equivalents for 'I,'" says the essayist Atsuharu Sakai. Euphemism is another delicate area: when speaking of the toilet, should one say *benjo*, "motion-place," or *gofujo*, "honorable impurity," or *habakari*, "impoliteness"? It depends on the company. In Japanese, synonyms multiply like Hondas: there are five words for "and."

These idiosyncrasies might nonetheless be tolerable; it is the rendering of them into writing that raises a higher language barrier to outsiders than any other major language in the world. The reason is historical. The ways of writing that existed in the world in the fourth and fifth centuries were essentially two: the logical sound-by-sound alphabets of India, Africa, and the West; and the memory-glutting ideographs of the Chinese, each of them standing for a whole word. As Professor Reischauer says, "Perhaps the greatest single misfortune in the history of Japan was that, because of her geographic position, Chinese characters and not one of the Western alphabets became the basis of her writing system."

In those centuries, Japan's great gulps of Chinese culture, particularly the scripture of Buddhism, put her in obvious need of ways to write. At first the intellectuals simply wrote in Chinese, until the temptation grew irresistible to make this script serve to write Japanese. The process took centuries of linguistic hammering. Adopting the Chinese character for a given noun together with the Chinese pronounciation (as nearly as it could be imitated in Japanese) was not too difficult. In other cases, applying the Chinese character to the Japanese spoken word worked well enough. But Chinese grammar, which depends on word order, lacked the connectives and suffixes that Japanese requires. In desperation, the scholars stripped many Chinese characters of their original meanings and turned them into Japanese connectives. Bit by bit, this process led to applying certain simplified Chinese characters to each of the forty-eight basic Japanese syllables, mostly made by placing one consonant in front of one vowel, thus creating a syllabary that could spell anything in the language.

That was a marvelous invention, as utilitarian as an alphabet. A few books were written in nothing but syllabary characters. But subtlety, complexity, even sheer difficulty for difficulty's sake, were more to the taste of the otherwise idle court littérateurs; they went back to drawing on Chinese for nouns and verb roots. They even set up a second syllabary that virtually duplicated the first, and used both of them for marginal explanatory notes when the going got too heavy in the Chinese ideographs. This hybrid writing system was their unfortunate bequest to those little boys and girls who nowadays must spend twice as much time learning language as do children elsewhere.

Then and now, the system screamed for simplification, and got a little. Beneficent scholars reduced the syllabaries to a few strokes for each letter, ending up with a cursive, feminine style for the *hiragana* syllabary, which is handy to write, and an angular, masculine style for the *katakana* syllabary, which serves for simple, punchy advertising signs, for transliteration of foreign words and names, and for the only kind of keyboard typewriter that can write Japanese. The three ways of writing the word *nihongo*, "Japanese language," in Japanese look like this:

CHINESE CHARACTERS	HIRAGANA	KATAKANA
日	に	ニ
本	ほ	ホ
語	ん	ン
	ご	ゴ

Chinese characters are called *kanji*, and the most elaborate Japanese dictionary of them contains 48,902 entries, far beyond any human being's memory capacity, and a heavy strain on printing, telegraphy, and cybernetics. In 1946, the American Occupation pressured the Ministry of Education to single out 1,850 commonly used Chinese characters, leaving the rest of the language to be spelled out from the syllabaries. The intent was eventually to shuck off Chinese writing entirely, but the Japanese dragged their feet—the more xenophobic among them *favor* a language barrier. The novelist Yukio Mishima deliberately used rare, old, discarded kanji. Now children must learn 881 kanji in the first six grades, the rest later. Characters requiring too many strokes (the most complex takes forty-eight) are being abbreviated.

Even though docked to 1,850, the sheer number of kanji in Japanese, taken together with the two forty-eight-character syllabaries, Arabic figures, the Roman alphabet, and assorted symbols, remains a high technological hurdle. The standard typewriter—*taipuraita* in Japanese—is large, heavy, cumbersome, and slow. It consists of a type case, bigger than a chessboard, that contains more than two thousand characters, and a cylindrical carriage, holding the paper, that can be moved anywhere—backward and forward, and from side to side—over the case. Having positioned the carriage over the chosen character, the operator presses the machine's single key, whereupon a mechanical finger reaches down, plucks out the desired type, impresses it on the paper through an inked ribbon, and replaces it. The type case is so hard to memorize and the process so inefficient that large business enterprises keep only a few machines, together with the skilled women who run them, for formal communications. Most letters are written by hand.

At the newspaper *Mainichi Shimbun* (which, with *Asahi Shimbun*, encouraged the 1946 language reform), I watched an up-to-date Japanese typesetting operation. The compositor sits at a panel a yard wide containing 600 postage-stamp-size keys, each showing four characters—2,400 in all (Chinese characters, syllabaries, Roman letters, figures, punctuation, stock-market symbols, etc.). A pattern of yellow squares among the white keys helps the operator to find his way around this sea of symbols. Pushing one of four foot pedals selects the top, bottom, right, or left character on the key, and pressing the key causes the machine to punch a particular pattern of holes into a continuous paper tape. This tape activates another machine, with a cylinder studded with type for each of the 2,400 characters; the cylinder whirs, shuttles, stops, and, one after another, stamps the indicated characters in series onto paper rolled around a platen like that of a Western typewriter. The resulting copy serves for editing, and the same tape, after correction, operates an automatic typecasting machine with a cylinder that is similar except that it contains molds. For standard newspaper use, this caster produces vertical lines of fifteen characters each and assembles these short lines side by side into a horizontal column. To correct or change copy thus set, printers with impressive memories hand-set type from wall cases bigger than a garage door, hopping nimbly back and forth in front of the 2,400 little compartments. Large headlines are cast from hand-set molds, but a case to hold all of them would be impossibly huge, so many are kept in drawers. For some purposes—printouts for editors, type for classified advertisements—*Mainichi* uses new, high-speed, computer-aided machines.

Traditionally, Japanese has been written from top to bottom, and the vertical lines thus formed arranged from right to left. This format in turn means that the pages of books, magazines, and newspapers are numbered in a way that Westerners would call back to front. I was amused in a subway once to watch a man and a girl sitting side by side with open books, flipping pages in opposite directions as they read, respectively, an Agatha Christie mystery in English and a novel in Japanese. But nowadays a lot of Japanese—in scientific books, telephone directories, and business letters, for example—is written in Western sequence. Whichever way Japanese is written, it comes in indented paragraphs of a number of sentences that are punctuated by conventional commas and ended by conventional periods. There are no spaces between words.

The chasm of difference between Japanese and Western languages raises intriguing questions. *How do you look up a telephone number?* The consulter of the Tokyo telephone directory faces a formidable needle-in-the-haystack task. Since the 1946 language reforms did little to simplify family and place names, the three-thousand-page phone book is written with a range of five thousand characters, of which more than three thousand are not taught in schools. But the first step in sorting out phone listings is literally as simple as ABC. At the beginning of the book is a list of forty-four sounds and the page numbers where names beginning with these sounds can be found. If, for example, you are looking for Suzuki, Shintaro, you would first find the page number where the *su* sound begins. Here the ABC analogy abruptly ends. Because Suzuki in Tokyo is as common as Smith is in New York, and because it also can be written in fifteen ways, you have no choice but to commence reading seventy columns of Suzukis, seven thousand of them altogether, carefully scrutinizing the intricate strokes of the characters until you find the one that fits your memory of the name. After fifteen minutes of doggedly scanning the character variations, you usually give up in desperation and dial 113 for the information operator. But if you have no inkling of Mr. Suzuki's address, even she can't help.

In writing, is one person's hand distinct from another's? Yes, but not enough to prevent forgery of signatures. For documents, people use special ivory or hardwood signature seals that can be inked and printed. The seal is initially given a sharp blow to damage it slightly, and thus make the print harder to forge. Some sign checks in Roman letters. I was told, by the way, that it is maddeningly difficult to write Japanese left-handed. In any case, most children are forced to learn to write right-handed. *Should foreigners learn Japanese before a tour of duty in Japan?* Perhaps they should, but they must set aside two years for nothing else if they want to do it right. Most don't. "Recently, it was said that no more than three out of eight hundred American businessmen in Tokyo knew enough Japanese to make an impromptu after-dinner speech," writes John K. Emmerson, U.S. minister in Tokyo from 1962 to 1967. *Dialects?* Universal compulsory education, the standardized speech on government radio and television, and the will to national unity cause the authorized Tokyo speech to be spoken and understood everywhere. Nevertheless, there are thirteen areas of distinctly different dialects, surviving weakly from earlier eras, and several of these are mutually unintelligible. *Personal names?* Before the Meiji Restoration, few persons were entitled to family names, and when they gained the right they mostly took names from places: Tanaka, "inside the paddy"; Matsumoto, "foot of the pine." Given names also have meanings, usually the qualities that parents presumably hope for: Hideo, "excellent male"; Sachiko, "happy child" (for a girl—most girls' names end in "ko"). The Japanese always say names with family name first and given name second (Doe John, as it were), but most books and publications dealing with Japan in English use the Western John Doe order, as I do in this book. Middle names are almost nonexistent. *Can the Japanese read Chinese?* To some extent. The Japanese and the Chinese can converse fairly well by writing Chinese characters, which they often do with imaginary strokes on the palm of the hand. A Japanese woman I met in Hong Kong, seeking a hairdressing shop, had no trouble making out the characters for "place of beauty" on a certain building. Unfortunately, it turned out to be a whorehouse.

Many have been the proposals to chuck the ideographs completely and romanize all writing, as Kemal Ataturk did in Turkey in the 1920s. In past centuries, the Portuguese and the Dutch invented passable forms of *romaji*, romanization, and three versions exist today, the commonest being the Hepburn system devised by an American missionary in 1867. As compared to highly intoned Chinese, Japanese is rather easily transliterated, a fairly simple exercise in phonetics. The Roman alphabet is, of course, the underpinning of Japan's attempt to make English its second language, and therefore it is familiar to everyone.

Romaji is deeply embedded in the Japanese culture. NHK is automatically referred to as "en-aitch-kay" by the announcers at NHK. Nobody calls JNR (Japanese National Railways), JTB (Japan Travel Bureau), JAL (Japan Air Lines) by anything but their romaji initials. Subway and railway signs are given in Chinese characters, the hiragana syllabary, *and* romaji (although the practice of including romaji is dropped in the distant provinces). Sometimes the signs are a trifle difficult to catch from a speeding train—there's a station near Osaka named HIGASHISUMIYOSHIKUYAKUSHOMAE.

Romaji alphabetical order determines the processional order of contestants in international beauty contests in Tokyo, and romaji supplies the symbols for teaching algebra. Building directories tell you what is on 1F, 2F, 3F, 4F, and so on. Internal mail can be addressed in romaji. The old Imperial Navy wrote its secret messages in romaji in order to code them—thus making it a little easier for American intelligence to decode them. Advertisers find it stylish to put brand names into romaji. A taxi is labeled just that, though sometimes, taking a cue from the reversibility of kanji, it may say TAXI on one side and IXAT on the other. (I also saw trucks labeled HSIF HSERF and GNINAELC YRD DNA YRDNUAL.)

Though indisputably complex, is the Japanese writing system all that bad? Learning kanji builds habits of study discipline, and makes reading an admired skill. When Admiral Yamamoto, of Pearl Harbor fame, was asked how he learned to play bridge expertly, he replied: "If I can keep five thousand ideographs in my mind, it is not hard to keep in mind fifty-two cards." Despite the complaints of some, Japanese is not impractical for technical use. Though free in borrowing Western terminology, the Japanese have also created from Chinese roots neologisms for "electricity," "airplane," "atomic bomb," and so on—words so useful that the *Chinese* have adopted them. If you read Japanese well, Reischauer told me, you can read faster than if you read English well. Kanji are subtly expressive, the Japanese say, full of what they call *deriketo na nyuansu*, delicate nuance.

It appears possible that using ideographs avoids the reading disabilities that American educators are so worried about. Dr. Kiyoshi Makita, of Keio University School of Medicine, has found that Japanese children suffer dyslexia one-tenth as frequently as Americans. He therefore proposes that the major cause of dyslexia lies not in the child or the teaching methods but in what he is supposed to read. Some suspicious weaknesses of the alphabet as used in English are: pairs of letters, like *b* and *d*, and pairs of words, like *saw* and *was*, that might tend to encourage mirror reading, a common form of dyslexia; confusing variants of spelling, like *i y igh eye ay ei aye ye ie* and *ais* for the same sound; and atomization of sound to the point that letters cannot be said, and therefore exactly related to a sound, but instead must have names like *bee cee el em* and even *doubleyou*. By contrast, Japanese's closest approximation to letters, the kana syllabaries, have no mirror-image shapes; the syllables' sounds are the same as their names, and they never vary; and kanji are relatively free of the problem of composing words from bits.

A couple of years after Dr. Makita published his observations in the *American Journal of Ortho-Psychiatry*, researchers at the University of Pennsylvania chose eight intelligent second-graders who had failed to learn the most elementary English, and taught them thirty Chinese characters to which English meanings had been arbitrarily assigned. The children picked up this kind of reading in mere hours. The researchers concluded that an ideograph changes from printed symbol to meaning-in-the-brain in one leap, whereas English requires piecing together sound bits to a soundable word that then becomes meaning-in-the-brain, a double transaction.

Perhaps science will eventually prove that ideographs have decisive advantages over alphabets, and that Japanese, arguably the world's toughest major language, is also one of the best.

8 /

Maddened by Butterflies

BY MEANS OF ITS ART FORMS Japan holds a mirror up to itself and lets the world peek over its shoulder. Of course, art everywhere often falls short of its aspiration, which is to tell a pure truth, so we know that seeing Japan in reflection may give us a more or less distorted picture. To turn things around, the thought of a Japanese learning about America through Broadway, CBS, the Chicago *Tribune*, and the paintings of Larry Rivers would set any American to babbling a string of caveats and sentences beginning with "on the other hand." But perilous as it may be, this kind of examination is irresistible, and we find, again, that the crux of the matter is: East and West, ancient and modern, and how they harmonize in the world's most eclectic country.

Looking back on many hours spent in front of the rainbow colors of a Sony television set in Tokyo, hours of delight, bemusement, and perplexity, I summon to mind a kaleidoscope of images, a barrage of impressions that even in memory batter my sensibilities.

A samurai's hara-kiri . . . Yellow Tomato, a drama of love . . . the difficulties of driving a cab in London . . . Beeg Rotary Mazda . . . Susan Hayward and Gary Cooper speaking Japanese . . . bare-breasted girls at midnight . . . little green microphones in the hands of bouncy singers . . . an English instructor: "Won't you come in? May I take your coat? Will you have some tea?" . . . a geisha and her customer dancing to music from a samisen . . . bullet train streaks past a temple . . . "and now, the Peanut Sisters!" . . . "Promise me that you will leave me never / I will love you longer than forever"

135

. . . Sammy Davis Jr. prefers Suntory whiskey . . . a Buddhist priest as a figure of fun—drops fan while chanting sutras . . . the burial scene from *Aïda* . . . wise old Japanese eyes examine how the brewing of the sake is going . . . lacquered boxes, screens, and tea bowls, stunningly displayed and instructively explained . . . a series of girls remove dresses to show quality of bras and panties.

> *Hi ho hey hey*
> *Made in U.S.A.*
> *Hi ho hey hey*
> *Wrigley Chewing Gum!*

You name it—it's all there on Japanese TV, with a strong American accent. Seven tireless channels in Tokyo—fewer in the hinterlands—pump it out, and a higher proportion of the population than anywhere else spends a higher proportion of its time looking at the higher proportion of television sets that bring in the broadcasts. Virtually all Japanese households have receivers, and 75 percent have color sets. All the channels but two are private and commercial, permitted to broadcast as much advertising as they think the public can stand, and they think the public can stand plenty. The two noncommercial channels belong to puissant, publicly owned NHK—Nippon Hoso Kyokai, which means Japan Broadcasting Corporation.

NHK is a cautious colossus, plump with money, firsts, biggests, and prudence. Its statistics boggle the mind, but two will suffice: it has 16,500 employees and (in fulfillment of its legal obligation to cover Japan) 3,245 television transmitters. An American Embassy cultural attaché told me that NHK is "light-years ahead of us—the humblest family gets rich fare." NHK's two channels pour out education, science, language instruction, absorbing documentaries, fine music from its own symphony orchestra, historical drama of the same high standards as the British Broadcasting Corporation's. Significantly, NHK broadcasts the proceedings of the Diet, which gives the Japanese a much better chance than Americans get to watch their politicians in action.

Because "we are not a slave to ratings," as NHK's foreign-relations manager Hiroshi Shionozaki put it when I talked to him, the corporation can broadcast specialized programs for farmers, computer operators, businessmen, young people, and even for such tiny minorities as the deaf, dumb, and mentally retarded. NHK's general-interest channel gives about a third of its time to public affairs, another third to culture, and the remainder to entertainment plus a smattering of education. Sometimes when this channel has a gripping public affairs program going on at eight o'clock in the evening, it draws 15 to 20 million prime-time viewers and leaves the commercial channels to divide up the remaining 4 million. NHK's other channel, which devotes itself 85 percent to education (including *Sesame Street*, broadcast in English) and 15 percent to culture, is largely directed to the TV sets one sees in every Japanese classroom, coordinating with the curriculums of about four-fifths of all elementary schools—"the best developed school broadcasting system in the world," says John Scupham, former head of education broadcasting at BBC. Nationally standardized courses and a single national time zone are assets in this endeavor.

NHK's new broadcasting center, just occupied when I visited it, is a twenty-three-story building of bluish glass in west-central Tokyo. A computer guides the immensely complex operation: national and regional programing for both TV networks and some new ultrahigh-frequency transmitters, programing for one FM stereo and two AM radio networks and for international Radio Japan, and allocation of studios, personnel, props, and other "resources" for program production, work that when done by men required five thousand order slips a day. In the dim entrails of this building I saw a computer-run miniature railroad with a car that glides among hundreds of stored videotapes, chooses one needed for the next program somewhere in NHK, plucks it out with mechanical fingers, and carries it to the machine that plays it. Similarly, film projectors waiting in the dark turned themselves on and off at silent electronic bidding. Floor tiles when lifted reveal a squirming spaghetti of black rubber cables running everywhere. Happily, NHK's IBM 370 and its miles of wire are not infallible. One day while I was in Tokyo, the computer cut off every last radio and television program and, until the men at the broadcast control center sprang to their switches, patriotically played the national anthem on all channels.

Twenty television studios, the largest 156 feet long, 82 feet wide, and 50 feet high, occupy the first floor. I looked into one that was producing an episode of *Kunitori Monogatari*, a long-running drama of Japan's sixteenth-century civil wars, comparable to the BBC's *Henry the Eighth*. Against a background of live trees and grass, fierce armored samurai sat taking a break, some powdering their noses. Viewers follow this story with a printed history provided free by NHK, and having got hooked, flock to Gifu Prefecture to view the original setting of the action. In a smaller studio, rich with the smells of ginger and soy sauce, cameras peered into the bubbling pots of NHK's cooking school.

Against a wall on the fifth floor is the deliberately low-key desk and backdrop of the announcer of the 7 P.M. news, who, far from being a celebrity in the manner of Walter Cronkite, remains as anonymous as he can. Approximately one acre of machines, spread out over the floor, support him: projectors, viewers, still-picture file, switchboard, twelve-minute film developers, sequencers, a small computer to calculate timing. The news originates from 180 correspondents in Japan and twenty bureaus overseas. The foreign bureaus also produce half-hour documentaries—a look at Harlem, military life in Singapore—that go on the air right after the evening news.

NHK's product, the images it puts on the screen, is tasteful, instructive, exhaustive, objective, elevating, mercifully free of the abominable huckstering of commercial TV—and yet, somehow, the total is less than the sum of its expensive parts. A play-it-safe philosophy pervades its 100-percent Establishmentarian programing. The "entertainment" shows—cheerful, blue-jeaned, long-haired boys and girls, energetic choreography, moony ballads—are banality defined. "NHK has got the hardware," snorts a friend of mine who works for a Japanese commercial TV network, "but it puts on magic-lantern shows. In news reporting, a bloodless objectivity is everything for NHK. The announcers have to be masks."

My friend, as well as such critics as sociologist Takeshi Ishida and many others that I talked to, find the root of this devitalization in NHK's touchy relations with the government. Japan decided way back in 1922 that radio would follow "the general pattern of government sponsorship of public services," as José María de Vera explains it in *Educational Television in Japan*, and the militarists of the 1930s used NHK radio, founded in 1926, for blatant propaganda. The American-written constitution of 1947 encouraged NHK to convert itself into "an independent, public juridical person 'sponsored' by the nation" and supported (as before) by fees collected from its audience. Its official mission is to "present news, educational, cultural and entertainment programs in line with the requirements of the people and to contribute to the elevation of the cultural level of the nation," as well as to speak to the world through Radio Japan. Its ruling body is a thirteen-member board of governers appointed by the prime minister with the consent of the Diet. The board picks NHK's president, who runs the corporation from day to day. The government provides no funds for NHK, but the Diet must nevertheless approve its budget and its fees, which cannot be increased without permission of the Ministry of Posts and Telecommunications. These links, though designed to be minimal, seem to be sufficient to make NHK leery of experimentation that might stir up the conservatives in the Diet.

NHK's answer to this charge, as I heard it from Haruo Sato, assistant publicity director, is that the corporation in fact responds to what its viewers want. "We are in a unique situation, protected by the broadcast law from exterior pressures including the government's. We have obligations to twenty-four million households, and they do pour in requests and opinions and criticisms. We arrange eight thousand meetings a year between our staffers and the grass-roots public." He was proud that "NHK gets 80 percent of the knocks against television in the press *and* 80 percent of the raves." A further constraint against any kind of immoderation is NHK's awareness of its own strength. "NHK stays in the middle, knowing how frightening it could be if this powerful organization moved to the left or to the right. The reason we get our fees is that we please the silent majority."

But does NHK get the fees—all of them? Unlike European public corporations, which rely on the post office to collect television fees, NHK has its own ingenious combination of old and new technology: an army of two thousand house-to-house bill collectors guided by a computer that knows the name, status of television-set ownership, and newest domiciles of just about every potential subscriber in the country. Thus everyone with a black-and-white set (fee: $1.10 a month) or a color set (fee: $1.70) is going to be pestered to sign an NHK contract and pay. Most do, many by bank-account checkoff. But many thousands dodge, contending that they watch commercial stations only (not a legal excuse), or that they have conscientious objections to pay-TV (in fact, *Asahi Shimbun* once printed a ringing manifesto titled "Reasons for Refusing NHK Fees"). NHK's response is never to bring resisters to court, but merely to continue pressure to collect from what it suavely labels "possible future contractors."

If television has a mostly Western aspect, Japan compensates by preserving its own unique stage. The Kabuki-za, the classical Tokyo theater that is the stronghold and center of the art of Kabuki for the whole country, looks (though the present building is a 1950 reconstruction) exactly as Oriental as it should: three blue-roofed gables with ski-jump curves, cream-colored concrete columns made to resemble the huge cypress trunks that hold up temples, railings that cross and rise at the corners, red, white, and blue suspended banners; and inside, a square room, seating 2,600 people, under a long, ribbed ceiling that slants down from the second balcony to the top of the low but wide proscenium opening, all gold and red and lighted by

Japanese lanterns that line the balcony rails. Opening off the hushed corridors are Japanese and Western restaurants, a tea parlor, and a bar, for sustenance during intermissions. Here is a home for great art.

Great art? My notes from one performance read: "one musician now making snoring sound," "bent-kneed walk, pitter-patter steps," "strangled singing," "is this where Gilbert and Sullivan got their ideas?" " 'yow,' 'ow-w,' 'ooh,' 'yoh,' sing the chorus," "actors roll heads a lot—sob, wail—pat teary eyes with tip of sleeve," "quavery tuneless music," "much performance done kneeling," and "two-man chorus sounds like starving huskies in *Call of the Wild*."

This performance ran from 4:30 P.M. until 10 P.M., with four leisurely intermissions, the one at six o'clock being long enough for a meal of tempura noodles. Kabuki is always a variety show: this particular evening I saw two brief dances, a one-act play, and two single acts extracted from long classical plays. In one dance, first performed in 1742 and set in a garden of foot-wide tree peonies, a geisha becomes possessed of the spirit of a lion and, "maddened by butterflies" (paper replicas made to flutter on the ends of wands), she whirls and charges. In the other dance, a top-peddler spins like the toy that he sells. The one-acter was a 1923 version of an Irish play—old fire-watchman meets young fugitive, conversation conveys that they are father and long-lost son, they part without either acknowledging the other. In one of the excerpts, a samurai thrusts a bamboo spear through a paper wall—and kills his mother, rather than the enemy whose shadow he thought he saw.

Kumagai Jinya, the other excerpt, dates from 1751 and has the most preposterous plot I know of, even though it is based on a historical incident. In an ancient battle, the samurai Kumagai, following an enigmatic order from his commander, decapitates his own sixteen-year-old son rather than behead his enemy's son of the same age. He compounds this absurdity, later in the play, by showing the head of his son to his commander and to the mothers of both boys, while all pretend that the head is that of his enemy's son. At story's end Kumagai decides that he will war no more. Stripping off his armor, he reveals the shorn head and white garments of a priest; he is going to enter a temple. He leaves the stage by the traditional Kabuki runway, which goes out into the audience at the left, and there, to the heartbreak of every spectator, *including me*, he blinks away tears and recalls his son: "Sixteen years . . . a dream! only a dream!"

Why am *I*, who was mentally jeering at this spectacle a few minutes before, now so moved? I am moved because Kabuki is anciently wise in the magic of the theater. I am moved for the same reason that Metropolitan Opera audiences, overlooking the contrivances of stilted acting, fat heroines, and communication by song in foreign languages, are moved when Mimi dies or Violetta catches tuberculosis. And the more moved because Kabuki works against a higher barrier of contrivances. Banshee voices, men performing as women, warriors mincing around in silken pajamas with ten-foot trouser legs that trail like wedding-dress trains. Highly visible prop men, wearing all-over black as a code to suggest that they are really not there, popping on stage to insert seats under hunkering lords and lieges. Acting stylized to absurdity: static recitations, knife stabs that miss the victim by yards (he dies anyway), oscillation of fans to connote despair. Archaic language that modern Japanese cannot understand. But much of the artifice is entrancing. The turntable stage, a Kabuki invention, brings into view sets of ravishing color and imaginative detail. You see typhoons, fireflies, snowstorms, bamboo forests, real-water pools, street scenes, and palaces. Costumes, wigs, and props are stunning. The acting, however formal, however immobile those plucked and whitened faces, ultimately communicates authentic sorrow, love, menace.

I'm mad about Kabuki.

Kabuki acting is a family profession. Utaemon VI, most famous of the great Nakamura family, is probably the leading female impersonator. He has done plays by the late Yukio Mishima at the Kabuki-za. With poor-little-me willowiness, he danced the butterfly-tormented geisha that I saw, dressed in a gorgeous red-lined black-and-silver robe, small face a chalky mask with high, thin, questioning eyebrows, quintessentially Japanese eyes, two dots for nostrils, and a short dash of scarlet lipstick for a mouth.

Nizaemon Kataoka, leading actor of the Osaka Kabuki, is officially designated by the government as a Living National Treasure. Kuroemon Onoe, incumbent star of a formidable acting family, who has taught Kabuki in the United States, emphasizes the dedication and discipline that the profession requires. He tells American students that "Kabuki cannot be taught by words or books. What is needed is to master control of the movements of the body including the eyes and fingers. Subtle movements of the minor parts of the body give the audience an ineffably strong impression."

Kabuki originated in Kyoto at the end of the sixteenth century, as between-the-acts diversions to relieve the seriousness of the Noh drama. Picturing the lords of the time as stupid whoremongers, Kabuki attracted prostitutes as actresses, which led to the banishment of the plays as too erotic, which led to companies formed only of boys, which proved even more immoral, which led to a more serious Kabuki played only by men (nowadays, a few women get parts).

Noh itself dates back a century earlier, ancient juggling acts and buffoonery having somehow metamorphosed into solemn court masques. Serious it was, and serious it remains. One judicious commentator remarked that it has "great impelling qualities that thrill the devotee and weary the uninitiated." The stage is an eighteen-foot square, the backdrop a painting of an ancient pine. Actors enter on a runway from the left. The plots, usually something to do with a priest and the ghost of a samurai, are acted out with cadenced choreography and languorous, vibratory speech. The actors walk in squared patterns, waving fans, flinging sleeves, kicking their superlong trousers at the corners. The interpretive music has an Andean sound —the whistle of flutes, the chanting of the chorus, the uncoordinated clack of drums. Noh is the theater of masks, some of them carved false faces, and some the actual countenances of the imperturbable actors. I felt that understanding Noh would take more time than I was prepared to invest.

Song and dance, vaudeville and girls, shows with overwhelming "production values," dominate Tokyo's nonclassical legitimate stage; the city has nothing to equal Broadway for "what literature does at night." A tireless musical perennial is the Takarazuka Grand Theater, which has four companies constantly touring Japan; here, in answer to Kabuki and Noh, the players are all girls, the elite among them being those who act the parts of men. Lately a Honolulu girl, Margaret Akita, daughter of Japanese history professor George Akita of the University of Hawaii, became the first American to pass Takarazuka's tough tryouts, and at five feet eight inches she is tall enough to aspire to wear a tuxedo and twirl a cane.

The elemental truth about Japanese music is that it's not much good. "Traditionally the Japanese failed to explore the possibilities of harmony and polyphony," writes historian Reischauer, and so Western music has put the Japanese "on the verge of rout." At a guess, only a tenth of the music on radio, television, and the stage is Japanese. All the Muzak that I can remember was Western.

In a sense, Japanese music does not give itself a chance. The octave divides into five basic tones, and subdivides into twenty or thirty, which sacrifices the discipline of the twelve-tone scale and leaves the ear in limbo. "One is unable to walk out of a concert whistling or humming a melody that has caught the fancy," comments musicologist Howard Nelson. Moreover, the music is mostly played in primitive linear form, one note at a time, like Gregorian chant, rejecting chords and harmony. This undeveloped style, in turn, requires only simple instruments, principally the three-stringed samisen, the koto with plus-or-minus thirteen strings, the *shakuhachi* bamboo flute, and drums, plus the voice. In order to divide the scale so finely, the stringed instruments do not use frets, and this makes mastery difficult. Notation is predictably complex. "On the piano, even a fool can play a number, as long as he knows which keys to punch," says the superb samisen player Chikuzan Takahashi, who is blind, like many Japanese musicians past and present. "The samisen is not like that. There is no end to how good a player may become, but in the same way, there is no end to how badly one can play."

The body of the samisen is made of wood from the mulberry or the Chinese quince, and the skin stretched over it comes from dogs or cats, trapped and killed by obscure wretches who make this their profession. The famed samisen-maker Asaji Ohashi says, "I go every year to Ekoin, a temple of Ryogoku, to a memorial service for the honorable cats who provide us with what we need to make samisen." The six-foot-long koto, called "the Japanese harp," "a zither with class," or "a surfboard with strings," gives out what has been described as a "dream-like, mysterious sound—which has the same effect on one's nervous system as pipe-smoking or breaking clods of earth with bare hands."

Gagaku, or court music, played by an orchestra of ancient lutes, gongs, reed instruments, and drums sometimes twenty-four feet high, exactly reproduces sounds first heard in A.D. 749 when the great image of Buddha in Nara was unveiled, and is thus the world's oldest living form of music, a museum of sounds, spooky but soporific. "Often the pulse is hypnotically slow," notes the *New York Times*'s Harold C. Schonberg. "Westerners usually doze off somewhere during the course of the program. Japanese are always asking visitors, 'Did you stay awake?'" Even more exotic are the silent concerts at Shinto festivals. "Both stringed and wind instruments are used in this concert; but it is held that the sanctity of the occasion would be profaned, were any sound to fall on unworthy ears," reported Basil Hall Chamberlain in *Things Japanese*. "Therefore, although all the motions of playing are gone through, no strains are actually emitted."

German bandmasters, brought in about 1880 along with other Prussian military trappings, and the first phonographs, imported in 1896, helped to get Western music established in Japan. Now, musically speaking, Japan is a Western nation. In Tokyo during one week in April 1973, one could have heard: the Tokyo Symphony playing Liszt's *Christus*; Sergio Mendes and *Brasil '77*; pianist Minoru Nojima in Scarlatti and Schubert; Daniel Barenboim conducting the NHK Symphony and the English Chamber Orchestra, and in two piano recitals; Percy Faith and his orchestra; the Pittsburgh Symphony with Ravel, Mozart, Prokofiev, and Stravinsky; Quincy Jones and his orchestra; the Czech Trio with Mozart, Beethoven, and Dvorak; the Tokyo Philharmonic and Niki-Kai Opera Chorus in *Madame Butterfly*; and ten other serious performances. New York City has one important symphony orchestra; Tokyo has *seven*. Bach and Brubeck, plus some koto sounds, are the staples of the coffeehouses, where taped music is the chief attraction. Western musicals are also big. In Tokyo within one month in mid-1973, one could have seen *Applause, Mame, My Fair Lady* (on its fourth revival), and *Jesus Christ Superstar* (with King Herod riding in a rickshaw).

The standout Japanese masters of Western music are conductors, who have become a commonplace export, like Nikon cameras. Seiji Ozawa, born in Mukden, Manchuria, in 1935, and now conductor of both the Boston Symphony and the San Francisco Symphony, roams the world as guest conductor, typically directing *Così fan Tutte* at the 1969 Salzburg Festival "as if he had been born in a Mozartian city," in the words of *Realités*. The son of a Christian mother, Ozawa lived in a church for a year when he was fifteen, and there as church organist he learned "all of Bach's keyboard music." After breaking two fingers in a Rugby match, he turned to conducting. In daily life he wears espadrilles, red turtlenecks, and black cotton pants, and sometimes carries a leather purse suspended from a strap; he has been known to wear bell bottoms on the podium. The American Symphony Orchestra has imported Kazuyoshi Akiyama to be its conductor, and Hiroyuki Iwaki, permanent conductor of the NHK Symphony, is doing a three-year stint as the head of the Melbourne Symphony, an appointment that one Australian critic called "almost unbelievably good news."

The most noted composer, Toru Takemitsu, was once so avant that he made even John Cage seem old garde. Today he says that he aspires to "attain a sound as intense as silence." (Winthrop Sargeant reports that a Zen monk, taken to hear the Boston Symphony, reacted by exclaiming, "Not enough silence!")

Japan makes more pianos than any other nation (mostly at Hamamatsu, "the city of musical instruments"), and the sound of children practicing fills the neighborhoods. The violin is equally popular, partly because of the famous teaching method devised by

Shinichi Suzuki. This Montessori of violin instruction, now in his late seventies, discovered—through the homely observation that small children learn to speak complex languages—that children can learn to play the violin at ages as young as three. His technique, now widely used in the United States, is to start children on tiny violins, playing by ear rather than from a score, and acquiring skills through games, such as "windshield wiper." Many professional Japanese musicians accuse Suzuki of overapplying rote learning and of failing to produce stars, but he answers that he is trying only to hook children on the violin for their own satisfaction. Suzuki inherited a 1,100-employee violin factory from his father, but actually became serious about the instrument only after encouragement from his math professor in a German university, who, curiously enough, happened to be Albert Einstein.

"Summary: Seven fornications, one masturbation, one fellatio, one fetish, and one sado-masochistic act. Nudity throughout, breasts and butts galore, but no front shots below the navel and no pubic hair." So reads a scholarly report in *The Japan Interpreter* on a movie belonging to the new Japanese category *roman poruno*, romantic porn, the 1970s successor to the earlier, less salacious *erodakushun*, erotic production. Roman poruno is a legitimate subject of sociological inquiry simply because it is the predominant form of today's Japanese cinema, once so justifiably esteemed by the entire world.

The Japanese criminal code prohibits the public display of obscene materials, and in response to the law the Motion Picture Code of Ethics Commission bans depicting sexual organs or pubic hair, as well as full-length or close-up explicit shots of the sexual act. Consequently, Japanese poruno is not as pornographic as European or American, but it has its idiosyncrasies. A scene in one movie shows a girl in sexual ecstasy while her nonchalant lover drinks and listens to his transistor radio without missing a stroke; moments later, while being sodomized by another man, it is she who keeps her cool by casually slurping up a bowl of noodles. By the rigid poruno formula, some such excitement must come along every five minutes throughout the film. It is also decreed that blood must flow freely, sado-masochistically, and sanguineously red—all poruno movies are in color. Filming techniques range from pop art to James Bond, sometimes expertly done. Billboards and newspaper advertising of poruno films show approximately what the films themselves show; huge depictions of lustful, naked men and women are commonplace in the entertainment districts of the cities of Japan.

In general, Japanese moviemaking, like American, is in the doldrums, the profits knocked on the head by television, but it has an honorable past going clear back to the Kinetoscope in 1896. By 1903, Donald Richie writes in *Japanese Cinema*, "several years before England and America broke away from the store front nickelodeon, a permanent theater devoted entirely to films had been built in Tokyo." At first, Japanese directors used female impersonators instead of actresses, and employed commentators to travel with the films and explain them, rather than learning to let images tell the story. Toward 1930, however, they found an enduring theme: history—history as something alive and actual, the present as a continuum of the past. The first of the estimable directors—Kenji Mizoguchi, Yasujiro Ozu, and others—appeared, and the Japanese style developed: a seemingly paradoxical way of lingering over a scene (avoiding fast cutting), an apparent overexplanation that is actually a way of inducing the viewer to bring to his own mind many a subtlety that the director feels would be destroyed if he made it explicit. Critic Barbara Wolf compares these "longueurs in Japanese film" to Japanese painting, "full of empty space," in which the beholder must infer the significance of what is omitted, and to Japanese poetry, which takes the reader to a point and lets him "find his own way" on from there.

With Akira Kurosawa's *Rashomon*, in 1950, the world discovered that the Japaneseness of Japanese film, far from barring comprehension, was an invitation to powerful cinematic experience. Movie after movie showed, "for all who care to see, the most perfect reflection of a people in the history of world cinema," in the judgment of Donald Richie, who was until lately curator of the film department at the Museum of Modern Art in New York City. Along came Kurosawa's *Seven Samurai, The Throne of Blood, The Lower Depths,* and *Yojimbo*; Mizoguchi's *The Life of Oharu* and *The Princess Yang Kwei Fei*; Ozu's *Tokyo Story* and *The End of Summer*; Hiroshi Teshigahara's *Woman in the Dunes*; Kaneto Shindo's *Children of the Atom Bomb*; Shiro Toyoda's *Snow Country*. With the sure Japanese sense of design, they found that history had provided them with ready-made sets of great cinematic beauty—nothing is better composed than ancient Japanese temples, palaces, gardens, or ceremonial costumes. The directors themselves offered some of the most memorable images ever seen. Greed, war, seduction. An alcoholic doctor, a blind swordsman, a frenzied potter. A man and his wife teach their child to run in front of moving cars and get hit, so that they can collect damages. A man making love has—orgasm? no, brain stroke. It was a directors' cinema; only Toshiro Mifune, Machiko Kyo, and a few other actors and actresses ever became international household names.

Mizoguchi and Ozu are dead. After an attempted suicide, Kurosawa, once so lordly that his studio dared not complain even if he temperamentally stayed away from work for a week, has lately spent a year in Siberia working for Soviet Mosfilm to make the epic *Dersu Uzala*, about a great hunter of that name. Daiei, the studio that made *Rashomon* and *Ugetsu*, went broke in 1972; Toho and Shochiku diversified, moving into the parking-lot business in order to survive as studios. One former director became a horse-race announcer, and another a Buddhist monk. But cinema, in Japan as elsewhere, is an art of too many possibilities to become extinct.

The pointed brush. Ink made of soot and glue, to be dissolved in water. Painting as decoration for screens, scrolls, fans, or architectural panels, rather than as self-contained work to be framed. Oil paints, unknown. These were the parameters of fifteenth-century Japanese pictorial art, which still speaks eloquently, to the entire world, of nature's beauty transferred to silk and paper with enviable economy of stroke and color. The most talented artist was the Zen monk Sesshu (1420–1506), who went to Ming Dynasty China hoping to learn, but found "no master there who had anything to teach me." With dexterity acquired from incessant practice, Sesshu painted the daring, unretouchable single strokes that this instant art requires, modeling as well as delineating with swift certainty a roof beam or a bamboo shoot, a stream or a wading heron, graying the ink with precisely controlled wetting. Sesshu achieved his effects in large degree by what he left out. (But when he capriciously added a pagoda to a landscape of the village of Okitsu, his overawed patrons felt compelled to make the painting accurate by building a real pagoda there.)

Wood blocks. Drawing. Engraving tools. Everyday life. Colored ink pressed to paper. These were the elements of ukiyoe, the art of the "floating world," the eighteenth- and nineteenth-century life "of fugitive pleasures, of theaters and restaurants, wrestling-booths and houses of assignation, with their permanent population of actors, dancers, singers, story-tellers, jesters, courtesans, bath-girls and itinerant purveyors, among whom mingled the profligate sons of rich merchants, dissolute samurai and naughty apprentices," in the words of the historian G. B. Sansom. Ando Hiroshige (1797–1858), the man who depicted Tokyo's primordial department stores, was perhaps pre-eminent among the ukiyoe printmakers, though he sidled away from the floating world into the countryside and the world of peasants and wayfarers, his fame being rooted in a series showing the fifty-three stopping places on the Tokaido road between Tokyo and Osaka. One of the places Hiroshige pictured was Okitsu, the same village that Sesshu caused to acquire a pagoda.

Ukiyoe artists were adept at depicting stance and gesture even when their characters were completely tented in costumes or armor, and their ungeometric perspective charmingly widened, rather than narrowed, to the background. Ukiyoe required a guildlike collaboration between the artist who composed the original painting, the carver who made cherry-wood blocks for as many as twelve colors, and the printer who dabbed on pigment in subtle shades and pressed the blocks to paper.

Hiroshige—a man who loved his sake and feared his wife—was only one of several artists who each painted more than ten thousand scenes. His immediate predecessor, Hokusai, was equally famed in his time, and equally productive. He tended toward bolder patterns and fewer, simpler forms—people, flora and fauna, landscapes, grotesqueries. Because the paintings were so numerous and because each was reproduced at least two hundred times, ukiyoe was called a "vulgar" art; but for the same reasons it showed a society as a whole better than any other school of art in the world. Small-mouthed beauties, firefly-like nights, one samurai throttling another in armor as colorful as the King of Diamonds, snowstorms, moonlit nights in Kawasaki: the prints appeared like editions of newspapers, and the public loved them. Erotica formed an important subdivision of ukiyoe: kimonos falling askew to reveal colossal, hairy male genitalia thrust into distended female pudenda, the faces of the coupling pair expressing blank, whited lust.

Ukiyoe is the Japanese art the world knows best—and knew first. Ukiyoe prints arrived in Europe late in the nineteenth century, and their bold, flat color and strong patterning and often asymmetrical compositions delighted and influenced painters like Vuillard, Gauguin, Degas, Toulouse-Lautrec, van Gogh, and Whistler. Today New York's Metropolitan Museum of Art and the Boston Museum of Fine Arts own thousands of ukiyoe prints, and the Freer Gallery of Art in Washington has five hundred elegant ukiyoe paintings (the originals for prints). The Philadelphia Museum of Art has a collection of prints made not in Tokyo, the center of the art, but in Osaka, where for subjects artists overwhelmingly preferred slit-eyed, fierce-mouthed Kabuki actors—the ancestors of the Kataokas and the Onoes—in glorious dress. And despite this looting of ukiyoe by the West, Tokyo still has the vast collection of five thousand prints, many designated as National Treasures, from which the Riccar Museum draws its stunning, never-ending shows.

Sesshu and Hiroshige establish the two major landmarks in Japanese art, although much of interest comes before and between: ancient depictions of Bodhisattva (one who is eligible for nirvana but postpones it to help others achieve enlightenment) remindful of Byzantine icons, romantic illustrations for twelfth-century novels, temple murals of pussy-cat tigers (to Japan the tiger was as mythical as the unicorn), portraits of ferocious shoguns, scrolls narrating head-long battles, and, above all, innumerable lovely screen paintings of pines and plums and cranes composed on gold grounds that de-materialize space, or of vast castle towns and the wars around them (the museums of extant castles are full of these).

Perhaps the unifying characteristic of Japanese painting, as divergent from the Chinese, is an abiding instinct for the decorative, as opposed to the mystical and spiritual. The Japanese have always had a strong sense of the picture as a flat plane, where abstract forms have an authority of their own, over and beyond the subject depicted. The first known Japanese painting, one of a series dating from the early seventh century at the Tamamushi shrine in Nara, depicts the Buddha as Prince Siddhartha, who sees a starving tigress and her cubs and decides to give up his own life so that the tiger family can feed upon his body. He strips off his clothes and flings himself off a cliff to be devoured by the tigress and her young. The theme is im-ported from India via China, but the Japanese artist has changed the rocky cliff into a wondrous arabesque of abstract shapes, counter-pointing the three images of Buddha—disrobing, diving, being de-voured—into a cascade of linear delight.

Similarly, the Japanese took the Chinese hand scroll, which tended to be a meandering tour of a river valley, and made it into a dramatic narrative, boldly patterned. These hand scrolls, it should be explained, are designed to be unrolled from the left hand into the right, with the viewer seeing only the space comfortably held open between the outstretched arms, perhaps eighteen inches of a scroll that may be fifty feet long. Each of such views had to be self-contained, yet urge the viewer on to what was still concealed in his left hand. The progression was "musical" in that a scroll might begin with a quiet countryside, move on into the hills where (main theme, announced in dramatic red) a column of warriors moves, andante, through wind-ing paths, and, with a staccato of pine trees across a cliff, emerges on a quiet lake whose bridge leads to (clash of cymbals) a towering palace gate. The assault is a crescendo of tumbling forms, and a great blast of flames soars over the combatants. Then in flittering diminuendo, the defeated flee.

In the course of developing this style, the Japanese invented what they call *fukinuki yatai*, the simple but effective device of lifting off the roofs so that the observer can peer in from a diagonal bird's-eye view. Even then, the Japanese showed their interest in decorative pattern. The faces, in fact, are often reduced by what is called the technique of *hikime kagibana*, "a line for the eye, a hook for the nose."

From its earliest days, Japanese portraiture made almost more of the subject's robes than of his face, delighting in the powerful patterns they could produce by a swirl of cloth or the punctuation of a sword hilt. The portraits seemed to have been composed less as likenesses than as *pictures*. In one "portrait" of a poet, the robes are so effulgent that the lady's face is almost totally obscured.

This sense of painting as shapes on a flat plane carried on through Sesshu's monochrome style, whose roots were basically in China's southern Sung style. But where the Sung painters let their landscapes recede in plane after dimming plane into infinity, Sesshu and his Japanese compeers tended to reduce the planes to foreground and background, playing sharp against soft in an overall pattern.

The Japanese decorative spirit burst into its fullest bloom with the screens and wall paintings commissioned by the shoguns, feudal lords, and newly rich merchants of the Momoyama and early Edo periods (roughly, from the late sixteenth century through the eighteenth century). Where a European artist might have filled such huge spaces with a motley of busy figures, these great Japanese decorators—Sotatsu, Koetsu, Eitoku, Korin, Kenzan—dared to use a single huge pine tree soaring over immeasurable empty space. Or to set a field of irises dancing across yards of golden background. Stylized streams wound past plum trees. Bridges sprang from outside the picture frame, swept over it, and ended beyond the viewer's ken. Bamboo thrust into the picture frame or out of it. These painters, said Langdon Warner, "paint in the air, as it were, beyond the boundaries." The result was a decorative style that has never been surpassed. "Italy was never more sumptuous nor did Flanders render with greater literal truth," says Warner. It is this decorative tradition, with its emphasis on pattern, abstract shape, and flat color, that makes Japanese art speak more directly to the modern taste, schooled as it is to the art of Matisse and Miró and the latter-day abstractionists, than does its Chinese counterpart, which is essentially literary and mystical.

Beyond the decorators, there was another school, which, though minor, has a fascination all of its own. That is *nanban* ("southern barbarian") art, the West seen through the eyes of Japanese painters in the period between the arrival of the first Portuguese in 1543 and the closing of Japan a century later. With styles partly their own and partly copied from imported late Renaissance art, they painted St. Peter (the portrait was later made to serve as that of a Buddhist saint), Crusaders and Mussulmen, imaginary views of Rome and Lisbon, Portuguese sailing ships, and "the social customs of foreigners." The Kobe Municipal Museum of Nanban Art has a marvelous collection. When foreigners returned to Japan after 1860, it fell to the ukiyoe printmakers to depict the new barbarians in Yokohama. And there we are, exotic, with our muskets, canes, pipes, iron cookstoves, red beards, top hats, and perverse insistence on sitting in chairs.

But by the time Japanese prints caught the fancy of the West— Debussy used the unforgettable "Great Wave" by Hokusai as a sheet-music cover—printmaking had come into collision with the modern world. One of the last of the traditional prints, by Kiyochika Kobayashi, shows a newfangled electric-power pole and wires against a background of Mount Fuji. Not only had ukiyoe run its course, but Western art stood seductively at hand, with its oil paints, scientific perspective, the nude human figure as the most challenging subject, and even the exciting new style of Impressionism.

"History since ancient times amply shows that Japanese art achieved its own unique development, by ingesting, and assimilating in the process, stimuli from overseas. In modern Japanese art, contacts with art and artists overseas have been mainly with those of Europe," said the introductory notice to the Tokyo National Museum of Modern Art's 1973 show called "Modern Japanese Art and Paris." This provocative exhibit juxtaposed works by Degas, Matisse, Cézanne, Soutine, Dufy, Utrillo, Picasso, Monet, and Modigliani with works by dozens of Japanese who contemporaneously went to France—painters whom one Japanese critic called "cut flowers." The show deftly made its quiet point: one could never be very sure, on first glance at a painting, whether the artist was French or Japanese. Technique and style were thoroughly "assimilated."

At some point, however, according to all precedent, ingestion and assimilation are supposed to lead the borrowing Japanese (in any field—camera making, religion, calligraphy, whatever) to heights of their own, just as Sesshu surpassed his Chinese contemporaries. In tramping through galleries and talking to experts, I could not discover that this is happening today. In what I should think must be embarrassing conformity to international fads, Japanese painters are doing conceptual art, white-on-white canvases, surrealism, trompe l'oeil, pop and op, image and figuration. Perhaps because the Japanese have traditionally insisted on high technique and complete control of the material, with long apprenticeship under a master, the work I admired was superlatively carried out—I recall, in a show at the Kyoto Museum of Modern Art, Keiko Minami's droll prints of girls and ducks, Akira Tanaka's great gray fat faces, Key Hiraga's fantasies of copulation and fertilization. But in the West the idea is more important than the technique; have the Japanese got the priorities reversed?

Many modern Japanese painters are not only artistically in the West, but physically there as well, creating an ambivalence among their Japanese votaries. "It's great to be hung in the Museum of Modern Art in New York," one critic remarked to me, "but after a point you're not Japanese any more." Being indisputably Japanese is the pride of one school of painters, the producers of *Nihonga* art, which combines traditional Japanese paper and paint with modern themes and perspectives. "Western space and Japanese feeling— slick, pretty, slightly surreal," mused my critic friend. "Dreamy, lyrical, and maybe . . . sickening?" Nihonga has a big market; the imperial family patronizes it, and the empress goes to the openings. A number of wood-block printers survive prosperously, most notably Shiko Munakata, a man in his seventies who admires van Gogh and Toulouse-Lautrec, but, more than either of them, Hokusai.

Japanese sculpture—then and now, big and little, here and there —simply blows the mind. Imported along with Buddhism in and after A.D. 552 was T'ang Dynasty religious art, which the Japanese swiftly transformed into bronze Buddhas, Bodhisattvas, Amidas, and Kannons (goddesses of mercy) of lofty beauty and half-smiling serenity. From wood they sculpted temple-guardian deities and warriors with savage expressions and hair like flames. Wood (volcanic Japan has no sculptable stone) is also the material for beautifully draped statues of monks and princes and demons. At Nara and Kamakura ancient artists constructed *daibutsu*, sitting "great Buddhas," the first fifty-eight feet high and the second forty-two. For ten yen (three cents) one can climb inside the Kamakura daibutsu and marvel at the joinery of the heavy bronze castings that form it. In the seventeenth and eighteenth centuries the wandering Buddhist priests Enku and Mokujiki used wood sculpture to communicate their faith; a dazzling show of their work that I saw in Tokyo displayed scores of small (three-foot) figures whose smiles and scowls were equally engaging.

To judge from today's sculpture, the talent is still in the Japanese genes. World renowned Masayuko Nagare, who now lives away from urban stress on the island of Shikoku, last year finished a two-hundred-ton abstract in Swedish black granite and sent it to Manhattan for installation in the plaza of the World Trade Center. Nobuo Sekine is one of many confident and creative rising artists. A typical recent work is a huge ring of some rocklike material with the opening lined in stainless steel, all standing on edge like a picture frame for some quiet, universal truth.

To learn something about Japanese pottery, I talked to Sir Bernard Leach, and my notes show that he dwelled heavily on religion—which is to say that I learned something about pottery. Leach, who was eighty-six when I met him, is an English potter who first went to Japan in 1908 and formed a lifelong friendship with the Japanese potter Shoji Hamada, who is six years his junior. Together they spurred this folk art into a strong revival, which accounts for the worldwide popularity of Japanese ceramics. "The application of Zen to the arts," Leach said, "is that it is nonrealistic; it deals with emptiness; it doesn't say there isn't fullness, but rather that fullness equals emptiness, and therefore equals thus-ness, which equals God." A good understanding of this concept, I gathered, provides the mystical thus-ness that pottery, more than other arts, needs for superiority.

"Hamada is the leading creative artist in the whole world, in the applied arts," says Leach roundly. At the potter's wheel, Hamada "throws boldly and fast and turns great strips of shavings off when the clay is only just sufficiently dry to keep its shape on the chuck." He does his work at his small estate on a dusty road leading out of Mashiko, a village devoted to pottery located about fifty miles north of Tokyo. The main house has a soaring thatched roof, and firewood for the kilns lies among bamboo groves. Hamada's father was a Buddhist priest, who, Leach says, spent winters making huge charts of the narrow road to virtue and the broad one to vice, and in summer walked the roads of Japan to distribute his drawings and preach.

Hamada is, by the terms of the charming Japanese custom of officially singling out men as well as buildings and objects as cultural treasures, an important Intangible Cultural Property. His tea bowls and plates, heavy and simple, with abstract designs, show some of the Western influence that he absorbed while in England and France with Leach. These products bring staggering prices in Japan—as do Leach's. At his first show in a Tokyo department store, Leach told me, "everything was sold in eight minutes; at the next show in four minutes; at the third one, in seconds. I was pushed aside and half knocked over by the buyers."

"Whatever critics may say about the eclecticism in other fields of artistic creativity," writes the art historian Hugo Munsterberg, "in ceramics, at least, Japan is the leading country in the world, and it is America and Europe who are the imitators."

Architecture is an ancient institution in Japan, but *architects* are something new. The traditional house, with its posts and beams and tiled roof, needed only a master builder able to accommodate the occupant's preferences to the standard tatami-mat modules. Larger buildings, mostly temples, copied their plans from Chinese models, with priest-designers to look after the details. Japan built of wood, not stone or brick, and employed neither the arch nor the dome nor the glass window. Fortress-castles were impressive in their height and pagoda roofing, but there are no Japanese buildings that compare in grandeur with, say, an Austrian *Schloss* or the Alhambra. It was the Meiji-era zeal for "catching up" with the West, particularly in the construction of grand public buildings, that created the need for architects.

Unluckily, the search for architectural inspiration coincided with what Munsterberg calls "the most debased and eclectic period in the entire history of European architecture." Buildings went up in Classic Revival, English Gothic, German Renaissance, Italian Baroque. Some of the work was surprising. Tokyo's central station rose in the exact form of Edinburgh station; this quaint red-brick structure is still in service next to the high-rise expansion of it. A combination of Buckingham Palace and Versailles went up in central Tokyo's Akasaka district, originally to be the Detached Palace of the emperor, but now a forty-room official guesthouse, used in 1974 by President Ford and in 1975 by Queen Elizabeth. Japanese cities took on a schizophrenic look, the domestic architecture being native and the commercial and governmental buildings rendered in infelicitous Western style. The indubitable blessings of modern architecture arrived with Frank Lloyd Wright's Imperial Hotel in Tokyo in 1923, since dismantled and replaced by a skyscraper of the same name and purpose, but, marvelous to relate, being reconstructed at the Meiji museum-village near Nagoya.

The bombs of World War II, leveling vast swatches of every major city except Kyoto, gave Japanese architecture a chance—not too efficiently utilized—to make a new start. The profession also got a miraculous new tool: the computer, which could make the infinite calculations needed to build an earthquake-proof skyscraper. As a result, hundreds of handsome new office buildings, auditoriums, schools, libraries, stores, conference halls, and prefectural capitols have sprouted all over the country—amidst, it must be added, a far greater volume of ferroconcrete boxes and monotonously fenestrated cubes.

Many talented men have seized the chance to be modern Japanese architects, taking advantage of an abundance of clients and a clean slate for style. Kenzo Tange provided the amazing Olympic swimming pool in Tokyo, with its suspension-bridge roof; the Atom Bomb Memorial Museum in Hiroshima; the Dentsu advertising agency's well-muscled and grainy-textured headquarters in Tokyo; the raw-concrete Kagawa Prefectural Office on Shikoku; St. Mary's Roman Catholic Cathedral in Tokyo. He also designed the just-completed cluster of museums for the Minneapolis Institute of the Arts. Yoshinobu Ashihara, author of a sensitive book (published both in Tokyo and New York) on the psychology of space in designing building exteriors, put his thinking to work in such constructions as Musashino Art University in Tokyo, Komazawa Olympic Park in Tokyo, and the Japanese Pavilion at Expo '67 in Montreal. His Sony Building, in central Tokyo, divides the floors into quarters, each set five steps higher than the one behind, so that you ascend the building like a spiral staircase.

When I visited Ashihara's office one night at eight o'clock, he and his associates were still at work. I was curious about the effects of earthquakes on skyscrapers. Ashihara pointed out that quakes cannot tip a building over, no matter how tall it is, because the earth simply moves back and forth laterally. So the trick is to prevent the building from being shaken down, which is done by designing in enough flexibility to allow the skyscraper to become a standing sine wave as its foundation vibrates sidewise. Ashihara, elegantly casual in a blue sweater and seersucker trousers, his hair a mop of graying black, said that a greater hazard is typhoons. Violent winds make solid-glass siding on tall buildings a ticklish problem.

"We Japanese are very good on single buildings, but not so good in urban design," says Ashihara. To match the chaos of the cow paths that determined the plan of old European cities, Japan had the happenstance arrangement of truck gardens and rice paddies to make its town plans confusing. In attempting to combat this handicap, Ashihara's concepts of space begin with such simple but intriguing ideas as that when picnickers spread a blanket or lovers walk under an umbrella, they carve "exterior space" from nature. Similarly, the shape and placement of buildings create definable zones of space, positive and negative.

The economy and clean lines of the teahouse-based sukiya style have so much in common with modern Western architecture that architects are forever tempted to combine them. In many inns, restaurants, and luxurious residences, they have succeeded famously. Buildings that are more monumental face difficulties of scale, in attempting to be "Japanese," and of making concrete work like wood. But I saw three—the Kyoto International Conference Center, the Metropolitan Festival Hall in Tokyo's Ueno Park, and the National Theater in Tokyo—that come off with great Oriental flair and grandeur.

A couple of blocks off Tokyo's Ginza stands a grimy eight-story building that houses the headquarters of *Asahi Shimbun,* a newspaper with an unusually ambitious mission. *Asahi Shimbun* (meaning "Rising Sun Newspaper") is serious, influential, literate, intellectual, deliberately unsensational—and for this brain-testing package of news it manages to find readers enough to swallow the astonishing total of 10,000,000 copies a day. *Asahi* combines the sobriety and responsibility of such low-circulation serious newspapers as *The New York Times* (circulation 830,000) or Britain's *Guardian* (326,000) or France's *Le Monde* (347,000) with a readership vastly beyond such popular and pandering newspapers as the New York *Daily News* (2,103,000) or the London *Daily Mirror* (4,316,000). *Asahi* calls itself "the newspaper of the mass elite." But if it can justifiably boast of itself, *Asahi* must also admit its advantage of built-in opportunity. First, the homogeneity and geography of Japan—the concentration of reader interest on the country as a whole—favor national newspapers. Second, the economy is still at a level where newsboys can profitably provide intensive home delivery; only a tenth of Japanese readers buy from newsstands. Third, the massive growth of universities supplies readers who demand news of depth and intelligence.

The double goal of making a quality newspaper and doing it on a gigantic scale requires a huge organization. *Asahi* employs eighty-five hundred people, three thousand of them in the editorial process. Editors can pour hundreds of their one thousand reporters into top stories, often using the paper's ten airplanes and three helicopters. *Asahi* has nearly three hundred news bureaus in Japan, and fifteen abroad. All except the ranking reporters have to consider themselves lucky to get a few sentences per week into the paper. A typical *Asahi* reporting tool, used for riots, is a van with a telescoping mast that can lift a closed-circuit television camera high enough to look down upon the tumult; editors in the vehicle need only punch a button to produce printed photographs of what they see on the TV screen, and they can send these photos, as well as reporters' stories, by radio to the newsroom. One hundred and sixty presses all over Japan print the paper; remote plants get facsimiles of pages sent by radio.

Asahi starts its day before noon with the first of three editions of its evening paper, and goes on through nine more editions to be read in the morning. Two-thirds of its subscribers get both morning and evening editions, and the rest a combined edition. Including regional variations, 120 editions of the newspaper are produced every day. A reader who gets two editions is counted as one subscriber, and *Ashai*'s circulation, calculated this way, comes to 6,000,000. Only the Soviet Union's *Izvestia* (8,500,000) and *Pravda* (9,200,000) have more readers.

With unimportant variations, everything just said about *Asahi* can be said all over again about *Mainichi Shimbun* ("Every Day Newspaper"), which has 4,700,000 subscribers, of whom 2,900,000 also get the evening edition. Its enormous Tokyo office, separated only by a boulevard from the outer moat of the Imperial Palace, is the most elegant newspaper building I have ever seen, a pair of long, low (nine-story), glass-faced slabs set side by side, interlinked with two cylindrical towers for the elevators, and finished inside in stainless steel and edge-grain wood. In the newsrooms, as at *Asahi*, hundreds of writers and editors sit shoulder to shoulder as their flying pencils write the news with about twenty Japanese characters per small sheet of copy paper. *Mainichi*'s new Hamada presses in the cavernous basements of this building print, at a rate of forty a second from each press, 3,500,000 copies of the paper a day; the rest come from other plants. The date on the paper's first issue read: "No. 1, February 21, 5th Year of Meiji. March 29, 1872, by the Western calendar." (*Asahi* dates back to 1879.)

One more huge daily, *Yomiuri* ("News Crier"), completes the trio of great national newspapers, with 5,800,000 subscribers, of whom 3,500,000 also get the evening paper. Below the Big Three stand eighty regional and local dailies. Japan ranks just after the United States and the Soviet Union in aggregate circulation of newspapers, and grabs off an easy first in intensity of readership, with 550 copies per 1,000 population.

The Big Three also run English-language editions—*Asahi Evening News*, *Mainichi Daily News*, and *Daily Yomiuri*—and together with the independent *Japan Times* they supply Tokyo residents with a choice of more dailies with general news in English than even New Yorkers get. These papers, catering to foreigners, are edited by staffs that contain a sprinkling of Nisei but are mostly Japanese who have learned English well. The writing is surprisingly (but not entirely) free of Japlish, and the papers make far fewer typographical errors than American papers. They carry much American, British, and other international news, but their stance is Japanese; editorials criticize the government in the apparent expectation that politicians will read them. Foreigners often suspect that the big publishers take one attitude in their Japanese editions and another in English, but one *Asahi* editor assured me that his paper, at least, tried to make the *Evening News* a faithful, though condensed and not literal, reflection of *Asahi Shimbun*. The *Japan Times*, founded in 1897, is widely accused of having links to the Foreign Office that are too close for the health of its objectivity.

Most Japanese papers, and *Asahi* and *Mainichi* in particular, have for years opposed the government with criticism generally deemed to be healthy, sound, and moderate. A thoughtful high-ranking businessman made the point to me that the papers are a "force against war." Another plus: they open their columns to readers; letters to the editor are a serious outlet for public opinion. Economic journalism in Japan wins high marks for depth and intelligence. The International Press Institute says that the Japanese press is "free, powerful and conscious of its responsibilities to the life of society."

The salient defect of the newspapers is their unwillingness to rock boats. Editors do not demand investigative reporting; they think that investigation is a job for the police. In part, their very pride in their tools and techniques, in all those helicopters and field radios, seems to make newsmen forget the need for hard-hitting exposure. The exaggerated need to be politically impartial provides an excuse not to dig too deeply into one party or another's scandals; similarly, editors seem happy to believe that libel laws prevent them from exposing wrongdoers. *Asahi* has frequently appeased China to keep its correspondent in Peking, even as *The New York Times* was doing without, rather than accept China's conditions. In 1973, *Mainichi Shimbun* made a great fuss about the public's "right to know" in defending one of its reporters who had obtained some secret Foreign Office cables by seducing the secretary of the deputy vice-minister. The reporter's trial was billed as the Japanese version of the Pentagon Papers case. Forgotten in the furor was the fact that *Mainichi* editors had refused to print their reporter's scoop, and he was forced to turn the cables over to an opposition member of the Diet before the press got interested in the scandal.

Japanese editors sometimes delude themselves by stressing the need for hordes of young reporters, who swarm all over a story, instead of older, more experienced, and better-connected journalists who can get deeper into the news. At prolific news sources, such as the government ministries, reporters use the deplorable syndicate system: they have well-organized and exclusive clubs that pool questions and give them to a "captain" to ask, with everyone sharing the answers. The reporters mutually decide what, *and what not*, to use from interviews, and stipulate which edition a story will break in. All the clubs exclude foreigners.

Newsmen regard reporting as an apprenticeship, and editing as the prestige role. One editor told me with some regret that too many of his profession "play golf every day, won't mix with the man on the street, have no focus on the common people. The editor-in-chief doesn't even read the paper—he's too busy going to the weddings of zaibatsu families." Another result of complacency is sameness. Editors copy the most successful papers, rather than strike out to create something new. Moreover, Japanese papers, though vast in circulation and resources, are small in pages: twenty-four at the most, twelve for evening editions—newsboys could not carry papers bigger than this on their bicycles.

A piece of hypocrisy common to both the United States and Japan is the myth that editors can resist pressure from advertisers, but I found Japanese hanky-panky to be more blatant. I asked one adman what editors do when the message of a story conflicts head-on with the message of an advertisement, and got one of those unsettlingly soothing Japanese answers. "The editors usually feel that the paper must have harmony," he said, "so they remove the story."

The agency that dominates Japanese advertising, Dentsu Advertising, Ltd., is the biggest in the world, its billings of nearly a billion dollars having recently surpassed those of the American giant, J. Walter Thompson. Five thousand employees work in and out of Dentsu's fifteen-story building near the Ginza, and at seven o'clock on the evening I visited the agency, most of them were still on the job in enormous, open offices, beehives of paper and telephones. Yukata Narita, director of the print-media division, told me something of Dentsu's history. Modeling itself on France's darkly powerful Havas agency, Dentsu began in 1901 as a news service (the name is a contraction of the words for "telegraphic communication") supplied to papers in exchange for space that the agency sold to advertisers. This setup became onerous in 1936, when Japanese militarists demanded control of news, so Dentsu shucked off the reporting end of its operation to the agency called Domei, which was virtually the voice of Japan during the war. At war's end Domei died of overidentification with Japan's defeat, to be replaced by Japan's present news services, Kyodo and Jiji, which together, cozily enough, own one-half of Dentsu's privately held stock. After the war Dentsu diligently fostered the birth of commercial radio and television in Japan, which greatly helped the agency in its climb to the top.

Dentsu so dominates national newspaper advertising among regional and local papers that each of them must maintain a man in Tokyo to perform a function that translates as "Dentsu worship." Dentsu, whose accounts include not only Toyota but also Datsun and Mazda, runs a sophisticated, polished, technically excellent operation, and I did not get the impression that it interferes directly in the editorial affairs of newspapers. But a leading magazine editor told me that when the business establishment became worried that the press was abetting the anti-American riots of 1960, Dentsu was used to warn editors to cool it.

Foreign correspondents in Tokyo operate one of the last vigorous, enterprising, colorful press clubs in the world. A sign on the wall in the bar says: "O LORD, help me to keep my big mouth shut until I know what I am talking about." A decorous Mitsubishi Estate Company building in the financial district houses the Foreign Correspondents Club of Japan, but the club's mythical address, honored by the post office through several moves, is "No. 1 Shimbun Alley." James Michener lived at No. 1 just after the war, in a bedroom with a Turk, a Nationalist Chinese, a Korean, an American black, a Frenchman, and five girls cooking fish heads on hibachis. "This was thought to be immoral," he recalls, "so the hibachis were banned."

Kobo Abe, born in 1924 in Tokyo but brought up in Manchuria, took a degree in medicine from Tokyo University in 1948 and went at once into writing novels and plays. Of Japanese writers accessible to the West through translations, Abe is now the leading figure, partly due to the deaths in recent years of Yukio Mishima and Yasunari Kawabata. In the Shibuya experimental-theater district of Tokyo, Abe keeps a studio reached through an obscure entrance and containing its own tiny theater for rehearsals of his plays. He is an informal, confident sort of man, with a thatch of black hair and a predilection for dark, open-necked shirts and bulky jackets. Abe's hobby is sculpture, and he is also a talented photographer, who used pictures shot by himself to illustrate his new novel.

Abe writes in eerie parables, with the power to make insane situations as believable as blood from a stab wound. In *The Woman in the Dunes*, from which the much-admired movie was made, a hiking insect collector is tricked by spittle-dripping villagers into living with a woman who has a shack in a vertical-sided pit in western Honshu's dune country. Trapped and helpless, he has to spend whole nights shoveling sand to send up in buckets to the mad villagers. In *The Face of Another*, a man whose face has been blown off gets a new and different one of plastic. In *The Box Man*, the afflictions of the times lead one of their victims to take up residence in the cardboard box in which his refrigerator was delivered; again the absurdity is made plausible by Abe's brilliance and concern for detail.

In 1923, when Arthur Waley published his translation of *The Tale of Genji*, Western literary critics suffered a triple trauma. First, they took note that this Japanese novel was written about A.D. 1000, long before such classics of the west as *Don Quixote*, *Le Morte d'Arthur*, *The Decameron*, and *Gargantua and Pantagruel*. Second, they saw that it was a huge (1,135 pages in the Modern Library edition) and sustained work, rich in dialogue, description, and delight. And finally, they swallowed the fact that the author of this story of a prince at the old Kyoto court was a woman, a courtier named Lady Murasaki.

Over the centuries, similar thunderbolt novels appeared, but then the talent seemed to slacken. By the Meiji Restoration in 1868, in the estimate of Columbia University professor Donald Keene, "Japanese literature reached its lowest point." For a decade or so, some schools taught English literature but not Japanese. Result: in the past ninety years "Japanese literature has been intimately affected by all European trends and, in fact, may be regarded in effect as forming a part of the modern movement in Western literature," according to Keene. This may be the key to the pleasure and excitement Westerners get from reading modern Japanese writers.

The Japanese appetite for books is third in the world, after the United States and the Soviet Union. Around 27,000 titles appear each year (as compared to 35,000 in the United States), for a total of more than 500 million copies. Translated works sell furiously. John Kenneth Galbraith, chided by his translator for being too easy on the Japanese economy, is supposed to have joked, "How can I be tough on my best customers?" Japanese best sellers often run past 1 million copies. Titles on the list one week in 1974 included: *The Big Prophecy*, about Nostradamus; *We Comrades*, about the student uprisings of the 1960s; *The Ruling Family*, history of the shogun Tokugawa Ieyasu; *Thus Spoke Doctor Zhivago*, about "man's mind diseased by a huge mechanistic civilization"; *Poseidon Kamensai*, the "comical happenings on the night of a festival for the Greek god of the sea on an unknown small island"; *Japan Submerges*, science fiction about Japan sinking into the sea after earthquakes and volcanic eruptions; *A Fool Always Loses*, counsel for businessmen by the Japanese president of the McDonald hamburger franchise; and *Notes on Paris, Vol. 3, The Town and the Form*, the diary of a Japanese novelist in Paris. A big hit a couple of years ago was a gripping story about a Mafia family, rendered in romaji as *Goddofaza*.

9/

Irresistible Forces and Other Games

THE ROUNDABOUT ROUTE of my return from my last trip to Japan took me by train across Siberia, and I prepared to fend off boredom by stocking up on reading matter, which included the autobiography of sumo wrestler Daigoro Takamiyama. At Nakhodka, the port of entry near Vladivostok, a Russian woman customs inspector, herself somewhere in the three-hundred-pound class, minutely inspected everything I had with me. Peering into the bottom of an airline travel bag, she glimpsed the book jacket's four-color photograph of wrestler Takamiyama, a pink mountain of swelling flesh and gleaming skin.

"Aha!" she said, smacking her lips. "Pornography!"

As a matter of fact, sumo wrestlers—those men of oaken calves, hippopotamic hams, glutei maximissimi, and rain-barrel bellies—are attractive to most women. About a third of sumo audiences are women, and many geishas have taken to wrestlers as highly compatible off-duty bedmates. But all this is beside the point. Sumo is a battle and a pageant. It is a ridiculously gripping kind of fight, a contest between two men, stuffed like Strasbourg geese, which shows off not only the brute strength of those mastodon muscles but also their flashing speed. It is an eerie, dazzling pageant, attended by ancient though invisible gods.

The sensation when I was last in Japan was Hiroshi Wajima, "the man with the golden left arm," who had scrambled through the ranks in three and one-half years to Grand Champion, a position occupied in any given year by only three or four wrestlers. Like many sumo wrestlers, Wajima comes from cold northern Honshu, where the generally diminutive Japanese race seems to grow taller and burlier.

Not many wrestlers are university graduates, but Wajima crashed into professional wrestling precisely because he is one: he won the all-Japan college championship in 1969. From among the twenty-eight stables in Tokyo where wrestlers live and train, Wajima joined the Hanakago outfit, right next door to his university. With continuous exercise and by fighting many matches, Wajima thickened his belly muscles (that flesh is *not* fat) and strengthened his huge thighs to develop pushing power and—most important—lower his center of gravity.

The spirit of sumo is profoundly Shinto. It goes back fifteen hundred years to when the matches were a way of predicting crops: if you backed a winner you were in for the beneficence of the gods. The canopy over the ring copies shrine architecture, and the tassels at its corners represent the gods of the cardinal directions.

As a match begins, Wajima carries out the sumo/Shinto rituals with swaggering relish. At the edge of the ring, he purifies his body by washing his mouth with water, and purifies the ring by tossing a handful of salt into it. With a piece of tissue called "power paper," he wipes his armpits, which symbolically crushes any wickedness in the vicinity. He claps his hands, to summon the attention of the gods. He opens and rotates his outstretched palms, to prove that he carries no weapons. All the while, he and his opponent try to psych each other out. Sometimes Wajima glowers at the adversary with cold belligerence, and sometimes refuses to honor him with a look. Still warming up, Wajima grasps a knee, stretches his massive leg out sideways high over his head, then hammers the bare foot into the sanded clay of the ring. Resoundingly, he smacks his big, sweaty butt and the slablike sides of his thighs with his open palms. Two, three, four times, he and his opponent face each other, fists in the dirt like runners at the starting line, seemingly ready for battle, but each time they break away and return to the ringside for more posturing.

Fans love this suspenseful, swashbuckling buildup, but the clock watchers of the television industry have managed to put a four-minute limit to it. Wajima and opponent crouch again. By a backward flip of his fan, the referee, a small, nimble man in a gorgeous, fancy-belted kimono, indicates that time is up. But this is not quite the signal to start. By some mysterious telepathy, the warriors themselves decide precisely when to spring.

The match may end in one second—the time for one battler to charge and the other to dodge, so that the charger plunges on to lose by touching a foot outside the thick straw rope, half-embedded in the clay, that marks the circumference of the fifteen-foot ring. More commonly, the loser touches out because the winner shoves, pummels, or carries him out. If in this collision of irresistible forces and immovable objects a wrestler touches any part of his body except the soles of his feet to the clay within the ring, he loses just as certainly as if he were forced out. The rules forbid punching with a closed fist, strangling, gouging eyes, breaking bones, pulling hair, clapping both ears simultaneously, bending back fingers, and compression of the genitals. But wrestlers are free to butt, grab, trip, slap, straight-arm, punch with the heel of the hand, and push against the jaw. Most matches are over in ten seconds, but a few last five minutes (sumo wrestling is exhausting), in which case the referee calls a draw and rematches the wrestlers when they have rested up.

Wajima, like most lighter wrestlers (in his case, 260 pounds), shuns shoving in favor of throws. Here is where the sumo battler's belt comes into play. This garment of heavy silk is simply a sash about thirty feet long and two feet wide, folded in four to a width of six inches. Wrapped round and round the wrestler's middle, with an end drawn between the buttocks and legs as a *cache-sexe* and with some silk tassels hanging down in front, it serves modestly to preserve modesty; but in battle, to wrestlers of the Wajima style, the opponent's belt is as functional as the handle on a beer mug. Wajima consistently wins by hooking his left hand onto his adversary's belt under the arm; then he grabs the belt in front with his right hand, butts his head against the opponent's chest, and with a twist throws the helpless fellow down on his shoulder.

The Sumo Association officially lists seventy distinguishable ways of winning a match. The neatest switch in sumo comes when a man pushed to the edge of the ring digs in his toes against the straw rope and suddenly lifts his attacker, swings half a turn, and throws the embarrassed warrior outside. The referee calls the wins, but he can be overruled by the judges, who at major bouts number five, one of them using slow-motion television replays to observe close decisions.

Wajima rose so fast in sumo that he was entitled to fit himself out in the high-ranking wrestler's glossy, samurai topknot before he had grown enough hair to form one (he got a beauty parlor to fake it with a permanent wave). Reaching the Grand Champion rank entitled him to another sumo distinction, the right to wear at ceremonies a white rope belt made of three strands as thick as salamis, copied after Shinto shrine bellpulls and symbolizing guardian deities. Climbing into his white Lincoln Continental, Wajima promptly took the belt to Meiji shrine in Tokyo to have it blessed. Wajima likes golf, and has a drive like a siege gun. A straightforward and intelligent young man, Wajima is almost the only wrestler performing under his own name; the others adopt fighting names chosen for euphony and poetry. The name of the Grand Champion Kitanofuji means "north of Fuji," and that of Kotozakura means "harp of the cherry blossom." Kitanofuji, by the way, is an adept surfer—all these big men are balanced and graceful.

A sumo wrestler's income, made up of a small salary, allowances and expenses, reward money based on his win–lose record, donated prize money, gifts, and other emoluments, is something of a secret between himself and the tax collector, but experts say that even high-ranked men do not often top $50,000 a year, less than half of what good baseball players make.

An amazing addition to the world of sumo in recent years has been the American Jesse James Walani Kuhaulua, otherwise known as Daigoro Takamiyama, the cynosure of the aforementioned Russian customs inspectress. This battler was born (at 10 pounds 14 ounces) in 1944 to parents of Hawaiian descent in Happy Valley, on the island of Maui. He was playing tackle for Baldwin High there when Toshio Takizawa, athletic director of Meiji University in Tokyo, paid a visit to Hawaii and spotted Jesse as a promising broth of a freshman —he measured 6 feet 2 inches and weighed 280 pounds.

In February 1964 the head of the great Takasago stable in Tokyo brought Jesse to Japan. The Hawaiian suffered from the cold, from inability to speak Japanese, and, most of all, from his height and long legs. "I was top-heavy in a world of heavy bottoms," he recalls. Japanese apprentices, built close to the floor, toppled him so quickly that he was advised to concentrate on straight-arming and bulldozing his adversaries out of the ring. At first, too, he could not stomach the food. Sumo wrestlers build those middle-heavy bodies by eating a stew of carrots, cabbage, onions, and bean curd flavored with soy sauce and sugar, all varied and enriched by the addition of either beef, pork, chicken, or (mostly) fish. They eat only two meals a day, but shovel it in like coal, and supplement it with heaps of rice. The younger wrestlers prepare the food, becoming good cooks, which leads many sumo men to open restaurants upon retirement.

Jesse went through some hellish years. The exercise for an apprentice is tough (hauling a tire uphill with a man sitting on it, or carrying another wrestler on his back), and the trainers are rough (throwing salt in his mouth, or hitting him with bamboo sticks). But heavy exercise plus heavy food makes immense muscles just lightly layered with lard, and creates the Japanese paradox of the world's biggest giants walking in a land of mostly small, lean people. Sumo wrestlers are made, not born; recruits need weigh only 154 pounds and measure at least 5 feet 8 inches. A wrestler's ultimate weight is less important to victory than his skill; there are no light, middle, or heavyweight classes in the sport, and Jesse, at 365 pounds and 6 feet 4 the biggest and tallest man in sumo, occasionally takes beatings from men more than a hundred pounds lighter.

Pro sumo stages six fifteen-day tournaments a year, three in Tokyo's Kogugikan Arena (a sort of Astrodome in shrine style), and one each in Nagoya, Osaka, and Fukuoka. A fan can arrive at ten thirty in the morning, when the newest recruits battle, and might see as many as 150 bouts before the Champions and Grand Champions finish at six in the evening. A wrestler's win–lose record over the fifteen days of a tournament sends him up or down in the rankings.

Jesse Kuhaulua, always winning more than he lost, reached *sekitori* (full-fledged) status early in 1967, which entitled him to wear the wrestler's ritual brocaded-silk apron at ring ceremonies. Such aprons, gold-fringed and ornately decorated, cost easily a thousand dollars. Jesse got his as a gift from the 442nd Veterans Club in Hawaii, and it bore the motto of those vets' famed Nisei regiment of World War II: GO FOR BROKE. In 1972 in Nagoya, Jesse won sumo's highest award, the Emperor's Cup, presented by turns to the winners of each of the year's six tournaments. The award stirred apprehension among some superpatriotic sportswriters that foreigners might take over sumo. Matched against Grand Champion Wajima, Jesse frequently manages to win, but nevertheless he has never scored enough to reach Champion, much less Grand Champion (which requires winning the Emperor's Cup twice or more). In February 1974, at the New Otani Hotel in Tokyo, Jesse married a pretty, twenty-five-year-old dance instructor, and he plans to live in Japan the rest of his life.

One million balls! Or nearly.

It is mid-evening, and I am in the basement of a commercial building in Shinjuku, a Tokyo night-life center. From overhead, through a chute, comes a cascade of steel balls the size of marbles. They clatter into a throbbing stainless-steel machine, where they are . . . washed! Yes, washed; and sterilized. Then an endless chain of buckets carries them up, up, up—up to the room above the main floor, and there they roll in channels to fall into each of 335 apertures, arranged in rows.

This is backstage at a pachinko parlor, and the steel spheres are its life blood. A pachinko machine is a small vertical pinball machine, onomatopoetically named, and Japan has 1.6 million of them in 9,304 parlors (more than one-third run by Koreans). The *chink* of pachinko is a standard Japanese sound, and the playing of pachinko is a standard Japanese madness. An appalling madness: 15 million people, mostly men, play this inane game, mostly daily, and in many cases for hours on end. Elbow to elbow they stand in the pinball arcades, which are as gaudy as sunsets and as noisy as textile mills. The Japan Association of Game Machine Manufacturers reports that the populace spends more than $3 *billion* a year on pachinko. A young Japanese friend of mine, contemptuous of this lonely and mindless self-gratification, calls pachinko "Japanese masturbation."

At "Pachinko Jack," which was the name emblazoned in neon romaji on the parlor I inspected, owner Kei Kumagai explained the ins and outs of this amusement. The player buys a hundred balls for 300 yen ($1) and places them in a reservoir in the pinball machine. Flipping his thumb against a lever, with the gesture of a bank teller counting money, he fires the balls upward so that they descend among the pins. The trick is to cause one ball to trigger an aperture called, because of its shape, a tulip (*churippu* in Japanese) to open its petals for a moment so that the next ball can enter, bringing a jackpot of fifteen balls. A part of the pachinko player's skill is speed. Amateurs shoot slowly (thirty balls a minute) and watch mesmerized as each ball sails up and over; professionals shoot rapidly, avoiding the temptation to watch, and sometimes get all three of the machine's tulips open at once.

The winnings, if any, serve to buy trifling prizes—socks, cigarettes, flashlight batteries, orange juice; a total of two hundred items, all priced in balls—from a counter in the corner of Pachinko Jack. Payment in goods evades laws against gambling. But Kumagai told me that near every pachinko parlor there is a hole-in-the-wall shop that will buy back the prizes for cash. The repurchaser then sells them to a wholesaler, who sells them to the distributor who supplied them to the pachinko parlor in the first place. The aggregate cost of the prizes Kumagai hands out is 60 percent of the sum players spend buying balls. Kumagai told me that the best professional pachinko players learn to sniff out high-paying machines, and win enough to make a living; he fights the pros by constantly switching the machines from one location to another.

I often fancied in Japan that the people were worshiping a god about whom, for some occult reason, they would tell me nothing. His temples were visible on every hand, blank-walled buildings of two or three stories. Rising from their roofs like the campaniles of Siena were replicas of the god's modernistic totem, a soaring column knobbed at the top, drawn gracefully in toward the middle, thickened lower down, but narrowed to a delicate foot at the base. These strange symbols loomed in the cities, stood out against sunsets, nestled in the greenery of landscapes seen from train windows. In fact, Japan has about three thousand of them. They are supersize bowling pins, used to advertise the immense and ubiquitous arenas that have sprung up in the last half dozen years.

At first, bowling was so fashionable that people waited until eleven o'clock at night for a chance at a lane, or rose at 5 A.M. Then speculators rushed in and built an ultimate total of 122,000 lanes. Bowling soon lost its snob appeal, the popularity of the sport sinking in inverse proportion to the availability of lanes. The churches of the god of the bowling pin are now about as empty as the churches of most other religions. The Economic Planning Agency estimates that seventy thousand lanes will handle the needs of the serious bowlers of the future.

A reverent look skyward in Japan often also brings into focus another Western sport, one that is not a fad but a permanent and fixed obsession of the Japanese: golf. Atop many a lofty roof there billows a huge green net, held up by a great pipe frame. It is a practice driving range. On the ground these same artificial aviaries for wingless missiles, some with three decks of tees and perhaps three dozen swinging customers, disfigure villages, neighborhoods, and shopping centers.

Golf came to Japan in 1910, and by the beginning of World War II the country had sixty-five courses where the rich could knock around. The sport grew in rough proportion to GNP, or, perhaps more precisely, in proportion to the burgeoning of expense accounts, and in mid-1973, according to the Ministry of Construction, 681 courses were in operation, 214 others were being developed, and 532 more were planned. Such growth bucks a plain fact of geography in Japan: the shortage of flat land. From this fact flow strange consequences. For one thing, golf courses are fantastically expensive—typically, $10 million. Memberships, which in effect are shares (of limited number) in the enterprise, like shares in a cooperative apartment house, are much in demand, forcing up their cost and making them fabulous investments. Golf is a genuine threat to agriculture; authorities must battle constantly to keep golf links from swallowing up too much farm or building land. Golf architects have responded by becoming skilled at designing courses on mountaintops.

The land at Koganei Country Club, just west of Tokyo, where former Prime Minister Tanaka played Jack Nicklaus a couple of years ago, is worth $300,000 an acre, which means that the going price of one of its six hundred memberships, $110,000 in late 1973, was a bargain in terms of what the land would sell for if the club were dissolved. Even at quite ordinary clubs, memberships were worth from $4,000 to $30,000 at that time, and that represented a three- or fourfold increase from two years before. Club developers typically begin by selling memberships cheaply to get start-up money, and raise the price as the process of land acquisition and course building goes on, so that when the club opens the original investors already stand to profit hugely. Even non-golfers buy memberships for speculative gain. They call such investments *infure heji*, inflation hedges.

Headlong golf-course development causes head-on collisions with various levels of government. At Haramachi, on the Pacific coast north of Tokyo, a real estate company filled in five acres of rice paddies to make part of a golf course, violating laws requiring official permission to convert this valuable leveled farmland to other purposes. The Shizuoka prefectural government rose in anger against plans to add three courses to the seven already built in Oyama, which would have resulted in giving over no less than 9 percent of the township's entire area to tees, greens, roughs, and fairways. In Hyogo Prefecture, golf-course construction triggered a number of landslides, including one that buried thirty-five acres of paddies, and another that killed twenty-one people. Where built without such mishaps, though, mountain golf courses are ingenious adaptations of sport to terrain, sometimes utilizing escalators or funicular railways. A spectacular mountain course is that in Karuizawa, in central Honshu, with seventy-two holes.

I never asked a Japanese business executive about his hobbies without hearing in reply that he played golf. Much more even than in the United States, the golf course is where business contacts are made and deals arranged. One of the most exclusive courses around Tokyo is the Three Hundred Club, far enough south to have a good view of Mount Fuji over its artfully shaped trees and velvety fairways. Here crew-cut, elderly businessmen, T-shirts hanging casually outside their elegantly casual slacks, go round the links under yellow parasols, each with his *caddy-san*, a girl in a blue bonnet and white gloves. Japanese leftists oppose such exclusivity, and a while back the 180 big-business and big-finance members of the Three Hundred Club were put under heavy pressure by newspapers, and even by private threats, to amplify the membership. The club capitulated, allowing one hundred *nouveaux riches* to join the crusty original fat cats.

But even if many clubs are exclusive, golf really is a game for the masses in affluent Japan, as the abundance of courses shows. More than five million people flail away at it. Club members have to make reservations well in advance of playing on Sundays and holidays; often a thoughtful gift for the schedule maker helps to get the most coveted tee-off time. Oddly, Japanese companies have not yet captured the whole market for clubs, balls, bags, shoes, and clothing; 40 percent of these goods come from such foreign firms as Wilson, Spalding, MacGregor, and Munsingwear. The golf-equipment market tops $300 million a year.

Japan's most famous golfer is Masashi ("Jumbo") Ozaki, now in his late twenties. When I was in Japan, Ozaki won the Tokai Classic International Open in Nagoya, taking $18,000 in prize money plus a prize car, at the same time defeating Lee Trevino, a guest competitor, by one stroke. A big, powerful man, he is famed for long drives that may or may not be related to the fact that he was once a pro baseball pitcher.

Japanese baseball is as American as apple pie. One day, looking down from the monorail that runs between the airport and downtown Tokyo, I spotted five separate sandlot games. An *Asahi Shimbun* sportswriter named Junji Kanda observes that the Americans gave this game "rules more complicated than in any other sport. The Japanese, being passionate lovers of rules, find it very appealing." In 1973, Japan celebrated the centennial of the introduction of baseball by American missionaries and YMCA organizers. Universities took to the game first, and to this day, in the six-school Tokyo college league, the annual game between Keio and Waseda is a wild and gripping event. There are two professional leagues, the Central and the Pacific, with six teams each.

The Japanese have been leery of adding any heavy Oriental touches to baseball. Pro team names, which are spoken in English and spelled out in Roman letters on uniforms, mostly animalize the players American-style: Hanshin Tigers, Kintetsu Buffaloes, Taiheiyo Lions—though the Hiroshima Carp, Chunichi Dragons, and Taiyo Whales provide exotic switches. Clubs are not (with one or two exceptions) profit-making franchises; instead they are sponsored by corporate interests because they provide incessant and effective publicity. Hanshin, for example, is an Osaka railway company. Nevertheless, some clubs become identified with cities, American style. The Yomiuri (a newspaper) Giants is the team that stands for Tokyo, and the Nankei (a railway) Hawks represent Osaka.

At Tokyo's 50,000-seat Korakuen Stadium, the crack of the bat, the black suits of umpires, the swagger of the players, the look (but not the taste) of the hot dogs, the Xerox advertisement on the outfield fence, the calls of *puree booru* (play ball) and *fauru* (foul) are all more or less American. In contrast, you can buy box lunches of barbecued eel, and at amateur games the cheerleaders are likely to be kimonoed girls twirling parasols on top of the dugouts.

When American clubs play exhibition games in Japan, the Japanese teams win often enough, but American sportswriters generally equate Japan's baseball prowess with that of the American Double-A minor leagues. Most Japanese batters connect well enough, but cannot hit long. They get their share of home runs because the farthest fence in Japanese ball parks is only 340 feet away, compared to 400 in a big American stadium. The ranking batter, Sadaharu Oh, had hit his 634th homer at the end of the 1974 season, compared to Hank Aaron's 733 at that point, and since Oh is six years younger than Aaron, he seems sure to become the new world-record holder.

Japanese pitching is expert. Says Jim Lefebvre, the Los Angeles Dodger infielder who quit to play for the Lotte Orions in Japan: "Pitchers use more finesse—unbelievable control. They're not strong enough to be overpowering, but you might not get a good ball to hit all night." He hit twenty-four home runs during his best year in the United States; in his first year in Japan he led his team with twenty-nine but "was disappointed. I felt I could hit more over here." Lefebvre is one of a score of Americans playing in Japan under a rule that limits teams to two foreigners apiece. He makes $119,000 a year; others get from $17,000 to $130,000.

Fans enjoy the Americans: Don Buford, who used to play for the Baltimore Orioles, is the top draw of the Taiheiyo Lions. But there are tensions. The Americans could be hitting at the Babe Ruthian rate of sixty home runs a year if pitchers walked them less and officials gave fairer calls.

In 1943, as Japan's forthcoming defeat in war became foreseeable, the militarists who ran the country banned baseball as "a sport of foreign origin." Like many Japanese soldiers, an army pilot named Shin'ichi Ishimaru, a former pitcher, found it hard to give up the game. At idle times he continued to play catch, as a nostalgic touch of the beguiling American sport. At an airfield one day in the war, he put his arm through a series of satisfying pitches, the ball thunking solidly into the mitts. Then he got into his Kamikaze plane, took off toward the warships that had steamed to the shores of Japan from the homeland of baseball, and did his final duty for his country.

10 /

Outside Japan

ONE DAY A COUPLE OF YEARS AGO, Michio Nagai, now Japan's minister of education but at that time a world-touring journalist, was puzzled to notice twenty or thirty women in kiminos at the Stockholm airport. "Must be wives of a group of traveling executives from some Osaka company," he mused. Not even the samisens that they carried quite triggered recognition. But when they got into a chartered bus and drove off winking and waving, he realized that he had just witnessed what "had to happen": a group of prosperous geishas were out seeing the world.

The Japanese traveler has lately printed his image on the world much as the Americans did in the years after World War II. With swiftly rising affluence and relaxed currency restrictions added to the age-old Japanese trait of insatiable curiosity, the number of Japanese going abroad shot from fewer than half a million in 1969 to 2.4 million in 1974. The nation that until the coming of Commodore Perry spent two and a half centuries sealed off from the rest of the world has now produced the world's most avid tourists. Proportionately, more Japanese travel abroad every year than any other nationality. More Japanese tourists (roughly half a million a year) visit the United States than those of any other nation—although, to be sure, most of them come no closer to the American mainland than Hawaii or Guam. Nearly as many go to Hong Kong, and, in descending order, to Taiwan, Korea, the United Kingdom, and Thailand. About thirteen thousand go to the Soviet Union, and eight thousand to China. Japanese travelers currently spend about $1.25 billion a year abroad. Moreover, nearly a hundred thousand Japanese now live abroad as businessmen, students, diplomats, artists, or expatriates.

Once, they were wide-eyed innocents abroad. By contrast, in 1973, dining at the Angara Hotel in Siberian Irkutsk one evening, I was joined by Tomizo Kohata, a sophisticated electrical engineer from Yokohama. Into a five-day holiday he was cramming quick but serious studies of Irkutsk and Khabarovsk (a bleak eastern Siberian city so much visited by Japanese nowadays that it has posted signs in Japanese on the railroad-station doors). He talked of his interest in comparative world history, and of his plan soon to go to Rome, Greece, and Egypt to get a grasp of early Christianity and its predecessor religions. The world is Kohata's province, and so it is also for a substantial proportion of other Japanese travelers. The train in which I crossed Siberia carried dozens of blue-jeaned Japanese boys and girls intent on absorbing the culture of Russia and Western Europe. A year or so ago, a fifteen-man team of exuberant Japanese amateurs took a midget submarine to Scotland's Loch Ness and spent a couple of carefree weeks searching for the monster. The famed actor Utaemon VI, when not howling archaic Japanese on stage at the Kabuki theater in Tokyo, likes to play the games of chance in Las Vegas. The newest archeologists in Egypt are Japanese: at Luxor they recently uncovered a thirty-five-century-old brick staircase, painted with Nubian figures, that apparently led to a long-since-vanished sanctuary.

Seeing the world in such numbers may well produce a greater impact on Japan than any event since Perry's visit. The Japanese capacity for selecting from and absorbing the best of other cultures will get new scope. But so far the Japanese hegiras have affected the world more than they have Japan, in ways delirious, unsettling, and funny.

Some of the travelers from Japan have quickly built a reputation as the Ugly Japanese—a reputation composed about equally of truth, myth, and Japanese zeal to excel the Americans at everything. The biggest single source of foreign resentment against Japanese travelers is their clannishness. The great bulk of them find traveling alone unthinkable. All the middle-income people who now have money to go abroad "feel unique overseas, think that they are somehow going to goof, to feel laughable," one travel agent told me. Many of them have never seen an actual dollar bill or pound note. Traveler's checks, requiring signatures in Roman script and identification in (usually) English, are confusing. Language is a fearful barrier. So they go in groups: employees of the same company, or teachers from the same school, or, most visible of all, farmers from the same *nokyo*, or agricultural cooperative (the citizens of many countries of Southeast Asia employ the work *nokyo* to mean "Japanese lout"). Other groups are simply assortments of people drawn by the advertising of Japan Air Lines' JALPAK tours or Japan Travel Bureau's LOOK tours. Obviously, the tours benefit the tourists in many ways besides fending off solitude. Group organization, especially in Europe, is no doubt the best way to cram all the sights the tourists learned about in school into, say, eighteen days. By inflexible custom, each group's leader carries a flag bearing the heraldry of his tourist agency, and the members need only heed the leader's whistle and keep an eye on the flag to avoid getting lost.

Not only do clannish tourists find safety in numbers, but they also shun experimentation with foreign ways and customs. In the pattern of Conrad Hilton building American hotels all over the world, burgeoning tourism has inspired Japanese entrepreneurs to erect hotels in countries as distant as Bulgaria. Manhattan, Toronto, Amsterdam, and all the major cities of East Asia have Japanese hotels. Guam has five, Hawaii twenty-four. Eighteen Japanese firms have joined with Intourist to build a hotel in Moscow's Lenin Hills area that will have forty stories, a thousand rooms, and a luxury annex with 250 rooms—a "Japan Town" in Russia, or a homey stopover on the Tokyo–Europe route. Japan Air Lines Development Company is putting up a thirty-two-story hotel on the banks of the Seine, and there are a dozen Japanese restaurants in the French capital.

At his worst, the Ugly Japanese is not only clannish but also boorish. Japanese farmers and laborers are not only astonishingly affluent, but often uncouth, or at least earthy. They spit and shove and "run around in their underwear at Hiltons the world over," as someone told me. Because they never have to tip in Japan, they nervously tip too little or too much abroad. But, guided partly by government instruction on how to avoid "shaming the Japanese people," and partly by their own growing worldliness, gained to a great extent from television, the nokyos get more sophisticated every year, and even those who remain rough win respect abroad for their basic honesty and innate decency.

If obnoxious nokyos earn resentment-with-pity, the obnoxious rich earn resentment-with-envy—much as Americans used to. Perfume shops in Paris cadging foreign customers now have signs in Japanese, not in addition to, but instead of signs in English. "They buy diamonds, pork, works of art, fashions, lumber, factories—anything that is real and solid," says an American trade expert. "Most of the important gems that come on the market are leaving the country, more often than not to Japan," said Harry Winston, the Fifth Avenue jeweler, a year or so ago. The Japanese also buy antiquities, gold, incunabula, and Italian leather. "They walk into the store here, make a little bow, and say two words: 'Gucci shoe,'" reports a Roman shopkeeper. Japanese horse breeders in 1972 spent about $15 million for six hundred European and American brood mares.

Where Japanese rapacity shows itself greediest is in the buying of art. In the three years after the 1971 dollar devaluation, the Japanese rich, seeking inflation hedges, invested stupendously in painting, chiefly Western, and in sculpture and ceramics. The first splurge was for painters of the Paris school—Renoir, Rouault, Cézanne, Modigliani, Chagall, Miró, Picasso. Henri Rousseau's "Tropic Zone" (also called "Monkey in the Jungle"), which was "de-accessed"—to the accompaniment of angry criticism—by the Metropolitan Museum of Art for $1.5 million, fetched up as the property of Mitsui & Company in Tokyo, which paid about $1.7 million. A bit later in an auction staged by London's Christie Manson & Woods, Japanese buyers accounted for just under half of the sales, leading Christie's Tokyo man to remark: "Japanese taste has already become the main determinant of the prices of Impressionist paintings, Chinese potteries and porcelains, and Japanese art and craft items on the British market." In fact, Japan has got back a good deal of Oriental art made off with by Western collectors in the last century; one Japanese buyer acquired a print of Hokusai's "Great Wave" for $13,500.

The Japanese have also developed a taste for American paintings. At a Sotheby Parke Bernet auction, the *New York Times*'s Deirdre Carmody looked on mesmerized as two dignified men bid up the prices of modern American paintings (Kuhn, Levine, O'Keeffe, Shahn) in thousand-dollar jumps to staggering heights; both bidders were Japanese art dealers. An advertisement signed "Japanese investment group" in the same newspaper carried the blunt headline: UNLIMITED CASH AVAILABLE. For tax-dodging reasons, paintings acquired by Japanese buyers often go underground, with the unhappy result that they cannot be traced for loan shows or for reproduction in art books. A big show of Monet in Tokyo put together sixty-four of his paintings from all over the world, but did not include even one from the many that crafty local collectors presumably own.

Sightseeing is the prevalent motive when the Japanese tour Europe or the United States, and the groups include both husbands and wives. But many groups who go to nearby points in Asia are composed entirely of men, and the motive of their wanderlust is a little wander plus a lot of lust. They act in accord with a much-quoted Japanese proverb which says: "A person away from home is immune to shame." A Japanese newspaperman in Bangkok told me that group-tour guides there, with flags held high, commonly march their platoons into bordellos and crisply call out the numbers of the rooms to which each man has been assigned. It's a safe, orderly, accepted part of the tourist business. In Korea, Japanese men seek out *kisaeng* parties, kisaeng girls being the more pliable Korean version of the Japanese geisha. Japanese feminists have occasionally picketed the airport gates in Tokyo through which men bound for Korea pass; the girls carried signs pleading with the "sex animals" to "feel ashamed," and to cease and desist from "prostitution sightseeing." A JAL stewardess who flies to Taiwan reports that men on the planes unabashedly summon her to ask, "How much does it cost in Taipei?" A brothel just off Rome's Via Veneto, catering only to Japanese, was busted a while back after police received, in letters from Japan, a number of complaints—that the prices were too high.

Guam, 30 miles long, 8 miles wide, and 1,600 miles south of Tokyo, is the island whose airfields dispatched many of the B-29s that fire-bombed the Japanese capital on the night of March 9, 1945, incinerating sixteen square miles of houses and buildings. Now, on the same flyway, shuttling Boeing 747s carry as many as two hundred thousand Japanese to this member of the Mariana Island group each year. They like to tour the battlefields where the Americans bloodily won back the island from the Japanese in mid-1944, and they like to inspect the cave where the Imperial Army straggler Shoichi Yokoi lived for twenty-eight years until his reappearance in 1972. Each year, when Guam celebrates the anniversary of the American recapture, it flies the Japanese flag as well as the American. "The courteous thing to do," says one Guamanian, considering the friendliness and affluence of the vistors from Japan.

Japanese tourism's contribution to Guam's $80 million-a-year tourist trade has made the island a booming place. "Our growth has been indicated to be something in the neighborhood of 35 percent a year," says Governor Carlos Camacho, a former dentist who was appointed by President Nixon. One-fourth of Japanese tourists to Guam are middle-income newlyweds, constituting the biggest share of the more than one hundred thousand couples that take an "airplane honeymoon" abroad from Japan each year. Often young people do not wed before departure, but go to Guam (and elsewhere) to marry "Christian style" and escape the fuss, boredom, and expense of a traditional Japanese wedding. At such hotels as the Dai Ichi or the Okura, the brides and grooms enjoy the sand and swimming of tropical Tumon beach, a few miles north of Agana, the capital. In

Guam's restaurants they test the empanadas and tortillas that reflect ancient contacts with Mexico, when the island was a stop on the Spanish galleons' Acapulco–Manila route. The older Guamanians speak passable Japanese, a heritage of two and a half years of occupation during the war. So attractive is Guam that one Japanese farmers' group has booked rooms at the Miami Beach–style Hotel Guam Kakuei for the next fifteen years. The spot in Guam where Japanese soldiers set up the first enemy command post ever placed on American soil now holds the Fujita Hotel, catering to Japanese tourists.

Saipan, 150 miles closer to Japan, is another of the Mariana Islands that seems in line to go back under Japanese domination, at least in spirit. This island was mandated by the old League of Nations to Japan, which kept it until an American armada seized it in 1944, with a toll of 33,000 dead, including thousands of Japanese soldiers and civilians who killed themselves by leaping from a precipice. The United States made Saipan into a B-29 base for bombing Japan, and after the war took it under American rule as part of the United Nations Marianas Trust Territory. A couple of years ago, a search party of twenty-four Japanese university students found the remains of 745 Imperial Army soldiers in the shadow of Suicide Cliff. They built a funeral pyre, placed sake, flowers, and rice on it, and set it ablaze to the sound of chants from a Shinto priest. Tourism is just revving up. The old bomber strip has been turned into an airport, and Japan Air Lines won from the Civil Aeronautics Board permission to fly into Saipan from Tokyo. Some experts guess that by 1976 vacationers, mostly Japanese, will begin arriving at the rate of two hundred thousand annually. Legally, the Japanese cannot own property or businesses on Saipan, but they use loans and credit to back Americans; such joint ventures plan to build two hotels on the island, plus an eighteen-hole golf course on the site of a base where the CIA once trained guerrillas for Chiang Kai-shek. A lot of other islands in Micronesia, notably Ponape and Yap, face similar quasi-Japanese futures.

Some even odder places have heavily Japanese presence. Tanque Verde Ranch, near Tucson, gets lots of Japanese dudes. The China International Travel Service reports rather ruefully that the Japanese are No. 1 among foreigners who scribble on the Great Wall. An outfit called Japan Golf Promotion, Inc., of Osaka, has ties that enable its members to play on ten courses in California and Oregon. I saw a band of Japanese Buddhist monks riding in a chartered bus in front of "Mariposa de Vida—The Aphrodisiac Restaurant" in Manila. Ginza bar girls drink in bars in Los Angeles. Club Méditerranée Japan takes its members to a vacation village in Tahiti, among other places, and another resort company runs a villa for Japanese vacationers on Mana Island in the Fijis. Even after Japan broke relations with Taiwan, fifty thousand Japanese per month sought out a half-hidden Tokyo office (ostensibly a branch of the Taiwanese Embassy in Korea) to get visas to go to Taipei. But no Japanese has ever, according to reliable reports, visited Tokio, Arkansas (population approximately thirty).

The Japanese go to Hong Kong, at the rate of a thousand a day, not only to buy tax-free Swiss watches, but also to buy tax-free Japanese watches, which cost three times as much at home. They also buy Courvoisier, Johnnie Walker Black, and expensive golf clubs. Seoul is just a weekend trip, or a two-day excursion. Any morning, Seoul's dilapidated airport is a mob scene of departing Japanese, taking direct flights not only to Tokyo but also to Osaka and Fukuoka. Many Japanese drive to Korea—there's a car ferry between Shimonoseki and Pusan. Even the humblest Japanese seems to be able to see the world these days. The man who peddles vegetables to some friends of mine in Kamakura mentioned casually not long ago that he had just returned from his vacation in the south of France.

The men who, beginning about 1950, carried the Japanese presence abroad on behalf of its outthrusting exporters and investors were not really the first Japanese businessmen abroad. The huge Mitsui trust, for example, kept three hundred men working in the United States in 1935, and suave Japanese bankers and salesmen operated in every European capital. But the postwar effort that made Toyota, Sony, Yamaha, Nikon, Datsun, Seiko, and dozens of other trade names familiar to the whole world was incomparably bigger. And it was mostly carried out by men who did not want to go. "There is no alienation, loneliness or irritability comparable to that of the Japanese whose work takes him to a foreign country. 'They've probably completely forgotten me,' and 'That colleague of mine back home has probably played his cards so well that he'll be a manager in no time'— such apprehensions suggest the atmosphere built around himself by the Japanese exile," writes sociologist Chie Nakane. I know, from interviews, that many Japanese businessmen have now learned how not to be miserable abroad, but the adjustment is precisely opposite to that of Englishmen, who would rather go abroad than stay home.

In my travels I met a number of men who more or less bracket the feelings of the overseas Japanese businessmen. Take youthful

Atsuo Okazaki, assistant manager for the Asian & Euro-American Merchant Bank Limited, on bustling Shenton Way in Singapore. He felt gung-ho about his work, and he had found an attractive, five-room apartment, in a building with a swimming pool, only twenty minutes' drive from the office, at a rent he could afford—all conditions that he admitted would be hard to duplicate in Japan. His English is good; he has "no trouble in conversation with foreigners." He knows the conditions of life in Tokyo: "Lot of tensions there: getting up early to catch a comfortable commuter train, taking one, two, three hours to drive to a golf course." Moreover, "for me, to be abroad is sometimes good—living in foreign countries is not a bad thing." But on balance he yearns intensely to be back in Japan. "If I were there I could be buying a golf-club membership by installment, a wonderful investment. The television there is so much better; Singapore won't have color TV for a year yet. If you go abroad you lose fringe benefits, like use of the company's villa in Karuizawa, or a company loan to buy a house. Twenty years after the war I thought going abroad was a privilege of the rich and the powerful, and therefore enviable. Now people think going abroad is bad for them, bad for their overall prospects."

Or take Tetsuro Iwabe, special assistant to the president of Mitsui & Company (U.S.A.). On rainy spring days in Manhattan, Iwabe wears a cowboy hat to work, and on sunny summer days he strolls to his office in the Pan Am building in *geta*, the Japanese thonged clogs. Ted Iwabe found corporate life in Japan suffocating. "In Japan, Japan comes first, the group comes first, the company comes first— you have to be a Japanese before you are an individual," he grumbles. "If I raised issues with my superiors, they thought I was not 'co-operating.' You can't have an original idea—that's why the Japanese can perfect but not originate." He revels in working and living in the United States and never wants to live in Japan again.

Another New Yorker is Gohsuke Shibayama, general manager for Mitsui O.S.K. Lines, who occupies a chamber high in 17 Battery Place that has a view of New York Harbor clear to the Verrazano-Narrows and Kill van Kull bridges, a wall-filling track chart of all the oceans, and a Japanese geisha doll in a glass case, just like those one sees in virtually every important businessman's office in Tokyo. Shibayama, who was born in Tokyo just after the 1923 earthquake, has his wife cook Japanese food at home, but does not put on any such Nipponese airs as switching to a kimono when he arrives home from the office—"Western clothes are more convenient." He finds that "New York and Tokyo in the daytime, doing business, are the same, but at nighttime Tokyo is much safer."

In my conversation with him, Shibayama raised a problem that all Japanese abroad take seriously: schooling for their children. He considered himself lucky because his offspring are girls, and he thinks that American high school and college education is adequate for girls, though not good enough for the young Japanese male. "A boy who graduates from a high school here can't pass the exams to get into a good Japanese university," said Shibayama. Most businessmen abroad make some arrangement to leave their sons in Japan for high school and college, for to make them attend foreign universities would be to handicap them for life, at least in Japan. The only part of foreign higher education the Japanese respect is postgraduate work.

Wherever there is a sizable colony of Japanese businessmen abroad, they have set up their own lower schools. On Bukit Timah Road in Singapore, I noticed cute little Japanese girls in flowered hats being chauffeured to their school, which has two hundred pupils. The equivalent school in Hong Kong has four hundred students, running through junior high school. "No use keeping children here after that," Kentaro Aono, chief representative of NHK there, explained to me. "They must go back to Japan and prepare for exams." About four thousand Japanese live in Hong Kong, he said, but many businessmen leave their wives and children in Japan so that the children can get a proper education.

Even more annoyingly than with tourists, Japanese clannishness among businessmen irritates the citizenry of many countries. Bangkok, where anti-Japanese feelings have been fervent in recent years, has an enclave of Japanese establishments around Rajadamri Street that could easily be mistaken for a district in Tokyo. Closely grouped here are the Amarit Hotel, the Daimaru department store, the office of the Japan Export Trade Organization, and several restaurants clearly intended for Japanese customers only. "The Japanese businessmen here are single-minded about their work, won't adapt to Thai life, don't mix socially," observed a Japanese news correspondent to whom I talked in Bangkok. "It's a question of our language, and our homogeneity, and our nationalism." A Japanese visiting professor at a Thai university was able to compile a list of two hundred reasons why the Thais resent the Japanese. Three of the reasons were: "They don't try to learn our language. They urge us to master Japanese at their offices. They are very poor speakers of English but criticize our way of speaking English." Still, the Japanese like Thailand, one of them told me, "because it is a monarchy, like Japan." They also remember it as one country that sided with Japan in World War II.

Southeast Asians compare the Japanese unfavorably to the "overseas Chinese" businessmen, who traditionally learn native languages, marry, and settle down for good. A Westerner who has observed the Japanese in many countries says: "Many Japanese live a life sealed off from the local society. They eat, play golf, go to parties with a small group of Japanese." They stick close to their local Nippon Clubs, and avoid admitting foreigners into them. On Java, people have never forgotten a certain Japanese golfer who, furious that someone had landed a shot on the green while he was putting, hurled the offending ball into the rough. It turned out to belong to the mayor of Surabaya.

Understandable, but harder to sympathize with, is foreign resentment that the Japanese among them are too diligent. "They walk so fast, they work so hard," a Bangkok waitress told me. A Japanese executive boasted that "when the lights are on in a New York office building late at night, you find either a cleaning woman or a Japanese businessman." Someone who saw a couple dozen Japanese businessmen in the Frankfurt airport, all dressed in dark suits and about to catch a JAL plane for home, remarked: "Not only do they look like an army in uniform, but also you suspect that they've just held a secret meeting." In Southeast Asia, the Japanese still have to overcome war memories. On the waterfront in Singapore stands an immense granite monument so specifically remindful of Japanese atrocities that Japanese residents openly suggest that it should be torn down. "But we leave it there," a Singapore Chinese told me. "It's good for them to remember what happened." At Fort Santiago in Manila, Japanese visitors attentively read a sign that says: "In the dungeons of this fort, Americans, Filipinos, Spanish and Chinese political prisoners were tortured during the Japanese Occupation."

Officials in the Foreign Ministry and in big corporations in Tokyo are quite aware of resentments against the Japanese abroad, but their concern is not deep and their solutions cosmetic. "Nothing much can be done about it," one high diplomat said with a shrug when I asked him about the problem. The Japan-Thailand Cooperation Committee of the Federation of Economic Organizations induced some companies to take down overly conspicuous advertising signs after a student dustup about Japanese economic domination in Thailand. Still, the first billboard that hits the eye when one leave the Bangkok airport plugs Toyota, and it is followed by Komatsu Koya, Subaru, Mazda, Sanyo, and Nissan. In Hong Kong, first-glimpse signs give an impression of landing in Japanese territory, and the most unignorable neon visible from the top of the Manila Hilton promotes Sanyo and Mitsubishi. When he was in office, Prime Minister Tanaka pleaded with Japanese business not to put up any more billboards in Southeast

Asia, and Toyota obligingly dismantled an electric sign on top of Djakarta's highest building.

But the dynamics of sending battalions of businessmen overseas are forcing some changes that will better the reputation of the Japanese. Tours of duty in the United States, says Mitsui O.S.K.'s Shibayama, are being lengthened from an in-and-out two or three years to twelve or thereabouts, long enough to learn the customs and the language. Talented young employees are taking foreign assignments successively in various countries, and training themselves to be flexible and cosmopolitan. Many get an education for foreign experience at the Institute for International Studies and Training, administered by Douglas Overton, formerly an American diplomat and later head of the Japan Society of New York. Supported by Japanese big business, the institute enrolls 120 young men, mostly newly hired corporation employees, and gives them a year of intensive English, the basics of still another language (Chinese, Russian, French, German, or Spanish), and various kinds of area studies. Located on the slopes of Mount Fuji, the institute physically removes its students from their homes and plants them in its ample new dormitories for day-and-night effort. When I visited the school, Overton said that "even the modern young men here hate to go abroad if not in groups." One student, headed for Phoenix, asked me hopefully whether he would find other Japanese in Phoenix.

INTERLUDE

11 /

The Ever-Present Japanese Past

$\mathbf{A}$ T THIS POINT, we turn from examining the people of Japan—their society, their way of life, their customs, their arts and professions and entertainments—to an exploration of the places of Japan. These places possess a singular common denominator: history, extraordinary history extraordinarily little known outside Japan. Every city, every valley, nearly every crossroads is weighted in every Japanese memory with its own history and its place in the nation's history. Far more than Americans, the Japanese carry with them a sense of time past, of what happened in what place, and how and when and why. This sense of the past informs the present, and haunts and vitalizes every particular locality.

The pivot of Japan's modern history is the year 1853, and the responsibility for this turning point lies with the United States of America. For nations so vastly separated in space, this has been a curious and fateful concatenation: since that date, one way or another, these two widely disparate countries have been inextricably and (once) mortally interlocked. Seen in this light, the rather private history of the Japanese archipelago takes on new relevance and fascination.

Eighteen hundred fifty-three.

In the United States, the all-compelling issue was slavery, with that newly published tract, *Uncle Tom's Cabin*, helping to push the nation toward civil war. Such was the emotion and turmoil over slavery that it tended to obscure a deeper trend in the nation: its bursting growth and expansion. Immigrant ships poured Irishmen,

187

Germans, Swedes, and Poles onto the wharfs of Boston and New York. The iron horse, first made practicable only twenty-three years before, already chuffed along fourteen thousand miles of track, in every state east of the Mississippi. With the addition of Texas, California, and the Oregon, Utah, and New Mexico territories, the area of the United States had grown in size by a third in only eight years, although the "Great American Desert" and the Rockies were generally thought to be worthless. But California was already a state, and ambitious expansionists had no trouble at all in thinking of the Pacific Ocean beyond this coast as an American lake. In fact, some decades had passed since a congressman in Washington first pronounced that "geography points us to China, Persia, India, Arabia Felix and Japan."

Japan? To most Americans in 1853, Japan was a tantalizingly remote country. In an unmatched act of self-isolation, Japan had, from about the time the Puritans were getting established on the Massachusetts coast, sealed itself off from the rest of the world. Only one small window was left open: the Dutch trading post on the islet of Deshima in Nagasaki harbor. To be sure, books published in the West occasionally described Japanese government and society with a rough measure of accuracy and detail. In 1847 the author R. Montgomery Martin, a member of the Legislative Council at Hong Kong, praised Japan as ranking "high in the scale of civilization" through its mastery of astronomy, medicine, trigonometry, civil engineering, maps, clocks, almanacs, music, metal blending, wood engraving, copper engraving, watercolors, prints, lacquerware, printing, and bookselling. Martin even noted hints of friendliness toward foreigners: "One of the cures adopted by our sailors for scurvy—namely, burying a man up to his neck in fresh earth—cannot be resorted to on the coast of Japan, as the Japanese prohibit our people landing; but the villagers bring off large casks full of earth for the seamen to be embedded in."

Now, of course, historians have made much clearer what kind of nation it was that lay beyond those misty shores upon which some British tar may have gazed while reposing in a tub of fresh earth. This was the Japan of the Tokugawas, the line of shoguns who decreed the closure of the country in 1639 and had since ruled it with an autocratic benevolence that produced a longer period of absolute peace than in any other nation with a history of record. The population was stabilized (by the practice of infanticide) at 30 million, as compared to 25 million in the United States. The capital of the Tokugawa shogunate was Edo (now Tokyo), and in 1853, with roughly 1 million people, Edo was the largest city in the world.

The Tokugawa sociopolitical system was pure feudalism, although that oppressive word obscures the vitality, prosperity, grandeur, and frequent gaiety of the nation. The shoguns—including such luminaries as the ninth Tokugawa, "the bed-wetting shogun"—prevailed over 265 local domains by requiring that their lords spend half of each year in Edo and leave their families permanently in the capital as hostages, making insurgency impossible. The warrior class, the samurai, deprived of the delights of bloodletting in battle because of the general tranquility, had metamorphosed into suave governmental bureaucrats and judges—though they did retain their ancient privilege of packing two swords, and their right to use these weapons instantly to decapitate disrespectful commoners. The feudal lords paid the samurai to govern the lesser classes, the peasants, the artisans, and the despised but necessary merchants. The emperor was maintained in harmless splendor in the Imperial Palace in Kyoto, exercising even less power than he does today.

The Tokugawas promoted the Confucian philosophy of the ruler and the ruled, of a harmonious social order wherein each person stayed strictly in his place. But Shinto was simultaneously sustained and even encouraged, as a kind of national heritage. Buddhism, though demoted in importance, was used to ensure the obliteration of Christianity, every person being forced to register with a temple. But these stresses on propriety did not dampen the impulse for gaudy, sensual pleasure among the city dwellers—the merchants, artisans, and even disguised samurai. Under the Tokugawas flourished the "floating world," the world of geishas, restaurants, baths, lewd books, and the "nightless city" of Yoshiwara (Happy Fields), the notorious brothel district of Edo. On a higher plane of gratification, painting, woodblock printing, and the realistic novel flowered. The brilliant and rousing Kabuki theater was invented, and soon outshone the older, more somber Noh drama. Puppets were popular; balladeers sang; the haiku was born. In Kyoto, the populace busied itself with the manufacture of needles, lumber, Buddhist prayer beads, jade sculptures, and tobacco products, while black smoke poured from the pottery kilns and the shopkeepers on Gokomachi sold eyeglasses and papier-mâché toys.

At the same time that Newton was writing his *Principia*, Japanese intellectuals posed for themselves such metaphysical questions as, "Why do eyes not hear and ears not see?" and earnestly sought answers. The world of thought was conformist without being closed to innovations: the influential Peers' School, where princes studied, was founded in 1845 as a modernizing step. Dutch books, imported through Deshima, brought news of Western progress in the study of anatomy, gunnery, smelting, botany, and shipbuilding; and scholars at the Office for the Interpretation of Barbarian Books learned the "strange language written sideways" to translate these works. In consequence, Tokugawa Japan progressed remarkably in technology and commerce. By 1850, Japan had big textile mills and reverberatory furnaces. By 1853, as the Light Brigade charged in Crimea with cannon to the right of them and cannon to the left, armorers in Japan were casting cannon just as lethal as those of the Russians. Japan had the most advanced economy in Asia, with banks, letters of credit, busy coastal shipping, and the buying and selling of futures in commodities like rice. The technical gap between Japan and the West was less one hundred years ago than the gap between the West and most of the rest of Asia today.

Daily life was, by Western standards, exotic, but not incomprehensibly so. The memories of Yukichi Fukuzawa, as a young boy in a samurai family in the 1840s, included: helping his mother pull lice from a beggar's hair as an act of charity; watching a workman make a file; substituting ordinary stones for holy stones in a Shinto shrine and snickering at the hoaxed worshipers; crimping a nail so as to pick a lock. He recalled that his class-conscious father reproached a modern-minded teacher who instructed young Fukuzawa in arithmetic: "It is abominable that innocent children should be taught to use numbers—the tool of merchants!" Fukuzawa got a lifelong taste for wine because his mother gave him sake to soothe the pains of shaving his head in order to make a proper samurai topknot. At a sort of boarding school that he attended, he remembered, the dinners consisted of boiled potatoes and sweet onions on days whose dates contained the number 6, shellfish soup on dates containing 3 or 8, and bean-curd soup on dates divisible by 5. Fukuzawa was one of those bright young Japanese assigned to learn Dutch; of his first lesson, he wrote, "I could hardly believe these ABC's to be signs of a language." He learned to improvise quills from crane feathers, because copying Dutch with a brush, Japanese style, was too difficult. Soon he was able to read a book on the fascinating subject of electricity.

With so much input from the West, informed Japanese in 1853 were quite aware that seclusion as a policy would not serve much longer. Moreover, the Dutch traders at Deshima, stirring from lazy afternoons of puffing cigars, went to Edo that year (as was their annual custom), crawled in ritual self-abasement to the shogun's throne, and warned that continued isolation probably meant war with the West. A Japanese fisherman, who had been blown into the sea, rescued by a Yankee whaling ship, taken to Massachusetts, and eventually returned to Japan, informed the shogun that the United States had acquired California as a shipping base and needed North Pacific ports, such as Japan's, for coaling stations.

In 1853 such was Japan—vital, bustling, quintessentially Oriental; whiffing the winds from the West with both fear and fascination. Then, on July 8, an American naval officer named Matthew Calbraith Perry abruptly ended the centuries of isolation by anchoring four black-painted U.S. warships off Uraga, at the mouth of Edo Bay.

Perry, a commodore when that was the United States Navy's highest rank, was the most forceful and imaginative naval officer of his time, outshining his older brother, Captain Oliver Hazard Perry (who coined "Don't give up the ship!" and "We have met the enemy and they are ours"). As an administrator, Calbraith Perry helped banish dueling, scurvy, and grog from the fleet. In West Africa he chose the site of what was later to become Monrovia, capital of Liberia. Almost single-handed he pressured the navy to switch from sail to steam, and he commanded the first successful steam naval ship, *Fulton II*. In the Mexican War, he subdued Tabasco and bombarded Veracruz. But in his career at sea he was always less a shot-and-shell commander than an executor, or perhaps even a creator, of national policy. As a sort of rehearsal for opening Japan, he collected $1,750,000 in American claims from the Neapolitan government by sailing one ship after another into Naples harbor until the overawed authorities conceded.

Forcing the door to Tokugawa Japan had been the goal of many men before Perry. Catherine the Great sent a young Russian naval lieutenant to Japan's northern island in 1792, and a British frigate invaded Nagasaki harbor in 1808, causing the local magistrate to commit suicide for having permitted Japan's isolation to be breached. The shogun thereupon ordered Japan's coastal gunners to fire on sight at future invaders. Nevertheless, an American commodore named James Biddle put in at Edo in 1846, with two ships. Aware that a Philadelphia Biddle must not be too haughty toward foreigners, he overreacted with a naïve agreeability that cost him all respect from the Japanese. They scornfully towed his ships to sea and sent him away.

In that self-righteous age of Western colonialism, actual or economic, Japan's turtlelike posture was maddening. "The Japanese undoubtedly have an exclusive right to the possession of their territory";

fumed the *Edinburgh Review,* "but they must not abuse that right to the extent of debarring all other nations from a participation in its riches and virtues." Protestant-ethic Americans, imbued with the doctrine of Manifest Destiny, saw Japan's refusal to trade as just plain morally wrong. It took no particular initiative for that forgettable President, Millard Fillmore, to order Perry in 1852 to open Japan by a show of American might—a task much to Perry's taste.

Perry prepared for his assignment with all his well-honed military-diplomatic skills. From Holland, for $30,000, he bought Dutch charts of Japanese waters. He saw to it that Fillmore's letter to the Japanese emperor (composed by Daniel Webster and inscribed on vellum) and his own credentials were sealed in gold boxes that were placed inside a rosewood box with gold locks and hinges. He spent weeks selecting appropriate and instructive gifts for the Japanese. For his flagship he chose the side-wheeler *Susquehanna,* which, along with the similar *Mississippi,* could (and did) unnerve the Japanese by steaming into the wind, towing the two sailing frigates that made up the rest of the flotilla. For purposes of dealing with the Japanese, Perry blandly raised his own rank to admiral.

As if to show that Perry's arrival had been synchronized with the occult workings of the entire universe, a brilliant meteor swept across the Edo skies the night the ships anchored. When the news of his arrival reached the city, thirty miles to the north, the "tramp of war-horses, the clatter of armed warriors, the noise of carts, the parades of firemen, the incessant tolling of bells, the shrieks of women, the cries of children," wrote a Japanese observer, "made confusion worse confounded." Less hysterical Japanese at once perceived the strategic meaning of Perry's presence: these men-o'-war could starve out Edo by blocking the coastal shipping on which the city depended for its food.

Perry, wary of repeating Biddle's error, resolved to meet "no one but a Mandarin of the highest rank." Therefore he stayed in his cabin for several days, leading the Japanese to call him "the High and Mighty Mysteriousness." Meanwhile, wood-block prints of the black ships, hastily engraved and circulated like newspapers, informed all of central Japan that the country's quarantine was over. Nobody dared tell the shogun, who somewhat overbilled himself as the "Barbarian-Subduing Generalissimo," but he overheard the news while at the theater—and died several days later, presumably from emotional shock.

On July 14, Commander Franklin Buchanan, captain of the *Susquehanna,* became the first of the Americans to set foot on the shores of Japan, while onlooking samurai growled in displeasure. Behind him three hundred more men of the squadron—marines, sailors, bandsmen playing "Hail Columbia"—came ashore from boats under the looming cone of Mount Fuji. Perry, in full dress, ascended the beach flanked by two muscular blacks. Five thousand Japanese archers, lancers, and cavalrymen lined the shore, many armed with brass-bound muskets. For this unwelcome but inevitable encounter, the Japanese had thrown up a temporary hall, thatch-roofed but elegantly hung with violet silk and paintings of cranes. There, in a frigid ceremony, Perry turned over the President's letter to a lowly provincial governor masquerading (like Perry) as someone more important—in this case as First Councillor of the Empire. No matter: the point was made. Under the floor of the hall, unknown to Perry, nine samurai lay in hiding, ready to slay the American if he got belligerent.

Fillmore's letter, noting that "our steamships can go from California to Japan in eighteen days," proposed, as bluntly as any Yankee profiteer could have wished, that "our two countries should trade with each other." Perry gave notice that he would return for Japan's response, and the following February sailed into Edo Bay with eight ships, one-fourth of the United States Navy. With much palaver, he persuaded the Japanese to open Shimoda, eighty miles southwest of Tokyo, and Hakodate, in southern Hokkaido, as "ports of refuge" for shipwrecked Western sailors—a foot in the door. Then, with relish, he presented his thoughtfully chosen gifts: two electric telegraph instruments, 110 gallons of whiskey, four volumes of Audubon's *Birds of America*, eight baskets of Irish potatoes, and a real steam train, built to one-fourth scale, with 350 feet of circular track.

Before heading home, Perry sailed to Hakodate for a look at what his bargaining had acquired, inspiring someone there to write a rueful haiku—

> *Four steam vessels*
> *Disturb our sleep*
> *Like four cups of tea.*

Perry's return to America was hardly noticed in a nation preoccupied with the approach of war, and he died in 1858.

Every October, the city of Kyoto stages a resplendent Festival of the Ages, a two-mile parade in which each troop of cavalry, or company of swordsmen, or brigade of bowmen—all interspersed with armor-clad samurai, mounted princes in dazzling robes, court ladies with whitened faces, and sandaled peasants—represents an era of

Japanese history before Perry. The newest era comes first, the oldest last, so that the onlooker can see antichronologically back, back, back into Japanese history. It is a splendid spectacle, a dazzling history lesson. The Western viewer becomes aware that history is the great engine of tradition in Japan.

And it is exotic history, even bizarre: one general stirred up his troops for battle by dancing in front of them with a fan. Yet several factors make this history easy to get a rough grasp of. First, it is short, much shorter than Western history: everything before the sixth century is too primitive, tribal, legendary, and misty to dwell upon, in particular the unlikely myth of the creation of Japan, something about a husband-and-wife team of incestuous gods who crystallized the Japanese islands out of drops of sperm falling from his "jeweled spear"—surely history's most spectacular case of coitus interruptus. Second, the colonization was a slow spread from the western island, Kyushu, to the east and north; Hokkaido, the northern island, was still a frontier only a century ago. Third, the post-primitive history can be tidily classified into just three stages: early flowering of the court, the bureaucracy, and the arts, sixth through twelfth centuries; the feudal era (including the Tokugawa period), from then until Perry; and the nation-state, from Perry until now.

Archeologists have dug up ancient stone tools which show that some sort of hominid lived in the Japanese archipelago more than a hundred thousand years ago, having doubtless crossed on land bridges that then connected the islands and the mainland. Beginning about twenty thousand years ago, proto-Negroid and proto-Caucasoid people pushed eastward from south-central Asia, the former to become the ancestors of the Melanesians, and the latter to become the ancestors of the Aborigines of Australia and the Ainus of northern Japan. After that, Mongoloids, also from the west, overran these two stocks in eastern continental Asia and spilled on into Japan, coming by boat a few thousand years after the end of the last ice age had raised the sea over the land connections. Then incursions seem to have ceased, and by the third century after Christ, the present Japanese race was already a homogeneous people, descended from a fairly small group of progenitors: Japan really is a nation-family.

By that time, the Japanese had already established a civilization of some sophistication. They had irrigation, wheel pottery, bronze and iron, harnessed horses, political unity, and quilted clothing—as is demonstrated by the socket-eyed clay *haniwa* figurines that have come down to us. At the time that Constantine was calling the Council of Nicaea, the Japanese were building keyhole-shaped tombs, as rich in artifacts as King Tut's, and bigger in bulk than (though not so spectacular as) the pyramids; the greatest of them lies, sealed off from the public, just south of Osaka. Recently an 1,800-year-old house of the period, built of wood in gable style, was unearthed by archeologists on the island of Shikoku. Shinto had by then developed all the religious features that it still has. The royal house was occasionally headed by warrior queens.

The splendor and brilliance of China's Tang Dynasty (618–907) inspired Japan to dispatch ambassadors to study and emulate Tang culture. A chief import was Buddhism, which, through its focus on the life of the mind, served as a vehicle to draw ideas about architecture, city planning, medicine, and bureaucratic rule. Other importations were the calendar, Confucianism, and Chinese ideographs. The Japanese borrowed art techniques, too. Recently, in an excavation near Nara, scholars noted that murals depicting seventh-century Japanese court attendants were painted in a style precisely like that of similar Tang Dynasty figures uncovered at about the same time in Shensi Province. "It is difficult to find anywhere in the history of the world any other such successfully planned importation of civilization by a sovereign nation," wrote Ruth Benedict.

In those days, the emperor still ruled, in splendor and in fact, from the ancient capital of Kyoto. Then, in the ninth century, a clan by the name of Fujiwara moved in on the imperial family, using a combination of charm and superior political wisdom. Fujiwara regents dominated boy-emperors until they were old enough to marry Fujiwara brides (fifty-four of them, over the centuries) and rule thereafter under the thumbs of Fujiwara fathers-in-law. Buddhist nonviolence combined with Fujiwara political skill brought three centuries of stability propitious to the ripening of an age of great refinement, romance, and subtlety: the perfumed Heian period (794–1184) documented in the great novel by Lady Murasaki.

By the twelfth century the court in Kyoto had become so obsessed with cultivation and elegance that it forgot to maintain peace. The rising class of knights called samurai began to form into small groups to protect the holdings of local lords. The mystique of the samurai ("one who serves") developed rapidly. Samurai, or at least the richer among them, grew up on horses, carried bows so powerful that it took a couple of men to bend and string them, and used two-handed swords much stronger and sharper than those of Toledo—swords that they tested on the corpses of beheaded criminals, swords capable of slicing crosswise through a man, pelvis and all, at hip level. Samurai armor, in contrast to European plate, was made of lacquered iron scales stitched together with bright silk—strong, flexible, light, and as brilliant as the King of Hearts. The samurai warrior fought man to man, without a shield, and before the slashing began, he announced his pedigree: "I am Takezaki Suenaga, distinguished in several battles, but of little personal worth, and I care nothing whether I live or die in today's conflict."

The ambiguous privilege of self-disembowelment—typically to avoid capture—was a right that the samurai reserved for their own class. One samurai, perturbed that his master hesitated to commit hara-kiri when the occasion demanded it, showed the coward how easy it was by slitting his own stomach and expiring on the spot. Still, the samurai class had its little foibles. Some decapitated friends or allies, just to come back from battle with a head. Many loved a lovely boy—in fact, regarded pederasty as a virtue, and sex with a woman as a weakness. Sometimes clan members fought on both sides in a battle, to make sure of being on the winning side.

By now Japan was in effect divided between two feudal military families, the Minamotos and the Tairas, who between 1156 and 1185 fought in the streets of Kyoto and back and forth across the country for domination of the court. Of this time it was said, "Those who win are the emperor's army, while those who lose are the rebels." A furious naval battle in the Inland Sea elevated a Minamoto named Yoritomo to supremacy, and he took the title of shogun, meaning generalissimo. Japan thereupon went under double governance: the formal reign of the emperor in Kyoto, a carefully maintained illusion; and the effective, private, military government of Yoritomo, the first of many shoguns, ruling from Kamakura, a city thirty miles south of present-day Tokyo.

The Kamakura period initiated seven centuries of militaristic society in Japan—the force of arms being first used to repel invasion, and then to fight civil wars, and finally to seal off Japan and impose the more than two centuries of peace and orderliness of the Tokugawas. In 1274, Kublai Khan, whose hard-riding grandfather, Genghis Khan, had extended the Mongol Empire from the Black Sea through all of China and Korea, prepared to add Japan to his dominions. In 450 ships, Kublai's armies sailed across the Korean Strait and landed in Kyushu. The Mongols had weapons never seen in Japan: crossbows, flaming projectiles, explosive missiles. But the local samurai had their deadly swords, and used them. At the end of the first day both sides withdrew, the Mongols to their ships, which, struck by a storm, sank or blew back to Korea. Kublai girded for a new try, and sent envoys with an ultimatum; Kamakura gave its answer by beheading the envoys. In 1281, in a second attempt, 140,000 Mongols came from Korea and China in two fleets. On the shores of Kyushu the battle swayed for fifty days. Then a two-day typhoon wrecked the invasion ships, and the samurai mopped up the marooned Mongols. The Japanese named this storm Kamikaze, "divine wind," and the belief that providence favored Japan endured clear through to the conception of the Kamikaze suicide pilot in the last days of World War II.

The civil wars, fought with an ever swifter rhythm from 1333 to 1568, were basically conflicts between weak shoguns and restive local lords. Despite the strife, one line of shoguns, the Ashikagas, managed to move from Kamakura to Kyoto and preside over a great flowering of culture, refining the tea ceremony, painting, flower arrangement, and gardening, and building most of Kyoto's handsomest temples. Meanwhile, Japanese seafarers set up small colonies as far south as Sumatra, and, beginning about 1514, they began to sight northbound Portuguese carracks. The first Westerners, three Portuguese, touched Japan on the little island of Tanagashima, south of Kyushu, in 1543, bringing smoothbore muskets that the Japanese bought for models and copied in quantities.

Three formidable warriors then came on stage, one after another, to unify the strife-split country: Nobunaga, Hideyoshi, and Ieyasu. Nobunaga welcomed the Jesuit missionaries who had been led to Japan by Francis Xavier, and soon many of his soldiers were Christians who went into battle with crosses handing from their necks. He pacified most of Honshu, and was departing for similar chores in Kyushu when he was assassinated. The first act of his successor, Hideyoshi, was to build a great castle in Osaka (it still looms over the modern city), and by reducing other castles while defending his own, he made himself master of Japan.

Hideyoshi is the only man in all Japanese history of Napoleonic stature. At first he tolerated the new Christians and their faith, except for its insistence on monogamy. "If this could be changed," he said jovially, "I will become a convert." But he grew fearful that missionaries constituted a fifth column for military conquest, as they had in the Philippines, and in 1597, with conscious irony, he crucified six Spanish Franciscans and twenty of their Japanese friars and lay brothers. By then Japanese Christians numbered three hundred thousand, but subsequent persecution drove them all to recant, depart, or go underground. For Hideyoshi, fear of conquest by foreigners was no reason not to try some conquest of his own. In 1592 he sent two hundred thousand soldiers across the Korea Strait to conquer China.

They rampaged through Korea to the Yalu River. There, just as when General Douglas MacArthur reached the Yalu in 1950 during the Korean War, the Chinese marched a big army to the front and turned back the invasion. A few years later Hideyoshi tried another attack, and, failing again, died.

Now came Ieyasu, a loyal lieutenant to both Nobunaga and Hideyoshi, who while waiting to rise to the top had built himself a power base in Edo (which, as things turned out, is why Tokyo is now the capital and major city of Japan). His family name was Tokugawa: he was the founder of the line of shoguns who sealed off Japan by forbidding the Japanese to go abroad, banning all immigration, and prohibiting the construction of oceangoing (as opposed to coastal) ships. It was Ieyasu who devised the mechanism that kept all other lords helpless against the Tokugawas, requiring them to build palaces in Edo and leave their families there as hostages. Thus began what Richard Halloran calls "the world's most ambitious effort to make time stand still"; and when it turned out, as it always does, that time will not stand still, Japan was ripe for Perry.

To Japan, Perry represented the threat that the nation might be hacked up into foreign concessions, like China, or worse, to be made a colony, like India. The reaction of the shogunate—which was near collapse anyway from inflation, indebtedness, and decadence—was to flounder for a decade or so and expire. The disintegration left the once subordinate local lords free to maneuver for power, and some of them recalled that, formally speaking at least, the emperor had all along been the head of the Japanese state. The formula that they devised for the defense of Japan was: "Venerate the emperor and expel the barbarians"—barbarians being their chosen epithet for the Westerners. Few, if any, of these samurai defined "expel" as the simple ouster of the handful of traders in Yokohama, Kobe, and Nagasaki; nor did they really expect to seal off Japan again. Instead, the word increasingly took on the meaning of studying the West to use the West's own techniques of industrialization and warfare in order to keep Japan independent.

In 1860 a large delegation, including Yukichi Fukuzawa, the boy who had learned Dutch in order to study electricity, undertook the high adventure of becoming the first Japanese mission to visit the United States. In San Francisco, Fukuzawa was astonished at iced champagne, ballroom dancing, wastefulness in the use of iron, and the lack of reverence for the descendants of George Washington. Some of the touring samurai went on to Washington (via Panama) to ratify the first Japanese-American treaty. The gentlemen from Japan were by no means overawed—a session of Congress seemed to them "like the fishmarket in Edo"—and they returned confident that Japan could hold its own with the West.

In 1868, after unbelievable complications (which included the elimination by death of two shoguns and an emperor), Japan's men of power had come to agree in a typical Japanese consensus on the concept of an imperial restoration, to unify Japan and exploit the West in order to contain the West. Sir Harry Parkes, the British ambassador, perceived that if the emperor was about to regain importance, it would be useful to have an audience with His Imperial Highness. Ushered into the Kyoto court, he was shocked to find a boy of fifteen, dressed in white brocade and trailing crimson trousers, face whitened and cheeks rouged, one lip painted gold and the other red, teeth blackened, eyebrows shaved and replaced with painted arches—a kind of stylized and archaic toy-man. This was the Emperor Meiji, in whose name and under whose authority Japan was to be transformed yet again. Nothing could dramatize that change better than the subsequent change in the emperor himself. Only a few years later he was making public appearances in Western military regalia, with braid and sash and medals and white gloves—a truly imperious man with fearless, intelligent eyes, a heavy circumflex mustache, and thick black eyebrows.

A children's "civilization song" written shortly after the Meiji Restoration listed ten Western artifacts that Japan ardently wished to acquire in short order: gas lamps, steam engines, horse carriages, cameras, telegrams, lightning conductors, newspapers, schools, a postal system, and steamboats. But of course the goals of the emperor —or, more precisely, the dedicated young ex-samurai around him— were more profound than mere imitations. They proposed a top-to-bottom modernization of Japan, and they carried it out with skill, hard-headedness, and remarkably few mistakes.

As a sign of new times, the crown moved from fusty Kyoto to Edo, which was renamed Tokyo, "Eastern Capital." In 1871–73, Tomomi Iwakura, a young court noble who helped engineer the fall of the Tokugawa shogunate and went on to become a ranking minister of state for more than a decade, led a mission to the United States and Europe, and came back with the heartening word that the Western governments were only a little ahead of Japan in understanding the nature and uses of power. The mission spurred Japan to shop the world for expertise and technology. Importing thousands of advisers, the country learned about universities, medicine, and civil service from the Germans; government, armies, and the law from the French;

agriculture, post offices, lower schools, and diplomacy from the Americans; railroads, telegraphs, and navies from the British; techniques of painting and sculpture from the Italians.

One reason that Japan modernized so rapidly was that it was able to take over, full-blown, institutions that other nations had developed by trial and error. Example: central banking, modeled on the U.S. Federal Reserve System. Japan swiftly adopted the Gregorian calendar, confusing peasants accustomed to planting and harvesting by the Chinese lunar calendar used since the sixth century. Thus to the Japanese, accustomed to taking the first and fifteenth of each month as days of rest, came the concept of the seven-day week, with Sunday off. One day in 1872, flouting Buddhist precepts, the emperor ate beef, and shortly afterward somebody invented sukiyaki. Japan got the metric system in 1886, Tokyo was wired for electricity in 1887, and a store in Nagoya installed a Western-style counter in 1905 (before that, seller and buyer sat on the floor). In the realm of manners, the Japanese adopted fancy-dress balls, social clubs, toothbrushes, sewing circles, and woolen clothing. But within a decade or so, sensing a loss of Japanese values, they pulled back from excessively aping Westerners.

This wrenching turn from Tokugawa days was an authentic revolution, even though it came from the samurai level, the old top class of society, rather than from the downtrodden proletariat. Some innovators offered proposals as radical as the Social Darwinist idea of large-scale intermarriage with Westerners to change the national gene pool. Others suggested abandonment of the Japanese language as too difficult and arcane. Still others urged Christianizing the entire nation, on grounds that Christianity was the secret of Western success. These projects were all prudently rejected, but the Meiji revolutionists did propose and put across, to some degree at least, a liberal and democratic Charter Oath, in the emperor's name, with clauses that said: "Deliberative assemblies shall be widely established and all matters decided by public discussion"; "The common people . . . shall each be allowed to pursue his own calling so that there may be no discontent"; and "Evil customs of the past shall be broken off and everything based upon the just laws of Nature."

One amazing development was that the feudal lords were readily induced to give back the land they had for so long held in fief, so that it could be subdivided among its actual tillers, the peasants. Another key Meiji switch, breaking sharply with the Tokugawa past and still prevailing in the present, was to let any man rise in society on his merits. In terms of radically changing daily life, the imposed

Meiji revolution was more effective than the violent, popular French Revolution.

For the first few years, Iwakura and other young revolutionary ex-samurai ran the government by means of various councils and legislatures copied half-understood from Western governments. But the idea of representative government was alluring. Though utterly lacking in any tradition of rule by the ballot, the Japanese were well enough educated by this time to grasp the merits of it, and they knew that the exemplary nations of the world—Britain, France, and the United States—practiced it. Again, the idea of a parliamentary government came from the top instead of from the grass roots, and it was adopted slowly and with mistakes both foreseeable and unforeseeable. The first constitution, in 1889, provided that if the newly created Diet (parliament) did not approve the administration's budget, last year's budget would prevail. At once, the administration ruefully discovered what everyone knows nowadays, that it could never get by with as little money as the year before, and therefore had to compromise with the Diet to get funds. The most tragic mistake, which stemmed from copying the Germans, was to make the military accountable to the emperor rather than to civil government. This was the seed of Japanese fascism in the 1930s.

In his travels abroad, Yukichi Fukazawa reported, he had "learned that there were bands of men called political parties—the Liberals and the Conservatives—who were always fighting each other in the government." Japan obligingly acquired some parties of its own. Their arena was the new Diet, and over the ensuing years the parties slowly wrested away from the emperor's advisers the right to fill cabinet posts. In 1918, Hara Kei, the "Great Commoner," was appointed prime minister, the first man not an oligarch or a titled bureaucrat to hold the post.

Despite its adoption of Western political institutions, the Meiji modernization was aimed specifically at "noncolonization," at making the West remove its sticky fingers from Japan. The Americans, British, and French had imposed upon Japan (as they had in China) the concept of extraterritoriality—that is, refusal to allow Japan jurisdiction over foreign citizens living in Japan. If such Westerners were accused of any offense, they were to be tried in their own consular courts. In 1899 the Western nations duly allowed this "fungoid and poisonous growth," as the *Tokio Times* described it, to die. Yet Japan's social and political accomplishments were not crucial factors in the demise of extraterritoriality. Japan had become too impressive an industrial economy to be treated with the arrogance Westerners adopted in dealing with less developed countries. And it had built a military power that demanded respect.

The most intriguing factor in Japanese industrialization was . . . postal savings. The government took upon itself the basic task of getting new industries going. To raise money, it prudently shied away from getting into hock with foreign bankers. Instead, the government raised funds by making it easy for the common people, poor as they were, to practice the Confucian exhortation to save. The industries the government founded with funds collected in this Operation Bootstrap—shipbuilding, mining, machine tools, cotton spinning, woolens, glass—were blatantly sold off to businessmen-insiders at scandalously low prices. But they were nevertheless sound enough to thrive for the national good. Silk reeling and papermaking prospered on their own. Cotton spinning and weaving, employing in slavelike conditions an unending supply of girls from the hinterlands, grew in Osaka and elsewhere. Weaving cheap textiles for Asia came to be a major export industry.

The docile masses were the prerequisite of the Japanese industrialization, but the business houses that took on the infant industries— Mitsui, Mitsubishi, and others—contributed the indispensable elements of shrewdness and patriotism. Unlike the American robber barons of the same era, these Japanese capitalists shunned yachts and mansions and plowed back all their profits. The bad reputation of Japanese manufactured goods in later decades was a consequence not of Japanese incapacity but of the world's desire for cheap goods, particularly during the Depression. Concluding that the West did not want quality, Japanese manufacturers deliberately produced what they called "Yokohama junk."

The modern military machine that the Meiji restorationists began to build from their first days in power quickly demonstrated, as Hideyoshi had, that Japan would not stand for foreign domination but did not mind attempting some domination of its own. As early as 1876, Japan forced Korea to open its ports for trade, much as Perry had forced Japan. Quick learners, these Japanese; soon they were swarming all over Korea. In 1894, when the Chinese (who contended that Korea was a Chinese vassal state) sent troops to quell a rebellion, Japan responded by doing the same, and easily won the ensuing clash. By the peace treaty, Japan won hegemony over Korea, possession of Taiwan, and (Japan thought) a valid claim to the Liaotung Peninsula in Manchuria, site of the Chinese naval base Port Arthur. But the Russians, also coveting Port Arthur as an ice-free base on the Pacific, led France and Germany in forcing Japan to return the peninsula to China—whereupon Russia leased Port Arthur from the Chinese.

Furious at such trickery, Japan in 1904 invaded and seized Port Arthur from the Russians. Russia had already dispatched her Baltic fleet around the Cape of Good Hope to protect Port Arthur. On May 27, 1905, it met the Japanese navy in Tsushima Strait, the southern entrance to the Sea of Japan. Admiral Heihachiro Togo, schooled by the English at Portsmouth, performed a classic "crossing of the T," positioning his warships to fire broadside at the oncoming Russian line, which in turn could bring only its bow guns to bear. Only three of forty-five Russian ships reached Vladivostok; five thousand Russian sailors died, compared to just 117 Japanese. Against mighty Russia, upstart Japan scored the most crushing naval victory in all history. President Theodore Roosevelt, at the Treaty of Portsmouth (New Hampshire), gave Japan supremacy in Korea and Port Arthur— which left Japan violently unhappy, because it wanted reparations too. In 1910, Japan outrightly annexed Korea.

Nominally one of the Allies in World War I, Japan declared war on Germany and with little fighting plucked off choice German-held real estate (Tsingtao and other parts of the Shantung Peninsula) in nonbelligerent China. At the Paris Peace Conference, as a full-fledged big power, Japan also took over Germany's former possessions in the Caroline, Marshall, and Mariana Islands. In Paris, Japan's sense of being the target of racial discrimination caused her to propose an equality clause in the League of Nations covenant. The United States and Britain, fearing Oriental immigration, rejected this suggestion, which fed a slow-growing hatred of the West among the Japanese. (This did not deter the Japanese from swallowing American pop culture in large gulps. Even while their leaders were denouncing Western race prejudice, the Japanese people were singing "Desert Song" and "My Blue Heaven," and raving about Clara Bow in *It*.) During this decade, the military, feeling that civilian government had let the navy down by agreeing to a 5-5-3 ratio for British, American, and Japanese capital ships at the 1922 Washington Naval Conference, increasingly took charge of the nation's foreign affairs. In 1930, naval captain Isoroku Yamamoto, who was to be the mastermind of the attack on Pearl Harbor, went to Washington, dined at the White House, cozied up to President Herbert Hoover's naval aide, and proceeded to negotiate a 10-10-7 ratio at the London Naval Conference.

The military was clearly feeling its oats. The next year, middle-rank officers stationed near Port Arthur blew up a stretch of the South Manchurian Railway and, blaming the Chinese, seized all of

Manchuria. The emperor and the civil government not only felt unable to admonish the army for this breach of discipline, but also went along with the renaming of Manchuria as Manchukuo and setting up a puppet emperor there. Many Japanese, in fact, looked with favor on the army's expansionism. They felt that big Western "have" countries with plenty of room and resources of their own had grabbed colonies all over Asia (the Philippines, Indochina, Indonesia, Malaya, and so on) with much less need for them than "have-not" Japan. The military, pressuring Japanese big business to invest in Manchukuo, soon made the puppet land the most heavily industrialized area of mainland Asia.

All this created the justification, when some never-identified Chinese soldiers fired on Japanese troops at the Marco Polo Bridge near Peking in 1937, for the beginning of the great Japanese attempt to conquer all of China—in effect the beginning of World War II, or, as John Toland puts it, "the first giant step to war with America," China's ally. In fifteen months, the Japanese took Peking, Tientsin, and Hankow, penetrating more than five hundred miles into China and overrunning almost the whole northeastern quarter of that huge country. At Nanking, in a deliberately intimidating display of brutality scarcely ever surpassed anywhere, Japanese soldiers and sailors, full of freely dispensed sake, murdered 150,000 Chinese and raped 5,000 women.

In this brutality, the Japanese showed, besides the universal cruelty of war, their own particular proneness to lose humanity when their specific and customary rules of behavior do not seem to apply. Yet many present-day Japanese, and not only superheated nationalists, look back on the late 1930s and find a strong note of "purity." The soldiers were mostly rugged, simple peasants' sons, and in their young officers they thought they found allies against wicked big business and corrupt politicians. The military was "sincere"; the military fought social injustice; the military supported and adored the godlike emperor and the Japanese spirit that he stood for; the military signified the stern virtues of the samurai code.

More realistically, this was a time when Japan went half insane, perhaps subconsciously sensing the doom ahead. As novelist Junichiro Tanizaki shows in *The Makioka Sisters*, millions of sensible people went about their ordinary lives and worried about such problems as unmarriageable kin, but all the while young army extremists killed politicians for incomprehensible motives, the "thought police" tried to prevent the thinking of "dangerous thoughts," and secret societies with names like Black Ocean or Black Dragon hovered over the nation like the Ku Klux Klan. Pusillanimously, political parties threw in the towel, racing to see which could be quickest to join the Imperial Rule Assistance Association, a "reasonable facsimile of the Nazi party," formed in 1940. Children on the streets called every Westerner a "spy." An Irish priest who lived through this time told me that "on a ten-kilometer train trip, you had to tell the police where you were going, and tell them again, and still get checked over and over as you went."

As they looked around the world, the Japanese armed forces, the big businessmen, and even the common people were horrified by the growth of Communism. Not sufficiently confident of their own democracy, stunted as it was by the military, they resignedly admired the strength and authority of Communism's enemies, Nazism and Fascism. Japan renounced the game of golf, took down the signs in English in the railroad stations, and gave up ballroom dancing.

By 1941, the military-dominated Japanese government had come to think of all East Asia as Japan's own province, and casuistically conceived of Japan's war in China as a positive boon to the Chinese. Whether for racial, paternalistic, or merely acquisitive reasons, many Japanese had decided that it was their fate to save Asia for the Asians. For this purpose they had created what was grandly called the Greater East Asia Co-Prosperity Sphere—a sort of Oriental Manifest Destiny. Taking a leaf from their new ally Nazi Germany, the Japanese also talked of the need for *Lebensraum* on continental Asia for the over-crowded Japanese islands.

By the momentum of their own rhetoric, by the ambitions of their military, by the illogic of racism and of misunderstood history, the Japanese pressed toward Pearl Harbor and a confrontation that they could not win. The military hoped that the blow would wound the United States so seriously that Japan could fortify its conquered territory strongly enough to force the Americans to seek peace. The Japanese badly miscalculated the American character as they have so often miscalculated the reactions and personalities of other peoples. One might say that the Japanese thoroughly understand only the Japanese.

From these extraordinary ambitions, these preferred but unaccepted empathies with other Asians, these miscalculations of the American opposition, Japan pulled down on its head much of what it had so painstakingly built up since Meiji times. The structure that has arisen from the ashes of that cataclysm is the extraordinary land that is modern-day Japan.

PART TWO ❧ *Places*

12 /

A Ride on the Pea-Green Line

MODERN TOKYO, the Tokyo that invented itself after the disaster of the firebombs, is a gaudy city, green, lilac, and scarlet, dignified here and disheveled there, vertiginous, sprawling, poisonous, and lovely— all at once. If London seems a genial old trollop, and New York a high-fashion model, then Tokyo is a strident hoyden. In bursting change and constant fascination, Tokyo rivals any city in the world. It is obscenely addicted to neon and advertising hoopla, but to those lucky enough not to read Japanese the hustle is pure heraldic pop art: bright, many-charactered royal banners hang four stories long from the department stores, and the fluorescent escutcheons of bars and night clubs glow in countless alleys. Tokyo has Big Money, Big Government, Big Garbage. Tokyo has geishas, rivers, palms, mansions, monorails, and a genuine emperor. It also has an awful lot of crows.

The American fire-bombers left Tokyo's old wooden residential areas a flattened expanse of ashes and 72,489 bodies, punctuated by three kinds of blackened metal: sewing machines, safes, and machine lathes—lathes that had been used in cottage industry for the Japanese war effort. Now, scanning the city from the 750-foot-high observation deck of Tokyo Tower, a super-Eiffel shaft supporting television transmitters, you see no sign whatsoever of damage, but instead a megalopolis of Western-style buildings and—a surprise to me—trees and grass. The dry statistics prove that Tokyo devotes a far smaller proportion of its surface to greenery than, say, New York, but there are parks and parklets, 250 of them, and temple gardens, and playgrounds, and hundreds of paulownia-lined streets, and a large, looming isle of verdant peace smack in center city, the Imperial Palace. Off in the distance are the gardens of Meiji shrine, with lotuses and fish in its ponds, and a dazzling display of irises every June.

Prodigies and spectacles and curiosities smite the eye in Tokyo. Vast commercial villages, little subcities really, have been carved out underground, and you can stroll for many kilometers in these caves. Looking up from the streets, you see huge numbers—13, 5, 21, 17— floating in the air, like some surreal Steinberg cartoon: they turn out to be signs on the roofs of skyscrapers indicating the order of their acquisition by an ambitious real estate firm, which now owns twenty-five major Tokyo buildings. A shower starts, and suddenly Tokyo is a moil of umbrellas—pink, polka dot, orange, striped, black, peach, chartreuse. I remember glimpses of a parade with the all-Japanese band playing "The Marine Hymn," of the slimy black mud of a building excavation, and of lanterns floating on the palace moat during the annual festival for the souls of the dead.

Just after the war, devastated Tokyo, which has intermittently been the world's largest city for centuries, held only 3,500,000 people. Its growth since then to the point of containing one-tenth of the whole Japanese population is a measure of the astonishing energy poured into reconstruction and of the irresistible allure of the big city's jobs, its bright lights, and its 102 universities. Is it again the world's largest city? Its twenty-three wards (*ku*) contain 8,800,000 people, fewer than the 10,820,000 in Shanghai and more than the 7,895,000 in New York City and the 7,570,000 in Peking, the next-ranking cities according to the figures in the United Nations *Demographic Yearbook*. But the Tokyo Metropolitan Government, which is the basic unit of government in the sense that the five-borough government of New York is, includes areas that build the total population to 11,600,000. And physically contiguous, though governmentally separate, are Kawasaki, a sort of bigger, unglorified Newark, with 1,000,000, and the port of Yokohama, with 2,500,000. In any case, no city, least of all Tokyo, wants to be No. 1 any more; the Tokyo Metropolitan Government, swamped already with the environmental problems of excessive population, hopes to contain the city's growth at 12,180,000 people in 1990. Nearly 750,000 move into Tokyo from other parts of Japan every year, but they are balanced by an equal or larger number who move out, many of them disillusioned and defeated by the difficulties—bad housing, high prices, and pollution —of metropolitan life.

In the most desirable business districts of Tokyo nowadays, land sells for so much that a piece as big as the page you are reading, were it possible to buy such a snippet, would cost $400. Multiplied out, this means that a square foot costs $1,500, an area the size of an average American house lot $15 million, and an acre $66 million (as compared to $100 per square foot on Fifth Avenue in Manhattan). Some consequences are that the land under an ordinary residence (though of course far cheaper than business-district property) is worth many times as much as the building; that developers suffer in trying to piece together a site for skyscrapers, because any owner of a single lot in a jigsaw pattern of land can afford to hold out for a higher price; and that Tokyo is compressed and miniaturized by the exorbitant value of space. People sit thigh to thigh at bars because the bar stool occupies a surface area worth a couple of thousand dollars. Houses even in the periphery stand eave to eave because of the price of land.

Precisely because it is compacted, Tokyo's vast physical size is all the more awesome. The metropolis of Tokyo occupies 796 square miles (compared to Los Angeles' 458), and any of its twenty-three wards would make a sizable city if transplanted elsewhere. Tokyo's 2.4 million cars drive on 12,000 miles of roads that cross 5,800 bridges over 1,300 miles of canals. There are 50,000 bars and 32,500 restaurants.

If crowding leads to crime, as Western sociology would have it, Tokyo should be a death trap. But Tokyo has the lowest crime rate of any major city in the world, and the rate is dropping. In 1973, Detroit, with 1.5 million people, suffered 741 homicides; Tokyo, with seven times as many, had 213. In New York City in 1970, 538 persons were murdered with handguns; in Tokyo, in the same year, 3!

Why this happy situation? In the background are such crime-reducing factors as low unemployment, racial homogeneity, high education, traditional respect for law and order. More concretely, Toyko has 42,420 policemen—somewhat more, proportionately, than New York—and these well-trained, cool-headed men know their beats intimately. Police stations, instead of being large and few, are small boxes so numerous (1,242) that one can always be found in a couple minutes' walk. Working out of these boxes, largely on foot, policemen have specific responsibility for about 150 households each. Visting each household twice a year, the Tokyo policeman keeps close tabs on his neighborhood, and when a crime occurs, the cops usually know whom to arrest.

One day while I was riding an elevated train of the Yamanote Line in Tokyo, a courtly gentleman in his sixties sat down beside me, introduced himself by presenting a card that identified him as the overseas trade manager for a large gauge-manufacturing company, and remarked in antebellum English: "Very brave for foreigner to go on electric train!" Not at all, I assured him, not at all, for by then I had discovered not only that the pea-green cars of the Yamanote (Uptown) Line were safe, and non-electrocuting, but also that they constituted the organizing principle of the geography of Tokyo.

The Yamanote Line, which is part of the Japanese National Railways, forms a rough circle—twenty-one miles of double track that touches or encloses all that is most interesting about Tokyo. Its twelve-car trains, painted pea green as a color code to distinguish them from those of tangential lines that share various stretches of the route, go endlessly round and round in both directions, one every two minutes and forty seconds, stopping at twenty-nine stations and taking an hour for the circuit. On a map, the Yamanote Line looks like a wheel drawn by a Cubist, with the Imperial Palace as the off-center hub. Subways, like spokes, give access to the enclosed city.

The pea-green line begins, if a circular railroad can be said to have a beginning, at one of Tokyo's new skyscrapers, the World Trade Center Building, terminal of the monorail from Haneda Airport, which is on Tokyo Bay to the southeast. Take the train going north. The first stop is Shinbashi, a glitteringly dowdy district where dozens of plastic surgeons stand ready to do round-eye jobs and breast amplifications. The next stop is Yurakucho, where the pace, diversity, and excitement of this dizzying city begin to rise like heat from a summer pavement. Two blocks west is the landmark Imperial Hotel, a Hiltonish hulk much favored as a rendezvous. Right at the Yurakucho exit sits the bulky, vaguely Moorish building that houses the stripteases and other piccadilly titillations of the Nichigeki nest of theaters. Next to it is the somber pile of the newspaper *Asahi Shimbun*. Like many solid, old Tokyo structures, the buildings of Nichigeki and *Asahi* date from before the war; firebombs did not greatly damage heavy masonry. This small Times Square is, naturally, equipped with a vertical ribbon sign up which skitter incandescent ideographs giving the news. On rooftops are a nostalgic His Master's Voice dog advertising the products of the Victor Company of Japan, and other fantasies of neon art. At the nearby Sony Building, a car can plunge underground, spiral down through several floors of a parking garage, and fetch up in front of . . . Maxim's of Paris—a nearly exact copy of the famed *fin de siècle* restaurant at 3 rue Royale.

A few steps along the broad street leading east, and one arrives at the Ginza, and in a few steps more, at that architectural delight, the Kabuki theater. The Ginza is a district with a split personality:

the daytime's sedate, eight-block main avenue, and the nighttime's tangle of tiny streets just off it. Fronting the avenue, which is lined with handsome, neo-Oriental mercury lamps, are the substantial Greek, Italian, and modern buildings of smart fashion shops, modish international restaurants, jewelers, tailors, and six massive department stores. At the curbs, black-uniformed chauffeurs flick feather dusters over waiting limousines, and on the sidewalks American Hare Krishna monks in saffron robes jangle tambourines and chant. Even the most dignified stores temptingly set out merchandise on the sidewalk—toys and flowers and children's clothes in little white wire carts. The Ginza of the night contains 1,600 night clubs and 1,500 restaurants, mostly in rather ramshackle buildings that sit on top-price land. Many are cheap and good, but the cabarets with hostesses prefer customers with large personal fortunes or inexhaustible expense accounts: roughly $1 million per night is dropped in this communal seraglio. The hostesses are pretty, complaisant girls who profit according to the number of drinks they can induce a man to buy.

Someone told me that the three main themes of Japanese popular music are rain, harbors—and bar hostesses. Hostesses light your cigarettes, bring tidbits of raw octopus, and tell you, perhaps, about their aspirations to rise from daytime occupations as beauty operators to full ownership of a beauty parlor. Ginza chic requires paying whatever bill the proprietor presents, and, just to be droll, bars favor "wild" prices like $50 for a whiskey. "There's no relationship between how much the customer drinks and how much the bill will be," says one bar owner. "The only consideration is how much the customer seems to be able to pay." Incidentally, Tokyo also has ten bars that offer hosts instead of hostesses. In one of them, 130 men stand ready to dance with or talk to any girl who has enough money to pay for the costly drinks.

Ginza Avenue's northern extension crosses a wide canal on Nihonbashi bridge, which was such a focus of the bustling life of old Edo that distances to all parts of Japan were measured from there. I made a point of standing on Nihonbashi for half an hour. The present bridge, built in 1911, would look well over the Seine, with its bronze lions and lanterns and lovely entrance gardens at both ends. But a new expressway, constructed over and along the canal, makes a sort of roof for both the canal and the bridge, and the noise in this echo chamber brings to mind Cole Porter's "roaring traffic's boom." The canal itself, with waterbugs skating on it, is the color of used lubricating oil, as foul as a Bangkok klong. This is bank and broker country; the canal is walled in by building after muscular building of Japan's most substantial companies. But just behind the ponderous stone façades of finance I could see slatternly houses stilted over the canal, with laundry flying and garbage tossed overboard. Tokyo is a spicy stew.

Tokyo Station, next north on the pea-green line, is the vast terminal for innumerable trains (including bullet trains) that go to Nagoya, Osaka, Kyoto, and the west of Japan. By its very presence, the station has generated the biggest of Tokyo's underground shopping cities. This arcade is named Yaesu, which is the Japanese pronunciation of Jan Joosten, the name of a Dutch sailor who was shipwrecked in 1600 and drifted to Edo. He lived on this spot and served as a consultant on European affairs for the shogun. Like other underground cities in all big Japanese cities, this one occupies several acres of space dug out from under streets and plazas, and includes part or all of the basements of adjacent buildings and the station, which thus provide entrances to it.

These subterranean palaces of commerce flourish, despite dangers from earthquakes and fires, because they let shoppers avoid wheeled traffic and pick up purchases quickly on their way to or from the station. At Yaesu, to the sound of Hawaiian ukuleles on the Muzak, I stepped off five hundred paces in a straight line, passing stores selling candy, cameras, art, shoes, clocks, telescopes, Gordon's gin, and Arrow shirts. Then, wandering the air-conditioned corridors, I counted ninety-three restaurants. Every major stop on the Yamanote Line has a similar arcade for spelunking shoppers.

Only three blocks west of Tokyo Station lies the moat of the Imperial Palace, embanked with huge stones laid in a herringbone pattern. Along this waterfront, which reminds one of the Seine, runs an eight-lane boulevard back of which stand massive office buildings mostly just exactly 101.68 feet (31 meters) high. These rectangular buildings, plus nearly identical ones on the streets between the moat and station, make up Marunouchi (Ma-ru-no-u-chi), Tokyo's headquarters area for five thousand Japanese and foreign corporations, large and small. It was here, in Edo times, that feudal lords from the provinces built their obligatory mansions, to house their hostage families. The Emperor Meiji turned the area over to Baron Iwasaki, founder of the Mitsubishi trust, to develop.

"Marunouchi was a London idea, imported during the Meiji period," architect Yoshinobu Ashihara explained to me, meaning that the area was to be stately and dignified. The first buildings were behemoths in red brick, but they have nearly all been replaced by even solider structures of steel, glass, glazed brick, and marble. The area's present heir and owner, Mitsubishi Estate Company, quietly boasts that this sixty acres is the most valuable swatch of land in the world, being worth perhaps $2.4 billion without including its buildings. Grassy strips, planted with azaleas and carnations interspersed with intriguing small modern sculptures, line the middle streets, which throng at noon with the half a million people who work here, among them hundreds of Japan's highest business executives. Wildenstein, Alfred Dunhill, Georg Jensen, St. Laurent, and similar gentry (discreetly identified; bold signs would be in bad taste) keep store in Marunouchi, and airline offices occupy the fringes. Such exclusive cliques as Tokyo's Union Club—a hushed salon with gold-striped carpeting and walls of diagonal cypress planks —have their being in the upper floors of Marunouchi buildings. Amid the humdrum traffic, splendid but sober-colored American cars, with left-hand steering wheels, roll in stately dignity along the streets of what is sometimes called "Mitsubishi Village," projecting the aura of dignitaries who expect the common pedestrian to bow as they pass.

The uniform eight-story height of many of Marunouchi's buildings obeys old laws to reduce possible earthquake damage, but the Diet abolished the restriction in 1963. Since then, thirteen buildings between ten and twenty-five stories high have gone up in Marunouchi. For its own use, Mitsubishi put up an enormous fifteen-story building of hammered granite and precast concrete, and in the new structure's basements installed equipment to heat and air-condition all the buildings in the area.

The pea-green train continues north and passes Kanda, which Tokyo proffers as its version of Paris's Latin Quarter or Munich's Schwabing. One hundred thirty bookstores, mostly dealing in rare and antique volumes, stand door to door here in one of the few unbombed old areas of Tokyo, and no less than eleven colleges and universities surround and patronize them. Many book publishers center in Kanda.

Ueno, still farther north, is the Tokyo terminal for trains to northern Japan. Right at the station door, in Ueno Park, are the Metropolitan Festival Hall, a sort of one-building Lincoln Center, and the city's four main art and science museums, plus the zoo. Connoisseurs tell me that the Tokyo children's zoo outdoes San Diego's. The pandas, Kangkang and Lanlan, gifts of Chou En-lai, loll around in air-conditioned quarters with bulletproof glass, a pool, and—just in case—a delivery room. Back beyond the park is Tokyo University.

The shop-lined passageway called Nakadori is a choice example of a narrow Tokyo shopping street: I spotted Ecuadorian bananas, Apollo 17 billed caps, live squid, Parker pens, and even such a bizarre item as a copy of *Uniforms and Badges of the Third Reich.*

Eastward lies Asakusa, redolent of ancient sin. For centuries, in Asakusa's walled brothel area, a network of streets that were collectively called Yoshiwara, samurai and merchants and Kabuki playwrights picked and chose from girls displayed in cages, girls engaged in nothing so crass as whoring but rather (as the Japanese word puts it) in "selling spring." Yoshiwara was the first part of Tokyo rebuilt after the earthquake in 1923, and again after the bombing in 1944–45, whereupon the men of the American Occupation gave it one last wild fling. When the Diet outlawed prostitution in 1958, Yoshiwara became the home of many establishments labeled with the English word "Turkey," this being the accepted rendition of "Turkish bath." In a street of dim violet light from the neon of these massage parlors, taxis roll up all evening long to discharge men who desire the ministrations of the girls upstairs.

Asakusa teems with shopping arcades and stalls. I happened to see some visiting turbaned Sikhs, with wives in saris, poking around among meat cleavers, plastic abacuses, geisha shoes, playing cards depicting Japanese animals, and cakes shaped like pagodas, baked in front of one's eyes. To make ends meet, the Asakusa Hongan-ji Buddhist temple incorporates a hairdressing parlor and a kindergarten, and offers lessons in flower arrangement and the tea ceremony. Right across the street from the temple is one of Tokyo's innumerable modern and respectable-looking hotels that specialize in letting rooms—some with mirrored ceilings and vibrating beds—for two hours of dalliance. Rate, $6—bring your own girl.

From Ueno the pea-green trains run north, west, and then south, through eight miles of city containing 67,000 people per square mile, and reach Shinjuku, directly across the wheel from Tokyo Station. The Tokyo Station area and Ueno were parts of old Edo; Shinjuku was an independent village, a day's travel to the west for the litter-born traffic of the times. Shinjuku means "New Town," for the unarguable reason that it was new when established in 1699. Now Shinjuku is new in another sense: it threatens Marunouchi-Ginza as the most important center in this capital of many centers. Tokyo's center of gravity is gradually moving westward. Ten years ago, Shinjuku still seemed villagy. Then bulldozers, cosmetizing Tokyo for the 1964 Olympics, flattened the dreary houses west of the station, and the metropolitan government decommissioned an adjacent reservoir. The luxurious, 1,057-room Keio Plaza Hotel, forty-seven stories high, went up where water aerators had once spouted. Opened in 1971, this lofty slab, full of tapestries and sculpture, is popular with Americans and airline crews. The Sumitomo business group soon surpassed the Keio Plaza with a small-windowed, fifty-two-story tower built on a triangular base, and capable of swaying six feet at the top in a strong earthquake. Mitsui Real Estate Company later topped Sumitomo with a fifty-story X-braced building, the tallest in Asia.

Shinjuku Station is the busiest in Japan. It is the doorway to the central city for 3.5 million commuters a day (as compared to 200,000 at Manhattan's Grand Central). They come on a major artery of the Japanese National Railways and on three private railways, each terminating in one of the banner-bedecked department stores that flank the station plaza. Enormous sculptures like a steamship's stacks embellish this square; and under it is another square, a pedestrian mall; and under that another, a huge parking garage. Long subterranean streets branch off to the lower levels of stores and office buildings in the vicinity. The place seethes with humanity. One night I saw fifty or sixty alpinists, shod in heavy hiking boots, sleeping on the floor of an underground passageway at Shinjuku as they waited for a train to the mountains.

The Tokyo tippler who can't afford the Ginza goes to Shinjuku. Near the station are bright Babylonian warrens of *boîtes*, theaters, bathhouses, pachinko parlors, hotels, student dives, and faintly sinister mah-jongg gambling dens. Several times I went "ladder drinking" (to use the Japanese expression for bar hopping) in Shinjuku with friends. The saloon called Donzoko has bars on three levels interconnected by a tight little spiral staircase; college students jammed into them were singing "Que Será, Será" and drinking diluted whiskey. Happy Jack's was what Shinjuku calls a "mammoth bar": 160 boys and girls, all aged around twenty-five, sat at counters and in booths swilling beer under a black ceiling; an upstairs café presented, under purple lights, a guitarist and orgasmic photographs of Marilyn Monroe. At Teatro, stone-walled and hung with nautical ropes and lanterns, a singer sang a song of Sartre and Marx and of the unpredictability of the world. Somewhere along the line I spotted a nude statue of Raquel Welch, doubtless unauthorized. Many homosexual men sauntered along the sidewalks. At Don Taro, tiled, strung with ears of corn, and ornate with ironwork, lovers sat smiling at one another, while a girl in a canvas apron labeled "Tomato" served them drinks. We ended the night at midnight—that is to say, early, like all Japanese ladder hops—at one of many bars in Shinjuku run by Okinawans, drinking that island's *awamori*, a brandy made from rice or sweet potatoes.

Shibuya, just south of Shinjuku, is another once-ratty area of Tokyo transformed by prosperity and the Olympics. Its Yoyogi Park is the site of the nautilus-shaped stadiums put up for swimming and basketball, plus running tracks and other sports settings. NHK's chamfer-cornered high-rise headquarters and its Music Hall raise Shibuya's tone by many notches. Nearby a branch of San Francisco's Joseph Magnin sells handbags, jewelry, and high-fashion ready-to-wear—priced from $200 to $700—in the first American retail store opened (in 1973) in Japan. Under the beamed ceiling of the Play Bach night club, not far away, I noticed a Japanese in a tight red jacket with blue and white stripes, a striped gray shirt, and a knitted green tie with an enormous knot—a coiffed and brittle young dandy, obviously intending to be seen, drinking Scotch at $3.30 a shot. Seductive hostesses lounged at low, flute-legged walnut tables, awaiting invitations. In small dark streets off the station plaza, fortune-tellers sat at tiny tables and read palms by flashlight. Such is Shibuya.

Near the southernmost curve of the Yamanote Line, the pea-green trains pause at Gotanda (Five Rice Fields), where we lived for several months. Like most station plazas throughout Japan, Gotanda's is broad, open, clean, decorated with a few pieces of sculpture, awash with buses and taxis, and crossed by a set of pedestrian overpasses. Fronting the plaza are a bakery, a sumptuous confectionery, a small supermarket, a well-patronized store selling sake and beer, a film and camera shop, and a stand with pyramids of tangerines. Politicians shout in the plaza, and causists press their causes. One day earnest young men were handing out pamphlets urging the extinguishing of gas stoves during earthquakes. Nightly a noodle vendor sets up his stand and lights his gasoline lantern. Enticing alleys, their pavements regularly wetted, lead off the plaza past the glowing Japanese lanterns into a maze of broiled-chicken-on-a-stick counters and tiny dives. In their midst stands a six-story building containing floor upon floor of assorted bars and restaurants, topped by a beer garden, a zephyrean aerie with fir trees, director's chairs, a waterfall, and a good view of the flashing neon sign advertising the neighborhood two-hour hotel.

It takes seven minutes to walk from Gotanda Station along a broad avenue for a few blocks, then uphill through narrow, crooked streets, to the Japanese-Western cottage where we lived. The clamor of the plaza dies away. Many of the houses of this middle-level neighborhood seem to be imitations of Southern California imitations of the Spanish-American *casa*. The colors are the porous creaminess of the volcanic stone of the walls that surround each residence, and the greens of ivy and bayonet palms. The commoners who are the parents of the crown princess live somewhere nearby, I was told. One neighbor liked to walk his monkey in the quiet streets.

On those summer days when we were there, the sun rose at five thirty, and the squeal of the newsboy's bicycle brake served like an oboist sounding his A to start an orchestration of natural sounds, dominated by one specific bird and one specific insect. The standout bird was one of Tokyo's multitudinous crows, flapping and cawing in the trees above us. The standout insect was the cicada, "the large and lazy cicada," as Lafcadio Hearn wrote, "sipping only dew, and singing from dawn till dusk." The Japanese cicada, a filmy-winged beetle two inches long, is really more than a singer; he is a national treasure. Each morning crickets, doves, tomtits, jackdaws, chipmunks, and the plunk of a dripping air conditioner joined this auroral concerto, working up to an unbelievable rustic din—all well within the boundaries of heavily urbanized Tokyo. We breakfasted as the day's growing heat muted the birds and the bugs, and then I generally walked to the station and caught the pea-green train east and north to Yurakucho or Tokyo Station.

Inside the loop of this string-of-pearls railroad, there is a single block, in front of the Ministry of International Trade and Industry (MITI), from which in a two-minute stroll one can see all the power points centered in the great and potent district of Tokyo known as Kasumigaseki: the ziggurat-towered Diet building, which is across the street from the prime minister's official residence; the Ministries of Finance, Foreign Affairs, Education, Construction, and Health and Welfare; the Metropolitan Police Department headquarters; the garden-surrounded Kasumigaseki Building, which plays a role something like Rockefeller Center's NBC Building, and is a neighbor of the U.S. Embassy; the potent Mitsui Bank; Marunouchi's sedate financial centers; and the moated grounds of the Imperial Palace itself.

In other words, great Tokyo, extending farther than the eye can see from the tallest tower, has a heart, and Kasumigaseki is its name. And the heart speaks a message: power must be concentrated—or, at any rate, is concentrated. Government, diplomacy, finance, commerce, the gendarmerie, and the imperial symbol of the state are pulled together in one place, Kasumigaseki. Thus by its geography Tokyo demonstrates the kernel of truth in the concept of Japan, Inc.

The business tycoon who wants to see the prime minister, the ambassador who wants to see the foreign minister, the banker who wants to see the finance minister, the exporter who wants to see the MITI minister—and vice versa in each case—are all physically near one another.

The potentates of Kasumigaseki do much business after hours in teahouses and restaurants, and nearby Akasaka provides plenty of them. Flamboyant new hotels line the main avenue through this quarter, and the U.S. government still hangs on to an old hotel, the Sanno, an Occupation-era landmark, as a billeting place. Dollars and cents, not yen, are the currency in its bars and dining rooms. Foreigners, particularly rich Americans, tend to live in Akasaka and the expanse on southward to another sub-center of this segmented city, Roppongi ("Six Trees"). Nights at Roppongi Crossing, the hub of the district, are incandescent, by any definition and at any time of the year. The broad windows of the five-layered restaurant buildings are like bright-colored ukiyoe prints of gluttony, sophistication, energy, gaiety, and animation. The costumes of the passing girls one July night included halters, hound's-tooth caps, tank tops, kimonos, postage-stamp miniskirts, demure knee socks, and a black-and-white-checkerboard skirt suit; and of the men: ice-cream suits, umbrellas furled London-style, and (on one Nipponese dude) buckled knee boots, blue jeans, checkered shirt, shades, and cowboy hat. Blond Swedish girls walk by with bearded American blacks. The light from flashing signs turns faces green and lemon. One restaurant advertises with the silhouetted likenesses of twelve huge lambs—it serves mutton, one presumes.

Away from the crossing runs a street marked with a wooden historical-information post that identifies the area as the Edo-period Toriizaki (Hill of the Shrine Gate); the former estate of Baron Iwasaki, founder of the Mitsubishi zaibatsu, lies to one side. At the end of Toriizaki, on a cross street called the Juban, people flock on Tuesday nights, to an Edo-style street fair. They buy wind-bells, birdcages, pet shellfish that can climb ladders, and plastic kits to build models of the World War II aircraft carrier *Kaga*, sunk at the Battle of Midway.

Tokyo as outlined by the pea-green trains, Tokyo as towns grown together in the manner of Kensington, Westminster, Southwark, and the City of London, Tokyo as a nucleus defining a metropolis as Manhattan defines New York City, Tokyo as a geographical personality, a "downtown," a power center—this Tokyo measures only about thirty square miles, one twenty-fifth of the area of the whole metropolis. What meets the eye in the expanses beyond, according to a note I made on some Tokyo commuter train that reminded me of a Port Washington express whooshing through Queens, is "one-fourth greenery, one-fourth dark wood, one-fourth masonry, and one-fourth Coca-Cola signs." Some planning and some rebuilding—chiefly the broadening, straightening, and interconnecting of the many main avenues—went into central Tokyo after the war, but very little into the suburbs. "We Japanese are very bad at overall planning; our technique is addition," remarks architect Ashihara; but that's not a dead loss, he adds, because the result is humanistic and has a discernible internal order.

Villages-within-the-city, like northwestern Jujo, a long train ride from the Ginza but yet nowhere near the edge of the built-up megalopolis, are sociable and livable; children play under the sun, advertising banners suspended from balloons float in the sky, and the fruit-store man is obviously a local celebrity. Well-to-do Denenchofu, to the southwest, has streets shaded by ancient cherry trees, a quaint Scarsdale-like railroad station, and tennis courts where Davis Cup matches are played, reminiscent of Forest Hills. By contrast, Takashimadaira, thirty minutes by subway north of the Imperial Palace, sacrifices human scale to pack 36,000 people into the sixty-six 14-story buildings of a *mammosu-danchi*, mammoth housing project. You can stroll endlessly among these buildings, but the view is always the same: the Mondrian pattern of rectangular concrete, housewives thumping comforters hung from balconies, babies learning to walk in paved geometrical gardens. Each end wall carries a large number to help residents find their way home. "Takashimadaira, is it good?" asks a note I made to myself while viewing it, and answers, "Well, people have to live."

Dense, conglomerated Tokyo contains yet one more surprise: emptiness. Three hundred and forty-six thousand—repeat, 346,000— farmers raise crops on land enclosed by urbanization in the metropolitan area. Out westward, one notes that a goodly number of the residents of Tokyo are Holstein cows. These city farmers hang on to land in the perfectly valid expectation that the price of it will rise to delirious heights as the pressure grows for more space for housing. Odder yet, there are parts of Tokyo that lie a thousand miles from the city: the Tokyo Metropolitan Government has jurisdiction over the Seven Islands of Izu, pleasant recreation spots stretching 150 miles south into the Pacific, and south of that, the Bonin Islands, including Iwo Jima, scene of the famous American-flag-raising after one of the war's bitterest battles. The United States returned the Bonins, which measure only about twenty-seven square miles in total area, to Japan in 1968. The Japanese figure there are about twenty Bonins (they call them the Ogasawara Islands), but the number varies as volcanic action raises one out of the sea or drops another back—a new one was born in December 1973. Tokyo's islands altogether hold eleven thousand people, but only thirteen hundred of them live in the Bonins.

It is said that a seventeenth-century shogun decreed a higgledy-piggledy pattern for Edo streets and banned street names and numbers to prevent his enemies from finding his palace. Streetly anonymity prevailed until the American Occupation, which found a way to designate avenues from A to Z and streets from 1 to 60. When the Occupation ended, Tokyo quietly ditched this tidy system, but the city fathers did give names to each main boulevard, or *dori*. They are, moreover, labeled in Roman letters as well as ideographs. Thus: Sotoboridori for the outer ring avenue around the Imperial Palace, Shinjukudori for the avenue that runs from the palace to Shinjuku. But Tokyo is a city of crooked streets off avenues, and winding alleys off streets, and lanes off alleys, and passageways off lanes—and almost none of these have names. Finding a strange place can be maddening. A major function of the cops in all those police boxes is to give directions. Neighborhoods display prominent signboard maps showing individual houses and the names of the occupants.

If it is often hard to find an exact address in Tokyo, it is rarely hard to get near. The 94-mile-long subway system (in 1985 the mileage will be 200), which crisscrosses the area within the Yamanote loop and pushes some tentacles out beyond, is spotlessly clean, mostly new, and easy to travel. Machines sell tickets priced from thirteen to forty-three cents, depending on the distance to be traveled, and the gatemen, mostly young fellows with long hair flowing from beneath their uniform caps, stab the tickets with punches clicking like castanets. The trainmen have a certain gallantry: as the tail end of a train whips out of a station, the conductor and the platform man exchange military salutes (a signal, I was told, of the transfer of legal responsibility for the passengers).

The famous Tokyo *rushawa* (rush hour) crush seems to be succumbing to the amplification of services, but by diligent searching I found one at eight thirty in the morning on the central Tokyo interchange station called Akasakamitsuke. Throngs were spewing out of Marunouchi Line trains, arriving every two minutes, in numbers too great for Ginza Line trains, departing every two minutes, to carry away. But just before eight thirty, a couple of dozen white-gloved young men materialized on the platforms. These were the notorious "pushers," mostly students working part-time. They courteously formed the incoming throngs into three-abreast columns spaced as far apart as train doors, and guided the surge when a train arrived. When the car was packed, the pushers began to push, and managed to force in thirty more passengers per car. Then the pushers leaned against the last boarders until the doors closed, something like a zipper sealing an overstuffed suitcase. I lined up and got pushed aboard, and found the ride safe (not a chance of falling down) and tolerable (I could breathe). The rushawa lasted just about one awa. On subway rides at other times, most people find it possible to sit down on the velvet-upholstered (and, tribute to Japanese lawfulness, rarely slashed or burned) seats and read (books, not newspapers), or cat-nap.

While Tokyo waits for completion of its new International Airport in Narita, forty-one miles northeast of the capital, it has to make do with one of the least adequate big-city airports in the world, Haneda. On 874 acres of man-made land in Tokyo Bay, an area one-eleventh as great as Washington's Dulles International Airport, Haneda handles 460 flights daily. Not only do 44,000 people arrive and depart every day, but 20,000 more people, following an obsessive Japanese custom, throng the airport to shout "Banzai!" at departing friends and relatives. Queuing for check-in takes an hour, and queuing for departure takes another. Phones, lobbies, restaurants, and restrooms are jammed. "Haneda Airport pain in ass," says one of my notes.

The essence of phrases in Japanese often gets minced in English rendition, but maybe it's better that way. What could be more felicitous than "Association to Create Bright Progressive Politics in Tokyo" as a description of the coalition that keeps Tokyo's Governor Ryokichi Minobe in office, and will continue to do so until at least the end of his third four-year term in 1979?

Minobe, born in Tokyo in 1904 and graduated from Tokyo University with a doctorate in economics (specialty, statistics), comes from a famous family. During the 1930s, his father, who was dean of law at the same university, propounded a constitutional view that the emperor was merely an "organ" of the government. This demoted the emperor from the category of god, and the militarists who were leading Japan to war in China needed a god for whom men would fight. Minobe was forced out of his deanery and attacked (unsuccessfully) by an assassin. Thus the son lived in the shadow of the father's reputation, and for years, as the Japanese would say, adopted a low posture.

Until he was sixty-three years old, the younger Minobe led an unrenowned professional life of teaching economics at the Tokyo University of Education while moonlighting on many government councils dealing with health, science, industry, and administration. But he carried the liberal coloration and the noted name of his father, and in 1967 a coalition of "progressive" parties, including the Socialists and Communists, nominated him for governor of Tokyo (the office is governor rather than mayor because the Tokyo metropolis constitutes a prefecture as well as a city). By a smashing 1,800,000-vote margin, he defeated the conservative candidate, a former Metropolitan Police chief, and became the first socialist (with a small s—he belongs to no party) chief executive of Tokyo.

Years before, Minobe had married the sister of a prominent conservative politician and fathered three sons; but he divorced her and for the next twenty years established himself in the public mind as a free-wheeling bachelor who liked movies, the theater, sports, and pretty women. Despite, or because of, that image, women voted for him in droves; but in 1970, with another election coming up, and under criticism from the women's rights movement, he again took on the respectability of marriage by wedding his former secretary. Then he announced that they would live separately as long as he was governor, because he was "too busy."

Tokyo likes its governor, a spare, angle-browed man, dressed in suits the color of a mouse. In this land of fixed, inexpressive smiles, his is sincere, if slightly rueful, perhaps because of the frustrations of the job. He tries to represent human values in a vast, indifferent metropolis; his political creed is populism. He is not greatly influenced by his Communist support, which brings benefits (in votes) only about as large as its liabilities (in votes scared away), but he has enjoyed harassing the American military from time to time. Laborers and clerks and intellectuals vote for him. His reaction to the thought of governing such a huge city is that "world's biggest" is too big. When President Ford visited Tokyo late in 1974, Minobe asked him the question that no one else in the Japanese government dared to ask, for fear that the answer would be yes: Do American warships bring nuclear weapons to Japan? Ford was noncommittal.

To Minobe's frustration, the party of his opponents, though not strong enough to control the Metropolitan Assembly, is the ruling party in the national government, whose power outweighs the prefectures much more than Washington outweighs the American states. Minobe has only partial control over the Tokyo police, public housing, antipollution regulations, even his own revenue. "He sees Tokyo and its citizens as misused and exploited, serving as a locomotive for the Japanese economy but without maintenance or lubrication," says the Boston *Globe*'s correspondent Crocker Snow. Working without sufficient authority, Minobe has performed creditably in keeping the city's problems at bay, and fighting them back a little.

Pollution is the worst of the problems, and one of its most troublesome manifestations is in the form of garbage. Garbage creation in Tokyo is exponential: it grows in proportion to the fast population rise multiplied by the fast increase (caused by affluence) of garbage per person. Each Tokyo resident now throws away about four times as much as he did in 1960. It all comes to thirteen thousand tons a day.

Modern, grass-bordered incinerators burn nearly half of it, but the rest goes into three thousand blue-and-white trucks that all bear down on the unfortunate eastern ward of Koto. Through its narrow streets, stinking and dripping, they converge on a smoking, squishy, fly-swarming landfill in Tokyo Bay with the honeymoon name of New New Dream Island (two "News" because New Dream Island, which was an extension of Dream Island, has been filled to the limit with garbage). This land-building, with the promise of parks to go on the islands, seems no bad thing. But the people of Koto cannot stand the traffic, and in 1966 they touched off Tokyo's famous "garbage war," which continues to this day. In one battle, when the western ward of Suginami balked at installing an incinerator, Koto residents physically blocked Suginami garbage trucks from New Dream Island; after three days of waste piling up, Suginami caved in and voted to put up a disposal plant.

Governor Minobe wants each ward to handle its own garbage, and one day not long ago smilingly revealed the plans and model of a sixty-story incinerator to be built among the skyscrapers in the stylish new metropolitan subcenter in Shinjuku. This "Environment Center Building" would look like a hotel and, in fact, be quite near the luxurious Keio Plaza Hotel. The big incinerator would generate steam for regional heating and air conditioning. But the fashion shops and real estate men of the neighborhood shrieked "Horrors!" and promised to fight it. Minobe has also commissioned incinerator manufacturers to design systems for removing garbage in pipes by vacuum or compressed air, instead of trucks. In a way that would be a loss. Tokyo children adore toy garbage trucks, romanticizing them as the front-line tanks of the much-publicized garbage war.

An ancient bas-relief in Italy's Villa Albani shows Diogenes in conversation with Alexander the Great, and the dialogue is supposed to have gone like this:

ALEXANDER: "What single boon would you most like me to confer upon you, Diogenes?"

DIOGENES: "Just please stop standing between me and the sun, Alexander the Great."

One hundred seventy-seven thousand five hundred and thirty-four citizens of Tokyo, at least, share Diogenes' dedication to what they call "sunshine rights." According to a petition they submitted to the metropolitan government, they want Tokyo's tall buildings to stand aside, or, rather, never to rise high enough to block the sun in the first place. The petitioners, united as the People's Union Against Building Pollution, succeeded in persuading Minobe's administration to draw up an ordinance that would in general limit buildings to maximum heights determined by the length of the shadow they would cast when the sun crossed the Tokyo meridian at 11:40 A.M. on the winter solstice. In effect, the rule would prevent buildings higher than three stories in residential districts. Howls from construction interests scuttled this idealistic proposal, but the concept often prevails: builders modify plans to meet the neighbors' demands to keep Japan from becoming "the land of the shut-out sun." Minobe had one official building redesigned after five children appealed to him to protect their grandmother's right to see the sun, feeble though it may be under the Tokyo smog. Discouraging high-rise apartment buildings obviously prevents Tokyo from accommodating more people in better housing—which is why Minobe thinks growth should stop.

As a result, the skyline of Tokyo, conforming to all these pressures, is low and undistinguished. Quite a few buildings in the twenty- or thirty-story range push up into the murky atmosphere, but Japanese architects mostly favor horizontal lines. Strange-shaped lots make strange-shaped buildings—there are all kinds of polygons. One sees structures hardly wider than a man's outstretched arms but nine stories high. Lots of dot-size windows is a common style, and an abnormal number of buildings are finished in flat or glossy *black*.

The fear of earthquakes is rooted deep in the psyche of the Japanese. The pseudonymous Isaiah Ben-Dasan, author of *The Japanese and the Jews*, says that the Japanese "list of frightening things, as often given in their traditional literature, goes thus: earthquake, thunder, fire, and the Old Man"—the latter being patriarchal authority. "Of the four things most feared, the most terrible is earthquake, for it comes totally without warning and wreaks some of the most tremendous havoc known on earth. The Great Kanto Earthquake of 1923 caused more damage to Tokyo and Yokohama than did all the holocaust of atomic bombs in Hiroshima and Nagasaki."

Clearly a disastrous earthquake will someday strike Tokyo (just as one will someday hit all the cities in the circumpacific earthquake belt). This fate, this certainty that Tokyo will once again suffer devastation, lives in the back of everyone's mind. People keep rope ladders and small stores of food in their houses. Families agree on an exact spot to meet after the catastrophe. The fine wires that hold down precious pots inside the glass cases of museums speak quietly of the possibility of violent earth movement. Inconspicuous little automatic windlasses stand near windows in some office buildings, ready to lower the occupants to the ground. More fundamentally, the government's Geographical Survey Institute is establishing, by means of a laser range finder, 38,000 triangulation points all over Japan that will be accurate down to less than one millimeter per kilometer. Frequent remeasuring of the distances between these points will show the earth's expansion and contraction, and possibly provide data for earthquake prediction.

The Kanto earthquake killed 140,000 people. A shake equal in strength, 7.9 on the Richter scale, would be far more devastating now. Fire, rather than the collapse of buildings, is the major peril. Tokyo has about two hundred times as many cars now as in 1923, and "every car is a potential bomb in an earthquake," one gas-and-oil expert told me. Tokyo taxis run on liquefied petroleum gas (LPG), and when the city's Fire Defense Agency set afire a simulated neighborhood of prefab houses lining a street on which twenty-nine cars were parked, all the vehicles burned like torches, and the six among them fueled by LPG exploded. I heard, authoritatively, that a depot of 45,000 tons of liquefied petroleum gas in Kawasaki, just across the Tama River south of Tokyo, could ignite that whole industrial city if a quake ruptured its pressurized tanks.

Traffic trapped on Tokyo's elevated expressways, with their limited exits, could provide fuel for miles of linear fires, with drivers and passengers facing a choice between death by immolation and death by jumping. Bullet trains toppling from their tracks when they are going 125 miles an hour might kill every last passenger (although the trains are fitted with breakers that have so far successfully stopped them during minor quakes). Charcoal braziers, which, lighted to cook lunch, caused most of the fires when the Kanto earthquake struck at noon on September 2, 1923, are no longer used in Tokyo, but their replacements—kerosene stoves for heating and pressurized gas for cooking—are even more incendiary. One guess is that they would light 30,000 fires. Home extinguishers might put out many of them, but the Metropolitan Fire Board estimates that 2,500 of the blazes would require fire engines, and the fire department would be strained to put out as few as 150 simultaneous fires. Half a million people might die.

Then Tokyo would pick itself up, dust itself off, and start all over again.

13 /

Ticky-Tacky Tokaido

WHO'LL PAY THE LUNCH BILL?

The Tokyo man, sensitive and wary of being shamed, tries to find a way to pay it without hurting the feelings of the others.

The Osaka man, practical and money-conscious, proposes a Dutch treat.

The Nagoya man, conservative and yen-pinching, contrives to let someone else pay for all.

Wheezes like this are generated all over the world where cities have a simultaneous sense of competition and community. In Japan this sense comes to these three cities from sharing destinies on the legendary Tokaido corridor, which runs from Kyoto to Tokyo, along the underbelly of Honshu.

Japan can be sliced up in various ways. One way is by the forty-seven prefectures; but the Japanese feel that these states, invented after the Meiji Restoration, are too numerous and newfangled to bother about much in ordinary talk. They more often speak of historic regions, corresponding, perhaps, to New England or the Southwest. There are eight regions: Hokkaido, the northernmost island; Tohoku, or northern Honshu; Kanto, which is Tokyo and the Kanto Plain plus environs; Chubu, the plump middle of Honshu, including Nagoya, Mount Fuji, and the Japanese Alps; Kinki, centered on Osaka, Kobe, and Kyoto; Chugoku, the western end of Honshu, including Hiroshima; and the two other islands, Shikoku and Kyushu. But Tokaido is a different kind of entity, a once romantic and now frequently blighted belt of roads and commerce that might be called the spine of Japan. Tokaido is a route, a legend, and perhaps a future megalopolis, in the sense projected for the Boston–New York–Philadelphia–Washington area.

Ten centuries ago the center of Japan was Kyoto, and the Tokyo area was primeval country bordering on an immense ocean called the Eastern Sea. The Tokaido, the Eastern Sea road, penetrated to this frontier like a Nipponese Oregon Trail. Thus, historically, the Tokaido began in ancient Japan and fetched up as the conduit and creator of modern Japan. Decade after decade, warriors went up the road to press back the Ainu barbarians of northeastern Japan, making it feasible, in 1192, for the first shogun to turn far-eastern Kamakura into the military seat of government, while Kyoto remained the imperial and ceremonial capital. "Imagine England with a king in Edinburgh and a government in London; that was the situation that lasted in Japan for nearly 500 years. The road between the two became the nation's vital artery," writes Fosco Maraini in *Meeting with Japan*. Emissaries shuttled back and forth between the mutually suspicious military dictator and emperor, carrying hypocritical assurances of profound and continuing respect and good faith for one another.

The Tokugawa shogunate put the Tokaido road to the new service of keeping the nation in hostage. To prevent local lords from gathering forces for insurrection, the central government in Edo required these vassals to live in the capital. They could visit their domains only every other six months or a year, leaving wives and children as hostages in Edo. Now the Tokaido became what Oliver Statler, in *Japanese Inn*, called "the world's busiest highway, linking what were probably the world's largest cities." Surfaced with sand or stone, lined by rows of firs, this wide avenue carried a ceaseless two-way trample of runners, pilgrims, merchants, samurai, sumo wrestlers—all afoot or on horse; no wheels allowed. The finest sight was the passage of a lord traveling to or from his fief, borne in a stately palanquin by eight half-naked men, and accompanied by noblemen, porters, footmen, and soldiers.

The spur of mountains that runs into the sea from Mount Fuji forced the traffic to funnel through a high pass at Hakone, the same town now favored by Tokyo people for weekends. Here the instruction for the shogunate's guards was: "Watch for women leaving and muskets entering." No lord was to be allowed to smuggle his lady out of hostage, or bring arms into Edo. Fifty-three stations, set a day's travel apart, provided horses, bearers, message runners, and inns for the night. Evidently the maidservants contrasted strongly with the homely, middle-aged women who serve in present-day Japanese inns. Says a passage in *Japanese Inn*: She "helped him out of his travel kimono and into a fresh one provided by the inn, and when she tied his sash in back he thought that her hands fluttered over his hips for one unnecessary instant. . . . She smiled a promise."

Beyond doubt the Tokaido is still the world's busiest traffic corridor, for through it run the old road, unrecognizably rerouted and remodeled for car traffic, a new expressway, the Japan National Railways' original Tokaido Line, and the bullet-train route. Both rail routes go through the mountains at Hakone in separate four-mile tunnels. Forty-five million people, two-fifths of all Japanese, live in the Tokaido corridor, which means that it forms one huge, stretched-out city, with little open countryside anywhere along the route. Much of this superpopulation stems from the deliberate decision of the 1960 National Income Doubling Plan to concentrate on improving the Tokaido's communications and harbors. Now the megalopolis contains 70 percent of Japan's industrial production.

In parts of Tokaido, Japan the Beautiful dies a horrifying death. The sights are old factories built of grimy gray concrete, junked cars, hillsides scarred with highway cuts and quarries, TV antennas like a skyful of spiders, tall smokestacks in the worst old Birmingham tradition, wide-flung railroad yards. Perhaps the greatest offense to the eye is the electric power lines, marching across the countryside every which way, with poles and towers carrying as many as eighteen cables. It is a landscape festooned with wire. From the Yokohama station of the bullet trains I made a visual tour of the horizon and counted fifty-three power pylons. On the tops of factories—many of them, to be sure, bright, clean, and modern—signs shout the temptations that have replaced the complaisant maids of the Tokugawa inns: SANSUI HI-FI, MEIJI CHOCOLATE, KIRIN BEER. But they are none too visible through the smog. Mount Fuji, in legend the most divine sight along the Tokaido road, is only rarely seen, blocked out by air pollution.

On the Tokaido road, the city that seems to feel most comfortable with the corridor's dedication to industrious manufacturing is Nagoya. At the age of 365 years, Nagoya is something of an upstart to most of the rest of Japan. It heads the list of, and best epitomizes, the "average" cities of Japan. Foreign tourists do not often go to Nagoya. But when I visited, I found Nagoya to be surprisingly brighter and more pleased with itself than its advance notices had led me to believe.

Drawn by such targets as the Mitsubishi aircraft plants, which built the fearsome Zero, American World War II bombers in more than one hundred raids destroyed 23 percent of the city's area—and to top it off, an earthquake worse than the one in 1923 in Tokyo struck Nagoya in the midst of the raids in 1944. In rebuilding, Nagoya had a specific goal, which it has so far nicely carried out: to be the handsome and dynamic "managerial" center and seaport of a metropolitan region consisting of industrial satellite cities that are separated from Nagoya proper and from one another by the green rice and pines of the 25-by-50-mile Nobi Plain. "Nagoya is not as confined as Osaka and Tokyo," a cab driver boasted to me. "We still have space."

Nagoya's singular accomplishment in terms of reconstruction was to revise the whole street plan. Like bent wires stretched taut, old, narrow lanes were pulled into broad, straight avenues. The owners of raggedy-shaped properties fronting the old streets got new, squared, shrunken lots in approximately the same places. The proportion of the city's space devoted to streets rose from 14 percent to 27 percent, of that devoted to parks from almost nothing to 5 percent. An east-west boulevard was fashioned to cross a similar one running north and south in the city's center; broad arterial streets were laid out at one-kilometer intervals parallel to the boulevards. Inconspicuous low steel fences were installed to divide sidewalks from streets—a life-saving Japanese specialty. Together with parks, shrubbed center strips, globular street lights pocked like golf balls, and many clean-cut, horizontal-lined buildings of eight or ten stories, the street plan turned Nagoya into a city that is rational, even clinical, yet uplifting to the spirit, far from magical but a fine place to stroll, especially in the polychrome evenings.

The city of Nagoya itself has a little more than 2 million people, and comes after Tokyo, Osaka, and Yokohama in population rank. Its thirty thriving, busy satellite cities build the regional population to 5.6 million. These places, characterized by the old Japanese mixture of filthy canals, subcontracting industry, forlorn outdoor basketball courts, and houses with washing flying from their roofs, do the area's dirty, productive work. They turn out china, aircraft, petrochemicals, refined petroleum products. Tokai makes steel, Ichinomiya textiles. The satellite city of Toyota manufactures exactly what you would expect it to.

Nagoya dates back only to 1610, right around the beginning of the Tokugawa, or sealed-off, period of Japan. Osaka, by contrast, has origins too far back in time to trace with certainty. It was first of all a port—a good harbor on the Yodo River. Inevitably, it attracted habitation, and by the fourth century it was a national capital of sorts, the seat of the Emperor Nintoku. It was through Osaka that

Chinese travelers brought Buddhism to Japan in the year 552. As Japan developed a feudalism comparable to Europe's, Osaka, standing apart, created a role of its own as a free city of merchants and seafarers, like Genoa or Venice.

Some Southeast Asians called the Japanese "economic animals" because of their single-minded pursuit of profit in trade—a point raised when I talked to Toyosaburo Taniguchi, longtime head of Toyobo Company (cotton spinning) and a leader of two influential Osaka businessmen's organizations. "If the Japanese are economic animals, the Osakans have to admit that they are the prototypes," he said, a little ruefully. "We have lived for centuries bartering. But within the limits of the generally closed-in Japanese character, we do manage to meet foreigners more easily. Osaka represents the antithesis of the samurai warrior, and of his bushido code of behavior. During the Tokugawa period, the samurai in Tokyo were the governors, and we Osakans placed ourselves at the side of the governed. We obeyed the rulers—but we thumbed our noses at them behind their backs. The high-and-mighty feudal lords got rice from their fiefs, but they had to sell it through us, and buy our goods, and borrow money from us. So we became rich, and even if those samurai put merchants at the bottom of the social scale, we got control of the economy and much of the real power."

Taniguchi, a heavy-set man with bow-shaped lips and dabs of iron gray for eyebrows, told me how Osaka quite inevitably grabbed for itself the first Western-technology industry brought to Japan after the Meiji Restoration. "The government tried to set up cotton mills all over the country, but my predecessors at Toyobo had already gone to England and brought back ten thousand spindles—the first Japanese importation of foreign machinery. In twenty years, we raised the number to thirty thousand. And we stayed up to date. Our mills were lighted by electricity only six years after Edison invented the lamp."

Thus Osaka grew to be the textile capital of Asia. But now, says Taniguchi, textiles are in trouble. "The technology all over the world is not too different from one hundred years ago, and it is still a labor-intensive industry. So the American and the Japanese mills are vulnerable to Korea, Taiwan, Hong Kong, and Pakistan, where the wages are lower. But Japan professes free trade, and tremendous amounts of cloth are coming in here from Southeast Asia. We'll have to think of something new to do with cloth—maybe carpets for streets, or whole golf courses. In a day of men on the moon, we should be able to invent a machine that can take in a bolt of cloth and turn out finished shirts without any human hands. The governor of Texas came to see me recently, and proposed that we put up a mill in his state. But I found the Texans too complacent. They're still putting up cotton in bales—we move all of ours by pneumatic tubes. I told the Texans, 'Make the deal more appetizing.' "

Adapting to the times, chemicals, iron and steel, and machinery have now shouldered the traditional textiles aside as Osaka's leading industries. Osaka also makes beer, cars, vitamin pills, television sets, motorboats, bread, whiskey, cameras, refrigerators, farm machines, computers, clothing, and chocolate. "The city's factories turn out practically everything except for arms," says the municipal government's self-description.

The fiery surgery of bombing cost Osaka 310,955 houses, and 77,588 more were demolished to make wide firebreaks that to some extent contained the blazes. The city rebuilt on its old street plan, which in the city's center was a pleasing combination of a 1930s remodeling job together with the never-failing attraction of water, provided by the meandering Yodo River. In the heart of Osaka, a long island divides the river, like Paris' Île de la Cité. Twenty bridges lead to the important buildings that stand on the island: the city hall, the Bank of Japan, the Festival Hall, the Osaka University Medical School, *Asahi Shimbun*'s Osaka offices, and the Osaka Royal Hotel. Osaka's three-mile, gingko-lined main boulevard, Midosuji, which crosses the island in front of city hall, is a sort of cultural and economic dumbbell: the railroad station, banks, and department stores group at the stately northern end; theaters, arcades, pachinko parlors, and restaurants group at the raffish southern end. The Kabuki theater, scalloped in sixteenth-century style, is an architectural grace note there.

Osaka, Japan's second city, has 2.9 million people, having lost a quarter-million in ten years. This is the "doughnut phenomenon," they told me at city hall. "People are leaving the central city." They seemed relieved, because the outward move, far from bespeaking inner-city decay, provides a healthy reduction in population density in the overcrowded center. The small prefecture of which Osaka is the capital has sixteen other cities of between 100,000 and 700,000 people, so the metropolitan area spreads far and wide.

But not so far as Mount Koya, about thirty miles south of Osaka Castle. Koyasan, to give it the Japanese name, is a center of the spirit to balance Osaka's obsession with the profane. About four hours on a train, cable car, and bus gets you to Koyasan, altitude 2,858 feet. A friend of mine, the author Carl Solberg, went there not long ago, and described his visit in a letter. "Koyasan," he wrote, "is a monastic center of renown and sanctity founded in 816 by the revered teacher Kobo. There were once one thousand monasteries on the mountain, but today only about one hundred. Kobo, a Luther-like figure who fathered irrigation and education and was one of the three great calligraphers of Japan, retired on the peak to meditate and was never seen again. At one time a sizable part of central Japan gave its revenues to Koyasan. Until just one hundred years ago, no woman had ever trod on Koyasan, a veritable Mount Athos. Over the centuries the monks built a Buddhist tradition—in the West we would say a theology—at Koyasan."

Solberg visited Koyasan with his daughter-in-law, in midwinter. "We slogged about in the muddy paths, stood beneath pine trees taller and thicker than Minnesota's, watched a monk at dusk swing a huge tree-butt suspended by a rope that smote an immense bell, tried to photograph the massed lanterns glowing under the ancient eaves of a couple of the temples, and walked through a spooky, mile-long graveyard in the twilight. About half of the monasteries take paying guests, and this was what Gail and I pointed for at the end of the day. There are three ranks of monks, students, practitioners, and itinerants. The practitioners are men of mature age and emanating authority. Their vocation is not to 'do,' but only to 'be.' We dealt with the students. They had not only a record of our phone call for reservations, but, greatly to Gail's disillusionment, a Diners Club sign on their entry window."

Like Tokyo with its Yokohama, Osaka is today a minor seaport that relies on a nearby major seaport, Kobe, to handle most of its ocean commerce. Similarly too, Osaka and Kobe have grown to be a continuous urban area although their centers are twenty miles apart. Moreover, Kobe, like Yokohama, had its beginnings only a century ago, when the Japanese government grudgingly assigned it to be the port and place of business for Western traders, far enough away to keep them from contaminating Osaka. Then, again like Yokohama, Kobe turned out to have an unexpected asset, the deep water needed to dock the new iron steamships. On its waterfront, early English traders built godowns of red brick imported from Glasgow as ballast for tea ships, and set about, as was the Englishman's wont, to establish an enclave that was a little bit of Old England. Soon they were playing cricket and putting on theatricals. A certain shady lady named Christine set up a discreet bordello in a building labeled "Import-Export," where the girls, who were not Japanese but foreigners, were reputed not only to wear flesh-colored stockings, but to roll them down below the knees. Thus did Christine put her son through one of the best schools in England. One of the early English firms was M. Samuel & Company, which exported scenically painted Japanese sea shells to be sold at English bathing beaches. When Samuel & Company later went into the oil business, it took the shell for a trademark—the Shell now seen on countless gasoline stations everywhere in the world.

The ambiguous merits of urban renewal by bombing—five-eighths of the city area in this case—let Kobe grow into its present clean-lined, cosmopolitan, but rather soulless self as Japan's sixth-biggest city (population 1,330,000). Thirty thousand foreigners live there. Restaurants with names like Texas Tavern and King's Arms reflect a feeling that Kobe is very much in touch with the world.

A snake of a city, Kobe is nine miles long and one mile wide, compressed between the sea and steep mountains. As a consequence of this bind, machines have been set to chewing at the mountain to produce rock that is cast into the sea as fill for a broader plain. A conveyor belt in a tunnel under the city hustles the material from hill to waterfront. Still, the blue-green Rokko range, which is rather too large for ready destruction by dynamite and bulldozer, remains the city's pride. Aerial trams climb its sides to parks, temples, inns, spas, golf courses, and a revolving observatory.

Merely by dint of being seen by so many millions from so many train windows, Tokaido sometimes seems the stuff and substance of Japan, just as Boston-to-Washington sometimes masquerades as the whole United States. But near the western end of ticky-tacky Tokaido, there stands in serene contrast to slam-bang, workaholic Osaka and Nagoya an imponderable city full of ghosts and ethereal beauty. This is Kyoto, and for westbound travelers on the Tokaido road, reaching Kyoto has always—whether now or a thousand years ago—been an occasion for excitement, pleasure, and relief.

14 / 🌸

Kyoto the Microbeautiful

WHICH AMONG THE FABLED CITIES of the East is the richest in ancient glories? Jungle-covered Angkor? Kublai Khan's Peking? Agra, with the Taj Mahal? Surprisingly, perhaps, the answer may be Kyoto, which was, by way of evidence, already in its fifth vigorous century when China's Forbidden City was built. Kyoto does not flaunt bedazzlements, like the Great Mosque at Delhi or the fantasy temples of Bangkok. Restraint, not bedazzlement, is the Japanese way, and Kyoto contains countless restrained treasures and an overpowering sense of unbroken history.

Although the 1,450,000 citizens of this immemorial city manifest as much energy as the people in any other part of the country, Kyoto's role in exploding Japan is to stand as a subtle exception. The nation thrives on combining the old and the new, and this city is the citadel and symbol of the old. At its founding, Kyoto loomed as an island of culture in a primitive world, like Athens twelve centuries earlier. Its early Fujiwara regents could have been, in their sophistication and political manipulation, models for the Medicis eight centuries later. Kyoto, prizing this past, has changed less between then and now than any old city of Europe. Kyoto gives Japan its sense of continuity. From Kyoto comes the whole marvelous world of Japanese esthetics.

For further distinction, Kyoto lies in a lovely setting, often compared to that of Florence, with forested hills to east, north, and west. Kyoto is, in fact, officially a sister city to Florence, as well as to Boston, Paris, Cologne, Kiev, and Sian—mostly meaningless relationships, but suggestive of Kyoto's vision of itself. A symmetrical,

237

temple-dotted mountain called Hiei, 2,784 feet high, guards Kyoto on the northeast, the malignant quarter of the compass in ancient belief. On the slope of a smaller, nearer hill, a startling, 524-foot-high representation of the Chinese character for "great" is branded into the forest by fire. Each year, at the equivalent of Halloween, this character and lesser ones on other hills are set ablaze to guide the souls of the dead back to the world beyond, after their annual brief visit to earth—a fine fiery show, watched by Kyotans from rooftop beer gardens. Kyoto's winter sometimes brings a light snow, delectably beautiful on the soaring roofs of the Gold Pavilion. Spring produces a unique lavender mist, and the chills of late fall turn the surrounding maples a vivid vermilion.

The founding of Kyoto was a case of the willed creation of a great capital, like Washington or Brasília in later eras. Until the year 710, Japanese emperors changed their seats of government with every succession; then, for seven reigns, until 784, the capital remained at Nara, thirty miles south of present-day Kyoto. Suddenly the Emperor Kammu, feeling suffocated by the power of the Buddhist priesthood at Nara, resolved to move away. Three hundred thousand men were set to work building a city at Nagaoka, to the north. Kammu moved there at once, and for ten years construction continued. Just as the job was nearly done, Kammu, sensing ill omens, abandoned Nagaoka, and in 794 started all over again at what is now Kyoto. The builders laid out a rectangular city, three by three and one-half miles. On the south was a 75-foot-high-gate-labyrinth, which by the twelfth century had turned into the crumbling repository for abandoned corpses described in Ryunosuke Akutagawa's novel *Rashomon*.

For 1,066 years, Japanese emperors reigned from the Imperial Palace of what was first called Heian (Peace and Tranquility) and later simply *Kyo* (capital) *to* (city). By the year 1000, it had half a million inhabitants, making it one of the largest cities in the world. Kyoto always built with wood, not masonry, and as a result its noblest buildings have all through history been going up in flames. So Kyoto does not *feel* old in the marbled way that Rome does. Instead, strangely, the sense of age seeps up from the very streets, for the city plan was taken over from the formidable Sui Dynasty capital Ch'ang-an, now Sian. Somehow this has the effect of stretching the sense of Kyoto's antiquity back further than its actual founding. Moreover, though the existing wood of a given temple may be only a century old, the building is usually a faithful reconstruction of its burned-down predecessor, which may have been a reconstruction of an earlier one. Gardens, too, survive in the same form from as long ago as the fourteenth century. As a result, the visitor gets the feeling of a city with a continuous history going back to well before the time (about 1300) when Marco Polo relayed to the West what he had learned during his long years in China: that there was an island nation still farther to the east, a nation by the name of Cipango.

American bombing during World War II could certainly have shattered this continuity, but Kyoto was spared. This was due to the intervention of Secretary of War Henry Stimson, a cultivated man who knew Kyoto firsthand, and made the decision to strike it from the list of B-29 targets—and later of atomic bomb targets—on grounds that Kyoto "had been the ancient capital of Japan and was a shrine of Japanese art and culture." Many Kyotans, puzzled over their city's exemption from attack, concluded that the Americans wanted it as a residential area for the conquering Yanks after the war.

Americans and Europeans seem to sense Kyoto's charms from afar, to smell it like some Oriental incense borne across the oceans, without ever having bothered to read about it in their geography books. Like those visitors to Italy who glance around Rome and hurry off to Florence, Westerners often give Tokyo a once-over and catch the bullet train for Kyoto. There they may find themselves in for a thudding initial disillusionment.

Whatever Kyoto may be when examined in detail, seen panoramically it turns out to be *un*magnificent, *un*imposing, *un*majestic. Across the station plaza the infelicitous five-hundred-foot spire of the Kyoto Tower Hotel stabs the sky, holding aloft some ungainly balloonlike platform. The downtown buildings are of drab brick and tile, or spoliated concrete. Overhead power lines run like railroad tracks against the sky. The Chinese street plan, though blessedly easy to get around in, is mostly a monotonous grid. Because it is rigidly oriented north-south and east-west, it ignores the possibilities of accommodating to the mountain setting.

As a civic sight, it is no Florence. The Kamo River, diked against occasional high water from a typhoon, usually runs in a shallow trickle through flats of mud and gravel. Its bridges, unlike Florence's several glories, are undistinguished. Small tributary streams, oily and noisome, are bottomed with rusty cans and old umbrella frames. Along such shopping streets as Kawaramachi and Shijo, and among the pretentious government buildings on Karasuma street, or on the campuses of the city's eighteen universities, the Western-style buildings are blocky, badly fenestrated, disconcertingly eclectic, or downright shoddy. Cramped wooden Japanese-style stores and houses of weathered aspect and poor repair are spotted among filing-cabinet Western buildings in such disarray that each makes the other look out of place.

Yet to say all this is to miss the point about Kyoto. Kyoto does not boast of itself as a stately Buenos Aires or a bespired Prague or a monumental Manhattan. Its treasures are small ones, even tiny ones; its beauties are hidden, though susceptible to discovery; and it contains art beyond any visitor's capacity ever to absorb. It is a jewel box of gems badly mounted.

Kyoto must be scrutinized close up. It comes retail, not wholesale. It has hardly any proper parks, for example, but almost every random, six-foot scrap of land left by the vagaries of urbanization is rented and put into flowers by someone who lives nearby. Kyoto has to be walked, not seen from a car. Turning from such a street as Higashioji, gray and uninteresting, you are suddenly on narrow Pottery Lane, climbing the flank of the eastern hills, so steep that here and there it requires steps. The street, a major passageway though narrow, is a river of animation, a torrent of faces, picture-pretty in the opening perspectives of its twists and slow curves, color-bright from signs, awnings, roof tiles, and schoolchildren's caps. On each side, shops sell blue-and-white Kiyomizu porcelain, made nearby, and shell-thin Kyoto cookies that sniff of cinnamon. How did the nondescript city of a few minutes ago suddenly produce this perfect example of the genus *little winding street*?

The contradiction of the microbeautiful and the macro-ugly nagged at me the whole time I was in Kyoto, and I asked constantly for explanations. Few Kyotans could even comprehend the puzzle that bothered my Western mind. One tentative answer was that Buddhist belief sees life on earth a sort of hell that is not supposed to have a pleasant appearance, and that when man does try to create a patch of heaven on earth he must do it on the scale of a temple or a tearoom, not an entire city. Or perhaps the explanation could be found in the late journalist Nyozekan Hasegawa's assertion that in esthetics the Japanese have simply never wanted to overwhelm. Another insight is that the Japanese ability to appreciate beauty is complemented by an equal ability to ignore the ugly.

Kyoto is a big city, though not overwhelming, and it has no heavy industry. The central occupation of Kyoto is the cultivation of taste —taste in the diminutive rather than the grand. Taste in handicrafts and home industries, taste in customs and festivals and entertainments and ceremonies, taste in food, taste in shops. Taste often flawless, taste sometimes cerebral or sterile, taste occasionally extravagant or egregious. Example: the Kyoto branch of Takashimaya, the department-store chain, annually displays the work of the city's foremost cake makers in its seventh-floor art gallery. I went hardly knowing what could be done to make a cake a work of art, aside from putting pastel icing and a bride and groom on it. Part of the answer, as the first glance around the show demonstrated, is that in the hands of a Kyoto artisan, cake becomes sculpture or jewelry, fashioned with such skill, finish, and taste in hue and form that it nearly overrides the question, "Is this worth doing?" Before your eyes lie astoundingly realistic creations in sugar. Miniature full-rigged ships. Sea urchins. Pagodas and castles. Hawks and cormorants. Petunias. An ear of corn charred by fire, with a grasshopper to admire it. Who likes this sort of thing? Answer: nearly every Kyotan. *Throngs* of aficionados of the cake art are on hand, their trained eyes intent on each delicate detail, Nikons ready to record this comestible sculpture on film. Is it ever actually eaten? Sad to say, yes—at wedding parties and other grand occasions.

Silk weaving, dating clear back to the city's founding, is Kyoto's main industry—a cottage industry, mostly. In the one-story wooden houses of the Nishijin district, houses so narrow and deep that their inhabitants call them "eel sleeping-places," machine looms clatter behind every latticed façade. Bigger shops employ the principle of the Jacquard looms, imported from France in 1872: coded punch cards on a chain work the harnesses to determine the pattern of the textile, while the weavers deftly supply variously colored cross threads from memory. But much design weaving is still done on small handlooms, the weavers filing their fingernails like combs to pull the filling threads tight. Kyoto silk comes as a dappled white, but much of it is hand-dyed in splendid colors and fixed by being hung out like banners along the Katsura River, a branch of the Kamo. Kyoto supplies the bulk of the flamboyant costumes used in the Noh and Kabuki theaters. The curtain of the Kennedy Center Opera House in Washington is made of Kyoto silk.

Similar feverish care goes into jewelry, wood carving, fan making, paper folding, pottery, damascene, cloisonné, and embroidery. From high-flaming furnaces, workmen pour bronze to cast temple bells or Buddha images, with priests on hand to recite sutras as the metal cools. Lacquerware makers, working in utter concentration and total silence, sift flakes of gold onto wet surfaces to achieve the typical Kyoto coloration. Other artisans fabricate exquisite dolls no taller than a sake bottle, in extravagant kimonos, with pencil-line eyebrows and glossy hair. Some craftsmen are so specialized as to make only dolls' eyes.

The people of Kyoto adore these little creations. One night, at a tiny bar where light from the paper panes of a bamboo-framed lamp shone softly on the fragrant cedar walls, I met Kimosuke Usui, who publishes a magazine devoted to Kyoto's unabashed self-worship. Usui, a fragile man in his habitual black kimono, explained that Kyotans put a distinctive stress, beginning in childhood, on training the eye to drink in beauty in a manner at once thirsty and yet quietly pleasurable. Something of this is obvious to anyone watching a woman buying dolls, or a connoisseur in a shop where fine tea bowls are sold, or even a barmaid arranging a plate of pinhead mushrooms.

The aspect of Kyoto that gives the discerning eye its greatest scope is the architecture of its 1,598 Buddhist temples, 253 Shinto shrines, and four palaces, together with the gardens that surround them. Though impossibly numerous, these gems are all behind walls, only fractionally visible from the streets of Kyoto. They must be sought out, and entered, and examined. Taken together, they embody the whole delight and exaltation of the world's finest and oldest wooden architecture, with its curving tiled roofs and soaring ridges and Chinese-puzzle timbering. The material is often cypress, cut from a tree big enough to provide columns as massive as the Parthenon's, strong enough to support tall pagodas, and so resistant to weather that examples thirteen centuries old can be found. Cypress bark makes an impermeable roof, thick and gray, and is sometimes used instead of tile.

By a set of curious chances, we lived in a Buddhist temple while in Kyoto. This city is the center of authority for eleven sects of Buddhism in Japan, and its temples are grouped in headquarters compounds of half a dozen to forty separate buildings. Some of the lesser temples in these compounds serve in effect as rectories, and the occupant priest sometimes separates off an apartment to rent for extra income (one priest even rents the temple grounds as a parking lot). A friend had located such an apartment for us in the seventy-four-acre compound of thirty-seven temples, sub-temples, and monasteries known collectively as Myoshinji—Temple of the Wondrous Spirit. Outside the wall was a narrow street with heavy traffic, tangerine vendors, and noodle shops; inside were serene, straight, stone-paved lanes running in rectangular patterns between whitewashed walls that were topped by ornate tiles and pierced by elaborate roofed gates. Behind one of the gates was our temporary home, a large, square, one-story building. Tudor-like in its post-and-beam timbering intersticed with white plaster, it was roofed in rippling tiles the color of iron, which rose at the lofty ridgepole ends to support fine sculptures of lion heads. Our landlord turned out to be a kindly, cultivated priest named Joyu Kimura. With his ever-smiling wife, he occupied most of this subtemple as the living quarters due him for his services as a professor at nearby Hanazono University, theological school for much of Japanese Buddhism.

Myoshinji, founded in 1308 by the Emperor Hanazono, is headquarters for the nine Rinzai Zen sects in Japan, and has 3,500 subsidiary temples throughout the country. Walking the peaceful lanes in the next few days, I learned of some of Myoshinji's marvels. The central temple, the Dharma Hall, square and about sixty feet on a side, displays on its high ceiling a fine painting of a writhing dragon. It is said that the artist commissioned to paint it, in the sixteenth century, complained, reasonably enough, that he had never seen a dragon. The abbot, employing Zen techniques, told him to "become a living dragon, and paint it."

"How?" asked the artist.

"Retire to your private room," replied the abbot, "and concentrate your mind on it. The time will come when you will become a dragon."

Myoshinji is planted with maples, bayonet palms, and tall, gray-barked pines. A benevolent atmosphere prevails; neighborhood children play under the trees as bent-over monks shuffle by. Occasionally a sprig falls in your path and you look up to see the small figure of a gardener high in a pine, pruning it to preserve its spare shape, and even plucking individual needles that grow like an unwanted beard from the bark of the main branches.

Yet no one rates run-of-the-mill Myoshinji as Kyoto's most famous treasure, or anything like it. That distinction belongs to an all-by-itself temple only twenty years old, the Gold Pavilion. A fourteenth-century shogun—one of the Ashikagas—built the original Gold Pavilion for a villa, and although it still seems a villa, sitting reflected at the edge of its Mirror Lake, it was soon afterward turned into a temple. Three-storied, double-roofed, and surfaced with gold foil, the pavilion is perhaps the most beautiful single building in Japan. What artistic audacity—to gold-leaf an entire building! The eye critically seeks for —but cannot find—any part of the building that is out of harmony with the rest. Atop the peak of the highest roof, a copper-and-gold phoenix, with wings like flames and glaring eye, unwittingly symbolizes the history of the pavilion itself, which rose from its own ashes after being burned to the ground by an apprentice priest in 1950.

Such sacrilege is rare in Japan. The motive of the arsonist is still unknown, but his mother's atoning act of suicide caused the life sentence proposed for him to be reduced to eight years. The crime inspired Yukio Mishima's novel *The Temple of the Golden Pavilion*, which explains the arson as postwar nihilism ("I could hardly feel the heat," the young priest says. "When I saw that the steadfast flames had moved to the offertory box, I felt that everything was going to be all right"). The abbot of the Gold Pavilion managed to raise funds and get it rebuilt, foil and all, in five years. Japanese department stores sell plastic kits from which children build detailed models of the pavilion.

After the Gold Pavilion, the next most striking feat of architecture around Kyoto is in nearby Nara, Kyoto's predecessor as Japan's imperial capital, and now only fifty minutes away by train. This building is the Hall of the Great Buddha, a double-roofed, horizontal structure the equivalent of fifteen stories high, reputedly the biggest wooden edifice in the world. It is a powerfully dramatic temple, massive and emphatic, but seemingly resting lightly on the ground. Its centerpiece is a huge and famous sitting statue of Buddha. The statue stands 71 feet high, including the pedestal, and the bronze in it weighs 450 tons, as compared to 225 tons of metal in the Statue of Liberty. A century ago an astonished Englishman wrote of it as "a bronze idol, the dimensions of which may be estimated, when one man failed to grasp with his two arms the thumb of the right hand." And it was all cast when Charlemagne was a little boy. Currently, the Hall of the Great Buddha is being rebuilt, a six-year job. An iron-framed canopy, modestly described as "not as big as the Astrodome in Houston," covers the whole huge wooden structure like a hat.

Being even older than Kyoto, Nara has buildings put up almost fourteen hundred years ago, probably the oldest wooden structures in the world. Chief among them are the temples of the Horyuji compound, which contains a dozen or so works of art—Buddha statues, gates, entire buildings—of the kind that the Japanese solemnly, but properly, label "National Treasure" or "Important Cultural Property" in accordance with the Cultural Properties Protection Law of 1950. This ancient city, one must add—grimly—also has a Disneyland-like entertainment park with a peculiarly Japanese attraction, an Ancestor Land.

A frightening case of overdoing things from seven centuries back is Kyoto's Sanjusangendo, a Buddhist edifice 390 feet long, with a corridor along one side for the slippered feet of pilgrims, and along the other side thirty-three bays divided by columns. Back of the columns, on ten stepped tiers, stand rank after rank of human-size statues of the goddess of mercy, Kannon: five hundred on one side of a central sculpture (an oversize statue of the same lady) and five hundred on the other. Each of the thousand statues has a dozen or so pairs of arms, and each statue, the mind boggles to note, is slightly but significantly different from any other.

Gardens in Kyoto have nothing whatsoever to do with green thumbs, or mucking around in black loam with trowel and bag of fertilizer—hardly anything to do with flowers, for that matter. The English or Italian garden imposes order on unruly nature, and boasts about it; the Japanese garden also imposes man's art, but then—almost—conceals the imposition. The Western garden is based on color; the Japanese on shape. The Western garden is painterly; the Japanese sculptural.

The best Kyoto temple gardens go back to three or four consummate geniuses of the fourteenth to seventeenth centuries, who perfected the underplayed and asymmetrical arranging of rocks, moss, trees, sand, water, stepping stones, and monolith bridges. The goal of the garden, derived from Zen, is to be a setting for contemplation and, more than that, to offer material for contemplation. Often some small drama is depicted. Daitokuji temple, for example, has a garden no bigger than the floor of a bus wherein two boulders lie half submerged in coarse sand that is kept raked in concentric circles around them. The drama: a big stone makes larger ripples than a small one. Thus, the big stone has more power, and . . . but carrying the obvious to the mysterious is a task for the Zen mind. Anyone, though, can sense the bellow of the blast suggested by a pine pruned to seem gale blown, or the passage of the centuries in an ancient cherry tree with branches thoughtfully propped up by poles and crutches, like a nonagenarian with a cane.

The epitome of Kyoto's gardens is at Ryoanji temple, where the esthetics of spareness has been taken to such an extreme that some moss and lichens are the only living things. Fifteen stones, chosen for form and texture, sit like islands in a rectangle, smaller than a tennis court, of raked white pebbles. A fairly faithful replica of it can be seen in the Brooklyn Botanic Garden in New York City. Many Westerners find the garden affected or intolerably sterile, but enraptured Japanese viewers have been known to perceive among the stones such extravagances as a mother tiger swimming with a cub on her back. More restrainedly, the abbot of Ryoanji, Joei Matsukura, says, "We can view the garden as a group of mountainous islands in a great ocean, or as mountaintops rising above a sea of clouds. This garden is such a profoundly meaningful one that it might better be called 'Garden of Nothingness' or 'Garden of Emptiness' than

'Garden of Stones.' " The critic Sacheverell Sitwell pronounced Ryoanji to be "among the most original conceptions of the human intellect." And so it is. The sense of exact proportion among the stone groupings, of mathematical tension so precise that no stone could be moved, much less removed, reverberates in the eye and gut of the viewer and produces a supernatural calm.

Reverberates, that is, when the verandah of Ryoanji temple is not so crowded with jostling tourists that one has to look at the garden over somebody else's shoulder. Sometimes Ryoanji in reality does not work as well as Ryoanji in photographs.

Some Kyoto temple gardens are landscape pictures, copying some Sung Dynasty painting with symbolic stones (chosen with much fuss and brought from afar, wrapped in silk) and shaped trees and shrubs. Or sometimes a replica of an actual Japanese landscape, abstracted and miniaturized. The lines of sight are so carefully thought out that one should view these re-creations kneeling, not standing, on the temple verandah. But the outer corridors and the short bridges between temples also link up with the garden perspectives, so that walking along these ambulatories is a visual entertainment. Monks preserve the gardens by consulting notebooks as much as five hundred years old.

Kyoto's Shinto shrines lack the intellectual content of the Buddhist temples, but the more important of them, being large and colorful and open to the street, give the city some needed embellishment. Orange-painted Gion shrine, in the geisha sector, becomes at night a sorcerer's demesne, with paper lanterns shedding soft light on the parklike surroundings and fortunetellers lurking in dark corners. Another Shinto center, the Heian shrine, Kyoto's greatest (and almost only) unwalled spectacle, is a three-fifths-scale copy of the first Imperial Palace, built in 794. The present building dates back eighty-one years, having been put up on the 1100th anniversary of Kyoto's founding. Crimson lacquer, blue tiles, extensive gilding, and embossed brass fittings make this big edifice scintillate. Kamigamo shrine, on Kyoto's northern edge, *is* old, older than the city, having been the shrine of an ancient tribe. On May 5 each year, ten horses are raced at Kamigamo, and all are deemed to win, for the gods of the shrine hate a loser.

Shinto shrines and Buddhist temples resemble one another in architecture, and frequently stand side by side. But shrines are often painted, while temples are a weathered brown; and shrines always have *torii* gates, consisting of two pillars of wood or granite, slanting slightly inward and topped by a double beam.

The palace that the imperial family left behind when the crown moved to Tokyo in 1868 stands empty but maintained, as though ready to house the emperor again if the march of history returns the capital to Kyoto. It is an unpalatial place, low-built and highly inflammable, though its handsome green grounds provide the city with the nearest thing to a Central Park. The adobe-colored buildings, though high-ceilinged, are single-storied, and mostly thatched, like a farmhouse, with cypress bark. Falling fireworks ignited this roofing on one building in 1959 and destroyed it—but then imperial palaces in Kyoto have burned down half a dozen times since 794.

In pondering Japan's political history, it is provocative to compare the Imperial Palace with Nijo Castle, the Kyoto residence of all the mighty shoguns from 1603 until it was handed over by the deposed last Tokugawa in 1884. Not only is Nijo more gorgeous in entrances and painted screens ("worthy of a Doge," wrote Sitwell), but it is also fitted with secret chambers for guards to protect the shogun, a person acknowledged to be more worth protecting than the emperor. The passages are floored so that a footfall causes them to emit a sound like birdsong. The people of Kyoto call these "nightingale floors," although a similar corridor in one temple is thought by discriminating critics to sound more like the call of the bush warbler. In any case, assassins could not sneak up on the shogun. I assume that this pretty little story is true, since making floors so uniformly squeaky without intending to would seem improbably sloppy for the meticulous Japanese.

Trod by tireless Japanese sightseers, so numerous that Nijo Castle requires several acres of parking space for tour buses, the nightingale floors tirelessly chirp a song of Kyoto's past. Yet this is not by any means a dying museum town. Fully half its fascination comes from its animated present, from a sense of liveliness uninterrupted since the eighth century. Some of the street scenes speak less of a haughty imperial city than of a comfortable village multiplied many times. Lovers scrawl their names on walls, not inside a heart but under a stylized umbrella. Railroad crossing gates are made of bamboo, painted alternately yellow and black in accordance with the joints. Signs everywhere warn against drunk driving. A rusty air-raid siren on top of a building is a reminder that, although spared, Kyoto lived in fear of incendiary bombing; the broad firebreaks it cleared for this contingency now serve as boulevards. Aboard every bus, a tape-recorded female voice, triggered over and over by the opening of the doors, warns passengers not to get on with cans of gasoline or other high explosives, for the safety of everybody.

On the streets there are Shinto priests in getups like Druids, unctuous young men in neat, quiet pinstripes, blue-jeaned hippies. There are crones only three and a half feet tall, bar hostesses with hair bleached red, kimonoed ladies in gauze masks. There are throngs of commuters who work in the offices of Osaka, twenty-six miles away, and Kobe, forty-seven miles. There are fat babies, and parades of schoolchildren, and courtly old men in tailcoats and striped pants. Away from the center you see shopping housewives wearing baggy black pants, tied at the ankles, over their kimonos, and white-aproned pushcart vendors tootling musical horns to sell bean curd, and girls holding pieces of newspaper under defecating dogs (it's the law). Perhaps the commonest figure of all in this Vatican of Buddhism is the black-kimonoed monk or priest. And sometimes the shaven-headed, black-robed monks whom tourists from the United States gawk at on Kawaramachi street turn out to be their own countrymen. "Now why would an American boy do a thing like that?" asked one matron who had gone out for a walk from her room at the Kyoto Holiday Inn. The abbot of a temple in Daitokuji, quoting a lad who applied for Zen studies there, supplied a typical answer. "He told me that in America, people are ants working for the sugar of affluence. But the sugar is no longer attractive to some ants and they are beginning to wonder what they need more than sugar. That is why he is here to learn about Zen."

Kyoto is a patrician city, a Boston to Tokyo's New York. Kyoto cannot forget that it was Japan's capital for a thousand years. Tradition lies heavy on it. Unlike elsewhere in Japan, pedigree counts for something in Kyoto. People trace themselves back to formidable samurai, or cite connections with the royal family. Kyotans move a little slower than other Japanese. They speak with a more elegant accent, which sounds somewhat effeminate to their countrymen. They are more sophisticated and enigmatic. The people of Tokyo say of the people of Kyoto (in an ironic echo of what Americans say of all Japanese): "You can never tell what they're thinking!"

In strange tandem with this aristocratic bent goes Kyoto's spirited position in the left wing of politics. Part of the explanation, one politician told me, is that the loss of the capital to Tokyo a century ago still rankles, so Kyoto "has a tendency to be against the federal power in Tokyo," which is conservative. More profoundly, Kyoto's leftism derives from the work of a Kyoto aristocrat, a professor at Kyoto University named Hajime Kawakami. In 1927 he translated *Das Kapital* into Japanese, thus making Marxism a significant and respectable political philosophy despite the fascism of the times.

Socialist thought appealed to the workers in Kyoto's cottage industries, which, in contrast to the corporate industry elsewhere in the country, do not pay high wages. Professor Kawakami created a leftist tradition that is still demonstrated by the left-wing coalition majorities in the Kyoto city and prefectural councils of recent decades—a pattern similar to, but stronger than, that of Governor Minobe's backers in Tokyo. The most dominant leader of the left in the Kyoto area is the prefectural governor, Torazo Ninagawa, who has been in office now for twenty-five years.

Ninagawa, who is in his late seventies but looks fifty, perfectly embodies the aristocratic Marxist. His ancestors were not merely samurai but full-fledged *daimyo*, feudal lords. He calls himself a progressive, which is the Japanese catchword for the leaders of coalitions that include Socialists and Communists; of these supporters it is the Communists who are his warmest admirers. He holds a doctorate in economics from Kyoto University, and specialized in statistics. In April 1974 he won election to a seventh four-year term as governor. To show what Kyoto thinks of Tokyo, Ninagawa refuses to go to the capital, ever. To show Ninagawa what Tokyo thinks of Kyoto, the powerful central government effectively prevents any Marxist alterations to the prefectural government or economy. So Kyoto struggles with bourgeois problems in a bourgeois way. Housing is as bad as the national average, and the sewer system covers only 40 percent of the city. Buses and streetcars run a $6-million deficit each year; the federal Finance Ministry has approved the idea of a subway, and Kyoto is appealing to the national government for funds to build it.

In world recognition, however, the most celebrated citizen of Kyoto is not a politician but the physicist Hideki Yukawa. In 1949 he won the Nobel Prize for deducing the existence of the meson, subsequently found in cosmic rays—an outstanding example of the application of mathematical reasoning to physical problems. The scope of his thinking has now grown far beyond pure physics. He is obsessed with the wrenching question of how the scientist, sworn only to know more and more, to pursue truth in nature, should behave when he discovers that his truth can be used for terrible ends. "Newton constructed his system and nothing very serious happened during his lifetime, and he was happy," Dr. Yukawa contends. "Later, of course, his discoveries were the basis of the satellites and the trips to the moon, which are not necessarily bad. But Einstein discovered that a small mass could be changed into a large amount of energy, and had to live to see the atomic bomb."

"Japanese scientist" is something of a contradiction in terms, as Yukawa himself has acknowledged: "The Japanese mentality is unfit for abstract thinking . . . the indifferent pursuit of truth" does not appeal to it. In his own case, the paradox is resolved by his background and brilliance. Long ago he spent five years at Princeton and four years at Columbia, absorbing Western thought—although his wife complains that in Manhattan he used to walk the streets several steps ahead of her in the old Japanese style. To his Japanese mentality and his experience in the West, he adds an intellect powerful enough to synthesize the twain. A by-product is that he is deeply interested in the philosophical differences in Eastern and Western thought and, by extension, the mysteries of intuition and creativity. He also composes haiku.

Yukawa is a quietly forceful man with a large, square countenance. As he and his wife sat side by side in their book-cluttered, Western-style living room, they emanated serenity. Servants brought tea and grapes, which Yukawa ignored as he continued to talk about the consequences of science. Nuclear researchers first began to feel deep alarm, he said, after the American bomb test at Bikini in 1954, when the Japanese fishing boat *Fortunate Dragon* was caught in the fallout and its sailors came down with a mysterious and deadly disease. Scientists had simply not known "how dangerous the fallout was going to be," Yukawa said. He was particularly apprehensive about the leakage of radioactivity from atomic electric-generating plants.

But how can a scientist call off an investigation into the unknown when the dangers that it might create are by definition unknown? Dr. Yukawa thought that for trained scientists working in developmental research, the perils would be visible in time. "We must warn as early as possible. We should not balance off the good and bad, but completely avoid the bad."

In temple-dotted Kyoto, of course, scientists have to share respect with abbots. A courtly and learned representative of this profession is Boku-o Seki, head of suburban Tenryuji temple. I talked to him one noon as we lunched on pink rice from lacquered trays on the tatami-mat floor of a large ceremonial room. The occasion was the anniversary of the founding of the temple in 1339, and perhaps a hundred lay and religious worthies sat on their heels around the edge of the room. All of them made a point, by turns, of approaching Seki on their knees to bow low, hiss with indrawn breath, and pay their respects to the abbot.

Between these devoirs, I asked the abbot, a tall, bony man with a kindly air, whether some sort of revelation or profound spiritual call had drawn him to the priesthood. Not at all, he said, and went on to explain that, at the age of twenty-three, while a student at Tokyo University, a girl he loved suddenly jilted him. His despair made him resolve to be a monk—and what city could be better for that purpose than Kyoto? Following the ancient custom, he stood outside the gate at Myoshinji, waiting to be called in and given vows. No one called. So he went to Tenryuji, was taken in, and rose over the years to abbot. As it happened, he then found a woman who pleased him, and married her.

"The way to ruin a man is to introduce him to Gion," say the matrons of Kyoto. One of the more memorable pleasure quarters of the world, Gion is a Place Pigalle with geishas, a Rio with rickshaws, a Kasbah with Japanese lanterns. The life centers in the teahouses, rows and rows of them along the dim side streets. Behind brown latticed doors with frosted-glass panes are little gardens, paper walls, mazes of small rooms, much polished wood. The ideographs on the lanterns beside the doors spell out their naïve names: Happiness Hall, Turtle and Crane, Pleasure Dome. Strangers cannot just walk in; introductions and invitations are required. Nearby there are three- and four-story buildings entirely occupied by numerous tiny walk-up bars, of which some prefer to serve only their regular clientele, and others welcome anybody.

But primarily Gion is famed for its geishas. They are considered Japan's most beautiful, accomplished, and diverse. Even Tokyo firms bring their best customers to Kyoto's Gion for special occasions. According to the highest geisha tradition of the past—and Kyoto's is the highest—a girl set out on the road to geishahood at the age of six years six months, when her geisha mother started her training. She learned to play the samisen, to sing, to make up her face, to do her hair, to wear her triple kimonos with grace, to arrange flowers, to perform the tea ceremony, and to read and converse intelligently (the word "geisha" means "art person"). Between the ages of twelve and eighteen, she served as a *maiko*, an apprentice, attending to the bath and dress of an older geisha and silently pouring sake at parties. After some rich man with a taste for defloration ended her virginity, she went into the full practice of her profession, adopting some such *nom de guerre* as Clever Girl, Little Sleeve, Golden One, or Flower Willow.

Nowadays, though there are still some dynastic geishas, any girl with an elegant kimono, some piquancy, and a smattering acquaintance with song and dance can become a geisha. I heard of a girl

whose experience as a bus tour guide proved ample for the transformation to geisha. Thoroughly modern geishas play golf, go on
strike, and drive to work in their own cars, instead of taking the
hallowed rickshaws. They even wear panties, something older geishas
find unthinkably newfangled. A common misapprehension outside
Japan is that geisha is just another name for prostitute. Some of them,
in truth, are rightfully called Daruma geisha, after the small spherical
Daruma dolls that can so easily be rolled onto their backs. Many
more settle for long-range mistress relationships with rich patrons.
But lots of them live two or three together in apartments with an old
mamasan to care for and dress them, and they are often home in bed
by ten o'clock.

The spread of amateurism among geishas makes them difficult
to count. A fair guess is that there are 35,000 and that their number
is growing because of Japanese affluence, despite the boldly carnal
competition they get from bar hostesses.

A geisha party is an early-evening teahouse dinner enlivened by
drinking and made amusing by the girls. In bunned hair, whitened
faces, and brilliant kimonos, they sing to the thin notes of a samisen,
play the flute, spin fans, make risqué puns. They dance alone,
or with the male guests, who are usually businessmen for whom
geishas (as one of them put it) "are the necessary bridge between their work and home." After much sake, the men and girls
play silly games like blind man's buff or passing straws held between
the upper lip and the nose. Western businessmen, attending these
parties as expense-account guests of Japanese executives (cost: $70
to $100 per man), find them an ordeal. "Embarrassing and unbe-
lievably boring," writes the Australian iconoclast Hal Porter, who
described the geisha as "a cross between a cheer-leader and a practical
joker," and deplored her "boomps-a-daisy party games." The girls are
essentially teases. Eroticism is mostly confined to pats, squeezes, and
bottom slapping. Japanese men, who appreciate the tradition and
savor the jokes, obviously have more fun at geisha parties; but their
pleasure comes also from a certain crepuscular silliness that sometimes overwhelms an otherwise earnest people. S. I. Hayakawa theo-
rizes that these men may be acting out "the Japanese male's desire
to return to childhood."

In *The Mikado*, Koko asks Katisha if a woman improves with
age. "Is a maiden all the better if decayed?" Kyoto opinion holds that
a geisha can readily serve until she is forty-five, and even after that
she can go on displaying her professional charm as proprietress of
some comfortable little bar. The most famous geisha in Kyoto history

was a girl named Oyuki (Honorable Snow), who in 1903 bedazzled a nephew of J. P. Morgan when the young man stopped in Kyoto on a round-the-world tour. He married her, after in effect buying her for $50,000 from those who had paid for her education as a geisha. The couple lived in New York and France until he died in 1913. Years later, she returned to Kyoto, and with Morgan money financed the construction of a Roman Catholic church that still stands near the Gold Pavilion.

The moon that shines over Kyoto is the same moon that shines over Kraków or Keokuk, but by an ancient rite Kyoto makes the moon its own. This is the bacchanale known as moon viewing. The invitation for the one that I attended gave the address in a couple of scrawled ideographs, indecipherable to me. But I showed them to a cab driver, and in a few minutes we pulled up in front of the high, closed gates of a Buddhist temple which I recognized as the famed and ancient Ninnaji. I discovered a small entrance to one side, went in, and saw . . .

Well, what I saw was by no means what I thought I might see, a handful of connoisseurs of lunar beauty, silent, heads upturned, awestruck, murmuring their delight, perhaps, as the full moon peeked through passing clouds. My solemn expectations may have been stirred by memories of reading the last words of Princeton-educated Rear Admiral Tamon Yamaguchi, who went down with the carrier *Hiryu* (after Americans dive-bombed it at the Battle of Midway), remarking to the ship's captain: "There is such a beautiful moon tonight. Shall we watch it as we sink?" No, what I saw was another kind of lunacy entirely. On the temple's broad, mat-floored verandah, a throng of happily pickled guests sat cross-legged at low tables forested with tall porcelain bottles and thimble-size sake cups, plus dainty wooden picnic boxes half-emptied of rice and radishes and raw fish. These revelers were mostly white-shirted businessmen, together with a few bureaucrats, doctors, and writers, plus some comely bar hostesses picked up on the way to the rite. One group was singing "Auld Lang Syne." Three men, each having discovered what really wonderful chaps the others were, had collapsed in tipsy hilarity into one another's arms. Elsewhere, a man had risen to sing some old samisen song and dance to it, geisha style.

But my host, a real moon man, had not come just for food and drink. He led me off round a corner of the verandah, and we were suddenly in a silent moonstruck world of light and shadow. Ninnaji has historically alternated between roles as a palace and a temple;

full moons have shone down upon it since the year 888. Emperors and retired emperors beyond recollection have viewed the moon, presumably with imperial sobriety, at Ninnaji. We looked out over silvery raked gravel to misty shrubs and beyond to trees pruned to sharp black silhouettes against the luminous sky, and only reluctantly departed.

Back at the gate two of the guests, in business suits, were lying, cheerfully full of sake, on their backs on the pavement. Indubitably the best position for viewing the moon, they explained. Oscar Wilde would have understood. "We are all in the gutter, but some of us are looking at the stars," says a character in *Lady Windermere's Fan*.

15 /

The Outer Spaces

WHEN I WAS VERY YOUNG, my atlas showed Japan colored all green, and I imagined Japan as a land green underfoot, green to the horizon, green like the Emerald City, green in detail, greenly lighted, green if seen from high above. When I finally got to Japan, decades later, this green vision was, for the most part, pleasantly confirmed.

The green of well-watered Japan is essentially the yellow-green of rice in the leveled alluvial bottoms plus the deep green of forests that dress the mountains that rise in four-fifths of the country. What gives the Japanese landscape its special character is the special character of rice—it must be grown in a one-inch-deep pond of water. The Japanese have met this demand by laboriously dividing, flattening, terracing, and diking nearly all of what once was green rolling country. From an airplane Japan's lowlands are an infinity of small verdant mirrors, flashing the sun back to the eye. Japan's greatest asset, and greatest investment, is these thirteen thousand square miles of green land leveled in little square terraces by the strong backs of generations long gone.

Terraced up some tiny valley, the paddies make a geometry of different hues of green, set against the blue-green of the background mountains or, down-valley, against the white-capped aquamarine of the sea. Seen from eye level, the green stems of the rice harmonize with the azure of the sky reflected in the paddy water. Seen from on high, the paddies form patterns of varying green according to how they are contoured, or arbitrarily parallelogrammed, or blocked into the surveying-instrument rectangles of the postwar land reform. Near villages, the paddies, bordered by banks and ditches, make the green squares of a checkerboard, alternating with the iron gray of the roof tiles of the intermixed housing lots. In industrial areas, patches of green rice relieve the blasted landscape.

The green of the forests that cover Japan is a green of varying textures. Through one long, dreamy September afternoon, we rode on a train southward along the east coast of verdant Kyushu. At first, as we climbed a spur of the mountains, the forest was all bottle-green conifers, dense enough to raise the speculation that no man had ever set foot there—until we noticed that the trees were lined up in perfectly straight rows. The green of Japan's mountains is mostly the green of tree farms rather than the green of wilderness; the Japanese love of the touch and look of wood in houses has long since cost the country most of its natural forest. On the hillside plantations, the black-green crowns of the mature cypresses made a pattern like the warp and woof of some nubby fabric. Separated by ruler-straight borders from these trees ready for harvest were logged-off patches of mottled-green seedlings and underbrush, and next to them the shiny green of well-pruned half-grown trees poking upward like rows of daggers. The train speeded down the other side of the spur, its draft flattening and fluttering the oily green leaves of a junglelike deciduous forest. Turning west, we crossed the high center of Kyushu through misty evergreens mixed with snippets of rice paddy, and sighted the Fuji-shaped, blue-green slopes of Mount Sakura-jima, a volcano-peninsula in the shimmery turquoise of Kagoshima Bay.

The commonest Japanese tree is the cedar, generally debranched in the lower trunk to make it grow straight and knot-free, and rising to a tuft that makes rounded hills look as though they were clothed in soft green fur. It is the flat green of cedar leaves that colors the mountains north of Kyoto. At mills and sheds in the harmonious little towns of the twisting valleys, women scrape the red cortex from the slender young trunks to make naturally fluted columns for the alcoves of sukiya-style houses. In the lofty, green-canopied cedar forest on Mount Koya, near Osaka, men climb huge cedars three hundred years old to get seeds from which to plant more such big trees, which will presumably be needed two or three centuries from now for pillars in the rebuilding of temples and shrines. Under the green mushrooms of their crowns, similar cedars stand like ghosts in the gloomy natural forests of Unzen National Park, with a tangle of vines and bushes at their feet.

Japan's other evergreens are silver fir, white fir, larch, hemlock, spruce, and several kinds of pine. Patient gardeners dote on pine, for by plucking some needles before they can grow into branches, while leaving others to form green branch-tip clusters, and by training trunks and boughs into grotesque twists and loops, they can make the pine into a living sculpture.

And yet more green: the green of the bamboo's feathers, and of the dull oval leaves of the persimmon displaying yellow-orange fruit like Christmas globes. Green of palms and weeping willows. Green of corn, grape, maguey, mulberry, tobacco, Chinese cabbage; of tea shrubs shaped like shaggy boulders, just uphill from the paddies, and above the tea, the glossy green leaves of tangerine trees. Green of algae in fish ponds, and even of the potted plant that the captain keeps in the wheelhouse of the ferry to Miyajima.

The green archipelago of Japan, with its four large and 3,918 small islands, has a total land area of 142,726 square miles; it is somewhat smaller than Montana, Paraguay, Spain, or Sweden, and somewhat larger than New Mexico, the United Kingdom, Italy, or New Zealand. Honshu, the main island, is 800 miles long, site of all the major cities, and the home of 85 million people. On a map it looks like a circus seal, head to the north, tail curving off westward toward Korea; and the ball that it balances on its nose is the South Carolina–size island of Hokkaido, Japan's far north, with more than 5 million people. Under the seal's tail is dumbbell-shaped Shikoku, a little bigger than Connecticut, with 4 million people; and at the tail's end is Kyushu, the size of New Hampshire plus Vermont, with 12 million people. Two long spurs of the archipelago form the Ryukyu island chain, notably Okinawa, between Kyushu and Taiwan, and the Bonins, notably Iwo Jima, poking southward into the Pacific from central Honshu.

If the Japanese islands were swept straight eastward until they overlaid the Atlantic coast of the United States, they would run from Montreal to Tallahassee. Sapporo, the capital of Hokkaido, would lie on top of Syracuse; Tokyo would be near Durham, North Carolina; Kyoto and Osaka near Charlotte; and Kitakyushu, the biggest city of Kyushu, on top of Atlanta. The climate is not quite a match. Sapporo in winter is a few degrees warmer than Syracuse; Kitakyushu in summer is a few degrees cooler than Atlanta; and all points of Japan have as much as 50 percent more rainfall. Tokyo in the summer is oppressively hot, all sweat-in-the-small-of-the-back between stops in air-conditioned places.

Geologically, the Japanese archipelago is a huge upsurge of volcanoes forming an arc that touches the Asian continental shelf on both ends and encloses the Sea of Japan. The mountains are, in actuality, all the higher because they drop off eastward into the Japan Trench, which at 35,000 feet is the third-greatest ocean deep in the world (after the Mindanao and Marianas trenches). What makes the Japanese islands so precipitous is the fact that they are the summits of underseas mountains. The oldest and lowest rocks are metamorphic schists, pierced by volcanic action that pushed up masses of granite and diorite to form the highest peaks. All over Japan, tombstones, stepping stones, and stone lanterns speak of the abundance of granite in the country. Some of Japan's 150 volcanoes are still active. One of them, Mount Aso in Kyushu, has a crater with two-thousand-foot walls and an area of ten by fourteen miles. In many parts of the country, hot springs bubble and steam.

Mount Fuji, Japan's loftiest mountain at 12,397 feet, is more than a mere mountain. It is perhaps the world's most perfect volcanic cone, symmetrical as a diagram. From nearly sea level, it rises in splendor and isolation out of the Kanto Plain, site of Tokyo, and can be seen for miles around in a way that Mount Everest cannot, nor the Jungfrau, nor Mount Whitney. Mount Fuji is a major image in Japanese painting and printmaking, symbolizing something mystical and proud, an immaculate (at least from a distance) presence detached from human weaknesses, near yet far, and definitely Japan's own. Geologically, Fuji is relatively young, having been formed only three hundred thousand years ago. It last erupted in 1707, covering Tokyo, sixty miles to the east, with six inches of ashes.

Three north-south ranges, lying roughly parallel to one another but well west of Fuji, divide the thick middle of Honshu. They are the Japanese Alps, and dozens of their peaks rise higher than eight thousand feet. The top of Fuji is barren lava cinders, but the peaks of the lesser mountains grow alpine plants. In some places, volcanic craters, ripped by terrible explosions, make a scalloped skyline, but spectacular cliffs, bare pinnacles, Grand Canyons, and snowy sierras are not in the Japanese style of mountains. Their beauty is of a gentler kind, the simple, peaceful presence of round forested knobs forever within view, almost no matter where one is, divided by cozy, steep-sided, V-shaped valleys cut by rushing streams.

The streams carry to the coastline the sediment that has formed Japan's minuscule plains, which are so few and so vital for rice that they are carefully named and ranked. The biggest, seventy-five miles square, is the Kanto Plain, surrounding Tokyo. Sapporo, in Hokkaido, lies at the edge of the second-largest plain, the Ishikari; and Osaka and Nagoya lie in lesser plains. For many miles along the Sea of Japan coast, the narrow plains are made up of dunes, the closest thing to a desert in green Japan, but out of the desperate need for productive land, farmers are stabilizing the sand with vegetation and turning the dunes into orchards. This western coast is relatively unindented, measuring 2,887 miles, as against the 10,562 miles of bays and peninsulas of the Pacific coast, where the sinking of the land has dropped many valleys into the sea. But both coasts—except where industry dominates—are continuously pleasant, ornamented by caverns, natural bridges, islands just big enough for one house, wind-eroded fantasies, and landlocked bays that are any sailor's dream.

Japan was sufficiently connected to the rest of the world by prehistoric land bridges and by stepping-stone islands to have been reached by all the standard animals; the mystery is that so many species, including all big animals, are missing. One sole primate, apart from man, made the immigration: the pink-faced Japanese macaque, and this doughty little monkey lives as far north as the snowy tip of Honshu. Deprived of glamorous beasts, Japan is left with a rather pedestrian population of bears, badgers, foxes, otters, martens, squirrels, moles, and bats, mostly smaller than their mainland counterparts. Deer, tame and fed by tourists, overrun the temple grounds at Nara, but elsewhere they are rare. I kept seeing snakes in cemeteries, but barring the deadly *habu* of Okinawa, the Japanese snakes are harmless, and the largest is only five feet long. The flora, which also arrived by island hopping, are standard and mostly unspectacular; the greenery of Japan is a bulk product, not the sum of beautiful minutiae.

To see green Japan, a good way to start is to take the Romance Train, so designated to single it out from the humdrum commuter trains at Tokyo's Shinjuku Station. A silvery streamliner, its engineer's compartment is molded atop the front of the head car, like a Boeing 747, so that children can sit in the nose of the train and shriek their delight at its speed as it races from Tokyo southwest to Odawara. At Odawara you transfer to a romance train of another kind, a Toonerville Trolley that toils at precisely twelve kilometers per hour through many switchbacks to the mountainside town of Gora, where tourists buy butterfly nets and tomato juice. The next form of transportation is a cable car that hoists itself to a high pass and deposits you at the terminus of an aerial tramway. The child buried in every Japanese adult adores "ropeways" like this, and they are so common that sometimes Japan seems like one immense Disneyland. In jumps of more than a mile, this one crosses several deep valleys, one of them called "Valley of the Greater Boiling" because hot water and sulfur fumes spout from it everywhere. The ropeway alights on the shore of a crater lake called Ashi, and there you board another toy, a ferry got up as a pirate ship, and sail to the tourist town of Hakone, where great lords once passed in their litters on the Tokaido road between Edo and the west. (There are, to be sure, several highways that reach Hakone—the tram-ropeway-ferry route is mostly for fun. But railways bypass Hakone in tunnels about two thousand feet below.)

Hakone is a place that shares atmosphere with both the south of France and the more expensive parts of the Catskills. We stayed at the Hotel de Yama, in a tatami room opening onto a garden of flowering shrubs with Mount Fuji as the backdrop—an almost surrealistically perfect example of Japanese loveliness. On this site once sat the country villa of Mitsubishi's Baron Iwasaki. The service seemed as if it were still patterned after what the great baron expected and got. I counted twenty-seven separate receptacles brought to serve the two of us our evening meal in our room (the hotel, like not too many other Japanese inns, has a dining room, but the classical way is to eat in one's own quarters). There were china dishes both square and round, and other vessels of glass, pottery, and wood, all intentionally in many patterns, rather than forming a matching set. Breakfast consisted of fish paste with horseradish, raw egg and pickles, seaweed in a bowl of brine, a cucumber-lettuce-and-carrot salad with dressing, dried salmon, rice, soup, and tea. We took a large, comfortable, but all too prosaic bus down-mountain to Atami, a seaside resort spiritually akin to Brighton or Atlantic City, and there caught the bullet train back to Tokyo.

This sort of excursion is the way millions of Japanese escape the trials of life in Tokyo, or, more generally, the whole Kanto region. To the Japanese, Kanto stands for wealth and power. It includes not only rich Tokyo-Yokohama, but also the nation's largest stretch of farmland. North of Tokyo the flat land goes on for mile after mile like northern Oklahoma put into rice paddies, but instead of farmers driving tractors you see straw-hatted figures cultivating the black earth between rows of leafy vegetables. Most of the ample wooden or stucco farmhouses have, as a second story, one single bedroom, with views in all four directions—an attractive arrangement. Amid these farmlands is the city of Utsunomiya, near the edge of the plain. Utsunomiya has lately provided itself, in a setting of small houses and dusty streets, with a perfect diamond of an art gallery, the Tochigi Prefectural Museum of Fine Arts. The building is a tall cube of glass sliced here and there into angles and overhangs, with rough white-marble brick for some of the inside walls. The 317,000 people of

Utsunomiya can enjoy paintings and graphics by Japanese artists who have worked at home, in the United States, and in Europe; one handsome set piece is a series of Picassoesque Buddhist saints by Shiko Munakata.

Nikko, not strictly on the Kanto Plain but up in the mountains just beyond Utsunomiya, is a banal tourist magnet that really is marvelous in a gaudy sort of way. Nikko is first of all a shrine town, built three and a half centuries ago to provide a mausoleum for Ieyasu Tokugawa, the iron leader who sealed Japan off from the West. The shrine's fifteen thousand designers and carpenters utterly abandoned the restraint that characterized the bulk of Japanese temple architecture until then, and put up twenty-two buildings of riotous lacquerwork, fantastic carving, and gold-leaf ornamentation. Nikko is both Buddhist and Shintoist, the two faiths jumbled happily together. The planners drew from Chinese models as well as from the earlier Momoyama ("Japanese Baroque") style, and gave Nikko dragons, reliquaries, crests, phoenixes, and angels. Here is the original of the much-reproduced "simian trinity"—the carved hear-no-evil, speak-no-evil, see-no-evil monkeys, who hold their hands, respectively, over their ears, mouth, and eyes. A blue-and-purple five-storied pagoda is barely taller than the great cedars beside it; and thirteen thousand other cedars, planted in 1625, line twenty-three miles of avenues in Nikko. I know of no other structure in Asia, except the wats of Bangkok, that surpasses Nikko shrine in imagery and brilliance.

A whole other side of Nikko is the scenery of the national park that surrounds it. Two dizzying roads (one up, one down) connect the town to cold, blue Lake Chuzenji, elevation 4,171 feet. The down road, on a grade as steep as 14 percent, has forty-eight hairpin curves, most of them swinging more than 200 degrees.

In a brewing typhoon one July afternoon, a friend who lives in Yokohama showed me Japan's biggest port (and the world's second biggest, after New York), just south of Tokyo. Twelve thousand oceangoing ships call here each year, as well as ninety thousand coasters and other smaller vessels. This port moves nearly 200 million tons of Datsuns, soybeans, machinery, chemicals, and other goods a year. Yokohama was invented as Japan's response to Western demands for trade more than a century ago. The idea was to get the British, the Americans, and the French away from Tokyo by planting them among a straggle of fishermen's huts along the western coast of Tokyo Bay, hard by a salt swamp and a tidal creek.

At what is now Yokohama the government built a substantial custom house, granite jetties, a stone wharf—and more. "The Japanese officials," wrote the outraged bishop of Hong Kong after a visit, "have also endeavoured to render Yokohama an attractive locality to young unmarried foreigners by establishing at the edge of the settlement and on a site approached by a narrow drawbridge over the canal, one of those infamous public institutions . . . containing its two hundred female inmates dispersed over a spacious series of apartments and all under government regulation and control." Even more solicitously, the government arranged for permanently settled foreigners to acquire mistresses by direct negotiations with the custom house.

Largely because the Americans were having at one another in the Civil War, the British took preeminence in Yokohama (as in Kobe), in best colonial style. They attended to business in their warehouses from ten to four, with two hours off for lunch at the club; they hunted foxes and enjoyed the airs of the regimental band at dinner parties. The 1923 earthquake devastated Yokohama even more thoroughly than it had Tokyo, but the indomitable populace threw the rubble into the sea as landfill, and had the city nicely rebuilt in time for the bombing in World War II to flatten it again. As re-rebuilt, Yokohama looks like Liverpool with palms. The legendary British trading firm Butterfield & Swire still has offices on the waterfront Bund, an ornamental esplanade that lets Yokohama look at the bay. On the rainy day when I looked at it, the harbor was a drenched scene of gray ships half visible through the wet; and up on the Bluff, where foreigners live, the rain dripped down the stone Christian crosses of the Foreign General Cemetery. On one tombstone I read: "To the loving memory of Charles Davys Moss, Late of Her Britannic Majesty's Court for Japan"—Her Majesty being Victoria.

Yokohama suffers from the inner-city decay that affects American cities, but near Yokohama Station several new department stores (making a total of five side by side) showed that businessmen have faith in the city. But being so young, in Japanese terms, Yokohama is, despite its big population (2,430,000), less a city than a facility. It has no major temples, shrines, art galleries, or historical sites. One of its few conspicuous buildings turned out, when I asked about it, to be not precisely Yokohama's but rather the capitol of Kanagawa Prefecture, whose 6 million people make it the third most populous prefecture, after Tokyo and Osaka.

Kanagawa contains horrors and treasures. The major horror is Kawasaki, a smoky wasteland of chimneys, factories, and warehouses that nestles noisomely against Tokyo on its north and Yokohama on its south. The major treasure is Kamakura, a city of 147,000 enclosed by jungled hills except where it fronts on Sagami Bay, the ample indentation just west of Tokyo Bay. In the thirteenth century, when Kamakura was the de facto capital of Japan under the first shoguns, a skilled sculptor of the era, using 247,000 pounds of bronze, cast the Kamakura Great Buddha, the equivalent of four stories high and to this day one of the must-see sights of Japan. The temple built around it was fortunately carried away by a tidal wave a couple of centuries later, so that now it stands, epicanthic and bemustached, in open air against a wooded knoll. Sixty-five temples and nineteen shrines survive, giving Kamakura its fine flavor of religiousness and antiquity.

But twentieth-century Kamakura is largely a Tokyo commuter town. As commuters, we stayed for a month in a grand Japanese-Western house on one of Kamakura's rim hills, rocked once or twice by the mild earthquakes that are so commonplace throughout Japan. In this gentle spot thirty miles from the Ginza, one bright morning I saw nearby: a gardener digging sweet potatoes out of the wet earth, moss and lichens growing on blackened masonry, vines lushly clothing trees and bushes, carpenters building a house; and, more distant, the glittering Pacific; and, farther yet, Mount Fuji. Somewhere a garbage truck played nursery-rhyme melodies on chimes, to advise of its approach. Somewhere a priest chanted sutras. Japan is always more, much more, than bustle, commerce, and pollution.

A thermometer ten stories high on the side of a building in Sapporo, capital of Hokkaido, demonstrates succinctly how this northern island differs from most of the rest of Japan. For the thermometer can register as low as −20° C., which is −4° F., enough to cause plenty of snow. This is the cold island, the only one that ever had an ice age. Sheet metal, brightly painted, is the common roofing material in Hokkaido, because shoveling off the winter's six feet of snow (to prevent the building from collapsing) would damage the clay tiles used elsewhere in Japan. Hokkaido houses have furnaces or large stoves, and therefore chimneys; to someone accustomed to Tokyo, the sight of them comes as a shock. The tall orange-and-white stack of a central steam plant stands in the center of Sapporo. Sporting-goods stores display sturdy ski boots; one of the ski jumps used in the 1972 Winter Olympics virtually overlooks the city. Families can easily work in an hour of skiing before dinner, and mothers pull children on sleds while shopping.

Hokkaido was frontier country as recently as Kansas was. Until a century ago, the island's dominant inhabitants were the Ainu, Japan's aborigines. They believed that they had descended to earth from outer space, which might have seemed logical to the Japanese, who found them utterly exotic—round-eyed, big-nosed, hairy of face and body, swarthy in complexion, and stout in build. But apparently the truth is that they came seven thousand years ago to Hokkaido and northern Honshu from northern Asia after originating in the Caucasus, like the white race, and with the same basic genetic makeup. Pushing the Ainu back, the Japanese got a toehold on Hokkaido in the fifteenth century, but never fully occupied the island.

Immediately after the Meiji Restoration, the Tokyo government deemed it fitting to establish a colonization commission, chiefly to make it utterly clear to the Russians that Hokkaido was part of Japan and not part of Siberia (it is separated from the Russian island of Sakhalin by only thirty-five miles). For advisers to the commission, the government imported seventy-six foreigners, more than half of them Americans. Most influential were Horace Capron, a former U.S. commissioner of agriculture, and William Smith Clark, president of the Massachusetts Agricultural College, who founded what became the University of Hokkaido. As a bequest of these stern, bearded Americans, Hokkaido today has Iowa-style silos and Pennsylvania-Dutch barns (minus hex signs). Subsidized settlers poured into the island, and the government also sent a couple of thousand soldier-farmers, who milked cows and scared away Russians.

Capron, helping to found Sapporo, gave it a characteristic identical to every Kansas town that was being planned at the same time: a rigid grid of numbered streets at right angles to one another. In some other ways the city also seems American. The park in front of the prefectural capitol looks like Washington's Lafayette Square, and the phalanxes of government employees going to work at 8:50 A.M. similarly resemble those of the American capital. Sapporo, however, with 1,118,000 people, is considerably larger than Washington, with 756,000. The University of Hokkaido, with a grassy, poplar-lined campus like that of American land-grant schools, has exchange programs with the University of Massachusetts and Portland State College in Oregon—Portland being a sister city of Sapporo. Of Hokkaido U's ten thousand students, three-fourths study science, engineering, and agriculture.

Little touches make Sapporo seem surprisingly modern. The automated subway, like some other installations here and there around the world, uses magnetically coded tickets, which cleverly signal padded barriers to imprison anyone who tries to get out of a station without paying full fare. Outside the business area, the rubber-tired trains run for miles protected from snow by a windowed, above-ground tunnel of aluminum, which Sapporans call "the longest building in the world." The pedestrian Walk/Don't Walk signs play a tune that grows premonitorily louder as the light is about to change.

Sapporo specializes in a barbecue of bean sprouts and mutton (Hokkaido is chock-a-block with sheep). This dish is called Genghis Khan; for some peculiar reason, Hokkaido feels a particular affinity for the great twelfth-century Mongol who pushed his empire as close as the part of continental Asia (now Siberia) that lies two hundred miles to the west. Sapporo is also noteworthy for its cuckoos, which sojourn there in their migrations between Siberia and New Guinea. For some sappy Sapporan reason, billboards advertising porno movies have black patches pasted over the *eyes* of the naked girls. The Japanese penchant for fantasy is realized here during the winter ice carnival in massive snow sculptures set out on the promenade: gelid Buddhas, castles, temples. Of real castles and temples, all Hokkaido has only one of the former and few of the latter. Religion lays a light hand on this island; the people seem to prefer to attend the many bright-colored drive-in restaurants set out spaciously along the smooth new highways.

The feel of physical Hokkaido is the feel of Tasmania, Patagonia, Scandinavia, Alaska—nothing between here and the pole, though Sakhalin and other parts of dreary Siberia do lie farther north. National parks cover four large swatches of the island, preserving lakes (no outboards allowed), volcanic areas (vendors are forbidden to boil eggs in the bubbling water), and primeval spruce and fir like British Columbia's. Brown bears, which sometimes kill people, are in turn freely killed as dangerous pests. Its northerliness notwithstanding, Hokkaido's main crop is rice, but it also raises wheat, corn, apples, onions, potatoes, beans, oats, and sugar beets. Television commercials in Tokyo like to show Marlboro-country Japanese cowboys pounding leather in Hokkaido, but most of the cattle are really not ornery beef steers but peaceable moo-cows, yielding one-fifth of Japan's milk supply. Dairying makes good profits, and the government encourages farmers to shift from rice to cows. In a formidable set of stone buildings at Yoichi, Nikka whiskey is distilled from Hokkaido barley dried by burning Hokkaido peat.

Eighteen thousand Ainu survive in Hokkaido, fishing and truck gardening along the southern shore. Like American Indians, they sometimes don their traditional costumes, made of bark cloth or skins with geometrical designs, and some of the elders wear the foot-long beards of the "hairy Ainu," supposedly the world's most hirsute race. But just as white Americans have shattered the native Indian's culture, the Japanese have stamped out Ainu ways. The Ainu have been forced to take Japanese names, speak Japanese, farm instead of hunt. The last Ainu who could recite the race's epic poem died a couple of years ago—and the Ainu have no written language. Predictably, the younger Ainu, formed into the Ainu Liberation League, are angry. One of them lately stabbed a village mayor who proposed to group the local Ainu in a settlement, complete with straw houses and dugout canoes, that would attract tourists from Tokyo.

Shikoku is the smallest, the least populated, and the least important of the four major islands of Japan, but its people argue plausibly that, more than any other part of the country, it encapsulates the true and authentic Japan. Scenically, it performs the indispensable function of framing and forming the lovely Inland Sea, which is not so much a body of water as a piece of the Japanese psyche. The island's shores and mountains are unremittingly pleasing, and its cities proudly provincial. Historically, some of the most potent "outer lords" of the Tokugawa period were those who dominated what are now the four prefectures of Shikoku; nowadays, some of the most potent politicians in Tokyo come from Shikoku. In Matsuyama, the biggest city (population 340,000), in the northwestern corner of the island, I had the good fortune to meet Masaki Ohnishi, a young employee of the city government. He put down his pencil, put on his jacket, plunked me into the front seat of his car, and, while showing me around, told me about the city and the island.

"Matsuyama was badly bombed during the war"—it suddenly came home to me that the Americans bombed virtually every Japanese city of any consequence at all—"but it was rebuilt with a master plan under the New Towns Law. Now we have a bright and pretty city, but the new boulevards leading out of it are so inviting and efficient that everyone lives in the suburbs, and so we have to dig underground parking garages near the offices, and traffic accidents have become one of our biggest problems.

"The mountains around Matsuyama protect the city from typhoons, and the climate is almost tropical, so retired people come here from Tokyo to enjoy the good food and the cheap housing. Young men and women leave here for better jobs in the capital, but some of them—quite a few of them—come back in a couple of years. We call them 'U-turn workers.'

"Five million tourists a year come to Matsuyama, quite a few of them on foot," Ohnishi continued. "Ishite temple here is number fifty-one on the walking tour of eighty-eight temples around the island of Shikoku, which about seventy thousand Buddhist pilgrims make every year. They wear white robes and straw sandals. It takes two months. They are copying the great priest Kobo, who made the walk twelve hundred years ago. Sick people hobble clear around Shikoku, and then throw away their crutches at the last temple, like Catholics at Lourdes."

The pilgrims who circumambulate Shikoku, I learned, find themselves mostly in village country—only six cities have more than a hundred thousand people. Along the shore there are tiny shipyards, conical islets, fishing boats riding the blue water; inland, the customary haze makes the mountains appear to be cardboard cutouts placed one behind the other. Power plants mostly have three-legged smokestacks, painted with red and white stripes, looking like missiles on a launching pad. The south-coast city of Kochi stages fights that pit a rooster against a dog, and the east-coast city of Tokushima puts on a riotous festival in which the people dance all night in the streets and sing a song that has been translated as "Fools we are who dance, fools they are who watch us prance. Since a fool I must be, I want to be a dancing fool." At Takamatsu, a banking center on the northeast coast, the people like to view the Inland Sea from nearby Yashima Hill. There I saw laborers in undershirts eating grilled octopus or ice cream or a hard-boiled-egg-on-a-stick, as the Muzak played ". . . when we're out together dancing cheek to cheek."

Ohnishi told me, though, that not every pilgrim sees the sights of Shikoku on foot. "Lots of them take taxis or trains, and get clear around the island in a couple of days," he said with a broad smile. As he took me to my hotel on the night of our tour, he gave me a final injection of civic pride. "Matsuyama's castle, which is here on this hill, is the great original castle in Japan, because most of the others, you know, have been reconstructed in reinforced concrete. This one is made of wooden beams and stone masonry. The stones were all carried up the hill by women." The castle, floodlighted on top of the pitch-dark hill, seemed to be hovering in the sky, like a flying saucer got up in early Tokugawa style.

The astonishing spectacle nowadays on the Inland Sea between Shikoku and Honshu is the unending parade of big tankers, the stern of one not far ahead of the bow of the next, on water where pirates sailed four hundred years ago. This narrow sheet of ultramarine is 260 miles long and so shallow that the big ships clear the bottom by only ten or twenty feet. But it is generally smooth sailing because its four entrances from the ocean are so narrow that no high seas can get through. Hundreds of islands, little cones and steep-sided mounds, fill the sea like peppercorns.

Across this slender sea, an hour on the hydrofoil from Matsuyama, is Hiroshima and the seal's-tail appendage of Honshu that it dominates, the Chugoku region. Sand, sea, pines, and a sky full of hawks are trademark characteristics of Chugoku's Sea of Japan coast; they are happily combined with fifty temples and villagey little houses in the town of Hagi, where we stayed a day. Hiroshima itself is the place where the Mazda, the first practical rotary-engine car, is manufactured. Bright, trim buildings, distinctly new and running about ten stories high, occupy its broad downtown streets. A looming billboard on one of them, facing Peace Boulevard, proclaims the imperial rubric XEROX. In part of the area devastated by the Bomb, Hiroshima has one of Japan's liveliest "night industries," a warren of bars, cabarets, inns, and restaurants. Shopping centers glitter. A maypole of plastic flags dances over a used-car lot, together with a sign depicting a thumb and forefinger forming a circle, to suggest the flawlessness of the automobiles being offered. Mayor Setsuo Yamada is proud that Hiroshima has "markedly advanced manufacturing" and sorry that "cultural facilities are inadequate." The number of inhabitants recently hit 741,000, a swift ascent from that day in August 1945 when a 500,000-degree fireball killed 82,833 people and dispersed so many others that the population fell from 400,000 to 190,000.

Before the Bomb of August, Hiroshima had been raided only lightly. The people cherished a rumor that the city was being spared because President Truman's mother lived somewhere in Hiroshima. Then the Americans, "without stopping to think fully about what they were doing," as Reischauer puts it, dropped the bomb. The Atomic Bomb Memorial Museum in Hiroshima shows unforgettably what this weapon did. The most awesome and informative display is a mockup, as big and round as the Piccadilly fountain, of the city just after the bombing, centered on ground zero. At the bull's-eye, even streets are obliterated out to a radius of half a mile. All is wreckage and cinders, except for some reinforced concrete buildings, out to a mile. Beyond that, making an amazingly exact circle, houses not hit hard enough to collapse form a low wall around the edge of the display. Here and there, even in the smashed area, stands a chimney, untoppled because it got blast pressure equally from all sides. For the same reason, and because it was precisely beneath the parachuted bomb, which exploded at 1,980 feet of altitude, the substantial Industrial Exhibition Hall stands, in small replica, just as it stood after the detonation, damaged, even slightly melted, but not leveled. In rebuilt Hiroshima, this shattered building, with the bare-bones iron ribs of its lofty dome, remains where it was that day, now as the center of Peace Memorial Park.

As you can see from their solemn and puzzled demeanor, the Japanese and American tourists who look at these ghastly exhibits (after checking in at the posh Hotel New Hiroshima, right next door) are numbly debating all over again whether the bombing was justified. John Toland points out, in *The Rising Sun*, that Japan was beaten long before the Bomb; the fire storms of Tokyo had irrevocably settled that. The options were to fight on to national suicide, compelling an American invasion, or to surrender with maximum advantage (meaning, chiefly, that the emperor would not be hanged or even dethroned). The leadership angled for mediation by the Soviet Union to avoid unconditional surrender. Russia's hard answer was to declare war on Japan in the three days between the bombing of Hiroshima on August 6 and the bombing of Nagasaki on August 9. Precisely one minute before the Nagasaki bomb went off, Prime Minister Kantaro Suzuki was telling military leaders in Tokyo that Japan had to accept Truman's terms. Whether atomic bombs really ended the war will always be a razor-edge question—and in any case a further consideration intrudes: Would the world have accepted the present nuclear standoff if there had not been at least one horrifying example of the bomb's devastation? Maybe Hiroshima, unwilling and unknowing, sacrificed itself to world peace—or, more precisely, to an effective mutual acceptance of the balance of terror.

Not long after the war, a high official of the Japanese Foreign Ministry said bitterly: "President Truman boarded a train for hell when he ordered that the bombs be dropped." Nowadays, the quality of anger is restrained. As a Hiroshima high school teacher says, "Man can forget anything. When I read my diary and come across a phrase like 'The whole sandy beach was covered with dead bodies,' I can hardly believe that I actually wrote it."

Yet that single bomb loosed from the bay of the B-29 *Enola Gay* nearly thirty years ago still kills, by long-range effects, around ninety people a year in Hiroshima; still affects the lives of all the people there in social and pathological ways, some drastically; and still promises to do a lot of dirty work among the chromosomes of succeeding generations. On a green hill that overlooks the Hiroshima hypocenter stand the barrel-roofed buildings of the Radiation Effects Research

Foundation, a collaborative effort of the American National Academy of Sciences and the National Research Council, and the Japanese National Institute of Health. Neither of the American components is a governmental organization, but they get funds from the Atomic Energy Commission and the Public Health Service.

The foundation's goal, in blunt words, is to take advantage of the great pool of bomb survivors to learn about the long-range medical effects of exposure to radiation, anticipating that humanity will need such knowledge in using nuclear energy. To get a large statistical sample, the foundation more than two decades ago sought the cooperation of one hundred thousand residents of Hiroshima and Nagasaki who had been exposed to the bomb within two kilometers, or more distantly, or not at all. For eighty thousand of these people, the foundation's main interest is in their life span; when they die, the foundation records the cause of death and age at death in relation to extent of exposure. For the other twenty thousand, the foundation adds thorough, twice-a-year diagnoses in the wards and laboratories of the headquarters hospital, for adult health studies. In huge file rooms, I saw samples of the histories kept for this group; every single one of them contains, for instance, a diagram showing the angle and distance of the victim's position in relation to that bomb up in the air, and his shielding, if any, by walls or roofs. In the months just after the bomb fell, the visible effects were diarrhea, bleeding gums, and falling hair. But the permanent damage lies in the areas of cancer, genetic change, and, probably, rapid aging. By now the foundation's work has gone on long enough to produce some conclusive, if mostly predictable, results.

More radiated people die of cancer than those not exposed. Leukemia kills bomb survivors at a rate four times greater than that of the Japanese at large, and thyroid cancer is notably commoner. These observations derive from statistical, not clinical, studies, and are reinforced by the correlation between the number of cases and the nearness of the victims to the bomb; but they do not demonstrate that any individual victim got his disease specifically from the bomb. Similar population studies give the bomb the blame for higher incidence of Hodgkin's disease, myelofibrosis, lymphosarcoma, hardening of the seminal tubes, degeneration of blood vessels, and eye cataracts.

"It was known at the time of the bombs that genetic effects are like an iceberg—if there were any results of the atomic bombs, only a small part would be apparent in the first generation born after the bombs; the rest would become apparent in later generations," says a foundation report. "And the changes are likely to be deleterious," one scientist told me matter-of-factly. Radiation is a mutagen, a gene changer, just as thalidomide is a mutagen. He stressed that the results of this study will serve the whole world, but to the people of Hiroshima and Nagasaki, the invisible changes within their own cells are the seeds of personal tragedy. Mothers exposed to heavy radiation early in pregnancy gave birth to some children with small heads and mental retardation, but over the years the foundation found no significant shifts in such genetic indicators as the ratio of the sexes among children born to irradiated parents, or the rate of still-birth, or weight at birth, or infant mortality.

Now the crucial second generation is coming along. "In four or five years," I was told, "we will know whether more mutations have occurred than normally." Analysis of blood proteins will be the tipoff to genetic change; yet, maddeningly, no individual man or woman will even then be able to know for sure whether the *Enola Gay*'s bomb destined his or her child to be, perhaps, a tiny-headed moron. But the fear is strong. The children of irradiated parents are less marriageable than other Japanese, just as the outcasts are less marriageable. Some try to "pass" into untainted society by moving to Tokyo and hiding their origins.

When animals are experimentally irradiated, they age faster than normally. The disasters-of-war irradiation of Hiroshima and Nagasaki provides science's first chance to discover whether men age faster, too. In one sense, exposure inevitably shortens life expectancy, since the victims of leukemia and other deadly diseases die sooner than they would have. But the questions are subtler: whether radiation accelerates death even if it is not the cause of death; and whether, even in cancer deaths, speeded aging brings on a proneness to cancer (essentially a disease of age) faster than it might have come normally. The foundation has found no statistically valid proof for this suspicion, but believes that it is on to something solid that may test out with more data. "Gerontology is a very young science," a recent foundation report points out.

In their relations with the Radiation Effects Research Foundation, the survivors of Hiroshima are torn between feeling like guinea pigs and desiring to know what it can tell them about their lives and futures. Some feel that the American scientific community is with all too much alacrity utilizing for research the consequences of a horrible act of the American politico-military community. Yet the people of Hiroshima and Nagasaki have courageously collaborated with the project in one way that particularly violates Buddhist precepts and Japanese sensibilities, by permitting autopsies on about half of all bomb survivors who die, as a benefaction to humanity. Amid the sterile stainless steel and clinical white of the foundation's laboratories there is one thoroughly Japanese room of paper walls and satiny wood, where relatives can sit on tatami mats and meditate while an autopsy is being performed.

"Ladies and gentlemen, we shall soon make a brief stop at Nagoya," says a woman's voice with a British accent, on the public-address system of a bullet train on the world-famed Shinkansen (New Cut Line) system. "Please check your belongings and be ready to alight."

Alight is right. In the buffet car, you watch the needle of a specially installed speedometer drop smoothly down from 200 kilometers an hour, to reach 10 just as the head car enters the station. Politely slow, so as not to bowl anyone over, the train glides along the platform and stops with each of its sixteen numbered cars precisely adjacent to a sign with the corresponding figure. The doors slide open; people "alight"; but almost at once the departure warning bell begins. Somehow the boarding passengers all manage to get on without fuss by the time the bell stops, forty-five seconds later. Ten more seconds pass; the doors close; the train starts. A glance at the platform clock shows that the train is neither one second early nor one second late, but exactly on schedule. Still politely, the train moves slowly until the last car clears the station. Then current surges into the high-torque motors on every axle, and in the buffet car the speedometer needle sweeps smoothly up to 200 again. Nagoya falls behind, and from the windows you can soon see the shadow of the pantograph, sucking in great drafts of power from the overhead wire, racing through the rice paddies at airplane speed.

Shinkansen trains are not to be compared for luxury with the trains of the dead-and-gone past like the Twentieth Century Limited or the Super-Chief. Shinkansen's byword is efficiency, nothing more and nothing less. Its dining cars offer plain food like beef stew and pork cutlets, and two buffet cars on each train provide sandwiches and other fast food. The cars were built with airplane-fuselage technology, and they pack people in, three on one side and two on the other, only a little less compactly than, say, a Boeing 707. (Two first-class cars per train, with two seats on each side, are more spacious.) As on all Japanese National Railways trains, a computerized, airline-style reservation system provides guaranteed seating on the Shinkansen, but four cars are left open for all comers. The fare between Tokyo and Osaka on ordinary cars is $13.70. The average speed, including stops, is 101 miles an hour (thus Tokyo to Osaka, 320 miles, takes three hours and ten minutes by superexpress). This means that the train usually travels at 125 miles an hour and hits peaks of 131—the world's fastest railroad.

Speed notwithstanding, the most impressive characteristic of the Shinkansen system is frequency of service. Every seven and one-half minutes from 6 A.M. until 10 P.M. a train leaves Tokyo headed west, and Osaka headed east—more than one hundred departures each way each day. Inaugurated in 1964 as a Tokyo–Osaka shuttle service, Shinkansen in 1972 began running fast trains westward to Okayama, a hundred miles beyond Osaka, and in March 1975 it opened service with twenty-three trains a day all the way to Fukuoka, in the western-most island of Kyushu, using a tunnel to go under the strait between Honshu and Kyushu.

Since it started running, Shinkansen has carried more than 700 million passengers, lately at a rate of a quarter-million a day, with no accident worse than a single derailment of an empty train in a switchyard. Sophisticated computers, which control traffic and train operation, account for part of the safety record, and meticulous main-tenance for the rest. When a train has done half a million miles, it goes into the shops for ten days of disassembly, inspection, overhaul, repainting, and reassembly. Much of the roadbed, not only in cities but even among rice paddies, is a continuous elevated bridge of heavily reinforced concrete, ensuring dead-accurate tracks. Shinkansen makes no compromises with mountains—it just goes through them. Thirty-five miles of the 100-mile track between Osaka and Okayama are in tunnels.

For the future, Japan is still putting its chips on railroads, in astonishing contrast to the faint-hearted Amtrak effort. Eight hundred feet below the level of the sea in Tsugaru Strait, between Honshu and Hokkaido, men are digging a railroad tunnel (to be finished in 1979) that surpasses the long-proposed English Channel tunnel in length (thirty-four miles) and difficulty. Shinkansen trains will streak through this burrow far below the keels of the Russian freighters that use the strait as one of Vladivostok's few outlets from the Sea of Japan to the Pacific. Another branch of the Shinkansen will go straight across Honshu in ninety minutes to Niigata (population 400,000), on the Sea of Japan, through twenty-five tunnels now being dug, the longest fifteen miles, two others eight each. Also under construction is a stretch of high-speed track between Tokyo and Morioka, in north-ern Honshu. Maximum speed will rise to 163 miles an hour. Trains from Tokyo will reach the most distant parts of the country, northern Hokkaido and southern Kyushu, in seven or eight hours. A comparable train would cross the United States in one day.

Yet to the Japanese National Railways, the Tokyo–Osaka bullet trains are already beginning to seem a little out of date, not fast enough. Yoshizo Kinoshita, a company official, told me that in ten years traffic on that route will reach half a million people a day, and the company plans to get them between the big cities in just one hour, at three hundred miles an hour. The vehicle, already tested in proto-type, does not run on wheels but is levitated on a cushion of magnet-ism that floats it on its rails. A linear, rather than a rotary, motor pulls it; that is, coils in the guideway provide a fast-moving field of magnetism that sucks the train along with it.

"With the problem of moving all those people," said Kinoshita dryly, "we had to invent something better than the airplane."

The first bullet trains will roll into Nagasaki in 1979, and this historic port awaits the event with all the suspense of old Abilene anticipating the arrival of the Kansas Pacific. From the far western end of Japan, Nagasaki faces the East China Sea, and dreams of its future while reflecting upon its past. Behind it lies receptivity to the early Portuguese traders and missionaries, several centuries as sealed-off Japan's lone window to the world, the inspiration for the opera *Madame Butterfly*, and destruction by a pillar of fire and thunder. The future promises rich bustling commerce with a presumably more accessible China: Shanghai, five hundred miles to the west, is closer to Nagasaki than Tokyo is. But mountain-walled Nagasaki first needs fast and modern communications to the rest of Japan. The old con-necting roads and railroads, twisting and tunneling, seem more like barriers than arteries. The nearest airport is twenty-five sinuous miles away, and only this year was it rebuilt with runways long enough for jets. The Trans-Kyushu Expressway will reach Nagasaki in 1977, linking the port to Beppu, on the island's eastern coast. But it will take the bullet train to end Nagasaki's isolation decisively and to make it Japan's gateway to China, as it was in the sixteenth century and before World War II. So Nagasaki sits and sings "Waitin' for the Train to Come In."

With a population of 430,000 people, Nagasaki falls well behind industrial Kitakyushu (1,050,000) and political Fukuoka (900,000) among the cities of Kyushu, but it surpasses them in interest and significance. The setting, steep-sided green and purplish bluffs drop-ping into the indented shores of the mouth of the Urakami River, compares to San Francisco, Sidney, or Rio de Janeiro. In fact, all the western face—it can't be called a coast or shore—of Kyushu is spectacularly cusped and crenelated. The peninsulas have peninsulas that have peninsulas. Sugar-loaf islands and islets, tantalizingly close to one another, create charming straits and passages. Roofs colored tangerine or pink make accents on the shores. No better yachting grounds could be imagined. Ferries go every which way, and bridges jump from island to island. S-shaped Kammon Strait, only a few hundred yards wide, is all that separates Kyushu from the mainland of Honshu; the railroads tunnel beneath it, and a new suspension bridge carries cars over it.

The languor of the high-ceilinged Bank of Tokyo branch in Nagasaki reminded me of some old Far Eastern factoring house in a story by Somerset Maugham, but actually the city is very much alive. The historic Mitsubishi shipyard, which built the World War II superbattleship *Musashi* and two other battlewagons, has been expanded into the world's largest. In a drydock three-fifths of a mile long, this yard mass-produces 260,000-ton mammoth tankers three at a time, as effortlessly as Ford makes Mustangs. The buyers are Exxon, British Petroleum, Shell. The yard employs sixteen thousand people, who with their families form a fifth of Nagasaki's population. The city is building a new bridge over the Urakami River so that Mitsubishi's men and women can get to work more easily. Nagasaki also fishes, in the East China Sea, which means that the fish it sends to Osaka and Tokyo are not contaminated by any of the disease-causing pollution of some of the fish caught in Japanese coastal waters.

Nagasaki's third-biggest industry, after shipbuilding and fishing, is Puccini. Well up on the city's South Bluff, in a tulip garden, stands a dwelling so out of place that the mind reels: an ample, one-story English bungalow with verandahs, shutters, fanlights, and fireplaces. This is the Glover House, built by a Scottish wheeler-dealer who came to Nagasaki in 1859 to make a fortune, which he did by selling weapons and warships to both sides in skirmishes that accompanied the fall of the Tokugawas. Thomas Glover, bald, big-nosed, and bemustached, then went on to start a mint, open a coal mine, build a railroad, and set up a shipyard that evolved into the present Mitsubishi operation. Marrying a Japanese woman, he founded a famous family dynasty, although in the process the name Glover had to give way to the more pronounceable Kuraba.

Glover's house, along with his shipyard, passed into Mitsubishi's hands, and in 1957, to honor the "father of shipbuilding," Mitsubishi gave the house to the city. Then a bolt of inspiration struck the city fathers. If there ever had been such a lady as Madame Butterfly, the tragic heroine of Giacomo Puccini's opera, she would most certainly have lived in a house like Glover's. (Puccini got the plot from a play, produced in New York and London, which in turn came from a story by John Luther Long, who got his theme from Mrs. Irwin Corell, wife of an American missionary in Nagasaki. Mrs. Corell undoubtedly knew about Glover's house.) Indeed, the view from the garden, over the harbor to the quaint hills beyond, is only a little less stylized than the set that the Metropolitan Opera used for years. The Japanese never much cared for the opera, neither the beginning, where the American naval lieutenant Benjamin Franklin Pinkerton takes the geisha Cio-cio-san (equals Butterfly) for his mistress, nor the end, where the cad returns with his American wife to take away his and Cio-cio-san's baby, causing her to commit hara-kiri. But now it became clear that Nagasaki could forget these scruples and hook itself, together with "the cottage where Madame Butterfly supposedly lived," to the world-famed opera and reap heaps of tourist money. If people go to Elsinore to walk where Hamlet walked, they'd come to Nagasaki to take in Cio-cio-san's view. The idea was, and is, irresistible.

When the dictator Hideyoshi turned suspicious of the Roman Catholics centered in Nagasaki in 1597, supposing them to be a fifth column aimed at giving Manila-based Spanish power a foothold in Japan, he executed or ousted not only priests from Spain and Portugal but also traders from those countries. By then some traders from Holland had reached Nagasaki. "What's your religion?" Hideyoshi's minions asked. "Dutch," the traders replied, and proceeded to grab the Nagasaki concessions. Even after succeeding shoguns closed Japan's doors to the world, they let the Dutch stay on in Nagasaki, though confined to a tiny man-made island, called Deshima, a few yards offshore from the port's business district. The traders' strange customs amazed the Japanese. It was solemnly reported that "the Dutch, apparently because the backs of their feet do not reach the ground, fasten wooden heels to the backs of their shoes."

Swilling Holland gin and dallying with girls sent out from the town, the Dutch East India Company's agents remained for more than two centuries, providing Japan with its only news of the West, and vice versa. Around 1770, for example, the Dutch imported a copy of *Ontleedkundige Tafalen,* a Dutch translation of what was then the finest Western treatise on anatomy. Painfully learning Dutch, a Japanese scholar named Gempaku translated it into Chinese (which all well-educated Japanese could read). The book rapidly brought Japanese medicine abreast of the West. Doctors were surprised to learn that Japanese hearts, livers, stomachs, and intestines were just like anyone else's. Previously, going by the texts imported from China, the Japanese had found their own internal organs so different from those pictured in the Chinese diagrams that they had concluded—a little proudly, one suspects—that they were anatomically different from other humans. Between 1823 and 1830, the Dutch brought in a doctor named Philipp Franz von Siebold, who was allowed to set up a villa outside Nagasaki. He treated patients and taught Western clinical medicine to Japan. A naturalist as well as a physician, Siebold married a Japanese woman named Otaki, introduced the Japanese hydrangea to the rest of the world, and honored his wife by giving this flower the name *Hydrangea otakusa*. Siebold was expelled when, in an excess of zeal, he collected some forbidden Japanese maps and clothes bearing the Tokugawa crest. But Nagasaki, remembering him warmly, has put up a statue of him and made the hydrangea the city flower.

At 3:49 A.M. on August 9, 1945, the B-29 *Bock's Car* took off from the Island of Tinian, just north of Guam. In the plane's belly was the "Fat Man," an iron spheroid ten feet eight inches long: the plutonium bomb, even more devastating than Hiroshima's uranium bomb. *Bock's Car*, though deprived of the use of six hundred gallons of its gasoline by an inoperative valve, flew on through the dawning hours toward Kokura, a port in northern Kyushu, now incorporated into the city of Kitakyushu. Three times *Bock's Car* made passes over the hazy target; three times the bombardier said, "I can't pick up the aiming point." "Roger," replied the pilot. "Proceeding to Nagasaki."

Clouds also covered the aiming point in Nagasaki, the city center, but suddenly an opening revealed the oval of a stadium on the banks of the Urakami River, two miles northwest of the target. Militarily, the stadium was not a bad target, lying as it did near two Mitsubishi war-goods plants. But *Bock's Car*'s crew did not debate the point—it was eleven o'clock by then, and the plane did not have enough fuel for a second pass. Down went Fat Man, by parachute, to explode at an altitude of 1,600 feet. These were the happenstances that made Nagasaki the second, and so far the last, city in the world to take an atom bomb, and that placed the bomb off-target, with such wry benefits as the survival of Madame Butterfly's house.

"Nagasaki never got as active as Hiroshima in protesting against the atomic bomb," one city official, Noburu Tasaki, told me. "We don't have resentment or hatred. We said: 'Hiroshima in anger,

Nagasaki in prayer.'" Prayer is more a Christian ritual than a Buddhist one; but then Nagasaki is still the capital of Christianity of Japan, and, to top it off, Christians there had ironic cause for prayer. The most notable single building destroyed near the epicenter of the bomb from Christian America was the Urakami Roman Catholic Church, the biggest Christian church in the Orient.

The small "Relics of A-Bomb" museum, on two floors of the six-story International Cultural Hall at one side of Peace Park, shows (chiefly in pictures) the effects of the bomb on human beings more bluntly than Hiroshima's museum. "Boy lying dead on verandah as if basking in sun," reads one caption. One photograph shows the deformed head of a child born with no brain to an irradiated mother. The museum also displays the variously headless, handless, or noseless statues of the saints from Urakami Church, and a vast collection of clocks stopped at 11:02—one of them, all flying springs and blasted rims, has been so frequently pictured as to become a sort of city escutcheon.

A simple, square, black stone column, in a park where people picnic and children play, marks the precise epicenter of the bomb. Not far away is sculptor Seibo Kitamura's thirty-two-foot-high bronze Statue of Peace, depicting a seated man who points with one hand to the sky from which the bomb fell, and with the outstretched other hand, palm down, makes a gesture of benediction for peace. His eyes are closed in prayer for the Nagasaki dead, but the tension of his Herculean muscles and the grim look of his mouth and chin roar a message: "Never again!" The Nagasaki bomb killed 73,884 people, injured 74,909, and destroyed or badly damaged 18,409 houses.

Nagasaki neglected the opportunity to rebuild on a modernized city plan, but, being mostly new, has a trim, modern, high-rise look in the city center. And the city's Catholics have rebuilt the Urakami Church just as it was. But the human suffering goes on. Noburu Tasaki told me briefly about his brother, who on the "day the sun fell" (as one Nagasaki writer put it) was working in a factory within blast range; he received bad keloid burns—clawlike excrescences—and now, ever weaker, fears leukemia. "Like thousands of others," said Tasaki laconically.

Kyushu constitutes a busy and substantial portion of the Japanese nation and economy, even though it looks and feels provincial and faraway. It is rich in rice, sunshine, volcanoes, and national parks. Pittsburgh-like Kitakyushu operates some of the world's biggest blast furnaces. Fukuoka, energetic and well dressed, is a hinterlands Tokyo.

Kyushu is where Japan began: the several waves of Mongoloids who were pressed eastward from China most probably crossed the Tsushima Strait from Korea to Kyushu. The mythology surrounding the origins of the imperial family places the first emperor, Jimmu, in what is now Miyazaki, in southeastern Kyushu, although he moved to the Nara area on Honshu in 660 B.C. to set up his court. By the beginning of the fourth century A.D., the Japanese were burying their high-ranking dead in huge mounds, and, appropriately, Miyazaki has one of the most impressive, opened some years ago and put on public display. The most fascinating of the contents are the haniwa figures, sculptures from two to four feet tall, made of low-fired, reddish-brown clay. The typical haniwa figure is a soldier, helmeted and armed, but there are also women, with beads, and many humans of no clear profession or sex, as well as animals and artifacts. The haniwa ("clay cylinder") trademark is the eyes and mouths, simply holes punched into the hollow interior of the statues, making the figures look horrified, shrewd, sad, laughing, or calm, depending on the shape of the holes, but always unearthly. The figures are invariably distorted, most commonly by tiny arms and thick legs like twin fire hydrants, but it is clear that the distortion is the result of conscious art, not lack of technique.

Haniwa sculptures also represent material goods—armor, swords, houses—probably providing a way of symbolically burying an important man's possessions with him without actually losing the use of the goods themselves. Ancient tradition held that burying figures of soldiers and servants was similarly symbolic, avoiding the need to bury real people alive. But new archeology has disproved the theory, and no one really knows what the motivation was. In spite of this mystery, haniwa art, well preserved in many of the ten thousand burial mounds scattered over all but northern Japan, provides an extraordinarily detailed and accurate record of protohistoric Japanese life. How horses were harnessed, types of armor and dress, the many-gabled construction of houses, the placidity of cows—all these and many other aspects of life are shown with a clarity equal to the representations on Greek vases or Egyptian friezes. In a park in Miyazaki—which also contains what was begun in 1940 as a war monument but was rebaptized after the war as a peace monument—four hundred reproductions of haniwa sculptures of humans, animals, and artifacts have been set up amid trees and shrubs.

The Japanese archipelago, the Japanese countryside, is like the Japanese people, homogeneous. The monochrome greenness accounts for that, and so does the uniform geology. Though Hokkaido and northern Honshu have their snows, and southern Kyushu verges on the subtropical, the climate, evened out by the deep-blue Kuroshio Current flowing around the islands from the Philippine Sea, lacks much variety. Moreover, the island mentality prevails everywhere, for the sea is nowhere more than a hundred miles distant. The long seclusions of history have further unified these islands, and the collapse of empire after World War II defined more sharply than ever the irreducible homeland. By the same token, the one noncontiguous part of Japan has to be a spicy exception to Japanese homogeneity. That exception is Okinawa.

16 /

Okinawa Redenta

Is OKINAWA JAPANESE? The answer of course is yes. Ethnically it has been Japanese since prehistoric times, and politically it has been Japanese for going on four centuries. But Okinawa—400 miles south of Kyushu, and the only sizable (67 miles long, 3 to 13 miles wide) and important member of the 73-island Ryukyu chain—does not *seem* Japanese. World War II, a disaster for Okinawa, wiped out its grandest castles and 94 percent of all other structures. In place of them, during its long career as an American colony and bomber base, Okinawa acquired Cuddle Clubs, barracks, Mt. Sinai Baptist Churches, well-mowed towns for officers and their families, and strips of auto dealers. With their unerring proclivity for finding the condescending word, the American military people prefer to call the islanders neither "Japanese" nor "Okinawans," but rather "Orientals." Yet perhaps by its very unspecificity the term does convey the orphanlike quality of Okinawa.

But then, Okinawa did not seem Japanese even before the war. The highly developed ability of the Japanese to think themselves superior made them, and still makes them, look down on Okinawans, even though Okinawans and main-island Japanese share common racial origins. Part of the reason for the prejudice is that the Okinawans talk funny. Their language, Ryukyuan, has the same roots as Japanese, but it evolved in a different way beginning about sixteen centuries ago, so that now it compares to present-day Japanese roughly as Chaucerian compares to present-day English. Just before the war, the militarists who ran Japan posted signs in Okinawa

281

that said: "Be Japanese! Speak Japanese!" If Okinawan draftees could not speak Japanese, how could they understand the orders of officers from the mainland? True, said some Okinawan skeptic, but then why not run a similar nationalism campaign on the island of Hokkaido, way off to the north. "Ah, but that's part of Japan," replied the officer in charge.

So Okinawa took to speaking standard Japanese in addition to Ryukyuan. And even little girls fought the Americans to the point of suicide during the 1945 invasion. But Okinawa still doesn't have the air of main-island Japan. Discussing Okinawa's identity confusion with me, Seishiro Hokama, the astute editor-in-chief of the major daily, *Ryukyu Shimpo*, compared Okinawa to such varied places as Hawaii (sugar-raising island province far from the national mainland), Korea and Taiwan (historically prey to conquest from the Japanese main islands), and the Saar (shifting nationalities according to international power games).

Okinawa has been a victim of geography and history and nature, victim of war and circumstances, victim of the Chinese, the Japanese, and the Americans, and is all set up to be a victim far into the future. Ming Dynasty China made Okinawa a tributary province in 1372, and enthroned the first Ryukyu king in 1429. Though very much under China's thumb, the Loo Choo islands (as Okinawa and neighboring islands were called in Chinese; "Ryukyu" is the Japanese rendition of the same name) prospered satisfactorily for a couple of centuries. "To make a tribute to China was to make a fortune," editor Hokama pointed out. "You sent bananas and got back gold." China supplied Okinawa with the sweet potato and the techniques of sugar making. In 1609, the lord of Satsuma, a province in southern Kyushu, dispatched three thousand warriors and one hundred warships to take over Okinawa, and then, incredibly, *concealed* his victory from the Chinese. Okinawa thereupon entered two and a half centuries of pure schizophrenia, of double subordination. In those times both China and Japan had tightly restricted commerce between their countries, but Japan, supposing Okinawa to be hers, allowed trade between Okinawa and China.

Like Nagasaki, Okinawa was a small door from the outer world to closed-off Japan. Part of the commerce was in Japanese swords, but Okinawans were forbidden to carry them. For self-defense, Okinawans invented the martial art of karate—the word means "empty-handed." But this middle-man business made Okinawa a madhouse. When China sent delegations to coronations, the Okinawans had to remember not to speak any Japanese and the Satsuma samurai had to lie low in farmhouses in the countryside. Conversely, when the Satsuma samurai wanted to take a group of Okinawans to Tokyo to prove their domination of old Loo Choo, they forced the islanders to wear Chinese clothes. Commodore Perry, after his first contact with Japan in 1853, wintered at Okinawa, and could not at first decide whether it was Chinese, Japanese, or independent, but concluded that it should be American, a base for whalers. President Millard Fillmore found the proposal "embarrassing"—a little bit too imperialistic, presumably.

After the Meiji Restoration, the government abolished tribute to China, dethroned the island king, made Okinawa into a prefecture, and forced the people to change their names from Chinese to Japanese. Kyushu and Osaka merchants dominated the island as an economic colony, and main-island Japanese treated the Okinawans as country cousins. Signs in Osaka storefronts said: "Help Wanted (No Koreans or Okinawans)." Many Okinawans emigrated to Hawaii, the Philippines, Brazil, and Argentina. At a fair in Osaka in 1904, two Okinawan women were put on display as curiosities in a Hall of Races. Thus Okinawa coasted along, meek and miserable, until 1945, when the island loomed out of the map as the staging area that the American armed forces had to have for the invasion of the main islands of Japan.

On Easter Sunday of that year, sixty thousand American soldiers and marines landed unopposed on the western coast of Okinawa north of Naha, not far from where the Kadena Air Force Base's golf course is now. Marines quickly overran the northern stretch of the island. But the resistance soon became ferocious as the Japanese strategists realized the peril to Japan itself if Okinawa were overrun. In this last convulsive effort, 1,005 brave Kamikaze pilots flew to their foreknown deaths, as part of attacks that sank thirty-six American ships and damaged 369 others.

On land, the battle turned into an effort by General Simon Bolivar Buckner Jr. to drive Lieutenant General Mitsuru Ushijima off the southern tip. The Americans rapidly built up forces to 170,000, and pushed the 110,000 Japanese fighting men past their defenses in a four-mile waist of the island to a tiny area on the southern extremity. There a coral escarpment stood like a wall in front of the Americans, and Ushijima set up headquarters in a well-protected cave, facing the ocean, just under the brow of a cliff that angles a couple of hundred feet into the water. Bloodily, with grenades, flamethrowers, and artillery fire, the Americans worked their way up the escarpment. One day General Buckner climbed a tiny coral knoll near the front, and for an hour watched the action. As he started down, a Japanese shell blasted the coral, and a fragment of it crashed into Buckner's chest and killed him. By June 22, after eighty-three days of the "typhoon of steel," Ushijima knew that he was done for. He knelt on the floor of the cave and ripped his stomach open with a knife. Thus, by the Philippine Sea, within four days and three miles of each other, died two brave enemies.

Okinawa was the bloodiest battle of the Pacific war. American dead and missing totaled 12,520; Japanese 185,000, including 75,000 Okinawan civilians who got in the way of bombs and shells.

Nowadays the point where Buckner died is marked by a low concrete fence and littered with beer bottles; neither the Americans nor the Japanese on the island take responsibility for keeping it neat. The clifftop near Ushijima's cave, by contrast, is a well-kept, palmy park, with elaborate monuments set up by all the Japanese prefectures to commemorate their dead. The bluff is cut with caves and passages; glimpses of light come up from openings beneath one's feet. Tranquil and clear is the view of what someone has called "the sea of seven colors"—it must have been a beautiful place to die. Enormous parking lots accommodate the buses of the Japanese tourists and the soldiers' survivors who visit the battlefield, especially in June. The public-address system there frequently plays a recording of "Umi Yukaba," the official song of the old Japanese Imperial Navy, the words of which are:

> *Across the sea, corpses in the water;*
> *Across the mountain, corpses in the field.*
> *I shall die only for the emperor,*
> *I shall never look back.*

For a few fleeting months after the war, the Okinawans entertained the idea of annexation by the United States, whose conquering soldiers had proved uncommonly kind. Washington properly decided that annexation would amount to territorial aggrandizement, against the grain of Allied and United Nations ideals. For three years thereafter, years made ugly by the arrogance, crime, and corruption of the third-rate American troops sent to this "rock" to replace the original invaders, the United States simply hung on to Okinawa. The islanders speedily reversed themselves and clamored to be returned to Japan. Then the cold war clanged its loud alarums, and John Foster Dulles found a formula, written into the U.S.–Japanese peace treaty, that proposed a United Nations trusteeship for Okinawa, but meanwhile left the island in American hands. Not by accident, "meanwhile" stretched out through the cold war and the Indochina war as well.

Okinawa became the only colony in the world created since World War II. Huge, fenced-off bases, the largest American military establishment outside the United States, covered no less than 23 percent of the island's surface, forcing rice farmers to give up flat land for airstrips and move to the mountains to grow pineapples.

War became the main industry and source of prosperity, and per capita income reached levels about two-thirds as high as the rest of Japan's. The Americans built the University of the Ryukyus. A rapid succession of American high commissioners, military officers usually doing their "sunset tours," preferred not to rock the boat by encouraging the rapid return of local self-government. The officer-commissioners were so suspicious of Tokyo's interest in Okinawa that for years they restricted the amount of "foreign aid" that the Japanese government could send to the island. In point of fact, Japanese politicians were pressing hard for Okinawa's return. One of them, to drive home how Americanized the island had become, once showed Senator Edmund Muskie a certain coin and told the senator that it was Okinawan money. "Why, it looks exactly like an American dime!" Muskie exclaimed. Supposedly the high commissioners operated under a written charter for Okinawa, but it was stamped "Classified." "The world's only secret constitution," an American newsman in Okinawa called it.

Once again, Okinawa became the victim of its geography: the U.S. Air Force used it to supplement Guam as a base for B-52s bombing Vietnam—the bombers that appeared at Kadena Air Force Base were said to be "dodging typhoons." Lyndon Johnson sent fifteen thousand troops and large quantities of supplies from Okinawa to Indochina. Friction never stopped. American servicemen and civilian employees committed 446 "atrocious and violent" crimes against Okinawans in a typical year, 1966. A C-130 cargo plane accidentally dropped a trailer from its hatch and killed a schoolgirl; a B-52 blew up on takeoff and its bombs exploded, injuring several persons. The Americans, though they denied it, stored nuclear weapons and poison gas on the island. Louder and louder, the Okinawans cried for reversion, flying the Japanese flag on holidays and restoring the teaching of Japanese culture in the schools. American military rule ultimately made the nearly 1 million Okinawans into superpatriotic Japanese. Their patriotism reached the point of anger at the "home" government for not negotiating reversion faster.

"Five years too late for it to be a graceful gesture," as Frank Gibney wrote in *Foreign Affairs*, the United States agreed in 1969 to negotiate a deal in which the United States would give up governing Okinawa, while retaining the bases for use with the same restrictions—chiefly, no nuclear weapons—that apply to American bases on the Japanese main islands. By then, the reversion issue had become so hot that the American Embassy in Tokyo feared rioting by students and leftists, but when he prepared to negotiate, President Nixon had an entirely different concern in his mind. The American textile industry, which had contributed heavily to Nixon's 1968 campaign, was crying for protection from Japanese competition. So Nixon traded American control of Okinawa, hitherto described as vital to the national security, for what he took to be Prime Minister Eisaku Sato's promise to restrict textile exports to the United States. As an extra irony, Sato failed to make good. Nixon, furious, unilaterally put a quota on Japanese textiles, and refused to attend the signing of the Okinawa treaty.

"Happier the eve than the holiday itself," says a Japanese proverb. Reversion, which took place May 15, 1972, at once cut into Okinawa's standard of living in the shift of currencies, because the dollar, which until devaluation some months before had bought 360 yen, had dropped to 308. Being again part of Japan, Okinawa had to start eating high-priced Japanese rice instead of the cheap rice it had imported from California. The wages of sugar-cane cutters rose so high that the cane went uncut. Many Americans in Okinawa, living in what they call their Golden Ghettos, smugly assumed that after these pocketbook blows the Okinawans would be sorry they demanded reversion. But the polls taken by Hokama's *Ryukyu Shimpo* show that the bulk of the people are glad to be Japanese again. Ambivalently, they oppose the continued presence of American bases while welcoming the bases' payrolls and purchases, which equal one-fourth of Okinawa's gross income.

The American military, too, finds advantages in reversion. One colonel told me: "When the water system broke down, people used to come to the Americans to fix it. Now we say, 'Go see Governor Yara.'" Putting servicemen under Japanese law for off-base offenses ended charges that military courts went easy on Americans accused of crimes against Okinawans. American servicemen on Okinawa number 38,000 and their dependents 22,000, for a total that is more than 6 percent of the island's population. The confrontation between the Americans and the Okinawan-Japanese is grumpy, full of ignorance and misunderstanding, much on everybody's mind, but not profoundly bitter.

Governor Chobyo Yara seemed a grandfatherly man, mild and low-voiced, fingering a button on the jacket of his well-cut gray suit as he sat in his ample office in the prefectural capitol in Naha. As the air conditioner hummed and Governor Yara told me of his modest aspirations for Okinawa, I smiled to recall that this small, moon-faced man, with his meticulous tie clip and glass-doll cuff links, was the radical who enraged one American high commissioner after another before Okinawa's reversion.

I had noticed on Yara's office wall bright-colored maps of the grounds for the International Ocean Exposition, then in the planning stage. Yara is well aware that if the United States ever does remove its military bases, it will pull the props from under the Okinawan economy. While contending that he wants the bases out, he realizes nervously that Okinawa will need new sources of employment. He therefore proposes—unsocialistic as it may be—to accommodate Japanese big business in ways that will build up the economy. Expo '75 is part of the accommodation. "Okinawa feared that its lack of electricity and water made it unattractive to industry," editor Hokama explained to me. "The future looked gloomy. So we thought, 'Let's sell the ocean. Let's get the Japanese government to agree to support a big international exposition that will draw attention to our ocean resources.'" The Establishment in Tokyo was only too happy to oblige, and pushed Expo '75 with $66 million and so much zest as to make many of Yara's supporters suspect that he was selling out, or being sold out. The governor found himself torn between fears of exploitation and his obligation to promote prosperity, but he finally came down heavily in favor of the fair.

Expo '75, which compares in scale with Seattle's fair of 1962 or Montreal's of 1967, benefits Okinawa in several ways: construction boom, profitable tourism, international attention. The location, on northwest-jutting Motobu Peninsula, draws Okinawa's center of gravity toward the backward, mountainous, nonagricultural north. The exhibits—a floating artificial city, a marine-life zoo, an enormous aquarium of fish, pavilions on ocean science and technology, a display of ships—will drive home the point that Okinawa lies amid a great resource, the sea. When Expo '75 closes, the two-and-one-half-mile, arc-shaped waterfront site will become an industrial area to produce whatever Japanese big business deems suitable, and developers from Japan will move in to make the neighboring mountains and beaches into resorts and golf courses.

The probable future of Okinawa is to continue, however reluctantly, as the major American military bastion in the far Pacific; to become the world's largest depot for oil storage and transshipment; to have its land bought up and subdivided by the big Japanese recreation and other light industries; and to be inundated with Japanese tourists. Porfirio Díaz said of his country, "Poor Mexico, so far from God and so close to the United States." One is tempted to echo: Poor Okinawa, so far from God and so close to Japan, China, and (influentially, at least) the United States.

INTERLUDE

17 /

Defeat and Transfiguration

OKINAWA WAS NOT ONLY the bloodiest battle of the Pacific war; it was also the last, its multitudinous graves a melancholy monument to the tragic adventure by an essentially unadventurous people. Defeat left the military discredited and the Japanese people chastened. Yet even today there are Japanese who think that they might have gotten away with establishing their hegemony over all the western Pacific and creating the Greater East Asia Co-Prosperity Sphere of the militarists' dreams, if only they had not been so foolhardy as to challenge the mighty United States with their savage attack on Pearl Harbor.

Pearl Harbor, more than most crucial events, is a tantalizing story of "what ifs." What if the United States and Japan had had more respect for each other? What if Americans had not believed such propagandistic taradiddle as that the Japanese built warships that foundered upon being launched? What if the Japanese had not thought the United States to be the feeble giant described in a Japanese book called *America on the Verge of Collapse*? What if Franklin D. Roosevelt had not been influenced by a Japanese fellow student at Harvard who told him of a supposed hundred-year Japanese plan of conquest of nations as far away as Peru? What if Emperor Hirohito had asserted himself to prevent war as forcefully as he later did to end it? What if Roosevelt had not put the pre-Pearl Harbor negotiations in the hands of that maddeningly moralistic Tennessee politician Cordell Hull, and what if Hull had not chosen for his adviser the old China hand Stanley Hornbeck (who scoffed, "When did a nation ever go to war in desperation?")? What if the Japanese army, which wanted to fight the Soviet Union, had prevailed over the Japanese navy, which wanted to fight the United States? What if that brilliant loony, Foreign Minister Yosuke Matsuoka, who was raised by an American woman in Portland, Oregon, had succeeded in his effort to stop the alarming Japanese occupation of French Indochina after the fall of France in 1940? What if the ABCD (American, British, Chinese, Dutch) countries had not responded by cutting off the oil, mostly Indonesian, that Japan and particularly its navy needed at the rate of twelve thousand tons a day? What if Chiang Kai-shek had not pressured Roosevelt to forgo his planned meeting, in Juneau, Alaska, in the fall of 1941, with Prince Konoye, the Fujiwara-descended Japanese prime minister who had been put into office to try to head off war?

The biggest what-if is: What if Cordell Hull had made perfectly clear that the United States insisted on Japan's withdrawing from China *but not Manchukuo*? Hull assumed Japan knew this; the Tokyo militarists thought "China" meant all of China. For them, to pull back from the quagmire guerrilla fighting in central China would have been a great relief, though humiliating. But to quit Japanese-developed Manchukuo was unthinkable. In any case, perhaps in the greater dynamics of world events, particularly the unrelenting American move westward so pertinently symbolized by Commodore Perry, the United States and Japan were destined to clash.

Admiral Isoroku Yamamoto, who had been educated at Harvard, knew one simple fact very well, and he stated it publicly and often before and during the war: that American industrial power would ultimately and inevitably overwhelm Japan's. Nonetheless, he spent 1940 and 1941 devising, developing, and training for a secret attack on Pearl Harbor "in diametrical opposition to my personal beliefs." To bring it off was an act of professionalism for Yamamoto. Still, he hoped against hope that Pearl Harbor might make Americans think the Japanese were too crazy and reckless to take on in a fight; but of course what the Americans did was to declare war on Japan, Germany, and Italy. Moreover, since the U.S. Navy had sent the aircraft carriers *Enterprise* and *Lexington* to sea a few days before the attack, the Japanese bagged only old battleships, and by miscalculating their priorities they failed to hit Hawaii's oil tanks, a blow that would have forced the American fleet back to the west coast of the United States. Pearl Harbor was a disaster—for Japan.

Yamamoto had predicted that the first year of the war would go well for Japan, and, indeed, the Imperial Army and Navy needed only five months to assemble the biggest empire in world history, stretching four thousand miles from the Manchuria-Siberia border and the Aleutians to the middle of New Guinea, and six thousand miles from the Gilbert Islands west to where Burma touches India. But even before the conquering Japanese reached the outer limits of the domain, the first chords of eventual doom were sounding, like the death theme in *Carmen*. Aboard his flagship, the new superbattle-ship *Yamato*, Yamamoto learned early in May 1942 that the carriers *Yorktown* and *Lexington* had turned back the Japanese navy in the Coral Sea, ending the threatened invasion of Australia. Three weeks later, Yamamoto, on *Yamato*, moved out of the Inland Sea with 106 other warships toward Midway Island. Two ghastly surprises awaited Yamamoto there. First, American cryptanalysts had cracked the Japanese code and knew the invaders were coming. Second, *Yorktown*, heavily bombed in the Coral Sea, had been repaired by four-teen hundred Pearl Harbor workmen in an incredible forty-eight hours; she joined *Enterprise* and *Hornet* in repulsing the Japanese (and, it must be added, was sunk in the course of the battle). Yamamoto despondently played chess while four Japanese carriers went to the bottom, taking down with them many of Japan's best pilots —those fellows who brought you Pearl Harbor. When it was over, the commander of the Pacific fleet, Admiral Chester William Nimitz, pronounced that the United States was "about midway to" avenging Pearl Harbor. Yamamoto said that he would dictate the peace terms in the White House, where he had once dined; in Japanese belly talk, this far-fetched boast was a warning to his colleagues that Japan had bitten off too much.

Now the men and women of Japan, dressed for the duration in grim, mustard-colored tunics, settled down for a long series of defeats announced as victories. Slowly, what they at first called the Great Asian War turned into the less boastful Pacific war. Elevators, steam heating systems, funicular railroads, park railings, and bronze name-plates went to foundries to be made into munitions. Japan learned how to make auto tires and railway tracks out of wood. Month by month the cadenced chords rang louder. The turning point of ter-ritorial conquest came early in 1943 at Guadalcanal, where American tanks mangled Japanese bodies until the treads looked like meat grinders. After the Battle of the Bismarck Sea had heralded the Allied recapture of New Guinea, Emperor Hirohito judged in private that "we have suffered what can only be described as a disaster."

In April 1943, American decoders discovered that Admiral Yama-moto was making a flying inspection tour of the Solomons, and P-38s shot down his Mitsubishi bomber. A million people lined the streets of Tokyo for his funeral. "We knew we were going to lose the war after that," a professor who was then an intelligence officer told me. More doomsday chords: Tarawa, Eniwetok, the "Marianas Turkey Shoot," Saipan, Leyte. Before dawn one morning in November 1944, an American submarine skipper sank *Shinano*, a newly launched *Yamato*-class superbattleship being converted into the world's largest aircraft carrier, as she fled for safety from Tokyo Bay to the Inland Sea. By now, Japan's oil reserves were almost gone, Midway alone having used a year's supply. Soshitsu Sen, the tea-ceremony master, then a naval pilot trainee, recalls how hard it was to start airplane engines fueled with a mixture of gasoline and pine-root oil.

Next Iwo Jima fell, and, in March 1945, the Japanese resisted eleven days before surrendering at Corregidor, the island fortress in Manila Bay, which they had captured three years before in eight days. General Curtis LeMay's bombers incinerated Tokyo. *Yamato* went down in the seas north of Okinawa; it seemed symbolic that the ship's name was the ancient word for "Japan." But by then the Japanese navy's task was to shoot up the enemy and get sunk, since the ships were worthless without fuel. "The three biggest follies in the world are the Great Wall of China, the Pyramids, and *Yamato*," said disillusioned young officers of that anachronistic battlewagon. In Kure I met a middle-aged man who told me that in those last desperate days of the war he took up the family sword and made his way to join Tokyo students who were going to fight the Americans hand to hand to the bitter end. He passionately remembers the "pure" feeling he got from this act, and still bitterly resents the Yankees' confiscation of his sword.

"I wish the war would come to an end soon," said Hirohito to one of his senior statesmen, and after Hiroshima and Nagasaki, it did.

Flying toward Tokyo to accept the surrender of Japan, General Douglas MacArthur peered down at Mount Fuji and remarked, "It's always good to look at." Within a few days, young American naval officers were sitting on the banks of the Imperial Palace moat and lunching off K-rations. The only decoration at the surrender ceremony on the decks of the *Missouri*, in Tokyo Bay, was the same American flag that Perry had flown on the *Susquehanna*, ninety-two years before. The war had cost Japan 1,850,000 lives, 668,000 of them from air raids.

After the war, the International Military Tribunal prosecuted twenty-five government officials for "war crimes," in a two-and-a-half-year trial of dubious legality (the justice from India dryly suggested that "only a lost war is a crime") and fairness (the justice from the Philippines had been a Bataan death marcher). All twenty-five were convicted and seven were hanged, most notably General Hideki ("The Razor") Tojo, wartime prime minister and war minister, who before the trial began had bungled an attempt at hara-kiri. Whatever the defects of the trial, it produced valid evidence of Japan's wartime atrocities, and among the Japanese the realization grew that it had lost its way, had suffered a national moral sickness, and that losing the war was good for both Japan and the world.

Defeat ended the long era of heady expansion in which Japan met and mastered Western technology and dreamed its dream of mastering Asia. It was a kind of death, and like death, it brought about a transfiguration—from a militarist bully power to a democracy, from a devastated land to an industrial giant. The war left Japan a land of half-charred and half-depopulated cities, with a standard of living comparable to that of the Andean Indians. The people lived, squalid and demoralized, on fifteen hundred calories a day. One statesman had predicted that if Japan lost the war, "we will simply have to sleep in the woodshed and eat bitter fruits for a few decades." But his gloomy prognosis omitted two factors. The first was the realism of the Japanese, their ability to face consequences, draw a lesson from them, and act accordingly. Totalitarian government and aggressive war had brought catastrophe, and therefore the nation needed diametrically different directions. No use licking wounds or cherishing resentments, the Japanese said; let's rebuild the nation. "The emperor told them they were licked and to cooperate. They've done this in what seems a much more manly way than the Germans," wrote Harvard's Langdon Warner. Kyoto University historian Masataka Kosaka adds that Japanese situation ethics relieved the people from feeling war guilt (though lacking Dachaus and Buchenwalds, they had less guilt to feel).

The second factor was the enlightened humanity of the American Occupation, probably the most singularly constructive occupation of a conquered nation in history. Columnist Art Buchwald remarked in the late 1960s that the way to end the Indochina war would be to fly a planeload of Japanese businessmen and bankers to Hanoi and let them explain to Ho Chi Minh the advantages of losing a war to the United States. The fact of the matter was that between the end of the war and the signing of the peace treaty, Japan changed from a foe to a kind of victim, then to a ward, a protégé—and now, even a challenger.

The Occupation succeeded because planning for it had started back in early 1942, even as the Japanese conquerors were parachuting into Sumatra in their southward rampage, and because Douglas Mac-Arthur, then and later the unassailable idol of the American right, turned out in Japan to be, as Reischauer puts it, "the most radical, one might even say socialistic, leader the United States ever produced." Swiftly six million overseas Japanese were pulled out of the collapsed empire and returned to their small home islands. MacArthur abolished the "thought police," released political prisoners, and restored press freedom and civil rights. MacArthur's closest friend and chief aide, Brigadier General Courtney Whitney, got his staff to draft, in just nine days, the amazing Japanese constitution that still prevails, and on April 10, 1946, the populace cheerfully voted ratification, asking only, "Has it been translated into Japanese yet?" It had, of course, although with some difficulty in finding a word precisely equal to "civilian" as the necessary qualification of future prime ministers. Shifting the whole theoretical basis of Japanese law from duties to rights, the constitution de-deified the emperor to the status of "symbol of the state and of the unity of the people," set up a full-fledged British-style parliamentary system, and renounced war and the maintenance of "land, sea, and air forces." Constitutionally and otherwise, the Occupation also:

> Broke up the huge zaibatsu, the commercial and industrial trusts, chiefly Mitsui and Mitsubishi (they regrouped later).
> Encouraged the formation of unions to the point that Japanese labor became more intensively organized than labor in the United States, with many unions under Communist control.
> Disbarred from public office 210,000 Japanese, including all military officers, and many businessmen.
> Enfranchised women and broke up the patriarchal family system.
> Halted flaring inflation by an austerity budget, facilitating Japan's later export boom.
> Purged textbooks of imperialist and totalitarian indoctrination, and gave Japanese education a democratic and even radical-left stance.
> Disestablished Shinto as the state religion.
> Abolished the tenant farming system that had grown up since Meiji times, letting sharecroppers buy the land they farmed for about a hundredth of its realistic value, thus creating Japan's present-day well-to-do farmer class.
> Imposed steeply graduated income and inheritance taxes.

The Occupation also introduced that inimitable slice of Americana, the Parent-Teacher Association, and the PTA has been going strong in Japan ever since.

After this euphoric beginning, whose goals were achieved by the end of 1947, the Occupation authorities began to pull back from their reforms. They dabbled in press censorship, halted the zaibatsu breakup, "depurged" many of the purged, and started purging Communists. The Japanese left, which had been figuratively singing "God Bless America," cooled off, and the right, which had been fretful, began to see merits in the Americans. All this was a consequence of the beginning of the cold war; the Occupation's worry point shifted from right to left, and its concept of Japan changed from a Switzerland in Asia to a bastion against Communism. With U.S. entry into the Korean War, MacArthur created the 75,000-man Japanese National Police Reserve, which looked rather like the kind of armed force banned by MacArthur's constitution. Nevertheless, MacArthur was able to present the Japanese with one last lesson in democracy, however inadvertent: in April 1951 he was fired by President Harry S. Truman, and accepted (though not humbly) the decision of his civilian superior. Two million amazed Japanese turned out to see him off.

Just after the war, the United States demanded $670 million in reparations from Japan, but shortly reduced the figure to $450 million, to $180 million, and to zero. This forgiveness was really an act of common sense, since in the same period the United States was sending aid to Japan to the tune of $350 million (at first in food for starving people), then $470 million, then $550 million, and, by the end of the Occupation, a grand total of $2.1 billion. In San Francisco on September 8, 1951, Japan, the United States, and forty-seven other nations signed a peace treaty that, basically dealing with territory, confirmed Japan's loss of its empire. The war was over; Japan was free to make a new life for itself.

During the Occupation, politics hardly mattered. Of one proposed prime minister, MacArthur asked only: "How old is he?" and "Does he speak English?" In May 1946, however, the Diet chose (with MacArthur's assent) the man who was not only to lead Japan strongly for most of the next eight and a half years but also to cast Japanese politics into the conservative shape that it still has in 1975.

Shigeru Yoshida, then sixty-seven, was a career diplomat who appealed to the Americans because he had been ambassador to London in the late 1930s (his English was fluent and terse) and because he had been jailed, though with notable brevity and comfort, toward the end of the war as the leader of the peace faction within the government. Actually, Yoshida had been a wartime hawk, though dubious about attacking the United States, and the peace faction was not a nest of doves but a devious way of salvaging something out of defeat. Yoshida dragged his heels at zaibatsu busting and other liberal acts of the early Occupation, so MacArthur did not object when the 1947 election put the Socialist Tetsu Katayama, a Christian and a Japanese version of Britain's Clement Attlee, into office for a while. But when the Americans grew more conservative, Yoshida came back in 1948 and comfortably carried on, with MacArthur his firmest backer. Once Yoshida stopped his official car to pick up a hitchhiking GI, who offered the prime minister some candy and gum —the kind of postwar incident that led Yoshida, a good-humored, stumpy man who always had a cigar in his mouth, to comment on the "comic helplessness of being Japanese."

In the election that Yoshida called in 1949, his Liberal Party won decisively, thus sealing Japan into the capitalist-conservative ideology that is still in control. Productivity and exports—textiles, cameras, motorcycles—started to grow. The Korean War, during which the United States spent $4 billion in Japan for military procurement, produced a boom in trucks, ships, and other heavy industry. Yoshida, negotiating the 1952 security treaty with the United States, resisted pressure from Secretary of State John Foster Dulles to create a new Japanese military establishment. But once he was free to act on his own, he followed his conservative proclivities and turned the National Police Reserve that MacArthur had created into the present Self-Defense Forces, with ground, sea, and air arms.

From 1952, when Japan resumed its own sovereignty, until 1972, the three most prominent prime ministers were men of the "Yoshida line," that is, conservative bureaucrats who had risen to the cabinet. Nobusuke Kishi (1957–1960), who served as minister of commerce in Tojo's wartime cabinet, had been openly surprised that he was not indicted as a war criminal, although he was purged (and later de-purged). Such are the miraculous powers of rehabilitation that, as prime minister, Kishi was invited to address the U.S. Congress, and did; students that I talked to in Tokyo still hoot at the irony of it. Under Kishi came the 1960 riots, when, to clear the decks for a scheduled visit by President Eisenhower, Kishi rammed through the Diet a widely hated revision of the United States–Japan security treaty, extending the right of the American government to station forces in Japan. The operative word in this clash was not "hated" but "rammed." By staging a wee-hours surprise vote in which the Liberal Democratic majority approved the treaty, Kishi violated the strong Japanese conviction that in a democracy the minority must be heard. The Communist-Trotskyist-anarchist Zengakuren, the Federation of Student Self-Government Associations, demonstrated so frighteningly at this outrage that Kishi had to un-invite Eisenhower. Thus shamed, Kishi fell ignominiously from office.

The administration of the next Yoshida-line prime minister, Hayato Ikeda, got off badly when the far-right son of a Self-Defense Forces colonel stabbed to death the leader of the Socialist party, as the whole nation watched on television. Ikeda, cold-hearted, blunt, close to big business, imitated President John F. Kennedy ("to the moon by 1970") by making his goal the doubling of the national income in ten years. Japan dutifully stopped rioting and turned to, and was within easy distance of reaching the goal only four years later, when Ikeda stepped down because of a cancer that soon afterward killed him.

For the next 2,797 days, which is almost eight years and the second-longest incumbency in the nation's parliamentary history, easy-laughing Eisaku ("The Quick-Eared") Sato served as prime minister. He was in the Yoshida line, and more particularly in the ultraconservative Kishi branch of it, for Kishi was Sato's admired elder blood brother. (Kishi, born a Sato, was adopted into the Kishi family in accordance with a custom common among prewar patriarchal families in need of a male heir. In fact, Kishi's father had been adopted by the Satos from the Kishis.) Sato perfected Liberal Democrat toryism so skillfully that he could have taken out a trademark on it, although his administration was sometimes clouded by the "black mist," as the Japanese call it, of corruption. Sato's leadership stretched out Japan's period of one-party rule to an overlong twenty-four years (which the present administration continues); it put the whole government at the service of business and neglected people-related problems; but it nevertheless represented the democracy that Japan had aspired to since the Meiji Restoration. Under Sato, the Japanese economic miracle grew even more miraculous. And it was Sato who in 1969 persuaded the United States to return Okinawa and its million people to Japan. "It is quite an achievement to do that without war, through peaceful negotiations," he remarked. The Okinawa settlement won Sato a decisive victory in elections that year.

President Nixon, angry because Sato did not curb competitive Japanese textile exports to the United States in the way that he thought Sato had promised in exchange for Okinawa, pointedly refused to go to Tokyo and consult with Sato before announcing in mid-1971 that he would visit Japan's big neighbor—one of the so-called "Nixon shocks" to Japan. Nonetheless, Good Soldier Sato, anti-Communist and undeviating supporter of Chiang Kai-shek's Taiwanese

Republic of China, allowed himself to be point man in the futile American-coached effort a few months later to keep the People's Republic of China out of the United Nations. Japanese wags joked that his name should be spelled eisakUSAto. When businessmen clamored that Japan had to recognize China to get trade advantages like the Americans', Sato's anti-China record prevented him, try as he might, from getting an invitation to Peking; so in 1972 he made way for a prime minister who could. After he left office, Sato mused, "I feel I stuck it out a little too long." To cheer him up, a friend of his named Morinosuke Kajima, who is chairman of Japan's largest construction company, enlisted the services of a former Japanese ambassador to the United Nations in a long international lobbying effort that culminated in the choice of Eisaku Sato for the Nobel Peace Prize. The rather negative argument for this astonishing award was that during his term of office Sato had done nothing to change Japan's long-standing policy of shunning nuclear weapons. He died in mid-1975.

Occasional headlines ("Fiery Rampage in Tokyo") and occasional whipped-up demonstrations and occasional nervous comparisons (Marxism is much more intellectually articulate in Japan than in the United States) have in the last three decades obscured the bed-rock fact that Japan is a stable, conservative country, with conservative people, run by a conservative Establishment for the benefit of conservatives. Riots and the *demo* (to use the Japanese word for demonstration) have never significantly deflected this course. It is part of the Japanese psychology that most people over college age would rather take their chances with the system than with a revolution. The system has responded with a 200-fold growth of gross national product, which multiplied the standard of living (as measured in money) 150 times. Though Japan today has a sufficiency of worries, old and new, this skyrocketing economic performance, turning desperation into pride, has sapped leftist criticism. The Datsun, not the demo, best symbolizes postwar Japan.

PART THREE 🌸 *Power*

18 /

Hirohito

WHO RUNS JAPAN? Any account of power in Japan today must still start with the emperor—though in reality he is more a pressure than an active power. As of New Year's Day 1946, the emperor of Japan has been, by his own declaration and by Occupation fiat, a "human being," rather than the Shinto deity that he was before then. God or man, he remains a pervasive figure in Japanese life and government. With ancestors dating back to the dawn of Homo sapiens in Japan, Hirohito is the incumbent monarch of the world's oldest royal house. His reign, which will reach half a century if he is still on the throne on December 25, 1976, is longer than that of any of his 123 predecessors, having in 1972 surpassed the standing record set by his grandfather, the Emperor Meiji (1867–1912). At seventy-five, he remains an intelligent man who keeps well informed about government, and can—through the complexities of the ways in which politicians must deal with him and relate to him—topple cabinet ministers and cause political turmoil. His vast secluded palace grounds, occupying a place of prominence in Tokyo comparable to Central Park in Manhattan, constantly remind the capital's millions of his teleological Presence. To Americans, who saw him as Gerald Ford's host in late 1974 and who were scheduled to receive him on a historic first tour of the United States in October 1975, he is coming into focus as the quietly dignified symbol of an ever-less-ignorable nation.

Far from monarchic in appearance, Hirohito looks like a small-town pharmacist, perhaps, or a grade-school principal. All his life he has suffered from a slight motor malfunction of the legs, which together with nearsightedness causes him to walk carefully and hesitantly; nevertheless, he says, "If there's anything strong about me, it's my legs." Edwin O. Reischauer, the Harvard historian who was American ambassador to Japan from 1961 to 1966, found the emperor to be a "painfully shy and nervous man," with little capacity for small talk or eloquent expression. During his postwar efforts to meet the common people of Japan he became known as "Mr. Ah-so-desuka?" ("Is that so?") from his customary response to whatever he was told. When he visited Hiroshima after the atom-bombing, he remarked, "There seems to have been considerable destruction here."

The imperial institution costs the Japanese people more than $15 million a year. Yet Hirohito's life style is more conspicuous for its unpretentiousness than for any grand show. Hirohito lives in the Western manner, except that he has been gradually giving up Western food for a heavily vegetarian Japanese diet: sushi, sweet potatoes, pumpkins, noodles, all set off, sometimes, by a dish of eel. He used to employ food tasters, to foil poisoners, but doesn't any more. In public he wears only Western-style clothes, and he lives in only Western-style rooms; in fact, his private residence, Fukiage Palace, deep inside its walled and moated park, is a simple, white, fifteen-room building with just one Japanese-style chamber. He never wears a crown (the Japanese monarchy does not have such a thing), and he is never called "the mikado" (that word went out of use long ago). Once a year, in an act of symbolic identity with the nation's farmers, he puts on rubber boots and sets out rice plants in the palace's royal paddy. At the fall equinox he offers the harvest to the main Shinto shrine, at Ise, two hundred miles southwest of Tokyo.

Ceremony requires him, on January 2 and on his birthday, April 29, to greet between one and two hundred thousand flag-waving well-wishers from a low balcony of the official Imperial Palace (shielded by bulletproof glass ever since someone sling-shotted a steel ball toward him in 1969). Other New Year's functions, put on early in January, are formal lectures to their highnesses by noted scholars (1974 subjects: Goethe, social legislation, and natural science), and the Imperial Poetry Party, where the ten best wakas (thirty-one-syllable poems) from among thirty thousand entries are read, together with the emperor's own poem, which in 1974 was:

> *Beyond the hills*
> *In twilight looms*
> *The islet of Toshima*
> *In the sea of morning calm.*

Hirohito is a biologist of recognized merit. Half a dozen botanists advise and assist him at his laboratory in a wooden building in the corner of the Fukiage gardens, where he studies flowers and weeds. Newsmen who cover the emperor recall trailing along through the woods at his villa a hundred miles north of Tokyo as Hirohito, dressed in beige sport shirt and a Panama hat, called out the names of all the flowers, even identifying a certain creeper "although it happens to be standing up straight." But his specialty is marine biology. In a two-story museum in the Fukiage gardens, he has a collection of four thousand aquatic specimens from Sagami Bay, south of Tokyo. He gets credit for twelve books, with names like *The Opisthobranchia of Sagami Bay* and *Some Hydrozoans of the Amakusa Islands*, but only two are really "By Hirohito, Emperor of Japan"; in the others he is "the collector." The University of Hawaii published in English his book on shellfish.

By ancient custom, Hirohito was taken from his parents shortly after birth and brought up until almost school age in the Japanese-style villa of a stern and vigilant admiral, a couple of miles south of the Imperial Palace. The young prince got his education at the rigorous Peers' School, founded in Kyoto during the late Tokugawa period to train the children of the nobility and of high government officials and business leaders. The headmaster, who laid down Hirohito's courses, was General Maresuke Nogi, who four years earlier, in 1904, had led the Japanese forces in capturing Port Arthur. Nogi forced Hirohito through such tests as standing naked under an icy waterfall. After Nogi and his wife committed double suicide as a duty to the Emperor Meiji upon his death in 1912, the great Admiral Heihachiro Togo took charge of Hirohito's schooling. He left the task mostly to various barons, viscounts, and professors, who kneeled before the prince and delivered lectures.

Hirohito also learned those obligations of royalty, riding, swimming, and golf. In 1921, after voyaging through the Indian Ocean escorted by a squadron of battleships, he made a five-month tour of Europe, staying in Buckingham Palace ("Everything satisfactory, me boy?" bellowed King George V), and in Paris walking the streets alone for the first and last time in his life. He still cherishes an aging Metro ticket as a memento of that liberating trip. When he returned to the palace, Hirohito had to take over the imperial duties of his father, the Emperor Taisho. Once an intelligent, strong-willed man, Taisho had gone balmy after a brain thrombosis in 1919. On one occasion, when he was supposed to address the Diet, Taisho rolled up the script of his speech and, holding it like a telescope, peered interestedly around the chamber. Another time, receiving the credentials of a kneeling Belgian ambassador, he playfully patted the diplomat's bald head.

When the 1923 earthquake shook Tokyo, Hirohito fled from the Imperial Palace and found the ground outside moving so violently that he could scarcely stay on his feet. At that time he had been preparing to marry Nagako, a prince's daughter and a childhood friend to whom he had been betrothed since she was fifteen and he seventeen—an engagement that had survived a court scandal when it was first proved and then disproved that Nagako carried the genes of color blindness and would damage the royal blood. Out of respect for the quake victims, Hirohito postponed his wedding until the next year. There followed nine years of waiting for a male heir. The empress gave birth to Princess Shigeko, then to Princess Sachiko, then to Princess Kazuko, then to Princess Atsuko. Rumors spread that the emperor might have to take a concubine from among the court ladies, some of whom were Bryn Mawr and Radcliffe girls—though why they should have a better chance of producing a boy was never made clear. But Hirohito preferred monogamy, and on December 23, 1933, Nagako gave birth to a son, Akihito. Then, for insurance, she had another son, Masahito, in 1935, followed by one more daughter, Takako, in 1939.

Hirohito installed his first telephone in 1928, but in many ways the throne remained a medieval institution clear through to the end of World War II. The emperor's portrait was deeply revered; when *Time* printed it on the magazine's cover in 1936, Japanese officials implored the editors to advise readers not to place such objects as beer bottles and ashtrays on top of the picture. Commoners were not supposed to say the word "Hirohito" or to look at him—they had to avert eyes, turn away, pull windowshades. John Nance Garner, the brash Vice-President of the United States in the 1930s, once proposed, just before calling on Hirohito, to flash a dollar watch in the emperor's face and say, "Your Majesty, here's one thing you folks can't imitate and undersell!" If he had carried through, the imperial aide who allowed Garner to call would have had to commit suicide. (What's more, the Japanese were making the same watch for thirty cents.)

Despite his insulation inside the palace walls, and despite the distortions that deification no doubt imposes on a man's perceptions, Hirohito managed to keep a lively, intelligent, day-to-day grasp on the affairs of Japan and the world. Did he therefore lead Japan to war? Japan-born David Bergamini, who after his release from a wartime Japanese concentration camp in the Philippines went on to become a Rhodes scholar and a *Life* magazine correspondent, argues in *Japan's Imperial Conspiracy* that "Hirohito was a formidable war leader: tireless, dedicated, meticulous, clever, and patient. He had inherited . . . a mission, which was to rid Asia of white men." Bergamini depicts Hirohito in the months before Pearl Harbor as "immersed in the pros and cons of war," inquiring into such details as how much rubber the United States could get from South America if cut off from Malaya and Indonesia. Quoting the diaries (published in 1967), of Hajime Sugiyama, who was army chief of staff, Bergamini shows that on November 3, 1941, the emperor was one of the first to get a copy of Admiral Yamamoto's Order No. 1, the detailed plan of attack for Pearl Harbor, the Philippines, Hong Kong, Singapore, and Indonesia. During the war, Hirohito more and more frequently attended meetings of the chiefs of staff and cabinet ministers, and to break down the stultifying formality of such contacts, the meetings were redesignated as Political-Military Liaison Conferences Which Happen to Take Place Before His Majesty.

Whether this adds up to an imperial conspiracy is highly dubious: Hirohito seems mostly to have put his seal on the decisions of others, and in the end he asked Japan to "bear the unbearable" and surrender. Nevertheless, he symbolized the war effort, and his name was used endlessly to spur on the troops. In the depths of desperation on Guadalcanal, Lieutenant General Hitoshi Imamura urged the men to "set His Majesty's heart at ease" by retaking the island. General Tojo said, "It is only when I am exposed to the light of His Majesty that I shine." At the same time, Japanese soldiers generally believed that the emperor did not like war and would not have permitted his people to be dragged into it if he could have helped it. Obviously, he was on Japan's side, and hoped to win, not lose, the war, but only for a month or two at the beginning did he let himself believe that Japan might really win. After that, his overriding concern was worry over losing. In many conferences with officers and officials, Hirohito pointedly refrained from intervention, giving assent to decisions only by his silence. Hirohito's own summation, to MacArthur, of his wartime attitude may not be far off the mark: "It was not clear to me that our course was unjustified. Even now I am not sure how future historians will allocate the responsibility for the war."

At length the time came to acknowledge, as Hirohito tactfully put it in his surrender speech after two atomic bombs had massacred 157,000 people, that "the war situation has developed not necessarily to Japan's advantage." From his study the emperor removed a bust of Napoleon and replaced it with one of Lincoln. In the delicate surrender negotiations, the deepest concern of the Japanese was that the Allies might dethrone, or even execute, the emperor. Neither Winston Churchill nor Harry Truman seriously considered such measures; the American government was following the advice of its Ethnogeographic Board, a group of anthropologists who as early as 1942 were saying, "Don't attack the emperor—we are going to need him to end the war." Contrarily, Australia angrily argued that "the visible dethronement of the system is a primary means of shaking the faith of the Japanese in the heavenly character of the emperor in whose name they have committed many atrocities."

MacArthur settled the matter, exculpating the emperor, and argued that Hirohito should be retained as a symbol uniting the Japanese. Otherwise, MacArthur told Washington, "I believe all hope of introducing modern democratic methods would disappear and that when military control finally ceased some form of intense regimentation probably along Communistic lines would arise from the mutilated masses." This concept prevailed, which merely reflected the strange but indisputable fact that for two millennia the emperor—strong or weak—has been the legitimizer of the power of others. And for these reasons the emperor escaped indictment as a war criminal. When, at the Tokyo trial, General Tojo implicated Hirohito by saying that "there is no Japanese who would go against the will of His Majesty," consternation reigned. A week later Tojo was induced to amend his testimony and say that "because of the advice given by the high command the emperor consented, though reluctantly, to the war."

Of the whole issue of the emperor's guilt, one prominent Australian, Sir William Flood Webb, president of the Tokyo war crimes court, ultimately wrote: "I suspect that, had Hirohito sat in the dock in 1946–1948, I would have had a higher regard for his character than I had for that of most of the other Japanese war leaders. Indeed the worth of Hirohito as a statesman appears from the position of his nation today, which, under his rule, has reacted to war and defeat by making herself the third industrial power on earth."

When the journalist John Gunther visited Hirohito in 1950, the emperor seemed a humbled and uncertain man, eyes cast down, dressed in an ancient suit, repeatedly pulling up a garter that slipped down his leg. Since then, by careful coddling, he has regained a position of dignity and confidence. The coddlers are the Grand Steward, the Vice Grand Steward, the Private Secretary to the Vice Grand Steward, the Grand Chamberlain, and the other 1,148 officials and employees of the Imperial Household Agency.

One of the agency's headaches in recent years has been the rise of skyscrapers around the edges of the palace grounds, in violation of an ancient rule that no one should look down upon the emperor. When an official armed with a pair of binoculars discovered that from the observation room on top of the Kasumigaseki Building he could look directly into Hirohito's living room, the household agency planted some tall trees around the emperor's house to block the view. Construction of the Tokio Fire & Marine Insurance Company skyscraper in Marunouchi was stopped for months on grounds that the household agency disapproved, but resumed after the emperor allowed that he would not mind a few tall buildings to look at. When the emperor and empress visited the renovated headquarters of the Metropolitan Police Department a couple of years ago, the problem was how to arrange for the superintendent to see their imperial highnesses into the elevator on the first floor and be present to greet them on arrival at the third floor. It was generally acknowledged that the superintendent was too old and fat to run up the stairs faster than the elevator, and consulting engineers found no way to slow the machinery. After much debate, the household agency gravely decreed that it would be permissible to hold open the door of the emperor's elevator for a moment while the superintendent rode to the third floor in another elevator.

Hirohito's palace, opened in 1967 to replace the building fire-bombed in the war, is a two-story, 300-foot-long building of brown masonry in modern Japanese style, capped with a curving roof of green copper. As the seat of the Tokugawa shoguns before 1868, the palace grounds contained in various epochs a five-story castle, nineteen donjons, a treasury, two palaces, and dwellings and stores. If it was townlike then, it is parklike now. Only three donjons, lovely small white castles of two or three stories, remain: one is called Fujimi Yagura (Can-See-Mount-Fuji Donjon). The original outer moat has long since been filled in and turned into space for office buildings, but about six miles of moat still surround and divide the palace grounds. Many broad avenues, marked with 30-kilometer-an-hour speed-limit signs, provide communications within the grounds. But traffic is light; silence prevails, and only the fingerlike new skyscrapers on the horizon betray that this sanctuary lies in the heart of a great city. In these quiet precincts I saw maples, cherries, willows, pines, a lotus pond, an English garden, and pheasants and white herons living in the half-wild reediness of an empty moat. Coolie-hatted women volunteers, who apply six months in advance for the privilege, come great distances to weed the gardens and sweep the streets of the palace grounds, and in return the emperor, in a brief audience, gives each of them a pack of cigarettes printed with the imperial chrysanthemum crest.

The 1947 constitution reduced the imitation-Western Japanese nobility, founded under the Emperor Meiji, to commoners. Japanese royalty now consists of the emperor and his brothers, their wives and children (except women married to commoners), the wife and children of the crown prince, and the wife of the crown prince's younger brother —eighteen persons, all told.

Their various highnesses occupy themselves in assorted ways. Prince Mikasa, Hirohito's younger brother, is the knowledgeable president of the Japan Society of Orientology and a lecturer at Tokyo Christian Women's University. He likes folk dancing. His son Tomohito got a degree in English history at Oxford, wrote a book called *Tomohito's Lovely English Life*, worked for a time as an ordinary salary man, and wears a tidy chin beard. Empress Nagako, who with Hirohito lately celebrated the golden anniversary of their wedding, is a talented painter in traditional Japanese style, whose works have been shown at the Japan Academy of Art. Hirohito calls her Nagamiya (roughly, Princess), and she calls him Okami (Honorable Supreme). She has more poise and humor than her husband. She has been known to make fun of supersolemn court occasions by catching the eye of some dignitary and giving him a long, slow wink.

Akihito, first in line to succeed Hirohito, is described as "utterly suave compared to his father, but no conversationalist either." The crown prince was educated at the Peers' School, and tutored from 1946 to 1950 by the American scholar and author Elizabeth Gray Vining. He took a degree in political science and economics at Gakushuin University (as the Peers' School has been renamed) in Tokyo in 1956. One day, playing tennis, he met Michiko Shoda, pretty daughter of the president of a flour-milling company. Soon afterward, a woman private detective named Midori Sato got a request from a mysteriously unidentified client to run a check on Michiko. The girl proved out to be unflawed, generous, sophisticated, and a good student in English and physics at Sacred Heart Women's University. The crown prince married her in 1959. They have traveled widely on every continent—even to Nepal, Ethiopia, and Peru. Their oldest son, who might well become the 126th emperor, is Prince Hiro, born in 1960. He is going through the lower schools that are attached to Gakushuin University, and gets so-so grades. Akihito and Michiko, who are now both in their early forties, pack up their children and dine with the emperor and empress every Wednesday evening. Akihito, conscientious, serious, and thoughtful, is reportedly much interested in politics, and on the throne he may try to enlarge the influence of the emperor.

"The emperor is revered by older people—and the young people make jokes about him," I was told by an official of the Ministry of Foreign Affairs. It seemed to me that these observations, while valid and true, did not catch the quiet intensity of feeling about the emperor that I discovered in asking many people about him. A conservative banker held stoutly that the monarchy should be abolished, blaming Hirohito as the willing tool of the war criminals. A political scientist noted that "in Japan, it is difficult to embody authority in a prime minister, and we haven't got a president. So the emperor is a convenient 'hat' for authority." A bright young career girl thought that the emperor "is harmless, and even useful as a symbol." A historian held that "people who suffered from the war blame the emperor for not preventing it, but people too young to have experienced the war are proud of the emperor because the monarchy *is* ancient and makes a good 'center' for the country."

A few years ago, China's Hsinhua news agency called Hirohito "the No. 1 hangman whose hands are stained with the blood of the people of Japan and Asia"—a blast that the Japanese press, which generally treats the emperor in a kindly and reverent way, obligingly suppressed. Now China feels more tolerant. Premier Chou En-lai, bidding farewell to Japan's Prime Minister Tanaka after Tanaka's historic first visit to China, genially inquired after the emperor's health. "Give him my best regards," said Chou.

19 /

The One-and-One-Half Parties

LET US NOW SING a (necessarily) brief paean of praise to Japanese democracy.

It is, to begin with, still amazing that the Meiji-era leaders could have imported so forthrightly and effectively such Western political institutions as a constitution, a parliament, elections, ministries, and parties. It is paradoxical but admirable that Japan should have proceeded, on orders from the American Occupation, to put real flesh on the bones of this imported democracy. It is politically unnatural but pragmatically praiseworthy that the Japanese nation should still be comfortable living under their American-written constitution, which to Japanese ears does not sound literary, or even well translated.

Yet Japanese democracy works. Japan vies in the responsiveness of its parliamentary government with France, Italy, and Western Germany, and it puts the rest of Asia, as well as all of Latin America, not to mention Africa, to shame. Votes count in Japan, and the Japanese believe that votes count: 73 percent of the electorate voted in the mid-1974 election, as compared to 38 percent in the November 1974 American elections. Just as in the United States or England, the electorate can change the government whenever it decides to. The Liberal Democratic Party has ruled Japan since 1948 precisely because most Japanese favor the way it governs.

The structure of Japanese democracy is sound, a clear division of powers into legislative, executive, and judicial, as in the United States, that nevertheless incorporates the British principle of fusion, wherein the legislative parliament elects a prime minister, who forms an executive cabinet that (among other duties) chooses the judicial branch's judges. The constitution contains a long and modern list of civic rights, surpassing America's. But it provides no states' rights, because Japan's unitary system makes the forty-seven prefectures merely arms of the central government.

The Diet divides into lower and upper houses, the 491-seat House of Representatives and the 252-seat House of Councillors. The House of Representatives is the more powerful, for it can repass by two-thirds vote any bill that the House of Councillors rejects; wags say that the basic power of the councillors is to eat lunch every noon. Representatives are elected from local constituencies for four years or until dissolution of the house. Councillors serve an unqualified six years, half the house being elected every three years. One hundred and fifty-two of them come from local constituencies, and one hundred from the "national constituency," which is Japan at large.

The cabinet of ministers, which supervises the writing of the bills (by the bureaucracy) and sends them to the Diet to be passed, is the power center of Japanese politics. The prime minister, who appoints the cabinet usually (but not necessarily) from among the members of the Diet, is himself elected by a majority of both houses, and he and his cabinet must resign if the House of Representatives passes a no-confidence resolution.

End of paean.

In almost every respect except these basics, Japanese democracy takes on Oriental traits of its own. The Anglo-American concept of democracy stresses majority rule; the minority is supposed to concede in a sporting way and play along, at least until the next election. The Japanese concept stresses that democracy must first of all protect the weak and downtrodden, and allow their views to have some weight in great decisions. Democracy is not, to the Japanese, a game with winners and losers, but a way of achieving the consensus that the whole society prizes. Undemocratic behavior in the Western world is anything that tends toward dictatorship and tyranny, but in Japan it is whatever ruptures harmony. Democracy in Japan applies less to the structure of government than to human relationships, and while the concept protects dignity and human rights, it does not make men social equals, which is impossible in a hierarchic society.

The practical workings of consensus democracy, once a Diet is elected, require that the minority opposition parties get their say, in a style and tradition that is for the most part exceedingly civilized, though every so often riotous and even bloody. It is bad form for the majority simply to outvote the minority without hearing out the minority position and making some compromise with it. The pictures of Diet members scuffling, overturning desks, or strangling one another that occasionally get into Western newspapers usually depict what happens when the majority tries to ram a bill through the house. The opposition's more serious ultimate threat is to boycott sessions of the Diet, which immobilizes it. The necessity for the majority to concede something to the opposition molds the consensus. Election victors, even if they win big, cannot assume that they have a mandate to trample on the losers. The majority's leaders must humbly subject themselves to questioning by the minority. Even when the minority favors a majority bill, the minority wants to, and gets to, make points and take exceptions.

The voting law, which is easy to state and fiendishly complex to work with, is another idiosyncrasy of Japanese democracy. Each of the 124 electoral districts sends between three and five members to the lower house. (In the upper house, the electoral districts are the prefectures, each of which, depending on population, sends between one and four councillors to the Diet.) Each voter may vote for only one candidate, a considerable deprivation. Typically, the voter may believe that a certain five candidates, out of perhaps ten, should become the Diet members from his district, but since he is allowed to vote for only one, he can only hope that other like-minded voters will elect the other candidates that he favors. For the political parties, putting up candidates under this "multi-member, single-vote" system is an even more tantalizing problem. The sheer realities compel a party to estimate how many votes it will get in a district, and present just enough candidates to take all those votes. With too few candidates, it wastes votes by allowing its winners unnecessarily large victories; with too many candidates, it may spread the sure votes too thin and lose them all. In other words, candidates from the same party, if too numerous, are in effect forced to run against one another, rather than against the opposition.

The Japanese political party—faction-ridden, Tokyo-centered, shallowly organized—is a third peculiarity of this nation's democracy. Parties were born in Japan in 1872, nearly two decades before there was any Diet to which candidates might be elected. On behalf of sectional, rural, or popular interests, they tried to influence the governmental bureaucrats who were carrying out the Meiji revolution. These parties thus stood ready to share political power upon the establishment of the Diet in 1889, but only slowly did the high officials who ran the government begin to join and use the parties. Japan had barely achieved the selection of a popular (rather than aristocratic or military) prime minister in 1918 when the newly emerging big business trusts took effective control of the parties—Mitsui of the Liberals, Mitsubishi of the Progressives. In the mid-1920s, Socialist and Communist parties managed to organize and sputter along, but conservatism ruled the field. During World War II, the parties were dissolved and remolded as the war-supporting Imperial Rule Assistance Association. The American Occupation energetically revived them, but only the Communists have created a wide-scale membership organization. The other parties are federations of factions, each led by a prominent politician. The parties seem to be the property of the politicians rather than of the people.

The Japanese say that they live under the "one-and-one-half-party system," the one party being the Liberal Democratic, and the one-half being the four opposition parties taken together. The Liberal Democrats have had the necessary majorities in the Diet to rule for the last twenty-seven years, but their insurance policy for power has been the dogged disunity of the opposition, which cannot coalesce because each party wants a greater share of the cabinet ministers, including the prime ministership, than the other parties are willing to concede. But the opposition is not helpless: Japanese consensus politics gives even half a party the power to delay and modify legislation. And in one supremely important matter this half-party has profoundly affected Japan. The initiation of constitutional amendments requires a two-thirds vote in both houses of the Diet. By voting against the Liberal Democrats in numbers always greater than one-third, the opposition has defended the constitution against the Liberal Democrats' favorite project, which is to strike out the article that renounces war and the maintenance of armed forces.

A fourth singularity of Japanese politics is the shameless use of money to win campaigns. "We have Watergate here all the time," one editor told me gloomily. Many Liberal Democrats estimate campaign costs at 1,000 yen, or $3.30, per vote, compared to $1.50 per vote for the most extravagant American senatorial campaigns. Typical expenses for an incumbent member of the lower house are $330,000, and a challenger, attempting to establish his identity, may pay twice that much. In getting ready for the mid-1974 upper-house election, the Liberal Democratic Party reportedly accumulated a fund of $100 million; one faction leader had $33 million for his own people, and one candidate scraped together $2.3 million. In 1972, the expenses of one candidate included $10,000 for a picnic at a hot spring for three thousand elderly voters; $40,000 for twenty thousand umbrellas distributed as gifts; $30,000 for a luncheon for five thousand members of his Association of Supporters; $33,000 for ten thousand sets of table utensils distributed as gifts; $37,000 as giveaway money for prefectural, city, and town politicians capable of rounding up votes; $100,000 for posters; $50,000 for headquarters and staff.

Unlike American corporations, Japanese companies can legally provide campaign funds for political candidates. In the 1974 election, Liberal Democratic secretary general Tomisaburo Hashimoto got each major business firm in the country to take responsibility for getting a specific candidate elected. For example, Kajima Corporation, a big construction company, undertook to back Shinji Sato, son of the former prime minister, by building up support organizations and pressuring its own employees to vote for him. The Sumitomo group took on Iichiro Hatoyama, also the son of a former prime minister. Mitsubishi assigned 107 of its executives to form an organization to elect a former police official. (Sato and Hatoyama won, but Mitsubishi's man lost.)

Cornucopia spending by candidates violates the law, which limits upper-house campaign expenses to $65,000; the Japanese call it the "bamboo-basket law," because it is so leaky. Even more blatantly, politicians sidestepped another clause of the law, which restricts campaigning to twenty-three days before the vote. Theoretically, short campaigns focus the voters' attention; in actuality they serve to prevent issues from being developed and to keep incumbents in office because challengers cannot establish themselves in the electorate's mind. Parties dodge this time barrier in two ways. Long before elections, they put up posters picturing candidates and purportedly advertising books they have written or lectures they will give; in mid-1974, one could see posters in Wakayama advertising lectures to be given (by national-constituency candidates) in Tokyo, four hundred miles away. Alternatively, the parties pick celebrity candidates who are already famous, particularly to run in the national constituency. Novelists, coaches, comedians, singers, and television emcees are put up as *tarento* (talent) candidates. One of them in 1974 was a young man who, putting on a gray wig and a kimono, played the title role of Nasty Grandmother in a TV serial. Another won election to this Japanese equivalent of the House of Lords in 1968 on the popularity he had earned with his "octopus dance," in which he waved his arms limply like tentacles. The Liberal Democrats also try to get votes by running prominent Buddhist and Shinto leaders.

The actual campaigns, formal and perfunctory, are hardly more to the point. At railroad-station plazas, one sees candidates standing on top of Toyota Hi-Ace vans fitted with two-thousand-watt loudspeakers, flanked by a couple of local supporters and bellowing damnations against pollution and inflation to apathetic audiences of half a dozen. By inflexible custom, candidates paste up portrait posters, beautifully printed in four colors at a cost of $1 apiece, on specially allotted squares on specially designated political billboards—the combined effect is like an enlarged sheet of postage stamps.

In sum, voters usually have to go to the polls with slight knowledge of the candidates' views and stances. But that hardly matters. One votes for a candidate not in hopes that he will represent his constituency, but only in the expectation that he will follow his party's line. "You don't write your congressman in Japan," Masaru Ogawa, a commentator for the *Japan Times*, pointed out to me. "It wouldn't do any good. He has to vote the way the party tells him to." So in effect the voter chooses among parties. And in this choice he gets a large range: the cautious, historic, dominant, business-first Liberal Democratic Party, the labor-oriented Japan Socialist Party, the unignorable and serious Japan Communist Party, the Nichiren Buddhist Komeito (Clean Government Party), and the small and moderate Democratic Socialist Party.

The price of rice—what's that got to do with politics? In the case of the Liberal Democratic Party, plenty; although the party of business, it stays in power by keeping farmers happy. The party's two antecedents, the Liberals and the Democrats (then called Progressives), traced back to a couple of strong feudal clans, the Tosa and the Hizen, which provided the leaders for agriculturally based political parties for a dozen years after the Meiji Restoration in 1868. When revived after World War II, the Liberals and the Democrats enjoyed a windfall of support from the strength, independence, and prosperity that the American Occupation's land reform provided for the Japanese farmer. Soon Liberal Democratic governments were subsidizing farmers by guaranteeing to buy rice at support levels and by fencing out competitive foreign farm products with high tariffs. Nowadays, rice in Japan costs three times as much as the international market price, and a duty-paid American grapefruit goes for between $2 and $5 in Tokyo, to keep this citrus from competing with Japanese mandarin oranges (tangerines). Farmers gratefully give the bulk of their vote to Liberal Democratic legislators, who are as a consequence known as "rice Dietnam."

Farmers, of course, comprise only about a tenth of the working population, and to compensate for this shortcoming the Liberal Democratic Party utilizes a legal loophole that makes each farmer's vote count for the votes of as many as five city dwellers. For three decades, voters have been moving in large numbers from the country to the city, but the allocation of Diet seats to electoral districts remains what it was in 1950, because the Liberal Democrat-controlled Diet has quite intentionally failed to reapportion seats. Relatively depopulated farm districts elect just as many Diet members as heavily populated urban districts. In a recent election, it took 1,033,267 votes to win a seat in Kanagawa Prefecture (site of industrialized Yokohama and Kawasaki), but only 203,111 to win in rustic Tottori, on the Sea of Japan. A Liberal Democratic candidate won a seat with 128,591 votes in Kochi, on the island of Shikoku, while a Socialist lost with 640,893 votes in Tokyo. In 1974, the Supreme Court upheld these disproportionate seat allocations on grounds that they are not serious enough to be unconstitutional—a far cry from the U.S. Supreme Court's "one man, one vote" ruling. About the same time, the Liberal Democratic government rewarded farmers with their annual steep rise in the price of rice; subsidies now run around $4 billion a year. In years past, the Liberal Democrats commanded absolute popular majorities; now they stay in power by winning Diet majorities with popular pluralities.

The Liberal Democrats' strong base of rural votes (magnified by misapportionment) plus the conservatism innate to the countryside make the party the natural ally of business, and businessmen big and small supply the other main bloc of the party's votes. After taking care of the farmers by voting rice supports, the party concerns itself chiefly with coddling big business. What the party expects and gets from big business in this bargain is huge torrents of money. The voice of big business in dealing with the Liberal Democratic politicians is the Keidanren, the Federation of Economic Organizations. One recent Keidanren president, Kogoro Uemura, who while vice-president was specifically the channel of donations to politicians from business, makes no bones about Keidanren's role in financing the Liberal Democrats—he only complains that the party wants too much. Steelmakers, banks, and power companies are the party's major contributors. For its money, big business gets a philosophically sympathetic government, specific legislation, and many smaller kindnesses. Throughout the 1960s, the business elite, through its friendly politicians, successfully opposed social welfare spending not only as a government economy but also to force the Japanese people to save in order to finance much-needed extra old-age income, creating savings accounts that provided banks with funds for business to borrow. Business demanded and got the merger of the Liberals and the Democrats in 1955 as a way of unifying and insuring its power base.

Keidanren's charter flatly says that the business group "will not only submit motions and resolutions to the Diet and the government, but will also cooperate in carrying out measures that are considered necessary."

Favors like these involve the bureaucracy—and the talented, well-educated, and predominantly Liberal Democratic bureaucracy, two million strong, is very much a part of this relationship between business and government. The Diet often relies on the ministries for drafts of proposed laws. The middle-level bureaucrats who write these drafts have three reasons to make them acceptable to business. First, they generally agree with the conservative thinking of the political–business Establishment. Second, they thus make contacts with members of the Diet, which often leads to political careers. Third, bureaucrats who help business can retire from government service in their late forties (particularly if they have hit a dead end in promotion) and "parachute" into good jobs in corporations. One hundred and eighty high-ranking government officials made the "celestial descent" in a typical year, 1973, according to the National Personnel Authority. These fallen angels serve their new companies by dealing with their former colleagues in the ministries—in friendly games of golf, of course, or night-club binges; never anything so gauche as calling on them in their offices.

With an eye to such future favors, bureaucrats award franchises, expedite licenses, decide on bids, "interpret" the antitrust laws, and even make high policy, for the cabinet depends heavily on the bureaucracies for advice. In fact, the elite Japanese bureaucracy runs the government day by day, providing continuity while the cabinet serves as an executive committee. About a third of the Liberal Democratic members of the Diet are usually former bureaucrats. Once elected, they quickly win places on Diet committees dealing with their former ministries. "You can't, for example, be a member of the Diet committee on finance without the kind of experience you'd get serving in the Ministry of Finance," one high government official explained to me. "And this lines you up to become minister of finance, heading your old organization."

Sheer expertise, though, is not enough to shoot a man into a cabinet minister's job; and without holding several successive cabinet posts, no man can hope to become prime minister. The successful bureaucrat-turned-politician must learn how to form a faction and to ingratiate himself with the businessmen who will give him money. But a faction leader who is also a cabinet minister often has regulatory and other powers over business, which makes it easier for him to solicit funds. All this adds up to a howling scandal—open, above-board, accepted, but a scandal nonetheless. The Liberal Democratic politicians are bought and paid for. "Everyone knows," writes Robert Guillain, that contributions from businessmen are "the prime reason for the long reign of the Right. Ministers are virtually the delegates of the managerial class, their representatives in power."

One reason that the Japanese for years tolerated their purchased-politician system is that the resulting government was sensitive, constructive, and accommodating. Columnist Joseph Kraft observes that former prime ministers Kishi, Ikeda, and Sato, "unlike conservatives in most countries, have had both a liking for government and real feeling for it." The conservatism of the Liberal Democrats has until lately been pragmatic, Keynesian, paternalistic, tolerant, democratic, and carefully in tune with public opinion—all attitudes that reflect the intelligent and patriotic self-interest of the best of the business managers. The party is neither radical nor innovative, but it has had a way, one bureaucrat told me, of "sensing the feelings and hopes of the people faster than the opposition parties." Contrarily, the Liberal Democrats often let the opposition develop an issue, wait for a consensus in favor of it, and then co-opt it. During the 1950s and 1960s the party stood for high industrial growth at any cost in pollution and social welfare; but now, sensing public discontent, the tories are lifting leftist ideas, talking about curbing property rights and supporting a guaranteed annual income. Even the most conservative of the factions proposes to replace "government for material affluence" with "government for spiritual happiness."

Like the Republicans in the United States, the Liberal Democrats in Japan readily overcame their anti-Communist scruples when the time was ripe to recognize the People's Republic of China. By its willingness to move with the times, while retaining conservatism's basic appeal of prudence and stability, the Liberal Democratic Party regularly wins the support of the all-important independent voters—the white-collar people, for instance, who live in those towering new public-housing apartments.

The many years of Liberal Democratic success in Japanese politics stem in part from the fact that a lot of its politicians are men of considerable intelligence and sophistication. Leonine, elegantly dressed Wataru Hiraizumi, a member of the House of Councillors, is typical. He travels frequently to the United States and Europe, talks easily of world politics and the politics of other nations, and has a specific vision of what Japan should be. "We are trying," he told me, "through a mixture of our own values with what we admire in the West, to create something new. We are producing Nobel Prize scientists, the result of absorbing Western culture with our own. This new balanced society that we hope to create in the next twenty years could become the vanguard of the coming world. We are getting far more international than, say, America, Britain, or France."

As the party of conservatism, the Liberal Democrats include the far-right extremists who symbolize the threat of a Japan turned once again to authoritarian government. The mainstream members of the party, out of prudence and pragmatism, fence the hawks out of cabinet positions and generally contrive to give the party an image of moderation. Yet it often seems that though the party's head is in the center, its heart is on the right. A sputter of events and indications continually betrays the Liberal Democrats' emotional sympathy for the hawkish position. The main case in point is the party's yearning to rewrite the constitution, doing away with its prohibition against maintaining armed forces and restoring some power to the emperor. Former prime minister Nobusuke Kishi heads the National Conference for the Establishment of an Independent Constitution, which advocates revision.

In a drumfire of smaller moves, the Liberal Democrats press other nationalistic causes. In 1966 they restored the holiday of February 11, which until the Occupation banished it had been part of the emperor-worship syndrome, since it was supposedly the anniversary of the accession of the nation's first ruler to the throne in 660 B.C. Former prime minister Kakuei Tanaka wants full legal (instead of traditional) status for those two reminders of militarist days, the rising-sun flag and the old national anthem, whose ambiguous four lines go like this:

> *May Thy peaceful reign last long!*
> *May it last for thousands of years!*
> *Until this tiny stone will grow into a massive rock*
> *And the moss will cover it all deep and thick.*

The Liberal Democrats also flare up over the dangers of leftist influences among teachers, and many of them propose to restore the 1890 Imperial Rescript on Education, a vaguely worded document that stresses filial piety, "perfect moral powers," and loyalty to the throne. The party also wants to pass a new, tough penal code that would, for example, heavily punish industrial espionage, clamp down on pornography, jail those who "insult" foreign heads of state, and even penalize people who "abuse an automatic vending machine."

Finally, the Liberal Democrats continually press a project known as Nationalization of the Yasukuni Shrine. A vibrant symbol of fighting and dying for Japan, Tokyo's Yasukuni shrine, containing a roll of honor of 2.4 million war dead, is the country's most impassioned glorification of militarism. It was, for example, natural for a young clerk to choose Yasukuni as the place to disembowel himself one day recently, leaving a note praising right-wing causes. Built in 1879, Yasukuni shrine was part of the deliberate revival of state Shintoism to foster nationalism; but at the end of the war, Article 20 of the MacArthur constitution ("No religious organization shall receive any privileges from the State") deprived Yasukuni of government funds. The Liberal Democrats, partly to get the votes of the Japan Society of the War Bereaved, the War Veterans Association, and the Military Pensioners Association, perennially try to pass a bill that would provide funds for ceremonies at Yasukuni expressing the nation's "gratitude and respect for the spirits of those who died for their country in war." In 1974, the party rammed its Yasukuni bill through a committee of the lower house in four minutes, causing the opposition parties to boycott the Diet. After a week, the Liberal Democrats agreed to shelve the bill. Eventually they will get it through.

Suspicions of neofascist leanings in the Liberal Democratic Party center on a group of thirty-three young right-wingers in the Diet who in 1973 nicked their little fingers with razor blades and like ancient samurai signed themselves in blood as members of the Seirankai, a sort of Japanese John Birch Society. The name means "Summer Storm"—the kind that "refreshes the scene," says its inventor, Shintaro Ishihara. Ishihara is one of the Beautiful People of Japan, talented, clever, handsome, and cosmopolitan—he has visited the United States a dozen times, and in 1973, for a lark, he joined the Japanese search for the Loch Ness monster. His main profession is writing novels, thirty of them in the eighteen years since he was twenty-four-years old (in one, a couple manages to copulate through a hole punched in a paper wall). Born rich, he stays rich enough from royalties to afford a country house and a yacht—a couple of years ago he came in second in the South China Sea yacht race between Hong Kong and Manila. He acts, sings, and directs films. His *tarento* made him so popular that he won election to the House of Councillors in 1968 with 3 million votes, a tidy 1 million more than any other candidate had ever got. In 1972, he decided to move to the more powerful lower house, and won big in a Tokyo constituency. The Liberal Democratic organization chose Ishihara as the only man who might defeat the nearly unbeatable incumbent governor of Tokyo,

Ryokichi Minobe, in the April 1975 election, and though he lost Ishihara managed to pile up 2,336,359 votes against Minobe's 2,688,-566.

To Americans, Ishihara speaks of the Japanese constitution as "your" constitution. He calls it "clumsy" and "stupid" and adds: "I think we should have a defense army of our own no matter what your constitution says." He believes that the reorganized armed forces should have "clean" nuclear weapons. Ishihara was a good friend of fellow-novelist Yukio Mishima, but sounds less fanatic. He insists, for example, that "Seirankai is not an anti-Communist group. We did not oppose the establishment of diplomatic relations with China. We are simply opposed to those things that erode the national interest of Japan." He wants to develop the "foundations of a new morality," and contends that "our children are aimless—they believe in nothing."

Seirankai predictably stands for rewriting the constitution, restoring "morality" and conservative thinking to education, elevating the importance of the throne, strengthening the military, and providing state support for Yasukuni shrine. At least one member talks ominously of the "trouble" that Japan's "absolute power of freedom of the press and speech" causes. An undertone of vote-cadging populism runs through the Seirankai position: criticism of "excessive capitalism" and support for more equal distribution of wealth. Seirankai also demands respect for the aged ("We want young people to give up their seats to their elders on the train," says one Seirankai official), but not in politics. Its youngish members wish devoutly that the Liberal Democrats' senior officials, some of them old fellows in need of hearing aids and secretaries to help them walk, would give way to what Ishihara has dubbed the "new generation" of party politics. "These young hawks in the blood society have no chance of becoming cabinet ministers, and they're frustrated," one political science professor told me. Their frustration leads them to touch off some of the roughest punching, kicking, choking, and furniture busting seen in the Diet.

Seirankai probably will not endure as an organization, but in a few years many of its members will move up to greater power in the Liberal Democratic Party, and they may well carry Japan toward more nationalistic and authoritarian government.

The plight of the opposition parties in Japan's central government is paradoxical: jointly they come tantalizingly close to power, but they are decisively barred from taking it. Taken together, the Japan Socialist Party, the Japan Communist Party, the Democratic Socialist

Party, and Komeito won half a million *more* votes than the Liberal Democratic Party in the December 1972 election for the lower house of the Diet. If they could count on the votes that went to independent candidates, 5 percent of the total, the leftist parties would have a solid 53 percent popular majority. But so far any dreams of coalition power based on a high combined vote have been doomed as fast as they were concocted. First, the parties cannot drop their differences and make an alliance that sticks. Second, the unfair apportionment of lower-house seats as between country and city enables the Liberal Democrats to keep power in the Diet. So near and yet so far—that is the leftists' predicament, all the more frustrating because if the leftist parties could just once gain power they could reapportion the electoral districts and deprive the Liberal Democrats of their automatic majority in the lower house. And if they had a majority in the upper house, they could reject Liberal Democratic bills sent over from the lower house, where, in turn, they could deny the Liberal Democrats the two-thirds vote constitutionally needed to repass bills over the upper house's veto. This possibility was the main point of the close-fought mid-1974 House of Councillors election, but the Liberal Democrats, though badly set back, managed to hold a three-seat majority.

Lord Acton said, "Power tends to corrupt, and absolute power corrupts absolutely." The Japan Socialist Party seems to assume that the corollary to this dictum would be, "Lack of power tends to purify, and absolute lack of power purifies absolutely." The Socialists, an American Embassy analyst told me, would be "horrified" if they achieved power. Without the responsibility of power, the Socialists can smugly preach the adage that "the government party is the party of corruption; the opposition party is the party of principle." The principles the Socialists offer to the people of Japan are: (1) abrogation of the Japan–United States Security Treaty, (2) permanent renunciation of nuclear weapons, (3) abolition of the Self-Defense Forces, (4) reapportionment of electoral districts, (5) 100 percent support for the existing constitution, (6) strict application of the antimonopoly laws against big business, (7) nationalization of the coal-mining industry, (8) restrictions on economic colonization abroad by Japanese corporations, and (9) the thirty-five-hour work week and other employment benefits. This program seems to be sufficiently unexciting to save the Socialists from any danger of being elected to power. In the 1972 election, the Japan Socialist Party won 11,478,600 votes, 21.9 percent of the total, and thus acquired 118 seats in the lower house of the Diet.

Socialism came to Japan from the United States, brought by half a dozen Japanese who had worked or studied there—one of them grasped the principles of Marxism while working his way through Yale as a dishwasher. One day in 1901 they organized Japan's first socialist party, and the very same day the government banished it. Some of the Japanese socialists then retreated to the United States and kept the idea alive in Japan by propaganda. During the 1920s and 1930s a few socialists won election to the Diet, and the popular vote rose to 900,000. The party's high point was the April 1947 election, which put Socialist chairman Tetsu Katayama into office as prime minister over a coalition government that lasted ten months. A split in the party itself brought down Japan's first and only Socialist government, and splits have rent the party ever since.

Most of the party's votes and funds come from labor, specifically the 4,200,000-member Sohyo, the biggest of Japan's labor federations. But labor is growing disillusioned with its big pet poodle of a party, because it is now clear that in the 1960s the Socialists, by schisms and disdain for power, blew a good chance to attract more of the voters then moving from the countryside to the cities. Lately the party has had to send speakers to Sohyo conventions to plead with the unions for their continued exclusive support. Even though it makes the Socialists a class party, this support is vital: the only other Japanese who vote Socialist are low-level employees of government and business who are well enough educated to be open to the intellectual attraction of Marxism and so low in organizational rankings that they feel frustrated. Because of splits, excessive Marxist theorizing, and the prosperity of capitalism as fostered by the Liberal Democrats, the Socialists have lost strength steadily from their peak of 166 seats in 1955. Now, working within the curious confines of the multi-member, single-vote election law, the Socialists dare not nominate enough candidates to win even half of the Diet seats. In sum, the Socialists are beaten before they start. Still, they are good, considerate people. When they paint political slogans on the sides of railroad cars and locomotives, they do it in whitewash, and clean them off a few days later.

The Japan Communist Party is the world's first and only self-proclaimedly "lovable" Communist Party. History taught it that it had better be that way. In 1951, Joseph Stalin ordered the Japanese Communists to shoot for a violent revolution, and they obediently rioted in the Imperial Palace Plaza on May 1, 1952, in protest against the just-signed Japan–United States peace treaty. This bloodiest of postwar demos (two killed, two thousand injured) and the implicit "Molotov-cocktail strategy" went down so poorly with the public that the Communist Party lost all its seats in the lower house at the next election. After Nikita Khrushchev de-Stalinized the Soviet Communist Party, the Japanese party gave up the strategy of revolution by violence and began to shape the image it now has: sweetly reasonable, national-istic, and above all committed to attaining power only through the ballot. Just what conservative Japan needed—a conservative Commu-nist Party.

As ward heelers, the Communists are Japan's best. The party recruits doctors and lawyers to give free medical and legal aid to the poor. "Absentee husbands," conservative corporation men away from home until midnight entertaining clients for their employers, often discover to their chagrin that their forsaken wives have found a measure of solace in joining the Communist Party's New Japan Women's Organization. Other party organizations court students with dances and picnics, and render aid to 210,000 small businessmen. If a householder finds that his sewer is clogged, the Communists can find someone to clear it. Communists install free telephones in the houses of the aged and lonely, and then call them daily. *Akahata* (Red Flag), the Communist newspaper, shuns dull ideological preach-ments in favor of cartoons, detective stories, and entertaining cultural news; its popular Sunday edition sells 2.8 million copies.

In 1973 I got a taste of how lovable the Communists can be by attending an outdoor fair staged by *Akahata* at a public park in Tokyo's western outskirts to mark its fifteenth anniversary and raise funds for the party. Twenty thousand high-spirited lower- and middle-class people were there drinking beer, bouncing babies, and picnicking under the pines. The booths sold pottery, pins, Pepsi-Cola, and alumi-num rings "made from B-52s shot down over North Vietnam." One gentle old man wore a jacket entirely covered with antiwar buttons from all over the world, including the United States. The inevitable university student who wanted to practice his English assured me that everyone present was a convinced Communist, but to me it seemed that the climate of the fair was far more Japanese than Communist.

The strategist of Communist lovability is sixty-seven-year-old Kenji Miyamoto, presidium chairman of the Japan Communist Party and "the greatest living Japanese politician," one political commentator told me. A judo champion in high school, he went on to Tokyo Univer-sity, and has old-school links to some of his dearest political enemies, in the same way that British politicians of all stripes keep up friend-ships made at Oxford or Cambridge. He spent the years between 1933 and 1945 in jail. Miyamoto's wife is president of the Parent-Teacher

Association at the high school their teen-age son attends. Fleshy-faced Miyamoto is proud that "whenever we show weaknesses or make mistakes, we analyze them. We never skirt problems." The secretary general of the Japan Communist Party is boyish Tetsuzo Fuwa, another Tokyo University graduate. He is in his mid-forties, "clean-cut, no long hair, like Nixon's Bob Haldeman," one Japanese professor told me. With a pleasant irony, the Communists call their up-and-coming young officials "princes," and of them Fuwa is "the crown prince." The third major Communist leader is Central Committee chairman Sanzo Nosaka, born in 1892, and a graduate of Keio University. He attended the 1935 Comintern congress in Moscow and then smuggled himself into California, where he laid hands on some Japanese printing type and published a Communist newspaper shipped clandestinely to Japan. He spent the war with Chinese Communists under Mao Tsetung in Yenan, fighting against the Japanese Imperial Army. Says he: "The Communists are the sole clean political party, having no financial support from the business world."

The Japan Communist Party is more than half a century old, but its history during the 1920s and 1930s is little more than a series of purges, jailings, and obliterations. The "dangerous thoughts" suppressed by the prewar "thought police" were mostly Communist thoughts. The Communists' record of standing up to repression won them, after MacArthur freed them to maneuver, the respect they needed to move into influential posts in journalism and education. The Communists got 3 million votes and thirty-five Diet seats in the 1949 election. But with the outbreak of the Korean War, the American Occupation mounted a "Red purge" of 20,997 supposed Marxists from government, newspapers, broadcasting, and industry, and the Communist Party had to go underground.

International events—Mao's victory in China in 1949, China's attack on India in 1962, the split between China and the Soviet Union in 1963—racked the Japan Communist Party. At one point, the Communists broke up the annual anti-nuclear bomb demonstration in Hiroshima by defending China's right to possess and test bombs—even though the prevailing winds inevitably bring the fallout to Japan. Not until 1973 did the Japan Communist Party denounce the testing of nuclear weapons by China and Russia. In the 1960s, too, the Japanese Communists had to endure the comparison between Communist China's disastrous Great Leap Forward and capitalist Japan's doubling-plus of everybody's income. Now the party, completely "naturalized" to Japan, claims independence from both the Chinese and Soviet Communist parties. In fact, the Japanese Socialists are on friendlier terms with Peking and Moscow than the Communists. The first Communist Chinese ambassador to Tokyo looked up the head of the Japan Socialist Party and pointedly thanked him for helping the two nations to reestablish relations, and Prime Minister Tanaka quoted Chou En-lai as saying that the Japan Communist Party was "no good."

With no hope of winning majority power by ballot, the Japan Communist Party's platform tells only what it would attempt in coalition with other leftist parties. The Communist proposals are scarcely more revolutionary than the Socialists'. The Communists would abrogate the Japan–United States Security Treaty, but would not be averse to maintaining a minimal armed force if the other parties in the coalition want it. They would not nationalize any industry, but would group all the present private-enterprise energy industries—electricity, gas, coal, oil, nuclear power—in one publicly owned corporation. Big business would come under "democratic restriction" that would lead to a "welfare-first economy." The Communists would buy land held for speculation at "fair prices," and then freeze land prices. They would hope to continue the present huge trade with the United States. Far from keeping the constitution sacred, as would the Socialists, the Communists vaguely guarantee that it would not be amended "for the worse." Communist members of the Diet boycott opening sessions in the presence of the emperor, on grounds that the constitution does not provide for him to be there, but the party no longer wants to abolish the monarchy. "We will not give the emperor harsh treatment. We will act according to the national sentiment," says the editor of *Akahata*. Finally, the Communists assure all sumo wrestlers, professional bowlers, and baseball players that their livelihoods would be inviolate under a leftist coalition.

Anti-Communists in Japan describe this mild parliamentary revolution—indeed, the whole concept of lovable Communists—as a deceptive foot-in-the-door strategy that would lead, as soon as the other parties duly withered away, to a rigid, one-party dictatorship of the proletariat. That may be so, but for the time being the Communists have smoothly announced that all they seek in Japan is a "regency" of the proletariat.

Unlike the Liberal Democrats or the Socialists, which are small groups of politicians rather than mass parties, the Communists strive to sign up card-carrying, dues-paying members, and claim three hundred thousand of them. The members—as well as pro-Communist voters, who are nearly twenty times as numerous—come from among intellectuals, salaried workers, and union laborers stolen from the Socialists. Each member contributes 1 percent of his salary to the party. This income, plus profits from *Akahata* and book publishing, totals more than $14 million a year, making the Communists Japan's second-richest party (after the Liberal Democrats). The Japan Communist Party gets some of its votes from Liberal Democrats who would be horrified if it won—they merely want to make their own party a little humbler. "I voted for the Communist to scare the Liberal Democrats," reported the daughter of a Tokyo millionaire after the mid-1973 municipal election. "But I'd rather die than see the Communists take over."

Lovable Communism has no pull at all on Japan's far-left young extremists. These are the members of the Red Army, who instead love violence, and take part in a great deal of it. Their strength is unknown, but they probably number only in the scores. In 1970, Red Army boys and girls hijacked a plane to North Korea, where they met fanatics of the Arab Popular Front for the Liberation of Palestine. Two years later three of these Japanese—one of them carrying Rimbaud's memoirs in his pocket—staged the atrocious massacre of twenty-four innocent airline passengers at Lod Airport in Tel Aviv. Before that, Red Army murderers tortured and killed fourteen "deviating" members of their own group at various places in Japan. Recently a girl named Misako Sugizaki, who showed up in court wearing well-combed long hair and a white cardigan, was sentenced to twelve years at hard labor for ice-picking one deviator to death and strangling another. Early in 1974, four Red Army men blew up a Shell oil storage tank on an island in Singapore harbor; later in the year, three of them seized the French Embassy in The Hague, and after five days released nine hostages, including the French ambassador, in exchange for $300,000 and a flight in an Air France jet to haven in Damascus. Within Japan the shrewd and diligent police seem to have controlled these left extremists, chiefly by arresting and convicting their leaders of murder.

Komeito may literally mean Clean Government Party, but what it more precisely stands for is militant Buddhism, and that is both its strength and mortal weakness. Komeito was created a decade ago as the political arm of the laymen's association Soka Gakkai, the postwar burgeoning of the ancient Nichiren Shoshu sect of fanatically proselyting Buddhism. When the Japanese public began to fear that Komeito would try to establish Nichiren Shoshu Buddhism as everybody's religion, Komeito ostensibly broke away from Soka Gakkai by forcing the leaders of the party to resign their positions as leaders of the lay organization. Nobody swallows this distinction, and Komeito probably touched the outer limits of its political power when it elected forty-seven members to the lower house of the Diet in 1969. A best-selling book called *I Denounce Soka Gakkai* by a cantankerous political science professor and social critic named Hirotatsu Fujiwara heavily damaged Komeito, arguing that "it is a major and obvious premise of government in modern states that, since religion and politics have entirely separate domains, they should be separated. Komeito dares to ignore this basic principle." In 1972, Komeito fell back to twenty-nine seats in the house.

In ideology, Komeito stands in the middle of the Japanese spectrum. It is populistic, moralistic, and proud of being native Japanese. Domestically it seeks law and order, and better living standards (typically, cheaper fish, delivered more efficiently) for its underdog members, but no radical changes. It vaguely opposes "misimprovements" to the constitution. Soka Gakkai's president, Daisaku Ikeda, who runs Komeito from behind the scenes, is perhaps comparable in his conservatism and traditionalism to Alabama's George Wallace. Internationally, Komeito early on favored Japan's recognition of China, and party chairman Yoshikatsu Takeiri, a good friend of Prime Minister Tanaka, made several trips to Peking to help arrange Tanaka's historic 1972 visit. Losses in the 1972 election jarred Komeito into lining up with the leftist parties in supporting "immediate abrogation" of the Japan–United States Security Treaty. Komeito usually wins around 4.5 million votes that would otherwise go partly to the Liberal Democrats but mostly to the Socialists.

The fourth, and smallest, opposition party is the Democratic Socialist Party. It was born in 1960 when thirty-three Diet members who belonged to the right wing of the Japan Socialist Party defected over the party's rabid objections to the Japan–United States Security Treaty. Less a party than a splinter, the Democratic Socialists nevertheless recruited and nurtured the labor federation called Domei, which is smaller (2 million members) and more moderate than the Japan Socialist Party's Sohyo. The Democratic Socialists have a plan to "make people four times as happy in five years," using indices to measure air-pollution abatement, housing quality, and other components of happiness. As for the security treaty, the anti-Communist Democratic Socialists now propose to modify it so that American forces would be stationed in Japan only during emergencies. They have lately won more than 3.5 million votes, about 7 percent of the total.

Japanese political strife lacks the kind of nip-and-tuck national battles fought out in the British or American two-party system, but the presence of five parties offers its own kind of drama by raising an infinity of possible recombinations of the component parts of the electorate. Two trends now point to a dramatic change in Japan's leadership by the end of this decade. One trend is the Liberal Democrats' slow hemorrhage in popular votes, a loss that comes to less than 1 percent a year but seems inexorable. The party has lately had to dragoon thirteen independents into its majority to give it a sufficient edge; next time around, the Liberal Democrats might fail to win a majority of lower-house seats, and might therefore have to form a coalition with another party—probably the Democratic Socialists—to govern. The other trend is the growing understanding of the opposition parties that they must finally coalesce, an understanding that they have demonstrated by actually coalescing in many local elections.

The list of cities where leftist coalitions control municipal governments is a roll call of the metropolises of Japan: Tokyo, Yokohama, Kawasaki, Nagoya, Osaka, Kobe, and Kyoto. Around 130 other, smaller cities, out of Japan's 643, have also elected left-wing mayors. Leftist governors preside in seven prefectures: Okinawa, Okayama, Kagawa, Kyoto, Osaka, Saitama, and Tokyo (which is a prefecture as well as a city). Altogether, these mayors and governors are in power over about two-fifths of the Japanese population. Seemingly, the Liberal Democrats can no longer win majorities in big cities. This leftward swing has come about rapidly; as recently as 1967 Kyoto's perennial governor Torazo Ninagawa was the only Communist- and Socialist-backed official in a high position. But while these pro-leftist victories, together with probable wins soon in other prefectures, prove that coalitions of the Communist, Socialist, Komeito, and Democratic Socialist parties can attract voters, they do not give the left much real power. Local and prefectural governments are weak relative to the central government. Even though the Occupation destroyed the prewar Home Ministry that used to appoint all governors and police all cities, the "Home Ministry syndrome" still prevails because the national government controls needed funds. Governors have to kowtow to cabinet ministers.

Tokyo's governor Ryokichi Minobe speculates that the many local coalitions of the left could be confederated into a national coalition, a "people's front" against the Liberal Democrats. But something the Japanese call "opposition ego" stands in the way of a national coalition. In the gubernatorial and mayoral elections that leftists so often win, the voters choose between two specific men, one being the Liberal Democratic candidate and the other usually a political independent of leftist inclinations—like Minobe or Ninagawa

—whom the opposition parties all find acceptable. In national elections, the voters merely elect Diet members who in turn pick the prime minister. In the case of the Liberal Democrats, the voters clearly understand, as in England, that the Diet members will elect the party leader, and so the campaign presents one clear-cut, tangible personality to vote for. If the leftists ever want to match this advantage, they will have to settle on a single candidate in advance and commit themselves to him. So far the opposition leaders would rather lose than close ranks around one or another—which is, of course, one secret of the Liberal Democrats' long and happy life in office.

But this egoism is apparently coming to an end. The Communists, having gained lately at the cost of the Socialists, are trying to seduce the other leftist parties into coalition by proposing a broad, joint platform of abrogation of the Japan–United States Security Treaty, smashing of the power of big business, and "defense of democracy." The little Democratic Socialist Party speaks of itself as a "catalyst" to consolidate "constructive, reformist forces dedicated to parliamentary democracy." The Buddhist Komeito proposes a coalition in which the Socialists would serve as a "bridge" between Komeito and the Communists. For their part, the Liberal Democrats contribute to the likelihood of a big power shakeup about 1978 because of the growing distance between the party's center and its right wing; in other words, its factions may cease to collaborate.

When all is said and done, the two parties that currently count most in Japan are the Liberal Democrats and the Communists. Partly because the Japanese Communists strive so hard not to look or act Red, and keep a cool distance between themselves and the other Communists of the world, they give promise of gaining in numbers and influence. A Liberal Democratic politician says self-critically: "If a fire breaks out, the Liberal Democrats will visit the victims and take two bottles of liquor with them. The Socialists will not bring anything and the Democratic Socialists will not even visit the sufferers. Members of Komeito will spend a day clearing debris from the fire. The Communists will take care of the sufferers to the very end." I heard one observer muse that "the Liberal Democratic Party is like an old-line family in decline. It won't accept its losses gracefully. But it will lose its Diet majorities, and will have to realign itself and retitle itself."

20 / 🌸

A Gallery of Politicians

THE RAIN HAD STOPPED, and the late afternoon sun flooded through the broad window of Takeo Miki's private, unofficial office suite in Tokyo, picking out the green of a woodsy painting on the wall. Miki, now prime minister but at that time deputy prime minister, looked at me quizzically over horn-rimmed glasses and reminisced about a career in politics that goes back nearly forty years, farther than any of his colleagues in the Liberal Democratic pentarchy.

With such experience, Miki, as Japan's sixty-sixth prime minister, is supposed to be the man best able to keep the Liberal Democrats from any further loss of strength that might force them to coalesce with opposition parties—or to form the coalition, if it comes to that. His qualifications are that he is a centrist rather than a rightist, that he does not belong to the "Yoshida line," and that his background includes no instance of corruption like that for which some of his Liberal Democratic colleagues were in the past indicted and even jailed. Former prime minister Kakuei Tanaka gave Japan its own Watergate; Miki is the Liberal Democrats' response to the party's need to look a little cleaner. All this makes Miki the head man in the gallery of five politicians who presently hold Japan's political future in their hands. Expectably, all five of them are Liberal Democrats. Time may bring Japan a prime minister from the opposition, but just who he might be cannot yet be foretold.

Technically, Miki is prime minister because he was elected to that position, on December 9, 1974, by a majority of the members of both houses of the Diet, the procedure set down in the Japanese constitution. These majorities consisted of members of his own Liberal Democratic Party, which has ruled Japan since 1948 under Yoshida,

Hatoyama, Kishi, Ikeda, Sato, and Tanaka. The Diet members, under iron party discipline, chose Miki because he is president of the party. And he is president because over the years he has carefully built up and maintained a large faction of followers among Liberal Democratic Diet members, which gave him ample status when the party had to pick a new leader upon Tanaka's fall. All prime ministers in recent decades have been Liberal Democratic Party presidents, and all party presidents have won that post by heading potent factions.

Understanding factionalism is the key to understanding Japanese politics. The pattern of the faction is that staple of Japanese society, the hierarchical pyramid. "Feudalism has not completely disappeared in Japan," one political commentator remarked to me wryly, meaning that in its mode of operation and stress on reciprocated fidelity, factionalism resembles a feudal lord's relationship with his samurai, and their relationship with their peasants. Faction leaders have something in common with Boss Tweed, Mafia leaders, benevolent despots, and family patriarchs. The system is based on Confucian precepts of loyalty to one's parents, superiors, or masters. Politically, a faction leader qualifies himself by a long series of elections to the Diet and by acquiring rich sources of campaign funds from among businessmen. Thus in return for his followers' loyalty he can give them the money they need to get elected. A follower cannot shift factions without bringing his fealty into question, and without going back to square one in his own quest for eventual leadership.

Thus the criterion for belonging to a Liberal Democratic faction is neither geographical, economic, nor rigidly ideological—the factions do not stand for ideas or programs. What a faction's members have in common is loyalty to their leader. Other parties have factions that do tend to be ideological, but since other parties cannot manage to get into power, it has been the factional struggle among Liberal Democrats that for decades has determined who runs Japan.

The number and strength of Liberal Democratic factions shift as leaders arise or die, and the party's approximately 420 members in both houses of the Diet have sometimes been divided as many as eight ways. At present there are five main factions, and their leaders' names form a roster of the big guns of Japanese politics, the men with the brains, strength, leadership, and political cunning to keep themselves at the top. They all have high positions, because no matter how hard Liberal Democratic factions fight among themselves, they also pull together after party-president elections. That is, the winner takes the prime ministership and gives good jobs to the losers, who serve him and ponder how to unseat him the next time around. By name, these potentates are: Prime Minister Takeo Miki, Deputy

Prime Minister Takeo Fukuda, Finance Minister Masayoshi Ohira, Liberal Democratic Party secretary general Yashuhiro Nakasone, and former prime minister Kakuei Tanaka.

Prime Minister Miki at sixty-eight has a grandfatherly air, with deep lines beside the nose that run down past the corners of a broad mouth. He reads Toynbee, but gets his political philosophy from the Analects of Confucius: "The most important thing for a politician is the trust of the people." Miki's father was a well-to-do farmer-merchant dealing in fertilizers, pharmaceuticals, and liquor on the backwater island of Shikoku, who sent his son to nine years of law at Meiji University in Tokyo, and then gave him $2,500 to tour the world. Miki got his taste for power and politics not in Tokyo but by observing the 1930 disarmament conference in London, and added to his education by taking law at the University of California at Berkeley, where he supported himself by giving lectures to Japanese residents in San Francisco.

Miki's wife, Mutsuko, is the daughter of Nobutero Mori, founder of Showa Denko, Ltd., huge manufacturer of chemicals, fertilizer, and aluminum. The Moris thus symbolize the parvenu glamour of recent wealth, and they have intermarried with similar families, one of them being the flour-milling Shodas, who supplied Prince Akihito with his bride, Princess Michiko. This link to the imperial family makes Miki something of an aristocrat in terms of modern Japanese society, but he has nevertheless stood aloof from the "in" people of his own party, the scions of the Yoshida line.

It was in 1937, after returning to Japan from the United States, that Miki, at the age of thirty-seven, ran for the lower house of the Diet from Shikoku, and got elected for the first of fourteen consecutive terms. He publicly argued that Japan should not go to war with the United States, and remains decidedly pro-American to this day. In the course of a career that included holding ten cabinet posts, he acquired such influential financial supporters as Shigeo Nagano, chairman of Nippon Steel Corporation, Kazutaka Kikawada, chairman of Tokyo Electric Power Company, and Tahei Morinaga, president of Morinaga Milk Industry Company. Thus backed up, he built a faction big enough for others to reckon with, but until 1974 never strong enough to carry him into the Liberal Democratic Party presidency and the prime ministership. He was the "permanent underdog," the intentional outsider.

Calling himself "a child of the parliament," Miki broke, one after the other, with all the recent prime ministers, who were (except Tanaka) children of the bureaucracy. He broke with Kishi in protest of his repressive police law, with Ikeda over his resistance to party reform, with Sato over the terms of the reversion of Okinawa to Japan, and with Tanaka over his heavy-money political style. He also took to campaigning American-style, making speeches to grass-roots voters when he might better have been bargaining for votes in the party caucus, Japanese style. In one speech he said: "It transcends the world's understanding that Japan should boast of being first or second in shipbuilding, steel, automobiles, and chemical industries, while letting pollution run riot, while disregarding the living environment, destroying nature, permitting bad housing, bad roads, impossible traffic, and inadequate social welfare." One of Tanaka's first acts as prime minister had been to appoint Miki director general of the environment agency (as well as deputy prime minister). Talking to Miki, I kept in mind the pressures from big-business polluters that must bear on him, and the need of the Japanese to form a consensus before acting in concert on such a problem as the ills of the environment. "We are in the process of changing course—a tremendous change in mentality," he said. But as for concrete results in forcing industry to clean up, he shunned credit and gave it instead to effective citizens' suits in the courts.

Miki is sometimes called "the Sea Anemone," in reference to his figurative ability to watch what floats by and swallow what he wants. His chance to swallow the prime ministership came because he protested Tanaka's peccadillos so spectacularly (resigning his post as Tanaka's deputy prime minister), and because as far back as a decade ago he was rumbling about the need to clean up Liberal Democratic politics. Obviously, he did not succeed in that reform; equally obviously, he has—by cultivating his own set of big-business backers and factional followers—been willing to play the game in the old-fashioned way. And he has become rich enough to own a house worth $460,000, the company that operates the four-story building where I met him, two villas, and assorted other property. Still, to the Japanese, who have seen so much "black mist" floating around high Liberal Democratic politicians, Miki is Mr. Clean. Now he has a chance, depending on how long he can keep the Diet's confidence, to carry out the five goals he set for himself upon taking office: drastic reform of the Liberal Democratic Party, a strong battle against inflation, truth and candor in public utterance, a diplomatic policy of international harmony, and close dialogue with the opposition parties.

Takeo Fukuda stirred the Diet to laughter a few years ago by a revealing slip of the tongue: "As I said in my administrative policy speech, I mean my speech on the government's financial policy . . ." Only prime ministers make administrative policy speeches—and Fukuda has wanted to be prime minister from the day in 1929 when he entered the Finance Ministry as a young bureaucrat just out of Tokyo University. He is ruthlessly ambitious, deeply conservative, and a demanding administrator who took the bureaucratic route to succeed. Thrice he raised the cup of power to his lips, and thrice it was knocked from his hand. Yet he remains in contention, because he has a big faction and a strong will. His age is against him—he would be more than seventy-five years old by the time he retired from office. But as deputy prime minister and director general of the economic planning agency, he is now the second most powerful man in Japanese politics.

Fukuda's father was a farmer—a rich one. At four, Fukuda could already play *go,* a Japanese game as difficult as chess. Though he walked ten miles a day to and from school, he was sickly—they called him "Pale Takeo." When Fukuda went to Tokyo from his birthplace in Gumma Prefecture, a hundred miles or so north of the capital, it was not to work, but to attend the now defunct First National High School, a feeder for Tokyo University and a breeder of young politicians. In the Finance Ministry, he slogged upward through such thuddingly boring jobs as chief of the document section and chief secretary to the chief of the secretariat. During World War II he served as financial adviser to the puppet Chinese government in Nanking.

Au director of the Finance Ministry's budget bureau in 1948, Fukuda suffered a serious setback. He was indicted for taking bribes from Showa Denko, Ltd., the chemical firm run by Miki's father-in-law. The scandal brought down the regime of a now-forgotten prime minister who had got briefly into power, and the government suspended Fukuda from service. Four years later, the voters in Gumma Prefecture decided that Fukuda's sweet-and-sour background fitted him for membership in the House of Representatives and duly elected him, then and nine times since. In 1958, after the Tokyo high court at long last cleared him of the bribery rap, he began to move up in the Liberal Democratic party organization, serving as policy board chairman and secretary general, and in the government, as minister of agriculture, forestry, and fishery. As right-hand man for the 1957–60 prime minister, Nobusuke Kishi, Fukuda vied for the prime minister's job in 1960, but lost to Hayato Ikeda because the Showa Denko scandal still besmirched him.

Smarting under Ikeda's hatred and ascendancy, Fukuda organized the Moral Reform League within the Liberal Democratic Party, and this group lifted Eisaku Sato into power in 1964. Sato made Fukuda finance minister and later foreign minister, and politicians called Fukuda "the crown prince of the Sato cabinet." In 1971 Sato assigned Foreign Minister Fukuda on a mission to confer with Nixon, and later to accompany the emperor and empress on their tour of Europe—both signals that Fukuda was the successor-designate. Again he felt that the top job was at his fingertips. But in the event, Sato overstayed his peak of power and could not hand party leadership to Fukuda in mid-1972. Just before the vote, Fukuda said of his opponent Tanaka, sardonically but nervously, "I believe he has the power of a young Hideyoshi." After young Hideyoshi won, Fukuda at first took only a minor cabinet post, so as not to share blame for the crash of the Tanaka administration, which he foresaw because he perceived its weaknesses. When late in 1973 he accepted the finance post, Fukuda—who is sometimes called "the Eel"—assumed the role of an expert come to clean up a mess. "I will operate on my own responsibility," he said.

Of the Liberal Democrats' Big Five faction leaders, Fukuda is the farthest to the right. Only belatedly did he agree to Japan's inevitable reopening of relations with China, and he never approved of breaking with Taiwan. Conservative big business prefers Fukuda to all others. Fukuda holds typically tory views, such as "Young people are too egocentric. They tend to cherish their own interests and forget about society and the country." He has urged bigger armed forces for Japan. He says that the economy should run on the stable "Fukuda rails," and implies that it would not hurt to have what he calls the "Fukuda locomotive." His advisers propose a modest "three-year Japan archipelago clean-up program," which would curb inflation, hold down land prices, and prevent more contamination of the environment. Accommodating to obvious pressures from voters, Fukuda also promises support for democratic principles and human rights; a policy of shunning the possession, production, or introduction of nuclear weapons; and stepped-up social welfare and more equitable income distribution. He pragmatically argues that the Liberal Democratic Party should not hesitate to "preempt any good point in the Communist Party's thinking."

Fukuda is a hard-boiled, self-disciplined man with hooded eyes, lips stretched over strong teeth, and black, parenthesis-shaped eyebrows. Yet he has an exuberant side. He relishes the swordplay in samurai movies, the Japanese equivalent of westerns. Once, when someone remarked, "Mr. Minister, I suppose you're expecting another difficult day today," he grinned, made a gesture like drawing a sword, and cried, "I'll be like Chuji!"—Chuji Kunisada being the legendary Robin Hood of his native Gumma. He married for love in a time when love marriages were rare; his seniors at the Finance Ministry many times tried to arrange a suitable society marriage for him, but he spurned them all and married the daughter of a postmaster. Now she beats him at golf three-up in nine holes. They have three sons and two daughters, and live in a 1920s stucco house in western Tokyo.

Says Takeo Fukuda: "I believe the day will come when Japan really needs a man named Takeo Fukuda."

Still another farm boy who came from the provinces to high office is Masayoshi Ohira, the finance minister, a man known in capitals all over the world for his sleepy-eyed quick-wittedness. Serious, dignified, shrewd, unsmiling, yet not unfriendly, he has the face of a contented cantaloupe. When he was foreign minister, diplomats called him a "formidable negotiator," but he says of himself: "I am an ordinary man. I want to do ordinary things." He is well-read and contemplative, maintains a global point of view, and has a way of quickly putting world events into historical perspective.

Ohira was born in 1910 in the Inland Sea town of Toyohama, on Shikoku. As a child described as "never naughty," he became a Christian, a little-league sumo champ, and No. 2 in his high school class. After his father died, when he was sixteen, his well-off older brother put him on a night train to Tokyo, where he went directly from the station to Hitotsubashi University and passed the entrance examination. In the familiar pattern, he went to work in the Finance Ministry after graduation, married, fathered two sons and a daughter, served as a bureaucrat through the war, and by 1952 was ready (under the auspices of the future prime minister Hayato Ikeda, his admiring superior in the Finance Ministry) to run for the House of Representatives, winning that and eight subsequent elections.

Ikeda, during his 1960–64 administration, appointed Ohira foreign minister, and Prime Minister Sato added to Ohira's experience by making him minister of international trade and industry. By then Ohira headed an influential faction of the Diet, but judged himself not quite first in line for the prime ministership, and in the 1972 contest for the presidency of the Liberal Democratic Party he threw his support on the second ballot to Tanaka, in hopes that Tanaka would be able to return the favor. Unluckily, in 1974 this obvious deal tied Ohira too closely to the tainted Tanaka, and the party elders felt they had to choose Miki instead. Now the owlish Ohira runs his potent ministry and waits, at sixty-five, for Miki to make way.

Strong vibrations of celebrity, power, ambition, and even mystery come from Yashuhiro Nakasone, the de facto boss of the Liberal Democratic Party, who in the Japanese political context is a boy wonder, only fifty-seven years old. He is the man Most Likely to Succeed to the prime ministership—later if not sooner. I called on him when he was minister of international trade and industry, and found him sitting in the large chamber of burlap walls and light green carpet where many of the most crucial decisions of the Japanese economic miracle were sealed in recent years. Nakasone, dressed in an elegant blue suit, proved to be a lithe, graceful, unflustered man, with the peculiarly Japanese kind of smiling eyes that take a ski jump upward at the outer corners.

What is mysterious about Nakasone is why he changes ideologies so readily, and where he stands now. After he graduated from Tokyo University Law School in 1941 he moved leftward, but as he climbed the ranks of government, beginning with election to the House of Representatives in 1948, then on to cabinet-level jobs as director general of the science and technology agency and minister of transport, he edged steadily to the right. Between 1967 and 1971, he was president (though still a member of the Diet) of right-wing Takushoku University and developed connections with right-wing extremists. Overlapping with this job came his service in the cabinet as director of the defense agency from 1970 to 1972.

While thus in charge of Japan's military, Nakasone so doggedly pressured for building up the forces that China's Premier Chou En-lai denounced him as a military expansionist. He favored revision of the Japan–United States Security Treaty by 1975 in order to let Japan create an "autonomous defense" and thereby wipe out the impression that Japan is a tool of American strategy in the Far East. He thought that if the United States was a "spear," Japan should be a "shield." He toyed with the idea of nuclear arms for Japan, but decided "at least for the time being" against that step. Someone suggested that he appeared to be striving to be a Japanese de Gaulle. He replied, "Thank you very much for the compliment." But Nakasone could not sell his aggressive-sounding policy to the rest of the cabinet. He spoke of his failure to his friend Yukio Mishima, whose flashy hara-kiri a few days later stemmed in part from realization that Japan was not ready to rearm.

By standing aside from the 1972 election for Liberal Democratic leadership, Nakasone facilitated the victory that made Tanaka prime minister. Tokyo political reporters say that Tanaka gave the Nakasone faction more than $2 million for this favor, as well as a promise of bossing the Ministry of International Trade and Industry. In this post, Nakasone tried a new tack toward the prime minister-ship. He climbed on the bandwagon of those who say that net national welfare now has to be put ahead of gross national product. Government, labor, and consumers, he says, have a right to intervene in business management in the public interest, dealing with problems like high land prices, the energy pinch, and commodity shortages. Nakasone proposes to conduct a "natural resources diplomacy"; by showy missions to the Middle East, he made himself the first important Japanese to side with the Arabs, and thus became a symbol of protecting Japan's access to Middle Eastern oil. As for Japan's military stance, he has come around to the position, as he told me flatly, that "Japan does not need nuclear weapons."

Nakasone's thoughts about his fellow countrymen are these: Their assets are their homogeneity ("one race, one language, no religious conflict"), their island situation making Japan a maritime country some distance from the continent, their generosity, their shunning of extremism ("this comes from Buddhism"), and their curiosity and eagerness to learn. Their shortcomings, he believes, are that they sacrifice rationalism to emotion, get excited over projects quickly but lose interest quickly, pay too much attention to the opinion of outsiders, and lack self-confidence. His fellow countrymen's thoughts about Nakasone are that he is brilliant, compelling, and effective, but maybe, someone told me, "a little too obviously fancy."

Kakuei Tanaka is a Japanese tragedy, and his story is an Oriental parallel to the fall of Richard Nixon. Tanaka came to power as prime minister in 1972 on a tide of euphoria. He was something different. Against a tradition of old men holding high office, he was only fifty-four years old, the youngest of Japan's postwar prime ministers. In contrast to his suave predecessors, he was a rags-to-riches, self-educated swashbuckler. His university-graduate colleagues regarded him as a boor who not only failed to follow their elaborate code of behavior, but did not even know the code. He was the "computerized bulldozer," and he had a glamorous "Plan for Remodeling the Japa-nese Archipelago." He came to office with an easy diplomatic triumph awaiting him: the renewal of Japan's diplomatic relations with China. Within two and a half months, Tanaka was toasting Chou En-lai in Peking.

Riding high, Tanaka would pounce on the microphone in the Diet, tilt his head up and to the right, jut out a jaw like a boxing glove, and fire off a speech with all the pace and force that he had adopted when young as a cure for stammering. He traveled the world, and in the presence of the greatest leaders of the greatest nations he put across—with his small, self-assured smile and his jaunty walk —his conviction that he was the equal of anyone, and Japan the equal of any nation. He had a touch of the actor—Japan smiled at his minstrel-show recitals of *naniwabushi*, epic poems of gamblers and outlaws in Japan's feudal period.

But he soon proved to be flawed by his utter obsession with money —money for his faction, money for his party, money for himself. In what they candidly admitted was an imitation of the American press's exposure of Watergate, the editors of the respected monthly *Bungei Shunju* published sixty-one pages of investigative reporting called "An Anatomy of Kakuei Tanaka, His Money and His Men." The article compared, for example, Tanaka's declared income of $280,000 for 1972 with his purchases that year of land worth $1,660,000, and asked, "Did or did not Kakuei Tanaka make use of the huge political funds (untaxed) to buy the above-mentioned real estate for his own benefit?" A couple of years earlier a group of angry protesters had marched on Tanaka's ostentatious, two-story, Western-Japanese house in Tokyo with the threat to catch and eat the collection of carp (he is a connoisseur of this fish) that he kept "while the people groan under inflation." *Bungei Shunju* revealed that Tanaka had paid as much as $3,300 each for these carp, which can be valuable collector's items in Japan. *Bungei Shunju* also told of Tanaka's "Melancholy Queen," a former bar hostess who, having his total confidence, handled the whole flow of billions of yen used to lubricate his faction. Big business has always provided money for Liberal Democratic politicians, but the magazine suggested that under Tanaka the nature of the money had changed from bribery by business to extortion by politicians. Jumping into the fray, the Japan Communist Party named thirteen business enterprises that, it said, Tanaka or his family and associates owned or controlled.

Not only personal financial scandals afflicted Tanaka. His remodeling plan, set down as a book, named specific sites for new cities to be built in the process of redistributing population, and this invited much unhealthy land speculation, chiefly by the trading and real estate companies of the large business conglomerates. On backwater Shibushi Bay, at the southern tip of Kyushu, the cost of land jumped to ten times what it had been. Mitsubishi Estate Company bought up hills east of the Tanaka-designated town of Tsuyama, and watched the value jump even more. Out-of-sight land prices threatened to make housing just as costly in new towns as in old cities, leaving the average man once again the victim of the big companies. Meanwhile, a hectoring Communist member of the lower house forced Tanaka to admit, red-faced from anger rather than embarrassment, that he kept a mistress (not uncommon in Japan), by whom he had two children.

Tanaka's impatient, bullying, impulsive manner of administration, studded with "surprise attacks" on minor officials summoned by telephone over the heads of their bosses, earned him the opposition of the potent and intelligent bureaucracy, that clique of Tokyo University alumni already unhappy with an outsider like Tanaka. His popularity in *Mainichi Shimbun* polls sank from 53 percent to 16 percent. Even his mother was not much of a comfort. From the family home, she phoned him regularly to say, "Your reputation is bad these days." At length, in November 1974, a couple of days after having received Gerald Ford on the first visit ever made by an American President to Japan, Kakuei Tanaka resigned, saying, "I feel deep political and moral responsibility for the current political confusion, which has in large degree resulted from problems pertaining to myself." He remains a member of the Diet, and controls the biggest of the Liberal Democratic factions.

With his checkered career, Tanaka is the most interesting and unusual of recent prime ministers. He was born in 1918 on a farm in the prefecture of Niigata, facing the Sea of Japan, the son of a man who failed in turn as animal dealer, carpenter, and dairy farmer. Diphtheria at two made Tanaka an indoor, literary type of boy. He went to school only until he was fourteen, then worked for a while as a construction laborer. To relieve his mother of supporting him, he moved at sixteen to Tokyo. While employed successively as a clerk, as a reporter for a business magazine, and with a construction firm (and all the time going to night school), he wrote a novel that won a prize of $2.50. He fought in 1939 against the Russians at Nomonhan, on the border between Outer Mongolia and Manchuria (then Japan's Manchukuo). This little-remembered skirmish was Japan's way of helping its ally Germany by pressuring Stalin from the rear so that he would sign, as he shortly did, a nonaggression pact with Hitler, which freed Germany to go to war with France and England. The next year Tanaka returned to Japan on a stretcher, nearly dead of pneumonia.

Starting a construction company of his own, Tanaka wangled

profitable contracts for building factories in Manchuria and Korea during the rest of World War II. In 1942, he married the daughter of the owner of the lodging house where he lived, a divorced woman eight years older than he, who asked of him only two favors: "Please, do not kick me, as my first husband did," and "When the day comes to cross the bridge to the Imperial Palace [for attestation as a cabinet minister], please take me with you." By 1945, his firm was accounted one of the fifty biggest construction companies in Japan, and he had made himself a fair amateur architect in the process.

Rich at the age of twenty-eight, Tanaka adapted readily to the new, postwar Japan. He ran for the Diet from Niigata under the slogan "Cries for Young Blood." He failed on the first try, but his wealth successfully bought him election in 1947, and in all ten elections since then. In the late 1940s, Tanaka, who was by then parliamentary vice-minister for justice, was arrested for accepting bribes in a coal-mining scandal. He filed for reelection from a cell in Kosuge prison in Tokyo, and won; later he managed to get cleared of the bribe charge. In his first cabinet job, minister of posts and telecommunications, Tanaka legalized commercial television as a competitor for NHK. Once, as minister, he did one of his naniwabushi turns on radio, a lapse from ministerial dignity that won him renown, admiration, sympathy, and votes. He followed up, during three years as minister of finance, by appearing weekly on television to give explanations of the policies that were then helping Japan to double its gross national product in seven years, explanations that the electorate found eminently pleasing. Tanaka spent the last half of the 1960s mostly as secretary general of the Liberal Democratic Party, fathering "growth" bills to develop hydroelectric power, new industrial cities, and water resources. As minister of international trade and industry under Prime Minister Eisaku Sato, Tanaka salvaged the best deal he could for Japanese textile exports to the United States, after the "Nixon shock" restrictions that resulted from the President's anger with Sato.

For this favor, Sato did not thank Tanaka. Rather, upon announcing that he would step down, the prime minister let it be known that of the Big Five he favored fellow Yoshida-liner Fukuda. But Tanaka had decided a year earlier to have a hard go at the party presidency. The members of his faction had disbursed promises of high positions and envelopes full of yen among members of other factions, in blatant attempts to win them over. All the other major faction leaders were participants in the party election, in which Liberal Democratic Diet members and the heads of all of the party's prefectural chapters were the voters. Fukuda, Ohira, and Miki competed as candidates for the presidency against Tanaka, and Nakasone stood aside in a conscious effort to win Tanaka's favor. On the first ballot of this round of what the Japanese call "the Kaku-Fuku war," Kakuei Tanaka got 156 votes, Fukuda 150, Ohira 101, and Miki 69. On the second ballot, Miki and Ohira hardheadedly shifted their votes, or most of them, to Tanaka, who beat Fukuda by 282 to 190, and thus won the Liberal Democratic presidency, and the prime ministership, for the term that was to end with Tanaka's throwing away the party's popular support at a spendthrift rate. In the July 1974 elections for the upper house of the Diet, the voters left the Liberal Democrats with a majority too skinny to rely on.

In grasping the opportunity for Japan to resume its fraternal relationship with China, Tanaka earned himself a niche in history comparable to Nixon's. His other contributions were sadly inadvertent. He weakened the Liberal Democrats enough to bring closer the day when the land of one-and-one-half parties becomes a land of two parties. And in so weakening his party, he alarmed its other leaders to the point of starting a serious reform.

21 /

Japan, Inc.

JAPAN HAS WATER: four feet of rainfall a year, on the average. Japan has mountains, which leave it with precious little arable land for the rainfall to irrigate, but which do provide productive forests and sites for power plants that use the plentiful water to generate some of the nation's electricity. Japan has small deposits of iron, copper, zinc, chromite, and lead ores, and a dribble of petroleum. Thus green Japan is not penniless in natural resources, though it pointedly lacks any such small-nation riches as Sweden's iron, Argentina's pampas, Malaysia's tin, or Indonesia's oil. And yet, as Japan's climb from postwar penury to economic giant shows, lack of natural gifts scarcely matters a whit. For Japan has a resource that no other nation can ever acquire: 111 million Japanese, with their unbeatable virtues of homogeneous harmony, willingness to work, thrift, education, intelligence, and—most overlooked and most important—boldness.

Bombed and burned, hungry and broke, Japan after the war looked gloomy even to the wisest foreign observers. Wrote Reischauer: "The economic situation in Japan may be fundamentally so unsound that no policies . . . can save her from slow economic starvation." The *Official Guide* at that time mourned that "the Japanese economy is essentially weak," and listed scarcity of land and resources, overpopulation, impoverished farm villages, and outmoded industry as causes. The panicky advice of many was that Japan should settle for being a low-wage, labor-intensive workshop producing toys and trinkets and cheap textiles—should be, in sum, just another forgettable, teeming Asian nation. But in a delectable irony, the American

346

Occupation's purge of prewar industrial leaders left Japanese business in the hands of bold young men who had been waiting to take over and make Japan great again. Toyosaburo Taniguchi, the Osaka spinning tycoon, told me that "the basic reason for economic progress after the war was the purge."

Cool, daring, and shrewd, these new leaders, men mostly in their forties, chose for their model the American economy, with its heavy industry and high technology. They made such amazing assumptions as that this land of little iron ore and no coking coal could rank (with 119 million tons a year) alongside the United States (136 million) and the Soviet Union (131 million) as the world's biggest steel producers. They put across what became known as Japan, Inc., which placed politics, the government, and the bureaucracy at the service of business, and they recruited labor and all the rest of the population to work in harmony for the survival, growth, and worldly prestige of Japan. Far from pleading for foreign investment, as "developing" nations do, the Japanese fended off outside capital with the deliberate intention of keeping foreigners from controlling the economy. They also raised tariffs, so that Japanese manufacturers had a virtual monopoly in many industries for many years before tariff walls came down under worldwide free-trade pressures. Spunky, even arrogant, behavior for a defeated nation.

To raise capital, Japan harnessed the astonishing capacity of its people to save even on small salaries, in bank accounts or postal savings. Bankers then supplied money to industry with a daring that Westerners called recklessness, commonly lending more than their total deposits. The money went into building modern factories, scamping "unnecessary" social expenditures, such as housing; the shortage of flush toilets and sewers in Japan is a direct consequence of pouring all available funds into refineries, blast furnaces, and ship-yards instead of amenities. The energetic, dedicated, purposeful people cheerfully paid this price, and they also took to utilizing abortion on a large scale to keep their efforts at economic growth from being swamped in a tidal wave of new babies. Uncomplainingly, they accepted low wages and worked efficiently over long hours.

The world, luckily, found new sources of raw materials—iron ore and bauxite in Australia, petroleum in the Middle East—and Japan got the benefit of them. For technology, Japanese industrialists shamelessly ransacked American and European patents, chose with great shrewdness exactly what they wanted, and bargained hard to buy them. Japanese businessmen selected the nation's portfolio of industries with ruthless objectivity, discarding, for example, the traditional silk as a major field for competition, and singling out electronics, cameras, steel, cars, and chemicals as products in which Japan could excel. Freed to start afresh, the Japanese made such logical decisions as locating the steel industry at sea level, creating sixteen mills where ore and coal carriers drawing fifty feet of water could unload their cargoes at one end and freighters could take away the finished steel in bars or rolls or plates at the other. Always a people of high standards, the Japanese overcame their prewar reputation for producing imitative junk by shooting for quality. Finally, they turned their recent conquerors, the Americans, into an avid market for their exports, the main point of which was to earn dollars to pay for the vital imports of raw materials.

The moment when this effort began to succeed may have been signaled to the West in 1950 when *Life* magazine photographers David Douglas Duncan, Carl Mydans, and Alfred Eisenstadt abandoned their German Leicas and equipped themselves with Japanese Nikons. The young executives' wager that Japan had to grow spectacularly (or turn moribund) started to pay off with compound-interest acceleration. Gross national product, which was the sole barometer of success for the Japanese for several decades, grew from $10 billion in 1950 to $375 billion in 1973. From 1950 to 1973, the rate of increase averaged 11 percent a year, two or three times as much as in most Western countries, and in 1968 Japan supplanted West Germany as the world's third-biggest economy, after the United States and the Soviet Union. Japanese GNP grew to be double that of all Latin America, quadruple that of all Africa. The greatest single accomplishment came in shipbuilding: each year Japan launches half of the world's new tonnage, around 10 million tons, compared to runner-up Sweden's less than 2 million. Almost monotonously, Japan is also out in front in pianos, cameras, sewing machines, motorcycles, television sets, electronic microscopes, tape recorders, transistor radios, and rayon and acetate. Its merchant fleet is the biggest after flag-of-convenience Liberia, and its people ride more trains more miles than anyone else. Japan ranks second in the production of cars, bicycles, watches, copper, aluminum, and zinc. It has more telephones and drives more cars than any nation except the United States, and catches more fish than any nation except Peru.

This economic miracle, this Japanese improvement on West Germany's famous *Wirtschaftswunder*, paid off precisely where it was supposed to: in material gains for each and every Japanese. Annual rises in real wages, made possible by continual jumps in productivity, have averaged 12 percent a year. From a stark $17 a year just after the war, per capita income rose quickly past that of all the rest of Asia, and then, one after another, topped those of the Soviet Union, Italy, the United Kingdom, Australia, Norway, and France, and lately has approached that of West Germany and Canada. At $4,500, Japanese per capita income is now three-fourths as great as that of the United States. No nation in history has ever raised its income so fast. In its air-conditioned subway stations, its gleaming Toyotas and Nissans, its good wool suits and pretty dresses, its opulent department stores, Japan shouts out a story of unprecedented material accomplishment. Japan's has become the kind of profligate society in which it is possible, as happened recently, for someone to throw away a nearly new washing machine because a few coins had clogged the drain.

But as every Japanese schoolboy knows, when his eyes sting from photochemical smog on his way home from classes, Japan's material miracle has cost the nation too much in environmental damage. It became clear, too, beginning in the late 1960s, that the national policy of putting all its money into the tools of production had gone on too long, at the expense of social needs like housing, health, schools, sewers, parks. The Japanese now say, "We are choking on our GNP." A vast change in priorities, from mere economic survival to building a more habitable nation, lies ahead. That vital Japanese prerequisite, consensus for change, has been achieved. And the same resources that built the economic miracle—the diligent and disciplined Japanese people, and their subtle and efficient techniques of management and organization—are already being put to work.

Japanese workers, I noticed while visiting factories, shipyards, and offices, in no way resemble the flying-fingered automaton on the assembly line in Charlie Chaplin's *Modern Times*. They work from a work ethic, from Confucianism-cum-Calvinism; they work continuously and seriously; but they also work in a relaxed, secure, and ungrudging manner. It is as though the choice between working hard or not had been left to each employee, and each had opted for hard work because of loyalty to his group within the company, to the company itself, and finally to the nation—and having made the choice, was happy with it. Obviously, the Japanese are not monolithic in their attitudes: polls and other evidence show that a sizable minority of workers scoff at such idealistic motivations, saying that they work for the pay envelope alone. Not long ago, in a Tokyo office building, a young employee of a shipping company beat to death his superior (who belonged to the revered category of middle management that the Japanese denote by the title "section chief") after a quarrel over the job.

Nevertheless, hard facts prove the reality of hard work. The work week, now about forty-two hours in manufacturing, exceeds America's by only a couple of hours, but days off are rarer and vacations shorter —six days a year until the tenth year of employment, then two weeks (compared to an average four weeks off in Europe). Moreover, not taking one's vacation is commonplace, as a sign of loyalty to the firm (or lust for advancement). Overtime, unpaid in the case of management, is customary. About half of the Japanese work force still works five and a half or six days a week. At each of twenty thousand Quality Control Circles in companies all over Japan, workers meet regularly with foremen after hours to correct flaws in working methods and devise improvements in production. Japanese workers, somebody told me, have "fingertip fineness" in precision work and an "insistent perfectionism." Company spirit, the sense of sink-or-swim together, has a hold on the Japanese that is laughable or even ridiculous to Americans, who refuse to deify corporations. Most companies put on morning inspirational assemblies. At the Kyoto Ceramics Company, for instance, the employees, dressed in jackets displaying the company trademark, gather at 8:20 for exercises followed by a reading from a book of homilies composed by the president. At all the factories of Matsushita Electric Industrial Company, the workers start the day with their famous song:

> For the building of a new Japan,
> Let's put our strength and mind together . . .
> Harmony and sincerity!
> Matsushita Electric!

In return for his loyalty, the worker gets the company's loyalty in a practical and substantial form: guaranteed employment. At the moment of hiring, the worker and the company make lifetime commitments to one another. Few Americans would want such a binding and immobilizing relationship with their employer, but the Japanese worker prizes his guaranteed job both for security and for the sense of belonging to a large human family. He is not only willing but proud to turn over his identity to a company: "I'm Nagai, of Mitsui." The company takes on the responsibility of paying wages through thick and thin, with never a layoff—an obligation frightening to typical American managers. Yet one secret of Japan's business success is that guaranteed employment profits the employer more than the employee.

Knowing that they will always have jobs, the workers never oppose efficient new machines that do work once done by men—there are no Luddites in Japan. Employers invest heavily in training their employees, certain that the workers, once educated, will stay with the company and not go job hopping. Much of the training, even for low-level craftsmen and artisans, is schooling in the goals and operations of the company, which gives an employee a creative understanding of his own function. Management trainees get higher education, or courses in Zen, or a tour with the Self-Defense Forces, to help keep the company intelligently open to changes and opportunities. Superior training thus becomes another asset of Japan, Inc. In the big conglomerates, moreover, personnel can be moved from one company to another—from shipbuilding, say, to aircraft, and then to electrical products—as needed, which lessens the handicap to the employer of guaranteed employment, and provides beneficial on-the-job training. A Japanese employer buys and shapes his labor; an American buys it (and demands it) ready-made.

Another boon of the Japanese employer toward his employee that is really more beneficial to the employer is the famous Japanese bonus, handed out at midsummer and year-end. A year's bonus often equals as much as a third of a year's pay, and though supposedly contingent on profits, bonuses are built so solidly into the remuneration system that employers give them even if they have to borrow money to do so. Bonuses touch off biennial spending binges, but millions and millions of workers simply add their bonus money to their savings.

Even more than lifetime employment and employee training, Japanese thrift is a key to the nation's economic success. The average Japanese family saves 17 percent of its income, exceeding all other nations and tripling the 5.7 percent saved by Americans. Banks hold $200 billion in personal savings; postal savings accounts hold another $40 billion. The average household has $8,000 in savings. Even though saving at interest of 6½ percent is a losing proposition when the rate of inflation is much higher than that, the Japanese go on saving. The motivation is basically to conserve money for what a more socially conscious government would provide: tuition for their children at private universities, and nest eggs to fill out inadequate pensions. Japanese savers also take a patriotic pride in providing funds for the growth of the country. With the private savings of these ordinary citizens as the main increment, Japan can invest more than one-third of the gross national product in expansion of the economy—double what the United States does.

Isn't the Japanese worker appallingly exploited? Shouldn't he rise in revolt? He is, and he should, but he won't. The intensity of advertising, the seductions of the department stores, and installment buying all massage men with the message: work, earn, save some, spend the rest.

Guaranteed employment, seen another way, is guaranteed slavery. An Irish Catholic priest, a long-time resident of Japan, told me, "The factory or the office or the bank—they seem to own their employees body and soul." Whoever dares to break away from one company and ask for a job at another is looked upon as a leper. The worker is asked not only to give his brains, time, and loyalty to his company, but also to save from his still-none-too-lavish salary or wage to finance Japan, Inc. And he does, and, in general, he is happy about it. Writes Professor Maurice Bairy: "The achievement and welfare of every individual Japanese is identified with the greatness of Japan itself."

Within this Japan, Inc. psychology, labor unions have generally shaped themselves as management's ardent friends and allies. Unions —originally organized as something called the Friendly Love Society —first scored in a defiantly successful dockyard strike in Kobe in 1921, and union membership reached 8 percent of the industrial work force by 1931, before the military effectively zapped the movement. The Occupation authorities, determined to give Japan unionism American-style, in 1945 promoted a bill patterned on the Wagner Act of 1935 (with rights to organize, to strike, and to bargain collectively), and in 1949 another bill copied from the Taft-Hartley Act of 1947 (which cut back on said rights). The American innovations served as the base for growth in union membership to nearly 12 million now, but the nature of unionism is nothing like that of the United States. Of the 34 percent of Japanese workers who belong to unions (compared to 29 percent in the United States and 36 percent in West Germany), four-fifths are members of no less than 64,000 separate company unions, which include all of a given firm's shop and office workers. Only two occupations, seafaring and mining, are organized into across-the-board industrial unions. The company unions belong to federations (railwaymen, steelworkers, chemical workers, teachers, and so on), and the federations belong to confederations, notably the Socialist-dominated Sohyo (General Council of Trade Unions) and the Democratic Socialist–dominated Domei (Japan Confederation of Labor). But the federations have no authority over the locals, and serve only as coordinating headquarters.

In the past from time to time a company union has gone on strike only to find that another union in a competitive factory was still toiling away. The strikers have usually conceded defeat at once and rushed back to work, for the good of the company. To prevent such piecemeal losses, all unions for the last twenty-one years have agreed to strike, or to threaten to strike, jointly in March and April, a ritual called the Spring Struggle. The struggle begins with months of muscle-flexing by Sohyo and Domei and their opposite number in management, the Federation of Employers Associations—all in the awareness by everyone that employers traditionally pass out raises in the spring, and that inflation catch-up and readjustment of labor's share of gains from increased productivity entitle workers to a big pay rise. The isolated and sporadic strikes that follow are mostly intended as "reminders" to management, and do little harm. Newspaper printers strike for two hours, and then work like blazes in order to get out the next edition on time. Strikes begin after work on Saturday afternoon and end before work on Monday morning.

Strangely, the greatest violence is precipitated by a union that is forbidden by law to strike, the public employees of the government-owned Japanese National Railways. Their slowdowns sometimes cause commuters, panicked at the possibility that they will not get to work, to explode in riots and break train windows, shouting, "Kill anyone with a JNR uniform!" Mostly, though, it is hard to tell that a slowdown is on. One night while in a sleeping car tearing through northern Japan, I waked with a sense of contradiction which I soon isolated as a recollection that the railwaymen were, by their own announcement, on slowdown. "Japanese workers work hard when not slowing down and even harder when slowing down," I wrote in my notebook. Marvelously to Americans, who are underprivileged in mail service, a slowdown of Japanese postal workers (who are also forbidden to strike) means that deliveries drop from three to two a day, and none on Sunday. In cold statistics, the Japanese lost only 4 million man-days of work to strikes in a typical year (1970), while the United States lost 66.4 million.

During the 1974 Spring Struggle, the most militant yet, newspapers printed, under the headline "Schedules of Major Strikes During the Week," a calendar with gray and black squares to denote slowdowns and strikes for commuter trains, bullet trains, buses, taxis, airlines, postal service, and telecommunications. The government of France had at that time sent the "Mona Lisa" for display in a Tokyo museum, and labor's public relations men seized the chance to use her visage, with her enigmatic smile changed to a pout and a shopping basket hanging from her arm, to illustrate a widely displayed poster expressing labor's woe at high prices and the need for higher wages. Strikes harassed the public for several days, and nearly shut down all transportation for several more. The break came when the Central Labor Relations Commission negotiated a 30 percent raise for employees of privately owned railroads, which run about a third of Japan's trackage, thus setting a pattern for all the rest of labor. Besides higher wages, labor had also been seeking the right to strike for public employees, a right taken away from them in 1947 by General MacArthur. The government, blandly closing its eyes to the fact that a lot of public employees *had* been striking (if only briefly), agreed to think about it.

The average railway worker or steelworker raised his wages about $100 a month by the 1974 Spring Struggle, bringing them to $535. The gain, which easily topped the up-to-20-percent raises of earlier struggles, was mostly compensation for the previous year's inflation, and the rise in real terms was about 5 percent. Exchange-rate fluctuations complicate dollar comparisons between Japanese and American wages, but broadly, in late 1974, Japanese industrial wages averaged between $500 and $600 a month, including bonuses, but not including the value of fringe benefits, such as low-rent housing and discount-price company stores. Americans probably average about 40 percent greater wages and benefits than their Japanese counterparts. American carpenters get $8 an hour, Japanese $3; on the other hand, American and Japanese seamen earn virtually the same wages.

Of course, the fact that 34 percent of Japanese workers belong to unions means that 66 percent do not. Non-union labor does not make headlines by strikes or political pressures, and its wages run to only three-fourths, or even one-half, as much as union labor, with few fringe benefits. The bulk of these employees work for small and primitive side-street factories, notably subcontractors for big industry, or little plants that make hardware, pencils, thermos bottles, gloves, cutlery, and so on. Alternatively, they work for big companies as "temporaries," ready to be laid off even as the companies boast of giving lifetime employment. Paternalism is not extended to these foot soldiers of the Japanese economy, and company loyalty is not much to be found among them. But the wages of employees at the lower level of the "dual structure" rise by at least the rate set by the Spring Struggle, while another factor tends to force them even higher. That pressure is full employment—one of those characteristics of the Japanese that makes them glad they are Japanese and not Americans.

Japan's postwar baby boom provided more than a million new workers a year during the late 1960s, and industry grew so fast that it soaked them all up—a nice match of supply and demand. A further increment came from farms, which employed 12 million people, or 26 percent of the labor force, in 1964, as compared to 5 or 6 million, or 11 percent, in 1974. But now only three-fourths of a million new workers come into the market annually, and some small businesses are going bankrupt simply for lack of labor. Many industrialists argue that Japan needs more people, more workers, but the national consensus favors holding population growth down. The labor pinch could reduce Japan's economic growth, or it could be solved in several ways. Japan could import workers—Koreans, perhaps, or Chinese—as West Germany does, though the Japanese fear that this solution would rupture their homogeneity. Employers could hire more women, raise the retirement age, or better utilize the labor they have. Though it makes no sense, even as industry seeks labor many people are doing inefficient or useless work. Japanese anti-crabgrass technology consists in hiring a group of straw-hatted women who, in sitting position, move across a lawn like so many amoebas and dig up the weeds blade by blade. The ticket punchers in railway and subway stations do work that could obviously be done (and here and there is done) by machines. In side-street lumber mills, men make boards with little band saws, moving every piece by hand. Such low-productivity employment stems from the admirable consensus that everyone deserves a job, but this kind of inefficiency seems obsolete in modern Japan.

The contribution of management to the success of Japan, Inc. is marvelously complementary to the loyalty and diligence of the work force. In diametrical contrast to the American concept of the executive as the Boss, a Horatio Alger-cum-John Wayne handing down brilliant commands from a position of lonely brooding, Japanese managers see themselves as mere encouragers of innovations from anywhere within the organization. This is the consensus system, involving much communication, much striving for everyone's consent if not approval, much stress on human relations. A key point is that no decision is taken until all opposition to it has been met and mollified. In a first-rate dissection of the Japanese system, Stanford University professors Richard T. Johnson and William G. Ouchi, authors of *Made in America (Under Japanese Management)*, make a point of analyzing the significance of the unpartitioned offices of Japanese corporations. Even the few top executives who have private offices often use them only for ceremonial occasions,

> preferring to remain at their working desks in the large open areas where the management of Japanese companies takes place. . . . The section head . . . sits at a desk that adjoins a long working table. Around the working tables are his subordinates—assistants, researchers, and secretaries—working side by side like college freshmen at the library during exam week. There is little that the section head does

during the day that his subordinates are not aware of. And there are many such section groups in one large room. Since one section head is just a twist of the swivel chair from another, as a problem arises, one turns to the next and discusses it. . . . And since the boss of the section heads and even the department head are also nearby, they too are kept in constant touch. Thus all see one another and have a relatively high level of awareness not only of the issues facing the organization but of the problems and perspectives of others. [This scheme] is an important factor in the way Japanese firms motivate employees. In the open work-space, there is no concealing an individual who is not taken seriously, whose opinions are disregarded or ignored. . . . In these ways, the Japanese system integrates, motivates and evaluates its employees.

In contrast to the American manager who fumes, "I didn't get anything done all day, people kept interrupting me," the Japanese manager regards getting interrupted as a central feature of his job.

To a degree that astonishes Americans and Europeans, Japanese executives take on obligations that modify or even conflict with the goal of "maximization of profits" that Westerners cherish. "Japanese companies just cannot be explained in terms of profit for the stock-holders," the economist Masaya Miyoshi told me. "Their goals involve cultural and social factors. Their executives are aware of the welfare of their employees and of the nation. They want prestige, more than money, for themselves." An American business leader with whom I talked in Tokyo commented: "It's rather refreshing to hear Japanese businessmen say, 'We can't do that—it wouldn't be good for Japan.' " Predictably, such idealism is honored in the breach nearly as much as it is honored in the observance: Japanese corporations have com-mitted harrowing social crimes in pollution and land speculation, and the Japanese public does not universally knock its head on the ground in reverence for the country's corporations. Yet tempering profit with moral values is too strong a tradition—going back to the feudal samurai and to the unified nation-building effort of the Meiji Restora-tion—to erode in foreseeable times.

Sociologist Chie Nakane says flatly: "Whether the feeling of love of company thrives or not is the barometer of the ability and talents of the management staff." Companies often provide housing for their employees, ranging from dormitories for single men and women, to cheap land where an employee can build his own house, to ample residences supplied free for ranking executives. In various combina-tions, companies offer clinics, clubrooms, vacation houses, sports fields, schooling in technical or cultural subjects, and bashes as costly as taking the whole staff to Hawaii. High executives must play father in such personal ways as attending—or even arranging—weddings, going to funerals, and drinking with the staff on Saturday night. A company president has to temper his power with his duties and avoid flashy charismatic behavior. Says Soichiro Honda, founder of Honda Motor Company: "An employer like me has a job just like everyone else in the plant. It is my job to foresee business trends, make plans to meet them, and thus keep all my men on the job. If I fail to do it, then it is I who should be fired, and not they."

Professor Reischauer observes:

> Japanese skills in minimizing the sense of personal alienation and reducing anomie in modern urban society should be of great interest to other countries. The worldwide pattern of great factories and huge corporations appears to be an inevitable product of the new technology, but within this general framework the Japanese, drawing on deep cultural traits, have developed extremely distinctive and effective relationships between management and labor, between business and government, and between various business groupings.

Most top-level Japanese executives—variously wispy, solemn, shy, liver-spotted, or furrowed in the forehead—do not look like confident plungers, but their bold willingness to put all their bets on imaginative projects has been an indispensable factor in the economy's growth. In 1957, for example, while the London *Times* was commenting that 100,000-ton tankers "will never form more than a small proportion of the world ship-building programme," Japanese managers were planning the docks that could, and did, build 476,000-ton tankers, and can build million-tonners. Japanese imagination foresaw the market for electronics, the worldwide camera boom, the super-speed train, the seemingly limitless opportunities for department stores, the possibility of building a huge car industry.

As bold as the builders were the bankers. "The central fact about the structure of the Japanese economy is that Japan is a nation heavily in hock to its bankers," said *Fortune*, in an appalled tone of voice. A typical corporation's capital structure divides into 80 percent bank loans and 20 percent equity—a four-to-one ratio (sometimes ten-to-one) coolly maintained while American firms think that one-to-two is scary. In other words, Japanese corporate managers use borrowed bank money, rather than the sales of stock, to finance growth. For their part, Japanese banks lend money on a firm's sporting chance to grab a good share of the market, rather than on such conservative, American-style factors as return on investment and debt–equity ratio. Theoretically, if some tottery bank had to call in its loans, a chain reaction might wreck the whole economy. But this has never happened, because of luck, brilliance, and the Bank of Japan. This potent central bank, whose old main building just off the Ginza in Tokyo copies the Palladian architecture of the National Bank of Belgium (which Japan used as a prototype), has been rescuing overextended commercial banks ever since the Meiji period. In a sense, Japanese businessmen and bankers can take big risks because they know that ultimately the government bank will always bail them out. Who owns Japan? The banks own Japan.

The Bank of Japan is one of 739 large corporations that form Keidanren, the Federation of Economic Organizations, the interlocking coordinator of Japanese big business. Keidanren speaks to government and the politicians on behalf of business; when a cabinet minister is invited to one of its meetings, he is clearly expected to attend. Behind the façade of Keidanren's gleaming, glass-faced building, where leftist demonstrators frequently gather to protest big business's various malfeasances, expert economists work out "advice" for the government, advice that amounts to heavy pressure. Keidanren's president is a doughty, seventy-eight-year-old workaholic named Toshio Doko, who started his career as a turbine designer for Ishikawajima-Harima Heavy Industries, rose to the presidency of that company, and not only saved it from collapse but made it the world leader in launched tonnage. Called in then to salvage Tokyo Shibaura Electric Company (Toshiba), he doubled sales in three years. Among his Mao-like "Sayings of Doko" is this: "Ordinary employees should work three times as hard as before, and executives will work ten times harder." He begins and ends each day chanting Buddhist sutras.

Beginning in 1955, Japanese management has sent no less than ten thousand men abroad, mostly to the United States, to bring back techniques and technology—modern versions of the emissaries sent to China in the seventh, eighth, and ninth centuries for the same purpose. For a grand total of $2.5 billion, which is only a tenth of what the United States spends every year on research and development, these emissaries bought virtually all the technology of the Western world. American companies permitted this naïve giveaway on the bad advice of their accountants that royalties from licenses were windfalls. Japanese companies could hardly be blamed for exploiting the bargain, even though it stunted research and development in Japan and reinforced Japan's reputation as a nation of imitators. And the Japanese took pains to buy technology with cold cash, even when money was tight, rather than take it in the form of subsidiaries of the foreign companies that owned it. "Even today," writes Professor Robert J. Ballon, "the first reaction of a Japanese industrialist faced with a new product or process may be to investigate whether he can acquire the pertinent license or patent at what cost, and well before wondering whether he himself might not create a similar product."

But even when importing technology, the Japanese take care to criticize it and, usually, improve it: blast furnaces designed for 1,500 tons a day turn out 2,500 in Japanese hands. "The Japanese digest technology like a man digests a steak," Ballon told me. "What used to be a separate something outside the person—the steak—becomes an integral part of his body." Out of this kind of innovation, and out of fear that foreign corporations hit by Japanese competition may stop selling licenses, the Japanese are now building massive research and development facilities of their own. The share of gross national product going into research, which was 0.6 percent in 1955, is 2.26 percent now, and will rise to 3.79 percent in ten years. By comparison, the United States now spends 3 percent, West Germany 1.7 percent.

Some experts question whether the Japanese mentality will free researchers to take long-shot risks, whether businessmen will insist too strongly on applied research at the cost of pure research. Scarcely anything Japanese yet deserves the word "invention," but patentable permutations and variations are numerous: fatigue-resistant steel, the one-gun color television tube, the lightweight videotape recorder, the Esaki diode, the practical rotary gasoline engine, the electron microscope, pollution-free coal-burning power plants, and electric cars. "Japan is now the greatest power in the world in industry based on microbiology," says the Swedish Nobel Prize winner Arne Tiselius. Two Japanese firms have jointly devised a way of making paper from petroleum. Honda Motor Company developed the best pollution-free engine in the world, causing Ford Motor Company to go to Japan and beg for the secret. "That's like General Motors appealing to Harley-Davidson for technology," someone wisecracked. The 1974 Tokyo Motor Show exhibited dozens of practical electric cars. The government is building a bathyscaphe that will be able to descend to twenty thousand feet below the surface of the sea. The Japanese also do a lot of research on research; the circulation of scientific information in translations, abstracts, and specialized publications is exceeded only by that of the Soviet Union.

Japan's new home-grown know-how has become a $60-million-a-year export. Imports of technology still run eight times higher than exports, but one now hears talk that the country might be able to phase out purchases of licenses within a few years. Japan exports technology in chemicals, steel, automobiles, machinery, and phar-maceuticals. Asia gets about a third of it, the United States one-fifth. Ishikawajima-Harima Heavy Industries provided know-how, for ex-ample, for an iron works in Maine. Fujitsu, Ltd., the leading Japanese computer maker, sold its patented numerical control system to Bendix, from which Fujitsu had bought its original technology twenty-five years before. International Business Machines acquired nine hundred Japanese patents in computer technology. Nippon Steel Corporation has sold blueprints for supersize blast furnaces to five European steel-makers, including Krupp.

Everybody in Japan stands in awe of MITI, pronounced appropri-ately as "meaty." The Ministry of International Trade and Industry corresponds roughly to the U.S. Department of Commerce, but is far more powerful. Commerce issues recommendations; MITI issues or-ders. MITI is, in fact, the tough, ruthless driving force that executes the Japan, Inc. policy of collaboration between government and business.

MITI's prime job has been to direct Japan's growth and keep the economy rolling at high speed. In other words, MITI does a lot of planning. American laissez-faire free-enterprisers detest the idea of government planning, but the Japanese conservatives have made it the cornerstone of their success. Founded shortly after the war, MITI, always working hand in glove with businessmen and the Bank of Japan, made the daring decision that Japan would not be toymaker to the world but instead would plump for heavy industry. This choice, requiring heavy employment of capital and technology at a time when Japan lacked those two things, seemed irrational, but MITI's men faced up to the fact that Japan could never catch up to the United States and Europe without a solid economic base. MITI, providing its own research by setting up technological laboratories, thereafter kept scanning the horizons for further industries that Japan could develop to comparative advantage, while heartlessly discouraging bummers. The ministry does not directly create or debar any given industry or enterprise, but, working through the Bank of Japan, it can provide or cut off credit with much the same effect.

MITI has aggressively protected infant industry by many devices for keeping foreigners out; at the same time, MITI manages Japanese foreign aid so as to provide maximum benefits for Japanese suppliers. Planning Japan's next jet airliner, MITI chose Boeing Aircraft Cor-poration and an Italian firm as collaborators, and set specifications for the plane (medium-range, two hundred passengers). When a provincial gas company announced a reduction in service during the energy shortage, MITI, in a typical exercise of its stewardship of the economy, "summoned the company president to Tokyo [as *Mainichi Daily News* phrased it] and took him to task for announcing the supply cut without prior consultation with the ministry."

But MITI is always at the service of Japanese business, even when making demands on it, even when the minister (as he did lately) urges corporations to desist from paying high dividends and calls in high profitmakers to explain themselves. MITI provides business with order and with goals—which together amount to cartelization on a scale that competition-minded Americans profess to be shocked at. MITI bureaucrats preside at the secret meetings in which, for example, the steelmaking companies set quarterly production quotas. Who controls whom in this arrangement is not clear. Political scientist Chitoshi Yanaga draws an analogy between politicians-bureaucrats-businessmen and the old scissors-paper-stone game (scissors cut paper, paper wraps stone, stone breaks scissors). Keidanren, through campaign money, controls the Liberal Democratic Party; the Liberal Democrats, through lawmaking, control MITI; and MITI, through credit and subsidies, controls the Keidanren's members. But searching for dominances and conflicts within the Japanese politico-economic system obscures the underlying unity: all segments work not merely for themselves but also for Japan.

Putting an ideological label on this mixed economy is difficult, but "collectivist capitalism" might do. The planning and the control over the economy are as pervasive as in any Communist country, but the free-enterpriser willing to go along with the agreed goals, far from feeling the heavy hand of government, has liberty and support to be bold, to grow, and to make a profit. "The beauty of Japan is that it has produced unquestioned success by our criteria but with an ideology almost the opposite of ours," says the Harvard Business School's George Cabot Lodge. Japanese fiscal policy, incidentally, may be the best in the world; the Bank of Japan has no compunction whatsoever about belt tightening if circumstances demand it. Government also aids the Japanese economy by keeping taxes low. National and local taxes taken together amount to only 16 percent of GNP, as compared to 39 percent in Britain and 24 percent in the United States.

A friend of mine in Tokyo belongs to a family that owned an estate in the country until the American Occupation expropriated it and divided it among the sharecroppers who had farmed it. The former tenants, now owners of the land, still keep in touch with him, and the relationship has a residual master–slave air about it. Recently, one ex-tenant family visited him to ask for a job recommendation for their son. He gave it, and they backed away kneeling and bowing in gratitude and humility. "Then," he told me laconically, "they got into their Bentley and drove back to the farm."

Thousands upon thousands of Japanese farmers, who on the average own two and one-half acres of land, are downright affluent; the many horny-handed men and work-worn women one sees vacationing on the beach at Waikiki are typical examples. But how can anyone get rich farming what amounts to a large garden by American standards? The answer, of course, is that on the average Japanese farmers are not all rich (only a few have Bentleys), but merely well-to-do, and the visible big spenders are either from the upper end of the averages or are taking a once-in-a-lifetime fling. Moreover, the richest of them are often spending the profits from selling some of their land, the price of which may have multiplied a hundred times as expanding cities or industrial areas encroached upon it. Another secret of the farmer's prosperity is that he or other members of his household work part-time at city jobs. Some move seasonally, some commute from the farm, and the labor shortage provides good opportunities for temporary or seasonal work. In 1973, the average farm household took in $3,880 (plus most of the family's food) from farming and $4,360 from wages and salaries, for a total, including some other business receipts, of $9,000, which was $2,700 greater than all outgo. Furthermore, vote-seeking politicians subsidize the price of rice so that per-bushel payments to Japanese farmers are probably the highest in the world. Lastly, Japanese farmers know their business. Ladling on chemical fertilizer, they make 8 million acres of none-too-fertile paddy land produce as much as 14 million tons of rice per year. They grow up to 2.1 tons per acre, which compares to 1 ton per acre from North Dakota wheat land.

A share of the credit for this record of rural prosperity and productivity has to go to the 1946–50 land reform, which limited land ownership to seven and one-half acres by any one farmer, who must be a local resident and who may not rent more than two and one-half acres of his property. Tenants who under virtually feudal terms had been paying three-fourths of their crops to landlords suddenly became landowners whose work benefited only themselves, and almost all land is now farmed by its owners. With this incentive, and with advances in technology, production shot up. Japan, which before the war had relied on its colonies for much of its food, became (according to the government's 1972 white paper on agriculture) 74 percent self-sufficient. Just as important, the Occupation encouraged the growth of agricultural cooperatives, which traced themselves back to weak beginnings around 1900. Now the 17,820 Japanese *nokyo*— joined under four national organizations that take care of their coordination, purchasing and marketing, insurance, and banking— constitute an enormous business by anybody's scale. The trading arm —buying fertilizer, insecticides, and farm machinery, and selling farm products—did $9 billion worth of business in 1973. That is why farming is an integral part of Japan, Inc. One single *nokyo*, the Ihara Agricultural Cooperative Association of Shimizu, with about sixteen hundred members, fathered a fertilizer firm, the Ihara Agricultural Chemicals Company, which now has assets worth $100 million. For big business, farmers form a juicy market. Every last farmhouse has at least one television set, usually a color set, and most families have a car or a pickup or both.

But when the members of the co-op are not busy taking part in a group excursion by chartered plane, their work remains drudgery. At harvest time I've seen old women trudge into the paddies while the eastern sky was still an electric predawn green. The work is all the more onerous because any given farmer's few acres do not consist of one piece, but rather of separate basketball-court-size paddies, acquired helter-skelter, that may lie scattered as far as a mile from his house. Not only does this necessitate a lot of walking or driving, but also it largely prevents the use of big farm machinery. The work schedule varies by latitude, but in the rice lands around the Inland Sea, it begins in May with the planting of seed in a well-fertilized nursery plot in a corner of each paddy. While the seeds sprout, the rubber-booted farmer floods the paddy with four inches of water and plows it with his motorized rotary hoe. After three or four weeks, when the seedlings are nine inches high, the farmer drains the field to a depth of an inch and sets out the plants by hand on a five-inch spacing. As the stalks grow, he tills and sprays, and when they reach the level of his waist, he strings over the paddy bird-scaring streamers of twisted silver and gold metallic ribbon, which dance and glint in the wind. He also plants a scarecrow, not on a pole, but as though standing in the water, like himself, and the paddies take on a comical populated look, the men of flesh becoming indistinguishable from the men of straw.

As the heads form and droop, breezes comb the fields, and the play of sunlight shifts the rice's green toward chartreuse or toward viridian, in rolling waves. At harvest time, in October, the farmer drains and dries his paddies, and then steers his small motor mower while his wife forms sheaves and throws them to the stubble. The land rarely lies fallow; it is kept at work summer and winter.

The Japanese no longer want to depend so completely on rice for nutrition as they once did. Because of affluence, changing tastes, bigger meals, and population growth, Japan now imports 29 percent of what it eats. Bread has to some extent replaced rice as starchy food, the use of sugar is increasing, and meat consumption is rising fast. But Japan grows only 8 percent of its own wheat, and none of its own sugar, and it has to import a fifth of its meat. The Japanese, as everyone knows, love soy sauce, soybean soup, and bean curd, but they grow only a very small percentage of the soybeans used for these national delicacies. All told, Japan's imports comprise 10 percent of the food traded among the nations of the world, and Japan is the largest food importer. Curiously enough, Japan also exports food—$800 million worth a year in beer, sake, canned fish, and canned mandarin oranges, which at a production of 3.8 million tons a year is one of Japan's most visible crops.

In a world that suffers more every decade from food shortages, Japan's reliance on imports constitutes a possible peril. But any increase in food output will have to come from making existing farms produce more, for almost all the arable land, right up to the foundations of the farmhouses, has long since been put under cultivation. A further limitation is the scarcity, age, and balkiness of the farmers. The exodus to the cities has reduced the farm population from 10 million a decade ago to 6 million now. The men and women left on the land are middle-aged or more, and locked into the subsidized-rice system so tightly that they refuse to make any large-scale switch to wheat and barley. But the chance of national hunger may force some changes. Probably many rice paddies will be consolidated into big farms for wheat and similar grains. As a matter of fact, the pattern of larger farms has already been set in Hokkaido, where the land is laid out in squares of twelve and one-half acres. And in case farm labor grows too scarce, the government's Institute of Agricultural Machinery has already invented a sort of movable bridge that rides over rice paddies, suspending mechanical planters, cultivators, sprayers, and harvesters that can produce rice almost without human attention.

Industry's pell-mell pursuit of GNP had its painful price: Japan, Inc. turned the country into the world's most intensively polluted nation. With an eye only on the balance sheet, and resolutely ignoring the symptoms of blight, the Japanese Establishment in the late

1950s and the 1960s brought Japan to the brink of a kind of environmental hara-kiri. The Japanese steel industry is the classic example. Its furnaces make steel about 30 percent more cheaply than American or European furnaces partly because the Japanese steelmakers ran their many-colored smoke right up the smokestacks, instead of through expensive particulate eliminators.

Pollution violates Japan's beauty and sickens its trees, but the most resented and dramatic offenses have been against human health. The tragedy of Minamata (population 36,717), a seashore town facing the splendid islets off the western coast of Kyushu, recapitulates the dawning danger of Japanese pollution, the full-scale horror of it, and the slowly developing counter-attack against it. Minamata is a company town, 70 percent supported by Chisso Corporation, a big chemical firm that used to make vinyl chloride, base of plastics; but the town also has fishing cooperatives that send their boats out into neighboring Yatsushiro Bay. One day in 1956, Yoshimitsu Tanaka, a ship carpenter, dining with his wife and six children, slapped his five-year-old daughter Shizuko because she kept dropping her rice bowl. Ten days later another daughter, aged two, began to behave with similar lack of muscular control, and then the family's five cats died mysteriously, one after another. Other Minamata children suffered paralysis in their arms and legs, or developed deformities, or died writhing in undiagnosable pain. The doctor in charge of Chisso's company hospital guessed that what was coming to be called the "Minamata disease" might be some new and more virulent form of encephalitis, and suffering families were quarantined to stop the spread of infection.

The medical school of Kumamoto University sent in researchers, who over the next three years found traces of mercury in the brains of the dead. They surmised that it came from fish that got it from the Chisso plant's waste discharges: mercury, used in the process of manufacturing vinyl chloride, constituted 70 parts per million of the bottom silt in the region. The company fought this hypothesis, but agreed to pay small sums to any victims who would waive the right to sue. More victims died, lost eyesight, went through convulsions, or suffered brain damage that left them mute, mentally retarded, or bedridden. One of the older brothers of the two Tanaka girls was ostracized for fear he was infected, and a planned marriage fell through when the bride's family learned of his sisters' disease. Further research proved beyond doubt that Chisso mercury, spilled into the sea, was the sole cause of the Minamata disease.

The victims of this incurable malady—an ultimate total of 428, of whom sixty-nine died—and their families divided five ways over how to seek redress, but eventually one group sued Chisso, despite their waivers. Four years passed before the Kumamoto district court ruled, in March 1973. The judge declared that Chisso "could have foreseen the effect of the mercury-containing wastes on the human body," and awarded $3.7 million in damages. The verdict reinforced the claims of the four other groups, and Chisso became indebted for so many payments in death and disease compensations, annuities for victims, and establishment of medical facilities that to raise funds it had to sell off a subsidiary, Chisso Electric Chemical Company. And millions of tons of sludge, containing four hundred tons of mercury, still lie on the sea bottom off Chisso's plant (though it no longer makes vinyl chloride or discharges mercury). Fishermen, who have to avoid this patch of water, forced Chisso to negotiate compensation for their loss by scattering two tons of smelly dead fish around the company's Minamata offices. The government is pressuring Chisso to dredge up and dispose of the whole frightening mess.

Any menopausal woman who has at some time given birth to twins or triplets and has for more than thirty years eaten the rice grown near the lower Jinzu River (which empties into the Sea of Japan northwest of Tokyo) stands a better than average chance of coming down with itai-itai (ouch-ouch) disease. Why the disease prefers such women for victims is unknown, but what causes itai-itai is clear: minute amounts of cadmium poison the kidneys, and soften and weaken the bones by dissolving calcium. At first, bone pain restricts leg movements and the victim acquires a waddling gait. Ultimately, mere movement of the muscles snaps the victim's bones, causing horrible pain. The cadmium comes from Mitsui Mining and Smelting Company's Kamioka silver-lead-zinc mine, whose discharges of waste into the Jinzu caused cadmium to enter the irrigation water used on downstream rice paddies. The government stopped the pollution of the river in 1968, and two researchers report that chlorella, a dehydrated chlorophyll derivative developed for space travelers, purges cadmium from the body. The disease is now virtually contained. But it has claimed 155 victims, including thirty-two deaths. Mitsui was sued, and agreed to pay $1,330,000 in damages.

Japan's unhappy claim to be the world's most polluted nation rests on the Minamata and itai-itai diseases, not because they killed or maimed great numbers of people, but because they are a kind of shorthand that covers many maladies. So numerous and various are the poisons which can in infinitesimal amounts sicken human beings that the measure of them, "ppm," from the English "parts per million," is an everyday expression in Japan. An electric public-service sign near Shinjuku Station in Tokyo—only one of hundreds throughout Japan—reflects this awareness of the surrounding poisons by flashing the news that the air at the moment contains (for example) "SO_2 0.07 ppm" and "CO 12 ppm"—0.07 parts per million of sulfur dioxide and 12 parts per million of carbon monoxide. The people, knowing that the Environment Agency has set 0.04 ppm of sulfur dioxide as the desirable maximum, can only try to breathe a little less. "We are living in the ppm age," says one newspaper.

Triggered by the Minamata tragedy, the authorities began looking for mercury elsewhere, and found that most fish had at least some of it, which was passed along and concentrated in the food chain, so that most human beings and other animals also had at least some of it, though not necessarily in dangerous quantities. The Society for the Preservation of the Japanese Stork discovered that an injured bird caught in western Honshu had 1.06 ppm of mercury in its wing. In humans, mercury is easily detectable in the hair. Mercury in the hair of Shoichi Yokoi, the soldier-straggler who returned to Japan after twenty-eight years of hiding out in Guam, rose in seven months from 2 ppm to 8.2 ppm, which is about the Japanese average. For months while I was in Japan, the nation was in a turmoil over the discovery that a certain fishmonger had 64.7 ppm of mercury in his hair from daily consumption of two pounds of fish, which itself ran as high as 1.84 ppm. Sushi restaurants, which specialize in tuna, cuttlefish, mackerel, and shrimp, were in a panic. The fishmonger probably was in danger, but fortunately for fish restaurants, health authorities believe that the peril point is not reached until mercury in the hair measures 50 ppm. They also hold that fish are safe to consume if the mercury content in more than 80 percent of the fish population is less than 1 ppm, because the human body excretes ingested mercury over a period of time. The Ministry of Health and Welfare calculated that a person could safely eat forty-seven slices of raw tuna a week.

The sky in Tokyo comes in sinister colors: the off-white of photochemical smog, the tawniness of sand blown over from China, a sullen darkness at noon, a pullulating gray-on-gray. Sometimes something—cyanide? metallic dust?—adds a pale lemony tone, and even a lavender hue. Even on the better days the sun is a wraithlike gold-orange sphere, as though seen through smoked glass. Newspaper editorials cheer the rare times when Mount Fuji appears at the rim of a vault of blue—usually on holidays when millions have left the city for some festival, decreasing the sources of pollution. Rare too are the nights when one sees the stars in Tokyo.

Middle Eastern crude oil, source of three-fifths of Japan's energy, contains as much as 2.5 percent of sulfur, which means that 2,670,000 tons of sulfur (in the form of gaseous sulfur oxides) rise into the Japanese air every year. Predictably, the air also contains (from cars and airplanes) carbon monoxide, and the hydrocarbons and nitrogen oxides that cause photochemical smog when exposed to sunlight. Less predictably, the air also has hydrogen fluoride, chlorine gas, cement dust, and forty-three kinds of metallic elements. There is an unhappy city named Yokkaichi, across Ise Bay from Nagoya, where the government in 1955 decided to site the main complexes of the petrochemical industry on an old fuel depot of the Japanese Imperial Navy. Its citizens suffer the most from the air-pollution diseases that afflict millions of Japanese: sore throat, coughing, nausea, eye irritation, bronchitis, emphysema, and lung cancer. The Japanese call Yokkaichi "asthma city," but the asthmatic diseases are also the main ailments of ten thousand patients under the age of eighteen in the health centers of the Tokyo Metropolitan Government, which subsidizes their treatment as victims of one of society's mistakes. Asthma and its nasal counterpart, rhinitis, particularly afflict the young. When the oxidants formed in photochemical smog reach 0.16 ppm, Tokyo schools order children not to exercise outdoors.

In the acid-laced rain that falls on Shizuoka, in the brass doorknobs discolored by the gases from pulp mills in Yatsushiro, in the TURN ON LIGHTS—SMOKE ZONE AHEAD signs on expressways through Kawasaki, in the anger of fishermen who flooded polluting Sangawa paper mills by sandbagging their sewers—in these and many other signs one can see that the Japanese still have an uncomfortable lead in what they call *kogai*, environment destruction. The Inland Sea suffers seriously from spilled oil, and even on coasts elsewhere petroleum clots from the dumping of contaminated tanker ballast range in size from three-fourths of an inch to nearly two feet. Sometimes kogai gets almost comic: in Chigasaki, an air-monitoring van exploded violently, as though the pollution it measured had overstrained it (actual cause: leaking hydrogen).

Although the scandals of kogai continue, it probably began to decline as far back as 1970—perhaps at the moment a certain Tokyo coffee shop ceased to offer its customers an oxygen mask with every cup. Since then, to its credit, Japan has embarked upon a far-reaching, severe, and expensive cleanup program, which Herman Kahn estimates will eventually cost a trillion dollars. In the first phase, politicians have already enacted a large body of law that roughly resembles contemporaneous American legislation. The government has also implanted the "polluters pay principle," which means that industry must build antipollution facilities at its own cost, share in public-works expenses like green belts and sewerage, and pay for human damage even when completely inadvertent. This toughened attitude seems to have put backbone into the courts, and in a series of strong decisions (including the Minamata and itai-itai cases) judges have forced the polluters to pay.

Back of the government's antipollution effort lies a clear and massive public consensus. The Japanese people are fed up. A government white paper counted 820 civic antipollution organizations and 600 conservation organizations across the country. All the left-wing mayors and governors elected in recent years won partly by campaigning for "quality of life" measures and picturing the Liberal Democrats as a band of gouty poison merchants. Often the conflict pits Village Japan against Japan, Inc. The villagers in Rokkasho, in northern Honshu, are heroes for rejecting a joint government–industry project that would have made the area into a huge complex for casting pig iron, smelting nonferrous metals, refining petrochemicals, and generating electricity. Much in contrast to the United States, where labor is often willing to live and die with industrial poison rather than lose jobs, Japanese unions (knowing their employment to be guaranteed) often oppose pollution out of realization that such iniquity as mercury discharge in the long run injures the public, the unionists, and the industry itself. The head of the chemical union says that "at a time when pollution is killing or crippling people, high wages do not compensate for the workers' spiritual poverty." The railway workers' union (rather than management) decided to slow bullet trains from 110 to 62 miles per hour over a six-mile stretch in Nagoya where residents said the roar of trains at high speed created unbearable "noise pollution."

The most promising success to come from all this effort and protest has been the decrease of sulfur compounds in the air, gradual in absolute figures, but considerable when related to the simultaneous high growth in consumption of the fuel oil that spews this poison.

Thirty "disfloaters," steel-hulled catamarans that fly over the water collecting floating rubbish, are cleaning up Japan's ports, and Ishikawajima-Harima Heavy Industries is developing a similar skimmer to recover waste oil from the surface of the sea. Osaka has made itself a leader in pollution-free compacting and packaging of garbage, for use in landfills, and the city has a plan for cutting airborne nitrogen and sulfur oxides to one-fourth of present levels by 1981. MITI is pressing for three improvements in cycling: quieter motorcycling, more bicycling, and increased recycling.

╳ Still, the overall image of Japanese big business in relation to pollution is largely that of hedging, qualifying, setting conditions, and resisting. One recent Keidanren president defended a "certain amount" of mercury pollution, and another called kogai a "necessary evil." Toyota and Nissan, the Japanese giants, dragged their feet as badly as General Motors and Ford in trying to devise an engine that would reduce carbon monoxide and hydrocarbon emissions; and the whole car industry balked at cutting nitrogen oxides by 1976 to the levels required by the Environment Agency under the Japanese version of the American Muskie Act. One mining company, Toho Zinc, went so far as to exchange contaminated sludge from its plant with mud from nearby rivers to conceal pollution that caused a death from itai-itai disease; when exposed, the president resigned, saying, "Our company failed to regard the pollution problem seriously."

Only under pressure has industry begun to change. Kawasaki Steel's newest blast furnace is a Rolls-Royce of pollution-free metal-making. Nippon Steel has planted ten million trees around its eleven steelworks to "achieve indigenous, ecologically balanced vegetation." In the showcase Kashima industrial district, sixty miles east of Tokyo, an oil refinery, an ethylene plant, and a power station supply basics to twenty-three companies in one of the cleanest petrochemical complexes in the world; a big petroleum-desulfurizing plant is the key unit. Major firms in Japan now put a healthy 10 percent or more of investment into pollution-prevention equipment and devices.

22 / 🌱

Mitsui!

FROM A CERTAIN SPACIOUS ROOM on the thirty-fourth floor of the famous Kasumigaseki skyscraper in central Tokyo, a group of influential Japanese businessmen every so often look down, with perhaps a touch of monarch-of-all-I-survey in their bearing, on the Diet building, the Imperial Palace, the prime minister's official residence, NHK's broadcasting house, and many other Japanese power points. The chamber itself, which measures about thirty by forty feet, is simple, rich, and elegant. This is the meeting room of the Monday Club, the center of gravity of the Mitsui combine of finance, commerce, and industry—one of the world's oldest, strongest, most varied, and most voracious business giants.

Meeting first thing every other week, the Monday Club is made up of executives of higher than managing-director level from forty major companies of the Mitsui Group. The group is a somewhat amorphous conglomeration that numbers as many as sixty firms, ranging from such venerable heavyweights as Mitsui Bank down to such relative newcomers as Showa Aircraft Industry Company. In the ultimate frustration of the American Occupation's effort to break up Japan's old zaibatsu (meaning "financial cliques"), these officials thus keep in collusive contact with one another for the benefit of the group as a whole.

Yet the Monday Club is only a committee of coordinators compared to the Second Thursday Club, which meets for some inscrutable reason in the Monday Club's room on the *first* Thursday of each month. Its members are presidents or chairmen of the board of twenty-two companies of the Mitsui Group, selected from the Monday Club and centered on the old-line firms that contain the word "Mitsui" in their corporate names. These men, holding in their hands the Mitsui tradition going back to 1616, shape the broad course of the whole enterprise. In a typical piece of work not long ago, the Monday Club, faced with a stock raid on the group's Mitsukoshi department-store chain, fought off the raider by pooling funds to buy up shares and keep control. In a similarly typical piece of work about the same time, it was the business of the loftier Second Thursday Club to admit to full membership in the Mitsui Group the big-league Tokyo Shibaura Electric Company (turbines, generators, nuclear machinery—best known abroad for Toshiba appliances and electronics). Mitsui, biggest of the prewar zaibatsu, now stands second to Mitsubishi (which for its part is ruled by a Friday Club) in total volume of business; and the unignorable Sumitomo Group, also formed from an old zaibatsu, presses Mitsui hard from the No. 3 position. But Mitsui, with a history both proud and sinister, and with the boldness and imagination to keep reshaping itself for the future, most insistently commands attention.

Among Mitsui's grouped firms, a number are Japan's biggest of their kind, and one of these is Mitsui Real Estate Development Company. Its president, Hideo Edo, is therefore a ranking leader among those Second Thursday executives who glance down on the edifices of the Tokyo power axis. Edo exemplifies Mitsui's historic talent for developing creative senior men and then liberating them to make what they can of their jobs. He is complex. Born a bumpkin on a back-country farm in 1903, he picked up a Marxist social conscience at Tokyo University before entering Mitsui as first among 102 applicants. In 1939, while still a junior clerk, he proposed the structural change that converted Mitsui to weaponry for the duration of the war; and after Japan's defeat, he struggled hard against Eleanor Hadley, the redoubtable American Occupationeer who had been put in charge of trust busting, to keep the Americans from atomizing the combine (he failed, but he and Dr. Hadley later became friends).

In his mahogany-wainscoted, lace-curtained offices just under the roof of the former Mitsui Bank headquarters building, Edo still speaks with collegiate idealism of the need for business morals. "As businessmen, we have to pay attention to social contributions," he told me, closing his eyes and holding to his forehead a hand with an arthritically bent little finger. Yet Mitsui Real Estate, with Edo as president since 1958, contributed heavily to the esthetic destruction of the Tokaido corridor, particularly in converting charming inlets into reclaimed flatland for industry. "Japan has a long shoreline, almost equal to that of the United States, susceptible to filling for good industrial sites, and we helped with the job," Edo said, sounding both proud and regretful. Mitsui Real Estate owns land in Hawaii, Singapore, and Bangkok; took part in the impressive Makati suburb development near Manila; and is a partner in a joint venture with Cabot, Cabot & Forbes in an industrial park near Seattle. The company has also put up downtown structures all over Japan. "I built the Kasumigaseki Building," Edo told me casually, and described how he had found a professor who, by observing the structure of tall, five-hundred-year-old pagodas, had developed a theory for earthquake-proofing skyscrapers.

Ruthless and energetic, this remarkable man is also thoughtful, artistic, and broad-minded. Putting to use his university degree in English jurisprudence, he serves part-time as judge of a family court, probating wills and such. After five hours' sleep, he rises at dawn to tend radishes, celery, bulb plants, and flowering trees in a rooftop garden at his house in Tokyo's posh Mejiro section. At his villa in the resort town of Karuizawa, he watches birds as a hobby. A look of happiness comes over his face when he speaks of these "contacts with nature," and he writes perceptive essays on business's duty to preserve the environment. He has a hand in the Tokyo Gakuen School of Music, and his wife and daughters are skilled in piano and violin. But the balance of forces in Edo's personality—social conscience, artistry, loyalty to Mitsui—has not resulted in making Mitsui Real Estate a leader in solving Japan's worst problem, inadequate housing. In fact, Mitsui's land speculation helps keep house-site prices too high for aspiring homebuilders. Edo promises change. "We must build apartments and high-rises." Not that he himself would like to live so far above the soil. "I think the tendency is very sad," he says.

Purists maintain that modern Mitsui—or Mitsubishi, or Sumitomo—is not a zaibatsu, a word that suggests greedy wealth, monopolization, merchants of death, and the bad old American "trusts." They say that the proper word is *zaikai*, "financial circles." As between the prewar Japanese trust and the present conglomerate, there are clear distinctions. The core of the historic zaibatsu was a holding company, now banished, and the owners were single families, instead of the present more dispersed stockholders. Family members used to fill most of the executive positions; now hired managers, like Edo, run the show. Zaikai by definition includes postwar industrialists, like Soichiro Honda and Konosuke Matsushita, whose companies lack the background to be considered zaibatsu. The banks of the present combines tend to guide the group as a holding company might, but the banks by law may not own more than 10 percent of any of the group's member firms, nor can company members account for more than 15 percent of the banks' outstanding loans. Nevertheless, I found that in ordinary conversation the Japanese do not say zaikai but zaibatsu, for the reason that the similarities between present and historic zaibatsu are greater than the differences.

The essential characteristic of a zaibatsu, old or new, is that it consists of a set of matched companies. To name the major members of the Mitsui Group is to give the range of activity (and Mitsubishi or Sumitomo match them almost one for one). They are: Mitsui Bank; Mitsui Trust and Banking Company; Mitsui & Company (trading); Mitsui Real Estate Development Company; Mitsui Mutual Life Insurance Company; Taisho Marine and Fire Insurance Company; Mitsui Shipbuilding & Engineering Company; Japan Steel Works; Sanki Engineering Company; Mitsui Construction Company; Mitsui Toatsu Chemicals; Mitsui Petrochemical Industries; Mitsukoshi, Ltd. (department stores); Toray Industries (rayon and artificial fibers); Mitsui Mining Company (coal); Mitsui Mining & Smelting Company (zinc and lead); Tokyo Shibaura Electric Company (Toshiba); Hokkaido Colliery & Steamship Company; Mitsui Warehouse Company; Mitsui O.S.K. Lines (shipping); and Mitsui Wharf Company (port operations).

In their working relationships, guided by the Second Thursday Club, these firms are cemented together by interlocking directorates, preferential credit, overall coordinating committees, and mutual supply of raw materials and products. But perhaps the tightest bond is mutual ownership, which makes the profit of each firm benefit all the others. Although no one company can by law own more than 10 percent of another (and in practice usually owns less), the aggregate ownership of most Mitsui companies by other Mitsui companies builds up to as much as 50 percent (the rest being owned by the general public). The cumulative effect of this logrolling is to let the Mitsui Group act as one, while innocently protesting that it neither breaks the antitrust laws nor hoards the profits.

Mitsui Bank possesses a great Grecian block of a building, put up in 1926 by American architects, which stands in Tokyo's Nihonbashi area just where its forerunner did when the institution was founded in 1683, a decade before the Bank of England. The lofty, football-field-size banking floor, with its forest of thick, fluted, tan marble columns—thirty-six of them altogether—makes a space rather more impressive than the interior of St. Peter's Basilica in Rome. Before the war, Baron Mitsui occupied an office suite up in the heavens of this building, as does Hideo Edo now. But Mitsui Bank nowadays needs something larger for a headquarters, so the old classic has been turned into a branch, and the main office is a new, utilitarian block facing the Imperial Palace. There, after going through many hushed corridors where women receptionists bowed in unison from a sitting position, I met Goro Koyama, the current president of this sanctuary of the yen.

Koyama, a short, blocky man with a strong jaw, a graying pompadour, and a belt buckle embellished with an Old English *K*, is another aggressive Mitsui loyalist with a sentimental side. In his office and reception room, along with a Courbet and a Corot, hang creditable impressionist paintings done by himself—a lake in the Italian Alps, a Turkish coffee vendor, an Istanbul cityscape, all consequences of his world travels. "I'm not a Sunday painter," he says stoutly. "I *work* on Sunday. Or play golf. I paint at night, and I spend more time painting than banking. Banking is so abstract, just dealing in gold. We must escape dirty business and get into the spiritual. When I'm irritated, painting soothes me. I select a fantasy from memory, and paint it."

Mitsui Bank is the group's financial heart, but it has to vie with Mitsui & Company, the giant trading firm, as the group's most influential member. In function, size, and mode of operation, the incredible Japanese trading companies constitute a business tool found nowhere else in the world, with the possible (and smaller) exception of Britain's Jardine, Matheson and Company and Denmark's East Asiatic Company. What do trading companies do? "Buy it, sell it, represent it, store it, forward it, transfer it, guide it, plant it, consult with it, lease it, assemble it, organize it," runs one partial definition. Originally, and still essentially, trading houses work on commission to barter commodities. In fact, the word "trading" often takes on the more specific meaning of "barter." Explains the government's Japan External Trade Organization: "Trading companies are in a position to facilitate barter exchange. Countries experiencing balance-of-payments deficits or countries without foreign exchange have on occasion been able to pay for Japanese exports in terms of goods. For example, trading companies have exchanged steel products for coffee beans, a swap that only firms with the breadth of product portfolio possessed by the larger trading companies could perform."

Yoshizo Ikeda, appointed in 1973 as president of Mitsui & Company after thirty-seven years with the company, is a springy, forceful

Jack Dempsey of a man with eyes like bruised apples. In 1935 he was captain of the baseball team at Tokyo University that played Harvard —and lost. Ikeda worked for Mitsui & Company in New York in the 1950s, living in a big old house in New Rochelle, and for five years in the 1960s he ran the company's London office. "Ikeda is a very British Japanese," one of his underlings told me. Like most Japanese businessmen of high rank, Ikeda is open and articulate, and more than most Japanese he seems an individualist. But those who work for him told me that he is careful to run the business in the Japanese way: he courts a consensus from his vice-presidents, and does not act until he gets it.

The first Mitsui to go into business was a samurai who in 1616 had the wit to foresee that the rise of the Tokugawa shogunate, dominating all Japan, heralded a long period of peace during which soldiers like himself would be largely unemployed, if not downright hungry. Plummeting from top to bottom through class lines, he turned from samurai to merchant, brewing and peddling sake and soy sauce on the Ise peninsula, with a little usury on the side. He failed, but his son, packed off to found a dry-goods store right where the head emporium of Mitsui's Mitsukoshi department-store chain now stands in Tokyo, did so well that every succeeding chief of the clan (including the present one) has taken the name Hachiroemon Mitsui, after him. He branched into money exchange; soon the Mitsuis were financial agents for the shogunate and the emperor. Under the Tokugawas, merchants continued to be regarded as scum, and in order to prosper, writes John G. Roberts in his book *Mitsui*, "they had to be cringingly obsequious toward their superiors, ruthlessly competitive with their equals, and pitilessly grasping with people more helpless than they. In short, the accusations heaped upon the Jews of Europe applied equally to the merchants of Japan." By 1722, eight decades before the Rothschilds got well founded in Europe, the House of Mitsui was a tradition-encrusted group of a main family and eight related families, bound together by a solemn constitution that prevailed in principle until after World War II (except that the number of families was expanded to eleven).

By the second decade of the twentieth century, the Mitsui zaibatsu —trading, mining, industry, retailing—was the largest private economic empire in the world. Despite the fact that the Mitsuis were merchants and moneylenders, the Meiji-created nobility had long before begun to admit Mitsuis to the peerage, though only at the lowest rank, as barons. With the help of their new rank and their established wealth, Mitsuis were soon marrying the sons and daughters of counts and princes, thus establishing relationships with the imperial family and the surviving Tokugawas. When the Depression brewed a mixture of militarism, China conquest, and right-wing fanaticism in Japan, the Mitsui zaibatsu both profited and suffered. Mitsui made fortunes out of the Japanese army's adventure in Manchuria, and the combine also coolly sold war matériel to the opposing Chinese. The Mitsuis devoutly favored the militarists' war on Chinese and Russian Communism, but managed to profiteer so blatantly that ultranationalists pictured the zaibatsu as unpatriotic.

When the war ended, Mitsui had to write off its entire assets in Manchuria and China, but within Japan it was richer than ever from war profits. Its factories and office buildings were only lightly damaged. Mitsui contentedly looked forward to lucrative business in the reconstruction of Japan. Instead, eight weeks after Japan's surrender, two American military trucks backed up to Mitsui's main office and removed securities worth $281 million—the first act to result from President Truman's decision to break up the "notorious" Japanese zaibatsu.

The main effects of this trust busting were the permanent liquidation of the Mitsui holding company, the disjoining of 294 Mitsui subsidiaries and sub-subsidiaries, the purging of top executives and most ranking members of the family, a heavy capital levy on their assets, and a ban on the use of the name Mitsui. The present Hachiroemon Mitsui, who lost his title of baron in the dissolution of the peerage, salvaged 9 percent of his assets and a 1937 Bentley, but, lacking gasoline and tires, he had to ride crowded public transportation to go to his office.

The zaibatsu dismemberment, carried out by the radical, deviltheory faction of the Occupation officials, was astonishingly drastic and efficient. But it met powerful objections, not so much from the old Japanese owners as from Wall Street and conservative American politicians, notably California's Senator William Knowland, who saw in Japanese big business a bulwark against Communism. A Deconcentration Review Board appeared from the United States in 1948 to call a halt to trust busting. Soon it became plain that the forced public sale of stock owned by holding companies was not really dispersing ownership, because old zaibatsu employees, banks, and even dummies for the zaibatsu families were buying it up. Mitsui Trading started its comeback when twenty-two men, mostly from the old company's building-materials section, founded a tiny firm called Daiichi Trading. Daiichi prospered on American military procurement during the Korean War, and after the ban on the use of old zaibatsu names was revoked in 1951, Daiichi reincarnated itself as Mitsui & Company. Similarly, other Mitsui companies shucked off their postwar lie-low postures and pseudonyms, and the zaibatsu, minus its holding company and family ownership, was reborn.

Obsessive saving and bold loans financed Japan's postwar growth, and a thriving channel for this money has been Mitsui Trust and Banking Company. Running the company since 1971 has been Sen-kichi Shono, a slender, un-tycoonlike man who wears a Rotary button in the lapel of his smoothly tailored blue suits. He lights a lot of cigarettes, clenching them between his teeth and stubbing them out when only one-fifth smoked. When I saw him, the only decoration in his office was the much-reproduced photograph of John F. Kennedy strolling on a beach, and the only item on his desk was an abacus.

Shono's speech is full of the words "thousand billion" (avoiding "trillion" presumably because of imprecision: some countries, such as the United States, define a trillion as a thousand billion, and some, such as Great Britain, as a million billion). Mitsui Trust's outstanding loans, he said, were 2,000 billion yen, about $7 billion. Out of respect for the antitrust laws, only about 10 percent of that sum went to other Mitsui companies. "Before the war, that percentage would have been much higher," he said. Shono estimated the gross sales of all Mitsui companies as running about 8,000 billion yen a year, or $28 billion. "The whole Japanese gross national product is only about eighty thousand billion, or about ten times greater," he remarked, "although of course you cannot properly compare production and sales." But though he was aware of the Mitsui Group's total sales, he insisted that the links between companies are not tight and confining, that companies have great independence, and that this flexibility is more functional than the tight fetters of the old zaibatsu. "If a European wants to buy a ship," Shono pointed out, "he can order it from Mitsui & Company, which has big offices there and understands the technology. The trading company will then give the order to Mitsui Ship-building, which used to be a Mitsui & Company subsidiary. On the other hand, Mitsui Shipbuilding is set up to get business on its own, and could take the order directly. And it would be happy to build ships for Mitsubishi's N.Y.K. Line, for example. To go back to the tight bonds of the prewar Mitsui zaibatsu would not be good for the Mitsui Group. Society nowadays opposes immense trusts."

Unluckily for Shono's argument, a large part of Japanese society views the renewed zaibatsu with dark suspicion, born of monotonously regular scandals. Zaibatsu firms are caught cornering markets, hoarding, speculating, forming cartels, dodging taxes, bribing officials, and poisonously polluting. Mitsubishi and Mitsui petrochemical companies, for example, agreed under government pressure not long ago to stop conspiring to set high prices for polypropylene and polyethylene. Japan's Fair Trade Commission, though very much a paper tiger, managed to expose a secret cartel of aluminum smelters, and got twelve oil refiner-wholesalers to admit that they plotted together to raise the price of oil products five times in a year. Even such a friend of business as the minister of international trade and industry had to speak out against trading-company speculation in soybeans, wool, yarns, lumber, and raw silk; and at one point the prime minister summoned eighty business leaders to advise them to stop "price rigging."

In the most damaging disgrace of all, the trading companies set out in 1972 with the apparent intention of buying Japan itself—that is, to corner every inch of worthwhile land in the country. From heavy foreign trade that year, the companies were loaded with dollars just at the time that the government (so the firms' intelligence sources told them) was about to let the yen float in world markets. They rushed their dollars to the Bank of Japan and got more than 300 yen for each dollar, which a few days later, after the float, would have brought only 265. In the case of Mitsui & Company, about $875 million instantaneously became the yen equivalent of more than $1 billion, affording an irresistible temptation to break the rule of the old Mitsui family constitution that reads: "Avoid speculation of all kinds." The trading companies put their surplus yen into stocks and commodities, but above all into a spree of land buying, which is customarily the domain of private railroads, insurance companies, and real estate firms. In Kanagawa Prefecture, near Tokyo, the average price of land nearly doubled that year. The price of remote mountain land rose to between $40,000 and $80,000 an acre. No head of a family, needing land to build a house, could compete with the purchasing power of the money-heavy trading companies, and people grew bitter at watching their dreams of home ownership dissolve.

Feeling that it had to respond on behalf of the public, the lower house of the Diet in 1974 called in twenty-three top business executives and sat them down, like little boys, for three days of grilling by Communists and Socialists in front of television cameras. Mitsui & Company's Yoshizo Ikeda was one of the business leaders; a Socialist representative accused Mitsui Sugar Company, which is virtually a subsidiary of the trading firm, of deliberately raising the water content of sugar from 0.8 percent to 1.1 percent to increase its weight.

Ikeda humbly promised to look into it. Other presidents, similarly accused, gave equally Japanese responses, apologizing or promising to give back excess profits. It was an extraordinary show—but just a show. Liberal Democratic politicians and the bureaucracy cannot crack down on the business interests that have bought and paid for them.

"Big business's public image has reached a new low" in recent years, comments *Mainichi Daily News,* and big business knows that it must reform. Mitsui's Ikeda seems to be leading the way, perhaps because during the Depression the trading company got into even worse disrepute and successfully managed to whitewash itself by creating the Mitsui Repayment of Kindness Association, modeled on the Carnegie and Rockefeller foundations and based on the concept that the company should repay the people and the nation for their role in its prosperity. The repayment association gave money for leprosariums, museums, schools, and the Kyoto botanical garden. Ikeda proposes more modern goals, such as antipollution measures. Echoing the repayment concept, he says that the idea of profit as the only goal of an enterprise has to be revised, and that it should return some of the profit to the society that enables it to do business. Other top businessmen speak similarly of the need for "reflection" on their goals, and even of amending their yes-in-principle-but-no-in-actuality approach to social welfare. For that matter, Japanese businessmen have always been conscientious about guaranteed employment and their duty to the greatness of Japan. But profits are sacred, too.

In Kure, on island-dotted Hiroshima Bay, I went aboard the 476,492-ton *Globtik London,* which vied with its twin *Globtik Tokyo* as world's biggest vessel until mid-1975, when Kure topped itself with a tanker 7,885 tons bigger. Kure Shipyard is run by Ishikawa-jima-Harima Heavy Industries Company, a Mitsui Group affiliate.

Globtik London's size makes the brain disbelieve what the eye sees. Upended, its 1,340-foot hull would rise nearly as high as Chicago's Sears Building. From the bridge the forecastle, a fifth of a mile away, seems like an outlying village. Strolling from stem to stern took me eleven minutes. The thought crossed my mind that the ship could use a highway and a few automobiles, perhaps a small bus line. From keel to top of wheelhouse the ship's elevator makes stops on twelve decks. These ships are the biggest movable objects ever made— and their movements are controlled by steering wheels no larger than that of an ordinary truck. Ishikawajima-Harima Heavy Industries puts these big tankers together in a mere ten months.

The "tik" in *Globtik* stands for the little-known Kashmiri ship-owner Ravi Tikkoo, who first went to sea as a sublieutenant in the Indian navy at twenty-one and now, two decades later, rivals the fabled Greeks, Onassis and Niarchos. He operates out of London, built both ships to the standards of the British Department of Transport and Industry, mans them with English crews, and home-ports them in London, even though neither could enter the Thames without running aground. In fact, these mammoths, drawing 92 feet loaded, could not enter most of the ports of the world, or transit either the Suez or the Panama Canal, which have a 38-foot limit. But no matter: they are built to go nowhere else but back and forth between Kharg Island, the Iranian crude-oil loading port in the Persian Gulf, and Kiire, the discharging port in southern Kyushu, all for the account of Tokyo Tanker Company, a charterer.

Even before the Suez Canal was closed in 1967, Japan, more than any other nation, was ready to build the world's supertankers, because the shrewd Japanese oil tycoon Sazo Idemitsu had perceived the economies of size in big tankers. Ishikawajima-Harima has regularly been the builder of whatever tanker was biggest, and not only has drawn up plans for a 700,000-tonner but is quite ready to take on a ship of a million tons. Other nations did not even have docks big enough to build 100,000-ton ships until the mid-1960s; to this day the biggest ship ever built on the west coast of the United States measures only 80,500 tons. This train of events made Japan into far and away the world's most prolific shipbuilder.

Once, before I came to know Mitsui better, I asked a Mitsui Trust man why the group had no automaker, such as Mitsubishi Heavy Industries' automotive division, which makes the Dodge Colt. "Aha!" he replied. "We have Toyota!" Indeed, the huge Toyota Motor Company is a Mitsui semi-affiliate that may soon join the Second Thursday Club.

Japanese cars are so common all over the world nowadays that it takes an effort to recall that the industry really got going less than ten years ago—certainly one of the swiftest business expansions on record. Before 1966, the industry concentrated first on trucks needed for postwar reconstruction, and then on motorcycles or four-wheeled vehicles almost too small and flimsy to be called cars ("Buy two, one for each foot," the Japanese joked). That year, Japanese automakers realized with a shock that the average Japanese was becoming affluent enough to want a real car, that the highway system, overhauled for the 1964 Olympics, invited a boom in pleasure driving, and that the worldwide free-trade trend might eliminate the tariffs that kept out foreign cars. Up went giant new factories. Production rose from 810,000 in 1961 to 7,083,000 in 1973, and the mix shifted to three passenger cars out of every five vehicles manufactured. The vehicle population passed 10,000,000 in 1967 and stands now at 28,000,000, half of them trucks. For comparison, the United States has 118,000,000, and the whole vast expanse of the Soviet Union only 3,000,000. In density of cars, Japan has the world's highest, with twice as many per square mile as the Netherlands and ten times as many as the United States. The biggest automaker in the world, General Motors, normally produces about 6,500,000 a year; next comes Ford, with about 3,500,000. Nos. 3 and 4 are both Japanese: Toyota and Nissan Motor Company, builder of what is known outside Japan as the Datsun. Japan with its 7,000,000-a-year production is outranked only by the United States' 12,000,000 in a good year (West Germany turns out about 4,000,000, France 3,600,000, Britain 2,200,000, and Italy 2,000,000).

At Toyota's quarter-mile-long Takaoka plant, set among rice paddies twenty miles east of Nagoya, I watched Toyotas of mixed colors and specifications move at the rate of one a minute along a quiet and unfrantic computer-controlled assembly line, acquiring engines, wheels, seats, and even some gasoline in the tank. They arrived at the end with only one part missing—whereupon a nimble man reached into a parts box, picked up a steering wheel, hopped into the car (either on the right side or the left, depending on whether the car was for domestic sale or for export), bolted the wheel to the steering column, started the engine, and whipped the newborn auto over to the testing racks. The assembly line resembles assembly lines elsewhere, but at the end of my tour I got a reminder that I was still in Japan. Near the exit, on a tasteful pedestal, stood a lovely bowl of chrysanthemums.

23 / 🌿

The World's Second-Greatest Trading Nation

J APANESE FOREIGN TRADE boils down to this: Japan imports from elsewhere nearly all the raw materials and energy needed for its huge industrial machine. By adding the value of Japanese labor and brains to these raw materials, the machine raises their value to ten times what it was. Japan keeps nine-tenths of the finished products for its own use, and exports the other tenth to get money to buy the raw materials. Businessmen elsewhere may think of the Japanese as fiercely competitive exporters, but the Japanese think of themselves as desperately hungry importers. "We don't export for export's sake," a Japanese exporter of textiles told me. "Our exports increase only because our purchases of foreign goods continually increase."

Japan's exports, concentrated in highly visible lines—cars, steel, electronics, optics—are known to every last Oklahoman, Bolivian, German, Pole, and even Nigerian. But taken as a share of gross national product, Japan exports less (9.8 percent) than France (12.3), the United Kingdom (16.6), West Germany (18.8), Canada (20.6), Norway (22), or Belgium-Luxembourg (44.4)—less, in fact, than any major nation except the United States (4.4) and the Soviet Union. Japan is far less dependent on exports than it was in the 1930s, when as much as 40 percent of its gross national product was sent abroad, most memorably to Westerners as cheap toys, but mainly in the form of five-cents-a-yard textiles for the rest of Asia. Now the stress is on selling at home. "The size of the Japanese internal market is huge," one Tokyo economics reporter pointed out to me. "Many producers are totally uninterested in exporting to the United States." The Japanese are just as ardent in consuming the things that they also sell abroad—hi-fi sets, cameras, watches, cars—as their foreign customers are.

Japan imports all its petroleum, uranium, nickel ore, and aluminum ore; nine-tenths of its copper ore and iron ore; three-fourths of its natural gas; half of its lead and zinc.

Yet even though the proportion of Japan's foreign trade is small compared to the whole economy, the whole economy is so big that in absolute terms Japan is the world's second-greatest trading nation. This distinction comes in good part from the fact that it trades so much with the world's greatest trading nation, the United States. Japan is the United States' best customer, and the United States is Japan's biggest supplier. In 1973, for example, the United States bought one-fourth of what Japan exported and sold one-fourth of what Japan imported. No other nation is even close in either category.

Obviously this trade vastly benefits both countries, but it is too huge to be carried on without acrimony and belligerence over the terms and imbalances. At the bottom of Japanese-American trade conflict lies a paradox. To Japan, the United States is largely a raw-materials supplier, like various backward countries in Latin America or Africa. From the United States, Japan every year gets about $4 billion worth of grain, tobacco, soybeans, raw cotton, and coal. Huge amounts of timber, not sawed lumber but softwood logs, cross the Pacific to Japan from the ports of the American Northwest (sometimes to be sent back in the form of manufactured plywood). Three out of every five bushels of wheat grown in Montana go to Japan, the state's best cash customer. Of their own cattle, Japanese farmers joke that three legs of every animal are American, since the cows eat so much imported feed. That enormously popular Japanese dish, tofu, comes mostly from American soybeans, which rate as tastier than those from China. Something like two-fifths of American exports to Japan, it is true, are manufactured goods: sophisticated machinery, office machinery, medical items, prefabricated houses, enriched uranium, and (importantly) airliners—for lack of sufficient internal market, Japan has not been able to organize a big jet-aircraft industry. Only 3 percent of American exports are consumer goods: large television sets and refrigerators such as are not made in Japan, Tupperware, Instamatic and Polaroid cameras. In sum, the United States shares with Japan a great quantity of the products of American farms and forests and mines.

Japan's exports to the United States, on the other hand, are such as befits a modern industrial nation. Americans have become comfortably familiar with the names Hitachi, Datsun, Kawasaki, Mazda, Suzuki, Sanyo, Shiseido, Toyota, Panasonic, Subaru, Nikon, Sony,

Pentax, Yamaha, Canon, Noritake, Honda, Daiwa, Pioneer, Brother, Seiko, Olympus, Ricoh. If the basic lubricant of the American export trade to Japan has been Japan's fierce hunger for American raw materials and food, the basic incentive in the Japanese export trade to the United States has been the enlightened American commitment to free trade, meaning low tariffs and few restrictions. Thus arises the troublemaking equation that while American exports to Japan fill needs for goods not to be had there, Japan's exports to the United States compete hard with American automobiles, electronics, optical goods, textiles, motorcycles, and steel—things Americans used to like to think they were good at.

The cumulative effect of cunning and aggressive selling was to quadruple Japanese exports to the United States between 1964 and 1971. So swiftly did Toyota and Datsun both surpass Volkswagen as the leading imported car in America that the Japanese had to make a strenuous effort to build special car-carrier ships. They thereupon designed vessels that could cram in as many as six thousand cars, with roll-on, roll-off loading so efficient that a car could be moved from a dock in Japan to a dock in California for only $150 (as compared to $450 to take a car to Japan in a container). Datsun quickly grabbed the lead in sports-car sales away from Britain's MG.

This pattern of trade—the United States supplying much-needed food and other basics to Japan in return for a flood of competitive manufactures—created conflicts of three kinds.

First, many American firms went out of business, and others had to cut production. The International Brotherhood of Electrical Workers claimed that Japanese competition cost the union fifty thousand jobs. Understandably, the victims objected.

Second, Japan, more than any other nation, caused the big American trade deficits of the early 1970s. Of the $6.3 billion gap in 1972, trade with Japan accounted for $4.3 billion.

Third, the United States often withholds some commodity customarily exported to Japan, which makes the Japanese jumpy. Japan wants more American timber to build four million houses, but Oregon politicians say that Oregon's own mills should get its logs, and environmentalists all over the Northwest think the forests are being overcut. The American soybean embargo of mid-1973, though quickly canceled and ultimately meaningless (Japan got more American soybeans in 1973 than in any previous year), called forth calamity-crying headlines and complaints in Japan that the United States did not care—or perhaps even know—about Japan's dependence on this food.

In response to the tension caused by moving in on markets too fast and too hard, the Japanese yielded by devising the concept of "orderly marketing"—meaning holding sales down far enough to keep the United States and other trading partners from becoming too angry. The Japanese, says Kasuji Nagasu, professor of economics at Yokohama University, had not been "aware that Japanese exports could cause serious damage even in a country as large as the United States." Orderly marketing works partly through unabashed cartels, around two hundred of them, that assign maximum export quotas to all the manufacturers in a given industry. It is also achieved through "administrative guidance" (a euphemism meaning "orders") from the Ministry of International Trade and Industry. Orderly marketing is a practical idea, a realistic recognition that Japan cannot take over all markets everywhere.

Having made this concession, the Japanese feel entitled to taunt American competitors with the questions, "Why don't you people work harder?" "Why don't you sell more to Japan?" A small-town Japanese metalware manufacturer, visiting a Cleveland counterpart a few years ago, remarked flatly, "Japanese industries would go broke if they operated the way you do." Japanese textile men taken to South Carolina to be taught how badly their competition was hurting coldly noted that the American looms had been made way back in 1942. One Japanese airily speculated that the United States might begin to catch up with Japan "when Americans work six days a week and the Japanese work five." These men feel that it is unfair for Americans to ask the Japanese to be less productive in order for Americans to compete with them more equally.

As for selling to Japan, Japanese businessmen accuse Americans of scarcely knowing that the market exists, much less how to cater to it. Americans still look to China as the big ultimate Asian market, but "Japan, and not China, represents purchasing power with the dollars for American imports," says Keizo Saji, chairman of the board of Suntory Ltd. One reason Americans sold only 10,813 cars to Japan in 1973, while Japan was selling a million to the United States, is that American automakers supply cars too big for narrow Japanese streets, and fail to provide them with right-hand drive. Oregon could sell finished lumber rather than logs to Japan if mills would cut it to centimeter sizes—Japanese carpenters don't know what to do with a two-by-four. The Japan External Trade Organization, which for so long pressured the world to buy Japanese goods, now tries to smooth the way for the world to sell to Japan. One of JETRO's baby-talk booklets, *The Japanese Consumer*, points out, for example, that the electric-blanket market is wide open, but that the American maker must not forget one simple thing: to adapt to Japanese voltage, which is 100, not 110.

There is much justification for the Japanese charges, as United States Steel confirms by its advertisements arguing for higher American productivity. Comparing the quality of American and Japanese color television, one is tempted to agree with *New York Times* columnist Russell Baker's speculation that good old American know-how has changed its address to Japan. *Fortune* calls the attitude of American exporters "defeatist." The U.S. Embassy in Tokyo finds that American businessmen fail to come into Japan with the same competitive drive the Japanese show in American markets, and that they are too prone to blame their troubles on the many-level Japanese wholesaling system and on government red tape. In sum, Americans in Japan are often unimaginative, sometimes careless in fulfilling contracts, and perhaps a bit lazy.

Since, as Zbigniew Brzezinski notes, Japanese trade concessions have always been "made so gracelessly that they cease to look like concessions and begin to look like extortion," the "Nixon shock" brought about by the devaluation of the dollar in 1971 was from one point of view justified. But it was the most overt act of trade bludgeoning in recent years. Senator Mike Mansfield was led to speak out against using "devil-take-the-hindmost politics" toward Japan. The point here is that trade friction can dangerously injure American-Japanese relations, and that the right principles to follow in reducing friction are free trade and international division of labor. Further "shocks" from Washington, tempting as they might be in the light of the occasional obtuseness of the Japanese, would not reach to the heart of the matter, which is that each country should produce what it produces best, and exchange it freely for what the other produces best.

Trading in other directions—with its Asian neighbors, with Europe, and with the oil countries of the Middle East—Japan encounters in differing proportions the same mixture of welcome and suspicion. Like the United States, East Asia (not including China) takes about a quarter of Japan's exports. Indonesia, for example, sells Japan a billion dollars' worth of crude oil a year, receiving in return so many Japanese clocks, clothes, vitamins, and appliances that one Djakarta editor says of the typical local citizen, "The only Indonesian product in his home is his wife."

In the 1960s, using "kowtow diplomacy," in which Japanese businessmen dutifully denounced supposed Japanese "militarism" and got purchase orders from the Chinese in return, Japan took Russia's place as China's main trading partner. The trade has grown steadily since, with a particular boost after the two nations resumed relations in 1972, at which time Prime Minister Tanaka specifically promised that Japan would not act like an "economic animal" toward China. Now the trade runs to a two-way total of over $3 billion, even though it is still in its infancy and hobbled by government restrictions—for example, the Chinese are reluctant to buy or sell on credit. Until lately, Japan sent mostly petrochemical fertilizer and machinery, and got back soybeans and raw silk. Now some observers foresee a spectacularly amplified trade in which Japan will supply China with technology, manufactures, consumer goods, and a big steel plant, and in return receive oil, oil for the lamps of Japan.

China's exports of petroleum to Japan have already jumped sharply, because China has made itself more than self-sufficient by bringing in rich oil fields at Taching in Manchuria, Shengli on the Shantung Peninsula, and Takang on the Gulf of Pohai, all within a few hundred miles of Peking. Production reached 350 million barrels in 1973, about a tenth as much as the United States produces, though still equal to only about a fifth of what Japan consumes. As output grows, Japan plans to ask China for 70 million barrels a year by 1978. Chinese oil is low in sulfur—just what Japan wants. As with oil, China may also come to supply Japan with iron ore, at low freight costs. "It could be one of our biggest sources," a Japanese shipping man told me.

A British reader wrote to the London *Daily Telegraph*: "I went shopping for a new car. Not a single agent, for any make of British car, was able to give me any idea of a delivery date for the car I had chosen. The local agent for one make of Japanese cars offered immediate delivery—colour to choice. Needless to say, I now own, for the first time, a Japanese car."

Comments such as this on the ubiquity and quality of Japanese products in Western Europe reflect a prevalent impression, peculiarly combined with panic, that Japan is seizing Europe's markets. It's as though some part of the world is doomed to take a beating from Japan's export drive, now that the United States no longer seems willing to asborb so much, and therefore the gnomes of Tokyo have turned to their next victim. In fact, then Secretary of the Treasury John Connally in 1971 startled a group of European bankers by charging that their efforts to shut out Japanese goods had forced Japan to concentrate on the United States in the first place. "Let's face it. Japan is a headache for all the major nations of the world," a Common Market official agreed. Up against Japan's cheap and excellent Nikons, Pentaxes, Minoltas, and other cameras, such lordly German brand names as Zeiss, Compur, and Voightlander had to merge around Rollei Werke and move their manufacturing to the lower-wage country of Singapore. As the men at JETRO coolly commented, "The Germans were resting on their laurels."

At noon on a sweltering day in Tokyo, the blessed coolness of the Ginza subway station comes from air conditioning that comes from electricity that comes from generators fired by oil that comes from countries mostly as hot as noon on a sweltering day in Tokyo. For its energy, used either as a luxury or as a bedrock necessity, Japan has shaped itself since World War II as the country most desperately dependent on imported oil. Of the oil used in Japan, only one barrel in two hundred comes from Japan (the fields are on the Sea of Japan coast in northern Honshu). Oil, pending the development of other, home-supplied sources of energy, is what Japan would go to war for. (Part of the rationale for Japan's attack on Pearl Harbor was that it had to secure the oil of the Dutch East Indies.) Importing five million barrels of oil a day, 30 percent each from Iran and the Arabian peninsula and 20 percent from Indonesia, Japan suffers from what John K. Emmerson, former U.S. minister in Tokyo, calls "involuntary servitude to geography."

Japan was so indifferent to Middle Eastern politics and diplomacy ten years ago that on a famous occasion the foreign minister fell into a deep slumber while formally receiving the prime minister of Kuwait. In the early Arab-Israeli wars, Japan was solemnly "neutral." The oil crisis of late 1973, touched off by the October war, panicked Japan into a me-first stance. After the *Kuwait Times* accused Japan of keeping a "strange silence" over the war, Takeo Miki, at that time deputy prime minister, and MITI minister Yasuhiro Nakasone roamed the Middle East, promising loans and aid in establishing refineries and petrochemical industries. Did Saudi Arabia want a truck-building plant? Nissan (the Datsun maker) would be glad to supply it. Miki pronounced that "justice is on the side of the Arabs." Japan called upon Israel (whose trade with Japan is too unimportant to bother listing in the Bureau of Statistics monthly report) to withdraw from occupied territories, although at the same time the Japanese foreign minister worried about placating American Jews, who handle almost all the brokerage services required by American imports from Japan. When Henry Kissinger urged Japan to join the United States and Europe in confronting the Arabs, Japan reserved the right to carry out bilateral agreements with oil-producing nations. As a result, the Arabs classified Japan as "friendly," and soon every tank in Japan was brimming with oil. On form, if some kind of consumers' cartel to restrain oil prices becomes necessary to halt world inflation, Japan will be too self-centered to join, even though by then the price of energy may be too high to permit the air conditioning of the Ginza subway station.

British capital built American railroads in the nineteenth century, American capital built automotive plants all over the world in the twentieth century, and now Japanese capital is building a zipper factory in Macon, Georgia. Such a Japanese foreign investment as Benihana of Tokyo, a chain of restaurants in American cities, is so successful that it has opened an outlet in Tokyo called Benihana of New York. The trend has gone so far that a cartoon in *Punch* shows a Japanese businessman viewing his English factory from a tatami-floored office and saying into his telephone, "Most honourable Mr. Furnaceman, would you get your esteemed finger out and restore the smoke from number two chimney to the harmonious pattern of the other seven!"

Japanese capital began to move out into the world strongly only in 1968, with Japan's first postwar surpluses in its balance of trade. After running under $1 billion a year for several years, the flow surged to $2.3 billion in 1972, after revaluation of the yen, and $3.2 billion in 1973. That put Japan's overseas investments, now more than $10 billion, ahead of France's and West Germany's, though far less than Britain's ($22 billion) or the United States' ($86 billion). In 1974 Japan surpassed all other nations in investments in the United States, the Georgia zipper factory being only a small sample. For a while, bankers guessed that Japan's foreign investments might grow to $25 or $30 billion by 1980, but in 1974 the high price of oil reduced balance-of-trade surpluses and forced the Bank of Japan to rein in the outflow of capital. The brief concern that Japan would "buy up the whole world" subsided (to be replaced by fears that the oil-exporting countries would do the same thing).

The motivations behind Japan's foreign investments have been to secure and develop sources of raw materials for itself, to find cheaper labor and plant sites, to "export pollution," to overcome tariffs and other restrictions on its exports by manufacturing within a foreign country while still taking out the profits, and to cut down on its surpluses of foreign exchange.

Until recently the major impulse of Japanese investment has been to assure supplies such as Philippine copper, Brazilian minerals, and Australian cattle. But as labor at home grew costlier, Japanese manufacturers also began to move plants to nearby countries—"transferring industry to labor-intensive areas," in the jargon of the economists. "That means 'finding sweatshops abroad,'" one sour Filipino businessman told me. Even as Americans complained that Japan was flooding the United States with textiles, Japanese textile makers were carrying on the "creative destruction" of their industry that made Japan a net importer of silk textiles in the 1960s and cotton textiles in the early 1970s, and will probably make it a net importer of synthetic textiles in the late 1970s.

The magisterial think-tanker Herman Kahn argues that "the Japanese have a hinterland in non-Communist Pacific Asia of possibly 200 or 300 million people, many of whom they will simply incorporate, by one device or another, into their economic superstate even while not moving them geographically. In effect, rather than importing labor into Japan . . . the Japanese will export the work." In Korea, where Japan and the United States (oil companies, chiefly) vie as the biggest investors, hundreds of little Japanese-owned factories produce plastics, textiles, electronics, and other labor-intensive goods, often under supervision of bosses from Japan's big Korean community. "Korea's best resource is its literate population—people who are dexterous, have marvelous eyesight, and can learn a job fast," a Korean newsman boasted to me. Korea also has cheap land—such a factory as a dust-creating cement plant can find a large site there.

In Australia, one frequently hears the fear expressed that Japanese investments will make Australia into "Japan's other island" or, more pointedly, into "Japan's Canada" (a reference to the domination of Canada by American capital). "Beware the superjap," say some Australians. In point of fact, Japanese investment so far amounts to only $338 million. It consists, typically, of part ownership of Queensland coal mines that send their product to Japan, and the motivation is to assure Japan of stable supplies. Now, however, five Japanese companies, led by Nippon Steel, have joined with Australia's huge Broken Hill Proprietary Company, Australia's Pilbara Iron Limited, Great Britain's British Steel Corporation, and the United States' Jones and Laughlin Steel Corporation in a venture that plans to invest $1.3 billion in a steel plant in western Australia.

The American market remains the richest in the world, and any capitalist who wants a large share of it must sooner or later move into it physically, in the form of factories and distribution systems—there are political limits to the inroads that can be made with exports. Of the $6.8 billion in Japanese investments in the United States predicted for 1980, the Boston Consulting Group foresees that $2.7 billion will be in "export-substitution" industries which thus dodge tariffs and quotas, and also help to head off excessive imbalances of trade and charges (like those made by American garment workers) of depriving Americans of jobs.

Sony Corporation of America, with fifteen hundred employees (97 percent of them American) and plants in San Diego producing hundreds of thousands of color TV sets and Trinitron picture tubes every year, is an example. Another is Mitsubishi Aircraft International, of San Angelo, Texas. At a decommissioned air force base where bombardiers during World War II trained to blast Tokyo, MAI builds—in competition with Cessna and Beechcraft—the sweet swift MU-2, a propjet favored by American corporate executives as the company airplane. One of the biggest Japanese investments was Matsushita Electrical Industrial Company's 1973 purchase of the television branch of Motorola Inc., a deal that gave Matsushita three plants in the United States and one in Canada.

Is Hawaii the fiftieth state—or the forty-eighth prefecture? Whatever it is, Japanese investors own around $350 million worth of it. One flamboyant Japanese tycoon, Kenji Osano, owns most of the hotels in Waikiki. Land and property in the United States seem absurdly cheap compared to Japan, and two other states besides Hawaii have attracted hundreds of millions of dollars in Japanese investments. In California, Osano owns San Francisco's Sheraton-Palace Hotel, where Warren Harding died, and Los Angeles' Sheraton-West. In Alaska, Japanese interests virtually own the town of Sitka, near Juneau, where their Alaska Lumber & Pulp Company produces the raw materials for film and paper, and the spruce sounding boards used in Japanese pianos. The Japanese have fishery bases at Anchorage and Cordova, buy quantities of natural gas, and would dearly like to get some Alaskan oil when the pipeline is finished.

Whipped up by the yen revaluation that Nixon forced on Japan in 1971, Japanese investment in the United States already surpasses the slowly accumulated American investment in Japan, now about $2 billion. Back in Occupation times, General MacArthur favored keeping foreign capital out of Japan, fearing backlash if his regime should appear to be an economic colonization of Japan. Nevertheless, some foreign capital moved in. The major international oil companies got a strong foothold in Japan at war's end because Japan recognized that they controlled the world's petroleum and Japan had to have it. Caltex, Esso, and Mobil Oil grabbed the lion's share, but Japanese companies later managed to muscle in for about a third of the market. Also moving in early, with brilliant foresight, was Coca-Cola (Japan) Company. Helped by the example of Coke-swilling American GIs, it "totally smashed small-sized Japanese soft drink manufacturers," as *Mainichi Daily News* put it. Coca-Cola regularly appears at or near the top of the Tax Administration Agency's list of most profitable corporations. International Business Machines, which first came to Japan as a supplier for the Japanese National Railways in 1923, picked up again after the war because MITI economic planners foresaw that Japan would need computer technology as much as it would need oil. Later the government excluded computer imports and investments by other foreign computer companies. But IBM Japan, manufacturing within the country, dominated the market even after a home-grown computer industry got going.

The sensation of foreign business domination, so palpable in Latin America, Southeast Asia, and even Europe, is virtually missing in Japan. Before the war, it was said that the Tokyo manager of First National City Bank outranked the American ambassador in importance in Japan. Now the Bank of Japan supervises foreign-owned banks as rigorously as it does the domestic ones. One American banker described for me how the Bank of Japan issues "verbal guidelines— nothing written, nothing explained" that left him feeling "like a baby asking for candy from a firm, fatherly government." He complained that Japanese bankers in the United States are much freer, but then added: "There's no way that I can lose money. The government sees to that. The host treats the guest well." In fact, the present generation of foreign executives in Japan may be the last, for many big foreign companies are coming around to doing what the Japanese all along thought they should do: hire a Japanese for the job. Coca-Cola (Japan), IBM Japan, and Esso Standard Sekiyu K.K. (Japan's Exxon) all have Japanese presidents.

For years, liberalization of foreign investment in Japan inched along by ridiculous steps, opening up, for example, the ice-making industry or the mashed-potato industry. Now, by law, foreign capital can enter Japan as freely as Japanese capital enters the United States, except in the primary areas of agriculture, forestry, and fishing. Japanese industry will henceforth have to compete for its own home market. But though it may fade away, Japan, Inc., which in one sense represents an intransigent idea that foreigners should not be allowed to compete in Japan simply because they do not know the rules of the business–government game, will certainly not die at once. And any foreigners who move in now face mature and formidable Japanese competition.

One Japanese writer says that the pressures that finally forced this reopening of Japan (some Japanese businessmen call it "the return of the black ships") were Mr. Kakuei Tanaka, Mr. Strong Yen, and Mr. Multinational Corporation. Opening its own investment potential to the world's multinationals puts Japan on solid grounds for expanding some of its own corporations into multinationals. And this may be a good thing. By and large, the world's multinationals seem no less rapacious than national corporations, but they provide mechanisms for overcoming some problems that are becoming increasingly serious for Japan. Multinationals are, in effect, companies without a country. They do not have to bring profits "home." They can move capital freely, and produce their goods wherever it is most efficient to produce them. Thus they can build factories where the raw material is or where the market is, and in both places reinvest their profits. For Japan, this flexibility coincides with the fact that it has reached clear limits as an island workshop: its raw-materials suppliers growingly resent having no part in processing what they supply, and its foreign buyers keep up their guard against being flooded by Japanese goods. The multinational formula lets Japan ease tensions by sharing jobs—management jobs as well as factory jobs.

Matsushita, already manufacturing in twenty countries; Sony, with plants in Brazil as well as the United States; Hitachi, Nippon Electric, Toray Industries—these forerunners of Japanese multinationals suggest what is bound to become a powerful trend. Their meaning is that Japanese business does not intend to hog it all for Japan, and since trade and investment remain preferable to a state of war, that should be a relief to many nations.

24 / 中日

Tokyo, Peking, Moscow, and Washington

ON AN EXPRESS TRAIN bound westward from Tokyo to Shimonoseki, one July day in 1918, a bored passenger tried to strike up a conversation with a youth of twenty sitting opposite him. The attempt immediately hit a snag—the lad was Chinese, and spoke Japanese badly. But the boy was friendly, and offered to speak in English; they settled for a conversation in Japanese written in Chinese characters, on the subject of Chinese literature. And the youth gave his new-found Japanese friend a visiting card. The name on it was: Chou En-lai.

The present premier of China spent a year and a half in Japan, living frugally in a nine-by-nine-foot room in Tokyo, eating fish and bean curd, and attending Waseda and Hosei universities. The episode symbolizes the intimate intertwining of Japan and China against a two-thousand-year shared history, full of both affinity and bitterness, that brings to mind Rome and Greece. Nowadays these two nations, one the second-greatest international economic power and the other the world's most populous and geographically the third-largest, loom in a fascinating tandem over the western Pacific. Of this long-troubled yet highly magnetic relationship, Japan's Prime Minister Takeo Miki says: "Stability in the Pacific area cannot be achieved until lasting friendly relations are established between Japan and China, in the same way that stability cannot be expected in Europe without lasting friendly relations between France and Germany." In 1972, Japanese diplomacy, coming to life after twenty-six years in limbo, renewed official relations with China. In the long light of history, this was a truly momentous event.

The first Japanese culture-seeker visited China in 57 A.D., and the Han Dynasty rulers sent back gold seals as China's opening gift in what turned out to be nine centuries of mostly eastward cultural flow. Even during Japan's period of seclusion under the Tokugawa shoguns, China and Japan continued a trickle of trade through Nagasaki and Okinawa. But with the Meiji Restoration, Japan, hell-bent on matching Western prowess, turned scornful of its continental mentor, which had disgraced itself in defeats at the hands of the British and French and by submission to the opium trade. Contemptuously, Japan snipped off bits of China for itself. In conquered Taiwan, the Japanese banned foot-binding and pigtails as loathsome Chinese customs. Humbled, the Chinese in the early 1900s sent tens of thousands of students, like Chou En-lai, to study in Japan. Sun Yat-sen, the begetter of modern China, based himself in Tokyo for some years. Chiang Kai-shek studied at Tokyo's Military Academic College. In the 1920s and 1930s and during World War II, Japan continued to chew away at China, ultimately killing 15 million Chinese. Yet when the war ended, Chiang Kai-shek benevolently forgave the Japanese transgressions, and Mao Tse-tung's troops treated the defeated Japanese soldiers with a consideration much in contrast to the harsh handling they got from the Russians in Manchuria.

These gestures, followed by Mao's strong assertion of China's independence in 1949, revived Japan's ancient admiration for China. Many Japanese thought the American fear of Chinese Communism to be pathological; they were puzzled or amused by American resistance to the plain fact that Peking was the legitimate government of China. Pressed by the United States to help ring China with military power, Japan dragged its feet. The Japanese accepted China's explanation that its atomic bomb was a defensive response to the American and Russian nuclear threats. Japanese prime ministers silently shrugged off abusive Chinese propaganda. "The cultural attraction has been stronger than the political difference," Yashiharu Naya-Sen, the conservative and thoughtful president of a large Kyoto book-publishing firm, told me.

Long before the diplomatic thaw, influential Japanese politicians, businessmen, and intellectuals began visiting China to work for the restoration of relations. In recent decades Japanese tourists in China outnumbered those of any other nation; one of them, my Kyoto land-lord, the Reverend Kimura, related that in the late 1960s he went to Nanking on the 1100th anniversary of the death of Rinzai (the Chinese founder of Kimura's sect of Zen Buddhism) and while there prayed for forgiveness for the Japanese soldiers who took part in the notorious 1937 rape of the city. The Japanese also welcomed visiting

Chinese, and Japanese television comedies tactfully stopped portraying the Chinese as pig-tailed laundrymen. All the while, Japanese big business yearned to trade its industrial products for China's soybeans, minerals, and petroleum.

By 1972, after President Nixon visited Peking, Japan's desire for an opening with China grew overpowering, but Prime Minister Sato remained locked into his pro-Taiwan, anti-Communist policy. Takeo Miki, who had long since decided that Taiwan was "not qualified to represent China," went to Peking in April 1972 and brought back to Sato the message that the Chinese would not "normalize" while Sato held office. Sato obligingly if somewhat reluctantly made way for someone who could unfreeze Japan–China relations. In July 1972, Chou En-lai gladly invited Sato's successor, Kakuei Tanaka, to go to Peking to negotiate the reestablishment of diplomatic ties.

At the welcoming banquet, the orchestra played "Sado Okesa," a folk song of Niigata, Tanaka's birthplace prefecture. Toasting Tanaka, Chou En-lai took occasion to note that "owing to the Japanese militarists' aggression against China, the Chinese people were made to endure tremendous disasters," and added, "The past not forgotten is a guide for the future." Tanaka apologized: "Our country caused great trouble to the Chinese people, for which I once again make profound self-examination," and added, "We should not forever linger in the dim blind alley of the past." Later, Tanaka had a *mao tai* with Mao Tse-tung.

MAO: "You'd better not drink too much of that liquor."

TANAKA: "I know mao-tai is a rather strong drink. Sixty-five proof, isn't it?"

MAO: "No, no, who told you that? It's seventy-five proof."

Such is the small talk of the great.

Way back in 1951, according to the "never for public view" Foreign Ministry minutes (revealed by *Asahi Shimbun*) of a visit to Tokyo by John Foster Dulles, the American secretary of state had held Prime Minister Shigeru Yoshida's feet to the fire until Japan agreed to recognize only one China, Chiang Kai-shek's Nationalist government on Taiwan. The situation had become progressively unreal, and Tanaka realized it. At about the same moment when he and Chou brushed their signatures to the reconciliation agreement, Tanaka had the Foreign Ministry in Tokyo summon the Chinese Nationalist ambassador and break Japan's diplomatic relations with Taiwan. As Japan lowered the flag over its embassy in Taipei, eighty-five-year-old Chiang Kai-shek denounced Tanaka as a "short-sighted profiteer," and Taiwan television showed old clips of Japanese atrocities against the

Chinese during the war. Thus it came about that Japan's ultimate response to Dulles pressure was to leave Taiwan as Washington's hot potato, a problem to handle all alone.

Taiwan banana growers long gave $200,000 to $300,000 a year to buy the late Chiang Kai-shek the support of some right-wing members of the Japanese Diet, and these politicians bellowed their displeasure in a manner remindful of the old American "China lobby." Ignoring them, Japan and China proceeded to exchange ambassadors and news correspondents, put in fourteen telephone circuits, plan a new underseas communications cable, and set the Chinese yuan at 130 yen (about forty-three cents). Japan presented Chin Hua University in Peking with ten thousand books about Japan. In return, Liao Cheng-chih, the Waseda University-educated Chinese Foreign Ministry adviser who pressed hardest for the recognition of Japan, arrived in Tokyo in an Ilyushin 62 and gave Tanaka three pressed cherry leaves, four rolls of handwoven cloth, and six Chinese writing brushes. At the Sapporo Snow Festival in 1973, ice sculptors carved a huge replica of Peking's Gate of Heavenly Peace. The highest and most conservative Japanese businessmen went one after another to Peking, to be received attentively and gravely by Chou En-lai.

The only matter of political substance yet dealt with by Japan and China has been the negotiation of a civilian aviation agreement. To get Japan Air Lines into China was a top-priority goal of Tanaka's government. The importance lay not so much in Japan–China traffic, but in "fly on" rights—the rights each nation got to fly over the other to farther points in the world. Japan Air Lines thus acquired a promising route between Tokyo and London, with stops at Shanghai and Peking, some still-unchosen city in India, Teheran, some other point in the Middle East, and a choice of three points in Europe, including Paris. Civil Aviation Administration of China planes got a route to South America via Tokyo and Osaka, Vancouver, Ottawa, some point on the east coast of the United States, and Mexico. In the negotiations, China blandly demanded that Japan ask Taiwan to change the name of Taiwan's China Air Lines to something else, and stop using the Chinese flag as a marking on its planes. Japan compromised by pronouncing China Air Lines to be "nongovernmental." Insulted, orphaned, and furious, Taiwan cut air ties with Japan and forbade Japan Air Lines to fly anywhere near Taiwan, thus depriving JAL of its single most profitable route.

Ultimately, of course, Taiwan will probably again unite with mainland China—which should be interesting for Japan. Presumably the present huge trade between Japan and Taiwan will then continue under some pragmatic capitalist–Communist accommodation. The thought appalls the upper-crust Chinese mainlanders who moved to Taiwan with Chiang Kai-shek's Nationalist Chinese government-in-exile in 1949.

The view of Russia from Japan begins quite literally with the view from the easternmost point of Japan, Cape Nossapu, on the northern island of Hokkaido. Looking across three and a half miles of water, one can see Russian troops maneuvering on an islet that , is part of the dinky Habomai Islands. In fact, many thousands of Japanese tourists *do* see this spectacle, using the telescopes, maps, and models in the two-story concrete "Pavilion Overlooking the Homeland" that has been built for this purpose.

The Soviet Union seized the Habomais and the neighboring islands of Shikotan, Kunashiri, and Etorofu from Japan right after the bombing of Hiroshima in August 1945, on grounds that the Yalta Conference between Roosevelt, Churchill, and Stalin, earlier that year, had awarded "the Kuriles" to Russia. Soviet soldiers rounded up the sixteen thousand Japanese residents and packed them off to Nemuro, the nearest port in Hokkaido, where many still live, calling themselves displaced persons. But only Kunashiri and Etorofu are truly parts of the Kurile chain, which stretches from Hokkaido to Siberia's Kamchatka Peninsula. The Habomais and Shikotan had always been Japanese, administered as parts of Hokkaido Prefecture. Moreover, Japan had possessed and governed Kunashiri and Etorofu ever since 1855, when Russia gave up any claim to them in a treaty establishing rela tions between the two countries.

For thirty years now, Japan's demand for the return of these islands has prevented Japan and the Soviet Union from signing a peace treaty. The territory itself, though in total twice as big as Okinawa (that exemplar of a returned island), is not valuable, but the surrounding waters produce abundant salmon, cod, herring, and a particularly succulent seaweed. The Russians, who administer the islands from Sakhalin, a Siberian island that nearly touches the northern tip of Hokkaido, have run a veritable war on Japanese fishermen, firing on their vessels from helicopters, killing thirty-two men, and detaining more than twelve thousand while seizing thousands of their boats for sailing within the twelve-mile limit. Yet Japan wants these "northern territories" back chiefly for reasons of nationalism. No politician dares propose abandoning them, even if the supposed "national consensus" favoring their return has nowhere near the steam behind it that recovering Okinawa had.

The Russians hold on to the islands because they fear that changing any border settled by World War II would open the door to changing many of them, specifically parts of its border with China along the Ussuri River near Vladivostok. They also point out that if Japan gets the Kuriles, it gets almost total control of the sea approaches to the coast of Siberia; even as things stand, most Russian ships sailing from Vladivostok go through the narrow Tsugaru Strait between Honshu and Hokkaido, or through the Korea Strait within sight of Japan. Nevertheless, when the Soviet Union in 1956 signed the Joint Declaration with Japan that reestablished diplomatic relations, the Russians offered to promise to return the Habomais and Shikotan whenever the two nations got around to making a peace treaty. Japan, determined to get Kunashiri and Etorofu too, rejected the offer.

As this sour scenario suggests, the Japanese don't much like Russians, or vice versa. "We have to be afraid of the Russians," one foreign ministry official told me. "They have the strength, and they are close."

The equally realistic Russians find themselves forced to admire, and covet, Japanese technology and money. For between the Japanese islands and European Russia lies that stubborn, frigid, balky, but wealthy expanse called Siberia, which must presently be developed as one of the world's great natural resources. It ties naturally to Japan; the distance from Tokyo to Khabarovsk, the major city of eastern Siberia, is only one-sixth as great as the distance from Moscow to Khabarovsk. Already the Siberian and Japanese economies are linked to some degree; an impressive sight on the Trans-Siberian Railroad is the frequent passage of eastbound trains of tank cars carrying Russian petroleum destined for Japan. But to both the Japanese and the Russians, it is clear that the link could be much tighter. Like the United States in Alaska, Russia possesses, in cold storage as it were, a vast supply of buried mineral energy in Yakutia, the northeastern quadrant of Siberia. Far to the west, but still east of the Urals, Russia has the ten-year-old Tyumen oil fields, which for Japan represent an important possibility for diversifying its sources of imported energy. To open up Siberia in a hurry, the Russians urgently need Japanese capital, steel, and technology.

The possibilities of a bargain—balancing the Soviet Union's need for Siberian development against Japan's aspiration for the return of its islands—inspired Prime Minister Tanaka to go to Moscow in October 1973 and dicker with Communist Party secretary Leonid Brezhnev. But a couple of days before he arrived, the fourth Middle

Eastern war began, threatening Japan's supply of oil from the area. Brezhnev decided he could negotiate Siberian collaboration without any concessions over the two Kurile islands of Kunashiri and Etorofu. He unrolled a map and hinted that the Russians might return the Habomais and Shikotan, which count as two in the Japanese-Russian dialogue. Silently, Tanaka raised his hand with four fingers extended, meaning that he wanted Kunashiri and Etorofu too. Replied Brezhnev, "No matter how dictatorial you are, Tanaka, that's impossible." Said Tanaka later: "Being called a dictator in the Kremlin was not quite what I expected." When the Japanese group gave a luncheon for Brezhnev in response to a Kremlin banquet for Tanaka, the Soviet leader failed to appear. Still, Tanaka did advance the Japanese claim to the four islands by a vital inch or two. *Pravda* printed his speech referring to Japan's claims, thus violating the Russian position that the islands are a "non-issue." And the Russians agreed to "continue" talking about the islands. Ultimately, one side or the other will have to retreat.

When Japan looks west toward China and Russia, it gets daughterly cultural vibrations from the first and let's-do-business-with-the-enemy vibrations from the second. But when Japan tries to combine these reactions in a triangular diplomacy, it finds that any friendly gesture toward one of the two Communist enemies seems to the other like an act of hostility. When Tanaka reopened Japan's relations with China, Russia took the move as Japan's threat to side with China if Russia did not return the northern islands. With effective diplomacy, the Japanese soothed the Russians so thoroughly that the Russians got serious about negotiating the development of Siberia. Chou En-lai warned visiting Japanese businessmen that the Russians were sure to break their promises on delivery of gas and oil. Moscow's *New Times* answered that the Peking leaders want "to push Japan into a one-sided orientation on China, and at the same time drive a wedge into Soviet-Japanese relations, to hamper the process of their improvement."

As things stand, the Chinese are outwitting the Russians in maneuvers to gain Japan's favor. Several years ago, the Russians proposed a joint Soviet-Japanese venture to build a pipeline from the Tyumen oil fields to Vladivostok. This alarmed the Chinese, who perceived that the pipeline could carry fuel to Red Army troops stationed along the border. Before Japan could make up its mind whether to risk offending China by throwing in with such a plan, the Russians frightened the Chinese even more by deciding to build a second Trans-Siberian railroad instead of a pipeline (the oil would be transported in huge, 180-ton tank cars). Already under construction, to be completed in the 1980s, this line will run from Lake Baikal to the Pacific parallel to and several hundred miles north of the present railroad, which follows the Mongolian and Manchurian borders. A fast, large-capacity rail link to Europe carrying containerized cargo could be an asset for Japanese exporters, but it will be less efficient than a pipeline for transporting oil eastward, and militarily it threatens China (and Japan) by making Red Army troop movements easier.

Taking advantage of Japan's discontent with the railroad project, the Chinese quickly offered to let the Japanese share China's new oil production. It now seems that Japan will not participate in any venture aimed at getting more Tyumen oil to Japan. But the other proposed Japanese-Russian joint effort, the development of Yakutia, is prospering. Japan has agreed to lend $1 billion to finance Japanese-built equipment to mine and ship Yakutia coking coal to be used in Japanese blast furnaces, drill for Yakutia natural gas and transport it to Japan, and develop Yakutia lumber and pulp production. In sum, the Chinese believe, probably correctly, that they have headed off a Japanese-Russian economic collaboration that was tantamount to a Russian bear hug on Japan, a virtual alliance against China.

The corpus of Japanese-American relations is "like that of a perfectly healthy person with a predilection for allergies, boils, and skin irritations," an American diplomat in Tokyo told me. "Our relations are better than perceived, after twenty-nine years of intimate dealings, but they do indeed look troubled."

Japan's perennially ruling Liberal Democrats are the ideologically conservative brothers of the American Republicans, but in recent decades Japanese-American relations have fared much better under Democratic administrations in Washington than under Republican. President Eisenhower's cold-warring secretary of state, John Foster Dulles, nagged constantly at Japan to assume a militaristic stance against Asian Communism. President Nixon and Henry Kissinger treated Japan with a mixture of indifference, exasperation, and pressure. Japan has responded officially with undeviating loyalty to its American alliance, but not far beneath the surface one frequently finds fretfulness, suspicion, and anger toward Washington.

The United States has been generous to Japan in many ways since World War II: the unvengeful Occupation, financial aid, military protection, technology, access to the American market. In return, the United States expected Japan to stand on the American side in the cold war. Japan did so, with great submission, made tolerably palatable to the Japanese by the deep national sense of debt and obligation, and with many wily exceptions, such as staying out of the Korean and Vietnam wars. Visiting Japan in 1950, Dulles heatedly urged Japan to override its constitution and rearm, but failed because General MacArthur sided with Prime Minister Yoshida in opposing the idea, exclaiming, "The prime minister is right!" In September 1951, Dulles sat Yoshida down in San Francisco and had him sign not only a peace treaty but also a mutual security treaty, by which Japan accepted the military bases all over the country that had been set up by the Occupation. Three years later, when three Japanese cabinet ministers went to Washington to propose softening this "unequal treaty," Dulles scowled and for an hour lectured them that revisions were "premature." When Japan decided to attempt a peace treaty with the Soviet Union in 1956, one of two chief negotiators felt obliged first to consult Dulles, who said: "Be careful. The Russians are not above trying to sell you the same horse twice."

The revised mutual security treaty proposed in 1960 was supposed to propitiate Japan by providing that the United States would have to consult with Japan before using American bases there to attack other parts of Asia (as happened in Vietnam), and by removing a clause that permitted American forces to quell internal insurrections in Japan. But thousands of protesting rioters took the position that the treaty demeaned Japan because Japan was accepting it voluntarily, rather than as the conquered nation it had been in 1951. The proposed visit to Japan by President Eisenhower, which had to be canceled because of the riots, was the idea of Eisenhower's Tokyo ambassador, Douglas MacArthur II, nephew of the general, who was blind to the passion of Japanese anti-Americanism that year. But once the government rammed the ratification of the revised treaty through the Diet, the Japanese shrugged and accepted it.

To repair relations, President John F. Kennedy chose for ambassador the Japan-born, Japanese-speaking Harvard historian Edwin Reischauer, even though (as historian Arthur Schlesinger tells it in *A Thousand Days*) "Foreign Service officers trying to stop the designation . . . had gone to the length of extracting statements from the Japanese Embassy that it would be terrible to send to Tokyo an American ambassador with a Japanese wife." In the Camelot years, this appointment proved brilliant, though later Reischauer overextended himself—out of loyalty to his government rather than personal belief—in defending the American intervention in Vietnam. President Lyndon Johnson in 1966 replaced Reischauer with the hawkish careerman U. Alexis Johnson, who sternly talked Prime Minister Sato out of a plan for Japan to negotiate an end to the Vietnam War.

During the Nixon administration, on issues of the highest importance the President and Henry Kissinger took charge. They devised the "Nixon shocks": the announcement of the President's trip to Peking without notifying the Japanese government, and without having first visited Tokyo; the American import tax that forced revaluation of the yen; and the restrictions on Japanese textile exports to the United States. The China announcement hit hardest. Prime Minister Sato thought Nixon had agreed to consult with Japan on policy toward China. But in Washington, Assistant Secretary of State Marshall Green contended that Japan might not keep Nixon's plan secret, and Kissinger coldly observed that "the Japanese have no options." Nixon's 1973 State of the World speech, a document that went unnoticed by most Americans, upset the Japanese by the threat implicit in the President's statement that "economic disputes"— meaning Japan's heavily favorable balance of trade with the United States—could "tear the fabric of our alliance." The usually discreet Masayoshi Ohira, who was foreign minister at the time, wailed that "the United States does not understand us." Later in the year, greeting Tanaka at the White House, Nixon stressed that "we are equals." Tanaka and most Japanese seemed glad to hear of this equality, but the more sophisticated businessmen and elite Foreign Ministry people were furious. "Would Nixon dare tell the French president that he accepted France as an 'equal'?" stormed one former ambassador to Washington.

All these Nixon shocks severely battered the pro-American Foreign Ministry, which had taken pride in being the "caretaker of the alliance," and was known in Tokyo as "Foggy Bottom's Kasumigaseki branch." But the Foreign Ministry does not count for much, anyway; just as Nixon shoved aside the State Department, at least until Kissinger became secretary of state, Tanaka himself acted for Japan in foreign affairs, traveling widely and bypassing the ministry.

Former Harvard professor Kissinger gets bad marks from several American scholars and diplomats, Japanophiles all, to be sure. Reischauer says, "I'll attack my colleague Henry Kissinger quite directly" for his "disastrous" treatment of Japan; he argues that Kissinger "knows nothing" of Japan and is "Europe-oriented." Columbia professor James W. Morley traces American neglect of Japan to "the personality of Secretary of State Kissinger." George Ball, former undersecretary of state, points out that Kissinger's staff (before he became secretary of state) contained not one Japan expert among its 165 members. Others charge that when Kissinger turns to Asia, he is overimpressed with China's area and population, and underimpressed with Japan's economic power, which is greater not only than China's but that of all the rest of Asia put together. "Kissinger thinks a country has to have space to count, so Japan doesn't count," one professor told me.

Kissinger now admits that his failure to notify Japan of the American policy shift toward China was a fumble, and he denies "hating" Japan, although "whether I like a country is totally irrelevant because I hope that we conduct our policy on the basis of more permanent factors than the personal like or dislike of particular nationalities." Still, the "more permanent factors" of his Metternichian calculations seem to be that Japan needs the United States more than the United States needs Japan, that the Japanese have to be "shocked" from time to time, and that China bulks much larger in Asia than Japan.

The Japanese remain more pro-American than almost any other people in the world. Year after year, *Asahi Shimbun* polls show the United States leading the list of nations whose friendship Japan needs most. In the 1950s, America, as viewed from across the Pacific, enjoyed something close to adulation in the eyes of plain people in Japan. Since Vietnam and the assassinations and racial strife of American life in the 1960s, the Japanese have taken a more measured view, singling out for admiration American technological skill, modernity, and "fairness." In polls, schoolchildren say that the country they most want to visit is Switzerland, but the United States invariably ranks second. From their newspapers, which cover American news closely, the Japanese learn much more about the United States than Americans know about Japan. Book publishers annually translate about 2,400 titles from English, as compared to about 100 translated from Japanese into English.

The Japanese are also deeply interested in what Americans think of Japan, without being aware that most Americans rarely think of Japan, apart from a certain familiarity with name-brand products. The Foreign Ministry regularly commissions the Gallup poll to report on American attitudes; the latest poll shows that Americans regard Japan as a dependable ally and a stabilizing power in Asia. American scholarship on Japan, incidentally, is strong. The critic Donald Keene told me, for example, of a seminar in Kyoto on Japan in the fifteenth century that was attended by fifteen Japanese and fifteen American scholars; the Americans, he says, acquitted themselves as well as the Japanese in both knowledge and language.

What chiefly sours ordinary Japanese about Americans is the United States' 164 military bases on Japanese soil; they irritate the Japanese with what is called *kichi kogai,* base pollution. Most of the bases are insignificant—remote radar sites and the like—but a dozen or so are large, visible, and objectionable for logical reasons. During the Occupation, the Americans established twenty-one facilities in Tokyo, and the city grew outward to surround, among other installations, two air bases capable of producing ear-damaging noise for nearby residents numbering in the hundreds of thousands. Once, jet shock waves shattered the windows of a public bathhouse and showered the bathers with splinters of glass. At Grant Heights, on the site of an old Imperial Army airfield, the Americans flaunted 1,500 spacious houses on centrally located land sufficient to hold 25,000 Japanese-style units. Similarly, the American forces clung to four golf courses surrounded by tight-packed housing.

Kichi kogai has taken many other forms too. In the scenic tranquility of Kitafuji, near sacred Mount Fuji, American troops practiced shellfire and flamethrowing. An American fighter plane once dropped a bomb into a petrochemical plant—a dummy bomb, luckily. American soldiers dealt in drugs, stabbed bar girls, ran down old women with tanks. Stevedores in Yokohama charged that military cargo from Vietnam brought in hordes of giant cockroaches. In the ports of Yokosuka, Sasebo, and Naha, the Japanese nuclear revulsion heightened when American nuclear submarines visited—and was not eased when the Japan Institute of Analytical Chemistry, hired by the government to measure radioactivity in those ports, was caught falsifying its reports (apparently to avoid the expense of detailed monitoring).

Socialists, Communists, and extremist students used events at two U.S. bases in recent years to put on wild demonstrations. In one case, students and union members staged a ninety-six-day blockade to prevent the transport of M-48 tanks and armored personnel carriers, shot up in the Vietnam War, between Yokohama piers and the American Supply and Maintenance Depot at Sagami, where such vehicles were repaired. They had the backing of Yokohama's Socialist mayor, Ichio Asukata, who professed he was enforcing long-ignored laws limiting the weight and width of loads carried on local roads and bridges. At one point, students exploded Molotov cocktails in the repair shops. In the other case, thousands of leftists mounted protest rallies when the U.S. Navy designated the Tokyo Bay harbor of Yokosuka as the permanent home port of the huge, 4,500-man aircraft carrier that in an exquisite irony bears the name *Midway.*

To protesters, home-porting *Midway* in Yokosuka represented a buildup of American power in Japan at a time when the need for it seemed to be declining. Thousands of the crewmen's wives and children found homes and settled down in Yokosuka. Almost abandoned by the American navy a few years ago, Yokosuka is now one of the world's largest naval bases, home port for the whole Seventh Fleet.

When Japan ponders its heavy involvement with the United States in the light of its delicate relations with China and Russia, the ramifications lead off in every direction. For example, in fearing a Japanese-Russian effort to bring large quantities of Tyumen oil to the Pacific, China shares the concerns of the Pentagon, which worries that the oil can be used by Soviet warships to dominate the Pacific and Indian oceans. There are possibilities of future two- and three-way gangups: Japan-China holding Asia against the United States and the Soviet Union; a "Pax Russo-Americana" to dominate the Pacific; Japan–China–United States to oppose those numerous Russian divisions along the Chinese border; Japan–Russia–United States to develop Siberia, with the United States cast as guarantor of the agreement, on the theory that Moscow would not break promises to both Tokyo and Washington, and that China would not attack Russians *and* Americans. There is even Europe–United States–Japan against the remote possibility of a grand Chinese-Russian Communist alliance—this is what Henry Kissinger proposed in his Atlantic Charter concept.

Most of those considerations are far-fetched, and they all sound disadvantageous in one way or another to Japan. By contrast, the concrete reality of its present relationships with the superpowers is comforting to Japan, and for an extraordinary reason: the Japanese-American security treaty, long a dagger aimed at China and the Soviet Union, has miraculously become a boon to both of them, and the prerequisite of their closer relations to Japan.

For many years, in the 1950s and early 1960s, the treaty was an effective military alliance, which is why the protests against renewing it in 1960 were so vehement. The pact would have drawn a Chinese attack on Japan if Dulles' brinkmanship in the Taiwan Strait had gone over the brink. On the other hand, the pact provided Japan with a protective "umbrella"—the threat that the United States would nuclear-bomb any nation that attacked Japan.

A series of great events reduced both the effectiveness of American protection and Japan's need for it. First, the 1963 split between China and Russia undercut the power of either to attack Japan. Then the United States failure to win in Vietnam scaled back American zest for wielding power in Asia, which led to the 1969 Nixon Doctrine that the United States would not automatically come to the aid of an ally. This seems to mean that the security pact's promise of American nuclear protection for Japan is no longer necessarily valid. The practical effect of this interpretation has been to let China and the Soviet Union perceive Japan as less threateningly locked in military alliance with the United States, but at the same time— they note with approval—the treaty retains enough force to serve as a reason for Japan not to rearm on a large scale. Chou En-lai, who has a flawless understanding of Japan's place in the world, took this perception of the security treaty into account in initiating the resumption of relations between Japan and China.

Prime Minister Takeo Miki says blandly that the mutual security treaty can now become a mere "bond of friendship" between Japan and the United States. The leftist political parties, left with egg on their faces because they said in the 1960s that China would not renew relations with Japan until Japan abrogated the treaty, now oppose the treaty with less vim. For its part, Washington has been slow to recognize the changed nature of the treaty, and ambiguously pressures the Japanese to increase their military power and police East Asia—"provide more cops in their neighborhood," as Melvin R. Laird put it when he was secretary of defense. Laird went so far as to advise Japan to develop nuclear weapons and send a naval fleet to the Indian Ocean, and in 1969 Nixon plainly told Prime Minister Sato that Japan's military power ought to be increased. More recently, Deputy Secretary of Defense William P. Clements Jr., reminded by visiting Japanese businessmen that Japan's constitution banned the use of military force, replied with the ineffable statement: "Confucius say, rules made to be broken."

A militarily more powerful Japan, these American Republicans argue, would put an end to Japan's "free ride" in national security, whereby the United States, devoting 10 percent of gross national product to the military, defends both countries, while Japan spends only 1 percent of GNP for defense and uses the extra productive capacity to manufacture goods that compete against American products. Former prime minister Tanaka's response to this argument was that "the United States is obtaining bases in Japan that are unobtainable elsewhere." The Japanese contend that their country has been "used" as a shield for the United States. Kinhide Mushakoji, head of the Institute of International Relations at Sophia University, holds that Washington's argument fails to "face its own logic": that if Japan stops taking a "free ride," it will have to develop nuclear weapons to counter China's and Russia's.

From Burma to North Korea, East Asia (excluding China, Australia, New Zealand, and Japan) holds 345 million people on a total land area about twelve times bigger than Japan. Japan's relations with these countries—the relevant ones being Burma, Thailand, North Vietnam, Malaysia, Singapore, Indonesia, the Philippines, Hong Kong, Taiwan, South Korea, and North Korea—are something like the relations of the United States with the banana republics and other nations of Latin America. Most of them are to some degree economic colonies of Japan. Most of their people fear, envy, dislike, or outrightly hate the Japanese. Conversely, like Americans in regard to the Latins, most Japanese think about East Asians as little as possible, and when they do, they see them as racially different, backward, unable to govern themselves, and not very hardworking. The Philippines supply Japan with bananas, as Honduras supplies the United States. Indonesia sends oil, like Venezuela; Malaysia tin, like Bolivia; Korea wetbacks, like Mexico. North Vietnam is a sort of Cuba.

Just as the State Department and American businessmen are happier with the dictatorships of Latin America, so the Foreign Ministry and Japanese businessmen are more comfortable with the strong-arm governments of Korea, the Philippines, Singapore, and Indonesia. When the prime minister of Japan visits Southeast Asia, he usually gets mobbed and spat upon, like Nixon in Venezuela or Peru. Japanese investment in this area is huge, like American investment in Latin America, and the desire to make vast profits from it is so similarly blatant that in compensation for exploitation Japan feels obliged to concentrate its foreign aid in Southeast Asia, as a kind of guilt money. Finally, the nations of East Asia, like those of Latin America, are so different culturally, economically, politically, and socially one from another that they cannot combine to deal with Japan: the Association of South East Asia Nations (ASEAN) is alike in impotence to the Organization of American States.

A disturbing factor in the background of relations with these countries is the memory of Japan's wartime ambition to build a Greater East Asia Co-Prosperity Sphere among them. Though the name sounds simultaneously comic, naïve, and sinister, this federation was a serious attempt to build a league of yellow- and brown-skinned people against the European and American colonialists. Japan was to be the leader because she had qualified herself by shattering the white warriors of the Russian navy in Tsushima Strait in 1905 and by winning the early battles of World War II. The envisioned sphere included not only conquered Southeast Asia but also China and, at least in ambition, India. The rulers of the occupied countries then were puppets of Japan, but they had the backing of everyone who wanted to get the white man out of Asia. "One billion Orientals, one billion people of Greater East Asia!" exclaimed the Filipino delegate when the leaders of all these nations met in the Diet building in Tokyo in 1943. "My Asiatic blood has always called to other Asiatics," cried the Burmese representative.

The Japanese idea did lead to the end of colonialism in some places: Sukarno, who threw the Dutch out of Indonesia, was a Japanese protégé. But Japanese atrocities, Japanese defeat, and the superior force of nationalism over Pan-Asianism dissolved the Greater East Asia Co-Prosperity Sphere. Asians now remember it as Japanese colonialism—largely an attempt to capture markets and access to raw materials. Since that is a definition of what aggressive armies of Japanese businessmen have now accomplished in East Asia, the people and the governments of those countries are leery, rueful, and angry. With the exception of North Vietnam and North Korea, they also feel overwhelmed by the immense bulk of China, and therefore the trend among them, led by Malaysia's Prime Minister Tun Abdul Razak, is toward a cautious neutralism rather than alliance with Japan. As a result of renewed relations between Japan and China, the anti-Communist Asia and Pacific Council (ASPAC), of which Japan was a member, has in effect dissolved, and ASEAN has become more neutral. In such a climate, Japanese political leadership in this region cannot flourish any more readily than that of the United States, which threw away its credentials in the Vietnam War.

"Japan and the United States are equal failures at understanding Asian nationalism," an *Asahi Shimbun* editorial writer remarked to me. One Japanese foreign-relations specialist observes that "the psychological distance between Japanese and other Asians is greater than that between Japanese and Western nations"; the well-to-do, technologically advanced Japanese now regard themselves as the "honorary whites" of the Orient. Language, incidentally, is a mountainous barrier: not only are languages like Thai and Malay difficult for the Japanese to learn, but Japanese is so hard for other Asians that bringing them to Japanese universities for training and people-to-people friendship is impractical (although a few thousand go to Japan and take courses taught in English).

The only wide-open route for Japan to tighten relations and heighten stability in East Asia is to amplify foreign aid, to assume what has been called the "yellow man's burden." Japan reports that its "net flow of financial resources to developing countries" in 1973 reached $5.8 billion, or 1.42 percent of GNP. But this figure includes all Japanese private investment in these countries, which is dirty pool in the minds of such aidsmen as Robert McNamara, president of the World Bank. He points out that in altruistic, government-provided grants and low-interest, long-term loans—what the bank calls Official Development Assistance—Japan contributes only 0.23 percent of GNP, less than the bank members' average of 0.34 percent, which is still only half of the bank's goal of 0.7 percent. Moreover, Japan is just beginning to "untie" its government aid—that is, not to force the borrowers to use the money to buy Japanese goods, and not to condition loans on access to the borrower's natural resources. In a crucial "have"–"have-not" contrast, Japan is ever more the "have" that appears unconcerned with the neighboring "have-nots." One exciting project that does get Japanese aid is the Asia Trunk Line, a linkup of existing railroads that will ultimately run nine thousand miles from Singapore to Istanbul, thus connecting with all of Europe.

The fiery teen-age students of Bangkok have made Thailand the focus of Southeast Asian resentment against Japan. In late 1972 and early 1973, students touched off a boycott of Japanese goods that jolted Tokyo into propitiating the Thais by taking the strings off $210 million in Japanese aid money. A shrewd Japanese named Yuji Mineyama, secretary general of the Japanese Chamber of Commerce in Bangkok, remarked to me in August 1973 that to some extent the students were "just practicing" against the Japanese, their real target being the Thai military dictatorship. Sure enough, two months later, student demonstrations toppled Marshal Thanom Kittakachorn's government. Next the students took on Prime Minister Tanaka, during his imprudent visit to Bangkok early in 1974. They pummeled his car and waved signs that said JAP GET YOUR ASS OUT (English is the lingua franca of Japan–Thailand relations), leading him to offer to debate them in person. He did not win them over, though, because he told them the unpalatable truth that the Japanese work a lot harder than the Thais do.

In Indonesia, Tanaka was mobbed in even more violent demonstrations, aimed partly at the Japanese ("Is it really necessary for them to have Japanese *barbershops* here?" asked one Indonesian), but also at the too-rich Indonesian generals, the wealthy overseas-Chinese merchants, and the $95 per capita income. In Singapore, Lee Kuan Yew, the autocratic prime minister, has criticized Japan for not sufficiently counterbalancing China, which he hates and fears. A Singapore journalist sympathetic to him told me: "The Japanese bury their heads, and the smaller nations cannot count on Japan."

Lee has suggested, for example, that Japan, whose tankers cram the straits off Singapore as they voyage to and from the Middle East, could help Singapore defend these waters—an act that would flagrantly violate the Japanese constitutional renunciation of armed force. In the Philippines, the equally dictatorial boss, President Ferdinand E. Marcos, who fought the Japanese in World War II, says: "The Filipino is a strange animal. He respects a strong opponent. So he likes the Japanese." Here, as elsewhere, Japan runs an "information center" that tries to offset bad feeling with good movies and other attractions. "It's free! Come one, come all!" says the sign at the door.

North and South Vietnam have happier memories of Japan's wartime occupation than their neighbors: they feel that Japan was sincere in helping Indochina throw off French colonialism. During the Vietnam War, the Japanese government cooperated warily with the United States, letting the Americans use their bases in Japan for logistic support, and Japanese business made an estimated $11.5 billion profit out of American military spending and other war-related sales. The Japanese people, though fearful that the United States might draw Japan into the war, resolutely ignored the rights and wrongs of it. A 1968 poll showed that 44.5 percent favored ending the war so that "neither side loses face," and 30.1 percent held that it "doesn't matter how, just so long as it ends." As a result of this hands-off attitude, the belligerents in the war excluded Japan from the Paris peace conference in 1973 (although China, the Soviet Union, France, and Great Britain were invited). Nevertheless, other nations let Japan know that it had to contribute heavily toward rehabilitating both Vietnams when the shooting stopped. North Vietnam, which throughout the war had never stopped sending Japan anthracite and cast iron in exchange for textiles, chemicals, drugs, and machinery, resumed diplomatic relations in mid-1973.

Finally, Korea: 32 million people in South Korea ruled by the anti-Communist strongman Park Chung Hee, a wartime officer in the Japanese Imperial Army; 14 million people in North Korea ruled by the legendary dictator Kim Il Sung, who fought throughout the 1930s with the Chinese Communist army and during World War II with the Russian Red Army. When I was in Seoul one morning in mid-1973, sirens sounded, troops in camouflage uniforms took over the main streets, a sound like the whine of falling bombs filled the air, and red smoke drifted everywhere. "We are still a divided country," someone explained to me. "We practice for air raids and are ready for an attack at any time." Both sides put about 30 percent of their government budgets into arms. For Japan, the division makes the already touchy and intriguing problem of dealing with the Koreans just about twice as intricate. It took twenty years for Japan and South Korea to write a peace treaty—years spent waiting for the death of anti-Japanese President Syngman Rhee, who unrealistically insisted that Japan would have to recognize his government as the government of all Korea.

I had not been in Seoul more than three hours before a government official told me, in explanation of Korea's distrust of Japan: "You've got to remember that that Japanese scoundrel Hideyoshi invaded our country four hundred years ago." As in a bad old marriage, a lot of sour history hangs over the relations between Japan and Korea, which nevertheless need each other. The centuries-long flow of culture from China to Japan went through Korea, and the Koreans think they absorbed and adapted it better than the Japanese; the elegant National Museum of Korea in Seoul eloquently argues this point by its displays of beautiful ancient artifacts.

After annexing Korea in 1910, the dreaded Japanese police and troops killed twelve thousand protesters and proceeded to Japanize the peninsula by installing Japanese officials in most government posts, building a great deal of Japanese-owned industry, changing the country's name (to Chosen), imposing the Japanese language, and finally, as a World War II extreme, forcing Koreans to take Japanese names. A well-known journalist named Young H. Lee told me with unforgotten fury how "they made our family call ourselves 'Matsumoto.' " At the end of the war, the Russians, breaking the Allied understanding that Korea would become independent, swept down to the thirty-eighth parallel and created the division that prevails today. During the Korean War in 1950–53, Japan successfully avoided fighting but served as a "privileged sanctuary" for the American and South Korean forces (as did Manchuria for the Chinese and North Koreans). In fact, Japan served so profitably as to provide the Japanese economy with its historic takeoff.

Renewed diplomatic relations in 1965 touched off a huge new advance of Japanese private capital investment into South Korea, with heavy government-to-government aid as a sweetener. The economic embrace is so tight that the Koreans have had to resume teaching Japanese in schools, so that waitresses can take orders from Japanese businessmen and employees can understand what the boss is saying. In some ways, South Korea is a Japanese colony all over again, and Korean students demonstrate against their country's "humiliating political and economic dependence on Japan." In the countryside, people try to offset Japanese influence by carefully maintaining monuments put up to mark Japanese atrocities during the 1910–45 occupation.

For many Japanese, the fall of South Vietnam suddenly illuminated the possibility that South Korea could similarly fall to its Communist northern enemy, converting Japan's nearest neighbor from uneasy friend to unpleasant foe. Such an event would unquestionably step up pressures to remilitarize within Japan; for the Foreign Ministry, South Korea is now clearly the world's most worrisome flashpoint.

"Japanese diplomacy gives the impression of an interested bridge partner, waiting to follow the first good bid from the American side," wrote Frank Gibney in 1971. Others described this policy-of-having-no-policy in unkind phrases like "being the good boy of international politics," or "more like that of a trading company than of a nation," or "being easy to push around," or "juggling act," or "not getting boxed in." The critic Kei Wakaizumi observed that Japanese diplomacy had mastered the first lesson of judo, which is to "fall without being hurt" and be "ready for the next action." The security treaty with the United States, it was said, supplanted any need for an independent foreign policy, and ambassador to Washington was the pearl of jobs in the Japanese foreign service. One foreign minister, trying to wrench Japan from what has been called its "stifling tête-à-tête" with Washington, gulped and said: "I have always considered the United States a respected watchdog for Japan. We cannot forget our indebtedness to that watchdog for our security. But I know of no house that allows its actions to be determined by its watchdog, and I have no intentions of doing the watchdog's bidding." While India lectured the world, and Canada worked for Middle Eastern peace, and West Germany found its *Ostpolitik*, Japan remained a cipher.

But events of the last three or four years have put an end to putty diplomacy. The Nixon shocks cracked Japan's unquestioning trust in the United States. The security pact turned from an albatross into a dove. Tanaka's warmth toward Chou En-lai's invitation to renew relations with China, and the aviation agreement that followed, outstripped the American effort to get closer to China. Russia has shown that it needs Japan, and East Asia has demanded more sensitive attention from Japan. In response to these changes, Japan could have gone four ways. The leftist parties proposed neutrality, which is the preference of a majority of the people in polls. The Soviet Union pressed Japan to take the route of the "Brezhnev concept" of collective security: a multilateral treaty freezing the status quo; but for Japan to accept would renew tension with China and prevent the return of the northern islands. The American proposal was a "multipolar" balance of power: "a strong, healthy United States, Europe, Soviet Union, China, and Japan, each balancing the other, not playing one against the other, an even balance"; the United States and Japan would no longer be allies in this every-man-for-himself adversary relationship.

Instead of any of these positions, the Japanese have gradually devised a policy that draws elements from all three and adds a bold new idea: that Japan should champion and symbolize world peace not as pacifism or dreamy idealism but as the nation's hard-headed, self-interested path to survival. Only Japan can exemplify such a policy, because among the "poles" defined by Nixon, only Japan has (for all practical purposes) renounced military power and the Bomb. "We must become trustworthy internationalists," said Masayoshi Ohira when he was foreign minister. "Japan must think what the role of creating peace means. We must not lose sight of the goal of creating peace. There is no other way than this."

Minister of International Trade and Industry Nakasone declared that "Japan does not want to hang on to the outdated concept that economic great powers must necessarily become military great powers." But Japan will certainly use its economic power and technology, the vast proposed collaboration with the Soviet Union in Siberia being an example. A Japanese Self-Defense Agency strategist explained this kind of power to me as follows: "The big nuclear nations use 'punishment deterrence'—do what we say or we'll bomb you. We will use 'bonus deterrence'—don't hit and we'll help you develop your oil production." The policy entails diplomatic relations with all other nations, down to and including Albania. The main point is that Japan must import from and export to virtually the whole world to survive, and therefore any threat to peace anywhere is a threat to Japan.

Diplomacy without armaments puts Japan in the big-power game without the historic big-power concerns—international power plays, spheres of influence, territorial acquisition. It assumes that the hands of the superpowers are tied by fear of nuclear war, and that such worries as the "domino theory" are out of date or irrelevant. This policy also puts its bets on the United Nations (Japan is the No. 3 fund contributor), and seeks for Japan a permanent seat on the Security Council "in order to represent opinions of non-nuclear countries," as Kei Wakaizumi puts it. He deplores "the impression that nuclear armament is the passport to big-power status" created by the fact that all present permanent members of the council have nuclear weapons.

He argues that in elaborating its peace diplomacy, Japan must reduce stress on exports, bring trade into balance, give the full World Bank quota of 0.7 percent of GNP in government foreign aid, and shun economic neocolonialism. Japan must also simply look better in the world, by improving its dismal public relations effort. For starters, the government's new philanthropic arm, the Japan Foundation, has given $1 million each to ten leading American universities to finance Japanese studies, and Mitsubishi, Sumitomo, Nissan, and Toyota have made similar grants of a million or more apiece.

Can Japan show the world the way to peace? Partly because its diplomacy has been so nearly invisible for thirty years, and partly because leadership is not a Japanese forte, the idea seems far-fetched. But the world might as well give Japan a chance, in two ways. One is to let her become the only member of the United Nations Security Council that does not come to the table with nuclear weapons in hand. And the other is to make sure that Japan is not deprived of the imports of food and raw materials that this small, insular nation must have. What might happen otherwise is the·subject of the next chapter.

25 / 🎌

Tora, Tora, Tora?

IF INDIA HAS THE BOMB, can Japan be far behind?

As things stand, a Japanese specialist on national security affairs writes in *Asian Survey*, Japan is headed toward "an unprecedented experiment of becoming a new type of nonaligned superpower lacking military capability in defending itself against any large-scale aggression." But then he goes on to say:

> I must add as an exception that Japan could suddenly go in an unexpected direction due to an emotional overreaction to some shocking future event if such should occur. It might rush into a dangerous situation even if it knew that it might be dangerous to itself.
>
> Some conceivable examples of such a shocking event would be the deployment by any big power of its naval and air power so as to cut off Japan's sources of oil from the Middle East and its trade with Southeast Asia; submarine harassment by any big power within or outside territorial waters of Japan, such as attacking and sinking Japanese ships; or the precipitate conversion of the existing democratic system in Japan into a Communist system, with Communist control of the self-defense forces, should a Communist government or a coalition government headed by Communists be established in Japan. This might provoke an attempted military coup which would be supported by many Japanese people.

Ay, there's the rub. Japan's utter reliance on peace will work well if the world reciprocates and rationality prevails. But Japan is starvable—it cannot sufficiently feed or energize itself. And the Japanese, preferring emotion to reason, can be irrational. The country's swift 180-degree turns of policy—going into seclusion from the world, for

417

example, or coming out of it—are the trademarks of her history. If the world chooses to starve Japan of food or energy (and these are possibilities as resources diminish), Japan could swing, with the irrationality of desperation, from a policy of peace to a policy of war. History has proved that war merely as war has a dark hold on the Japanese psyche.

Novelist Yukio Mishima raged all his life against Japan's military weakness. A few days before his death, he wrote a furious lament over the "rottenness" of the Self-Defense Forces for lacking the "spirit of the samurai"; he wondered why no general had committed suicide in protest of the politicians' gutless agreement to the Nuclear Test Ban Treaty. In his speech to assembled soldiers minutes before he disemboweled himself, he shouted, "To defend Japan is to defend the traditions of our history and culture, centered on the emperor . . . If you don't rise now, forever and ever, you will be nothing more than an army that serves the Americans." The listening troops laughed; cabinet ministers quickly declared that Mishima must have been insane; yet all Japanese caught his message: Japan should give up its affluence and bourgeois pleasures and reach again for the values of yore, including the chivalry of bushido.

Lieutenant Hiroo Onoda of the Imperial Army demonstrated samurai fanaticism even more forcefully—and Japan in response bared its soul with a great emotional jag of admiration. In 1944, at the age of twenty-one, Onoda vanished from his friends and family— even from the meticulous public registration records—to be enrolled in the army's hush-hush intelligence school in a remote town in central Japan. There he learned everything in the book for spies: disguises, psychological warfare, and, handiest of all as it turned out, jungle survival. He was whisked to the Philippines even as Japan was cutting and running there, and on Christmas Day 1944 his superior officer, Major Yoshimi Taniguchi, sent him to the island of Lubang with the order (much in contrast to the usual fight-to-the-death command) to "sabotage and harass the enemy rear" and to "stay alive even if all Japanese forces are annihilated."

And so Onoda did, year after year, decade after decade, until March 1974, when ex-Major Taniguchi was taken to the area of Onoda's known hiding place and performed an exorcism by canceling the order. Onoda's possessions told much about how he had survived: two rifles, a sword, a bamboo fire-making device, a butcher knife, three pans, sleeping bag and tent, handmade mustache scissors, a pipe. He had supplies of smoked beef, rice, coffee, beans, and seasonings—all ripped off from the Filipino islanders, of whom he had reportedly killed about thirty. On a transistor radio he had kept up with world events, concluding after Watergate that Nixon was "no good." His first words, addressed to his brother, were: "Sorry I've been troubling you for a long time."

Does such a man deserve to be treated as a fool, a murderer, or a nut? With hardly any dissent, Japan instantly and gratefully made him a hero. (What's more, so did the Filipinos. President Marcos personally pardoned Onoda's crimes, accepted his sword in surrender, then gave it back to the "brave and gallant soldier." The Filipinos also proceeded to develop Lubang as a Japanese tourist attraction.) A Japanese Air Lines DC-8 fetched Onoda home. At Tokyo's airport, leading right-wing politicians crowded Onoda's eighty-eight-year-old mother out of the way so that they could congratulate him and give him their calling cards. When he at last reached his mother, who had set out food at Onoda's place at the table every day for thirty years, she said, "You are great. *Arigato.*" Later, Onoda returned to her the dagger she had given him to kill himself with, had suicide become necessary. But with stern bushido spirit, he declared that he had not thought of his parents while in the jungle, because "I had asked them to give me up for lost when I left them." Crowds waving rising-sun flags lined the route from the airport to the city. Prime Minister Tanaka received him (and, Onoda complained, "monopolized the conversation"). The Imperial Household Agency ruled that the emperor had better keep a little distance from this reminder of Japanese miltary fanaticism, but His Majesty thanked the Filipinos for cooperating in Onoda's rescue, and sent his wishes for Onoda's good health.

Wiry, toothy, shaven-headed, jaunty, and irreverent toward modern Japan ("Bullet trains? They are very fast, but that's all"; "TV irritates my eyes"), Onoda seemed an unlikely hero, far from a fierce and scowling samurai. He made no one yearn for the militarism of the 1930s. Some, indeed, refused to admire him. A war veteran said, "Onoda failed to evaluate the situation surrounding him and blindly stuck to the order like a robot." A professional man warned that "the Japanese idiosyncrasy for governmental authority may again result in re-creation of the situation that will claim victims like Mr. Onoda." But most Japanese felt surgings of what they call *yamatodamashii,* Japanese spirit. "I saw Lieutenant Onoda emerge from his hiding into this world of ours through telecast. He was in uniform and stood ramrod straight, behaving all the while like a typical soldier. The rifle he carried showed a shiny polish, reflecting his constant maintenance work for the weapon, which was regarded as a symbol of soldier spirit," wrote a reader of *Mainichi Shimbun*. The newspaper itself, "although in no way trying to idolize Onoda," said that "still he is a fine example of a human being living in extreme conditions. His life is a great contrast to that of the people who today weigh everything according to personal benefit."

In sum, by his demonstration of military fanaticism, Onoda created in the Japanese people a powerful nostalgia for the same old values that Mishima considered himself to be dying for: the sense of obligation to family, associates, company, the emperor, and the nation; love of country and the belief that the Japanese are quintessentially different—and better—than other races, so that only they can understand Onoda's experience; exaltation of the country over the individual; duty and dedication; and filial piety. Unluckily, all these values can still be put to the service of the kind of militarism with which Japan frightened the world in the 1930s. In his final speech, Mishima said, "The one thing more valuable than human life is neither freedom nor democracy, but Japan."

Finding evidence of the perdurable Japanese attraction to the warrior spirit is easy enough, and taken together it amounts to a trend. Mostly because one generation cannot take blame for the previous generation's transgressions, war guilt is gone. Revisionist histories and textbooks—taking, for example, a more sympathetic view of why Japan invaded Indochina in 1940—pour from the presses by the shelvesful. The martial arts of judo, karate, and kendo (fencing with bamboo staves) grow ever more popular, and swords flash endlessly in samurai dramas on television. The Buddhist-based preoccupation with proper treatment for the remains of the dead inspires solemn missions by the Ministry of Health and Welfare to bring back the bones and ashes of servicemen killed all over Asia. The rational policy of peace, however, is overwhelmingly stronger, in the opinion of most Japanese, than the irrational choice for militarism. Only drastic pressures, and probably only pressures from outside Japan, could make the nation change its mind.

Japan's policy of greatness without arms is not quite what it seems, for Japan has arms—the peculiar something called the Self-Defense Forces. Article 9 of the constitution says, as explicitly as can be, that "the Japanese people forever renounce war as a sovereign right of the nation and the threat or use of force as a means of settling international disputes," and that "land, sea, and air forces, as well as other war potential, will never be maintained." Yet with the extremely dubious interpretation that this ban does not preclude self-defense,

Japan has created the most skilled and modern military establishment in the Far East. In budget, $3 billion a year, it ranks sixth in the world, after the United States ($79 billion), the Soviet Union, China, Great Britain, and West Germany. The Self-Defense Forces have been built up in a series of five-year plans. They are now in the fourth plan, running from 1972 to 1977, and have 259,000 men under arms — 179,000 soldiers, 38,000 sailors, and 42,000 air force men.

The Ground Self-Defense Force, composed of five armies in thirteen divisions, has such weapons as 980 tanks, 780 armored cars, 690 self-propelled guns, 350 aircraft, and 48 Hawk surface-to-air missiles. The Maritime Self-Defense Force has 575 ships, the biggest of them being helicopter-equipped destroyers; there are no aircraft carriers. There are 16 submarines, plus many smaller destroyers, destroyer escorts, minesweepers, supply ships, and other auxiliaries, and about 300 aircraft, mostly antisubmarine planes. The Air Self-Defense Force has something like 600 jet fighters, the hottest being 50 Phantoms. It also has reconnaissance planes, trainers, helicopters, Nike Ajax surface-to-air missiles, and C-1 jet transports, but no bombers. In sum, a highly lethal aggregation of firepower. The number of men in the three forces has risen only slightly in the last fifteen years; all extra money has gone into the quality of weapons and training.

The distant origins of the Self-Defense Forces lie in the postwar friendships between former Japanese Imperial Navy officers and Admiral Arleigh A. ("Thirty-one Knot") Burke, who arrived in Japan soon after the war as deputy chief of staff for the United States Navy, Far East. He arranged for Japanese minesweepers, which had cleared their own waters of war-dropped mines, to sweep the seas off Inchon and Wonsan during the Korean War—Japan's first little brush with resumed military activity. Burke encouraged rebuilding the Japanese navy; some of its officers call him "the father of the Maritime Self-Defense Force." The more proximate fathers were several of his friends, Imperial Navy admirals who had quietly plotted to revive their service right after the war. The Imperial Navy always was the elite and sophisticated branch of the Japanese military. One former officer told me: "I was brought up in Manchuria and never learned a thing about human rights, liberty, or equality until I entered the naval academy. The navy taught me that."

Former Imperial Navy commanders and lieutenant commanders built up the Maritime Self-Defense Force, and it is emphatically a continuation of the old navy. By contrast, the Ground Self-Defense Force, formed in 1954 out of the National Police Reserve created to replace American Occupation soldiers sent off to the Korean War, broke away from the jackboot tradition of the Imperial Army even though a high percentage of its officers were depurged Imperial Army men. The United States provided $1.6 billion worth of training and weapons between 1954 and 1968. Seventy percent of all Ground Self-Defense Force officers were trained in the United States, and American officers still have intimate contacts with their Japanese counterparts. Not long ago, Lieutenant General James H. Doolittle (Retired), who led the famous "thirty seconds over Tokyo" raid in retaliation for the Japanese attack on Pearl Harbor, visited Tokyo and had a friendly lunch with two of the Imperial Navy fliers who led squadrons in the Pearl Harbor attack and later advanced to the rank of rear admiral in the Maritime Self-Defense Force.

The crucial difference between the prewar and postwar armies and navies is civilian control. Before the war, the army and navy ministers had to be military officers, responsible to the emperor rather than the prime minister, and they could (and did) bring down governments by withdrawing from the cabinet. This threat was, in fact, the mechanism that brought the military to total power in the 1930s. Now the prime minister (who under the constitution cannot be a miltary officer) is commander-in-chief, appointing and supervising the civilian director general of the Japan Defense Agency, who has cabinet status. (Not even the most hawkish Japanese politicians have yet dared try to raise the defense establishment from agency to ministry.) It is to the director general that the chiefs of staff for air, ground, and sea report; the prime minister rarely sees them. Civilians fill all high posts in the defense-agency bureaucracy. The job of director general is a political plum to be passed from one Liberal Democratic politician to the next: thirty men have held the position in twenty years. And as the final touch to the civilian mentality of the Self-Defense Forces, it is an all-volunteer outfit. Japan has no draft.

The Japanese have also shackled runaway militarism by a consensus that the Self-Defense Forces must not cost more than 1 percent of gross national product. In practice, the figure is even less, having dropped from 1.13 percent in 1958 to 0.87 percent in 1972. The basis of Japan's claim to be the world's most peaceable major nation is that this percentage is far lower than that of any other important country. West Germany, next lowest, spends 2.8 percent of GNP, three times as much. The superpowers spend much more: the United States 7.3 percent, China 10.7, the Soviet Union 15.7; and the belligerents of the Middle East rank incomparably higher: Egypt 21.7 percent, Israel

23.9. There is something a little specious about the Japanese claim, however: Japan's GNP has grown so stupendously that less than 1 percent of it provides a thumping $15 billion for the current five-year plan. Thus, on the one hand, Japan's sheer growth might haul her military expenditure higher than China's in a decade; but on the other hand, the Japanese will probably continue to spend more on geishas and other expense-account frivolities than they do on arms and soldiers.

The atmosphere of the new Japanese army is more boy scout than jackboot, yet nevertheless recruiting soldiers in a manpower-tight economy is difficult. Posters showing a gloved hand in salute under the headline "Come, young men, for the defense of your country" failed utterly, and were replaced by posters picturing a Rugby scrimmage with the catch phrase "Hot sweat! How refreshing! Kindle your passion together with your fellows," which worked better. The navy and air force, offering first-class technical training, come closest to filling their authorized quotas. The old Imperial Army trained men with kicks and blows; the Ground Self-Defense Force treats its troops with consideration, like the new American army. Many non-coms live with their wives off base, and drive to work in their cars. Privates whistle on duty and jokingly call the sergeant "uncle." The former Imperial Army officers have mostly retired at the compulsory age of fifty-eight; many colonels now are men who got their entire training since the Ground Self-Defense Force was formed, and by 1980 all generals will be postwar products.

Amid all the contradictions of a military establishment that is probably unconstitutional, that is conventional and non-nuclear to the point of being anachronistic, and that is too small to guarantee self-defense but too large to jibe with Japan's declared intent to be a great unarmed power, the precise role of the Self-Defense Forces becomes a puzzle. The clearest of the military's unclear goals is defense against the Soviet Union. Half of the Ground Self-Defense Force is stationed in Hokkaido, and this army's specialty is repelling landings. The Maritime Self-Defense Force's antisubmarine recon planes try to keep track of Russian nuclear submarines sailing in the Sea of Japan out of the vast naval base at Vladivostok. The Air Self-Defense Force's F-104s and F-86s scramble as often as twenty-four times a week to photograph Soviet Bear and Badger reconnaissance planes skirting both coasts of Japan. From Chitose base in Hokkaido, the Air Self-Defense Force also tracks Soviet and Chinese missile firings and Soviet military satellites.

No Japanese is so foolish as to think that the Self-Defense Forces could defeat the Russian navy, air force, and Red Army, which has thirty-three divisions in the Far East. "Japan hopes that while she holds on, the U.S. would fulfill her obligations under the Security Treaty, the United Nations would move to mediate, and international public opinion would be aroused," says the Defense Agency's policy statement. In other words, the Self-Defense Forces would be the trip wire that would summon help, and would buy time—one to six months —until it came. If no help came, official doctrine assumes that Japan would simply have to surrender; the Japanese forces have ammunition reserves for only thirty days of heavy fighting. One former director general of the Defense Agency, Naomi Nishimura, calls this plan "the strategy of limited response." I heard the Self-Defense Forces described as "the symbol of our will to defend ourselves" and "like locking your door against burglars—you just don't make it too easy for them." A leading military thinker told me, "We can't abolish our forces unilaterally, but we can't afford a strategy for *winning* any kind of war."

Defining the Self-Defense Forces as protection from the Soviet Union is just sufficiently reasonable to fall within the somewhat unreal standards that all nations use in rationalizing their military establishments. It is also just sufficiently unreasonable to lead to suspicions that the Self-Defense Forces' real role may turn out to be something else. The Japanese military is over-officered, which raises the possibility that it could quickly be expanded into a major and threatening force through the use of a draft. The Japanese call this theory of a nucleus army "kindling charcoal to make a fire." One also hears frequently in Japan that the authentic function of the military is to protect the vast, rightist, politico-business Establishment by staging a coup d'état if Socialists or Communists manage to win the government in elections. Prime Minister (1948–54) Shigeru Yoshida forthrightly favored authorizing the military to suppress any internal rebellion, and riot-control drills are part of Self-Defense Forces training. One Communist Diet member charges that Self-Defense Forces instructional material is biased against Communists; he cites a passage that says: "If we trust the [leftist] Japanese Teachers Union and permit them to teach Japanese youth, irrevocable things could happen."

As additional motives for opposing the leftist parties, military men know that the Socialist platform proposes the abolition of the Self-Defense Forces, and that the Communists propose what sounds like a much-deflated military establishment. But a Defense Agency strategy professor with whom I discussed this possibility pointed out that officers and troops of this civilian-minded army would not carry out a coup as readily as some Latin American army might. For one thing, they vote for Communists, Socialists, and Liberal Democrats in about the same proportions as the population at large. "The Self-Defense Force is too professional to side with any political party," said the professor. "Moreover, the Communist Party might even appeal to the military men, because it favors changes in the constitution that might include making the defense force clearly legal. And, after all, the old Russian czar's army, minus its officers, became what is now the Red Army."

In contrast to the Europeans, who still prize American defenders, the Japanese, surrounded by the sea, have never been seriously worried about the danger of attack from China or the Soviet Union, and this indifference has created pressure to make the 57,500 American servicemen still stationed in Japan less visible, if not to get them out. In fact, the U.S. Army is almost all gone from main-island Japan, and even in Okinawa there are only 9,000 soldiers, versus 2,000 sailors, 18,000 marines, and 9,000 air force men. This gentle ouster of American troops from Japan is not necessarily disagreeable to the Pentagon—to the extent that the Self-Defense Forces pick up what the American government has long urged, the "Japanization" of Asian security. But the two forces have different purposes: what the constitutionally shackled Self-Defense Forces can do is a far cry from what the free-wheeling Pentagon can do. For one thing, the Japanese army may not leave Japanese soil, even to serve on such nonbelligerent forces as United Nations truce-watching teams. For another, the Self-Defense Forces have not got the Bomb.

To repeat: If India has the Bomb, can Japan resist? Japan has resisted, Japan can resist, and Japan will resist. Although there are sound strategical reasons why nuclear weapons are counterproductive for Japan, Japan resists mostly for moral, diplomatic, and economic reasons. It would be hypocritical for Japan, the only nation that ever learned firsthand the grotesque terrors of a nuclear bomb, to prepare to inflict a Hiroshima on other nations. It would shatter Japan's diplomacy of peace. It would alienate approximately one billion actual or potential customers of Japanese goods around the world. But if West Germany, Italy, Iran, South Africa, Brazil, Israel, Australia, Argentina, Switzerland, Sweden, and Egypt all learn how to make nuclear weapons, Japan's moral, diplomatic, and economic qualms will lose their force. It is not hard to imagine a headline some years hence saying "Japan Becomes Eighteenth Nation to Possess Nuclear Bomb." If Peru gets the Bomb, won't Japan?

In several senses, Japan already has the bomb. These past thirty years, even as anti-bomb demonstrators gathered annually at Hiroshima and newspaper editors pleaded for "the total abolition of this terrifying means of mass destruction," the Japanese have enjoyed the protection of American nuclear weapons. During all this time a Chinese or Russian attack on Japan might have brought, and might still bring, nuclear retaliation from the United States. Many Japanese doubt this proposition, assuming that such a strike would bring Communist retaliation against the United States, and asking, "Would you *really* trade Chicago for Osaka?" But if the Japanese can legitimately doubt whether the United States would retaliate for an attack on Japan, any possible enemy of Japan must equally doubt that the United States would not, so that for practical purposes the deterrent works.

If the United States for some reason withdrew its umbrella, Japan might feel obliged to get nuclear bombs of its own. And—this is the second sense in which Japan in effect has the bomb—Japan could. Its technology is at the stage where making bombs is only the last step. The nuclear power industry produces lots of by-product plutonium; the universities graduate about three hundred nuclear scientists every year; and the government has plenty of money. Official policy is to keep Japan capable of producing a nuclear device within two years of starting an all-out effort. To that end, Japan already has centrifuges to make uranium-235 on a small scale. On the same dubious grounds that make the Self-Defense Forces constitutional, a government white paper has decreed that nuclear weapons for defense would also be constitutional. Legally, going to work on the bomb would require only a change in the Japanese Atomic Energy Act. Moreover, Japan could launch any nuclear warheads it might make. Its missiles for orbiting satellites have approximately the same propulsion, guidance, and reentry capabilities as American Minutemen IIs. The *Mu* rocket could easily hit China or eastern Russia.

In sum, there are two visible ways by which the world can push Japan toward acquiring nuclear weapons: widespread proliferation of the bomb, making the Japanese acquisition a matter of indifference amid general pessimism that humanity is determined to blow itself up; and withdrawal of American protection, making Japan feel abandoned and vulnerable.

In either case, Japan would be joining the "nuclear club" mostly for reasons of prestige and status—"to put backbone into Japan's diplomacy," as one retired general expresses it. A largely symbolic nuclear device would suffice. If Japan plunged for nuclear weaponry in the strictly military and strategic sense, it might (with some logic) go only as far as building an essentially defensive anti-ballistic missile system, or it might (with hardly any logic) produce a complete second-strike deterrent system. The glaring defect of deterrent for the Japanese is that its Tokaido-corridor industrial cities form the world's most vulnerable target, whereas its major conceivable enemies, China and the Soviet Union, are protected by their size and dispersion from all but American-size nuclear deterrence. The bombs and rockets needed for a second-strike force would cost Japan more money than it can afford, more organizational concentration than it could spare, and, of course, the respect of the millions who admire its attempt to be the world's great non-nuclear power.

26/ ⚜

Japanese Canary

"**J**APAN IS LIKE THE CANARY sent down into the mine to see if the air there will support life," says Hiroshi Kurematsu, a director of Mitsui O.S.K. Lines. He means that by leading the world in disease-causing industrial pollution and environmental destruction, Japan has been serving as an experiment in how far a nation might go before destroying itself. Perhaps I caught him on a gloomy day, but he went on to say, "Japan is now ill in the soul and the spirit. Profits first, people last. Japanese cleverness is not clever sometimes. We must have serious reform. China has what we need—a spiritual revolution. But we Japanese are not revolutionary." He shrugged.

My own guess is that the Japanese are not going to go down into the mine and die. To the contrary, the flow of national energy is so powerful that Japan will probably provide other nations with an admirable model of living in material and spiritual compatibility with nature. Nevertheless, it would be imprudent not to keep in mind some of the strains that might thwart the achievement of the "vigorous welfare society" toward which the Japanese government's Basic Economic and Social Plan aspires.

To begin with, the political consensus, represented by the Liberal Democratic Party, that has stabilized and directed Japan for thirty years is certainly going to fracture—perhaps into extremes. Journalist Robert Crabbe goes so far as to argue that "Japan today is sliding toward a head-on clash between people with very different ideas about what Japan ought to be." A fluky victory by the left could inspire a coup by the right. The emperor, by then probably the young and

428

energetic Akihito, might serve with renewed stature as the symbol of such a trend.

No one can safely overlook the persistent national embarrassment that the Japanese suffer from living under a foreign-written constitution, which in turn puts in question the genuineness of the Japanese attachment to democracy and human freedom. The Japanese indubitably admire authority, and from here and there (the right wing of the Diet, for example, or recent changes in what's taught in schools) the country sometimes emits a slightly disquieting smell of jingoistic nationalism. Still, the most likely prospect is that Japan will move toward centrist coalition governments that may not work in harness smoothly but will provide continued stability and democracy.

Moreover, for the foreseeable future, any cutoff in the supply of foreign food and raw materials could badly wound Japan. Those ships bringing oil and ore and wheat, and the other ships carrying away exports, must arrive and depart with clockwork regularity. Yet everyone knows by now that producing nations can quite capriciously refuse to export materials. A longshoreman's strike could stop every wheel in Japan. The reason for such dependence, of course, is dense population, and though the country's population growth is well restrained, Japan has not yet made a firm decision to bring it to a halt, or better, reduce the number of people, through low birth rates; dangerously increased population remains a possibility. In sum, although the Japanese can to some extent offset their dependence by conservation, ingenuity, and population control, their plans may be dashed by decisions made in other countries. If sharply frustrated, the Japanese might feel that they have no choice except to turn belligerent. "What if your oil is cut off?" I asked one leading businessman. His answer: "We'd have to go to war. The attitude of the people would change 180 degrees."

In diplomacy, too, Japan faces possibly crippling errors. Without aggressive arms, but wielding economic power so great as to constitute a weapon, Japan must preserve good relations with the United States, the Soviet Union, and China, the big powers whose territories approach one another most closely in that part of the world centered on Hokkaido. Some such forthcoming event as the death of Mao Tse-tung (with possible resultant Russian meddling in China) will require careful judgments by Japan. Ultimately Japan will probably have to be content to watch China, by then with a population of a billion, replace Japan as the world's No. 3 power, measured in economic strength. The United States must be kept as a friend while being detached as a military senior partner. Resentments between

Third World nations and Japan, seen by them as the heartless Rich Man of Asia, must not be allowed to get worse. A happy Japan set in a miserable Asia does not seem like a tenable vision. A fully re-armed Japan would set almost everyone's nerves on edge.

Some observers see indications that the values behind the Japa-nese miracle are breaking down. The Japan Productivity Center finds in its annual surveys of newly hired young employees that fewer and fewer believe their work contributes to the enrichment of society (though most of them also say that given a choice between working overtime and keeping a date, they would work). Postwar generations lack some of the loyalty to the national good that prevailed among the selfless builders of the miracle. Schisms may appear—for exam-ple, between organized and unorganized labor. Workers may come to resent the bondage of their lifetime employment, and employers may begin to covet the freedom to hire and fire at will. The "one big family" psychology of a company and its union is not so strong as it used to be. "Japanese egalitarianism is changing from passive to demanding," an official of the Federation of Economic Organizations told me. "And once protest gets going, it does not recede. This is a symptom of a high-income society." Lately most of the protest has been aimed at big business, essentially because many people think the zaibatsu are growing too powerful. Still, these hostilities run up against the all-important Japanese tradition of harmony, and the overriding need for harmony can be counted upon to neutralize many conflicts.

One pessimistic prophecy certain to come true is that some heavily populated part of Japan will suffer a devastating earthquake. It may cost hundreds of thousands of lives, and a year's increment to the GNP. Still, no nation knows better than Japan how to recover from disasters.

Equally certain is it that economic growth at 10 or 15 percent a year is gone for good—and no bad thing, either, in the minds of most Japanese, with the qualification that the economy must continue to grow at least 6 percent a year. Very probably it would drop well below that, or go into a painful decline, if the rest of the world, or even just the United States, falls into a deep and persistent depression. Similarly, internal factors could shrink the economy to a level lower than anyone desires. Pessimistic economists point out that Japan has lost many of the forces that made the miracle possible: the supply of farm-boy labor, the free flow of foreign technology, now about used up, the foreign-exchange rates that made Japanese products cheap abroad, cheap foreign raw material, and universal dedication to economic goals. By the workings of the seniority system, the costs of an aging labor force grow higher and higher. Bigger and bigger zaibatsu may turn into managerial impossiblities. Moreover, the country simply must put more and more capital into what is solemnly called "social overhead investment" by the government (environmental cleanup, schools, health, parks) and less into privately owned, growth-creating factories. Finally, Japanese inflation, higher than that of its foreign markets, could soon leave Japanese exports outpriced and unsalable, and the balance of payments would again turn against Japan. But again, the damage suggested by these trends may be illusory. The rapidly increasing Japanese research and development effort will inevitably supply much useful technology, and a more technical economy will need less labor. And, after all, the reality behind those words "social overhead investment" is a pleasanter, more cultivated, better-educated life for everybody.

What Japan may become, if it can sidestep most or all of these pitfalls, is fairly easy to suggest, at least in the economic sense, for many high-ranking Japanese are pondering the future and making plans to become the world's first postindustrial society. One of these men is Saburo Okita, managing director of a think-tank called the Japan Economic Research Center and a member of the future-minded Club of Rome.

Okita is a large and jovial brainstormer with a disarming kind of candor. When I asked him, "What is your hobby?" he bellowed, "Drinking whiskey!" He devised the successful 1960 double-the-national-income plan, and now, saying "Perhaps we overdid it," he has thought up a pollution-halving plan, to reduce sulfur dioxide in the air and biochemical oxygen demand in water by 50 percent in five years. The "Okita Index" of a nation is the GNP divided by acres or hectares of utilizable land. The higher the index, the denser the nation's problems, and Japan has the world's highest.

But Okita's perceptions of Japan's future are only incidentally linked to the problems of pollution, for he has a vision of a society in which the Japanese place less reliance on their ability to make and more on their ability to think. Having once deified GNP, he now believes that it should peak out ("we no longer need a high rate of growth") at its present high level ("if the economy is cut we produce another kind of pollution, poverty"). This new economy will be rich, unpolluted, and tailored to Japan because it will have "a high input of brains and a low input of materials." The Japanese will concern themselves, for example, with the most sophisticated computers, with excellent design in textiles and the like, with fine chemicals produced in small quantities. Having earlier been so bold as to build a steel industry in a land without iron ore, Japan will now be so bold as to curb its blast furnaces, and will import steel instead of ore. What is now a net importer of technology, a land of copiers, will become a land of inventors, a supplier of research and development. Hitherto Japan has been essentially an exporter of labor; now it will export brains.

"We will open up a new national style of high production and low pollution," says Okita. He does not foresee a Japan of utter security and lavish luxury. The world's grim shortages of food and energy will hurt Japan too. The new Japan will hold down on air conditioning, grain-fed meat, and automobile transport, but it will have agreeable work, shorter hours, clean air and water, and less dependence on a possibly more hostile world. Such are the thoughts of Saburo Okita as he sits in his gym-size office and gazes at the tapestries, landscapes, abstractions, and calligraphy on the walls, and at the potted plant, the ornate globe, and the dragon dolls that stand on the bookcases.

The notion of radically changing the industrial structure has such a hold on Japanese thinking that it seems certain to come about. Predicting that Japan will continue growing at its recent 15 percent a year is as absurd as predicting that on projection of current growth a boy of seven will be thirty-five feet tall by the time he is forty. MITI plans to try to hold growth to 7 percent a year for the rest of the 1970s, and to 6.5 percent from 1980 to 1985. By then, MITI predicts, the thirty-four-hour work week will be standard. Not only is it irrelevant to argue over whether Japan's GNP will be highest in the world in the year 2000, but it is probable that Japan (and other nations) will drop GNP as a measure of success and use net national welfare instead. In comparing itself to Europe and the United States, Japan will play down per capita income (although it may come to exceed that of the United States) and boast, perhaps, of its cleaned-up atmosphere, pollution-free mass transportation, new universities, and ample participatory sports facilities.

Speculation about the nature of Japan's future industries is diverse and intriguing. "Knowledge-intensive" electronics and computer technology for an "information society" will come in many forms. The futurologist Gene Gregory sees Japan developing automatic medical diagnosis, remote-control medical equipment for homes and hospitals, computerized shopping services, cashless and checkless banking, automatic gas- and water-meter reading, portable wireless telephones connecting directly to satellites, surgical lasers, robots with eyes, and manless warehousing. In other fields he predicts the development of magnetohydrodynamics (the generation of electricity directly from ionized gases), synthetic lumber, 220-mile-an-hour freight trains, electric cars, and artificial body organs. Already Japan has planned cities on and under the sea. The government's Machine Technology Research Center has built an experimental computer-controlled vehicle system of driverless taxis that read the destination from a magnetic ticket (which the customer purchases from conveniently located machines) and go to it by the fastest route while providing the passenger with a desk and a phone.

Many of these products will form the next generation of Japanese exports, supplanting color television sets, tape recorders, steel, petrochemicals, and cars. But two of the biggest future industries will mostly supply the Japanese market. One is pollution-control equipment, which has already become a $4-billion-a-year industry and grows at 40 percent a year. The other is social overhead investment; the housing industry has already hit 2 million starts a year, which greatly surpasses that of the United States in recent years. "The future does not lie in expanding trade," said former prime minister Eisaku Sato. "It lies in expanding welfare by improving housing and sewage and taking better care of the environment."

Big business seems willing not only to go along with this next-generation portfolio of industries, but also to plan for it and lead the way. The Study Group for Industrial Planning, which is loosely linked to the Federation of Economic Organizations, has published concrete lists of industries that should be abolished, restrained, or encouraged in the next ten years.

Some of the activities that have got to go, according to the study, are: oil and petrochemical refineries near big cities; petrochemical fertilizer plants; primary phases of steelmaking, such as sintering, pelletizing, and cokemaking; smelting of cadmium, copper, lead, and zinc; any industry that discharges large amounts of mercury, arsenic, or lead; papermaking from imported pulp or wood chips; and coal-fired power generation near cities.

Industries that must not expand are: nonbiodegradable petrochemical products, blast furnaces, smelting of nonferrous metals from imported concentrates, light gasoline-powered passenger cars, paper made from domestic pulp and chips, and oil- and natural-gas-fired power generation.

Industries to be encouraged are: low-pollution petroleum refining in lightly populated areas, alloy steel, electric-furnace steelmaking, steel from scrap, smelting of aluminum and nonferrous metals from imported ingots, electric and other nonpolluting cars, recycled paper, atomic power generation, and containerized transportation by sea, rail, and highway.

Finally, the study produced its own list of needed future industries: hydrogen fuel, solar electricity, power generation by ocean currents and the jet stream, undersea mining, fifty-story apartment houses, high-conductivity power transmission, fusing and recrystallizing rocks to make materials resembling metals.

Some sober observers charge that with pollution and the energy shortage, Japan has reached the height of its economic miracle. They are right, of course, and Japan knows it. So Japan has put its foot on the road to another and entirely different kind of miracle. The dismantling and restructuring of Japan, Inc. will make fascinating news in the next few decades. Japan will certainly be postindustrial, to use the economists' jargon, and it may be not only postcapitalist but also post-Marxist.

"To live in harmony with Nature is the necessary condition of survival," writes Arnold Toynbee, adding, "This is surely the teaching of Shinto." Historically, the Japanese have always understood the polarities of "follow nature" and "conquer nature," and not only the metaphysics of Shinto but also the esthetics of Buddhism have come down heavily on the side of "follow nature." But for three decades of filling bays with dirt and skies with soot and lakes with waste, the Japanese have been attempting to conquer nature.

Whether they can now go back to following nature (to use that phrase as shorthand for a life of greater amenity) is not as easy to foretell as possible developments in the economy. Continued economic success need not stand in the way. Herman Kahn points out that there is "a basic kind of insanity" in regarding "the quality of life" as jeopardized by high GNP. History, as usual, provides a clue to the question of the future of the Japanese spirit. Twenty or thirty years after the next-to-last 180-degree switch of national policy, that is, the Meiji-era decision to junk feudalism and borrow heavily from the West, the Japanese began to draw back from certain excesses of imitation—to put aside the frock coat and resume the kimono. Now about thirty years have elapsed since the most recent 180-degree turn, just after the war. Perhaps Japan will produce some intriguing new version of the Tokugawa period—zero population growth combined with cultivation of the arts and the sensitivities. The Japanese, more than any other people, seem to know when they have had it, when one policy is played out and it is time to change.

Says Saburo Okita, with a crinkly smile: "We may yet be the canary that survives." The Japanese have lived through many changes and survived. Canaries they are not. But like a healthy physique, each time they acquired a greater immunity to the assaults by foreign bodies or the internal disorders that all mankind is subject to. The homogeneous society can take terrific strains. The Japanese are—supremely—a nation of survivors.

Acknowledgments

THE NEARLY INVISIBLE but 100-percent-present partner in this book is my wife, Deborah, who has for many years had a consuming interest in Japan and the Japanese. A graduate of Sophia University in Tokyo, she went on to gain journalistic experience as a researcher for *Time* magazine, and then took a master's degree in Japanese and Chinese history at the University of Hawaii's East-West Center. Whenever I ground to a halt while I was writing, she quietly supplied a suggestion or a source or a guiding insight. She read widely among periodicals and, aware of the framework of the book, passed along what she knew I ought to read. Criticizing the manuscript, she found many ways to make points more precisely. Many of the people I met in Japan were her friends, or friends of her friends, or friends of theirs—she got the famous Japanese go-between system going for me. Finally, her ability to speak Japanese made it easy and journalistically productive to live and travel in Japan. I am the author, because I wrote the words, but the plain fact is that my wife's collaboration was indispensable.

I am also grateful beyond expression to Cass Canfield, Senior Editor of Harper & Row, who, though unaware that I had a collaborator well qualified for the project, singled out Japan as a likely topic for a book by me. His faith in me, and his tireless encouragement, were essential to the writing of the book. And it was he, personally, who stripped this book of a great deal of verbiage that I said goodbye to with no regrets. I respect him immensely. A. T. Baker, who like me is a former senior editor at *Time*, edited the book to the benefit of its style, organization, and lucidity. Two other old-*Time* colleagues,

437

Philip W. Payne and Carl Solberg, and my wife's father, Brigadier General Herbert A. Hall, read and usefully criticized the whole manuscript. Edwin O. Reischauer, the Harvard historian and former American ambassador to Japan, examined the first draft and sent back a long list of corrections and improvements. I would also like to single out three men who gave me extraordinary amounts of time and assistance in Japan: Yasuhiro Goh, a leading Tokyo businessman; Saburo Itoh, deputy manager of the foreign department of Mitsui Trust & Banking Co., Ltd.; and Henry Mittwer, a Japanese-American who chucked a good job in the California weapons industry to become a Buddhist monk and a tea ceremonialist in Kyoto. Peter Fairbarns, vice-president of Coca-Cola for Asia, kindly lent us a grand house with a view of Mount Fuji for our month in Kamakura.

All those who throughout this book are quoted as a result of interviews have my thanks, although except for some who helped me in additional ways I will not repeat their names here. Persons who aided me number in the many hundreds; I want to mention, as having been particularly helpful, the following: Tomoji Abe, George Akita, Kentaro Aono, Koichiro Asakai, Shinichiro Asao, R. Wickham Baxter, S. Chang, Lee Chia, Michael Cooper, Martin C. Davidson, James Doyle, Brigadier General Taro Edo and his family, Eiko Fairbarns, Anitta Feldman, David F. Fitzgerald, Masao Fujioka, Nancy Geiss, Herbert Glazer, Norishige Hasegawa, Isamu Hashimoto, Yuji Hayashi, Tatsuaki Hirai, Ikumi Hishino, Yozo Horigome, Richard Hughes, Hiroya Ichikawa, Shui Ikemiyagushiku, Takeshi Ishibashi, Susumu Ishiguro, Frank Iwama, W. Bart Jackson, Toshiaki Kaneko, Donald Keene, Dong Hi Kim, Joyu Kimura, Yoshizo Kinoshita, Young H. Lee, Eduardo Lichauco, Klaus Luhmer, Graham McDonnell, Theodore McNelly, Hiroyasu Maruta, Shigeharu Matsumoto, Fumio Matsuo, Yuji Mineyama, Ray Mlnarchek, Makota Momoe, S. Motokawa, Minoru Muramatsu, Toyotaka Murata, Kinhide Mushakoji, Michio Nagai, Juntaro Nazase, Yutaka Narita, Herman Nickel, Michio Noji, Masaru Ogawa, Hiroshi Ohki, Masaki Ohnishi, Atsuo Okazaki, Yoichi Okazaki, Saburo Okita, Minoru Omori, Robert P. Paus, Sir John Pilcher, Guiseppe Pittau, Jean-Jacques Rollard, Peter Sagaseta, Yoko Sakai, Hiroshi Sakamoto, Masakatsu Sakata, William C. Sherman, Toshiro Shimanouchi, Hiroshi Shionozaki, Noburu Tasaki, Yoshiaki Ueda, Moto Uwano, Bob Wales, Martin E. Weinstein, Koji Yada, Shin-ichi Yamashita, Yoichi Yokobori, Ansei and Evelyn Yokota, Tadaaki Yoshida, and Sumi Yukawa.

Bibliography

Books that I found useful are:

Abbate, Francesco. *Japanese Art and Korean Art*. London: Octopus Books, 1972.

Akita, George. *Foundations of Constitutional Government in Modern Japan 1868–1900*. Cambridge, Mass.: Harvard University Press, 1967.

Asahi Shimbun staff. *The Pacific Rivals*. New York and Tokyo: Weatherhill/Asahi, 1972.

Axelbank, Albert. *Black Star over Japan*. New York: Farrar, Straus & Giroux, 1972.

Ballon, Robert J., ed. *The Japanese Employee* Tokyo: Sophia University/Tuttle, 1969.

Barr, Pat. *The Coming of the Barbarians*. Tokyo: Charles E. Tuttle, 1972.

Beardsley, Richard K., and John Whitney Hall (with chapters by Joseph K. Yamagiwa and B. James George, Jr.). *Twelve Doors to Japan*. New York: McGraw-Hill, 1965.

Beasley, W. G. *The Modern History of Japan*. London: Praeger, 1963.

Benedict, Ruth. *The Chrysanthemum and the Sword*. Boston: Houghton Mifflin, 1946.

Bergamini, David. *Japan's Imperial Conspiracy*. New York: Morrow, 1971.

Black, C. E. *The Dynamics of Modernization*. New York: Harper & Row, 1966.

Bonet, Vicente M., ed. *Religion in the Japanese Textbooks*. Tokyo: Enderle, 1973.

Bowie, Theodore. *Langdon Warner Through His Letters*. Bloomington: Indiana University Press, 1966.

Brzezinski, Zbigniew. *The Fragile Blossom*. New York: Harper & Row, 1972.

Busch, Noel F. *The Horizon Concise History of Japan.* New York: American Heritage, 1972.

Campbell, Alexander. *The Heart of Japan.* New York: Knopf, 1961.

Conrat, Maisie and Richard. *Executive Order 9066.* Cambridge, Mass.: MIT Press, 1972.

Cooper, Michael, ed. *The Southern Barbarians.* Tokyo: Kodansha International, 1971.

De Vera, José María. *Educational Television in Japan.* Tokyo: Sophia University/Tuttle, 1967.

Doi, Takeo. *The Anatomy of Dependence.* Tokyo: Kodansha International, 1973.

Emmerson, John K. *Arms, Yen & Power.* Tokyo: Charles E. Tuttle, 1972.

Fairbank, John K., and Edwin O. Reischauer. *A History of Asian Civilization.* Vol. I, *East Asia: The Great Tradition,* and Vol. II (with Albert M. Craig), *East Asia: The Modern Transformation.* Boston: Houghton Mifflin, 1958, 1965.

Fodor, Eugene, and Robert C. Fisher. *Japan and East Asia.* Don Mills, Ont.: Hodder & Stoughton, 1972.

Fromm, Erich, D. T. Suzuki, and Richard De Martino. *Zen Buddhism and Psychoanalysis.* New York: Harper & Row, 1960.

Fujiwara, Hirotatsu. *I Denounce Soka Gakkai.* Tokyo: Nisshin Hodo, 1970.

Fukuzawa, Yukichi. *The Autobiography of Fukuzawa Yukichi.* (New translation by Eiichi Kiyooka.) Tokyo: Hokuseido Press, 1960.

Genji, Keita. *The Guardian God of Golf.* Tokyo: Japan Times, 1972.

Gibney, Frank. *Five Gentlemen of Japan.* New York: Farrar, Straus & Giroux, 1953.

Gibney, Frank. *Japan: The Fragile Superpower.* New York: Norton, 1975.

Guillain, Robert. *The Japanese Challenge.* Philadelphia: Lippincott, 1970.

Gunther, John. *Inside Asia.* New York: Harper & Row, 1939.

Gunther, John. *Twelve Cities.* New York: Harper & Row, 1969.

Hadley, Eleanor. *Antitrust in Japan.* Princeton, N.J.: Princeton University Press, 1970.

Halford, Aubrey S., and Giovanna M. *The Kabuki Handbook.* Tokyo: Charles E. Tuttle, 1956.

Hall, John Whitney. *Japan from Prehistory to Modern Times.* New York: Delacorte, 1970.

Halloran, Richard. *Japan: Images and Realities.* New York: Knopf, 1969.

Hanke, Byron R. *Urban Densities in the U.S. and Japan.* Washington, D.C.: Department of Housing and Urban Development, 1972.

Haring, Douglas. *Okinawan Customs Yesterday and Today.* Tokyo: Charles E. Tuttle, 1969.

Hasegawa, Nyozekan. *The Japanese Character: A Cultural Profile,* trans. by John Bester. Tokyo: Kodansha International, 1966.

Hayashi, Chikio, with Hirojero Hoyama, Shigeki Nishihara, and Tatsusuzo Suzuki. *A Study of Japanese National Character.* Tokyo: Shiseido, 1970.

Hellman, Donald C. *Japan and East Asia: The New International Order.* New York: Praeger, 1972.

Hirota, Naotake. *The Lure of Japan's Railways.* Tokyo: Japan Times, 1969.

Hokkaido Prefectural Government. *Relations Between Japan and U.S.A. in the History of the Development of Hokkaido.* 1960.

Hosokawa, Bill. *Nisei: The Quiet Americans.* New York: Morrow, 1969.

Ishida, Takeshi. *Japanese Society.* New York: Random House, 1971.

Itoh, Teiji. *Traditional Domestic Architecture of Japan.* Tokyo: Weatherhill/Heibonsha, 1972.

Itoh, Teiji, and Yukio Futagawa. *The Classic Tradition in Japanese Architecture.* Tokyo and Kyoto: Weatherhill/Tankosha, 1971.

Japan Travel Bureau. *The Official Guide.* Tokyo, 1955.

Johnson, Richard T., and William G. Ouchi. *Made in America (Under Japanese Management).* Palo Alto, Calif.: Stanford University Press, 1974.

Kahn, Herman. *The Emerging Japanese Superstate.* Englewood Cliffs, N.J.: Prentice-Hall, 1971.

Kaplan, Eugene J. *Japan: The Government-Business Relationship.* Washington, D.C.: Government Printing Office, 1972.

Keene, Donald, ed. *Anthology of Japanese Literature.* Tokyo: Charles E. Tuttle, 1956.

Keene, Donald, ed. *Modern Japanese Literature.* Tokyo: Charles E. Tuttle, 1957.

Kitano, Harry H. L. *Japanese-Americans: The Evolution of a Subculture.* Englewood Cliffs, N.J.: Prentice-Hall, 1969.

Koestler, Arthur. *The Lotus and the Robot.* New York: Macmillan, 1961.

Kuhaulua, Jesse, with John Wheeler. *Takamiyama: The World of Sumo.* Tokyo: Kodansha International, 1973.

Leach, Bernard. *A Potter in Japan.* London: Faber & Faber, 1960.

Leonard, Jonathan Norton. *Early Japan.* New York: Time-Life Books, 1968.

Levy, Howard S. *Oriental Sex Manners.* London: New English Library, 1972.

Lifton, Robert Jay. *Death in Life.* New York: Random House, 1967.

Livingston, Jon, Joe Moore, and Felicia Oldfather, eds. *Postwar Japan, 1945 to the Present.* New York: Pantheon, 1973.

McNelly, Theodore. *Contemporary Government of Japan.* Boston: Houghton Mifflin, 1972.

McNelly, Theodore. *Politics and Government in Japan.* Boston: Houghton Mifflin, 1972.

Maraini, Fosco. *Meeting with Japan.* New York: Viking, 1960.

Martin, R. Montgomery. *China: Political, Commercial, and Social; in an Official Report to Her Majesty's Government,* Vol. I and II. London: James Madden, 1847.

Michener, James A. *The Hokusai Sketch-Books.* Tokyo: Charles E. Tuttle, 1958.

Miki, Fumio. *Haniwa: The Clay Sculpture of Proto-Historic Japan.* (English adaptation by Roy Andrew Miller.) Tokyo: Charles E. Tuttle, 1960.

Minami, Hiroshi. *Psychology of the Japanese People*, trans. by Albert R. Ikoma. Tokyo: University of Tokyo Press, 1971.

Miller, Roy Andrew. *The Japanese Language*. Chicago: University of Chicago Press, 1970.

Minear, Richard H. *Victors' Justice: The Tokyo War Crimes Trial*. Tokyo: Charles E. Tuttle, 1972.

Mitsuoka, Tadanari. *Ceramic Art of Japan*. Tokyo: Japan Travel Bureau, 1964.

Mody, N. H. N. *Japanese Clocks*. Tokyo: Charles E. Tuttle, 1967.

Morley, James William. *Forecast for Japan: Security in the 1970's*. Princeton, N.J.: Princeton University Press, 1972.

Morison, Samuel Eliot. *"Old Bruin": Commodore Matthew C. Perry*. Boston: Little, Brown, 1967.

Morris, Ivan. *The World of the Shining Prince*. Baltimore, Md.: Penguin Books, 1964.

Morris, M. D. *Okinawa: Tiger by the Tail*. New York: Hawthorn Books, 1968.

Mosley, Leonard. *Hirohito, Emperor of Japan*. Englewood Cliffs, N.J.: Prentice-Hall, 1966.

Murata, Kiyoaki. *Japan's New Buddhism*. Tokyo: Walker/Weatherhill, 1969.

Nagai, Michio. *Higher Education in Japan: Its Takeoff and Crash*. Tokyo: University of Tokyo Press, 1971.

Nakane, Chie. *Japanese Society*. Berkeley and Los Angeles: University of California Press, 1970.

Okakura, Kakuzo. *The Book of Tea*. New York: Dover, 1964.

Olson, Lawrence. *Japan in Postwar Asia*. New York: Praeger, 1970.

O'Neill, P. G. *Japanese Names*. Tokyo: Weatherhill, 1972.

Porter, Hal. *The Actors*. Sydney, Australia: Angus & Robertson, 1968.

Reischauer, Edwin O. *Beyond Vietnam: The United States and Asia*. Tokyo: Charles E. Tuttle, 1967.

Reischauer, Edwin O. *Japan: The Story of a Nation*. New York: Knopf, 1970.

Reischauer, Edwin O. *The United States and Japan*. Cambridge, Mass.: Harvard University Press, 1965.

Reischauer, Edwin O. *See* Fairbank, John K.

Richie, Donald. *Japanese Cinema*. Garden City, N.Y.: Doubleday, 1971.

Richie, Donald. *The Inland Sea*. Tokyo: Weatherhill, 1971.

Richie, Donald, and Kenkichi Ito. *The Erotic Gods*. Tokyo: Zufushinsha, 1967.

Roberts, John G. *Mitsui: Three Centuries of Japanese Business*. Tokyo: Weatherhill, 1973.

Robinson, James C. *Okinawa, A People and Their Gods*. Tokyo: Charles E. Tuttle, 1969.

Sakai, Atsuharu. *Japan in a Nutshell*, Vols. I and II. Yokohama: Yamagata Printing, 1949, 1952.

Sansom, G. B. *Japan: A Short Cultural History*. Englewood Cliffs, N.J.: Prentice-Hall, 1962.

Scalapino, Robert A., and Junnosuke Masumi. *Parties and Politics in Contemporary Japan*. Berkeley and Los Angeles: University of California Press, 1967.

Schecter, Jerrold. *The New Face of Buddha.* Tokyo: Weatherhill, 1967.

Seward, Jack. *The Japanese.* New York: Morrow, 1972.

Seward, Jack. *Japanese in Action.* Tokyo: Walker/Weatherhill, 1968.

Sitwell, Sacheverell. *The Bridge of the Brocade Sash.* Cleveland and New York: World Publishing, 1959.

Statler, Oliver. *Japanese Inn.* New York: Pyramid Books, 1962.

Storry, Richard. *A History of Modern Japan.* Baltimore, Md.: Penguin Books, 1960.

Suzuki, Daisetz Teitaro. *The Training of the Zen Buddhist Monk.* New York: University Books, 1959.

Taeuber, Irene B. *The Population of Japan.* Princeton, N.J.: Princeton University Press, 1958.

Tanaka, Kakuei. *Building a New Japan.* Tokyo: Simul Press, 1972.

Tokyo Municipal Office. *The Reconstruction of Tokyo.* 1933.

Toland, John. *The Rising Sun.* New York: Random House, 1970.

Tolischus, Otto D. *Tokyo Record.* New York: Morrow, 1943.

Trezise, Philip. *Our Two Countries.* New York: Japan Information Service, 1972.

Tsuneishi, Warren. *Japanese Political Style.* New York: Harper & Row, 1966.

Varley, H. Paul, and Ivan and Nobuko Morris. *The Samurai.* London: Weidenfeld & Nicolson, 1970.

Walworth, Arthur. *Black Ships Off Japan.* New York: Knopf, 1946.

Watsuji, Tetsuro. *Climate and Culture.* Tokyo: Hokuseido Press, 1961.

Weinstein, Martin E. *Japan's Postwar Defense Policy, 1947–1968.* New York: Columbia University Press, 1971.

White, James W. *The Sokagakkai and Mass Society.* Palo Alto, Calif.: Stanford University Press, 1970.

Williams, Harold S. *Tales of the Foreign Settlements in Japan.* Tokyo: Charles E. Tuttle, 1972.

Yanaga, Chitoshi. *Big Business in Japanese Politics.* New Haven, Conn.: Yale University Press, 1968.

Index

Japanese words in the text are listed, with translations, in this index.

Aaron, Hank, 172
abacus, 66, 67, 90–91, 118, 378
Abe, Kobo, 160–161
Abegglen, James, 27
abortion, 39, 347
Acton, Lord, 324
acupuncture, 108–109
Administrative Management Agency, 17
advertising agencies, 70, 159–160
Agricultural Machinery, Institute of, 364
agriculture, 221, 255–256, 258–259, 260, 265, 296, 354–355, 361–364
Ainu, 63, 230, 264, 265–266
Ainu Liberation League, 266
Akahata, 326, 328
Akasaka, 220
Akasaka Detached Palace, 154
Akihito, Prince, 306, 310–311, 335, 429
Akita, Margaret, 142
Akiyama, Kazuyoshi, 144
Akutagawa, Ryonosuke, 238
Alaska, 7, 392
Alcock, Sir Rutherford, 67
alcohol, 74–76, 213, 217–218, 265
alcoves, 51, 70, 79, 80
Altaic, 127
Amaterasu-Omikami, 96, 97, 107
American Journal of Ortho-Psychiatry, 134
American National Academy of Sciences, 270
American Symphony Orchestra, 144
America on the Verge of Collapse, 291
Amherst College, 118
Amida, 98, 152
Analects of Confucius, 335
ancestor worship, 96, 107
animals, 23, 219, 259, 265
anthem, 321
Aono, Kentaro, 181
architecture, 77, 98, 99, 154–156, 242

arigato (thank you), 20, 74, 419
art, 99, 147–154, 189, 195, 197
  modern, 151–152
  museums and galleries, 89, 215
  painting, 147, 149–152, 189, 195
  pottery, 153–154
  sculpture, 152–153, 279
  wood-block prints, 147–149, 151, 152, 189
arubaito (part-time work), 40
Asahi Evening News, 157–158
Asahi Shimbun, 115, 122, 130, 139, 156–157, 158, 171, 212, 234, 397, 405, 410
Asakusa, 216
Ashi, Lake, 260
Ashihara, Yoshinobu, 155–156, 214, 221
Ashikaga, Yoshimasa, 77
Ashikaga shogunate, 197, 243
Asian Survey, 417
Aso, Mount, 258
Association of South East Asian Nations (ASEAN), 409
Asukata, Ichio, 406
Atami, 260
Ataturk, Kemal, 133
Atomic Bomb Memorial Museum, 155, 268
atomic bombs, 268–272, 277–278
Atomic Energy Act, 426
Atomic Energy Commission (U.S.), 270
Atsuko, Princess, 306
"Auld Lang Syne," 67, 253
Australia and Japan, 308, 381
automobile industry, 3, 160, 268, 300, 359, 370, 381–382, 385, 386, 388
aviation, 384, 392, 398
awamori (brandy), 218

Bairy, Maurice, 15–16, 352
Baker, Russell, 387
Ball, George, 404

Hepburn system, 133
Hester, James, 121–122
Heublein, 74
Hideyoshi, 77, 78, 105, 197–198, 276, 338, 413
Hiei, Mount, 237–238
High Energy Physics Institute, 121
hikime kagibana (art technique), 150
Hiraga, Key, 152
hiragana syllabary, 129, 133
Hiraizumi, Wataru, 60, 320
Hirata, Seiko, 99–100
Hiro, Prince, 310
Hirohito, Emperor, 9, 24, 67, 152, 204, 291, 294, 295, 303–311, 419
Hiroshige, Ando, 88, 147–149
Hiroshima, 155, 227, 268–272, 277–278, 294
hissing, 21, 250
Hitachi, Ltd., 394
Hizen clan, 317
Ho Chi Minh, 295
Hokama, Seishiro, 282, 286
Hokkaido, 7, 194, 257, 263–266
Hokkaido, University of, 117, 264
Hokusai, 148, 151, 176
holidays and festivals, 10, 12, 86–87, 143, 193–194, 238, 246, 253–254, 265, 267, 304, 321, 398
Holland and Japan, 109, 116, 124, 188, 189, 190, 192, 198, 276–277
homosexuality, 93, 196, 217
Honda, Soichiro, 357, 373
Honda Motor Company, 357, 359
Hong Kong and Japan, 173, 179, 181, 182
Honshu, 7, 163, 194, 197, 229, 257
Hoover, Herbert, 203
Hornbeck, Stanley, 291
Hornet, 293
Horyuji, 244
housing, 38, 50–57, 373
Hsinhua news agency, 311
Hull, Cordell, 291
Human Capacity Development Division, 60

Ichinomiya, 232
Idemitsu, Sazo, 381
Ieyasu. *See* Tokugawa
ikebana (flower arrangement), 77, 79, 80, 82, 99, 197
Ikeda, Daisaku, 330
Ikeda, Hayato, 19, 299, 320, 336, 337, 339

Ikeda, Yoshizo, 375–376, 379–380
Imamura, Akira, 75
Imamura, Hitoshi, 307
imitators, Japanese as, 24–25, 358–359
Imperial Hotel, 108, 154, 212
Imperial Household Agency, 308–309, 419
Imperial Palace (Kyoto), 246–247
Imperial Palace (Tokyo), 210, 212, 214, 219, 303, 304–305, 309–310
Imperial Rule Assistance Association, 205
incense, 82–83, 101
income doubling plan, 28, 231, 299
India, 97, 99, 100, 102, 107, 198, 294
Indonesia and Japan, 182, 183, 387, 389, 411
Industrial Exhibition Hall, 269
industrialization, 202, 233
infure heji (inflation hedge), 170
Inland Sea, 8, 266, 267–268, 368
Intangible Cultural Property, 153
International Business Machines, 360, 393
International Cultural Hall, 278
International Ocean Exposition, 287
International Press Institute, 158
International Relations, Institute of, 408
International Studies and Training, Institute for, 59, 183
International Trade and Industry, Ministry of (MITI), 6, 219, 360–361, 369, 379, 386, 393
Ise shrine, 97, 107, 304
Ishibashi, Shojiro, 126
Ishida, Takeshi, 33, 59, 138
Ishihara, Shintaro, 322–323
Ishikari Plain, 258
Ishikawa, Yoshio, 111
Ishikawajima-Harima Heavy Industries, 358, 360, 369, 380, 381
Ishimaru, Shin'ichi, 172
Ishite temple, 267
Israel, 389
itai-itai (ouch-ouch) disease, 366, 369
Italy, 109, 200
Italy and Japan, 176, 177, 200
Itoh, Teiji, 77
Iwabe, Tetsuro, 180
Iwaki, Hiroyuki, 144
Iwakura, Tomomi, 66, 199, 201
Iwasaki, Baron, 214, 220, 260
Iwo Jima, 221, 257, 294
Izu, 221